DATE DUE

NEW DIMENSIONS in
evangelical thought

Essays in Honor of Millard J. Erickson

David S. Dockery, Editor

InterVarsity Press
Downers Grove, Illinois

InterVarsity Press
P.O. Box 1400, Downers Grove, IL 60515
World Wide Web: www.ivpress.com
E-mail: mail@ivpress.com

InterVarsity Press® is the book-publishing division of InterVarsity Christian Fellowship/USA®, a student movement active on campus at hundreds of universities, colleges and schools of nursing in the United States of America, and a member movement of the International Fellowship of Evangelical Students. For information about local and regional activities, write Public Relations Dept., InterVarsity Christian Fellowship/USA, 6400 Schroeder Rd., P.O. Box 7895, Madison, WI 53707-7895.

ISBN 0-8308-1517-1

Printed in the United States of America

Library of Congress Cataloging-in-Publication Data

New dimensions in evangelical thought: essays in honor of Millard J.
  Erickson/edited by David S. Dockery.
     p.   cm.
  Includes bibliographical references.
  ISBN 0-8308-1517-1 (alk. paper)
    1. Evangelicalism.   2. Theology.   I. Erickson, Millard J.
  II. Dockery, David S.
  BR1650.N47   1998
  230'.04624—DC21   97-50064
                                                                        CIP

22   21   20   19   18   17   16   15   14   13   12   11   10   9   8   7   6   5   4   3   2   1

17   16   15   14   13   12   11   10   09   08   07   06   05   04   03   02   01   00   99   98

New Dimensions in Applied Theology

Bibliography

Preface

David S. Dockery

....

I WAS INTRODUCED TO MILLARD J. ERICKSON'S WRITINGS AS A BEGINNING theology student over two decades ago. His work *The New Evangelical Theology* (1968) helped me interpret the larger evangelical world. His three-volume *Readings in Christian Theology* provided a framework for learning to think theologically. Many young collegians and seminarians have had a similar experience, which has been multiplied many times over since the publication of Erickson's three-volume systematic theology in the 1980s.

I had a providential opportunity to become acquainted with Millard Erickson a dozen years ago at a meeting of the Evangelical Theological Society. Since that time the Lord has solidified a lasting and strong friendship bond—one in which Millard has been mentor and I his privileged student.

I have taught theology at undergraduate and graduate levels in several settings since 1984. Erickson's influence has been obvious. Many of the contributors to this volume can tell a similar story. All can testify to his influence on both Baptist and evangelical life in North America and around the world.

The contributors to this volume are some of the finest thinkers in the larger evangelical world. They include Erickson's mentors, colleagues, students and friends. The commonality that draws this diverse group together is an ongoing common respect and appreciation for Millard Erickson. Not all agree with Erickson's positions, of course. And at times he has disagreed with the writings of some contributors. They in turn have challenged his thinking. Some continue to carry on a conversation with him in the chapters in this volume. Everyone will probably find something to disagree with in this book.

Each contribution focuses on a particular aspect of theology, reviewing recent work and suggesting "new dimensions" in these fields. Each chapter is motivated by a deep admiration for Millard Erickson and is offered as a tribute and a gift to him.

Today, as I pen the words for the preface to this volume, Millard is celebrating his sixty-fifth birthday. Millard, we thank God for you. The faithful stewardship of your gifts and abilities has shaped a generation of theologians, ministers and students. The other contributors join me in thanking you for your valuable investment in our lives and for your contribution to the church of Jesus Christ. May God's gracious blessings and enablement continue to be yours. Happy birthday!

Chapter 1

Tribute to
Millard J. Erickson

William Hordern

································

IT IS A PLEASURE FOR ME TO WRITE A TRIBUTE TO MILLARD ERICKSON. I first came to know Millard when he entered the doctoral program at Northwestern University, where I was his adviser. I was a professor of systematic theology at Garrett Theological Seminary, which served as the graduate school of religion for Northwestern University. Garrett is a Methodist seminary, but its relation to Northwestern encourages it to have an ecumenical faculty, which explains why I, a Lutheran, was there.

Millard was a serious young man, but he had a good sense of humor. He was an excellent student and worked diligently at his studies. Even at that early period in his career, he showed promise of the fine theologian he would become. He had the ability to organize his materials, and he had a lively way of expressing himself, both on paper and in class discussion. He had an analytical mind that got to the heart of a subject, and he was always fair to positions with which he disagreed. All of these qualities have been evident in his later writings.

Millard's decision to come to Northwestern to pursue his doctorate tells much about him. He came from a background of conservative theology and remained firmly dedicated to it. But Garrett was a liberal seminary. My theology, rooted in Luther and Karl Barth, was considered by most of my colleagues to be unduly conservative. The fact that Millard came to Garrett revealed that he was determined to test his own theology in a context that was not congenial to it. He was open to learn from others, but he never tried to hide his own convictions.

I recall the oral defense of his doctoral thesis. The examining committee included professors from both Garrett and Northwestern. One of the Northwestern professors was a philosopher who had little patience with conservative theology. All too often in such a situation, the student attempts to say what the examining professors want to hear. But Millard did not tone down his convictions to please the philosopher. When Millard left the interview and the professors were deciding his fate, the philosopher shook his head and said, "I do not see how anyone can believe what he does." But he voted to pass Millard because he had to admire his courage and his capable defense of his position.

Millard's later writings illustrate the qualities that he displayed in his graduate studies. He has always demonstrated a willingness to learn from other positions even as he firmly expresses his own convictions.

These qualities were displayed in his first book, *The New Evangelical Theology*. He noted that the two sides in the bitter fundamentalist-liberal controversy withdrew from each other in the early twentieth century. The new evangelical theology arose as scholars who emerged from the fundamentalist background determined to enter into a new dialogue with liberals and with neo-orthodox who had broken away from liberalism. The new evangelicals recognized that they had to engage the other positions if a dialogue were to exist. Unfortunately, after J. G. Machen, few fundamentalists produced work that seemed worthy of scholarly discussion.

Between 1946 and 1948 there was an outburst of literary production from the new evangelicals. Scholars like Carl Henry and Harold Ockenga expressed the view that fundamentalism needed to undergo a change. They did not abandon the essential features of fundamentalism, but they did see a need for a new defense of their position. In the years following, an impressive group of scholars, including Bernard Ramm, Edward Carnell, Vernon Grounds and the evangelist Billy Graham, contributed to the growth of the new evangelical theology. By 1968, when Millard's book appeared, he saw a need for someone to analyze the new movement.

As his first book makes clear, Millard was not the pioneer of the movement. In a sense he belonged to its second generation and began the task of analyzing and evaluating it. This became his central concern and culminated in his three-volume systematic theology, *Christian Theology*.

The comment has often been made that the writing of systematic theologies disappeared after the time of scholars such as Barth, Brunner and Tillich. Most theologians contented themselves with writing books on particular aspects of theology without trying to produce a complete systematics. Millard went against this trend and produced for the new evangelical theology a definitive systematic theology. His work did for the new evangelical theology what Karl Barth's *Church Dogmatics* did for neo-orthodoxy.

Millard's methodology in his *Christian Theology* is well illustrated in his treatment of the doctrine of scriptural inerrancy.[1] He admits that there has been a heated debate about this doctrine, although it has always been a central concern to conservative theologians. He then describes seven different views of inerrancy, ranging from those who hold to absolute inerrancy to those who argue that inerrancy is an irrelevant issue. Each position is described succinctly and fairly.

Millard then sets the concept in historical perspective, showing that the trustworthiness of the Bible was a concern from Augustine through Luther, although the term *inerrancy,* as well as the concept, has been developed in recent times.

The doctrine of inerrancy faces problems of apparent contradictions in Scripture. Millard looks at five different positions on how to handle such problems. Again each position is treated fairly.

Finally Millard presents his own position on inerrancy. He sums it up with "In particular, inerrancy should not be understood to mean that the maximum amount of specificity will always be present. Rather our doctrine of inerrancy maintains merely that whatever statements the Bible affirms are fully truthful when they are correctly interpreted in terms of their meaning in their cultural setting and the purpose for which they were written."[2]

Millard's methodology of presenting fairly major alternatives to his own position has made his work valuable not only for new evangelicals but also for a wider audience. For example, his *Christian Theology* was used as a text for systematic theology in the Lutheran Theological Seminary in Saskatoon by a professor while I was there.

As already noted, Millard sees new evangelical theology as an attempt to defend the historic faith in a dialogue with other positions. His *Christian Theology* has done much to advance this. Personally, I would like to see this dialogue advanced in another area. The new evangelical theology could profit, I believe, from a dialogue with what I call the "old evangelical theology."

We Lutherans are much concerned with the term *evangelical.* The largest Lutheran church in the United States is the Evangelical Lutheran Church in America and the largest one in Canada is the Evangelical Lutheran Church in Canada. I was on the merger commission that brought this Canadian church into being from two smaller Lutheran churches. The commission members agreed that we had to keep the term *evangelical* in our name. It was suggested that given the wide use of the term to describe churches that are somewhat different from us, it might be confusing for us to use the term. However, we decided that this was not a sufficient reason to give up a term that we had used through the centuries.

For Lutherans, the term *evangelical* refers to our confession that the center of

---

[1]Millard J. Erickson, *Christian Theology* (Grand Rapids: Baker, 1983), 1:221-40.
[2]Ibid., p. 238.

Christian faith is justification by grace alone through faith alone. We interpret all other doctrines in light of our understanding of justification. This brings us into some significant differences with the new evangelical theology, although there are many areas of agreement as well.

Given their mutual regard for the term *evangelical,* it is surprising that Lutherans and the new evangelicals have not undertaken more dialogue. This is partly due to the fact that both the older fundamentalism and the later new evangelical theology have been influenced primarily by the Calvinist tradition. In his three volumes of *Christian Theology,* Millard refers to Luther and Lutheranism nineteen times. He refers to Calvin and Calvinism forty-six times. Such statistics do not prove anything but do indicate a trend in new evangelical theology. The lack of dialogue between the two groups may also stem from Lutherans' satisfaction with our interpretation of evangelicalism. This sense of satisfaction leads us to feel that we do not have much to learn from anyone else. In any event, I do hope for more dialogue between the old and the new evangelicalism.

To my Lutheran eyes, Millard's sections on salvation in his *Christian Theology* seem to adhere to the theme of grace alone through faith alone. This would serve as a good starting point for a dialogue. Rightly or wrongly, it often appears to Lutherans that the new evangelicalism does not believe in salvation "by grace alone" but in salvation by "grace and . . ." Starting from Millard's position, the two groups might find a new harmony.

After Millard graduated from Northwestern, I did not see him for many years, although we maintained some correspondence and he sent me copies of his writings. After I retired, I served with Millard on an accrediting committee of the American Association of Theological Schools. It was a joy to meet with him again. I was impressed with the graciousness and practicality that he demonstrated while serving on the committee.

Millard later invited me to lecture at Bethel Theological Seminary, where I saw another side of him. He was obviously a good administrator and had a positive, easygoing relationship with both students and faculty. Theologians are often accused of being impractical, so it was good to see that Millard administered as well as he theologized.

It always gives a teacher joy to see a former student become a noted teacher and thinker. Millard has more than fulfilled the promise that I saw in him as a student. In such a situation a teacher is always tempted by pride to take some credit for the student's achievements. However, such pride is misplaced. Since we teachers do not want to be held responsible for students who fail dismally, we cannot take credit for those who succeed. Millard would have succeeded no matter who his teachers had been. I am only happy to think that I may have contributed some small stimulus and encouragement to his intellectual journey in the faith.

Chapter 2

Millard J. Erickson: Theologian for the Church

David S. Dockery

·······································

THE EVANGELICAL MOVEMENT IN AMERICA DURING THE PAST FOUR decades has basically been a transdenominational movement. For example, Billy Graham and Carl Henry are more quickly perceived as evangelicals than as Baptists. The same can be said for many others. Some have even questioned if it is possible to be both an evangelical and a loyal denominationalist. Millard Erickson, by contrast, not only has become the most outstanding writing theologian in the evangelical world but has remained a loyal Baptist. Erickson's heritage is firmly rooted in Baptist life. This heritage, inherited from his Swedish grandparents, combined with his early attraction to "new evangelical" theologians like Bernard Ramm, Carl F. H. Henry and particularly E. J. Carnell, has resulted in a new model for Baptist and evangelical theologians.

Millard J. Erickson was born on June 24, 1932, the youngest of four children in Stanchfield, Minnesota, near Minneapolis. His father had come to the United States with many relatives, including his grandparents, when he was only six months old. His mother was born in this country only months after her parents arrived from Sweden.

Erickson was raised on the family farm, which produced enough food to feed the family of six, but not much more. A windmill provided running water, and the family had to heat water on the kitchen stove for their weekly baths. Erickson studied by the light of a kerosene lamp until he was in high school, when electricity finally came to the farm.

Erickson, a well-rounded student who participated in football, basketball, baseball and music programs, demonstrated superior academic abilities throughout his life. Beginning his education in a one-room school a mile-and-a-half walk away, young Erickson was double promoted in the second grade. He graduated valedictorian from Braham High School in 1949.

His family heritage is firmly rooted in the Baptist tradition. His grandfather and grandmother became active in a Baptist church quickly after settling in Minnesota. For five years his grandfather served as lay pastor of a Baptist church they organized in their house. In this church, as a young boy, in an unemotional experience, Erickson responded to the gospel message and was converted.

After high school Erickson enrolled at Bethel College. He originally planned to attend the University of Minnesota, but through providential circumstances and his pastor's encouragement, he decided to attend a Christian college. That summer his pastor received a concussion while participating in a church softball game and was unable to preach at the Wednesday-evening service. Millard filled the pulpit. The pastor was so impressed that he encouraged him to consider a commitment to full-time vocational Christian service. "I wondered at the time," Erickson relates, "if he had recovered from the blow on his head. But God planted the idea in my mind, and I could not ignore it." During his first year at Bethel College, following an important chapel message, Erickson knew God was calling him to preach. Though he was shy and afraid to speak in public, he privately responded later that weekend. That Saturday he told the Lord that he would serve him as a minister but that God would have to supply what was lacking.

Erickson spent two years at Bethel and then transferred to the University of Minnesota in order to gain a wider exposure to secular thought. He majored in philosophy and minored in psychology and sociology. Erickson graduated Phi Beta Kappa in 1953. He then returned to the Bethel campus to enroll at Bethel Seminary before transferring to Northern Baptist Theological Seminary in Chicago. While at Bethel Seminary, he met Virginia Nepstad, who was then a student at Bethel College. They were married on August 20, 1955. The Ericksons have been blessed with three daughters: Kathryn Sue, born February 23, 1959; Sandra Lynne, born May 1, 1962; and Sharon Ruth, born September 20, 1964.

Having encountered Bernard Ramm at Bethel Seminary, Erickson became attracted to the works of the new evangelical theologians, including Carl Henry and E. J. Carnell. He credits Carnell's works with shaping his theology and approach to Christian apologetics during this formative period in his life. His interest in these new evangelical theologians would continue to develop and became the subject of his Ph.D. dissertation as well as his first major publication.

After graduating from Northern, Erickson was invited to become pastor of the Fairfield Avenue Baptist Church, a multiracial congregation in Chicago. On March 21, 1957, he was ordained to the ministry by this church. Erickson's lifelong desire to make theology both biblical and relevant to contemporary forms of thinking and life experience grew out of this important pastoral experience. Here he was challenged to relate the Christian message to both the urban intellectual and the blue-collar worker. Erickson learned much from the correlation methodology of Paul Tillich while seeking to develop his own understanding of the theological task.

On completing his studies at Northern in 1956, he enrolled in a master's degree program in philosophy at the University of Chicago, graduating in 1958. Determining that he was more interested in theology than philosophy, Erickson decided not to pursue doctoral studies at the University of Chicago. Instead he enrolled in a joint Ph.D. program offered by Garrett Theological Seminary and Northwestern University, under the supervision of William Hordern.

After completing his coursework at Northwestern, Millard and Virginia, with daughter Kathryn, returned to Minneapolis, where he accepted the pastorate of the Olivet Baptist Church. There he completed examinations for the Ph.D. and in 1963 finished writing his dissertation on the theology of Henry, Ramm and Carnell. Though not without a genuine struggle and some misgivings about leaving the pastorate and a church he loved, Erickson, in 1964, accepted a position at Wheaton College as assistant professor of Bible and apologetics. He was elected to the department chair in 1967.

Erickson revised his dissertation and published it as *The New Evangelical Theology* (Westwood, N.J.: Fleming H. Revell, 1968). In 1969 he accepted a position teaching theology at Bethel Seminary, also serving as executive vice president and dean as well as professor of theology. Currently he serves the church as visiting professor and lecturer in various schools in North America and around the world. In addition to numerous articles, book chapters and reviews, Erickson has authored or edited numerous books, including the impressive three-volume *Christian Theology* (Grand Rapids: Baker, 1983-1985), which has become the standard systematic theology text in many Baptist and evangelical seminaries. Erickson also edited a trilogy, *Readings in Christian Theology* (Grand Rapids: Baker, 1973-1979), and has authored over a dozen volumes that are identified and discussed in chapter twenty-seven.

Erickson's three-volume theology has placed him among the leading theologians of the day. Volume one is dedicated to his first theology teacher, Bernard Ramm. The second volume is dedicated to his doctoral supervisor, William Hordern, who wrote a personal tribute for it. Volume three is dedicated to his postdoctoral mentor, the eminent German theologian Wolfhart Pannenberg of the University of Munich, with whom Erickson spent a sabbatical year in 1976 and who contributed an engaging chapter in this volume on theology and culture. The *Christian Theology* volumes developed out of what Erickson perceived to be an intense need for an up-to-date textbook in systematic theology. The project began June 1, 1982, when he started writing a chapter per week. He completed volume one by the end of November. Erickson finished the rough draft of volume two over the next ten weeks as he taught the subject matter during the winter quarter. He soon began volume three and completed it during his sabbatical that year. He used the following year to revise volumes two and three. Erickson estimates that in addition to his eighteen years of teaching, he invested over four thousand hours in what his family calls "the book."

Erickson's many theological interests are evidenced in his ongoing projects focusing on Third World theology, process theology, black theology, contemporary linguistic analysis, missions, postmodernism and postconservatism. Yet beyond this, he is primarily a churchman. He continues to serve interim pastorates, having served almost fifty churches in the past thirty years. He is in demand as a speaker and serves on important denominational committees and boards. For almost two decades Erickson has been active in Baptist work outside of his own denomination, serving on positions with the Baptist World Alliance and lecturing at various Baptist colleges, universities and seminaries.

This kind of commitment has made Millard Erickson one of the most respected Baptist and evangelical theologians of our time. His theological works will no doubt be used to shape the thought and life of the next generation of Baptist and evangelical church leaders.[1]

Shapers of Erickson's Theology

As indicated in the previous section, Erickson's theological thought and method have been shaped by his Baptist beliefs and practice. Beyond that, he has been influenced by his commitment to the church, his apologetic orientation adopted from Ramm and Carnell, and his desire to relate theology to contemporary forms of thinking, so as to be both biblical and relevant. Erickson is not a disciple, in the technical sense, of any particular theologian or theological school. His two years as a student at the University of Minnesota forced him to interact with contemporary philosophical currents. By his own admission, it was the writings of E. J. Carnell, particularly *An Introduction to Christian Apologetics* (Grand Rapids: Eerdmans, 1948), that shaped the apologetic orientation of his theology. It is important to note that Carnell, Ramm and Henry, the formative thinkers of the new evangelical theology, were all Baptists. However, they were evangelicals first and Baptists second. Erickson's Baptist heritage and commitments have both directly and indirectly taken a higher priority in his life and in his theology.[2]

While acknowledging his debt to Baptist theologians like John Gill, E. Y. Mullins and particularly A. H. Strong, Erickson's theology is not distinctively

---

[1]Much of the material in this section is drawn from "Millard J. Erickson," in *Baptist Theologians* (Nashville: Broadman, 1990), pp. 640-54, and personal conversations with Erickson.

[2]Erickson, conversation with author, November 1988. Also see Warren C. Young's observation in his "Review of *The New Evangelical Theology*," *Foundations* 12 (January 1969): 95-96.

Baptist. Erickson claims that his theology is intended to be broad in hopes of influencing an audience beyond the world of Baptists. His work is Baptist in its shape in the sense that it grows out of his church experience and commitments. In this he is not unlike theological giants Karl Barth and Paul Tillich. They were not Baptists, but their understanding of the theological task was largely influenced by their pastoral arenas. Erickson points out that Lutherans have Martin Luther, Presbyterians have John Calvin, and Methodists have John Wesley. But Baptists have "no one shining light" and in some sense do theology from "an ideological ghetto." Erickson believes that a theology emphasizing biblical themes with a corresponding commitment to the church will produce a theology emphasizing Baptist themes.

Erickson's theology has also been shaped by his mentors. From Hordern he received a concern for clarity of thought as well as a writing style worthy of emulation. From Pannenberg he learned to grapple fairly with differing positions. Erickson has only the highest praise for his teachers and claims that it is a demanding exercise to interact with Pannenberg, who "is in a league by himself." But from the beginning his work has been largely shaped by the influence of the new evangelicals. The rest of this chapter focuses on Erickson's major contributions to Baptist and evangelical theology, which are his concern for theological method and his articulation of the doctrine of Scripture.

Erickson's Context

Out of the bitter fundamentalist-modernist controversy of twentieth-century America emerged a theological movement known as the new evangelicalism. With roots in the Reformation, evangelicalism reached its zenith in the nineteenth century. In the early twentieth century, however, evangelicalism went into temporary eclipse. The success of the previous century had brought a material prosperity and a loyalty to the nation that was confused with Christian commitment. An overemphasis on individualism also hampered evangelicalism's advancement. The flood of new ideas such as Darwinian evolution, German higher criticism, Freudian psychology, Marxist socialism and an overarching naturalism undermined confidence in the truthfulness of the Bible and the reality of the supernatural. These ideological changes, resulting in the fundamentalist-modernist controversies, coupled with the two world wars, brought new challenges as well as new opportunities. Out of this void developed the *new evangelicalism,* a term coined by Carl Henry and popularized by Harold J. Ockenga in 1947.[3]

Erickson recognized that the new evangelical theology movement took issue

---

[3] See Millard J. Erickson, *The New Evangelical Theology* (Westwood, N.J.: Revell, 1968). The popular claim that Ockenga coined the term *new evangelicalism* is disputed by Henry. Henry wrote three articles related to the new evangelicalism that were published in *Christian Life and Times* in early 1948. See George Marsden, *After Fundamentalism* (Grand Rapids: Eerdmans, 1987), pp. 3, 167.

with the older fundamentalism.[4] The new evangelicalism created a third stream in American Protestantism that ran between simplistic fundamentalism and the sophisticated faith espoused by the majority of the nation's best-known theologians and denominational leaders. The new evangelical theologians argued that fundamentalism was wrong-headed in its suspicion of all who differed from them in the least detail. Fundamentalist strategy promoted a strict separatism that sought to produce a totally pure church, both locally and denominationally. Fundamentalism produced empty results. It did not turn back the tide of liberalism, it did not have an impact on the thought worlds of the day, and it did not deal with the social problems of its time.[5] E. J. Carnell insisted that fundamentalism was orthodoxy gone cultic because its convictions were not linked with the historic creeds of the church. It was more of a mentality than a movement.[6] Carl Henry contended that fundamentalists did not present Christianity as an overarching worldview but concentrated instead on only part of the message. Fundamentalists were otherworldly, anti-intellectual and unwilling to bring their faith to bear on culture and social life.[7]

The new movement emphasized several important themes such as social ethics, apologetical theology, evangelism, education and Christian unity. Erickson noted that the movement sought unity on the basis of biblical doctrine. One of the goals of the movement was to restate the faith in a way that would command intellectual respect and heal the schism between the theological right and the theological left, at least to point to where the two sides could pursue meaningful theological dialogue. These themes and emphases have characterized Erickson's own theological pilgrimage as evidenced in *Christian Theology*. Erickson summarizes these evangelical themes and emphases as

> a set of concerns and attitudes related to the needs of the present day, in continuity with vital orthodoxy of the past, and generally distinguishable from later fundamentalism, coupled with an orthodox Christology and an orthodox view of the scriptures.[8]

---

[4]Ibid., pp. 31-45. R. Hammer remarks that American evangelicalism can be identified with British fundamentalism, pointing out the distinctions between the American and British scenes. See Hammer, "Review of *The New Evangelical Theology*," *Expository Times* 81 (January 1970): 109-10.

[5]Erickson, *New Evangelical Theology*, pp. 22-30.

[6]See E. J. Carnell, *The Case for Orthodox Theology* (Philadelphia: Westminster, 1959).

[7]See Carl F. H. Henry, *The Uneasy Conscience of Modern Fundamentalism* (Grand Rapids: Eerdmans, 1947).

[8]As summarized in a review of Erickson's work by Richard N. Longenecker, "A Review of *The New Evangelical Theology*," *Christianity Today* 13, no. 1 (October 1968): 19-20. All reviews of Erickson's early work were quite positive. The issues that were raised tended to focus on the definition of the term *evangelicalism*. In addition to Longenecker, see Charles C. Ryrie, "A Review of *The New Evangelical Theology*," *Bibliotheca Sacra* 126 (January 1969): 81-82, and Ralph Martin, "A Review of *The New Evangelical Theology*," *Evangelical Quarterly* 42 (January 1970): 57-58. Also see Millard J. Erickson, *The Evangelical Mind and Heart* (Grand Rapids: Baker, 1993).

The Definition and Method of Theology

Erickson suggests that "the study or science of God" is a good basic definition of theology.[9] Beyond that, it can be said that theology is "that discipline which strives to give a coherent statement of the doctrines of the Christian faith, based primarily upon the Scriptures, placed in the context of culture in general, worded in a contemporary idiom, and related to issues of life."[10] Theology is biblical, systematic, related to the issues of general culture and learning, contemporary and practical.

One of Erickson's outstanding contributions to the evangelical and Baptist worlds is his development of theological method. His process of doing theology is thoroughly grounded in Scripture, but it moves far beyond a simple "proof-texting" approach to theology. His theology is contextually relevant while being thoroughly biblical. His methodology attempts to bridge the gap between then and now, a concern that developed in his pastoral days in Chicago.

Erickson acknowledges that theology is an art as well as a science and cannot follow a rigid structure. Yet procedures can be suggested. For Erickson, biblical theology is developed before systematic theology, making the sequence exegesis, biblical theology, systematic theology. Erickson recognizes nine steps in the process of doing theology.

Collection of biblical materials. This initial step involves not only gathering all relevant biblical passages on the doctrine being investigated but also identifying personal presuppositions in interpreting these materials. Erickson notes the importance of knowing the presuppositions held by writers of reference books. Narrative texts as well as the didactic passages of Scripture should be used.

Unification of the biblical materials. This means taking into account the whole of Scripture when trying to find a common theme. Avoid forced harmonizations.

Analysis of the meaning of biblical teachings. After attempting to find the common teaching on a subject, these texts must be analyzed by the question, What is really meant by this? The theologian must seek to put the meaning of the Bible into clear and understandable language.

Examination of historical treatments. A recognition that we are not the first generation to examine a particular teaching will provide insight beyond our own viewpoint. It reminds us that we stand on the shoulders of those who have gone before us and helps us to ask the right questions of the text. Perhaps as helpful as anything, this step, suggests Erickson, calls for a measure of humility in presenting our conclusions.

Identification of the essence of the doctrine. Many biblical truths are bound up within the culture and context in which they are communicated. This does not mean

---

[9]Millard J. Erickson, *Christian Theology,* 3 vols. (Grand Rapids: Baker, 1983-1985), 1:21.
[10]Ibid.

dismissing the "cultural baggage." It does mean, for example, separating what Paul said to the Philippians as first-century Christians living in Philippi from what he said to them as Christians. Similarly, the sacrificial system in Leviticus is not the essence of the doctrine of the atonement. What is the essence is the concept that there must be vicarious sacrifice for the sins of humankind.

Illumination from sources beyond the Bible. The point of this step is the recognition that God has revealed himself through general revelation as well as special revelation. The Bible is the primary source for Christian theology, but it is not the only source. Erickson, consistent with his new evangelical heritage, suggests that experience and the sciences may add clarity where the Bible sheds little or no light. It is important to recognize that general (universal) revelation and special (particular) revelation are ultimately in harmony when they are properly interpreted.

Contemporary expression of the doctrine. The theologian must be mindful of not only the biblical message but also the contemporary context or situation in which the doctrine is being communicated. Both horizons must be observed. Any theology that is designed only to meet the moods or issues of a particular time will quickly find itself outdated. Truths that can remain faithful to the biblical message and can communicate across different contexts, cultures or traditions will be enduring.

Development of a central interpretive motif. Like all coherent theologians, Erickson maintains that a particular theme or perspective should be formulated so that the various doctrines can be seen in relationship with one another. He warns that a central motif should never be used where it is not relevant, nor should eisegesis be used to make biblical teaching fit a particular system.

Stratification of the topics. The final step in Erickson's method is an attempt to distinguish major topics from subtopics. The doctrine of the Second Coming is a major topic, while the question of the timing of the rapture is less important and certainly less emphasized in Scripture. An outline can help show the relationship of the importance of one teaching to another and can help arrange the topics on the basis of their relative importance.[11]

Erickson develops his theology around the central motif of the "magnificence of God."[12] This motif imparts a sense of coherence to his system. Magnificence is understood as encompassing what has traditionally been associated with the expression *the glory of God,* but without the connotation of self-centeredness sometimes carried by that expression.

Erickson is not unaware of the problems involved in contextualizing the theological message, in developing a central motif or communicating these matters through religious language. While wrestling with these matters, he opts for restating

---

[11]Ibid., 1:66-79.
[12]Ibid., 1:78.

the classical themes of systematic theology without becoming overly creative so as not to overstep biblical revelation. He understands the difference between doctrine and theology and recognizes the necessity of permanence. His method lends healthy balance to his systematic approach.

Revelation

Consistent with his new evangelical heritage, Erickson presents God's universal and particular revelation as being in complete harmony with one another. There can never be any conflict between the Bible, properly interpreted, and natural knowledge, correctly construed. If all the data were available, Erickson maintains, a perfect harmony would emerge. This implies that it is possible to exhibit the truthfulness of the biblical view by appealing to evidence drawn from the created space-time universe.

This conception of revelation also produces a positive attitude toward culture. Thus his theology is culture affirming rather than culture rejecting. There is therefore a possibility of some knowledge of divine truth outside of special revelation. Erickson contends that God's universal or general revelation should be considered a supplement to, not a substitute for, special revelation.[13]

Because of God's universal revelation, Erickson believes God is just in condemning those who have never heard the gospel in the full and formal sense. He amplifies:

No one is completely without opportunity. All have known God; if they have not effectually perceived him, it is because they have suppressed the truth. Thus all are responsible. This increases the motivation of missionary endeavor, for no one is innocent. All need to believe in God's offer of grace, and the message needs to be taken to them.[14]

Erickson distinguishes between universal and particular revelation. Universal revelation "is God's communication of himself to all persons at all times and in all places."[15] God's particular revelation involves "God's manifestation of himself to particular persons at definite times and places, enabling those persons to enter into a redemptive relationship with him."[16] Particular revelation is available now only through sacred Scripture. Universal revelation is inferior to special revelation, in both the clarity of the treatment and the range of subjects considered. The insufficiency of the universal revelation requires special revelation. Because special revelation builds on the universal, special revelation requires universal revelation as well. Not only does Erickson propose the complementary nature of special and general revelation, but he also opts for a both/and answer to the

---

[13]Ibid., 1:173.
[14]Ibid., 1:174.
[15]Ibid., 1:153.
[16]Ibid., 1:153-54, 175.

question of personal or propositional revelation.[17]

Scripture

Since revelation includes propositional truths, it is of such a nature that it can be preserved, written down or inscripturated. Revelation is God's communication to humankind of the truth that they need to know in order to relate properly to God. Since God does not repeat his revelation for each person, there has to be some way to preserve it. Erickson differentiates between revelation and inspiration, noting that revelation is the communication of divine truth from God to humanity. Inspiration relates more to the relaying of that truth from the first recipients of it to other persons, whether then or later. "Thus, revelation might be thought of as a vertical action, and inspiration as a horizontal matter."[18]

Erickson wrestles with the issues involved in formulating a theory of inspiration, even raising the question of the legitimacy of doing so. He interacts with various theories and methods of formulating a theory of inspiration and concludes that it is possible to formulate a model of inspiration. To do so, he suggests that the church should construct its view of the inspiration of the Bible by emphasizing the teachings of the Bible regarding its own inspiration, while giving an important but secondary place to the phenomena of Scripture.[19]

Erickson maintains that inspiration involved God's directing the writers' thoughts so that they were precisely the thoughts that God wished expressed. At times these thoughts were quite specific, and at other times they were more general. When they were more general, God wanted that particular degree of specificity recorded and no more. Erickson contends that this specificity can extend to the choice of words but does not necessarily become dictation.

Erickson concludes that God's Word is inspired, thus preserving God's special revelation. Inspiration is God's way of assuring that the Word will not be lost but will be conveyed to God's people in all ages. The result of inspiration assures God's people that the Bible is truthful, trustworthy and reliable. Likewise, the Bible has the right to command belief or action, but this should not be equated with a forced compliance. The Bible is authoritative because it is the dependable Word of God.[20]

The dependability of God's Word makes the Bible fully truthful in all its teaching. The theological term for this is *inerrancy*. Erickson defines inerrancy as follows: "The Bible, when correctly interpreted in light of the level to which culture and the means of communication had developed at the time it was written, and in

---

[17]Ibid., 1:191-96.
[18]Ibid., 1:200.
[19]Ibid., 1:207-10.
[20]Ibid., 1:242-44.

view of the purposes for which it was given, is fully truthful in all that it affirms."[21] Erickson contends that inerrancy, while not directly taught in Scripture, is the proper implication of the Bible's own teaching about itself. He claims that while inerrancy can be misunderstood, it must be maintained. He argues for its importance theologically, historically and epistemologically.

Erickson carefully avoids building his case on the "domino theory." He does not argue that one error would invalidate all other biblical teachings. But he points out that the presence of errors in Scripture would make it more difficult to show why we should believe its teachings. His view seeks to include and account for the phenomenological language of Scripture. Erickson suggests that the Christian would be unwise to give up the affirmation that "whatever the Bible teaches is true."

God, Creation and Providence

Erickson approaches the doctrine of God from the perspectives of "what God is like"[22] and "what God does."[23] These discussions are investigated from an orthodox, trinitarian perspective. He chooses God's majesty as the central focus when dealing with the attributes of God. He suggests that this, rather than glory, is a more appropriate way of describing God's greatness. After skillfully evaluating the various ways of describing God's attributes, he opts for the categories of greatness and goodness.[24] His conclusions on these matters are in line with classical formulations, though they are nuanced to account for the biblical data and the challenges of process theology.[25]

Erickson deals with "God's plan" (traditionally defined as decrees) from a moderately Calvinistic model. He valiantly seeks to correlate human freedom and sovereignty. This balance and consistency are generally reflected in his doctrine of salvation as well.

In line with Ramm and Carnell, *Christian Theology*, in volumes one and two, adopts a progressive creationist position. Erickson believes that the Hebrew word for "day" *(yôm)* can mean a long period of time. Rejecting the flood theory on the one hand and macroevolutionism on the other, Erickson strongly defends the historicity of the biblical Adam and Eve.[26]

---

[21]Ibid., 1:233-34.
[22]Ibid., 1:263.
[23]Ibid., 1:345. See Millard J. Erickson, *God in Three Persons: A Contemporary Interpretation of the Trinity* (Grand Rapids: Baker, 1995).
[24]Erickson, *Christian Theology*, 1:266-67.
[25]Ibid., 1:267-300. For example, "God and time" (274-75), "constancy" (278-81), "faithfulness" (291-92), "love" (292-94), "love and justice" (297-98).
[26]Ibid., 2:473-93.

Humanity and Sin

Like Luther and Calvin, Erickson primarily opts for a structural and substantive understanding of the image of God, including relational and functional aspects, while tentatively suggesting a "conditional unity" as the best way to describe the constitutional nature of humankind.[27] In some of his most creative work, he devotes a chapter to the universality of humanity, extending to all races, both sexes, all economic classes, all ages, as well as to the unborn and unmarried. Additionally, he fully treats the social dimensions of sin.[28]

Erickson defines sin as "any lack of conformity, active or passive, to the moral law." Sin is seen in terms of its negative effects on the sinner and in terms of the sinner's relation to others, in addition to the separation of one's relationship with God. The essence of sin is a failure to let God be God. Regarding the transmission of sin, he opts for a conditional imputation calibrated according to an individual level of responsibility and maturity. He says that "human beings, while inheriting both a corrupted nature and guilt, first become guilty when they accept or are proved of their corrupted nature."[29]

Perhaps motivated by Baptist and pietistic concerns, Erickson maintains that salvation requires a conscious and voluntary decision on our part. While suggesting that infants and children begin life with the corrupted nature and guilt that are the consequences of sin, he nevertheless says that our Lord does not regard children as basically sinful and guilty. Thus the act that ends childish innocence is every bit as voluntary as the act of accepting the offer of salvation at the age of moral responsibility.

Christ, the Spirit and Salvation

Erickson's Christology reflects a thoroughgoing commitment to Chalcedon with attempts to translate the meaning of Chalcedon for contemporary hearers.[30] Although obviously aware of issues surrounding the contemporary and critical discussion, Erickson depends on the treatment of Jesus' self-consciousness in John's Gospel for developing his Christology.[31] The christological titles are thoughtfully treated, but their significance is not fully developed.

The work of Christ is treated around the themes of revealer, reconciler and ruler.[32]

---

[27]Ibid., 2:536-59.

[28]Ibid., 2:641-58.

[29]Ibid., 2:639.

[30]Ibid., 2:734-38.

[31]Millard J. Erickson, "Christology from Above and Christology from Below: A Study of Contrasting Methodologies," in *Perspectives on Evangelical Theology*, ed. Kenneth S. Kantzer and Stanley N. Gundry (Grand Rapids: Baker, 1979), pp. 43-55.

[32]Erickson, *Christian Theology*, 2:762-69. These are fully developed in *The Word Became Flesh* (Grand Rapids: Baker, 1991).

The various models of the atonement receive comprehensive attention, but primacy is given to the penal substitution model. Following his moderate Calvinism, he rejects particular redemption in favor of a universal atonement with limited efficacy. The decision accounts for a larger segment of the biblical witness with less distortion than does the theory of particular redemption. For Erickson, among the most impressive of the biblical statements in this regard is 1 Timothy 4:10, which affirms that the living God "is the Savior of all people, especially of those who believe" (NRSV). Apparently the Savior has done something for all persons, though it is less in degree than what he has done for those who believe.[33]

In one of his more controversial conclusions, Erickson suggests that Jesus' resurrected body did not undergo complete transformation until his ascension. This statement does not detract from the resurrection but somehow gives significance to the ascension. In a cautious and hypothetical manner, Erickson attempts to deal with the biblical teaching (Lk 24; Jn 20; 1 Cor 15) to show that initial resurrection is somehow distinct from the glorified body of the ascended and exalted Lord. This results in understanding the forty days as a time similar to a resuscitation, like that of Lazarus. Perhaps Jesus ate with the disciples out of a need to eat rather than as a concession while with them. Erickson suggests this as a hypothesis only and cautiously concludes:

> But just as the virgin birth should not be thought of as essentially a biological matter, neither should the resurrection be conceived of as primarily a physical fact. It was the triumph of Jesus over sin and death and all of the attendant ramifications. It was the fundamental step in his exaltation—he was freed from the curse brought on him by his voluntary bearing of the sin of the entire human race.[34]

The work of Christ applied by the Spirit to the believer ultimately brings about the restoration of a proper relationship with God. For Erickson, the Spirit of God initiates the Christian life through regeneration and conversion and continues with empowering, illuminating, reaching, sanctifying and granting spiritual gifts.[35] His conception of salvation follows a moderate Calvinistic *ordo salutis*. Yet he goes against his usual Calvinistic tendencies opting for the temporal priority of conversion to regeneration.[36]

Church and Eschatology
Concerning the organization of the church, Erickson clearly favors congregational

---

[33]Erickson, *Christian Theology,* 2:834-35.
[34]Ibid., 2:777.
[35]Ibid., 3:872-77. Erickson suggests that it is difficult to determine whether the contemporary phenomena are authentic. He decides that charismata are sovereignly given and are not to be sought.
[36]Ibid., 3:932.

polity, but with care, "since the evidence from the New Testament is inconclusive."[37]

His baptistic commitments are quite obvious in his discussion of the church. He sees baptism as a token, an outward testimony or symbol of the inward change that has been effected in the believer. Regarding the mode of baptism, immersion is affirmed, though without dogmatism since he demonstrates openness to other modes.

The Lord's Supper is a time of relationship and communion with Christ. In the celebration the Christian community comes with confidence to meet the risen Christ, for Christ has promised to meet with his people. The sacrament should be thought of "not so much in terms of Christ's presence as in terms of his promise and the potential for a closer relationship with him."[38]

While emphasizing the local church, Erickson strongly affirms the universal church of God. Beyond this, he recognizes the church as only one manifestation of the kingdom. He argues passionately for the unity of the church and rejects fundamentalism's emphasis on separation, which tends to lead to division.[39]

Erickson's eschatology follows the line of a classical historic premillennialism. He is clearly aware of the apocalyptic elements in the biblical teaching concerning heaven and hell and other areas of eschatology, including the messianic banquet of Revelation 19. Yet in no way does he hint at any form of universalism.[40]

Conclusion

Millard Erickson's contribution to the theological enterprise is a significant milestone in Baptist and evangelical thought. His careful work evidences diligent research, critical argumentation and a spiritually sensitive understanding of the biblical materials. His theology is of immense importance, pervaded with a coherent and centralizing motif.

Erickson's theology is faithful to his Baptist and evangelical heritage. It is both orthodox and contemporary, yet it is not faddish or overly innovative. Generally, on every major issue Erickson's theological construction can be considered biblical and

---

[37]Ibid., 3:1084.

[38]Ibid., 3:1123.

[39]Ibid., 3:1130-47. Also see Millard J. Erickson, "Separation," in *Evangelical Dictionary of Theology*, ed. W. A. Elwell (Grand Rapids: Baker, 1984), pp. 1002-3.

[40]Erickson, *Christian Theology*, 3:1206-41. Also see his extensive discussion of these matters in his *Contemporary Options in Eschatology: A Study of the Millennium* (Grand Rapids: Baker, 1977). This book grew out of a request made by Bethel Seminary students for a course that would examine thoroughly and objectively eschatological options for today's churches. For evaluations of and disagreements with Erickson's conclusions, see reviews by Anthony Hoekema, "A Review of *Contemporary Options*," *Calvin Theological Journal* 13 (1978): 208-11; D. K. Erlandson, "A Review of *Contemporary Options*," *Christian Scholar's Review* 9 (1979): 186-87; R. A. Coughenous, "A Review of *Contemporary Options*," *Reformed Review* 32 (1979): 181-82; John Walvoord, "A Review of *Contemporary Options*," *Bibliotheca Sacra* 137 (1980): 83-85.

classical. The true strength of his work lies in its overall concern for the church and in his doxological tone.

His most noticeable strengths are his balanced theological method, carefully nuanced view of Scripture and concern to relate orthodoxy to the contemporary issues of life. Also, he demonstrates the importance of coherence in systematic theology, the virtue of theological humility and the tension between timeless and time-bound biblical themes.

He continually reflects openness to various options and evidences a broad understanding of issues in contemporary theology. While his theology is obviously born in a teaching context, it characteristically is irenic, fresh and pastoral.

Erickson's major contributions, as noted, are the creative construction of his theological method and his doctrine of revelation. Overall, his theology is biblical, relevant and practical. He demonstrates openness to contemporary trends while being fully aware of the centuries of theologizing in the Christian church. He has managed to interact meaningfully with modern theological developments while remaining faithful to his Baptist and evangelical heritage.

The strengths of his work are many, and the weaknesses are few. There is room for improvement in Erickson's theology, but to this date there is no finer evangelical theological work available. His work is more encompassing than that of Donald Bloesch and less intimidating than that of Carl Henry, less daring than that of Hendrikus Berkhof and much less defensive than traditional evangelical theologies such as those of Louis Berkhof, J. Oliver Buswell, L. S. Chafer and Charles Hodge. His theology is far more readable than that of A. H. Strong or Helmut Thielicke, more engaging than those of Bruce Demarest and Gordon Lewis, more creative though less encompassing than that of his former colleague James Leo Garrett and more challenging, though less pedagogically friendly, than that of Wayne Grudem. Erickson's work is certainly faithful to Baptist emphasis, yet it demonstrates a greater comprehensiveness than that of W. T. Comer, E. Y. Mullins, Dale Moody or Morris Ashcraft. His work is a first-rate achievement, and the chapters that follow testify to the significance of Millard J. Erickson's contribution to Baptist and evangelical theology.

Chapter 3

New Dimensions in Old Testament Theology

Walter C. Kaiser Jr.

....

IN SOME WAYS THE STATE OF OLD TESTAMENT BIBLICAL THEOLOGY IS grim. This judgment is shared by many who contribute to the discipline, perhaps best exemplified by Gerhard Hasel in 1991: "Old Testament theology today is undeniably in crisis. . . . Though it is centuries old, OT theology is now uncertain of its true identity."[1] In 1970 Brevard S. Childs was the first to announce that the discipline was in a state of crisis.[2] Yet an unusually active publishing record has been maintained in Old Testament theology from around the world during this same period of time—the last quarter of the twentieth century.

All agreed that there was a crisis but could not agree what constituted it. James Barr was convinced that

> the crisis of biblical theology lay not, therefore, in the cessation of its activities, but in its loss of status, its loss of prestige, the loss of its power to persuade. . . . The sort of authority that biblical theology had seemed to wield, its ability to carry the day, its power to coerce opinion, was definitely and irrevocably destroyed.[3]

Clearly, the discipline had to rethink much of what it had taken for granted during its heyday of prominence.

---

[1]Gerhard F. Hasel, *Old Testament Theology: Basic Issues in the Current Debate*, 4th ed. (Grand Rapids: Eerdmans, 1991), p. 1.

[2]Brevard S. Childs, *Biblical Theology in Crisis* (Philadelphia: Westminster, 1970).

[3]James Barr, "The Theological Case Against Biblical Theology," in *Canon, Theology and Old Testament Interpretation: Essays in Honor of Brevard S. Childs*, ed. Gene M. Tucker, David L. Petersen and Robert R. Wilson (Philadelphia: Fortress, 1988), pp. 4-5.

Historical Overview

Somewhere between A.D. 1550 and 1650, the term *biblical theology* came into existence. It did not designate a distinct discipline at first. It meant a doctrinal theology that was biblical in character and opposed to the role tradition had assumed in shaping theology in that period. Thus the term *biblical theology* began on a polemical note as a part of the Reformation.

The first works of biblical theology began to appear in the seventeenth century.[4] It gradually moved away from the service of doctrinal theology (also known as dogmatic theology or systematic theology) to a form closer to the historical narrative in which the Scriptures were cast.

One of the most important practitioners of distinctly biblical theology was Johannes Cocceius (1603-1669), who became the father of "federal"[5] or "covenant theology." While Cocceius was trained in Old Testament and Oriental studies, he taught doctrinal theology toward the close of his career. He organized his theology around the covenants as a record of God's history of redemption as found in Scripture.

It was this shift from a doctrinal to a more historical orientation that gave the impetus for the new discipline of biblical theology. This trend gathered momentum in the eighteenth century, particularly as German pietism revolted against Protestant scholasticism, a theology that was filled with a speculative theology that was abstract and removed from the personal interests and needs of the laity. Their purpose was to set forth the teaching of the Bible free of the strictures that dogmatics had placed on theology.

J. P. Gabler (1753-1826) is traditionally credited with the inception of biblical theology as a separate discipline, especially in his inaugural lecture in 1787 at the University of Altdorf.[6] This was not quite the case, however, as many of the concepts Gabler set forth had already been published prior to his programmatic essay. For example, G. T. Zacharia authored a four-volume work entitled *Biblische Theologie oder Untersuchen des biblischen Grundes der vornehmsten theologischen Lehren* (1771-1775). In this work he distinguished between what belonged to the age in which it was written and what was binding for all time. His emphasis was on the descriptive and historical aspects of the work, but he clearly provided for a normative function as well.

Gabler drew similar distinctions: doctrinal theology had a didactic character to

---

[4]The first is usually said to be by W. J. Christmann, *Teutsche Biblische Theologie*, published in 1629.
[5]The word *federal* comes from the Latin *foedus*, "league, covenant."
[6]The title of his lecture in English translation was "Concerning the Proper Distinction Between Biblical and Dogmatic Theology and the Appropriate Definition of the Respective Goals of Both." See the complete translation in J. Sandy-Wunsch and L. Eldredge, "J. P. Gabler and the Distinction Between Biblical and Dogmatic Theology," *Scottish Journal of Theology* 33 (1980): 133-58.

it; biblical theology set forth what the writers of Scripture taught in the historical frame of reference in which it was written. The biblical theologian had two tasks: (1) the scholar had to learn what the biblical authors thought and taught by means of grammatical and historical exegesis, and (2) these biblical concepts had to be weighted to deduce from them the items that were normative for all times and places and were suitable for use in constructing a dogmatic/doctrinal theology.

This emerging definition enjoyed a brief period of ascendance before bowing to various pressures. As the eighteenth century gave way to the nineteenth century, rationalism overpowered biblical theology, forcing a philosophic grid over it and dominating it. Usually it was the Hegelian dialectic that formed the construct around which the materials of the Old Testament were gathered.

A conservative reaction arose around the middle of the nineteenth century, led chiefly by E. W. Hengstenberg (*Christologie*, 1829-1835). Between the rationalistic and conservative camps were some mediating scholars like G. E. Oehler, H. Ewald and E. Schultz. Especially memorable was the two-volume work by Oehler (published posthumously [1873-1874], as many volumes of Old Testament theology were in those days), which was the first German Old Testament theology to be translated and published in English. His was a history of salvation *(heilsgeschichtliche)* approach.

In the last quarter of the nineteenth century, biblical theology gave way to a history of religion approach. The rage now was the Graf-Kuenen-Wellhausen hypothesis that alleged, among other things, that the Prophets preceded the Law! The future of biblical theology was to belong to critical and historical studies well into the first third of the twentieth century.

The stranglehold of the history of religions approach persisted until the year 1933, which marked the emergence of a new day for Old Testament theology. Two works appeared, one by E. Sellin and the other by W. Eichrodt. Using the concept of the "covenant" as his unifying center, Eichrodt, the more dominant of the two, presented a cross-section of the theological concepts of the Old Testament in a systematic synthesis. This pattern set the mark for Old Testament theologies for the next three decades.

Over against Eichrodt, the name of G. von Rad stands for the other major option in Old Testament theology in the twentieth century. For von Rad in 1952,[7] Old Testament theology was historical, not systematic—the retelling of Israel's confessional story. Thus the history of Israel was to be bifurcated from this time forward, consisting of an actual history and a "kerygmatic" or confessional history (a word illustrating von Rad's dependence on dialectical theology). Just as Eichrodt's

---

[7]Gerhard von Rad, "Kritische Vorarbeiten zu einer Theologie des Alten Testament," in *Theologie und Liturgie*, ed. L. Hennig (Kassel, 1952), pp. 19-34, esp. p. 31.

original (1933-1939) three volumes were translated into English (1961-1967), so von Rad's two volumes were likewise translated and published in English (1961-1965). The issues that these two giants in the field brought to the table have yet to be resolved as we come to the beginning of the twenty-first century. Indeed, the publishing record in Old Testament theology grew enormously throughout the last third of the twentieth century—even after the discipline was declared to be in crisis, if not moribund, in 1970. But there have been few creative solutions, with most emphasis being placed on descriptions of the issues, descriptions originally formulated by Eichrodt and von Rad.

Consensus Position

Although most agree that a crisis exists, the cause of it is a matter of serious debate. Answers swing from the historical[8] to the theological side.[9]

Most agree on the key issues, if not any of the suggested solutions. The following five questions summarize the main problems in Old Testament theology: (1) Is Old Testament theology a purely "descriptive-historical" discipline, or does it also have a "normative-theological" role as well? (2) What is the definition and role of "history" in theological formulation? (3) Is there a "center" *(Mitte)* or "goal" for the entire theological content of the Old Testament? (4) Is Old Testament theology an exclusively "Christian" enterprise? (5) What are the "continuities and discontinuities" between the Old Testament and the New Testament? Here is where agreement exists: on the identification of the problems. It would appear that this generation is better at analyzing the problems than it is at offering solutions that command a broad consensus.

Given the fact that the older synthetic interests of former generations have eroded and are not shared by this generation, the focus in biblical theology has shifted to more analytical concerns. One of the major reasons for this shift in emphasis and type of research is the shift in hermeneutics. This is illustrated in the growing fragmentation witnessed in the results from the field of exegesis and the rift that has continued to increase between biblical exegetes and systematic theologians.

Biblical theologians mostly agree that the text of Scripture evidences a multiplex, multithemed approach that cannot be reduced to any single "center" other than, perhaps, the subject of the Testament is God.[10] This multiplicity of themes often was a mere collection of what was observed to be prominent concepts, now tending

---

[8]Brevard S. Childs, "Some Reflections on the Search for a Biblical Theology," *Horizons in Biblical Theology* 4 (1982): 1-12.

[9]Barr, "Theological Case Against Biblical Theology," pp. 3-19.

[10]As well illustrated in Gerhard Hasel, *Old Testament Theology: Basic Issues in the Current Debate,* 4th ed. (Grand Rapids: Eerdmans, 1991), pp. 111-14, 194-208.

to be arranged in a more dialectical or bipolar nature.[11] But most agreed that these themes must not be organized into any kind of single or overarching unity.

Almost all contributors to the field eschew the imposition of a systematic approach based on categories from dogmatic theology. This would be seen as a failure to deal fairly with the biblical material itself. Whether these same contributors would feel the same hostility to a potential organizing theme that came from the realm of ancient Near Eastern studies or modern philosophical roots or contemporary hermeneutical systems is not as clear.

Contemporary Trends in Old Testament Theology

At the heart of the crisis in Old Testament theology are a number of interrelated issues. When it was still relatively young, the discipline faced the problem of defining itself. Was biblical theology a historical description of the theological substance of the Old Testament as it was developed through the various epochs of time in the text of Scripture? Or was it a constructive theology compatible in some sense with the Bible? The answer to these two questions, from some perspectives, was equivalent to summarizing most of the efforts of the last two centuries in the discipline of biblical theology.

The issue of definition remains with us today because of the sharp distinction that Gabler introduced into the field. In hindsight, it appears that he separated historical-descriptive approaches to the text too sharply from constructive-normative ones. But these two aspects belong together, even though the way they relate to one another is very subtle and not artificially established.

If biblical theology is to be more than a systematic theology of both or either Testament, it must exhibit at least some of the characteristics of a diachronic pattern. It is true, of course, that the initial stages and first usages of the term *biblical theology* tended to be collections of "proof texts," known as *dicta probantia*. But in their case the emphasis fell on the adjective *biblical* as a protest against certain excesses observed in their day. There is no evidence that they were intentionally founding a separate discipline or another theological methodology for carrying out the exegetical task.

What was crucial to the emerging discipline, when it finally emerged as a new area of study in its own rights, was the concept of periodization; that is, it exegeted and grouped the theological content of Scripture in "periods of time" *(oeconomia temporum)* instead of formal logical or systematic categories. The work of Cocceius (1603-1669) is a good example of this deliberate rejection of the traditional

---

[11]See assessments by Walter Brueggemann, "A Convergence in Recent Old Testament Theologies," *Journal for the Study of the Old Testament* 18 (1980): 2-18; Bruce C. Birch, "Biblical Hermeneutics in Recent Discussion: Old Testament," *Religious Studies Review* 10, no. 1 (1984): 1-3; Charles H. H. Scobie, "The Structure of Biblical Theology," *Tyndale Bulletin* 42, no. 2 (1991): 179-87.

categories of systematics and the substitution of historical and temporal ones. In Cocceius's case, of course, the narrative history was the diachronic hook on which he hung his own "federal theology." He went to the other extreme of allowing his concept of biblical theology to usurp the role of systematics or dogmatic theology.

Central to many of these historical periodizations was the concept of the *organic* nature of Scripture. Cocceius spoke of the "inner-biblical progression" that was even more central to his interests than any mere historical process itself. It was this organic nature found in the texts that led early interpreters to emphasize that the earlier seminal concepts in the text experienced a development in their inner progression in Scripture throughout the epochs of revelation.

What has confused matters immensely is the dichotomization of the descriptive approach from the confessional. It has become almost a byword today to repeat this hiatus in the terms given to us in the famous Krister Stendahl article on biblical theology:[12] we must distinguish between what the Bible "meant" from what it "means" today. In Stendahl's hands, Old Testament theology was assigned the descriptive task of merely saying what the text "meant," leaving "what it now means" to doctrinal theology.

But there were major weaknesses associated with differentiating between "what Scripture meant" and "what it now means." It seemed to share the old Enlightenment mentality that assumed that "objectivity" in formulating the meaning of the text was not only possible but available. Now, almost thirty-five years later, that optimistic consensus has entirely evaporated under the pressure of postmodernist (if not deconstructionist) hermeneutical systems.

There was another sense in which the purely descriptive approach was inadequate. Even if some penetrated to the ostensive meaning of the words and clauses, had they arrived fully at the "original" meaning of the text that it as a document of faith aimed at calling forth from the reader and interpreter—a response to the message proclaimed in that text? The text implied a participation in the author's meaning from the interpreter and reader. Why, then, should what the text "meant" be thought to be so different and so removed from what it "means"? Then the meaning of the Old Testament must be essentially irretrievable and incomprehensible to the modern mind, presumably because ancient Semitic thought and culture is so radically different from Western thought. But James Barr and others have long since put those kinds of arguments to rest.[13]

---

[12]Krister Stendahl, "Biblical Theology, Contemporary," in *The Interpreter's Dictionary of the Bible*, ed. George A. Buttrick, 5 vols. (Nashville: Abingdon, 1962), 1:418-32.

[13]The questionable thesis that Hebrew thought is fundamentally different from Greek thought was introduced by Thorleif Bowman, *Das hebraische Denken im Vergleich mit dem griechishen* (Göttingen, 1952). James Barr strongly opposes this concept in his *The Semantics of Biblical Language* (London: Oxford University Press, 1961).

The role of history also raises questions. Should Old Testament theology focus its attention on the scriptural *text* or on the text as a witness to God's revelation in the *events of history* as recorded in Scripture? During the height of the biblical theology movement, George E. Wright could say, "Biblical theology is the confessional recital of the redemptive acts of God in a particular history, because history is the chief medium of revelation. . . . The Bible is not primarily the Word of God, but the record of the Acts of God, together with the human response thereto."[14] Clearly, the events of God working in history were the real focus of theological construction for Wright.

The word *history*, of course, has two different senses in this discussion. The Old Testament itself *is* a history in the scriptural text, but it also *has* a history in that it was written in our kind of space and time, giving us a history of its writing. It is the relationship between these two histories that is the issue.

Hans Frei grouped scholars into three groups, depending on how they used history: the precritical interpreters, who centered on the text of Scripture as the locus of meaning in the biblical narrative; the empirical practitioners, who focused on the external historical events as the locus of meaning; and the idealists, who majored in the "ideas" embodied in and referenced by the biblical text.[15] While the older Protestant interpretation, according to Frei, viewed the biblical narratives as a coherent world of their own that fits into our lives, this "precritical" reading was replaced by the other two forms after the rise of historical criticism. Meaning was hereafter to be identified with the historical events themselves (empiricism) or with the concepts to which the narratives referred (idealism). Regarding the internal claims of Scripture, the locus of revelation was in the text, not in the event or the ideas. This is not to say that Scriptures are not historically true; they are. But does the divinely revealed meaning lie in the events of Israel's history or in Scripture itself?

John Sailhamer has argued strenuously for finding meaning in the biblical narratives themselves, not in the actual historical events.[16] In his view, even as the critical understanding relocates meaning away from the text into the ostensive reference of reconstructed history, so also many conservatives replace narrative meaning represented by the texts with a reconstructed (albeit a subtle and often slightly different) version of the event as also known from archaeological, geographical, historical or even critical studies.

Although there is some validity in Sailhamer's charges, we should not abandon the empirical-historical paradigm for a completely literary paradigm. Despite the

---

[14]George E. Wright, *The God Who Acts: Biblical Theology as Recital* (London: SCM Press, 1962), p. 107.
[15]Hans Frei, *The Eclipse of Biblical Narrative* (New Haven: Yale University Press, 1974), p. 90.
[16]John H. Sailhamer, *Introduction to Old Testament Theology: A Canonical Approach* (Grand Rapids: Zondervan, 1995), pp. 36-85.

heroic efforts of Wolfhart Pannenberg to reinstate the unity of facts and their meaning,[17] some now want to replace the historical model with the "story" model.[18] This is reminiscent of von Rad's kerygmatic history in that it is a reaction to viewing the Bible purely in historical terms.

The issue of history is far from being resolved. How are we to relate text to event? Do events come with some meaning attached to them, as Pannenberg argues? And what of the question of truth? Must the text be read only at a prima facie level to be fair to what was meant by the original authors? What is the exact relationship between text and event?

Third, does the Old Testament have a central concept, a focal point or a unity to its message around some discernible plan? There have been many suggestions as to what that theme may be: God as Lord (Köhler, 1958), holiness (Hanel, 1931), covenant (Eichrodt, 1961-1967), Israel's election (Wildberger, 1959), the blessing/promise plan (Kaiser, 1978), the kingdom of God (Klein, 1970), communion with God (Vriezen, 1970), Yahweh (von Rad, 1963) and a score of others. No suggestion, however, has been able to attract anything like a consensus.

If there was to be a "theology" of the Old Testament, it would presumably imply the presence of some type of unity. Was it a unity of purpose, revelation, relationships with the people of God, an unexpressed higher unity or some alleged kerygmatic unity? Many now believe that it is a unity in diversity.

But that assertion was usually left to explain itself or was said to be in the fact that the Old Testament was about Yahweh. But in affirming that Yahweh was the center, it only raised another ancillary question: Yahweh is or does what? Here we were given a subject but no predicate. What was the verb and what was the object?

The materials of the Old Testament are, as Hasel has claimed so often, multiform and multiplex. But no one has yet titled a work in this area *OT Theologies,* the only honest title, if there were no integrating whole in the plan and purpose of the Old Testament.

It is not necessary to argue for a "static unity" to favor some organizing center, plan or narrative purpose in the entire Testament. Those who opt out of searching for a center or *Mitte* in the Old Testament are demonstrating their cultural captivity

---

[17]Wolfhart Pannenberg, "The Revelation of God in Jesus Christ," in *Theology as History,* New Frontiers in Theology 3 (New York: Harper & Row, 1967), p. 127. Pannenberg went on to say in that same context that "in principle, every event has its original meaning within the context of occurrence and tradition in which it took place." On page 269 he adds, "The knowledge of history on which faith is grounded has to do with the truth and reliability of that on which faith depends. . . . Such knowledge . . . assures faith about its basis." Sailhamer would agree, of course, but merely observe that Pannenberg is confusing apologetics, which is a legitimate discipline in its own rights, with the concerns of exegesis and biblical theology.

[18]For example, James Barr, "Story and History in Biblical Theology," *Journal of Religion* 56 (1976): 1-17; reprinted in Barr, *Scope and Authority of the Bible* (London: SCM Press, 1980), pp. 1-17.

to the prevailing contemporary preferences for diversity, pluralism and relativity more than a conscious effort to replicate what is observed in the text.

This raises the question as to what criteria would count in establishing a center, if one is to be identified as part of doing a biblical theology. Surely it must be one that arises from the text itself as part of the text's own self-conscious reflection on its own direction, purpose and motivation. It must also be one that is broad enough to embrace the variety of theological developments in all the canon. It must also be one that connects easily and organically with the center of New Testament theology. Furthermore, it must do more than merely state the subject or the object of the revelation found in the text. It must connect both the subject and object with a verb that identifies the movement and relationships of the subject(s) and object(s). In our judgment, all this is achievable.

Is Old Testament theology an exclusively Christian enterprise? To be sure, it had its roots in the Reformation and has most often been practiced by Christian scholars. The absence, for example, of Jewish scholars has been very noticeable until recently. In 1975 Goshen-Gottstein and in 1986, even more significantly, Matitiahu Tsevat entered the field.[19]

Nevertheless, neither Christians nor Protestants can claim exclusive rights of a revelation of God addressed to all people. What has hindered the wider entry into the field, particularly of Jewish scholars, can be found in two historical facts. First, Origen's designating the Tanakh as the "Old Testament"[20] tended to imply that the real testament was the New Testament. This was most unfortunate, since the whole idea came from a misunderstanding on Origen's part about the new covenant of Jeremiah 31: 31-34. He concluded that the new covenant was the New Testament God gave to the church. But in fact this identification was incorrect. Moreover, God never made a separate covenant with the church. The one referred to in Jeremiah 31:31 is specifically said to be made with Israel. If the "people of God" in the Christian era did not view their origins in the Abrahamic-Davidic-new covenant, the whole concept of the church lost grounding, roots or anchoring history. That is why Paul was so insistent on his imagery of the grafting in of the Gentiles to the roots and trunk of the Jewish olive tree in Romans 11.

Second, the church began as a type of messianic branch of the Jewish people. This state of affairs persisted, amid genuine problems. The newly named Christians finally left Judaism under the joint sponsorship of and failed revolt against Rome

---

[19]M. Goshen-Gottstein, "Christianity, Judaism and Modern Bible Study," *Vetus Testamentum Supplements* 28 (1975): 69-88; and Matitiahu Tsevat, "Theology of the Old Testament—A Jewish View," *Horizons in Biblical Theology* 8 (1986): 33-59.

[20]See Walter C. Kaiser Jr., *Toward Rediscovering the Old Testament* (Grand Rapids: Zondervan, 1987), p. 35.

by Rabbi Akiba and Simon Bar Kokba ("son of [the] star") in A.D. 135.[21] So horrific were those days that it would be centuries before a small ghetto of Jews (mainly in Eastern Europe) would countenance any messianic claims, much less those of Jesus of Nazareth. That would set back discussions of continuity between the Testaments and between Jews and Gentiles for generations—to the present day.

Some have attempted to explain the reticence of Jewish scholars to enter this field to the fact that Judaism is less theologically oriented, preferring to concentrate on right conduct and proper observance. But anyone who has read Abraham Heschel's work on the prophets [22] or Y. Kaufmann's treatise on Israelite religion[23] will want to modify such assertions immediately.

To the extent that divine revelation is addressed to all the peoples of the earth, to that extent biblical theology must not be the exclusive or private domain of any one group. It is just as wrong for "Christians" to abrogate the use of the Old Testament (Marcion, Schleiermacher, von Harnack, Frederick Delitzsch)[24] as it is to "Christianize" it by superimposing Christian meanings on the Old Testament, usually by means of allegory, typology, *sensus plenior* (early church fathers down to the present hermeneutical fashions). This, of course, raised the issue of continuity and discontinuity between the Testaments. The sharp dichotomization implied in the two positions just cited tended to cancel each other out. Bultmann asserted that the Old Testament served as a negative contrast to the New Testament and the Christian gospel, but it had no positive theological or normative use for today.

The judgment of history, however, is that the Old Testament is the master theological problem[25] because every time contemporary generations have decided to abandon part or all of its message, they have ended up with heresy or a weakened Christian message. For example, much of the quandary that the church and society find themselves in with regard to ethics may be directly traced to a decision to divorce the Mosaic covenant at Sinai from the New Testament's gospel of grace. The debate in missiological discussions about whether there is universal salvation for those who have never heard the gospel can be traced to an inadequate exegesis of the *object* of faith in Abrahamic and Old Testament times.[26]

The Old Testament is theologically significant and is an indispensable norm for

---

[21]See the forthcoming biography and theological exploration of this theme from Daniel Gruber, *Rabbi Akiba.*

[22]Abraham Heschel, *The Prophets,* 2 vols. (New York: Harper & Row, 1962).

[23]Yehezkel Kaufmann, *The Religion of Israel,* trans. M. Greenberg (Chicago: University of Chicago Press, 1960).

[24]Kaiser, *Toward Rediscovering the Old Testament,* pp. 14-15.

[25]Ibid., pp. 13-32.

[26]See the argumentation on this matter in Walter C. Kaiser Jr., "Salvation in the Old Testament: With Special Emphasis on the Object and Content of Personal Belief," *Jian Dao: A Journal of Bible and Theology* 2 (1994): 1-18.

Christian faith. The very fact that the New Testament contains almost three hundred direct Old Testament citations, along with fifteen hundred to three thousand Old Testament allusions, strongly argues for the fact that the soil in which the church was planted was the theology of the Old Testament. Only explicitly obsolete aspects of the Old Testament should be counted on the side of discontinuity. For example, the fact that the tabernacle, its priests and its services were to be built after the "pattern" of what Moses was shown in the mount (Ex 25:8, 40) clearly indicates that there was a time limit on them, since they were merely the "copies," "patterns," while the real remained distinct and a matter of later disclosure.

New Dimensions for Biblical Theology: Guidelines for Future Study

Each of the previously discussed five issues must be addressed if biblical theology is to move toward a new structure and recapture the respect it has lost in the recent, much discussed crisis. Contrary to many leading voices in the discipline, I urge giving more attention to synthetic and holistic approaches instead of proliferating more and more detailed analytical studies in the discipline. The presumption ought to be in favor of the idea that the sixty-six books do contain a unified plan and an organizing wholeness. The validity of this as a starting presupposition is rooted in the books' claim to being a revelation of the mind of God.

It is possible to argue for the moment that the collection of books in the canon is no more than odd, or random, thoughts of the divine mind given now and again in randomlike fashion with no definite direction, goal or plan intended. But that thesis runs counter to assertions to the contrary, that God did have a plan and that God was directing not only sacred history but all history toward a predetermined conclusion and ending point! Accordingly, there ought to be a working hypothesis in favor of the idea that within the inner progression of the text such a plan could be ferreted out and used as a synthesizing overview to the ordering of the theological development of the text.

But how can such a divine plan be unearthed from the text, temporarily granting that such a hypothesis may be in order? It may be done from two separate but parallel lines of argumentation: (1) an inductive and forward movement through the Old Testament and (2) a deductive and retrospective movement from the teaching of Jesus and the New Testament.

The inductive movement can profitably focus on the following repetitions in the text: (1) *terms* that frequently appear that begin to take on a technical status, (2) the similarity of the *content* of the covenants made with the patriarchs, Moses and David and evidenced in the new covenant, (3) *inner-textual exegesis* of citations or allusions from within the Old Testament as used by later writers and then the New Testament, and (4) concepts that are offered in the Testament as a *unilateral and unconditional* divine gift to mortals. When all four criteria are followed fully, it becomes clear that there was a divine plan that centered around the substance and content of the covenants repeatedly made in the course of Israel's history.

The deductive movement must substantiate the conclusions arrived at in the inductive study. Several concepts, terms and suggestions from the New Testament quickly emerge: the kingdom of God/heaven, justification by grace, and the promise of God. Only the last option, however, is able to equal the first two (or all other suggestions that have been made) and embrace all that they imply within its rubric.

The Greek term *epangelia,* along with its cognate expressions, occurs in almost every New Testament book. *Epangelia* summarizes the message of the Old Testament and involves around two dozen different subsets of theological ideas—all embraced within this one term!

Willis J. Beecher was the first to identify the promise as the center of the plan of God in the canon.[27] While he did not offer a complete biblical theology, he certainly laid out the guidelines for one. Beecher defined the promise in this way:

> God gave a promise to Abraham, and through him to mankind; a promise eternally fulfilled and fulfilling in the history of Israel; and chiefly fulfilled in Jesus Christ, he being that which is principal in the history of Israel.[28]

The apostle Paul, on trial for his life, cut to the heart of the issues that were at stake between him and his Jewish accusers by telling King Agrippa:

> And now it is because of *the promise* God made to our fathers that I am on trial today. This is *the promise* our twelve-tribe nation is hoping to see fulfilled as they earnestly serve God day and night. It is about this hope, O King, that the Jews are accusing me. (Acts 26: 6-7, my translation and emphasis)

To judge from the New Testament evidence, the promise plan of Old Testament theology is indeed multifaceted and all-inclusive, including the gospel, the offer of salvation to the Gentiles, the gift of the Holy Spirit, the resurrection from the dead, the kingdom of God—including God's rule and reign, redemption from sin, justification by faith and, preeminently, the promise of Jesus of Nazareth as the Messiah.[29]

This "promise plan" has nothing to do with the promise-fulfillment school, which focuses merely on the predicted Old Testament word and the fulfilling event in the New Testament without paying attention to the third element—the *means* by which God kept that word alive throughout the history of Israel while it awaited its final fulfillment (frequently in a pattern of an inaugurated eschatology).

The question of a center is central after all. Without it, I wonder if biblical

---

[27]Willis Judson Beecher, *The Prophets and the Promise* (1905; reprint, Grand Rapids: Baker, 1963, 1970), pp. 175-94. This publication was taken from Beecher's Stone Lectures at Princeton Seminary, 1904.

[28]Ibid., p. 178.

[29]See chapter titled "The Old Testament as the Promise-Plan of God," in *Toward Rediscovering the Old Testament,* pp. 83-100, and the bibliography mentioned there. This is the theme of my *Toward Old Testament Theology.*

theology is worth all the trouble it has caused the theological household! The guidelines offered here will have value if they serve as a way out of the quagmire.

The two parallel lines of argumentation have the capacity to serve as the wave of the future. In fact, the trend in hermeneutics, if not taken to excessive lengths, will overcome some of the prejudices that former generations held on this matter. Old Testament theology must include both a descriptive *and* a normative aspect if it is to be true to itself and to the needs of the believing community that awaits the results of its exegesis.

The issue that will be the most difficult to resolve is the question of the role of history. It may even be a new way of stating the question of the place of natural theology in special revelation. Is the sacred history contained in the text separate from secular history, or is God in charge of all history, making us responsible to view God's actions both in and outside the text? Do we need to use all tools, including cognate languages, archaeology and secular historical sources, to probe the history referred to in the text in order to understand and respond to it as we should in our day? The jury remains out on these mind-boggling questions. There are too many good points being made by both sides to award the case to one or the other. And new lines of argumentation may yet emerge. For example, the text-only argument of a Sailhamer, may, in the hands of some of its advocates, end up being a literary paradigm, or the detractors of that position may end up sponsoring a historical paradigm. Too often the pendulum swings to opposite extremes while the center goes begging for adherents.

At the end of the day, the guidelines for the future must concentrate on offering a suitable structure for Old Testament theology. In spite of the massive literature in this field, with its innumerable proposals and essays on one detail or another, relatively little attention has been given to the question of an organization and structure for doing biblical theology, whether Old Testament, New Testament or the whole canon itself. It is to this key point that we have focused our attention in this chapter.

Summary

Despite the obstacles that this relatively new discipline faces, the prospects for its usefulness are enormous. To the degree that it retains its emphasis on periodization and epochs of revelation, it can serve as a wonderful assistant primarily to the exegetical task. Most place biblical theology in the service of dogmatic theology, but that is putting the cart before the horse. Priority must be given to the exegetical task if the view that God has spoken in his revelation is correct. To make doctrinal theology queen of the sciences is not to assign her the place of priority in the order of theological tasks.

In and of itself, exegesis can be an arid and historically dated venture. Exegesis needs the assistance of informing theology of preceding periods when the same terms or topics, mentioned later, were cited or alluded to in previous texts. Because of the unity and organic nature of Scripture, exegesis is strengthened by employing this natural ally in the interpretive process. The text is living and growing and exhibits the same epigenetical relationships observed (though only by analogy) in the realm of biology. What was in incipient seed form sprouts to more mature growth in the inner progress of revelation.

To solve the problems offered by biblical theology is to make enormous progress in stating precisely where the continuities and discontinuities lie between the Testaments. It is no accident that the New Testament uses the various forms of *epangelia*, "promise" almost seventy times, chiefly to refer to the Old Testament in all but four or five New Testament books. Surely we can take such a clue as a working hypothesis as we continue to search whether the Old Testament has a center, a unifying plan and an organizing mind behind the entirety of its message. The benefits of viewing the parts of the message, of either or both Testaments, in terms of an overarching unity cannot be rivaled in the positive effects it has on the understanding, preaching and counseling of such a practitioner. In an age that has stressed specialization in theological studies (as is the case in most areas of the academy), one of the best correctives can be found in a proper study and use of biblical theology.

Resources for Additional Study

Anderson, Bernhard, ed. *The Old Testament and Christian Faith.* New York: Harper & Row, 1963.

Baker, D. L. *Two Testaments, One Bible.* Leicester, U.K.: Inter-Varsity Press, 1976.

Bright, John. *The Authority of the Old Testament.* Nashville: Abingdon, 1967.

Brueggemann, Walter. *Theology of the Old Testament: Testimony, Dispute, Advocacy.* Minneapolis: Fortress, 1997.

Childs, Brevard S. *Biblical Theology of the Old and New Testaments.* Minneapolis: Fortress, 1992.

Gilkey, Langdon B. "Cosmology, Ontology and the Travail of Biblical Language. *Journal of Religion* 41 (1961): 194-205.

Goldingay, John. *Theological Diversity and the Authority of the Old Testament.* Grand Rapids: Eerdmans, 1987.

Hasel, Gerhard. *Old Testament Theology: Basic Issues in the Current Debate.* 4th ed., rev. and exp. Grand Rapids: Eerdmans, 1991.

Kaiser, Walter, Jr. *Toward an Old Testament Theology.* Grand Rapids: Zondervan, 1978.

Maier, Gerhard. *Biblical Hermeneutics.* Translated by Robert W. Yarbrough. Wheaton, Ill.: Crossway Books, 1994.

Martens, Elmer A. *Old Testament Theology.* IBR Bibliographies. Grand Rapids: Baker, 1997.

Ollenburger, Ben C., Elmer A. Martens and Gerhard F. Hasel, eds. *The Flowering of Old Testament Theology: A Reader in Twentieth Century Old Testament Theology.* Winona Lake, Ind.: Eisenbrauns, 1991.

Sailhamer, John H. *Introduction to Old Testament Theology: A Canonical Approach.* Grand Rapids: Zondervan, 1995.

Chapter 4

New Dimensions in New Testament Theology

Thomas R. Schreiner

··

I AM PLEASED TO CONTRIBUTE AN ESSAY TO A VOLUME HONORING MIL-
lard Erickson. I served as a faculty member at Bethel Seminary when Millard was
the dean, and I joined the faculty during his tenure in that position. I have always
admired Millard for the clarity and brevity of his writing, which are the two qualities
that John Calvin praises in writers.[1] Some may question whether Millard's *Systematic Theology* actually has the virtue of brevity! I am convinced that it does in light
of (1) the number of subjects he covers and (2) the fact that twenty centuries of
Christian theology had to be brought within the scope of one work. Even John
Calvin's *Institutes of the Christian Religion* extended to the two volumes of today's
standard English edition. Perhaps I am also impressed with Millard's brevity
because my systematic theology textbook was the one written by Augustus H.
Strong.[2] The edition we used was only one volume, but it had three different sizes
of print, the smallest of which required a magnifying glass for reading.

Any essay on "new dimensions in new testament theology" is doomed to (in this
case premature) obsolescence. Yet it is imperative that evangelical scholarship
interact with contemporary culture and scholarship. Our response to current trends
in New Testament scholarship may well influence the direction that scholarship
takes in the future. Of course, I can scarcely catalog current trends in New Testament

---

[1]See the introduction to *Institutes of the Christian Religion,* ed. J. T. McNeil, trans. Ford Lewis Battles
  (Philadelphia: Westminster, 1960), pp. lxix-lxxi.
[2]Augustus H. Strong, *Systematic Theology* (Valley Forge, Penn.: Judson, 1907).

theology in one essay.[3] The sheer volume and diversity of the work being produced renders this impossible. The days seem to have ended when one scholar or group of scholars found it possible to control the direction of New Testament scholarship. The influence exerted by F. C. Baur and his school during the nineteenth century or by Rudolf Bultmann and his disciples in the twentieth century is not likely to be seen again.[4]

A dizzying variety of perspectives are now advocated, and New Testament scholarship is marked by a plurality of perspectives. Contemporary New Testament scholarship may aptly be described in the words of the author of the book of Judges, "In those days there was no king in Israel; all the people did what was right in their own eyes" (Judg 21:25 NRSV). For instance, the Pauline theology seminar held by the Society of Biblical Literature from 1985 to 1993 did not really accomplish much in the overall program of formulating Pauline theology.[5] Many stimulating papers were read, but the seminar group could not agree on the proper methodology for constructing Pauline theology, and thus many sessions concluded with a discussion on that subject with no solution forthcoming. The multiplicity of proposals represented the assorted agendas of the participants. Any attempt to formulate a Pauline theology is vain unless it is agreed that Paul had a coherent and consistent theology and that this theology can be discerned by reading his letters. The members of the Pauline seminar had differing opinions on this fundamental question, and thus it is no surprise that no consensus emerged. (Of course, achieving a consensus would be difficult even if there were agreement that Paul's theology was coherent.)

Some question the very desirability of New Testament theology. Heikki Räisänen, for instance, calls for a return to the study of New Testament religion and an abandonment of New Testament theology.[6] In doing so he calls up the ghost of William Wrede, who advocated the same perspective at the end of the nineteenth century.[7] Rejection of theology is evident in the title of Räisänen's book *Beyond New*

---

[3]For an older survey, see Gerhard F. Hasel, *New Testament Theology: Basic Issues in the Current Debate* (Grand Rapids: Eerdmans, 1978).

[4]N. T. Wright's project of writing a five-volume work titled *Christian Origins and the Question of God* on Christian history and theology represents an attempt to do the kind of synthesis that Bultmann accomplished, but it is doubtful that it will garner the agreement or even the reaction that Bultmann's work did. So far two volumes have appeared: vol. 1, *The New Testament and the People of God* (Minneapolis: Fortress, 1992), and vol. 2, *Jesus and the Victory of God* (Minneapolis: Fortress, 1996). I had the opportunity to read the latter volume only after completing this essay.

[5]Volumes issued so far include *Pauline Theology*, vol. 1, *Thessalonians, Philippians, Galatians, Philemon*, ed. J. M. Bassler (Minneapolis: Fortress, 1991); *Pauline Theology*, vol. 2, *1 and 2 Corinthians*, ed. D. M. Hay (Minneapolis: Fortress, 1993); *Pauline Theology*, vol. 3, *Romans*, ed. E. Elizabeth Johnson and D. M. Hay (Minneapolis: Fortress, 1995).

[6]See his book *Beyond New Testament Theology* (Philadelphia: Trinity Press International, 1990).

[7]William Wrede, "The Task and Methods of 'New Testament Theology,'" in *The Nature of New Testament Theology*, ed. and trans. Robert Morgan (1897; Naperville, Ill.: Allenson, 1973), pp. 68-116.

Testament Theology. On other fronts, however, New Testament theology continues to be pursued. Peter Stuhlmacher and Hans Hübner have both published volumes in their respective New Testament theologies,[8] and James Dunn is editing a series, New Testament Theology, which explores the theologies of the various New Testament writers.[9]

In this essay I want to survey and interact briefly with two recent issues in New Testament theology: the so-called third quest for the historical Jesus and the Pauline theology of the law. Both of these issues are at the forefront of contemporary New Testament scholarship, and rightly so, since our understanding of these issues has major implications for formulating theology and for the life of the church. In both cases the survey is not comprehensive; my goal is to survey some of the major trends in both areas and to prime the pump by suggesting some strengths and some weaknesses in recent studies.

The Quest for the Historical Jesus

The old quest. The old quest for the historical Jesus was carried out in the nineteenth century. Albert Schweitzer in his famous book *The Quest of the Historical Jesus* demonstrated conclusively that the quest was a dismal failure.[10] The fundamental problem was that liberal nineteenth-century Christians painted a portrait of Jesus

---

[8]Peter Stuhlmacher, *Biblische Theologie des Neuen Testaments, Band 1, Grundelgung: Von Jesus zu Paulus* (Göttingen: Vandenhoeck & Ruprecht, 1992); Hans Hübner, *Biblische Theologie des Neuen Testaments, Band 1, Prolegomena; Band 2, Die Theologie des Paulus und ihre neutestamentliche Wirkungsgeschichte* (Göttingen: Vandenhoeck & Ruprecht, 1990, 1993). See also W. Beilner and M. Ernst, *Unter dem Wort Gottes: Theologie aus dem Neuen Testament* (Thaur: Kulturverlag, 1993). For recent attempts to do a comprehensive biblical theology, see Daniel P. Fuller, *The Unity of the Bible: Unfolding God's Plan for Humanity* (Grand Rapids: Zondervan, 1992); Brevard S. Childs, *Biblical Theology of the Old and New Testaments: Theological Reflection on the Christian Bible* (Minneapolis: Fortress, 1993). See also *New Directions in Biblical Theology: Papers of the Aarhus Conference* (September 16-19, 1992), ed. Sigfred Pedersen (Leiden: Brill, 1994).

[9]A number of volumes have appeared in this series. Barnabas Lindars, *The Theology of the Letter to the Hebrews* (Cambridge: Cambridge University Press, 1991); Jerome Murphy-O'Connor, *The Theology of the Second Letter to the Corinthians* (Cambridge: Cambridge University Press, 1991); Judith Lieu, *The Theology of the Johannine Epistles* (Cambridge: Cambridge University Press, 1991); Karl P. Donfried and I. Howard Marshall, *The Theology of the Shorter Pauline Letters* (Cambridge: Cambridge University Press, 1993); Andrew T. Lincoln and A. J. M. Wedderburn, *The Theology of the Later Pauline Letters* (Cambridge: Cambridge University Press, 1993); J. D. G. Dunn, *The Theology of Paul's Letter to the Galatians* (Cambridge: Cambridge University Press, 1993); Richard Bauckham, *The Theology of the Book of Revelation* (Cambridge: Cambridge University Press, 1993); Frances Young, *The Theology of the Pastoral Letters* (Cambridge: Cambridge University Press, 1994); Andrew Chester and Ralph P. Martin, *The Theology of the Letters of James, Peter and Jude* (Cambridge: Cambridge University Press, 1994); D. Moody Smith, *The Theology of the Gospel of John* (Cambridge: Cambridge University Press, 1995); Joel B. Green, *The Theology of the Gospel of Luke* (Cambridge: Cambridge University Press, 1995); Ulrich Luz, *The Theology of the Gospel of Matthew* (Cambridge: Cambridge University Press, 1995).

[10]Albert Schweitzer, *The Quest of the Historical Jesus: A Critical Study of Its Progress from Reimarus to Wrede* (New York: Macmillan, 1910). Published in German in 1906.

in their own image. According to these classical liberals, the core of Jesus' teaching was the brotherhood of man and the fatherhood of God. The miracles and the supernatural elements of the Gospels' portrait of Jesus either were written off as unhistorical or were explained away rationalistically. Schweitzer brought the whole project to an end by confirming the eschatological dimensions of Jesus' message. Jesus believed that the kingdom of God was near and that the end of the world was imminent. His belief marked Jesus as a man of his time. The eschatological Jesus proposed by Schweitzer ended the old quest, for it convinced scholars that Jesus was not a nineteenth-century Protestant liberal after all. He was a first-century Jew who had to be explained in terms of the Hellenistic-Jewish culture of his day.

Schweitzer's own solution, unfortunately, was not very promising. He suggested that Jesus traveled to Jerusalem to suffer and die in order to compel God to bring in the kingdom. What Jesus envisioned and anticipated never happened, however. His death did not bring in the kingdom of God, and his hopes did not become a reality. In essence, Schweitzer's Jesus was a deluded fanatic who tried to usher in the end of history and failed miserably. It is difficult to see what message Jesus of Nazareth has for us today if he died a defeated and broken man and was never vindicated by God through the resurrection.

From Bultmann to the new quest. After Schweitzer, the attempt to plot out the life of the historical Jesus was virtually given up. Form criticism came to the forefront in New Testament studies through the work of Karl Ludwig Schmidt, Martin Dibelius and Rudolf Bultmann.[11] Most form critics sought to discover the setting of life in the early church that precipitated the Gospel traditions. Bultmann's influence was especially dominant. He was convinced that the four Gospels yield virtually no reliable information about the historical Jesus.[12] This did not prevent him from constructing a theology of the New Testament, for in his estimation the historical Jesus was merely a presupposition for the theology of the New Testament, not a central part of New Testament theology itself.[13] In Bultmann's opinion any attempt to ground faith in history was a massive error akin to trying to gain salvation by works instead of accepting justification by faith. Genuine faith, Bultmann asserted, did not try to gain security through historical research but trusted in God apart from the vagaries of historical research.

Some of Bultmann's disciples, on the other hand, became dissatisfied with the lowly place that the historical Jesus occupied in the Bultmannian scheme. Ernst

---

[11]Karl Ludwig Schmidt, *Der Rahmen der Geschichte Jesus* (Berlin: Trowitzsch, 1919); Martin Dibelius, *From Tradition to Gospel* (German ed. 1919; New York: Scribner's, n.d.); Rudolf Bultmann, *The History of the Synoptic Tradition* (German ed. 1921; New York: Harper & Row, 1963).

[12]See his Rudolf Bultmann, *Jesus and the Word* (German ed. 1926; New York: Scribner's, 1934), p. 9.

[13]Rudolf Bultmann, *Theology of the New Testament* (German ed. 1948; New York: Scribner's, 1951), 1:3.

Käsemann launched the new quest with his famous essay, which he read in 1953.[14] Günther Bornkamm wrote a stimulating book titled *Jesus of Nazareth,* and James Robinson sketched in the program for the new quest—the second quest—in 1959.[15] Despite the initial enthusiasm for the second quest, the historical harvest was disappointing.[16] The methodological and historical views of Bultmann were not really surrendered. Some scholars believe that the new quest continues to be represented today by the Jesus Seminar and by scholars associated with the Claremont Graduate School in California.[17] It is more convincing, however, to understand the Jesus Seminar as a distinct movement within the third quest.[18]

The third quest. It is difficult to date the beginning of the so-called third quest,[19] since there is some overlap with the second quest. Establishing the date of the third quest is not as important as realizing that it is a reality. In the 1960s and 1970s a small but steady stream of books on the historical Jesus appeared. By the 1980s and 1990s it had turned into such a torrent of books and articles that it is difficult for any scholar to keep up with the writings produced.[20]

Central conclusions of the third quest.[21] Although space limitations rule out considering the contribution of every scholar, I sketch the main conclusions of the third quest and then outline some objections to them. Finally, I try to show that agreement on these main conclusions should not be overrated, since several issues

---

[14]Ernst Käsemann, "The Problem of the Historical Jesus," in *Essays on New Testament Themes* (German ed. 1954; Naperville, Ill.: Allenson, 1964), pp. 15-47.

[15]Günther Bornkamm, *Jesus of Nazareth* (German ed. 1956; New York: Harper & Row, 1960); J. M. Robinson, *A New Quest of the Historical Jesus* (Naperville, Ill.: Allenson, 1959).

[16]For some other works in the new quest, see Hans Conzelmann, *Jesus* (German ed. 1959; Philadelphia: Fortress, 1973); Ernest Fuchs, "The Quest of the Historical Jesus," in *Studies of the Historical Jesus* (German ed. 1956; Naperville, Ill.: Allenson, 1964), pp. 11-31; Gerhard Ebeling, "The Question of the Historical Jesus and the Problem of Christology," in *Word of Faith* (German ed. 1959; Philadelphia: Fortress, 1963), pp. 288-304.

[17]So Markus Bockmuehl, "History and Faith: Jesus of Nazareth in Recent Debate," *Epworth Review* 21 (1994): 19-20; N. T. Wright, *Who Was Jesus?* (Grand Rapids: Eerdmans, 1992), pp. 10, 12.

[18]This has been effectively argued by Randy Nelson, a Ph.D. candidate at Rice University, in a preliminary version of the first chapter of his forthcoming doctoral dissertation on the Jesus Seminar.

[19]There is disagreement over whether recent scholarship actually constitutes a third quest. Whether this is the best term for recent Jesus research is not discussed here.

[20]Some popular writings on Jesus have advanced fantastic theories that appeal to the popular imagination. See A. N. Wilson, *Jesus* (London: Sinclair-Stevenson, 1992); Barbara E. Thiering, *Jesus the Man: A New Interpretation from the Dead Sea Scrolls* (London: Corgi, 1992); John Shelby Spong, *Born of a Woman: A Bishop Rethinks the Birth of Jesus* (San Francisco: Harper, 1992). For a devastating critique, see N. T. Wright, *Who Was Jesus?* (Grand Rapids: Eerdmans, 1992); see also Bockmuehl, "History and Faith," pp. 21-24.

[21]After I completed this essay, a most helpful survey and analysis of the third quest appeared. See Ben Witherington III, *The Jesus Quest: The Third Search for the Jew of Nazareth* (Downers Grove, Ill.: InterVarsity Press, 1995).

in Jesus research remain unsolved.[22]

First, the Gospels supply a good bit of knowledge about the historical Jesus. Some scholars have focused on events in the life of Jesus rather than his sayings. There is general agreement that more of the sayings are authentic than was contemplated by Bultmann and his school. The notable exception to this trend is the Jesus Seminar, which has provoked public reaction because its results have been reported in the media.[23] Some laypeople think that the Jesus Seminar represents the results of mainstream New Testament scholarship. In fact, the Jesus Seminar represents a small minority of scholars. The extreme skepticism that characterizes their research is not typical of New

---

[22]See the surveys by William R. Telford, "Major Trends and Interpretive Issues in the Study of Jesus," in *Studying the Historical Jesus: Evaluations of the State of Current Research*, ed. Bruce Chilton and Craig A. Evans (Leiden: Brill, 1994), pp. 33-74; W. G. Kümmel, "Jesusforschung seit 1981," *Theologische Rundschau* 53 (1988): 229-49; 54 (1989): 1-53; 55 (1990): 21-45; 56 (1991): 27-53, 391-420; Marcus Borg, "A Renaissance in Jesus Studies," *Theology Today* 45 (1988): 280-92; Marcus Borg, "Portraits of Jesus in Contemporary North American Scholarship," *Harvard Theological Review* 84 (1991): 1-22; Marcus Borg, *Jesus in Contemporary Scholarship* (Valley Forge, Penn.: Trinity Press International, 1994); Marcus Borg, "Reflections on a Discipline: A North American Perspective," in *Studying the Historical Jesus: Evaluations of the State of Current Research*, ed. Bruce Chilton and Craig A. Evans (Leiden: Brill, 1994), pp. 9-31; James H. Charlesworth, "Research on the Historical Jesus Today: Jesus and the Pseudepigrapha, the Dead Sea Scrolls, the Nag Hammadi Codices, Josephus and Archaeology," *Princeton Seminary Bulletin* 6 (1985): 98-115; James H. Charlesworth, "From Barren Mazes to Gentle Rappings: The Emergence of Jesus Research," *Princeton Seminary Bulletin* 7 (1986): 221-30; James H. Charlesworth, "Jesus Research: A Paradigm Shift for New Testament Scholars," *Australian Biblical Review* 38 (1990): 18-32; James H. Charlesworth, "Jesus Research Expands with Chaotic Creativity," in *Images of Jesus Today*, ed. J. H. Charlesworth and W. P. Weaver (Valley Forge, Penn.: Trinity Press International, 1994), pp. 1-41; James H. Charlesworth, *Jesus Within Judaism* (New York: Doubleday, 1988); Bruce Chilton and Craig A. Evans, eds., *Studying the Historical Jesus: Evaluations of the State of Current Research* (Leiden: Brill, 1994); Craig A. Evans, *Life of Jesus Research: An Annotated Bibliography* (Leiden: Brill, 1989); Craig A. Evans, "Life-of-Jesus Research and the Eclipse of Mythology," *Theological Studies* 54 (1993): 3-36; Paul H. Hollenbach, "The Historical Jesus Question in North America Today," *Biblical Theology Bulletin* 19 (1989): 11-22; John P. Meier, "Reflections on Jesus-of-History Research Today," in *Jesus' Jewishness: Exploring the Place of Jesus Within Early Judaism*, ed. J. H. Charlesworth (New York: Crossroad, 1991), pp. 84-107; N. T. Wright, "Quest for the Historical Jesus," in *The Anchor Bible Dictionary*, ed. David Noel Freedman (New York: Doubleday, 1992), 3:796-804; Bockmuehl, "History and Faith," pp. 18-31; Jacob Neusner, "Who Needs 'the Historical Jesus'? An Essay Review," *Bulletin of Biblical Research* 4 (1994): 113-26; Craig A. Evans, "The Need for the 'Historical Jesus': A Response to Jacob Neusner's Review of Crossan and Meier," *Bulletin of Biblical Research* 4 (1994): 127-34.

[23]See Robert W. Funk, Roy W. Hoover and the Jesus Seminar, *The Five Gospels: The Search for the Authentic Words of Jesus: New Translation and Commentary* (New York: Macmillan, 1993). For helpful critiques, see Robert W. Yarbrough, "The Gospel According to the Jesus Seminar," *Presbyterion* 29 (1994): 8-20; Jeffrey A. Gibbs, "The Search for the Idiosyncratic Jesus: A Critique of the Jesus Seminar's *The Five Gospels*," *Presbyterion* 29 (1994): 21-35. See especially Michael J. Wilkins and J. P. Moreland, eds., *Jesus Under Fire: Modern Scholarship Reinvents the Historical Jesus* (Grand Rapids: Zondervan, 1995). After I completed this essay, a devastating critique of the Jesus Seminar appeared by Luke Timothy Johnson, *The Real Jesus: The Misguided Quest for the Historical Jesus and the Truth of the Traditional Gospels* (San Francisco: HarperCollins, 1996).

Testament scholarship as a whole or the third quest in particular. Many scholars from a wide diversity of backgrounds now acknowledge that the Gospels have preserved reliable information about the historical Jesus.[24]

Second, most scholars agree that Jesus must be interpreted in terms of his Jewish background.[25] He was a Galilean Jew, not a Roman citizen or a Hellenistic philosopher. The social world of first-century Judaism must be excavated in order to understand Jesus of Nazareth. In particular, the Old Testament Scriptures and the Jewish literature of the Second Temple period are the main sources for the cultural and intellectual forces that shaped Jesus. The importance of the Old Testament Scriptures should go without saying, since they are often cited as authoritative in the Gospels. Our comprehension of Jesus' social world can be sharpened through studying the Apocrypha, the Pseudepigrapha, the Dead Sea Scrolls, Philo, Josephus and (used with caution) the rabbinic literature. It is now recognized that the criterion of dissimilarity has often been employed in a misleading way that severs Jesus from his Jewish roots. Discerning the "authentic" Jesus only in the sayings that distinguish him from his Jewish contemporaries leads to the strange conclusions that Jesus never agreed with his Jewish compatriots on anything and, even more startling, that Jesus remained absolutely separate from the history of his time and from his Jewish roots. These conclusions give us an ethereal and bloodless Jesus who passed through human history like a flying Superman, his feet never really touching the ground.

Third, most scholars agree that the Jesus of history was decisively influenced by Jewish apocalyptic thought. An eschatological Jesus has been accepted in New Testament scholarship since the late nineteenth century, when Johannes Weiss wrote his groundbreaking book *Jesus' Proclamation of the Kingdom of God.*[26] Albert Schweitzer took up this insight and demonstrated that the liberal image of Jesus was unhistorical because it ignored his eschatology.

Fourth, there is general agreement that one of the purposes of the historical Jesus was to restore or renew Israel. Many scholars concur that he followed John the Baptist and that like the Baptist he desired to see Israel renewed. They agree that he selected twelve disciples as a core group that was to embody the restoration of Israel. It is also acknowledged that Jesus spoke in parables, and an increasing number of scholars believe that Jesus performed miracles and thought of his mission in

---

[24]See, for example, E. P. Sanders, *Jesus and Judaism* (Philadelphia: Fortress, 1985), p. 2; Marcus Borg, *Jesus: A New Vision* (San Francisco: Harper & Row, 1987), p. 15.

[25]Jewish scholars have emphasized the Jewishness of Jesus. See, for example, Geza Vermes, *Jesus the Jew*, 2nd ed. (London: SCM Press, 1983); Geza Vermes, *Jesus and the World of Judaism* (London: SCM Press, 1983); Geza Vermes, *The Religion of Jesus the Jew* (London: SCM Press, 1993). A number of other Jewish scholars have engaged in historical Jesus research. For a survey and a perceptive assessment, see Donald A. Hagner, *The Jewish Reclamation of Jesus* (Grand Rapids: Zondervan, 1984).

[26]Johannes Weiss, *Jesus' Proclamation of the Kingdom of God* (German ed. 1892; Philadelphia: Fortress, 1971).

messianic terms. Recent research has looked at the temple incident in which Jesus cast out those who were working in the temple precincts. Scholars have attempted to discern the significance of this action for the subsequent death of Jesus.

Objections to the consensus. Research on the historical Jesus has progressed in many ways in the last thirty years. But some scholars continue to dissent from the four points listed above, insisting that (1) the Gospel of Thomas is as valuable as (or more valuable than) the four Gospels, (2) a Cynic background leads to a better understanding of Jesus than a Jewish one, and (3) the notion that Jesus taught an imminent eschatology should be abandoned.

First, some scholars have postulated that the Gospel of Thomas is a prime historical source for Jesus traditions.[27] Adding another source to the four canonical Gospels would have a major impact on historical research, to put it mildly. A careful sifting of the evidence demonstrates, however, that the Gospel of Thomas is a later document and that it hardly warrants consideration as a genuine historical source for the life and words of Jesus of Nazareth.[28] The idea that the Gospel of Thomas contains traditions that are equal to the Gospels is a decidedly minority opinion.

Second, a few scholars have questioned whether Jesus' Jewish background is fundamental to an understanding of him. They have suggested that Jesus was comparable to the traveling Cynic sages who called into question the practices of society.[29] The Cynic Jesus was a social subversive who uttered witty aphorisms challenging the social conventions of his day. Jesus mocked and ridiculed people's preoccupations to stimulate them to see that they were imprisoned by their society. Certainly some of Jesus' sayings are similar in style and content to utterances by Cynic sages.[30] Nor should we overlook the Hellenistic influences in Palestine in

---

[27]Two notable examples are found in the work of the Jesus Seminar (see note 19) and the recent work by John Dominic Crossan, *The Historical Jesus: The Life of a Mediterranean Jewish Peasant* (San Francisco: Harper, 1992). See also Helmut Koester, *Introduction to the New Testament*, vol. 2, *History and Literature of Early Christianity* (German ed. 1980; New York: de Gruyter, 1982), p. 152; James M. Robinson, "On Bridging the Gulf from Q to the Gospel of Thomas (or Vice Versa)," in *Nag Hammadi, Gnosticism and Early Christianity*, ed. C. Hedrick and R. Hodgson (Peabody, Mass.: Hendrickson, 1986), pp. 127-75.

[28]Bruce Chilton, "The Gospel According to Thomas as a Source of Jesus' Teaching," and Craig L. Blomberg, "Tradition and Redaction in the Parables of the Gospel of Thomas," in *The Jesus Tradition Outside the Gospels*, vol. 5 of *Gospel Perspectives*, ed. David Wenham (Sheffield, U.K.: JSOT Press, 1984), pp. 155-75 and 177-205 respectively. Christopher Tuckett, "Thomas and the Synoptics," *Novum Testamentum* 39 (1988): 132-57; John P. Meier, *A Marginal Jew: Rethinking the Historical Jesus* (New York: Doubleday, 1991), 1:123-39.

[29]For the view that Jesus was a Cynic, see especially Burton L. Mack, *A Myth of Innocence: Mark and Christian Origins* (Philadelphia: Fortress, 1988); F. Gerald Downing, *Christ and the Cynics* (Sheffield, U.K.: JSOT Press, 1988); F. Gerald Downing, *Cynics and Christian Origins* (Edinburgh: T & T Clark, 1992). This understanding is also evident in the work of the Jesus Seminar.

[30]But Jesus is better described as a teacher of Jewish wisdom. See Ben Witherington III, *Jesus the Sage: The Pilgrimage of Jewish Wisdom* (Minneapolis: Fortress, 1994).

Jesus' time.[31] Nonetheless, evidence for Cynic influence in Galilee, Samaria and Judea is remarkably lacking.[32]

Jesus' teaching differs from Cynic teaching in crucial respects. Some of the alleged parallels (such as Mk 10:28-29; Lk 10:5-6), when studied in context, are not genuine. A Cynic Jesus can only be accepted if his teaching is noneschatological. But we shall see shortly that a noneschatological Jesus is quite unlikely. The attempt to postulate a Cynic Jesus is redolent of the nineteenth-century quest, for this Jesus is strikingly postmodern. He was an unconventional man who criticized the social system of his day with witty sayings. One suspects that this construction of Jesus has fallen prey to Henry J. Cadbury's warning in his book *The Peril of Modernizing Jesus*.[33] We look deep down into the well and find that the Jesus we see is really a reflection of ourselves.

Third, Marcus Borg has challenged the consensus of the eschatological Jesus, questioning whether Jesus taught an imminent end of the present world order. Borg defines the kingdom of God in terms of mystical personal experience and the new life generated by the Spirit.[34] He doubts that the kingdom of God was the central theme of Jesus' preaching and argues that the centrality of eschatology is due to the crisis with Rome that occurred in A.D. 66-70, when Mark wrote his Gospel. In other words, the sayings that seem to point to an eschatological Jesus in Mark are inauthentic. They were put in Jesus' mouth during the crisis with Rome but do not represent the eschatological teaching of the historical Jesus. Similarly, the sayings that identify Jesus as the Son of Man are inauthentic.

Borg emphasizes that Jesus intended to transform the present world order.[35] He contends that Jesus was vitally involved in the political world of his time, for he challenged the social world that was dominant in Palestine. In Judaism holiness and purity were considered to be central, so that boundaries were erected between things and people that were holy and unholy. Jesus rejected this paradigm and taught

---

[31]See Martin Hengel, *Judaism and Hellenism* (Philadelphia: Fortress, 1974).

[32]See especially Witherington, *Jesus the Sage*, pp. 117-45; Paul R. Eddy, "Jesus as Diogenes? Reflections on the Cynic Jesus Thesis," *Journal of Biblical Literature* 115 (1996): 449-69; Richard Horsley, "Jesus: Itinerant Cynic or Israelite Prophet?" in *Images of Jesus Today*, ed. J. H. Charlesworth and W. P. Weaver (Valley Forge, Penn.: Trinity Press International, 1994), pp. 68-97, esp. pp. 68-78.

[33]Henry J. Cadbury, *The Peril of Modernizing Jesus* (New York: Macmillan, 1937). Cadbury himself does not escape from this charge, for his antisupernatural worldview informs the book.

[34]Borg has made this case in a number of places, but see his essay "Jesus and Eschatology: A Reassessment," in *Images of Jesus Today*, ed. J. H. Charlesworth and W. P. Weaver (Valley Forge, Penn.: Trinity Press International, 1994), pp. 42-67, and *Jesus in Contemporary Scholarship*, pp. 47-96. The Jesus Seminar (*The Five Gospels*, p. 4) also doubts the eschatological message of Jesus, but see Gibbs ("Idiosyncratic Jesus," pp. 29-30) for a response. Of course, Borg himself is a member of the Jesus Seminar and is sympathetic to its conclusions (*Jesus in Contemporary Scholarship*, pp. 160-81).

[35]For a fuller picture of Borg's view, see especially his *Jesus: A New Vision* and *Jesus in Contemporary Scholarship*.

that compassion rather than purity should be the basis of human relationships. Jesus as a subversive sage and prophet founded a new movement that was intended to place Israel's relationship with God and their relationship with each other on a new basis.

A number of elements in Borg's understanding of Jesus are suggesting and promising, but what we want to focus on here is his understanding of eschatology. We can grant that understanding Jesus' conception of the kingdom of God and eschatology is no easy task. Both the words *eschatology* and *apocalyptic* were rightly treated in a series of articles on "slippery words" in the journal *Expository Times* awhile back.[36] Borg rightly cautions us about accepting the idea that Jesus necessarily expected an imminent end of the present world order. I define *eschatology* and *apocalyptic* similarly for the purposes of this chapter—namely, Jesus taught that the present evil age would end and the age to come would become a reality. In that coming age God would fulfill all the promises made to his people. Of course, this definition leaves many details unexplained, but it does affirm Jesus' teaching that the kingdom of God would involve the inauguration of a new world order.

Borg underplays the future coming of the kingdom of God.[37] For instance, it is scarcely probable that Mark 9:1 (predicting the coming of Jesus to some of his disciples before they die) is inauthentic, for the very difficulty of the saying supports its authenticity. Indeed, many scholars appeal to the same saying in support of the idea that Jesus erred, for he promised he would come again before some of the disciples died and he failed to do so. My intention is not to propose a solution to the alleged error of Jesus here.[38] The early church would not have invented such a difficult saying and put it in Jesus' mouth. This suggests that Borg's attempt to strip the eschatological sayings from the historical Jesus must

---

[36]I. Howard Marshall, "Slippery Words, 1: Eschatology," *The Expository Times* 89 (1978): 264-69; Margaret Barker, "Slippery Words, 3: Apocalyptic," *The Expository Times* 89 (1978): 324-29.

[37]Bruce Chilton ("The Kingdom of God in Recent Discussion," in *Studying the Historical Jesus: Evaluations of the State of Current Research*, ed. Bruce Chilton and Craig A. Evans [Leiden: Brill, 1994], pp. 255-80) emphasizes that the kingdom of God is the dynamic rule of God. His view overlaps with Borg's, but he indicates (pp. 266-69) where he departs from Borg. For the idea that the reign of God is imminent in Jesus' thinking, see Ben F. Meyer, "Jesus' Scenario of the Future," in *Christus Faber: The Master Builder and the House of God* (Allison Park, Penn.: Pickwick, 1992), pp. 41-58; Ben F. Meyer, "Jesus' Ministry and Self-Understanding," in *Studying the Historical Jesus: Evaluations of the State of Current Research*, ed. Bruce Chilton and Craig A. Evans (Leiden: Brill, 1994), p. 344; Dale C. Allison Jr., "A Plea for Thoroughgoing Eschatology," *Journal of Biblical Literature* 113 (1994): 669-78. Witherington (*Jesus Quest*, p. 96) is more helpful in saying that Jesus saw the end as "*possibly* imminent" but not "*necessarily* imminent." For two surveys on the kingdom of God in the teaching of Jesus, see G. R. Beasley-Murray, *Jesus and the Kingdom of God* (Grand Rapids: Eerdmans, 1986); Dale C. Allison Jr., *The End of the Ages Has Come: An Early Interpretation of the Passion and Resurrection of Jesus* (Philadelphia: Fortress, 1985).

[38]For a brief discussion, see Markus Bockmuehl, *This Jesus: Martyr, Lord, Messiah* (Edinburgh: T & T Clark, 1994), pp. 98-102.

be judged unsuccessful.[39]

Tensions within the third quest. The four points of agreement may suggest a greater consensus than exists, for more detailed investigation reveals significant differences of opinion on matters of substance. There is remarkable diversity even among those who subscribe to most of the four points. For example, E. P. Sanders in his book *Jesus and Judaism* argues that what distinguished Jesus from other Jewish teachers was not that he offered grace, mercy and love to those who repented.[40] It was that Jesus accepted sinners *without requiring them to repent.* The verses in the Gospels that attribute to the historical Jesus the need for sinners to repent are deemed inauthentic. Sanders insists that Jesus did not engage in any substantial conflict with the Pharisees, nor did he speak against the law, nor did he ever speak of the Gentiles' place in the kingdom of God. All the passages that suggest the contrary he dismisses as having been created by the early church.

The pillar of Sanders's book, in fact, is his understanding of the temple incident in Mark 11:15-17. But again he can only sustain his thesis by insisting that verse 17 is inauthentic. Sanders has contributed substantially to the third quest and agrees with the four points noted above. But when we examine his views in more detail, we see that he differs in substantial ways from other scholars. The Jesus reconstructed by Sanders did not require sinners to repent, had no disagreements with the religious leaders on the law and was not involved in any significant controversy with the Pharisees. My purpose is not to interact in detail with the issues raised by Sanders. Scot McKnight has demonstrated severe methodological problems in Sanders's work and the lack of an adequate rationale for accepting some sayings as authentic and others as inauthentic.[41] The point I want to make is this: one can accept all four points of the third quest and still come up with a Jesus who diverges remarkably from the Jesus of the Gospels.

Richard Horsley[42] also subscribes to most of the points made above regarding the third quest. Horsley emphasizes the political and social dimensions of Jesus' message and life and argues that Jesus was a social prophet who came to renew Israel. Jesus' words of judgment were not directed against the common people but the rulers of Jewish society who exercised control over ordinary people. He desired to see unjust social structures torn down and a just society built up. According to Horsley, the just society envisioned by Jesus had no hierarchy at all. Jesus opposed the patriarchal family system of his day and established a new community based on

---

[39]See especially the helpful criticisms of Witherington (*Jesus Quest*, pp. 93-98). In particular, Witherington demonstrates that Borg's dismissal of the authenticity of the Son of Man sayings is unpersuasive.

[40]E. P. Sanders, *Jesus and Judaism* (Philadelphia: Fortress, 1985).

[41]See his review in *Trinity Journal* 6 (1985): 219-25.

[42]See Richard Horsley, *Jesus and the Spiral of Violence: Popular Jewish Resistance in Roman Palestine* (San Francisco: Harper & Row, 1987). See also the article cited in note 32.

equality.[43] Jesus jettisoned any form of hierarchy in the social sphere, for anyone's ruling over someone else involves oppression. What Jesus longed for was a new political system that did not distinguish between rulers and the common people. In short, Jesus wanted to establish an egalitarian social system.

The political glasses through which Horsley reads the Gospel accounts become apparent as he explains exorcising demons and forgiving debts. "The violent struggle between God and demonic forces was simply a symbolization or reflection of the violent social-political-religious conflict in which the people were caught individually or collectively."[44] The forgiveness of debts (Lk 11:2-4) does not relate to forgiving one another of sins. Rather, people in Jewish society were oppressing one another by not releasing fellow citizens from their financial debts. Jesus called on them to instantiate the new society by emancipating their fellow citizens from their financial obligations. While Sanders argued that Jesus' message was distinctive in teaching that sinners could associate with him without repenting, Horsley moves in a different direction and contends that there is no genuine evidence that Jesus especially associated with sinners, tax collectors and prostitutes.

Horsley's work is very stimulating. He rightly reminds us that any attempt to neatly separate religion and politics in Jesus' day would be impossible and that there were political ramifications to Jesus' message. He correctly discerns that Jesus relativizes the social structures of his day. But like Sanders, he dismisses as inauthentic the verses in the Gospels that cut against the grain of his political Jesus. He provides no careful methodological discussion that supports retaining some verses and excising others.[45] The Jesus reconstructed by Horsley looks suspiciously like a twentieth-century Marxist feminist. Indeed, his whole program is strikingly similar to that espoused by many university professors in the United States. Of course, Horsley can maintain this picture only by relegating the high Christology of the Synoptics to the evangelists rather than to Jesus himself. The Gospel of John is not even considered as a possible historical source.[46]

On the other hand, A. E. Harvey's book *Jesus and the Constraints of History* evidences a methodological rigor that is lacking in both Sanders and Horsley.[47] Harvey, like Sanders and Horsley, is in basic harmony with most of the four points. He argues that Jesus would have had to speak to the culture of his day and that we

---

[43]In this respect Crossan *(The Historical Jesus)* is quite similar to Horsley. Crossan's distinctive portrait cannot be examined here, but for a compelling and devastating review, see Robert H. Stein in *Word and World* 13 (1993): 205-6 and also Bockmuehl, "History and Faith," pp. 24-26.

[44]*Spiral of Violence*, p. 187.

[45]Borg ("Reflections on a Discipline," p. 27) says that scholars often rely on hunches, as well as on how a theory "fits," more than on constructing a careful methodology for their theory. Such an approach is an invitation to subjectivism.

[46]Horsley, "Israelite Prophet?" p. 94.

[47]A. E. Harvey, *Jesus and the Constraints of History* (Philadelphia: Westminster, 1982).

can form a clearer picture of Jesus when we consider the historical constraints of the time in which he lived. Harvey's work reflects the careful hypothesis building typical of British scholarship. However, N. T. Wright correctly observes that Harvey's understanding of the "constraints" of history needs to be broadened.[48] The conclusion of the book is rather disappointing, for he argues that Jesus did not consider himself to be the Messiah with a capital *M* and that the constraint of Jewish monotheism demands that Jesus understood himself to be God's nondivine agent. Therefore, Harvey interprets Thomas's words "my Lord and my God" (Jn 20:28) as confessing Jesus' divine agency, not his deity.

Evaluation of the Third Quest

I have briefly discussed these three writers for illustrative purposes. Each scholar attempts to get behind what the Gospel writers have written in order to construct the real Jesus, for they are trying to strip off later accretions of tradition and expose the bedrock of who Jesus really was. And yet the very diversity among various portraits of Jesus indicates that there will never be any consensus on who he was. No two scholars agree on what is authentic. One scholar says that Jesus was distinctive in accepting sinners without calling them to repentance, and another says that he did not associate with sinners in a noticeable way at all. Evangelicals should salute this attempt in some respects, for it is astonishingly easy to read the Gospels in such a way that we make a Jesus in our own image. But the Jesus we worship is a Jesus of history, and as historians we must distance ourselves from our own conceptions in order to grasp as fully as possible the Jesus of history.[49] Our first task, therefore, is not to "create" a historical Jesus that fits with our modern agendas but to "see" him as he is presented in the Gospels.[50]

---

[48]See Wright's review article on Harvey, " 'Constraints' and the Jesus of History," *Scottish Journal of Theology* 39 (1986): 189-210.

[49]Compare Adolf Schlatter, "The Theology of the New Testament and Dogmatics," in *The Nature of New Testament Theology*, ed. and trans. Robert Morgan (German ed. 1909; Naperville, Ill.: Allenson, 1973), pp. 118-19. Schlatter (p. 128) says, "The justification for a New Testament theology conceived as history is that the independent development of historical science gives a measure of protection, admittedly not infallible, against arbitrary reconstructions of its object. It secures us against producing a mixture of what scripture says and what the church teaches, or a mixture of the Bible and our own religious opinions, in which neither the one factor nor the other is correctly grasped and fruitfully applied."

[50]On the importance of seeing what is really there, see Schlatter, "Theology of the New Testament," pp. 122, 127, 129, 135, 136, 148-49, 151. He remarks, "The first task of New Testament theology consists in perceiving the given facts of the case, and it would be childish to worry that there is no more work left for us to do since countless scholars have been observing the New Testament for a long time now. That would show how little we were aware of the size of the task posed by the formula 'observation.' What has happened in the past far exceeds in its fullness and depth our capacity for seeing, and there is no question of an end being reached even of the first and most simple function of New Testament study; namely, seeing what is there" (p. 136).

It must be understood that "every" historical portrait of Jesus depends on certain theological and philosophical preconceptions.[51] Some contributors to the third quest betray a surprising naiveté in claiming that theological concerns do not inform their historical work.[52] But the cultural climate always informs historical research, and there is never any historical work that is not influenced by a theological agenda.[53] Adolf Schlatter rightly remarks, "We have to be clear that historical criticism is never based on historical fact alone, but always has roots in the critic's dogma, too."[54] Schlatter's words should not be interpreted as justification for any and every philosophical approach in Jesus research, no matter how arbitrary. He is attacking the notion that some scholars simply do "objective" history while others are adversely "influenced" by religious commitments. No one is exempt from a philosophical worldview. Those who believe their historical research is immune from any theological preconceptions are naive. In order to do historical research we must self-consciously examine and defend our own philosophical worldview, for it will inevitably affect our historical conclusions.

Scholars have always worried about accepting the four Gospels as history, since they were written by people who were not neutral observers. But we now know that there is no such thing as uninterpreted history—written from a neutral standpoint. No historian has the secure Archimedean standpoint from which to declare the truth of history. All historians must adopt a certain perspective and select certain events and speeches in order to write history. Thus we should not reject the Gospels merely because they contain interpreted history and are written by people with a certain point of view.[55] What we must decide is whether the story of Jesus of Nazareth presented and interpreted by the Gospel writers is credible, including the claim that he was raised from the dead.[56]

---

[51]Rightly Bockmuehl, "History and Faith," pp. 27-28.

[52]Walter P. Weaver, "Foreword: Reflection on the Continuing Quest for Jesus," and James. H. Charlesworth, "Conclusion," in *Images of Jesus Today*, ed. J. H. Charlesworth and W. P. Weaver (Valley Forge, Penn.: Trinity Press International, 1994), pp. xiv and 113-14 respectively; Evans, "Life-of-Jesus Research," pp. 15-17.

[53]Compare Schlatter ("Theology of the New Testament," pp. 123-27), whose insights on this issue are fundamental. For example, Sanders's work is influenced by the terrible history of the Holocaust and Christians' history of mistreating Jews. Compare the comments of Telford, "Major Trends," p. 59.

[54]Schlatter, "Theology of the New Testament," p. 155.

[55]Martin Hengel ("Aufgaben der neutestamentlichen Wissenschaft," *New Testament Studies* 40 [1994]: 329) remarks, "Unsere Disziplin würde sich selbst zerstören, wollte sie die vom paulinischen und johannischen theologischen Denken angestossene Frage nach der Wahrheit des geoffenbarten Gotteswortes aufgeben und sich in blosse deskriptive Religionsgeschichte verwandeln, in der diese Frage nicht mehr gestellt werden darf. Hier ist das Salz, das unserer Arbeit Würze und Existenzberechitigung gibt."

[56]Bockmuehl ("History and Faith," pp. 26-27) notes the inadequacy of Meier's work *(A Marginal Jew)*, for the latter brackets out the resurrection as a matter of historical research. A supernatural Jesus would seem to be excluded a priori on this scheme. Bockmuehl (*This Jesus,* pp. 145-63) is more courageous,

And yet to decide against the Gospel writers' depiction of Jesus is not merely a neutral conclusion of historical criticism. As Adolf Schlatter wrote,

> According to the sceptical position, it is true that the historian explains; he observes the New Testament neutrally. But in reality this is to begin at once with a determined struggle against it. The word with which the New Testament confronts us intends to be believed, and so rules out once and for all any sort of neutral treatment. As soon as the historian sets aside or brackets the question of faith, he is making his concern with the New Testament and his presentation of it into a radical and total polemic against it.[57]

I am not suggesting that faith in the Gospel writers is blind, for there is substantial evidence that they were concerned about historical veracity.[58] And anyone who rejects the Gospel writers' interpretations of Jesus' life has no secure basis for historical research into his life.[59] We have too little other evidence and insufficient historical tools to get behind their portraits to the "authentic" Jesus.[60] Thus different portraits of Jesus will emerge as scholars juggle the materials we have, determining whether this bit or that is authentic. The only Jesus of Nazareth we have is the one interpreted by the four Gospel writers, and there are good grounds for trusting their testimony.[61] This Jesus had a messianic self-consciousness, and the Gospel writers claimed that he was raised from the dead. Two scholars who have led the way in this direction are Ben F. Meyer in his book *The Aims of Jesus*[62] and Markus Bockmuehl in his more popular but

---

for he tackles and defends the idea of the resurrection and the divinity of Jesus head-on in his work.

[57]Schlatter, "Theology of the New Testament," p. 122. This is not a call for subjectivity on Schlatter's part. Many historians assume as a starting point that "history" is restricted to the horizontal sphere of cause and effect, so that divine intervention is ruled out a priori. Schlatter attacks a definition of history that excludes the possibility of the miraculous.

[58]See the six-volume series *Gospel Perspectives* (Sheffield, U.K.: JSOT Press, 1980-86); Craig Blomberg, *The Historical Reliability of the Gospels* (Downers Grove, Ill.: InterVarsity Press, 1987).

[59]It is interesting that in his summary of the historical anchor points for Jesus' life, Charlesworth (*Jesus Within Judaism*, p. 169) concludes with the death of Jesus and does not even mention whether the resurrection is historically credible.

[60]Compare Telford, "Major Trends," p. 59. My point is very different from that of Helmut Koester ("The Historical Jesus and the Historical Situation of the Quest: An Epilogue," in *Studying the Historical Jesus: Evaluations of the State of Current Research*, ed. Bruce Chilton and Craig A. Evans [Leiden: Brill, 1994], p. 540), who follows in Bultmann's footsteps and believes the quest should be redirected. I am suggesting, on the contrary, that the only Jesus we have—the Jesus of the Gospels—is an accurate assessment of Jesus as he really was.

[61]For an insightful methodological contribution, see Brice L. Martin, "Reflections on Historical Criticism and Self-Understanding," in *Self-Definition and Self-Discovery in Early Christianity: A Study in Changing Horizons*, ed. David J. Hawkin and Tom Robinson (Lewiston, N.Y.: Mellen, 1990), pp. 56-77.

[62]Ben F. Meyer, *The Aims of Jesus* (London: SCM Press, 1979). For a defense of his methodology, see Ben F. Meyer, *Critical Realism and the New Testament* (Allison Park, Penn.: Pickwick, 1989), and his more recent essay "Jesus' Ministry," pp. 337-52.

instructive work *This Jesus.*[63] I would not espouse everything they propose in their works, but their historical work is paradigmatic in reflecting a careful use of the historical method that takes seriously claims for divine intervention that are present in the Gospel materials.

Controversy over Paul and the Law

A reappraisal of the soteriology of Judaism. Our first task in interpreting the New Testament is to "see" what is really there, to discern the actual meaning of the text. Contemporary scholarship relating to Paul and the law poses that question anew, asking whether we have imposed our own vision on the Pauline writings.

Ever since the Reformation scholars have argued that Paul criticized the Jews for their legalism—their belief that doing the works of the law earns merit in the sight of God. In the early part of the twentieth century some scholars questioned the validity of this hypothesis and contended that Judaism was not a legalistic religion.[64] Their objections, however, largely fell on deaf ears, and the consensus that Judaism was legalistic continued to reign supreme in New Testament studies.

This consensus was shattered in 1977, however, with the publication of E. P. Sanders's *Paul and Palestinian Judaism,* the most influential book in Pauline studies in recent years.[65] Sanders conducted a careful inductive study of Jewish writings found in the Apocrypha, Pseudepigrapha, Dead Sea Scrolls and rabbinic literature. He concluded that the supposed legalism of Jews in Paul's day was a myth imposed on the evidence by Christian scholars who read the disagreement between Paul and certain Jews through the lenses of the struggle between Roman Catholicism and Protestantism.

The actual soteriology of the Jews, Sanders asserted, was not legalistic at all. Palestinian Judaism is better described by the term *covenantal nomism.* The covenant that God enacted with the Jews was based on grace whereby God elected them to be his people. God did not demand a certain level of works before entering into covenant with his people. God mercifully forgave their sins and entered into a relationship with Israel. How does the word *nomism* fit into Sanders's understanding of Jewish soteriology? Certainly the law was a central feature of Palestinian religion, but, says Sanders, the Jews never understood obedience to the law as a way of earning or meriting salvation. The observance of the law was a way of maintaining salvation once having been inducted into the covenant. Keeping the law, then, was conceived as a grateful response to God's covenantal mercy in redeeming his people.

Sanders's understanding of Judaism was an idea whose time had come, for I have

---

[63]See note 38 for bibliographic information.
[64]See Claude G. Montefiore, *Judaism and St. Paul* (London: Max Goschen, 1914); George Foote Moore, "Christian Writers on Judaism," *Harvard Theological Review* 14 (1921): 197-254.
[65]E. P. Sanders, *Paul and Palestinian Judaism* (Philadelphia: Fortress, 1977).

already noted that others before Sanders suggested that Judaism was not a legalistic religion, but their work did not exert a significant influence on New Testament scholarship. Sanders's book, however, has changed the direction of Pauline studies, for he has convinced many scholars that the traditional picture of Judaism constructed by New Testament scholars does not accord with Palestinian Judaism as it really was. The probative force of his work is partially due to the thoroughness of his research. The acceptance that his thesis has gained may be influenced by the fact that he wrote it after the Holocaust. Christians continue to be deeply troubled that the Holocaust could occur in a country deeply influenced by Lutheran theology.

Sanders's work on Judaism raised a fundamental question. In identifying Paul's opponents as legalistic Jews, have we been seeing correctly what is really there in the text? Or have we been imposing a traditional soteriological paradigm on the Pauline letters that blinds us to our own presuppositions and prevents us from understanding his message? Sanders's work has been helpful in provoking scholars to ask afresh whether we have been "seeing" what Paul actually says about Judaism or if we have been guilty of "creating" a polemic against Judaism that does not accord with the text.

A reappraisal of Paul's criticism of Judaism. Sanders's work has undoubtedly caused a paradigm shift in our understanding of Judaism. But if Sanders rightly describes Judaism, then how should we understand Paul's critique of the Mosaic law in his letters? If Paul does not attack the legalism of his Jewish contemporaries, what is his complaint with reference to the Mosaic law? A number of scholars have proposed answers, but three scholars—Sanders himself, Heikki Räisänen and James Dunn—have been particularly influential.

E. P. Sanders followed up *Paul and Palestinian Judaism* with a book titled *Paul, the Law and the Jewish People.*[66] In it he defends the thesis that Paul's soteriology led him to reject the law as a way of salvation. To be specific, Paul reasoned that since salvation was obtained through Christ, it follows that the law could not be the means to salvation. Sanders coins the phrase *solution to plight* to explain his understanding of Pauline soteriology. Once Paul believed that salvation was available only through Christ, he reflexively concluded that salvation was not available through the law, for if salvation is only through Christ then it could not be obtained via the law. Sanders's study of Paul leads him to dismiss the anthropological emphasis found in Bultmann and other scholars. He argues that the problem with the law is not that it was impossible for anyone to keep it perfectly. Nor did Paul believe that adherence to the law led to legalism and meritorious works righteousness. The law is set aside as a soteriological path for salvation-historic reasons. Now that Christ has come, salvation must be through him rather than through Torah.

---

[66]E. P. Sanders, *Paul, the Law and the Jewish People* (Philadelphia: Fortress, 1983).

In other words, the reason Paul rejects Judaism is that it is not Christianity.

Heikki Räisänen acknowledges his debt to Sanders and agrees that the latter has demonstrated that Judaism was not legalistic.[67] How does he then explain Paul? Sanders admitted that at times Paul's arguments in favor of his conclusions are tortuous and even inconsistent, but Räisänen moves even farther in this direction than Sanders. The notion that Paul was a great theologian and a profound thinker needs to be dispelled. On the contrary, Paul's theology is filled with contradictions and inconsistencies. In a number of texts Paul asserts that the law is abolished and should no longer play any role in the lives of believers (Rom 7:1-6; 2 Cor 3; Gal 3:15—4:7). In other texts, however, he claims that believers should fulfill the law (Rom 8:4; 13:8-10; 1 Cor 7:19; Gal 5:14). Both of these teachings, observes Räisänen, could scarcely be true at the same time. To say that the law is set aside and that believers should keep it violates the law of noncontradiction. Scholars have labored to harmonize these two different kinds of statements. Räisänen exhorts us to concede that Paul said different things in different contexts that do not cohere logically.

Similarly, Paul asserts strongly that no one can keep the law and that all fall short of keeping its commands perfectly (Rom 1:18-3:20; 3:23; Gal 3:10). And yet in Romans 2:14-15, 26-27 he claims that even non-Christian Gentiles are able to keep the law. This demonstrates, says Räisänen, that Paul argues inconsistently to accomplish his own purposes. When he desires to argue against the Jewish Torah in favor of Christianity, he claims that no one can keep the law. But his attack on fellow Jews who are devoted to the Torah becomes so all-consuming that he forgets to notice, when he says Gentiles can observe the law, that he has already previously denied that anyone can keep it. A troubling characteristic of Paul emerges here, according to Räisänen. He sharply attacks the Jews for violations of Torah and claims in contradistinction that Christians keep the law. But in matter of fact we see that Christians scarcely kept the law any better than Jews. An examination of 1 Corinthians alone seems to bear this out. Thus Räisänen concludes that Paul is guilty of blatant partisanship in trumpeting Christianity and denigrating Judaism.

According to Räisänen, Paul's explanation of the origin and purpose of the law is riddled with problems. Usually Paul says that the law comes from God, but he becomes so carried away with his argument in Galatians 3:19 that he even denies this and concludes that the law stems from the angels rather than God. Nor is Paul consistent as to the purpose of the law. In Romans 7:10 he says that the law was given to produce life, but in Galatians 3:19 and Romans 5:20 he says that God's intention in giving the law was to multiply sin. These two statements seem to be

---

[67]See Heikki Räisänen, *Paul and the Law* (Philadelphia: Fortress, 1983); Heikki Räisänen, *The Torah and Christ* (Helsinki: Finnish Exegetical Society, 1986).

directly irreconcilable. And even if one or the other of these two statements fits reality, other problems emerge. A God who gave the law to lead to life must be lacking in wisdom. A wise God would surely have foreseen that life would not be obtained through the law. On the other hand, a God who enacted the law in order to increase sin seems to be rather cynical. How could God be good and give a law that would increase misery for human beings?

Räisänen finds that Romans 2:12 and 5:13 are also contradictory. In the former verse Paul says that those who do not have the law will perish without the law. The thought seems to be that they will be judged in terms of their obedience to the unwritten law that is written in their hearts (Rom 2:14-15). And yet Paul says in Romans 5:13 that sin is not reckoned when there is no law. If sin is not counted against someone when there is no law, how can those who do not have the law be held responsible for their sin? Paul cannot have it both ways. Either people without the law are held responsible for their sin per Romans 2:12, or sin is not counted against those who do not possess the law. Paul says different things on different occasions and does not perceive that he actually ends up contradicting himself.

How can we account for such incoherent statements from Paul? Räisänen remarks that Paul's motivation was laudable, for he desired to see the Gentiles included among the people of God without requiring them to observe the Mosaic law. But at the same time Paul retained the idea that the law was authoritative. Attempting to hold both of these convictions at the same time proved to be irreconcilable for Paul, and yet he could not bring himself to admit, says Räisänen, what moderns do not find to be so unpalatable—that not everything found in the Old Testament is from God.

James Dunn also celebrates the new dimension that Sanders has opened up to New Testament scholars through his study of Second Temple Judaism.[68] He argues, however, that both Sanders and Räisänen have failed to take advantage of the paradigm shift when it comes to understanding Paul. In particular, the Paul reconstructed by Sanders is too idiosyncratic and arbitrary, for he rejects Judaism only because it is not Christianity. An analysis of the Pauline writings reveals, says Dunn, that Paul's criticism of Judaism was deeper than this. Paul's Christology was not the sole reason he criticized the law as a way of salvation. Nonetheless, Dunn concurs with Sanders that the Pauline critique of Judaism is not directed against Jewish legalism or inability to keep the law.

Dunn contends that we must remove our Reformation blinders before we interpret Paul. If Judaism was not legalistic and if the root problem of the Jews does not relate to inability to keep the law, then how can we account for Paul's critique

---

[68]See J. D. G. Dunn, *Jesus, Paul and the Law: Studies in Mark and Galatians* (Louisville, Ky.: Westminster, 1990); J. D. G. Dunn, *Romans*, 2 vols. (Dallas: Word, 1988).

of the Torah in his letters? Dunn suggests that the fundamental objection leveled against Torah observance is that thereby Gentiles were excluded from participation in the people of God. It is interesting that much of the controversy over the law related to circumcision, food laws and the sabbath. These functioned as boundary markers between Jews and Gentiles, and Gentiles felt that in subscribing to these requirements they were surrendering their ethnic identity and becoming Jews. Indeed, Dunn argues the term "works of law" in Paul (Rom 3:20, 28; Gal 2:16; 3:2, 5, 10) focuses on laws that create a sociological rift between Jews and Gentiles. What Paul opposed, then, was not legalism or meritorious works righteousness. He objected to the ethnocentrism and nationalism of certain Jews who were requiring Gentiles to become Jews in order to join the people of God.

An Evaluation of the New Perspective on Paul

The revolution in Pauline studies is salutary in that it stimulates us to examine the text afresh to discern what Paul actually says. The issues raised by Sanders, Räisänen and Dunn cannot be explored in detail here, although I have examined their contribution in more detail elsewhere.[69]

Sanders's work has provided an important service, for all too often Judaism and particularly the Pharisees are portrayed in a caricatured manner. The impression given is that the Jews were consumed with pettifogging legalism and trivia, while Christians are spared these faults. Reading the texts in this way blinds us to the fellow humanity of the Jews who are criticized. Nonetheless, Sanders goes to the other extreme when he attempts to establish the thesis that the Jews were not criticized for legalism at all.

Surely Sanders is correct in emphasizing that one reason for Paul's rejecting the law was the salvation-historic shift between the Testaments. However, his claim that Paul argued only from solution to plight is questionable, as Frank Thielman has demonstrated in his careful study of the Old Testament, Second Temple Judaism and Galatians and Romans.[70] Sanders is less convincing in his attempt to peel away any anthropological dimension to Paul's soteriology. Here the criticisms by Robert Gundry and Timo Laato have revealed a serious weakness in Sanders's study.[71]

Careful study of a number of texts (Lk 18:9-14; Rom 3:27—4:5; 9:30—10:8; Gal 3:1-14; Phil 3:2-11) indicates that there is a polemic in the New Testament against legalism. These passages cannot be explained away easily. Salvation history

---

[69]See Thomas R. Schreiner, *The Law and Its Fulfillment: A Pauline Theology of Law* (Grand Rapids: Baker, 1993). For a helpful analysis of the law in Galatians, see In-Gyu Hong, *The Law in Galatians* (Sheffield, U.K.: JSOT Press, 1993).

[70]Frank Thielman, *From Plight to Solution: A Jewish Framework for Understanding Paul's View of the Law in Galatians and Romans* (Leiden: Brill, 1989).

[71]See Robert H. Gundry, "Grace, Works and Staying Saved in Paul," *Biblica* 66 (1985): 1-38; Timo Laato, *Paulus und das Judentum: Anthropologische Erwägungen* (Åbo: Åbo Academy Press, 1991).

and anthropology are not at loggerheads—both play a role in Pauline theology. Our existential knowledge of human beings confirms what we read in the New Testament. Our fundamental problem is pride; we desire to be great and to be admired by others. Pride expresses itself in a variety of ways, one of them being religious observance. We are all tempted to esteem ourselves above our fellow human beings because we think we are morally superior to them. It would be very surprising if the Jews of Paul's day did not struggle with the same problem, for the desire to impress God and other people with our works is at heart a human problem that is not restricted to Jews. Sanders strains the natural exegesis of the text (see Rom 3:27—4:8; 9:30—10:8; Phil 3:2-11) in denying legalism, but he also seems oblivious to human pride, which C. S. Lewis calls the root sin.

Evangelical students are tempted to dismiss Heikki Räisänen's work, since he detects so many contradictions in Paul's theology. This would be a serious mistake. Räisänen raises all the right questions (even if his answers are flawed) and thereby helps us see problems in the text that we need to grapple with. Räisänen's fundamental problem is that he fails to read Paul sympathetically and contextually. Wherever he detects a logical problem in Paul's statements on the law, Räisänen concludes that a logical contradiction is present. But in virtually every case an examination of context resolves the alleged difficulties. For instance, Jeffrey A. D. Weima has demonstrated that the so-called contradictions relating to the law and sin yield a coherent sense.[72] And Frank Thielman, by studying the Pauline statements on the law in the particular context in which they were made, shows that his theology is consistent.[73]

Dunn's approach to Paul and the law is more promising because he attempts to understand and explain the Pauline theology of the law at a deeper level. Moreover, he correctly identifies a major theme in Pauline theology. The inclusion of the Gentiles in the people of God was a driving force in the Pauline mission, for it was Paul's ambition to plant churches where there were none and to bring about the obedience of faith among all nations (Rom 1:5; 15:15-21; 16:26). Paul passionately resisted Peter in Antioch (Gal 2:11-14), for Peter's hypocritical actions in effect excluded the Gentiles from the people of God unless they became Jews.

We can also agree with Dunn when he establishes a connection between the cessation of Torah and the inclusion of the Gentiles. Circumcision, food laws and sabbath were boundary markers that erected barriers between Jews and Gentiles. When Paul heralded the end of the Mosaic law (Gal 3:15—4:7; 2 Cor 3:4-18), one of his purposes was to tear down the dividing wall that separated Jews and Gentiles

---

[72]"The Function of the Law in Relation to Sin: An Evaluation of the View of H. Räisänen," *Novum Testamentum* 32 (1990): 219-35.

[73]Frank Thielman, *Paul and the Law: A Contextual Approach* (Downers Grove, Ill.: InterVarsity Press, 1994). For a fuller evaluation of Thielman's work, see my review in *Trinity Journal* 6 (1995): 101-4.

(Eph 2:11-22). The laws that signaled to all that Jews and Gentiles were profoundly different were now passé. Now Jews and Gentiles were fellow members of the body through the gospel of Christ which Paul was specially commissioned to preach (Eph 3:1-13).

Despite the strengths of Dunn's contribution, some weaknesses remain in his analysis. For instance, he has not sufficiently emphasized that "works of law" refers to the whole law and instead descries a focus on the laws that separate Jews from Gentiles. Joseph A. Fitzmyer has demonstrated that in the Qumran literature "works of law" refers to the law as a whole and that a restriction to or focus on a portion of the law cannot be sustained.[74] That "works of law" refers to the entire law is the most satisfactory way to understand Paul's usage of the term as well. Romans 3:20 and Galatians 3:10 are particularly illuminating here, for both of these verses indicate that failure to keep the works of the law is the reason people (including Jews) are guilty before God. The fundamental problem with the Jews, as Romans 2:17-29 confirms, is that they did not keep the law that they proclaimed and taught to others. The Jews are not primarily indicted for *excluding* Gentiles. They are condemned for disobeying the very law that they charged Gentiles with disobeying (Rom 2:1-2). Dunn wrongly makes the exclusion of the Gentiles the central fault of the Jews, when in fact Paul's central criticism is that they did not keep the law themselves.

Similarly, Dunn's contention that the problem with the Jews was ethnocentrism or nationalism rather than legalism is unpersuasive. He wrenches apart here what should be kept together, for the Jews believed that they were superior to other nations not only because of their ethnic identity but also because of their devotion to the Torah. This is reflected in the tradition that God offered the Torah to all nations and only Israel accepted it.[75] Paul takes aim at the same conception in Romans 2. He does not merely criticize the Jews for nationalism but also strikes at the root of their nationalism, a sense of moral superiority for adhering to Torah. The Jews did not believe that they were favored over the Gentiles by virtue of their Jewishness alone. What set them apart was their devotion to and observance of God's law. They were separate from the Gentiles both ethnically and morally.

Such a stance is not necessarily legalistic, for some people may well be superior to others morally. What both Old and New Testaments teach, however, is that moral growth is due to the powerful electing and sustaining work of God's grace, not the inherent virtue of human beings. Those who are chosen by God are easily inclined to believe that it is their own virtue and nobility that sets them apart from other

---

[74]Joseph A. Fitzmyer, "Paul's Jewish Background and the Deeds of the Law," in *According to Paul: Studies in the Theology of the Apostle* (New York: Paulist, 1993), pp. 18-35.

[75]See the reference in C. G. Montefiore and H. Loewe, *A Rabbinic Anthology* (New York: Schocken, 1974), p. 121; see also Sanders, *Palestinian Judaism,* pp. 88-89.

human beings. The temptation to praise self rather than God is always lurking at our side, and we may begin to think that God owes us something for our good works (Rom 4:4-5). In conclusion, Paul's indictment of Jewish nationalism cannot be separated from legalism, for the texts in question show that the Jews believed themselves to be better than the Gentiles because of their performance of the law. We need only remark again that the inclination toward legalism is not a Jewish problem per se. It is a fundamental human problem, for we are inclined to praise ourselves instead of the God who is the giver of all gifts.

Chapter 5

New Dimensions in Patristic Theology, 1980-1995

James Leo Garrett Jr.

....

THE ACADEMIC DISCIPLINE KNOWN AS PATRISTICS, OR EARLY CHURCH studies, has been undergoing changes that have been evoking some serious reflection as well as bibliographic surveys of the latest publications in the field. Thomas P. Halton and Robert D. Sider reviewed the entire range of literature produced during the 1970s,[1] and Frederick W. Norris surveyed the period from 1973 to 1988.[2] Jean-Daniel Dubois in a series of eight articles reported on new publications between 1982 and 1993,[3] and G.-M. de Durand reviewed in some detail publications in patristica from 1988 to 1991.[4] All of these embraced the entire field of patristics.

Charles Kannengiesser, S.J., of the University of Notre Dame, in two articles[5]

---

[1]Thomas D. Halton and Robert D. Sider, "A Decade of Patristic Scholarship, 1970-79," *Classical World* 76 (1982): 65-127; 77 (1983): 313-83. These two articles are organized by patristic authors, embrace the patristic era up to A.D. 451, include journal and dictionary articles as well as monographs, and normally provide a concise statement of the thesis of each book or article.

[2]Frederick W. Norris, "Recent Developments in Patristic Studies," *American Theological Library Proceedings*, 1988, pp. 104-18.

[3]Jean-Daniel Dubois, "Chronique patristique," *Études theologiques et religieuses* 57 (1982): 405-24; 60 (1985): 455-67; 61 (1986): 257-69; 62 (1987): 97-111; 63 (1988): 263-71; 64 (1989): 577-86; 66 (1991): 243-60; 68 (1993): 395-407.

[4]G.-M. de Durand, "Bulletin de patrologie," *Revue des sciences philosophiques et theologiques* 76 (January 1992): 117-54.

[5]Charles Kannengiesser, S.J., "Fifty Years of Patristics," *Theological Studies* 50 (December 1989): 633-56; Charles Kannengiesser, S.J., "The Future of Patristics," *Theological Studies* 52 (March 1991): 128-39. Kannengiesser describes patristics as including "philology, theology, biblical studies, Semitic languages, history, law, philosophy, spirituality, hagiography, [and] Gnostic studies." "Fifty Years of

assessed the last half-century (1940-1990) of patristic studies and posed questions about the future of patristic studies. In the last half-century patristics was European dominated, had access to vast manuscript collections and moved from the monasteries and seminaries to the universities.[6] It became more comprehensive and was extended to its social context.[7] "Patristics . . . has been reborn as nothing less than a hermeneutic of the historical foundations of European culture."[8] A decade earlier Elizabeth A. Clark had also noted the shift from seminary to university and from theology to history. She cited the subsidence of neo-orthodox influence, the dominance of Gnostic studies and studies of heresy (on account of Nag Hammadi and Walter Bauer), and the advent of women's studies.[9]

Now the giants of that era (Congar, de Lubac, Daniélou, Rahner, Cross, Urs von Balthasar, Grillmeier) have passed from the scene.[10] The study of patristics has expanded to North America and is moving to the Two-Thirds World. Kannengiesser sees in the postmodern era the importance of correlating more fully academic study and ecclesial use of the Bible, the interpretation of Christian origins and answering questions raised by contemporary women's studies.[11] According to Rowan A. Greer, patristics is following one of three methods: a focus on the doctrines of the early church, a focus on patristics as "an extension of New Testament studies" and a focus on the early church as a social phenomenon in the Roman Empire.[12] The first of these methods or subdivisions of patristics is the subject of this present inquiry—patristic theology.

The present investigation encompasses the fifteen-year period from 1980 to 1995. It excludes the texts of patristic sources, the translations of patristic sources, monographs on patristic ethics and on early church liturgies, as well as most biographies within patristics, so as to concentrate on the doctrines and the doctrinal controversies of the early church. Journal articles are not included.

Encyclopedias and Dictionaries
One major encyclopedia on the early church was published during the period being

---

Patristic Studies," p. 633.

[6]Kannengiesser, "Fifty Years of Patristic Studies," pp. 654-55, 641-42; "The Future of Patristics," pp. 128, 129.

[7]Kannengiesser, "The Future of Patristics," pp. 128-34.

[8]Ibid., p. 132.

[9]Elizabeth A. Clark, "The State and Future of Historical Theology: Patristic Studies," in *In Memory of Wilhelm Pauck (1901-1981): Memorial Notices, Liturgical Pieces, Essays and Addresses,* ed. David W. Lotz, Union Papers 2 (New York: Union Theological Seminary, 1982), pp. 46-56; reprinted in Elizabeth A. Clark, *Ascetic Piety and Women's Faith: Essays on Late Ancient Christianity,* Studies in Women and Religion 20 (Lewiston, N.Y.: Mellen, 1986), pp. 3-19.

[10]Kannengiesser, "The Future of Patristics," pp. 132-33.

[11]Ibid., pp. 135-39.

[12]Rowan A. Greer, "Reckonings in the Study of the Ancient Church," *Anglican Theological Review* 73 (Spring 1991): 234-35.

reviewed, and another appeared in English translation. Under the editorship of Everett Ferguson of Abilene Christian University and the associate editorship of Michael P. McHugh and Frederick W. Norris, the 983-page *Encyclopedia of Early Christianity*[13] appeared in 1990, the product of 136 authors having Protestant, Roman Catholic and Eastern Orthodox identity, the majority of whom are Protestants who live in the United States. About one-half of the encyclopedia was written by the three editors.[14] Articles normally "follow a standard format," namely, "definition or identification of the subject, chronological or topical sketch, and basic primary and secondary bibliography."[15] Reviewers have assessed the doctrinal articles as being of high quality[16] and have criticized the encyclopedia for deficiency respecting philosophy and pagan religion[17] and for failing "to reflect recent studies that show the diversity of Judaism in the first century A.D."[18]

In 1992 the two-volume *Encyclopedia of the Early Church,* which Angelo di Berardino edited in Italian under the auspices of the Institutum Patristicum Augustinianum, appeared in English.[19] In his foreword to the English translation W. H. C. Frend declared:

> While reflecting . . . in many ways the traditions of continental European patristic scholarship, it incorporates a far wider scholarly perception of the early Church. This is a result of the team of 167 scholars drawn from 17 countries and representing a cross-section of Christian traditions and authors. The range of coverage—archaeological, philosophical, linguistic, theological, historical, and geographic, is enormous.[20]

Most of these authors are Roman Catholic or Eastern Orthodox. Although numerous articles pertaining to patristic authors contain paragraphs on the doctrines of the given author, the major articles on patristic doctrine tend to be of modest length in view of the scope of the double-columned, two-volume work. For example, the article on God is two pages, the one on Christology runs two and a half pages, and the article on the Holy Spirit consists of three pages. The article on church buildings totals six and a half pages. Platonism and Neoplatonism are treated in detail. The doctrinal articles by

---

[13]Ferguson, McHugh and Norris, eds., *Encyclopedia of Early Christianity* (New York: Garland, 1990).

[14]Ferguson authored 156 articles, McHugh, 228, and Norris, 141. Edwin Yamauchi, review of *Encyclopedia of Early Christianity, Fides et Historia* 23 (Fall 1991): 80; Abraham J. Malherbe, review of *Encyclopedia of Early Christianity, Restoration Quarterly* 33 (1991): 106.

[15]E. Glenn Hinson, review of *Encyclopedia of Early Christianity, Review and Expositor* 88 (Fall 1991): 465.

[16]Henry Chadwick, review of *Encyclopedia of Early Christianity, Church History* 62 (June 1993): 244; Malherbe, review of *Encyclopedia of Early Christianity,* 107.

[17]Malherbe, review of *Encyclopedia of Early Christianity,* 108.

[18]Howard Clark Kee, review of *Encyclopedia of Early Christianity, Journal of Church and State* 35 (Spring 1993): 425-26.

[19]Angelo di Berardino, ed., *Encyclopedia of the Early Church,* trans. Adrian Walford, 2 vols. (New York: Oxford University Press, 1992).

[20]Ibid., p. ix.

Manlio Simonetti, Basil Studer and Agostino Trapé are especially noteworthy.

César Vidal Manzanares is the author of a brief Spanish-language patristic diction-ary.[21] The great majority of articles in the dictionary pertain to patristic authors and the first five ecumenical councils. There are no articles on doctrine per se.

General Monographs

One noteworthy monograph of a general nature has been issued during the 1990s. Stuart G. Hall, former lecturer in ecclesiastical history, King's College, London, authored a survey through 451, *Doctrine and Practice in the Early Church*.[22] Hall's references are mostly geared to two source collections, James Stevenson, *A New Eusebius*, and *Creeds, Councils, and Controversies*, as revised by W. H. C. Frend. According to Wolfram Kinzing, "It is neither a history of dogma nor an account of the development of the Early Church, even though it contains elements of both these genres. Rather, it focuses on the complex and complicated interactions between theory and practice."[23] But for Gerald Bray the "development of doctrine is the central theme of the book,"[24] and for Carl A. Volz "the primary focus is on the Trinitarian and Christological controversies" with "practice" not receiving "equal consideration."[25] The volume "seems to fall naturally somewhere between J. N. D. Kelly's *Early Christian Doctrines* and W. H. C. Frend's *The Rise of Christianity*," being "more readable than the former" and "more concise than the latter."[26]

Frances M. Young, Edward Cadbury Professor of Theology, University of Birmingham, authored a much-discussed handbook on patristic literature from Nicea I to Chalcedon that serves somewhat as a history of doctrine for the period.[27] It has been described as "much more readable than most histories of doctrine and much more intellectually stimulating than most church histories."[28] Young has treated fairly the leading authors, both "orthodox" and "heretical."[29] Her presenta-

---

[21]César Vidal Manzanares, *Diccionario de patrística (S. I-VI)* (Navarra: Editorial Verbo Divino, 1993).

[22]Stuart G. Hall, *Doctrine and Practice in the Early Church* (London: S.P.C.K.; Grand Rapids: Eerdmans, 1992).

[23]Wolfram Kinzing, review of *Doctrine and Practice in the Early Church, Journal of Ecclesiastical History* 44 (July 1993): 516. For a similar assessment, see Richard A. Muller, review of *Doctrine and Practice in the Early Church, Calvin Theological Journal* 28 (November 1993): 537.

[24]Gerald Bray, review of *Doctrine and Practice in the Early Church, The Evangelical Quarterly* 65 (January 1993): 87.

[25]Carl A. Volz, review of *Doctrine and Practice in the Early Church, Church History* 61 (December 1992): 439.

[26]Bray, review of *Doctrine and Practice in the Early Church,* 87.

[27]Frances M. Young, *From Nicaea to Chalcedon: A Guide to the Literature and Its Background* (London: SCM Press, 1983).

[28]Christopher Stead, review of *From Nicaea to Chalcedon, The Journal of Ecclesiastical History* 35 (January 1984): 147.

[29]Donald F. Winslow, review of *From Nicaea to Chalcedon, Anglican Theological Review* 66 (October 1984): 447.

tion of the trinitarian controversy has been criticized as being less adequate than her presentation of the christological[30] controversy. She is also said to have neglected Chalcedon.[31]

Christian Doctrine and Classical Culture

Two significant monographs correlating early Christian doctrine and classical culture were issued in the early 1990s: Eric Francis Osborn's *The Emergence of Christian Theology*[32] and Jaroslav Pelikan's *Christianity and Classical Culture.*[33] Osborn, emeritus professor, Queen's College, University of Melbourne, who had written *The Beginning of Christian Philosophy* in 1981,[34] focuses on five authors: Justin Martyr, Athenagoras, Irenaeus, Clement of Alexandria and Tertullian. These authors, according to Osborn, "had a Christian Bible to expound and New Testament ideas to exploit" and "had opponents to refute: pagans, Gnostics, philosophers [and] Jews." Hence they "developed a brilliant new synthesis." They "saw the one God as the first principle of physics (metaphysics), ethics, and logic; that is, the one God was being, goodness, and truth."[35] These authors combined Pauline and Johannine theologies[36] and sought rationality without surrendering "the gospel to Greek philosophy."[37] Faulted for neglecting modern studies of Gnosticism,[38] Osborn concludes that "second-century theology is better than, and preferable to, fourth-century creeds, councils, and controversies." His book could have been titled "The Second, Greatest of Centuries."[39]

Pelikan, Sterling Professor of History at Yale University, has published his 1992-1993 Gifford Lectures at the University of Aberdeen. They focus on four Cappadocians: Basil, Gregory of Nazianzus, Gregory of Nyssa and Macrina (the sister of Basil and Gregory of Nyssa). Pelikan "maps their movement from a natural theology used in apologetics to a presuppositional natural theology that is meta-

---

[30]Richard Bauckham, review of *From Nicaea to Chalcedon, Churchman* 98, no. 3 (1984): 261-62.

[31]Winslow, review of *From Nicaea to Chalcedon,* 448.

[32]Eric Francis Osborn, *The Emergence of Christian Theology* (Cambridge: Cambridge University Press, 1993).

[33]Jaroslav Pelikan, *Christianity and Classical Culture: The Metamorphosis of Natural Theology in the Christian Encounter with Hellenism* (New Haven, Conn.: Yale University Press, 1993).

[34]Eric Francis Osborn, *The Beginning of Christian Philosophy* (Cambridge: Cambridge University Press, 1981).

[35]Joseph T. Lienhard, S.J., review of *The Emergence of Christian Theology, Theological Studies* 55 (September 1994): 542.

[36]M. J. Edwards, review of *The Emergence of Christian Theology, The Journal of Theological Studies,* n.s., 44 (October 1993): 683.

[37]T. J. Gorringe, review of *The Emergence of Christian Theology, Expository Times* 104 (September 1993): 381.

[38]Edwards, review of *The Emergence of Christian Theology,* p. 683; Gorringe, review of *The Emergence of Christian Theology,* p. 381.

[39]Lienhard, review of *The Emergence of Christian Theology,* p. 543.

morphized by revealed theology." Part one repeatedly demonstrates "how these contextual theologians depended upon their Greek legacy: philosophical, rhetorical and poetic." Part two shows how the Cappadocians not only shifted natural theology to being the presupposition for Christian doctrine but also transformed it confessionally.[40] Pelikan's book has been highly praised as historical theology written "as intellectual history" and for the benefit of today's systematic or constructive theologians.[41] It has been faulted for failing to meet head-on the objections set forth by Adolf von Harnack, for disregarding chronology, for assuming that there was a unified Cappadocian theology,[42] for ignoring the Incarnation and for offering no assessment of the Cappadocian theology.[43] The very genre of which this volume is representative has been called into question.[44] But most likely theologians will continue to write theology and historians history!

Monographs on Specific Doctrines

Noteworthy also are several monographs devoted to specific patristic doctrines: biblical hermeneutics, theology proper, Christology, pneumatology, Trinity and eschatology.

Karlfried Froehlich wrote a brief introduction to patristic hermeneutics for a volume of translated patristic texts.[45] David S. Dockery's history of patristic hermeneutics through the fifth century emphasizes the dependence on Jewish hermeneutics but with a Christological focus (first century), the shift from functional hermeneutics to the authority of the rule of faith (second century), allegorical (Alexandrian), and literal-historical and typological (Antiochene) hermeneutics, and canonical and Catholic hermeneutics (Jerome, Augustine, Theodoret).[46] Manlio Simonetti issued an introduction to patristic hermeneutics that carries the history through the sixth century with both the major authors and the lesser-known exegetes being included.[47] Peter Gorday sought to show how Origen, John Chrysos-

---

[40]Frederick W. Norris, review of *Christianity and Classical Culture, Anglican Theological Review* 76 (Fall 1994): 528.

[41]Ibid., 529.

[42]Michel René Barnes, review of *Christianity and Classical Culture, Theological Studies* 55 (December 1994): 757-58.

[43]Christopher Stead, review of *Christianity and Classical Culture, The Journal of Theological Studies,* n.s. 45 (October 1994): 726.

[44]Barnes, review of *Christianity and Classical Culture,* 758.

[45]*Biblical Interpretation in the Early Church,* trans. and ed. Karlfried Froehlich, Sources of Early Christian Thought (Philadelphia: Fortress, 1984), pp. 1-29.

[46]David S. Dockery, *Biblical Interpretation Then and Now: Contemporary Hermeneutics in the Light of the Early Church* (Grand Rapids: Baker, 1992).

[47]Manlio Simonetti, *Biblical Interpretation in the Early Church: An Historical Introduction to Patristic Exegesis,* trans. John A. Hughes, ed. Anders Bergquist and Markus Bockmuehl (Edinburgh: T & T Clark, 1994).

tom and Augustine of Hippo related the content of Romans 9—11 to the content of Romans 1—11. Chapters 9—11 *"are* essential to the epistle by bringing to a clear focus the complex relationship between Jews and Gentiles which is presupposed but only obliquely stated in the preceding argumentation of chapters 1—8." While for Origen Jewish-Gentile relations were paramount in chapters 9—11, with Augustine these chapters became a freestanding tract on predestination. Common, however, to both and to a lesser extent to Chrysostom were certain themes.[48]

Robert M. Grant has studied the identities, the functions and the deeds of the pagan deities of the first and second centuries A.D. and has then expounded the doctrines of God, Christ, the Holy Spirit and the Trinity, together with the creeds through Origen.[49] In his interpetation of second-century Christology Grant treated the Gnostics, the apostolic fathers, Justin Martyr, Theophilus of Antioch and Irenaeus.[50] Aloys Grillmeier, S.J., having treated in his first volume the development of Christology through the Council of Chalcedon (451), has continued his interpretation of the history of Christological doctrine through the year 538. Almost a third of the volume is devoted to the delineation of the primary sources. The remaining interpretation centers in the activities of Emperor Marcian, Pope Leo I, Emperor Leo I and Emperors Basiliscus, Zeno, Justin I and Justinian I.[51] Basil Studer's monograph[52] was designed "to make clear how, in the first Christian centuries, the doctrine of the Trinity and Christology had developed in a complementary interaction."[53] Consisting of three parts ("the pre-Nicene period, the Nicene turning point, and the influence of Chalcedon"[54]), this volume "questions binitarian interpretations of Spirit Christologies and highlights the Trinitarian positions of Tertullian and Hippolytus."[55]

The relationship between the work of the Holy Spirit and Christian martyrdom

---

[48]Peter Gorday, *Principles of Patristic Exegesis: Romans 9-11 in Origen, John Chrysostom and Augustine,* Studies in Bible and Early Christianity 4 (Lewiston, N.Y.: Mellen, 1983), esp. pp. 11, 197, 231-37.

[49]Robert M. Grant, *Gods and the One God,* Library of Early Christianity (Philadelphia: Westminster, 1986).

[50]Robert M. Grant, *Jesus After the Gospels: The Christ of the Second Century* (Louisville, Ky.: Westminster/John Knox, 1990).

[51]Aloys Grillmeier, S.J., *Christ in Christian Tradition,* vol. 2, *From the Council of Chalcedon (451) to Gregory the Great (590-604),* pt. 1, *Reception and Contradiction: The Development of the Discussion About Chalcedon from 451 to the Beginning of the Reign of Justinian,* trans. Pauline Allen and John Cawte (London: A. R. Mowbray; Atlanta: John Knox, 1987).

[52]Basil Studer, *Gott und unsere Erlösung im Glauben der Alten Kirche* (Düsseldorf: Patmos Verlag, 1985); E. T., *Trinity and Incarnation: The Faith of the Early Church,* trans. Matthias Westerhoff, ed. Andrew Louth (Edinburgh: T & T Clark; Collegeville, Minn.: Liturgical, 1993).

[53]Studer, *Trinity and Incarnation,* p. xi.

[54]Everett Ferguson, review of *Gott und unsere Erlösung im Glauben der Alten Kirche, Church History* 57 (September 1988): 356.

[55]Frederick W. Norris, review of *Trinity and Incarnation, Theological Studies* 56 (March 1995): 161.

was the subject of William C. Weinrich's revised Basel dissertation.[56] Weinrich studied primarily the New Testament, the writings of Ignatius of Antioch and "other selected martyrologies," giving less attention to Tertullian. The stress is on the Holy Spirit's working "in and through the community of faith" rather than "spontaneously" or individually.[57] One reviewer reckons Weinrich's thesis to be "a re-examination of Karl Holl's argument that marytrs were ecstatics to whom revelation was given,"[58] whereas another finds it to be the shift from the earlier dependence of martyrs on the Holy Spirit and the Christian community to Tertullian's later understanding of martyrdom as "a gladiatorial combat which the believer faces alone in order to prove worthy of reward."[59] One negative assessment concludes that "the relationship of the Spirit to martyrdom is shown to be vague or non-existent in most of the sources studied."[60]

In his monograph on the doctrine of the Trinity, Millard J. Erickson has surveyed the patristic doctrine of the Trinity through the Cappadocians.[61]

Brian E. Daley, S.J., has produced a "handbook of patristic eschatology"[62] that has been called a "watershed in early Christian studies"[63] and is predicted to be "the standard reference on patristic eschatology."[64] Covering the period to Gregory the Great in the West and to John of Damascus in the East, the volume treats "in turn each patristic author whose views on eschatology are available" and allows its readers by use of the index to trace specific doctrines through the period.[65] According to Henry Chadwick, Daley is "as much at home in 2nd and 3rd century debates about the nature of the resurrection body as in 5th and 6th century explorations whether divine punishment is vindictive or remedial."[66]

But Robert M. Grant concluded that Daley's treatment of second- and third-century authors was "not as detailed as what Daley supplies for later

---

[56]William C. Weinrich, *Spirit and Martyrdom: A Study of the Work of the Holy Spirit in Contexts of Persecution and Martyrdom in the New Testament and Early Christian Literature* (Washington, D.C.: University Press of America, 1991).

[57]Duane W. H. Arnold, review of *Spirit and Martyrdom*, *The Greek Orthodox Theological Review* 31 (Fall/Winter 1986): 442-43.

[58]Jerome H. Neyrey, S.J., review of *Spirit and Martyrdom*, *The Catholic Biblical Quarterly* 45 (April 1983): 334.

[59]Carl Volz, review of *Spirit and Martyrdom*, *Word and World* 4 (Winter 1985): 103.

[60]Neyrey, review of *Spirit and Martyrdom*, p. 335.

[61]Millard J. Erickson, *God in Three Persons: A Contemporary Interpretation of the Trinity* (Grand Rapids: Baker, 1995), pp. 31-93.

[62]Brian E. Daley, S.J., *The Hope of the Early Church: A Handbook of Patristic Eschatology* (Cambridge: Cambridge University Press, 1991).

[63]Paul M. Blowers, review of *The Hope of the Early Church*, *Restoration Quarterly* 34 (1992): 255.

[64]E. Glenn Hinson, review of *The Hope of the Early Church*, *Review and Expositor* 90 (Winter 1993): 151.

[65]Richard Bauckham, review of *The Hope of the Early Church*, *Theology* 95 (March/April 1992): 142.

[66]Henry Chadwick, review of *The Hope of the Early Church*, *The Expository Times* 103 (December 1991): 89-90.

times."[67] Frederick W. Norris commended Daley for his inclusion of Syriac, Coptic and Armenian authors.[68] Daley has been faulted for not comparing the hopes of Christians with those of contemporary non-Christians,[69] for not providing data on the sources for patristic eschatology (that is, storehouses traceable to 4 Ezra/2 Esdras),[70] and for his assessment of the relationship of millennial doctrine to orthodoxy.[71] Daley's sixfold identification of common patristic eschatological doctrines and fivefold delineation of "areas of disagreement" in patristic eschatology will surely attract the attention of all who pursue this area of study. Norris concludes, "This is historical theology at its finest: careful, wide-ranging and useful for contemporary theology."[72]

Apostolic Fathers and Greek Apologists

The introduction to the apostolic fathers written by Simon Tugwell, O.P.,[73] is unique not in its exposition of the teachings of these authors but in its dating of four of these authors in the first century A.D.: *Didache, Epistle of Barnabas,* 70s, by the Barnabas of Acts 4:36; *Shepherd of Hermas,* late 60s or 70s; Clement of Rome, 69-70. Much of the scholarly work of the past fifteen years has centered on the *Didache.* Clifford N. Jefford in his published dissertation,[74] which addresses primarily the sources of the *Didache,* concluded that "the community which produced the *Didache* developed from one of Christian Jews still connected with the synagogue to one largely of Christian Gentiles" and its "theological orientation also shifted from a prominently Jewish concern for Decalogue, wisdom and land to a more Hellenistic Christian concern for Christology and ecclesiology."[75] In a book of essays edited by Jefford, Nathan Mitchell's chapter treats the community of the *Didache,* the sources of Christian baptism, and the baptismal practice according to the *Didache.*[76] The most comprehensive work on the *Didache* has been the German-language com-

---

[67]Robert M. Grant, review of *The Hope of the Early Church, The Journal of Religion* 73 (January 1993): 86.

[68]Frederick W. Norris, review of *The Hope of the Early Church, Journal of Early Christian Studies* 1 (Winter 1993): 444-45.

[69]Joanne McWilliam, review of *The Hope of the Early Church, Theological Studies* 53 (December 1992): 747.

[70]Bauckham, review of *The Hope of the Early Church,* p. 143.

[71]Grant, review of *The Hope of the Early Church,* p. 86.

[72]Norris, review of *The Hope of the Early Church,* p. 446. See also Charles Evans Hill, *Regnum Caelorum: Patterns of Future Hope in Early Christianity* (Oxford: Oxford University Press, 1992).

[73]Simon Tugwell, O.P., *The Apostolic Fathers* (London: Geoffrey Chapman, 1989).

[74]Clifford N. Jefford, *The Sayings of Jesus in the Teaching of the Twelve Apostles,* Supplements to *Vigiliae Christianae* 11 (Leiden: Brill, 1989).

[75]D. Jeffrey Bingham, review of *The Sayings of Jesus in the Teaching of the Twelve Apostles, Journal of Early Christian Studies* 1 (Winter 1993): 447, based on Jefford, *Sayings of Jesus,* pp. 143-44.

[76]Clifford N. Jefford, ed., *The Didache in Context: Essays on Its Text, History and Transmission,* Supplements to *Novum Testamentum* 77 (Leiden: Brill, 1995), pp. 226-55.

mentary by Kurt Niederwimmer,[77] which has a literary-critical focus.

In his monograph on the Greek apologists, Robert M. Grant explicates the theologies of Justin Martyr, Tatian and Theophilus of Antioch.[78]

Orthodoxy and Heresy in the Second Century

The lengthened shadow of Walter Bauer still lingers over contemporary scholarship, but his thesis relative to the antiquity and dominance of heresy has met serious challenges. Thomas A. Robinson offers a major critique. Examining the second-century evidence, he concludes that in most areas (Edessa, Egypt, Corinth, Rome, Jerusalem and Antioch) there is not sufficient evidence to sustain Bauer's thesis and that where evidence is ample (Ephesus and environs), the orthodox preceded and outnumbered the heretical.[79] Robinson's book has been compared with H. E. W. Turner's *The Pattern of Christian Truth* (1954) as an answer to Bauer.[80]

Robert M. Grant,[81] after studying the literary-critical methods of the Hellenistic and classical Roman writers, the heretical Christian authors and the orthodox Christian writers, concludes that "it was Christian 'heretics' who first took up criticism to prove the authenticity of their doctrines but that it was not long before their opponents used the same literary methods to demonstrate rather the superior claims" of orthodox Christianity.[82] Arland J. Hultgren has opted for a "normative Christianity," that is, "a rather broad stream of Christian traditions that coexisted prior to orthodoxy, and which together constituted major foundations for the latter." It "recognizes and preserves different expressions of Christian faith, while acknowledging that there are limits to acceptable diversity."[83]

Marcion and Gnosticism

R. Joseph Hoffmann has concluded that Marcion's struggle against his opponents was not initially about doctrine but about "the right" to the Pauline gospel or to Paul as "the sole infallible teacher." Moreover, "Marcion was much closer to the

---

[77]Kurt Niederwimmer, *Die Didache, Kommentar zu den Apostolichen Vätern*, vol. 1 (Göttingen: Vandenhoeck & Ruprecht, 1989).

[78]Robert M. Grant, *Greek Apologists of the Second Century* (Philadelphia: Westminster, 1988), chaps. 7, 14, 19.

[79]Thomas A. Robinson, *The Bauer Thesis Examined: The Geography of Heresy in the Early Christian Church* (Lewiston, N.Y.: Mellen, 1988).

[80]Frederick W. Norris, review of *The Bauer Thesis Examined, Themelios* 16 (April/May 1991): 35.

[81]Robert M. Grant, *Heresy and Criticism: The Search for Authenticity in Early Christian Literature* (Louisville, Ky.: Westminster/John Knox, 1993).

[82]Hall Partrick, review of *Heresy and Criticism, Church History* 63 (September 1994): 428.

[83]Arland J. Hultgren, *The Rise of Normative Christianity* (Minneapolis: Fortress, 1994), esp. p. 105. See also Rowan Williams, ed., *The Making of Orthodoxy: Essays in Honour of Henry Chadwick* (Cambridge: Cambridge University Press, 1989).

Judaism of the diaspora in terms of his biblical exegesis, theological and philosophical innocence, and ethical praxis, than were any of his orthodox opponents," and his concept of two Gods was a "deduction based on human experience" that was "in some respects closer to the gospel of the primitive Christian communities . . . than was the 'monotheism' of his orthodox opponents."[84]

Two English translations of histories of Gnosticism have theological content: Kurt Randolph's study (from the German)[85] and Giovanni Firolamo's (from the Italian).[86] Jean Magne sets forth the novel thesis that the Gnostic origin of the church and sacraments can be proved from the breaking of bread at the feeding of the five thousand and four thousand, at the Last Supper, with the Emmaus disciples and in the book of Acts. Moreover, "under the influence of Jewish apologetics," such "exegesis was turned upside down into Christian exegesis," and thus "the Gnostic movement evolved into the Christian religious movement through a gradual rejudaization."[87] Simone Pétrement, however, concludes that Gnosticism can be "explained on the basis of Christianity," especially the Pauline and the Johannine types, and hence there is no need to posit "a pre-Christian Gnosticism," Jewish or otherwise.[88]

Gnostic teachings and practices are amply treated in Benjamin Walker's survey,[89] in essays by George W. MacRae, S.J.,[90] and Birger A. Pearson,[91] and in the festschrift for Gilles Quispel.[92] One of Quispel's students has developed and sustained, by the

---

[84]R. Joseph Hoffman, *Marcion: On the Restitution of Christianity—An Essay on the Development of Radical Paulinist Theology in the Second Century* (Chico, Calif.: American Academy of Religion, 1984), esp. pp. 307-9. Georges Ory, *Marcion* (Paris: Cercle Ernest-Renan, 1980), offered a commentary on Lukan texts attributed to Marcion, and Adolf von Harnack's 1924 monograph appeared in English: *Marcion: The Gospel of the Alien God*, trans. John E. Steely and Lyle D. Bierma (Durham, N.C.: Labyrinth, 1990).

[85]Kurt Randolph, *Gnosis: The Nature and History of Gnosticism*, trans. P. W. Coxon and K. H. Kuhn, ed. R. McL. Wilson (Edinburgh: T & T Clark; San Francisco: Harper & Row, 1983), esp. pp. 53-272.

[86]Giovanni Firolamo, *A History of Gnosticism*, trans. Anthony Alcock (Oxford: Basil Blackwell, 1990), the format of which is more theological than historical.

[87]Jean Magne, *From Christianity to Gnosis and from Gnosis to Christianity: An Itinerary Through the Texts to and from the Tree of Paradise*, trans. A. F. W. Armstrong, Brown Judaic Studies 286 (Atlanta: Scholars Press, 1993), esp. pp. 5-6.

[88]Simone Pétrement, *A Separate God: The Christian Origins of Gnosticism*, trans. Carol Harrison (San Francisco: HarperCollins, 1990), esp. pp. 211-13, 482-86. Originally published as *Le Dieu séparé: Les origines du gnosticisme* (Paris: Editions du Cerf, 1984).

[89]Benjamin Walker, *Gnosticism: Its History and Influence* (Wellingborough, Northamptonshire, U.K.: Aquarian, 1983).

[90]George W. MacRae, S.J., *Studies in the New Testament and Gnosticism*, ed. Daniel J. Harrington, S.J., and Stanley B. Marrow, S.J., Good News Studies 26 (Wilmington, Del.: Michael Glazier, 1987), pp. 184-262.

[91]Birger A. Pearson, *Gnosticism, Judaism and Egyptian Christianity*, Studies in Antiquity and Christianity (Minneapolis: Fortress, 1990). Monographs on Gnosticism in/and the New Testament fall outside the scope of the present study.

[92]R. van den Broek and M. J. Vermaseren, eds., *Studies in Gnosticism and Hellenistic Religions: Presented to Gilles Quispel on the Occasion of His 65th Birthday*, Études préliminiaires aux religions orientales dans l'empire Romain (Leiden: Brill, 1981).

use of studies of the Samaritans, Quispel's thesis "that the concept of the Gnostic demiurge was forerun by Jewish ideas about the creative agency of the hypostasized divine Name and of the Angel of the Lord, who was the possessor of the Tetragrammaton."[93] Pheme Perkins interprets "Gnostic dialogue" both as a literary genre and a discussion or debate and rejects the view of Elaine Pagels that Gnostics were "champions of individual creativity against an increasingly repressive orthodoxy."[94] Gérard Vallée, in studying the successive anti-Gnostic polemic of Irenaeus, Hippolytus and Epiphanius, concludes that there was a decline in serious argumentation, a greater use of clichés and caricatures, and a broadening scope in the use of the heresy label. Orthodoxy, moreover, did not arise solely from antiheretical polemic.[95]

The Canon of the New Testament and the Apostles' Creed

The 1980s constituted a period of major productivity in the history and formation of the New Testament canon. Monographs were written by William R. Farmer and Denis M. Farkasfalvy, O. Cist,[96] Harry Y. Gamble,[97] Bruce M. Metzger,[98] Lee Martin McDonald,[99] F. F. Bruce[100] and Franz Stuhlhofer.[101] Geoffrey Mark Hahneman, following Albert C. Sundberg Jr., shifted the date of the Muratorian Fragment from late second century to early fourth century and its provenance from western to eastern (Syria/Palestine), a view that, if accepted, would tend to provide evidence against the idea that some kind of New Testament canon was in place before the end of the second century.[102]

Certain authors have issued new interpretations of the Apostles' Creed: Jan

---

[93]Jarl E. Fossum, *The Name of God and the Angel of the Lord: Samaritan and Jewish Concepts of Intermediation and the Origin of Gnosticism*, Wissenschaftliche Untersuchungen zum Neuen Testament 36 (Tübingen: Mohr, 1985).

[94]Pheme Perkins, *The Gnostic Dialogue: The Early Church and the Crisis of Gnosticism*, Theological Inquiries (New York: Paulist, 1980), esp. p. 205; Marvin W. Meyer, review of *The Gnostic Dialogue*, *The Second Century* 1 (Winter 1981): 251-53.

[95]Gérard Vallée, *A Study in Anti-Gnostic Polemics: Irenaeus, Hippolytus and Epiphanius*, Studies in Christianity and Judaism 1 (Waterloo, Ont.: Wilfrid Laurier University Press, 1981), esp. pp. 93-97. It is not possible to treat all monographs on the Nag Hammadi Library or on gender studies.

[96]William R. Farmer and Denis W. Farkasfalvy, O.Cist., *The Formation of the New Testament Canon: An Ecumenical Approach* (New York: Paulist, 1983).

[97]Harry Y. Gamble, *The New Testament Canon: Its Making and Meaning* (Philadelphia: Fortress, 1985).

[98]Bruce M. Metzger, *The Canon of the New Testament: Its Origin, Development and Significance* (Oxford: Oxford University Press, 1987).

[99]Lee Martin McDonald, *The Formation of the Christian Biblical Canon* (Nashville: Abingdon, 1988).

[100]F. F. Bruce, *The Canon of Scripture* (Downers Grove, Ill.: InterVarsity Press, 1988), pp. 115-297.

[101]Franz Stuhlhofer, *Der Gebrauch der Bibel von Jesus bis Euseb: Eine statistische Untersuchung zur Kanonsgeschichte* (Wuppertal: Brockhaus, 1988).

[102]Geoffrey Mark Hahneman, *The Muratorian Fragment and the Development of the Canon* (Oxford: Oxford University Press, 1992), esp. pp. 1-4.

Mili Lochman[103] and Hans Küng.[104]

Irenaeus, Tertullian and Cyprian

Yoshifumi Torisu has examined Irenaeus's "economic-trinitarian" doctrine of God over against Gnostic views of God and salvation,[105] and Antonio Orbe, S.J., has treated numerous doctrinal themes while setting forth the "spirituality" of Irenaeus.[106] But Terrance L. Tiessen in his quest[107] for support of Karl Rahner's "anonymous Christian" concludes that Irenaeus "did not address the contemporary [twentieth-century] issue," for Irenaeus made "a clear distinction between general knowledge of the divine and saving knowledge based on the revelation in Christ," the latter being dependent on acceptance of that revelation.[108]

Bernd Jochen Hilberath,[109] examining Rahner's suggestion that the modern meaning of the term *person* has rendered it "unacceptable" as a trinitarian term because it can lead to tritheism, has found Rahner's substituted language not to be viable and has turned back approvingly to Tertullian's use of *personae*, especially *Against Praxeas*, which usage avoids an "overly individualistic understanding."[110] The prophetic movement in Carthage in the third century has been described and analyzed by Cecil M. Robeck Jr.[111]

Typology and salvation history are pervasive in the study by John D. Laurance, S.J., of Cyprian's presentation of the "priest" (by which Cyprian means bishop) as a "type" of Christ as he leads the Eucharistic observance by an assembly *(ecclesia)* unified by love.[112] Laurance favors an "imitation-presence ontology,"[113] which

---

[103]Jan Mili Lochman, *The Faith We Confess*, trans. David Lewis (Philadelphia: Fortress, 1984).

[104]Hans Küng, *Credo: The Apostles' Creed Explained for Today*, trans. John Bowden (New York: Doubleday, 1993). Henri de Lubac's *La foi chrétienne* (2nd ed., 1970) appeared in English: *Christian Faith: The Structure of the Apostles' Creed*, trans. Illtyd Trethowan and John Saward (London: Geoffrey Chapman, 1986).

[105]Yoshifumi Torisu, *Gott und Welt: Eine Untersuchung zur Gotteslehre des Irenäus von Lyon*, Studia Instituti Missiologici Societatis Verbi Divini 52 (Nettetal: Steyler Verlag, 1991), esp. p. 231.

[106]Antonio Orbe, S.J., *Espiritualidad de San Ireneo*, Analecta Gregoriana 256 (Rome: Editrice Pontificia Universitá Gregoriana, 1989).

[107]Terrance L. Tiessen, *Irenaeus on the Salvation of the Unevangelized*, American Theological Library Association Monograph Series (Metuchen, N.J.: Scarecrow, 1993).

[108]Lloyd G. Patterson, review of *Irenaeus on the Salvation of the Unevangelized*, *Theological Studies* 55 (December 1994): 749-50.

[109]Bernd Jochen Hilberath, *Der Personbegriff der Trinitätstheologie in Rückfrage von Karl Rahner zu Tertullians "Adversus Praxean,"* Innsbrucker theologische Studien 17 (Innsbruck: Tyrolia-Verlag, 1986).

[110]Robert Kress, review of *Der Personbegriff der Trinitätstheologie*, *Theological Studies* 49 (March 1988): 172.

[111]Cecil M. Robeck Jr., *Prophecy in Carthage: Perpetua, Tertullian and Cyprian* (Cleveland: Pilgrim, 1992); Robert M. Grant, review of *Prophecy in Carthage*, *Church History* 62 (September 1993): 378-79.

[112]John D. Laurance, S.J., *"Priest" as Type of Christ: The Leader of the Eucharist in Salvation History According to Cyprian of Carthage* (New York: Peter Lang, 1984).

[113]Wayne L. Fehr, review of *"Priest" as Type of Christ*, *Theological Studies* 46 (December 1985): 751.

seems to deny an identification of the Eucharistic sacrifice with Christ's passion in Cyprianic theology.[114] In examining John Calvin's concept of the unity of the church universal, Anette Zillenbiller has delineated his extensive usage of Cyprian's concept.[115]

Origen

A major field of recent patristic research has been the theology of Origen. Joseph Wilson Trigg has produced a readable, balanced introduction to the interlaced life, writings and theology of Origen.[116] In the foreword Robert M. Grant identifies "the principal merit" of the book as "its catholic character." By this he means that Trigg "seldom neglects certain aspects of Origen's thought or overemphasizes others," with the result that we find not a Roman Catholic/Anglican Origen or a Protestant Origen but "one" Origen.[117]

The climax to a lifetime of scholarly work on Origen, Henri Crouzel's *Origen*[118] consists of four parts: personality, exegesis, spirituality and theology. Building on Lubac and Daniélou but not Nautin,[119] Crouzel offers "an *apologia* in favor of the Alexandrian's 'orthodoxy,' "[120] concluding that his condemnation as a heretic in 553 was "utterly unjustified."[121] He finds Origen resisting the determinism of the Gnostics and Marcionites and in his eschatology the "Chiliasts and Anthropomorphites."[122] He is critical of "Jerome, Rufinus, and other translators" for misunderstanding or misrepresenting Origen.[123] According to Robert M. Grant, Crouzel rightly depends on Greek texts and Latin translations, "treats" Origen "as primarily a theologian rather than a philosopher" and "insists on the permanent role of Origen as a teacher of Catholic theology."[124] Antonia Tripolitis has summarized the extant writings,[125] and John Clark Smith has produced a monograph on "the full spectrum of Origen's unique Christian vision," chiefly spirituality, with copious notes, exten-

---

[114]Frances M. Young, review of *"Priest" as Type of Christ, Expository Times* 96 (August 1985): 350.

[115]Anette Zillenbiller, *Die Einheit der Katholische Kirche: Calvins Cyprianrezeption in seinen ekklesiologischen Schriften,* Veröffentlichungen des Instituts für Europäische Geschichte, Mainz, Abteilung Religionsgeschichte 151 (Mainz: Verlag Philipp von Zabern, 1993).

[116]Joseph Wilson Trigg, *Origen: The Bible and Philosophy in the Third-Century Church* (Atlanta: John Knox, 1983).

[117]Ibid., p. 1.

[118]Henri Crouzel, *Origen,* trans. A. S. Worrall (San Francisco: Harper & Row, 1989); originally published in French as *Origène* (Paris: Editions Lethielleux; Namur: Culture et Vérité, 1985).

[119]Joseph W. Trigg, review of *Origen, Anglican Theological Review* 72 (Summer 1990): 340, 342.

[120]William David Kirkpatrick, review of *Origen, Southwestern Journal of Theology* 35 (Fall 1992): 67.

[121]Trigg, review of *Origen,* 341.

[122]Elizabeth A. Clark, review of *Origen, The Christian Century,* April 11, 1990, 372.

[123]Ronald E. Osborn, review of *Origen, Encounter* 51 (Autumn 1990): 416.

[124]Robert M. Grant, review of *Origen, Journal of Religion* 71 (July 1991): 400.

[125]Antonia Tripolitis, *Origen: A Critical Reading,* American University Studies, series 7, Theology and Religion 8 (New York: Peter Lang, 1985).

sive bibliography and each major topic framed in the form of a question.[126]

Robert J. Hauck's study of prophecy and inspiration in Origen and in Celsus concludes that prophetic inspiration was crucial to the Christian-pagan debate and that both Origen and Celsus were concerned for "the soul's ascent to God." Yet they differed as to the role played by demons among the Greeks and Jesus and Christians.[127] According to Karen J. Torjesen, Origen's biblical exegesis "is theologically determined by a specific understanding of the form in which Christ [the Logos] is present in Scripture, the role of Scripture itself in the process of redemption, and how the individual is related to the biblical text," all within the progress of the soul toward God.[128]

Peter Widdicombe traces the concept of the fatherhood of God from Origen through Athanasius via Dionysius of Alexandria, Theognostus, Methodius of Olympus, Alexander and Arius, contrasting Origen's and Athanasius's doctrines.[129]

Alan Scott, focusing on the concept of "living heavenly bodies" (stars as having souls), has traced the development of such thinking prior to Origen and interpreted Origen's use of it in his "cosmology, theodicy, doctrine of the Fall, and eschatology."[130] J. Rebecca Lyman,[131] focusing on the interaction of Christian theology and Greek cosmology in the forming of Christology, finds freedom versus fatalism to be a key issue and concludes that there were religious motivations in pre-Nicene cosmology.[132]

James A. Lyons, S.J., compares the concept of the cosmic Christ in Origen and in Pierre Teilhard de Chardin. He finds Origen to begin "from above" and with the help of Platonism to move with "exemplary and instrumental causality" and an ontology of being to *apokatastasis*. Teilhard de Chardin begins "from below" and with the help of evolutionary thought moves with "final causality" and an ontology of becoming to Omega. But both were "putting . . . the face of Christ on the Logos of the world."[133]

---

[126]John Clark Smith, *The Ancient Wisdom of Origen* (Lewisburg, Penn.: Bucknell University Press; London: Associated University Presses, 1992), esp. p. 11.

[127]Robert J. Hauck, *The More Divine Proof: Prophecy and Inspiration in Celsus and Origen*, American Academy of Religion Academy Series 69 (Atlanta: Scholars Press, 1989), esp. pp. 137-43.

[128]Karen J. Torjesen, *Hermeneutical Procedure and Theological Method in Origen's Exegesis*, Patristische Texte und Studien 28 (Berlin: Walter de Gruyter, 1986), esp. preface and pp. 121-24.

[129]Peter Widdicombe, *The Fatherhood of God from Origen to Athanasius*, Oxford Theological Monographs (Oxford: Oxford University Press, 1994).

[130]Alan Scott, *Origen and the Life of the Stars: A History of an Idea*, Oxford Early Christian Studies (Oxford: Oxford University Press, 1991), esp. pp. xv-xvi.

[131]J. Rebecca Lyman, *Christology and Cosmology: Models of Divine Activity in Origen, Eusebius and Athanasius* (Oxford: Oxford University Press, 1993).

[132]John J. O'Keefe, review of *Christology and Cosmology*, *Religious Studies Review* 20 (July 1994): 243; Gerald Bostock, review of *Christology and Cosmology*, *Expository Times* 105 (March 1994): 182.

[133]James A. Lyons, S.J., *The Cosmic Christ in Origen and Teilhard de Chardin* (Oxford: Oxford University Press, 1982), esp. pp. 211-19.

J. Nigel Rowe's dissertation deals with Origen's doctrine of the subordination of the Son to the Father.[134] Gerardus Q. Reijners, O.S.C., has studied the symbolism of the cross as set forth both by Origen's predecessors and by Origen together with Origen's use of other symbols of redemption.[135] Gunnar af Hällström has explored the faith of the ordinary Christians of Origen's day, especially their literal biblical interpretation, close adherence to the rule of faith and aversion to Origen's more speculative teachings.[136] The role of Origen's doctrine of the Eucharist in controversies between the Protestant Reformers and the theologians of Trent and between Orthodoxy and the Enlightenment has been thoroughly investigated by Lothar Lies, S.J.,[137] and the foundational relation of Origen's doctrine of *apokatastasis* to that of Karl Barth and Hans Urs von Balthasar has been studied by Werner van Laak.[138]

Elizabeth A. Clark has authored a detailed study[139] of the Origenist controversy of "the last two decades of the fourth century."[140] Her method is a combination of traditional historical-theological exposition and social network analysis. She includes the late-fourth-century iconoclastic controversy and stresses the role of Evagrius Ponticus as Origenist and iconoclast.[141] Clark's sympathies seem to be with "the losers: Evagrius, Rufinus, and the Pelagians," not with the anti-Origenists: Epiphanius of Salamis, Theophilus of Alexandria, Jerome and Shenute of Atripe.[142] For Clark the controversy of Augustine with the Pelagians was a Western "resolution to the Origenist controversy," and the condemnation of Origenism and Pelagianism opened the door for a dominant theology of "human sinfulness," "divine determination" and the mystery of God in the West.[143] Jon F. Dechow has produced a detailed study of the anti-Origenism of Epiphanius and that of Epiphanius's predecessors with stress on subordinationism, preexistence of souls and the resur-

---

[134]J. Nigel Rowe, *Origen's Doctrine of Subordination: A Study in Origen's Christology*, European University Studies, series 23, Theology 272 (Frankfurt am Main: Peter Lang, 1987).

[135]Gerardus Q. Reijners, O.S.C., *Das Wort vom Kreuz: Kreuzes- und Erlösungssymbolik bei Origenes*, Bonner Beiträge zur Kirchengeschichte 13 (Cologne: Böhlau Verlag, 1983).

[136]Gunmar af Hällström, Fides Simpliciorum, *According to Origen of Alexandria*, Commentationes Humanarum Litterarum 76 (Ekenäs, Finland: Ekenäs Tryckeri, 1984), esp. pp. 93-95.

[137]Lothar Lies, S.J., *Origenes' Eucharistielehre im Streit der Konfessionen: Die Auslegungsgeschichte seit der Reformation*, Innsbrucker theologische Studien 15 (Innsbruck: Tyrolia-Verlag, 1985).

[138]Werner van Laak, *Allversöhnung: Die Lehre von der Apokatastasis; Ihre Grundlegung durch Origenes und ihre Bewertung in der gegenwärtigen Theologie bei Karl Barth und Hans Urs von Balthasar* (Sinzig: Sankt Meinrad Verlag für Theologie, 1990).

[139]Elizabeth A. Clark, *The Origenist Controversy: The Cultural Construction of an Early Christian Debate* (Princeton, N.J.: Princeton University Press, 1992).

[140]Joseph W. Trigg, review of *The Origenist Controversy, Journal of Religion* 74 (July 1994): 389.

[141]Gerard H. Ettlinger, S.J., review of *The Origenist Controversy, Theological Studies* 64 (September 1993): 561, 562.

[142]Trigg, review of *The Origenist Controversy*, 389.

[143]J. Kevin Coyle, review of *The Origenist Controversy, Journal of Early Christian Studies* 2 (Winter 1994): 474.

rection.[144] Four colloquia or congresses on Origen have resulted in a profusion of published papers.[145]

Arius, Arianism and Athanasius

Considerable recent scholarly activity in this field has been evident. As to Arius himself, Rowan Williams has authored a monograph[146] that reviews the modern understandings of Arius since John Henry Newman[147] and then focuses on the background and doctrine of Arius, seeking not to attack or defend him but to understand him. Arius is seen as more the product of Alexandria than of Antioch and one who majored on God's "absolute unknowability," "absolute simplicity"[148] and freedom of will.[149] Williams does not treat the "neo-Arians" (Aetius of Antioch; Eunomius of Cyzicus).[150] Thomas Böhm's dissertation[151] deals with Arius's Christology, the latter understood as "the relation of the Son to the Father, primarily in terms of eternity and participation in creation." He does not find Arius linked theologically "with Origen, Lucian, or Paul of Samosata" or dependent philosophically on "Plotinus and Porphyry" but does identify the hermeneutic of Arius with that of Origen. For Böhm, Hellenization did not seriously alter the Christian faith.[152]

In 1981 Robert C. Gregg and Dennis E. Groh issued a monograph[153] that,

---

[144]Jon F. Dechow, *Dogma and Mysticism in Early Christianity: Epiphanius of Cyprus and the Legacy of Origen*, North American Patristic Society Patristic Monograph Series, no. 13 (Macon, Ga.: Mercer University Press, 1988).

[145]*Origeniana tertia: The Third International Colloquium for Origen Studies, University of Manchester, Sept. 7-11, 1981*, ed. Richard Hanson and Henri Crouzel (Rome: Edizioni dell' Ateneo, 1985); *Origen of Alexandria: His World and His Legacy*, Origen Colloquy, University of Notre Dame, April 1986, ed. Charles Kannengiesser, S.J., and William L. Petersen (Notre Dame, Ind.: University of Notre Dame Press, 1988); *Origeniana quarta: Die Referate des 4. Internationalen Origeneskongresses, Innsbruck 2-6 September 1985*, ed. Lothar Lies, Innsbrucker theologische Studien 19 (Innsbruck, Vienna: Tyrolia-Verlag, 1987); *Origeniana quinta: Historica, Text and Method, Biblica, Philosophica, Theologica, Origenism and Later Developments: Papers of the Fifth International Origen Congress, Boston College, 14-18 August 1989*, ed. Robert J. Daly, Bibliotheca Ephemeridum Theologicarum Lovaniensium 105 (Leuven: University Press, 1992).

[146]Rowan Williams, *Arius: Heresy and Tradition* (London: Darton, Longman & Todd, 1987).

[147]Frances M. Young, review of *Arius: Heresy and Tradition*, *Scottish Journal of Theology* 42, no. 2 (1989): 264.

[148]Gerald L. Bray, review of *Arius: Heresy and Tradition*, *Anglican Theological Review* 91 (Spring 1989): 203.

[149]Young, review of *Arius: Heresy and Tradition*, 265.

[150]Lloyd G. Patterson, review of *Arius: Heresy and Tradition*, *Churchman* 103, no. 4 (1989): 362-63.

[151]Thomas Böhm, *Die Christologie des Arius: Dogmengeschichtliche Überlegungen unter besonderer Berücksichtigung der Hellenisierungsfrage*, Studien zur Theologie und Geschichte 7 (Erzabtei St. Ottilien: EOS Verlag, 1991).

[152]Michael Slusser, review of *Die Christologie des Arius*, *The Journal of Theological Studies*, n.s., 45 (April 1994): 320-22.

[153]Robert C. Gregg and Dennis E. Groh, *Early Arianism: A View of Salvation* (Philadelphia: Fortress; London: SCM Press, 1981).

together with Thomas A. Kopecek's two-volume work[154] in 1979, constituted the first major work on the Arian controversy in English for nearly a century.[155] Abandoning the traditional view that Arianism was essentially cosmological, they advance the hypothesis that it was essentially soteriological.[156] Covering Arius, Eusebius of Nicomedia and Asterius,[157] the book finds that Arianism built on an adoptionist tradition from Paul of Samosata.[158] An exemplarist view of salvation,[159] wherein humans can also attain to adoptive sonship, characterized Arianism.[160]

Richard P. C. Hanson produced (and died only weeks later) a monumental history of the Arian controversy,[161] which has been acclaimed as "a great work of erudition," the fruit of two decades of research,[162] indeed Hanson's *magnum opus*.[163] The book's title aptly identifies its objective—the tracing of the fourth-century search "for an adequate doctrine of God,"[164] "rather than the defense of an established doctrine,"[165] which "turns out to be the Christian doctrine of the Trinity,"[166] as "finally formed" by the Cappadocians[167] and completed by Chalcedon.[168] At the outset it "was not clear how monotheism and the worship of Christ could be reconciled."[169] Moreover, the Homoeans are presented as "a true theological school,"[170] and the later so-called Arians are seen not to have looked back to or built on Arius.[171] Hanson's probable thesis, according to

---

[154]Thomas A. Kopecek, *A History of Neo-Arianism* (Cambridge, Mass.: Philadelphia Patristic Foundation, 1979).

[155]R. P. C. Hanson, review of *Early Arianism, Journal of Ecclesiastical History* 33 (July 1982): 431.

[156]Andrew Louth, review of *Early Arianism, Theology* 85 (March 1982): 139.

[157]Michael Slusser, review of *Early Arianism, Theological Studies* 42 (December 1981): 684.

[158]Hanson, review of *Early Arianism*, p. 432; W. H. C. Frend, review of *Early Arianism, Scottish Journal of Theology* 36, no. 1 (1983): 117.

[159]Hanson, review of *Early Arianism*, p. 432; G. C. Stead, review of *Early Arianism, The Journal of Theological Studies*, n.s., 33 (April 1982): 285; Everett Ferguson, review of *Early Arianism, Church History* 52 (June 1983): 201.

[160]Slusser, review of *Early Arianism*, p. 684.

[161]Richard P. C. Hanson, *The Search for the Christian Doctrine of God: The Arian Controversy, 318-381* (Edinburgh: T & T Clark, 1988).

[162]W. H. C. Frend, review of *The Search for the Christian Doctrine of God, Expository Times* 100 (August 1989): 421, 419.

[163]Christopher Stead, review of *The Search for the Christian Doctrine of God, The Journal of Theological Studies*, n.s., 41 (October 1990): 668.

[164]Gerald L. Bray, review of *The Search for the Christian Doctrine of God, Churchman* 103, no. 2 (1989): 178.

[165]Joseph T. Lienhard, S.J., review of *The Search for the Christian Doctrine of God, Theological Studies* 51 (June 1990): 335.

[166]Andrew Louth, review of *The Search for the Christian Doctrine of God, Theology* 92 (September 1989): 406.

[167]Stead, review of *The Search for the Christian Doctrine of God*, pp. 672-73.

[168]Louth, review of *The Search for the Christian Doctrine of God*, p. 406.

[169]Frend, review of *The Search for the Christian Doctrine of God*, p. 419.

[170]Lienhard, review of *The Search for the Christian Doctrine of God*, p. 336.

[171]Louth, review of *The Search for the Christian Doctrine of God*, p. 405.

Lienhard, is that Athanasius placed the mediatorship of the Son in the Incarnation, not in the Godhead.[172] Eleven essays on fourth-century Arianism, edited by Michael R. Barnes and Daniel H. Williams and written chiefly by Americans,[173] were designed neither for "rehabilitating Arius" nor for "revising 'Arianism' " but reflect "patient theological archaeology."[174]

Some attention is given to theological themes and controversies in Timothy D. Barnes's monograph pertaining to Athanasius.[175] Arian and Nicene doctrines were reflected in the papers presented at the 1983 Oxford conference on Arianism.[176]

Cappadocians and Cyril
Anna-Stina Ellverson has written about dual human nature (body and soul, flesh and spirit) according to Gregory of Nazianzus,[177] Michael Azkoul on Gregory of Nyssa's dependence on Philo, Plotinus, and Origen[178] and John Anthony McGuckin concerning Cyril of Alexandria in relation to christological controversy.[179]

Hermeneutics: Greek and Latin
The Old Testament hermeneutic of the Antiochene commentator Theodore of Mopsuestia is the subject of a delayed-in-publication dissertation by Dmitri Z. Zaharopoulos,[180] who shares Theodore's "antipathy" to Alexandrian allegorism and seeks to identify Theodore's method and that of modern historical-critical exegesis.[181] Reviewers have criticized the author for trying "too hard to portray Theodore as the precursor of modern biblical scholar-

---

[172]Lienhard, review of *The Search for the Christian Doctrine of God,* 336.

[173]Michael R. Barnes and Daniel H. Williams, eds., *Arians After Arius: Essays on the Development of the Fourth Century Trinitarian Conflicts* (Edinburgh: T & T Clark, 1993).

[174]Robert Butterworth, review of *Arianism After Arius, Expository Times* 105 (September 1994): 381.

[175]Timothy D. Barnes, *Athanasius and Constantine: Theology and Politics in the Constantinian Empire* (Cambridge, Mass.: Harvard University Press, 1993), esp. chaps. 8, 14-16.

[176]*Arianism: Historical and Theological Reassessments: Papers from the Ninth International Conference on Patristic Studies, September 5-10, 1983, Oxford, England,* ed. Robert C. Gregg (Philadelphia Patristic Foundation, 1985).

[177]Anna-Stina Ellverson, *The Dual Nature of Man: A Study in the Theological Anthropology of Gregory of Nazianzus* (Uppsala: Almqvist & Wiksell, International, 1981).

[178]Michael Azkoul, *St. Gregory of Nyssa and the Tradition of the Fathers,* Texts and Studies in Religion 63 (Lewiston, N.Y.: Mellen, 1995). See also Verna E. F. Harrison, *Grace and Human Freedom According to St. Gregory of Nyssa,* Studies in the Bible and Early Christianity 30 (Lewiston, N.Y.: Mellen, 1992), and Philip Rousseau, *Basil of Caesarea,* The Transformation of the Classical Heritage 20 (Berkeley: University of California Press, 1994).

[179]John Anthony McGuckin, *St. Cyril of Alexandria: The Christological Controversy; Its History, Theology and Texts* (Leiden: Brill, 1994).

[180]Dmitri Z. Zaharopoulos, *Theodore of Mopsuestia on the Bible: A Study of His Old Testament Exegesis,* Theological Inquiries (Mahwah, N.J.: Paulist, 1989).

[181]Celia E. Rabinowitz, review of *Theodore of Mopsuestia on the Bible, Theological Studies* 51 (June 1990): 369.

ship," [182] thus overstating his thesis[183]; for neglecting the relation of Theodore's exegesis to his theology[184]; and for favoring modern liberal biblical scholarship when conservative scholarship would be closer to Theodore.[185] Jerome's biblical exegesis is the stated title of Dennis Brown's monograph.[186] The book seems to offer more concerning textual criticism and Jerome's work as translator.[187] Brown "qualifies the widely held opinion that Jerome, around . . . 390, broke with the LXX tradition in favor of the Hebrew text." Jerome indeed used the Hebrew as a scholar and the LXX as a churchman.[188] As "an eclectic exegete,"[189] Jerome drew from Judaism and from Origen "even during the Origenist controversy."[190]

Augustine of Hippo

The literature on Augustine continues to be voluminous. This essay excludes works that pertain primarily to Augustine's philosophy and ethics and treats briefly the ones that are relative to his theology. Introductions to Augustine's thought have been authored by Henry Chadwick[191] and Kurt Flasch.[192] Warren Thomas Smith has produced a readable blend of biography and theology.[193] Biographies containing some theological material include those by David Bentley-Taylor,[194] James Joseph O'Donnell,[195] Agostino Trapè, O.S.A.,[196] Michael Marshall[197] and Mary T. Clark, R.S.C.J.[198]

---

[182]Ibid.

[183]Rowan A. Greer, review of *Theodore of Mopsuestia on the Bible, Anglican Theological Review* 73 (Winter 1991): 73.

[184]Ibid.

[185]James R. Payton Jr., review of *Theodore of Mopsuestia on the Bible, Calvin Theological Journal* 26 (April 1991): 238.

[186]Dennis Brown, *Vir Trilinguis: A Study in the Biblical Exegesis of Saint Jerome* (Kampen, Netherlands: Kok Pharos, 1992).

[187]C. Thomas McCollough, review of *Biblical Exegesis of Saint Jerome, Religious Studies Review* 20 (July 1994): 243.

[188]Enrique Nardoni, review of *Vir Trilinguis, Catholic Biblical Quarterly* 56 (April 1994): 323.

[189]Ibid.

[190]McCollough, review of *Saint Jerome*, 243.

[191]Henry Chadwick, *Augustine,* Past Masters (Oxford: Oxford University Press, 1986).

[192]Kurt Flasch, *Augustin: Einführung in sein Denken* (Stuttgart: Philipp Reclam, 1980).

[193]Warren Thomas Smith, *Augustine: His Life and Thought* (Atlanta: John Knox, 1980).

[194]David Bentley-Taylor, *Augustine, Wayward Genius: The Life of St. Augustine of Hippo* (London: Hodder & Stoughton; Grand Rapids: Baker, 1980).

[195]James Joseph O'Donnell, *Augustine,* Twayne's World Authors Series (Boston: Twayne, 1985).

[196]Agostino Trapè, O.S.A., *Saint Augustine: Man, Pastor, Mystic,* trans. Matthew J. O'Connell (New York: Catholic Book Publishing, 1986).

[197]Michael Marshall, *The Restless Heart: The Life and Influence of St. Augustine* (Grand Rapids: Eerdmans, 1987).

[198]Mary T. Clark, R.S.C.J., *Augustine,* Outstanding Christian Thinkers (Washington, D.C.: George-

Augustine's conversion draws the attention of several authors: Leo Charles Ferrari,[199] Robert Austin Markus[200] and Ann Hunsaker Hawkins (who compares Augustine with John Bunyan and Thomas Merton).[201] Others give attention to Augustine's *Confessions*, including Joachim Ringleben,[202] a volume edited by Donald Capps and James E. Dittes,[203] Margaret Ruth Miles[204] and Gillian Clark.[205] Colin Starnes[206] and essays edited by Joanne McWilliam[207] focus on both Augustine's conversion and his *Confessions*.

The three volumes in Villanova University's *Collectanea Augustiniana* series contain 185 articles, the majority of which are theological in content. These volumes provide major resources for the study of the theology of the bishop of Hippo.[208] A volume in French edited by Anne-Marie la Bonnardière[209] has provided "an ample and suggestive panorama of the relation of the bishop of Hippo with the Sacred Scripture."[210] Alfred Warren Matthews expounds Augustine's theology during the five-year period between his conversion and his ordination,[211] and Benedict J. Groeschl, C.F.R., interprets briefly his major

town University Press, 1994).

[199]Leo Charles Ferrari, *The Conversions of Saint Augustine*, Saint Augustine Lecture Series, Villanova University, 1982 (Villanova, Penn.: Villanova University Press, 1984).

[200]Robert Austin Markus, *Conversion and Disenchantment in Augustine's Spiritual Career*, Saint Augustine Lecture Series (Villanova, Penn.: Villanova University Press, 1989).

[201]Ann Hunsaker Hawkins, *Archetypes of Conversion: The Autobiographies of Augustine, Bunyan and Merton* (Lewisburg, Penn.: Bucknell University Press; Cranbury, N.J.: Associated University Presses, 1985).

[202]Joachim Ringleben, *Interior intimo meo: Die Nähe Gottes nach den Konfessionen Augustins*, Theologische Studien 135 (Zurich: Theologischer Verlag, 1988).

[203]Donald Capps and James E. Dittes, eds., *The Hunger of the Heart: Reflections on the "Confessions" of Augustine* (West Lafayette, Ind.: Society for the Scientific Study of Religion, 1990).

[204]Margaret Ruth Miles, *Desire and Delight: A New Reading of Augustine's "Confessions"* (New York: Crossroad, 1992).

[205]Gillian Clark, *Augustine: The Confessions*, Landmarks of World Literature (Cambridge: Cambridge University Press, 1993).

[206]Colin Starnes, *Augustine's Conversion: A Guide to the Argument of "Confessions" I-IX* (Waterloo, Ont.: Wilfrid Laurier University Press, 1990).

[207]Joanne McWilliam, ed., *Augustine: From Rhetor to Theologian* (Waterloo, Ont.: Wilfrid Laurier University Press, 1992).

[208]*Augustine: "Second Founder of the Faith,"* ed. Joseph C. Schnaubelt, O.S.A., and Frederick Van Fleteren (New York: Peter Lang, 1990); *Augustine: Presbyter Factus Sum*, ed. Joseph T. Lienhard, S.J., Earl C. Muller, S.J., and Roland J. Teske, S.J. (New York: Peter Lang, 1993); *Augustine: Mystic and Mystagogue*, ed. Frederick Van Fleteren, Joseph C. Schnaubelt and Joseph Reino (New York: Peter Lang, 1994). Of a general nature is James A. Mohler, S.J., *A Speechless Child Is the Word of God: An Interpretation of Saint Augustine on the Trinity, Christ, Mary, Church, Authority, Sacraments, Prayer, Hope and the Two Cities* (New Rochelle, N.Y.: New City, 1992).

[209]Anne-Marie la Bonnardière, ed., *Saint Augustin et la Bible*, Bible de tous les temps (Paris: Éditions Beauchesne, 1986).

[210]Félix-Alejandro Pastor, S.J., review of *Saint Augustin et la Bible*, Gregorianum 69 (1988): 576.

[211]Alfred Warren Matthews, *The Development of St. Augustine from Neoplatonism to Christianity, 386-391 A.D.* (Washington, D.C.: University Press of America, 1980).

writings.[212] Duane W. H. Arnold and Pamela Bright have edited a volume titled *On Christian Doctrine*,[213] and Eugene Kevane treats Augustine's work as catechist and the pertinent writings.[214]

Jaroslav Pelikan interprets in Augustine "the relation between classical views of eternity and Christian views of time, as these came together in his philosophical-theological interpretation of continuity."[215] Waltraud Maria Neumann deals with the proofs of God's existence in Augustine's *On Free Will*[216]; Robert J. O'Connell, S.J., examines the concept of the origin of the human soul in Augustine's later, not-so philosophical writings[217]; Mary C. Preus studies the human soul and self-knowledge as reflected in Augustine's *On the Soul and Its Origin*[218]; Edward Booth, O.P., treats Augustine's contribution to the Western tradition of self-knowledge[219]; Carol Harrison writes on beauty in Augustine[220]; and John Joseph O'Meara interprets the creation of humankind according to *De Genesi ad litteram*.[221] For Gillian Rosemary Evans, the focus is Augustine's concept of evil, especially the impact of Manichaeism and Pelagianism, the changes in his view and the creature-centered nature of moral evil.[222] Marty L. Reid examined Augustine's exegesis of Romans 5.[223]

The study of Augustine's use of *persona* as a christological term was the task of Hubertus R. Drobner,[224] and the study of Augustine's relations with Ulfilan

---

[212]Benedict J. Groeschl, C.F.R., *Augustine: Major Writings* (New York: Crossroad, 1995).

[213]*De doctrina Christiana: A Classic of Western Culture*, Christianity and Judaism in Antiquity 9, ed. Duane W. H. Arnold and Pamela Bright (Notre Dame, Ind.: University of Notre Dame Press, 1995).

[214]Eugene Kevane, *Catechesis in Augustine*, Saint Augustine Lecture Series, Villanova University, 1983 (Villanova, Penn.: Villanova University Press, 1989). William Harmless, S.J., *Augustine and the Catachumenate* (Collegeville, Minn.: Liturgical, 1995), has studied Augustine's work as catechist in relation to the Roman Catholic Church's Rite of Christian Initiation of Adults (1972).

[215]Jaroslav Pelikan, *The Mystery of Continuity: Time and History, Memory and Eternity in the Thought of Saint Augustine* (Charlottesville: University Press of Virginia, 1986).

[216]Waltraud Maria Neumann, *Die Stellung des Gottesbeweises in Augustins "De libero arbitrio"* (Hildesheim, Germany: Georg Olms Verlag, 1986).

[217]Robert J. O'Connell, S.J., *The Origin of the Soul in St. Augustine's Later Works* (New York: Fordham University Press, 1987).

[218]Mary C. Preus, *Eloquence and Ignorance in Augustine's "On the Nature and Origin of the Soul,"* American Academy of Religion Academy Series 51 (Atlanta: Scholars Press, 1985).

[219]Edward Booth, O.P., *Saint Augustine and the Western Tradition of Self-Knowing*, Saint Augustine Lecture Series 1986 (Villanova, Penn.: Villanova University Press, 1989).

[220]Carol Harrison, *Beauty and Revelation in the Thought of Saint Augustine* (Oxford: Oxford University Press, 1992).

[221]John Joseph O'Meara, *The Creation of Man in St. Augustine's "De Genesi ad litteram,"* Saint Augustine Lecture Series 1977 (Villanova, Penn.: Villanova University Press, 1980).

[222]Gillian Rosemary Evans, *Augustine on Evil* (Cambridge: Cambridge University Press, 1982).

[223]Marty L. Reid, "An Analysis of Augustine's Exegesis of Romans 5: A Hermeneutical Investigation into the Contributions of Augustine's Exegesis for Contemporary Interpretation" (Ph.D. diss., Southwestern Baptist Theological Seminary, 1986).

[224]Hubertus R. Drobner, *Person-Exegese und Christologie bei Augustinus: Zur Herkunft der Formel "una persona,"* Philosophia Patrum 8 (Leiden: Brill, 1986).

Arianism, in which it is argued that his debate with Maximinus was more important than his debate with Pascentius, has been undertaken by William A. Sumruld.[225] J. Patout Burns writes on the development of Augustine's doctrine of operative grace,[226] Johannes van Oort on the source for Augustine's concept of the two cities (which he found chiefly in "the archaic Jewish-Christian tradition," not in Mani or Tyconius[227]), and Robert Bryan Eno, S.S., on Augustine's embracing the cult of the saints (martyrs and other Christian dead).[228] Certain doctrinal articles are included in the papers of the Giessen symposium.[229]

Patristic theology has continued to attract the attention of serious scholarship, North American as well as European. It is being written even more intentionally in the context of the total lives of the patristic authors and in the larger context of the early church. Areas of intensive activity during the past fifteen years have been Gnosticism, the New Testament canon, Origen, Arius and Arianism, and Augustine. The future beckons as the contemporary church becomes more conscious of its debt to the early church.[230]

[225]William A. Sumruld, *Augustine and the Arians: The Bishop of Hippo's Encounters with Ulfilan Arianism* (Selingsgrove, Penn.: Susquehanna University Press; Cranbury, N.J.: Associated University Presses, 1994), esp. pp. 137-38.

[226]J. Patout Burns, *The Development of Augustine's Doctrine of Operative Grace* (Paris: Études Augustiniennes, 1980).

[227]Johannes van Oort, *Jerusalem and Babylon: A Study into Augustine's "City of God" and the Sources of His Doctrine of the Two Cities,* Supplements to *Vigiliae Christianae* 14 (Leiden: Brill, 1991), esp. p. 364.

[228]Robert Bryan Eno, S.S., *Saint Augustine and the Saints,* Saint Augustine Lecture Series 1985 (Villanova, Penn.: Villanova University Press, 1989). See also *Saint Augustine the Bishop: A Book of Essays,* ed. Fannie LeMoine and Christopher Kleinhenz, Garland Medieval Casebooks 9 (New York: Garland, 1994).

[229]*Internationales Symposion über den Stand der Augustinus-Forschung, vom 12 bis 16 April 1987 im Schloss Rauischholzhausen der Justus-Liebig-Universität Giessen,* ed. Cornelius Mayer and Karl Heinz Chelius, Cassiciacum 39 (Würzburg: Augustinus-Verlag, 1989).

[230]The author is indebted to Everett Ferguson, Kenneth Ray Parks and Steven Ray Harmon for bibliographic assistance and to Amy Karen Downey for secretarial assistance.

Chapter 6
New Dimensions in Eastern Orthodox Theology

Bradley Nassif

●●●●●●●●●●●●●●●●●●●●●●●●●●●●

WITH THE FALL OF COMMUNISM IN OUR GENERATION THE "EASTERN" isolation of Orthodoxy has come to an end in North America. At the same time evangelicalism is gaining higher visibility in Russia and Eastern Europe. In the wake of these new developments it has become painfully evident that an unfortunate legacy of mutual ignorance exists among Orthodox and evangelical students of theology. There is an urgent need on both sides of the Atlantic for the theological histories of these two traditions to be known and understood in relation to each other. Students of theology can no longer limit their studies to issues that dominate the Protestant and Catholic scene. An entire third tradition of Christian theology must now be figured into the equation of modern research.

The present chapter seeks to facilitate the birth of Orthodox theology into the world of evangelical scholarship. My purpose is to advocate a vigorous agenda of research on the Eastern Orthodox tradition among evangelical students of theology in this generation. This I will do by outlining an approach that emphasizes the principal features of Orthodox theology and the methodological pitfalls to avoid when studying it.

First I will answer the question, Why is study of Eastern Orthodoxy important to the future of evangelicalism? Then I will identify contemporary trends and changes taking place within evangelicalism with regard to its relationship with the

Orthodox Church. Finally I will offer four methodological guidelines for students to follow in their study of Orthodox theology. The guidelines are intended to serve as a map with footnotes that supply a selection of resources for advanced study. Future research on the fine points of theology can be conducted within the framework of the parameters outlined here. I make no pretense of proposing *the* method for studying Eastern Christianity, nor even a comprehensive methodology tailored to fit the doctrinal distinctives of every evangelical denomination. The most urgent need for students and teachers at this time is to put at their disposal a reliable map that will orient them to the theological terrain of the Eastern Orthodox Church and guide them through its rich complexities.[1]

Why Study Eastern Orthodoxy?
Why is the study of Eastern Orthodoxy important to the future of evangelicalism? Daniel Clendenin, an evangelical student of Orthodoxy and a former visiting professor of Christian studies at Moscow State University, gives at least three reasons that bear repeating here.[2] First, Eastern Orthodoxy is the fourth major religion in America, numbering more than six million adherents (at the high end). Worldwide, the church numbers around 185 million, of which seventy million are in Russia alone. Despite seventy-five years of political control in Russia and Eastern Europe, atheism could not erase the profound influence of the Orthodox Church in shaping those cultures. Those who attempt to engage these countries with the gospel, therefore, must know Eastern Orthodoxy as well as they would have to know Catholicism in Italy, Islam in Kuwait or Mormonism in Utah.

Second, Eastern Orthodoxy is a friend of evangelicalism because it defends the basic truths of historic Christianity. The Orthodox Church maintains a firm commitment to the major doctrines of the faith. The great ecumenical councils and creeds that defended the Trinity, the Incarnation, bodily resurrection and Second Coming were largely achievements of the Byzantine Orthodox Church. While there are important areas where evangelicals will disagree with Orthodoxy (such as sacramentalism, to be discussed at the end of the chapter), there is unanimous agreement on most essentials of the faith.

Third, Eastern Orthodoxy is strongest where evangelicalism is weakest. A growing number of evangelicals have complained of experiencing reductionism, barrenness or minimalism in their churches. They have perceived a weak sense of tradition and a lack of mystery in worship. In Orthodoxy there is a strong sense of the majesty and mystery of worship, and a joyful celebration of the gospel in liturgy.

---

[1] I wish to express my gratitude to Fr. Stanley Harakas for reading this chapter and offering helpful suggestions.
[2] Daniel Clendenin, *Eastern Orthodox Christianity: A Western Perspective* (Grand Rapids: Baker, 1994), pp. 17-24.

There is a deep commitment to "holy Tradition," that is, a heritage rooted in a historical consciousness of the Church Fathers, a legacy of faith tested by the fires of persecution, and an emphasis on some overlooked biblical truths (such as the theme of deification in 2 Pet 1:4). These hallmarks of Orthodoxy can strengthen evangelicals whose churches seem to be marked by an "a-historical" faith.

In addition to Clendenin's reasons, I would add two of my own. Evangelicalism can offer an intellectual credibility to the faith needed by modern Orthodox, especially in the area of biblical criticism. The unmistakable clarity with which evangelicals proclaim the gospel and the meticulous conservative scholarship some have employed in their interpretation of the biblical text are among the most important gifts they can give to the Orthodox. A knowledge of Orthodoxy and its intellectual needs in modern biblical scholarship will provide evangelicals with an opportunity to make a constructive contribution to the future health of the Orthodox Church in North America and abroad.

Fifth, a knowledge of Orthodoxy will enable evangelicals to evangelize nominal Orthodox Christians without being divisive and can strengthen both mainline and evangelical renewal movements within the Orthodox Church itself.[3] To the extent that they stress Bible reading, preaching and personal faith in Christ, these movements include the Zoe movement in Greece, the Lord's Army in Romania, the Orthodox Youth Movement in Lebanon, the Orthodox Brotherhood of Saint Symeon the New Theologian in America, and the Antiochian Evangelical Orthodox Mission (AEOM) (the name AEOM was recently removed to homogenize it with the rest of the Antiochian Churches). Each of the above reasons for studying Eastern Orthodoxy could be elaborated upon at length, but space has limited us to these brief remarks. An analysis of recent trends between Orthodox and evangelicals will explain further why the study of Eastern Orthodoxy is personally important to future students of theology.

Contemporary Trends

A brief survey of contemporary trends and issues will size up where things stand between Orthodox and evangelicals at present. There are several signs that Eastern Orthodoxy is gradually growing among evangelicals as an alternative to Roman Catholic and mainline Protestant Christianity. Over the past decade, evangelical clergy and laity have left organizations like Campus Crusade for Christ, Young Life, Youth for Christ, Vineyard fellowships, Anglicanism, the Evangelical Free Church, Baptist denominations, the Christian and Missionary Alliance and others to join the Orthodox Church. An analysis of perceived deficiencies in their previous Christian experience is beyond our purpose here.[4] Nevertheless, Millard Erickson

---

[3]See my article "Evangelical Missions in Eastern Orthodox Lands," *Trinity World Forum* (Winter 1996) and the Lausanne pamphlet "Witnessing to Nominal Orthodox Christians."

[4]No less significant would be to study the lives and reasons why Orthodox members have left their

describes the contemporary interest in "historic faith and more formal worship" as a small but significant movement that has the potential of greatly influencing the future of evangelicalism.

> An increasing number of persons, especially college students, are turning to denominations emphasizing tradition, historical connection, and liturgy. I have in mind the movement of people like Robert Webber and Walter Dunnett into the Episcopal and Anglican Churches. An even more radical step is the movement of evangelicals into the Eastern Orthodox Church. Peter Gillquist, a major leader in this movement, has described the journey of two thousand evangelical Protestants toward Eastern Orthodoxy. One issue of his magazine *Again* featured the testimonies of recent evangelical converts to Eastern Orthodoxy. Among the more conspicuous is Franky Schaeffer, son of the late Francis Schaeffer. A few, such as Thomas Howard, have even been attracted to Roman Catholicism.

> This movement is small, but it is real and of potentially great influence because it includes young people who could be the leaders of the evangelical movement in the years ahead. Unless mainstream evangelicalism finds ways to meet the needs of young people desiring some tie with the historic faith and with more-formal worship, more of them will leave for denominations that offer real alternatives to popular experience-centered worship.[5]

Though Gillquist and Schaeffer are quite serious in their call for authentic Christianity, graduate students are encouraged to move beyond their level of discussion. Neither man possesses a substantial theological education as reflected in their educational histories and oversimplified interpretations of church history and theology.[6] Their main contributions appear to lie in the evangelical impact they are

---

church to join evangelical denominations. The history of Orthodox converts to evangelicalism and their subsequent impact on the movement, as well as on their families still in the Orthodox Church from which they came, has never been written. Also significant would be a study of the contributions made by cradle Orthodox who have chosen to remain in their church after receiving spiritual help from evangelical believers.

[5]Millard Erickson, *Where Is Theology Going?* (Grand Rapids: Baker, 1994), pp. 41-42.

[6]See, for example, Peter Gillquist, *Becoming Orthodox: A Journey to the Ancient Christian Faith* (Brentwood, Tenn.: Wolgemuth & Hyatt, 1989); Frank Schaeffer, *Dancing Alone: The Quest for Orthodox Faith in the Age of False Religion* (Brookline, Mass.: Holy Cross Greek Orthodox Press, 1994). Father Eusebius Stephanou, a reform-minded cradle Orthodox who has promoted evangelical renewal long before Gillquist entered the church, has criticized Gillquist and Schaeffer for preaching Orthodoxy rather than Christ, viewing "everything in the Orthodox Church through rose-colored glasses." "Converts to Orthodoxy: A Grave Concern," *The Logos* 25 (November/December 1992): 1-2, 4. A historical evaluation of Gillquist and his followers' move into the Antiochian Orthodox Church in 1987 has been done by Timothy Weber, "Looking for Home: Evangelical Orthodoxy and the Search for the Original Church," in *New Perspectives on Historical Theology: Essays in Memory of John Meyendorff,* ed. Bradley Nassif, foreword by Henry Chadwick (Grand Rapids: Eerdmans, 1996), pp. 95-121. Gillquist's criticism of the way the Greek Archdiocese handled his group's trip to Constantinople (Weber, p. 113) should be balanced by the oral history of Fr. Gregory Wingenbach, a priest of the Greek Archdiocese who oversaw their visit.

making on the Orthodox Church itself—a renewed emphasis on the centrality of Scripture, the need for personal conversion and a clarion call for a faith that transcends ethnic boundaries.

In addition to popular expressions of evangelical interest in Orthodoxy, there are also scholars, mission agencies, seminaries and academic societies that are beginning to engage the Orthodox Church in unprecedented ways. Within the past decade, a variety of evangelical theologians—Calvinist, Anglican, Baptist, Free Church, Nazarene, Mennonite, Wesleyan and others—have widened their comprehension of theology through a knowledge of the Orthodox tradition. Included are Gerald Bray,[7] Thomas Oden,[8] J. I. Packer,[9] Kenneth Kantzer,[10] Carl F. H. Henry,[11] Norman Geisler,[12] Miroslav Volf,[13] Harold O. J. Brown,[14]

---

[7]One of the most experienced and linguistically competent scholars, fluent not only in the biblical languages but also in modern Greek, Russian and Arabic. "Eastern Orthodox Theology," in *New Dictionary of Theology*, ed. Sinclair B. Ferguson, David F. Wright, J. I. Packer (Downers Grove, Ill.: InterVarsity Press, 1988), pp. 215-18; "Justification and the Eastern Orthodox Churches," in *Here We Stand*, ed. J. I. Packer (Downers Grove, Ill.: InterVarsity Press, 1986); *Creeds, Councils and Christ* (Downers Grove, Ill.: InterVarsity Press, 1993).

[8]Among others, *The Word of Life: Systematic Theology*, 3 vols. (San Francisco: Harper & Row, 1989). Oden holds the conviction that the consensus of the Fathers on doctrinal issues in the first millennium constitutes an almost normative status of historic Christian faith for the contemporary church. He is now putting together a projected 27-volume collection of patristic commentaries on the entire Bible that will be published by InterVarsity Press, a leading evangelical publishing house (the Ancient Christian Commentary on Scripture). The future impact of this series on the evangelical community will probably be a two-edged sword. On the one hand, it will strip away naive assumptions about the extent of doctrinal unity among the Church Fathers on a number of issues. In so doing, it will prove the absence of any absolute doctrinal consensus external to and independent from Scripture. On the other hand, it will also support the thesis that despite the church's great diversity, there is no orthodoxy without tradition. There was and is a consistent and continuous history of apostolic faith handed down over the centuries. Just what that tradition is, however, will be debated. Inevitably, it will prompt evangelicals to explore in much greater depth the problems of defining orthodoxy and heresy in the early church, the ecclesial context in which this occurred and how all this impacts contemporary Orthodox identity.

[9]See the course team-taught with the author in July 1997 at Regent College, "Eastern Orthodox and Evangelicalism in Dialogue" (available on audiotape). J. I. Packer, "On from Orr: Cultural Crisis, Rational Realism and Incarnational Ontology," with Bradley Nassif, "An Eastern Orthodox Response to J. I. Packer," in *Reclaiming the Great Tradition: Evangelicals, Catholics & Orthodox in Dialogue*, ed. James Cutsinger (Downers Grove, Ill.: InterVarsity Press, 1997). See also Packer's "Christian Morality Adrift," delivered to the Faith and Renewal Conference. An Orthodox response was delivered by Fr. Stanley Harakas. *A Society in Peril*, ed. Kevin Perrotta (Ann Arbor, Mich.: Servant, 1989).

[10]Kantzer's interest has been expressed in his involvement with and endorsement of the Society for the Study of Eastern Orthodoxy and Evangelicalism (described below): "Nothing but good could come from serious conversations between Eastern Orthodox thinkers and conservative evangelicals. This society provides just such a forum."

[11]Carl F. H. Henry, "Discussion of Christology now may be on the threshold of an exciting new epoch involving Protestant evangelical and Eastern Orthodox theologians, and possibly Roman Catholic scholars as well." Carl Henry, *The Identity of Jesus of Nazareth* (Nashville: Broadman, 1992), p. 112. Also personal conversations with the author over the past decade.

[12]Norman Geisler, "Evangelicals would do well to familiarize themselves with this most ancient of

Donald Bloesch,[15] Grant Osborne,[16] David S. Dockery,[17] T. F. Torrance,[18] Randy Maddox,[19] Carl Braaten[20] and others.[21] Their works reveal a growing interest in investigating what influence the early and Byzantine church has had on issues facing the modern evangelical movement.

This interest seems to stem partly from the fact that evangelical theology has

---

Christian jurisdictions. Eastern Orthodoxy has many desirable tenets—historicity, continuity and doctrinal steadfastness being the most noticeable. We should indeed become acquainted with our brethren in the 'Church of the Seven Councils.'" Norman Geisler and Ralph E. MacKenzie, *Roman Catholics and Evangelicals: Agreements and Differences* (Grand Rapids: Baker, 1995), p. 442.

[13]Miroslav Volf, *After Our Likeness: The Church as the Image of the Trinity* (Grand Rapids: Eerdmans, 1997). Volf offers the most penetrating Free Church critique of modern Orthodox and Catholic "communion" ecclesiologies developed by John Zizioulas and Cardinal Ratzinger.

[14]Harold O. J. Brown, "On Method and Means in Theology," in *Doing Theology in Today's World: Essays in Honor of Kenneth S. Kantzer,* ed. John D. Woodbridge and Thomas E. McComiskey (Grand Rapids: Zondervan, 1991), pp. 147-69. Brown is one of a few evangelical students who did their doctoral work under Orthodox theologian George Florovsky. Brown has been an effective interpreter of Florovsky for the evangelical community, even though at times he seems to squeeze Florovsky into an uncomfortably tight pair of evangelical shoes.

[15]Donald Bloesch, "Salvation in Protestant Evangelicalism" (delivered to the Society for the Study of Eastern Orthodoxy and Evangelicalism, 1993—see below). And especially in Christian Foundations, vols. 1-3 (Downers Grove, Ill.: InterVarsity Press, 1992-). Also Robert E. Webber and Donald Bloesch, eds., *The Orthodox Evangelicals: Who They Are and What They Are Saying* (Nashville: Thomas Nelson, 1978).

[16]Grant Osborne, "The Many and the One: The Interface Between Eastern Orthodox and Protestant Evangelical Hermeneutics," *St. Vladimir's Theological Quarterly* 3 (1995).

[17]David S. Dockery, *Biblical Interpretation Then and Now: Contemporary Hermeneutics in the Light of the Early Church* (Grand Rapids: Baker, 1992). This demonstrates a recovery of the ancient exegetical tradition by a Baptist New Testament scholar.

[18]Among others, *Trinitarian Perspectives: Toward Doctrinal Agreement* (Edinburgh: T & T Clark, 1994). Torrance pleads for space in the evangelical establishment of North America partly because of his epistemology and his deemphasizing of propositional revelation. Nevertheless, his rare mastery of the language and literature of the Eastern Church (ancient and modern), coupled with his relatively conservative ecumenism from a Calvinist platform, makes it impossible to overlook his contributions. Evangelicals should interact with his proposals more thoroughly than they have to date.

[19]Randy Maddox, *Responsible Grace: John Wesley's Practical Theology* (Nashville: Kingswood, 1994). One of Maddox's goals is to find in Wesley an instructive integration of theological emphases that have traditionally separated Eastern and Western Christianity.

[20]Especially his editorial work with *Pro Ecclesia,* a journal that seeks to give contemporary expression to the one apostolic faith and its classic traditions, including Eastern Orthodoxy.

[21]Such as Daniel Clendenin's two-volume work, *Eastern Orthodox Christianity: A Western Perspective* (Grand Rapids: Baker, 1994); Daniel Clendenin, ed., *Eastern Orthodox Theology: A Contemporary Reader* (Grand Rapids: Baker, 1995). Clendenin's chief contribution is his synthesis of the essential points of Orthodox writers in the secondary literature. His *Contemporary Reader* includes an excellent selection of important essays. A second volume like it would be very useful. Also James Stamoolis, *Eastern Orthodox Mission Theology* (Maryknoll, N.Y.: Orbis, 1986). Stamoolis is dean of Wheaton Graduate School and a former Greek Orthodox. Gabriel Fackre, *The Christian Story*, 3rd ed., 3 vols. (Grand Rapids: Eerdmans, 1995). Fackre grew up with a father from a Middle Eastern, Orthodox home. Robert Rakestraw, "Becoming Like God: An Evangelical Doctrine of *Theosis*," *Journal of the Evangelical Theological Society* 2 (1994). Thomas Finger, "Anabaptism and Eastern Orthodoxy: Some Unexpected Similarities?" *Journal of Ecumenical Studies* (Fall 1995).

self-consciously adhered to classical orthodox belief in the trinitarian faith and the christological confession of Christ as fully human and fully divine, as revealed by Scripture and as later formulated by the Nicene Creed and Chalcedonian Definition. Protestant evangelicals have begun to make the connection between the ecumenical councils of Christian antiquity, which were largely achievements of the Byzantine Orthodox Church, and those councils' modern heir apparent—the Orthodox churches of Greece, Russia, Eastern Europe and the Middle East. This consensual tradition within the Byzantine church articulates certain conceptions of Orthodoxy that remain central and common to Orthodox and evangelical identity.[22]

On the missiological front the situation is less promising at this time. Walls of tension and hostility between Orthodox and evangelicals are rising in pockets of formerly communist countries in Eastern Europe. A staggering number of approximately seven hundred Western Christian agencies have been documented as presently at work in Russia and Eastern Europe.[23] But very few missionaries seem to operate with even a basic grasp of Orthodox history and theology, let alone an appreciation for the rich cultural impact it has made on these countries. As a result, Orthodox leaders have shown increasingly strong resentment toward missionaries who have attempted to convert or proselytize their parishioners.[24]

Turning to American seminaries, I can happily report that in the past five years a small number of courses on the Orthodox Church have been introduced as part of the curricula. All such courses are noteworthy, since, historically, evangelical seminaries previously offered them on an "on demand" basis only. A study of actual course offerings shows that at least one class, whether Introduction to the Orthodox Church, Spirituality of the Eastern Church, Evangelical Missions in Orthodox Lands, Syriac Church Fathers, or Eastern Orthodoxy and Evangelicalism in Dialogue, has been taught recently at Fuller Theological Seminary, Southern Baptist Seminary (Louisville, Ky.), Gordon Conwell Seminary and Trinity Evangelical Divinity School, to name only a few.[25] Seminaries that develop

---

[22]Some evangelicals may find offensive the use of the term *Orthodox* to describe the churches of the East, since evangelicals, too, consider themselves "orthodox." Moreover, the categories of "East" and "West" today refer only to the historical bifurcation which occurred in the Middle Ages. They now have little geographic and cultural significance.

[23]Sharon Linzey, Holt Ruffin and Mark Elliot, eds., *East-West Christian Organizations: A Directory of Western Christian Organizations Working in East Central Europe and the Former Soviet Union* (Evanston, Ill.: Berry, 1993).

[24]Regional efforts at cooperative evangelism by Russian Orthodox and evangelicals have been rare. The Moscow patriarchate has given almost no official sanctions to these activities, preferring instead the path of silence or outright opposition. The patriarch's endorsement of Charles Colson's prison ministry is a laudable exception. Colson encourages converts to remain in their local churches, be they Orthodox, Catholic or Protestant.

[25]Orthodox seminaries that offer courses on evangelicalism are further behind. Holy Cross Greek Orthodox Seminary (Brookline, Mass.) makes evangelical courses available to its students through its

curricular emphases in Eastern Christianity will be better able to offer a fuller perspective on global theology and will find themselves on the cutting edge of the future of theological education. It is perhaps worth noting in this regard that the Antiochian Archdiocese is discussing the possibility of starting new M. Div. and/or Th. M. programs in Eastern Orthodoxy with Fuller Seminary. The programs would be staffed with a distinguished group of Pan-Orthodox faculty and made available to Orthodox and non-Orthodox students. Should the plans materialize, the use of classical and contemporary methods of theological education (combining Orthodox mentoring with class lectures and modern media technologies) could provide the means for a solidly Orthodox renewal in North America and, eventually, abroad.

Three organizations have sprung up in the past decade to cultivate a variety of exchanges between Orthodox and evangelical leaders. In July 1995 the World Council of Churches sponsored its first international conference in Alexandria, Egypt, between representatives of Orthodox churches and people of evangelical commitment. At a follow-up meeting after the WCC's Canberra Assembly in 1991, it became apparent that evangelicals and Orthodox shared concern on a number of issues that challenged historic Christian faith. A small meeting between representatives of the Ecumenical Patriarchate in Istanbul (old Constantinople) and evangelicals was convened in Stuttgart, Germany, in 1993. Discussions and contacts continued, especially within the framework of the Central Committee of the WCC. A much larger consultation of forty participants, now published in *Proclaiming Christ Today*, was hosted by the Coptic Orthodox Church in Alexandria, Egypt, under the sponsorship of the WCC on July 10-15, 1995. A followup meeting was held in Hamburg, Germany, March 30-April 4, 1998.

Evangelicals for Middle East Understanding is a group of evangelicals based in Evanston, Illinois. The organization is dedicated to promoting a knowledge of the plight of Eastern Christians living in the Middle East today. Much of their work seeks to raise the level of consciousness among evangelicals of North America concerning this neglected and misunderstood Christian church. Through its annual meetings, consultations and study tours the organization focuses primarily on the practical, pastoral and regional realities of the Orthodox Church in the Middle East.[26]

---

sister consortium school, Gordon-Conwell Seminary. Saint Vladimir's Seminary (Crestwood, N.Y.) shows signs of interest among several of its faculty members but has gone no further. Saint Nersus, its sister school from the Armenian Orthodox Church, invited an Armenian evangelical, Joseph Alexanian from Trinity International University (Deerfield, Ill.), to teach a course on evangelism in the book of Acts in the summer of 1994. In August 1995 Metropolitan Philip Saliba of the Antiochian Orthodox Archdiocese took a bold step forward in this regard by offering an annual comparative theology course to his seminarians on Orthodoxy and American Evangelicalism in the Antiochian House of Studies (Ligonier, Penn.). Faculty exchange programs can break down caricatures and stereotypes.

[26]The Institute for East/West Christian Studies also provides valuable statistical and religious resources for Orthodox-evangelical relations (located at the Billy Graham Center, Wheaton, Ill.).

The most theologically focused group of Orthodox and evangelicals today appears to be the Society for the Study of Eastern Orthodoxy and Evangelicalism (SSEOE). The SSEOE is a learned society that meets annually at the Billy Graham Center, Wheaton College. Through its annual meetings and unpublished papers, it seeks to make the two traditions known and understood in relation to each other in the areas of history, doctrine, worship and spirituality.[27] It seeks to take a constructive approach to conservative Christian dialogue without minimizing differences. It includes a wide cross section of evangelical denominations and Orthodox jurisdictions. Institutions represented by students and faculty include Trinity Evangelical Divinity School, Wheaton College, Dallas Seminary, Fuller Seminary, Southern Baptist Seminary (Ky.), Eastern Nazarene College, Associated Mennonite Biblical Seminaries, Holy Cross Greek Orthodox Seminary, St. Vladimir's Orthodox Seminary and others.[28] Evangelical and Orthodox endorsements on the SSEOE have been given by J. I. Packer, Kenneth Kantzer, Ward Gasque, Kent Hill, Bishop Kallistos (Timothy) Ware, Father Stanley Harakas, Metropolitan Philip Saliba and Father John Meyendorff.

These and similar developments demonstrate that the study of Orthodoxy is fast becoming a vital issue in modern theology. An unprecedented opportunity for growth, reconstruction and renewal lies before us as we stand poised for one of the most intriguing theological encounters of the twenty-first century.

Guidelines for Future Study

There are various ways to study Eastern Orthodoxy. Not all are equally profitable. With so many different angles to consider, the beginning student needs to know which books and methods of study will promote the highest level of academic integrity. It bears repeating that none of us in theological education has a corner on the truth, including the present author. With that awareness, I offer four guidelines for students to follow in their initial studies. The first three specify some of the fundamental prerequisites for comparing Orthodoxy with evangelicalism which can lead to an understanding of the Orthodox tradition on its own terms. The fourth guideline identifies key areas of convergence and divergence between Orthodox and evangelical theology and offers suggestions and resources for advancing future research to a deeper level.

1. Clarify and compare the different meanings of "unity and diversity" within

---

[27]The papers may soon be collected in a book.

[28]For media accounts of the SSEOE, see "Scholars Hope for Thaw in Evangelical-Orthodox Relations," *Christianity Today*, October 25, 1993; "Peering over the Orthodox-Evangelical Crevasse," *Christianity Today*, October 9, 1992; "A True Meaning of Church Service," *Chicago Tribune*, October 1, 1993; "Orthodox and Evangelical Scholars Meet," *The Word* (Antiochian Archdiocese), February 1995; "Orthodox, Evangelical Scholars Meet," *The Orthodox Observer* 60 (April 1995): 1102.

Orthodox and evangelical theology today. No subject carries more consequence for modern discussions on Christian unity than recent scholarly investigation into the meaning of unity and diversity as found on the pages of the New Testament. A careful assessment of the current (sometimes lack of) scholarship on how unity and diversity are perceived in Orthodox and evangelical theology is an essential prerequisite for evaluating each other's differences. The results obtained on this topic will inform the degree of importance that should be ascribed to all other areas of doctrine. The conclusions will affect how we evaluate everything else. If theologians from either side choose to emphasize how different they are from the other there is no way for them to escape from returning to this point sooner or later. At present, it is self-evident that modern Orthodox scholars have not yet grappled sufficiently with such research in their recent ecumenical dialogues. There are very few published biblical scholars in English working in this area, and the systematic theologians writing in English as well as the European languages often engage in dogmatic *eisegesis* rather than authentic *exegesis* of the biblical text (despite pious protests to the contrary). We can only point out the deficiency, encourage them to catch up with the research, and invite them to offer their own constructive evaluations of it. (In New Testament studies, for instance, they will need to compare the different views represented by the somewhat more liberal James Dunn with the more conservative Ralph P. Martin; for unity and diversity in the early patristic period they will want to compare the liberal Walter Bauer with the conservative H. E. W. Turner.) Yet evangelicals need prodding as well. While many evangelical scholars have engaged the subject, very few have filtered their research down for local pastors and their interdenominational relations. Thus until Orthodox theologians catch up with the research and evangelicals begin to apply it ecumenically, we are forced to limit our comparative analysis to that theology which is currently lived out in modern Orthodox and evangelical church life. We hope that one day soon scholars and church leaders from both camps will make a concerted effort to translate their conclusions into applied theology.

What is that theology which is currently lived out within the churches? We will look first at general conditions. Since evangelicalism is a widely diverse movement, it is not possible to provide a detailed analysis between Orthodoxy and all evangelical denominations or all submovements which fall under its umbrella (such as charismatics, fundamentalists or neo-evangelicals). A series of specialized monographs covering separate denominations and movements would be required. If such a task could be undertaken it would be of enormous benefit. At this stage, however, we will want to access the publications of the Faith and Order Commission of the World Council of Churches for acquiring authoritative and mature conclusions reached by world Orthodoxy on a wide range of issues. The WCC has collected conclusions from bilateral dialogues between the Orthodox and specific Protestant denominations on an international level over the past two decades (e.g., the Anglican-Orthodox, Reformed-Orthodox, Lutheran-Orthodox, Methodist-Orthodox and Orthodox-Evangelical dialogues).

Although they possess less international participation than the WCC consultations, the most doctrinally developed resources for the Orthodox-Evangelical dialogue are annual papers delivered to the Society for the Study of Eastern Orthodoxy and Evangelicalism noted earlier. My colleague at Fuller, Cecil Robeck, informs me that additional material will be forthcoming after a series of dialogues has been held between Orthodox and Pentecostal groups, tentatively scheduled to occur over the coming decade.

As students develop their studies in relation to this past progress, they need to do something that has not yet been done. They need to specify what it is within Protestant theology that makes it "evangelical" and then (the new part) determine how those evangelical distinctives compare with Orthodoxy. When that is done we learn that there is a history of the definition of the term *evangelical* and that definition has widened over the past twenty years.[29] A wider diversity exists within evangelicalism today that was not fashionable to acknowledge in the recent past. Today historians of modern religion acknowledge Catholic evangelicals, Anglican evangelicals and Orthodox evangelicals (though some would argue that all such labels are tautologous). This diversity within evangelicalism should not leave us with the impression that it is disunited. On the contrary, Alister McGrath identifies a cluster of six controlling convictions upon which the entire evangelical movement rests. Each of these is regarded as being true, of vital importance and grounded in Scripture. They are not purely *doctrinal* realities but also *existential* in that they affirm the manner in which the believer enjoys a redemptive and experiential encounter with Christ. McGrath sets out these six fundamental convictions as follows:

1. The supreme authority of Scripture as a source of knowledge of God and a guide of Christian living.

2. The majesty of Jesus Christ, both as incarnate God and Lord and as the Savior of sinful humanity.

3. The lordship of the Holy Spirit.

4. The need for personal conversion.

5. The priority of evangelism for both individual Christians and the church as a whole.

---

[29]See *Varieties of Evangelicalism*, eds. Donald Dayton and Robert Johnston (Knoxville: University of Tennessee, 1991). This book shows how defining evangelicalism has become one of the biggest problems in American religious historiography. It also supports the thesis that there is an identity crisis in evangelicalism itself.

6. The importance of the Christian community for spiritual nourishment, fellowship and growth.

McGrath elaborates:

All other matters have tended to be regarded as "matters of indifference," on which a substantial degree of latitude and diversity may be accepted but a diversity that is itself grounded in the New Testament, in that responsible evangelicalism has refused to legislate where Scripture is silent or where it offers a variety of approaches. This is especially clear in relation to evangelical views on the nature of the church. . . . Yet these six points also represent distinctive *emphases* that are regarded by evangelicals as identity-giving. For example, many outside evangelicalism recognize the need for evangelism yet do not regard it as being particularly significant, let alone of defining importance. Equally, many Christians who would concur with the six points noted above might wish to add additional items of belief or practice that some evangelicals would regard as being of marginal importance, and that other evangelicals might regard as mistaken or unjustifiable.[30]

It is vitally important for us not to underestimate the common ground that is described in this definition of evangelical unity and diversity. Its substance, if not the exact wording, can serve as a theological reference point for comparing evangelical faith with Eastern Orthodoxy.

When comparing this definition one must first approach the Orthodox Church with an awareness of the internal and external diversity which exists within the Orthodox Church itself. Too often the Orthodox tradition is viewed as monolithic. Insufficient attention is given to its own divisions and tensions. For example, the Orthodox Church today is made up of thirteen or fifteen autocephalous churches (reckonings vary). Outside those boundaries there are *administrative* (not theological) differences between those churches and non-Chalcedonian or Oriental Christians. And there are *theological* differences between those two bodies and Eastern Rite Catholics who liturgically resemble the Orthodox but in fact are under the pope; and between the fifteen autocephalous churches and sectarian movements which broke away from them, such as Old Calendarists in Greece and America or Old Believers in Russia. Yet even with the fifteen autocephalous churches one can discern different *attitudes* which characterize each group. For those who have been

---

[30]Alister McGrath, *Evangelicalism & the Future of Christianity* (Downers Grove, Ill.: InterVarsity Press, 1995), pp. 55-56. Most other evangelicals would include belief in the Trinity, the Second Coming, the general resurrection of human beings and their final judgment and eternal consignment to heaven or hell as part of their identity—an important qualification not adequately recognized by McGrath. For a positive statement of the areas of agreement among evangelicals and a discussion also of their many differences, see Robert P. Lightner, *Handbook of Evangelical Theology* (Grand Rapids: Kregel, 1995).

personally exposed to the variety of Orthodox communions throughout the world, it is readily apparent that not all are alike. For example, without wishing to be judgmental, one can make a reasonable case for generalizing that the Russian Orthodox Church tends toward an austere, if not legalistic, posture toward the faith, while Arab Christians in the Antiochian Patriarchate of the Middle East and North America are more flexible in their attitudes. (Yet an aberration within the Antiochian Patriarchate can also be seen in some recent evangelical and Anglican converts whose exclusivist posture toward non-Orthodox Christians is more of an Orthodox version of Protestant fundamentalism than authentic Orthodox catholicity.) These institutional characteristics are important to keep in mind when interacting with questions of ecclesiology, ecumenism and nationalism. What some propose as Orthodox teaching may be nothing else than a disguised nationalism or an Orthodox version of Protestant fundamentalism. Keeping these distinctions in mind, it is best for students to confine their theological comparisons with evangelicalism to the main fifteen autocephalous churches wherein exists an undisputed unity of faith and order.[31]

2. *Avoid research methodologies and theological categories which lead to false or misleading conclusions about the character of Orthodox theology.* There are several methodological fallacies to avoid when studying Orthodox theology.[32] These include an uncritical acceptance of contemporary Orthodox church life as a reliable guide for understanding its theology, the failure to recognize the false dogmatism of popular Orthodox writers in the secondary literature and the use of research methodologies which can possibly be inconsistent with the theological character of the patristic sources (such as the use of scholastic, confessional or liberal categories used in Catholic and Protestant theology). We will examine each potential fallacy in turn.

One of the most prevalent methodological fallacies employed today by students is what may be called the "empirical fallacy." This is practiced widely by missionaries in Russia, Eastern Europe and the Middle East. The empirical fallacy bases its understanding of Orthodoxy chiefly on what is visibly observed and experienced in the Orthodox Church today. The fallacy of this approach would seem to be self-evident, but since it is so widely practiced today extra attention must be given to it. Two true stories from the Russian Orthodox Church illustrate the problem.

---

[31] A handy resource for clarifying the institutional complexities is Ronald G. Roberson, *The Eastern Christian Churches,* 5th ed. (Rome: Pontifical Institutum Studiorum Orientalium, 1995); also Timothy (Kallistos) Ware, *The Orthodox Church,* 3rd rev. ed. (New York: Penguin, 1993), for the best general introduction to all aspects of the Orthodox Church.

[32] Those who are concerned about historical fallacies in modern research methods in church history can do no better than James E. Bradley and Richard A. Muller, *Church History: An Introduction to Research, Reference Works and Methods* (Grand Rapids:, Mich. Eerdmans, 1995); David Hackett Fischer, *Historians' Fallacies: Toward a Logic of Historical Thought* (New York: Harper & Row, 1970).

In 1992 the author was invited by Dr. Ronald Nash to join Campus Crusade for Christ's Co-Mission project in Russia. Our task was to evangelize and then train Russian educators how to teach the ABCs of the Christian faith to students in the public school system. More than six hundred teachers arrived in Moscow. On the last day of the mission over a hundred of us gathered together to share our experiences. The reports of personal conversions were deeply moving. As one might expect, stories were told from every quadrant describing personal encounters with the Russian Orthodox Church. In one city an archbishop welcomed the Crusade team with open arms; in other cities priests publicly denounced the mission as a false religion inspired by the devil. One young priest was reported to have taken the team on a tour of his church to explain the role of icons in worship. He informed my unsuspecting brethren that icons were like the mediums of a séance. "We Orthodox pray to icons like devil worshipers conjure the dead," he explained. With a wry look on his face he gleefully noted that he himself had even contacted the devil on occasion through the medium of an icon, part of which included an image of Satan. Another group reported a widespread identification of Orthodoxy with Russian nationalism. Seeking to revive the former glory of the Tsarist days, a number of Orthodox people advocated an enforced policy of Russification. "Autocracy, Orthodoxy and nationalism" were the saving elements of old Russia that would now rescue the country from communism and the Christian heresies of the West. Orthodox fundamentalists denounced all Protestants and Catholics as raving heretics who lived outside the Orthodox Church in one great sea of undifferentiated darkness!

These two examples of popular theology could be multiplied time and again. They illustrate how serious misinformation can be taken as truth by relying on the empirical realities of the Orthodox Church as a trustworthy guide for understanding its faith. To be sure, such examples are quite reliable indicators of the lived theology of some priests and people, and the form of Christianity they inherited and continue to perpetuate. But such popular misunderstandings only serve to underscore the need for removing biblical illiteracy, superstition, ethnocentrism and bigotry. It cannot be emphasized strongly enough that a great many of the practical realities of the contemporary Orthodox Church are *not* reliable sources of its theology. Sadly, what one encounters on the local and administrative levels reveals a church that is woefully deficient in the apprehension of its own religion. It is imperative for evangelicals to be made aware that what some laypeople and church leaders may believe is not necessarily what the Bible, councils, creeds, liturgy and fathers of the Orthodox Church have actually taught. It is a critical interpretation of the *sources themselves* (patristic, liturgical, historical, etc.) which provides the *norms* of Orthodox doctrine and delineates the criteria for establishing a common faith and checking deviations and abuses. Consequently, the first requirement for an Orthodoxy that is rightly understood is to base one's interpretation on the primary texts and reliable secondary sources, not on folk theology.

A variant of the empirical methodological fallacy is the inability of a novice to recognize the false dogmatism of certain Orthodox writers who provide critically unreliable literature about the Orthodox Church. At present, this seems able to be cured only through the guidance of an experienced Orthodox theologian. Although the situation is rapidly changing for the better, the caliber of Orthodox scholarship worldwide is uneven at best. In America the quality of the secondary literature can be placed somewhere between adolescence and maturity. It is not uncommon to encounter spiritual romanticism (especially in the liturgical literature), esoteric philosophical treatises in works written by and for philosophers at the expense of theological clarity (such as the works of Christos Yannaras), sweeping generalizations which contrast Orthodoxy with a vague "West," or theologically imprecise, incomplete or inconsistent presentations of Orthodox doctrine. Some of this is a legacy of the nineteenth- and twentieth-century Orthodox theology, which has undergone a revival in the fields of philosophy, patristics and liturgics but not in other disciplines. As the new generation of Orthodox scholars emerge, one hopes that the Church will also witness a renewed interest in biblical and systematic theology.[33] As noted earlier, this is an area in which evangelicals can assist the Orthodox in coming to terms with modern biblical scholarship without opposing faith and criticism. The need for raising the standards of academic excellence in world Orthodoxy remains one of the greatest challenges for the Orthodox Church at the dawn of the third millennium.

Additional inadequate approaches to the study of Eastern Christianity arise from a lack of knowledge concerning the character of its theological history and the understandable propensity to systematize it in the familiar categories of Catholic or Protestant thought. The following approaches should be avoided unless one is able to modify them in a manner that is consistent with the Church's vision of the divine reality. They include the categories of "scholasticism," "confessionalism," and "liberal" versus "conservative."

The categories of "liberal" and "conservative" are less problematic than the scholastic and confessional approaches. The late Alexander Schmemann objected that the term *liberal* can be constructive if by it one merely means going beyond the fathers to create a "new synthesis or reconstruction" that would put theology into a new "key."[34] In his opinion the best proponent of this approach was the Russian theologian Sergius Bulgakov (despite Georges Florovsky's justifiably negative

---

[33]Outside the United States the situation is significantly sub par, due to the political and cultural conditions of formerly communist-controlled countries where theological education was severely curtailed.

[34]Alexander Schmemann, "Russian Theology, 1920-1972: An Introductory Survey," *St. Vladimir's Theological Quarterly* 16 (1972): 172-94.

assessment of Bulgakov's sophiological heresy). In a similar way, the *conservative* label can raise questions if one is referring to a narrow "theology of repetition" that seeks only to repeat the past as sufficient for the needs of the present. If, however, *liberal* is used to refer to departure from apostolic and patristic faith and *conservative* to faithful adherence to it, then such labels can be useful theological indicators of one's position. No false problems should arise if one takes care to define what is meant by these categories.

To gain perspective on these problems students should familiarize themselves with the history of Orthodox theology.[35] Along with learning the main outlines, they should immerse themselves in the primary sources and liturgical life of the Orthodox Church itself, as much as that is practically possible. Only then can the methodology and "ethos"[36] be understood, and the ways of Eastern theology be known and distinguished from the Western forms of Catholic and Protestant theology.

Once the student has acquired this background, he or she can understand why the "scholastic" method is also foreign to Orthodox theology. By *scholastic* I mean the importation into Orthodoxy of the abstract, propositional development of Western thought-forms, as exemplified by Thomas Aquinas and Protestant ortho-dox scholastics such as Charles Hodge, B. B. Warfield and the Princeton theologi-ans. These approaches are concerned to view theology *primarily as logically deductive systems of propositional truths or statements.* These modes of thought came to be built into the infrastructure of Roman Catholic and Protestant thought and provide a common epistemological framework for virtually all of Western theology today. An emphasis on abstractive formal relations began as early as Tertullian and Augustine,

---

[35]For a concise overview see Gerald Bray, "Eastern Orthodox Theology," in *New Dictionary of Theology,* pp. 215-18. For a fuller account see Jaroslav Pelikan, *The Spirit of Eastern Christendom (600-1700)* (Chicago: University of Chicago Press, 1974), pp. 146-98; Georges Florovsky, *Ways of Russian Theology,* vols. 5-6 in *The Collected Works of Georges Florovsky* (Belmont, Mass.: Nordland); and G. A. Maloney, *A History of Orthodox Theology Since 1453* (Belmont, Mass.: Nordland, 1976). See also John Meyendorff, "Light from the East? Doing Theology in an Eastern Orthodox Perspective," in *Doing Theology in Today's World,* pp. 339-58; the primer by Alexander Schmemann, "The Task of Orthodox Theology Today," in *Church, World, Mission* (New York: St. Vladimir's Seminary Press, 1979); and Stanley Harakas, "Doing Theology Today: An Orthodox and Evangelical Dialogue on Theological Method," unpublished paper delivered to the SSEOE, October 4-5, 1996.

[36]Ultraconservative Orthodox have placed too much stress on the value of "ethos" in the apprehension of the Church's faith. They equate Orthodoxy with the wearing of old Byzantine clerical vestments, the use of a specific brand of incense in worship and devotion, wearing ponytails and so on. To illustrate the point, a group of evangelical converts recently went on a pilgrimage to "Holy Russia" to better learn "the Orthodox way." They returned to America, legally changed their given names to saints' names and began wearing Russian monastic garments so as to be "more Orthodox." This is a tragic example from people who ought to know better. Any reduction of Christian truth to a particular historic form—be it Byzantine, Russian, Arab or American—presupposes a cultural reduction of Christian catholicity.

then Aquinas, and was further accentuated by the analytical tradition that comes from Descartes and the way of thinking in external relations that comes from Newton and Immanuel Kant—that is, the Enlightenment.[37]

The "confessional" way of doing theology (a cousin of the scholastic method) is also foreign to the mainstream of Eastern Christian thought. In the seventeenth century, Catholics and Protestants looked to the East for support in their doctrinal disputes with each other and asked the Orthodox to send their confessions of faith. The results were less than satisfactory. Through Patriarch Cyril Lukaris, a basically Calvinist "confession" of faith was produced in 1629 in opposition to Roman Catholic theology; other confessions were basically Latin and Tridentine in spirit, such as the "confession" of Peter Mogila in 1640 in his apologetics against Protestantism. During this "Western captivity" of the Eastern Church, as it is known, the Orthodox spoke to Protestants through the structures of Catholic theology and to Catholics through the structures of Protestant theology. In neither case were the Orthodox being true to their patristic past. In the twentieth century, however, respected men like John Karmiris from Athens still expound the coherence of Greek patristic theology through the Western confessional approach.

Many Orthodox, such as Schmemann and Florovsky, consider these systems a pseudomorphosis of the Church's theology. They and others have opposed such systems because they tend to claim exhaustiveness by covering up gaps and mysteries, or because practitioners tend to read into the system a presupposed theology, with the result that there seems to be a contrived interrelatedness of doctrines. While I agree that the confessional approach is indeed a pseudomorphosis, it is also true that *no* theological method (even the patristic one) is beyond improvement in this fallen world.

There are several guidelines, therefore, that may shape the making of a "Western Orthodox" systematic theology (in whatever form that might take). Such an approach should possess the following characteristics: (a) It should organize and present the data clearly, thereby serving as an effective pedagogical tool (and this is no small contribution, given the confusion that often reigns on the lay levels of Orthodox parishes). (b) Such an Orthodox systematic theology should be developed and accepted as true if it is constructed only at the end of one's research, not at the beginning. The Bible, always in dialogue with the Church's historical and dogmatic theology, should be the beginning and end of the hermeneutical circle. (c) Such a

---

[37]A penetrating analysis and critique of the whole of Western thought can be found in a masterful essay by T. F. Torrance, "Karl Barth and the Latin Heresy," in *Karl Barth, Biblical and Evangelical Theologian* (Edinburgh: T & T Clark, 1992). But Torrance goes too far by wanting to dispense entirely with the notion of propositional revelation. There *is* a place for propositional theology in Orthodoxy today, just as there was among some of the early Church Fathers such as John of Damascus and Gregory Nazianzen.

system should always be kept open to further change that may come from the conclusions of modern theological scholarship, such as liturgical history. (d) Such a system should acknowledge the limited nature of human knowledge, so that it leaves room for mysteries, not logical contradictions. In these ways, Orthodox theology today can be done so that it will result in neither a slavish allegiance to past patristic methods nor a hybrid compromise, but an authentic synthesis of our traditions.

3. Construct the research in a manner that is cognizant of Orthodox dogmatic values (as reflected in Florovsky's "neopatristic" synthesis)and builds on the advances made by modern scholarship. This point is a correlary to the one just stated above. Here the emphasis is not on what method to avoid but on what to pursue. As John Meyerdorff has pointed out, there is no one way of doing Orthodox theology today.[38] However, in my opinion Florovsky's "neopatristic" synthesis offers a reliable starting point for Westerners who do Orthodox theology today. Even if one disagrees with the details of Florovsky's program, I believe that a basic knowledge of the neopatristic synthesis ought to serve as an indispensable reference point for contemporary studies in Orthodox theology.[39]

What is this "neopatristic" synthesis? According to Florovsky, the patristic age cannot be abandoned, for it is the only solution for contemporary theology. A neopatristic synthesis means "a return to the Fathers"—that is, a conscious adoption of the classics of Christian antiquity, including their Hellenistic thought-forms[40] and dogmatic convictions. It endeavors to recover the "catholicity" of the Church in all the fullness of its biblical and ecclesial tradition—that is, its "common mind" or "universal tradition."[41] Not only Augustine and Cyprian but also Irenaeus, Athanasius, the Cappadocians, Maximus the Confessor, Symeon the New Theologian, Gregory Palamas and other Fathers provide a synthesis of truth that is essential for Christian identity, then and now.

It is not enough merely to know what the Fathers have said; one must also adopt their way of thinking as witnesses to the apostolic faith. " 'To follow the Fathers,' "

---

[38]Meyendorff, "Light from the East?" With all that is happening in Orthodoxy today it becomes all the more imperative for students of Orthodoxy to keep alive Meyendorff and Florovsky's vision of theology. They are the safest guides for all our work.

[39]A historiographical analysis of Florovsky with a selection of key sources can be found in my chapter "Georges Florovsky," in *Historians of the Christian Tradition: Their Theology and Impact on Western Thought,* ed. Martin Klauber and Michael Bauman (Nashville: Broadman, 1996).

[40]Florovsky rejected Newman's theory of "development in dogmas" and Harnack's thesis that Nicea and Chalcedon represent a "Hellenization of Christianity." Yet it is ironic that although he rejected Harnack's thesis, Florovsky actually advocated Hellenism as a permanent category for expressing Christian truth. Florovsky's position on the continuing value of Hellenistic categories should not be considered essential to the neopatristic synthesis.

[41]This is a contemporary theme repeated in Thomas Oden's call for a "return to the sources," to the "consensual" tradition of the first millennium.

according to Florovsky, "does not mean simply to quote their sentences. *It means to acquire their mind,* their *phronema.*"[42] The best way to acquire this mindset, of course, is to immerse oneself in the patristic sources themselves. The next best way is for students to observe how Florovsky applied this synthesis in his *Collected Works,* where he formulates specific doctrines such as ecclesiology, creation, christology, salvation and eschatology.[43]

In modern Orthodox literature, little sustained effort has been made to develop a method of theology that can accommodate both the neopatristic synthesis and the various branches of modern theological research. For the student of Orthodoxy, the task can never be carried out in isolation from an ecclesial context. The student must be clear about the symbiotic relationships that exist between biblical exegesis and the adjacent fields of liturgics, patristics, canon law and dogmatic theology. There is a qualitative difference in dogmatic values which must be observed between the Bible as the Word of God and the fathers, liturgy, canons and creeds of the church. Since students are more likely to know how to study the fathers and creeds than they are Orthodox liturgy and canon law, a brief orientation to the latter two will facilitate a safe entry point to the neopatristic synthesis in relation to these disciplines.

Liturgical theology is more developed in Roman Catholicism and high-church Protestantism than in evangelicalism. In evangelical seminaries the study of liturgics remains an optional extra, far removed from the core curriculum, mainly because of the high priority placed on Scripture in worship. According to Alexander Schmemann, however, liturgical theology is indispensable to the task of Orthodox theology: "Without liturgical theology our understanding of the Church's faith and doctrine is bound to be incomplete."[44] In addition to studying Schmemann, students will want to consult other specialists on the history and interpretation of the church's multicultural liturgical rites.[45]

---

[42] Florovsky, *Collected Works,* 4:18.

[43] Georges Florovsky, *The Collected Works,* vols. 1-14 (1-5 by Belmont, Mass.: Nordland, 1972-1979), 6-14 ed. Richard Haugh (Belmont, Mass.: Notable & Academic Books, 1979-). See also George Williams, "The Neo-Patristic Synthesis of Georges Florovsky," in *Georges Florovsky: Russian Intellectual, Orthodox Churchman,* ed. Andrew Blane (Crestwood, N.Y.: St. Vladimir's Seminary Press, 1993), pp. 287-340.

[44] Alexander Schmemann, *Introduction to Liturgical Theology* (New York: St. Vladimir's Seminary Press, 1975), pp. 15-16. See also Schmemann's *For the Life of the World* (New York: St. Vladimir's Seminary Press, 1973), *The Eucharist* (New York: St. Vladimir's Seminary Press, 1991) and *Great Lent* (New York: St. Vladimir's Seminary Press, 1974).

[45] Standard works are Robert Taft, *Beyond East and West: Problems in Liturgical Understanding,* 2nd rev. ed. (Washington, D.C.: Pastoral Press, 1997), *The Byzantine Rite: A Short History* (Collegeville, Minn.: Liturgical, 1992) and "The Epiclesis Question in the Light of the Orthodox and Catholic *Lex Orandi* Traditions," in *New Perspectives,* ed. Nassif, pp. 210-237. Taft, a Catholic of the Eastern Rite, is arguably the foremost authority on the history of Eastern Christian liturgy. Read anything he has written. Also, John Meyendorff, *Byzantine Theology* (New York: Fordham University Press, 1970), pp. 191-211; Hans-Joachim Schulz, *The Byzantine Liturgy* (New York: Pueblo, 1986).

In evangelical seminaries the science of canon law is studied even more rarely than liturgical theology. Dogmatically speaking, it plays a somewhat less important role in the theological formulation of the Orthodox faith than liturgics. However, even there the most erudite canon lawyers seldom study canon law against the background of biblical theology.[46] What is canon law? Canon law is the study of the norms or standards of Christian faith and order produced by ecumenical, provincial and local church councils and by individual fathers. Ecclesiastical canons can be distinguished between those of a doctrinal character, such as the natures and person of Jesus Christ, and those of a practical, ethical or structural character, such as the ethical behavior of church members or the ecclesiastical responsibilities and territorial boundaries of bishops and priests. Furthermore, the canons can be classified into two genres: those that are changeable, such as episcopal celibacy, and those that are not, such as those that affirm the full divinity and humanity of Christ. According to John Erickson, one of the most ecumenically minded lawyers today, common abuses of the canons come from "anarchists," who completely disregard the canonical corpus, and "legalists," who seek to proof-text the canons in their modern application without considering the historical and cultural contexts in which they were first written.[47]

4. Having studied Orthodoxy on its own terms with the aid of the three previous guidelines, students are ready to identify and compare areas of convergence and divergence between Eastern Orthodox and evangelical theology. Where do our common convictions and main differences lie? And what may evangelicals learn from the Orthodox tradition? It would be presumptuous for me to attempt an inclusive survey of all the possible areas in the remaining space allotted to this chapter. Although the full scope of these questions cannot be probed here, a careful comparison between Eastern Orthodoxy and evangelicalism reveals the sharing of much common ground, which I would like to briefly outline in a schematic way. Students may wish to expand, revise or correct these observations as they advance the field.

If one adopts Alister McGrath's summary of evangelical distinctives given earlier

---

[46]See, for example, John Erickson, *The Challenge of Our Past* (New York: St. Vladimir's Seminary Press, 1991). While this work is brilliant in historical analysis, one can find only a few scriptural quotations sprinkled throughout it. The essays are indifferent regarding whether or not the conclusions reached conform to Scripture. Such an approach can only be methodologically flawed in its presentation of Orthodox dogmatic values.

[47]See John Erickson, "The Orthodox Canonical Tradition," in *The Challenge of Our Past*, pp. 9-22; N. Afanasiev, "The Canons of the Church: Changeable or Unchangeable?" *St. Vladimir's Theological Quarterly* 2 (1967): 54-68; also works by Bishop Peter L'Huillier, especially *The Church of the Ancient Councils* (Crestwood, N.Y.: St. Vladimir's Press, 1996). Erickson and L'Huillier are two of the most active canon lawyers in North America. Modern English textbooks that provide a comprehensive presentation of the use of canon law, particularly in the Byzantine tradition, are nonexistent. The best available introduction is the chapter by John Meyendorff, "Ecclesiology: Canonical Sources," in *Byzantine Theology*, pp. 79-90. Also, Lewis Patsavos's lecture notes on canon law are available from Holy Cross Greek Orthodox bookstore in Brookline, Mass.

in this chapter, then it is safe to say that Orthodox and evangelicals are in complete agreement on the essentials of evangelical theology but not the fringes. This is no small matter for either side, since a common doctrinal core lies at the heart of both communities and provides solid ground for unity. Easterners can affirm the orthodox character of evangelicalism, and Westerners can rejoice in the evangelical character of Orthodoxy. The major differences between them on these points are the *emphases* that are regarded by both parties as identity-giving. Theologians in both traditions will want to reflect deeply together on what value the Orthodox *should* place on items of belief that some evangelicals would regard as being of secondary importance (such as the sacraments of baptism and Eucharist). That would uncover the fundamental differences between the traditions and clarify concretely what should and should not be regarded as of secondary importance.

Additional exploration may further enhance areas of agreement. As indicated in my treatment of Florovsky's neopatristic synthesis, Orthodox can join evangelicals in affirming the centrality and authority of Scripture. The doctrine of biblical inerrancy, however, has largely been a nonissue in modern Orthodoxy. With but a few exceptions (e.g., Origen), the Church Fathers assumed the total trustworthiness of Scripture in all its assertions on the literal level (e.g., Augustine, Jerome and Chrysostom). In the area of biblical hermeneutics, Orthodox and evangelicals hold different emphases with respect to the role of the church in exegesis, but both concur that exegesis is an individual and ecclesial event.[48] Unfortunately, evangelical biblical scholars have been the slowest to explore possible connections with Eastern Orthodoxy. One would think that their study of the history, transmission and exegesis of the biblical text would naturally raise important ecclesial questions that directly pertain to the history and theology of the Byzantine Orthodox Church. But this simply has not happened.[49] Scripture remains to be studied as an inde-

---

[48]The finest comparative analysis of the subject has been done by an evangelical New Testament scholar, Grant Osborne, in "The Many and the One: The Interface Between Orthodox and Evangelical Protestant Hermeneutics," *St. Vladimir's Theological Quarterly* 3 (1995): 281-304. For the problem of the text and boundary of the Old Testament canon, see Harold Scanlin, "The Old Testament Canon in the Orthodox Churches," in *New Perspectives,* ed. Nassif, pp. 300-312. This subject will become increasingly important as the dialogue progresses in light of more advances in OT scholarship.

[49]Donald Carson, for example, has the right idea in theory: "We should learn all the historical theology we can. One well-known seminary insists that proper exegetical method will guarantee such a high quality of exegesis that historical theology may be safely ignored. I can think of no better way of cultivating the soil that sprouts either heresy or the shallowest sort of traditionalism" (Donald Carson, *Exegetical Fallacies* [Grand Rapids: Baker Book House, 1984], p. 137). But one notable New Testament scholar, Dale Allison, has put this principle into practice by making a conscious effort to bring his exegesis into a thorough dialogue with the creeds, councils, fathers and liturgy of the Eastern Orthodox Church. See Dale C. Allison Jr. and W. D. Davies, *A Critical and Exegetical Commentary on the Gospel According to St. Matthew,* 3 vols. (Edinburgh: T & T Clark, 1989-), and Allison's unpublished paper "Biblical Exegesis and the Church Fathers: Some Personal Reflections," delivered to the Society for the Study of Eastern Orthodoxy and Evangelicalism.

pendent text uprooted from the historical soil in which it was canonized.

It is absolutely imperative for evangelical biblical scholars to widen their comprehension of the Christian faith by moving beyond the narrow confines of their own disciplines, important as they are. The failure to do so has resulted in a serious dichotomy between the biblical text and the modern heirs of the ancient community that originally recognized the canonical status of the apostolic documents. The hermeneutical criterion that will facilitate a common apprehension of Scripture by Orthodox and evangelicals is for evangelicals to agree to theologize out of the authentic biblical and theological tradition that the Church has maintained in roughly the first thousand years of its history (i.e., the neopatristic synthesis proposed by Florovsky or the consensual tradition suggested by Thomas Oden). In that context, Scripture then and now may serve as an internal norm to tradition, and tradition as the interpretive context of Scripture. In this way the consensual hermeneutics of the Church can provide the criterion for discerning and expressing the apostolic faith in today's world.

Orthodox and evangelicals also affirm a commitment to a strong Christocentrism within a trinitarian framework. Although there are differences in the fine points of patristic Christology and trinitarianism when compared to individual theologians within the various evangelical denominations (e.g., the Cappadocian theology of the Trinity compared with Augustine's notion of the divine "Persons" and his impact on the Reformers and their children), there remains a firm agreement on these essentials of classical theology (contra the radical antitrinitarian groups in Pentecostalism). For the Orthodox, however, the Trinity and Christology are not just items in a list of basic beliefs but the source and reference point from which all Christian truth and experience flow. Most evangelicals would agree, yet I think it is fair to say that these areas of theology have not affected evangelical spirituality and worship to the same degree as they have in Eastern Orthodoxy. Nor have they impacted evangelical reflection on the role of Mary in worship and devotion (a correlative discussion).

Concerning the need for personal conversion, the monastic tradition makes it clear that the Orthodox Church affirms that salvation comes through personal faith in Jesus Christ as Lord and Savior, apart from human merit.[50] In fact, I would

---

[50]Sadly, all too often the Pauline doctrine of grace is not made clear to Orthodox parishioners. The most balanced presentation on the relation between faith and works in Orthodox theology is by St. Mark the Ascetic. The treatise appears in one of the greatest spiritual classics of the Orthodox Church, "On Those Who Think That They Are Made Righteous by Works," in *The Philokalia*, comp. St. Nikodimos of the Holy Mountain and St. Makarios of Corinth, trans. G. E. H. Palmer, Philip Sherrard and Kallistos Ware (London: Faber and Faber, 1979), 1:125ff. Metropolitan Maximos of the Greek Archdiocese today cites Galatians 2:16 as a summary of the Orthodox patristic tradition. It is Christ's faith, not our personal faith or works, that saves since our own faith and works are flawed (phone conversation in January 1998).

propose that the monastic tradition itself provides the strongest link between the Orthodox and evangelical communities because Eastern monasticism is rooted in the Nicene and Chalcedonian faith while also being deeply evangelical at heart. The monastic fathers rooted their mystical experiences in the Scriptures and the church's doctrine of the Trinity and Incarnation.[51]

According to J. I. Packer, however, evangelicals have lagged behind in a mature theology of spirituality. In his inaugural lecture at Regent College in 1989, the title of his speech, as much as its content, reveals the utter impossibility of separating theology and spirituality: "An Introduction to Systematic Spirituality." In that lecture Packer urged evangelicals to rediscover their own heritage and develop forms of spirituality that are thoroughly evangelical in their roots and outlook.[52] McGrath echoes the same call: "This is one of the most urgent tasks we face. Unless something is done to promote evangelical spirituality, the present growth of the movement may not be sustained in the longer term."[53]

The unrecognized convergence of evangelical spirituality with Orthodox spirituality is fascinating to observe. Historically, Orthodox and evangelicals have shared a concern for orthodox doctrine and vital spirituality. In the spirituality of the Christian East, "mystical" theology is defined holistically as an inseparable union of head and heart, body and soul, doctrine and experience—not a subjective ordeal apart from God's revelation in Christ. The Orthodox monastic and Protestant evangelical traditions powerfully converge on this point to offer common ground for mutual enrichment.[54] Intriguing cross-fertilizations between the classics of Orthodox and evangelical spirituality eagerly await exploration.[55]

---

[51]Douglas Burton-Christie, *The Word in the Desert: Scripture and the Quest for Holiness in Early Christian Monasticism* (New York: Oxford University Press, 1993).

[52]James I. Packer, "An Introduction to Systematic Spirituality," *Crux* 26 (March 1990): 2-8.

[53]McGrath, *Evangelicalism and the Future of Christianity,* p. 137.

[54]The question whether there are distinctively evangelical approaches to spirituality is of considerable importance (Reformed, Puritan, Wesleyan, revivals of the eighteenth century, holiness and charismatic movements, etc.). In the past, evangelicalism has been associated with specific paths to the spiritual life, some heavily cerebral, such as the "personal quiet time" with God through Bible reading and prayer, known as "cognitive" spirituality. However, new approaches see the need for a "spiritual director" who will offer people guidance and support over a long period (akin to the Navigators' "discipleship" program). Since the history of evangelicalism is not devoid of spiritual counsel from great Christian pastors and guides, what is needed is a recovery of that heritage and its cross-fertilization with the "spiritual guides" (*staretz* Russian, *geron* Greek, *abba* Coptic) of the Orthodox tradition. See Timothy Ware, "The Spiritual Father in Orthodox Christianity," *Cross Currents,* Summer/Fall 1974, pp. 296-320.

[55]Among the many exciting possibilities, three suggested comparisons are between the holistic "hesychast" insights of St. Gregory Palamas (1347-1359) and evangelical "contemplative" spirituality; Symeon the New Theologian's (949?-1022) charismatic teaching about the "baptism in the Holy Spirit" and John Wesley's doctrine of sanctification (see collection of articles in *Asbury Theological Journal* 3 [1991]); and the spirituality of the icon and icon makers such as St. John of Damascus with Jeremy Begbie's *Voicing Creation's Praise: Toward a Theology of the Arts* (Oxford: Blackwell Press, 1991).

The Greek texts of Byzantium (in both the early and late periods, from the fourth to fourteenth centuries), as well as the Syriac and Arabic Church Fathers and liturgies, remain among the greatest treasures of the Christian East which have not yet been discovered by evangelicals. These materials literally need to be raided. In doing this, future researchers will want to be careful to commence their work from a firm grounding in Scripture, so that they may bring their conclusions into dialogue with the norms of biblical theology. The constant temptation to guard against in this field will be to substitute the materials of historical theology for the authority of Scripture.

Although there is a great deal of common ground, theological differences must never be minimized for the sake of unity. Significant differences separate us. Among the more important is the theology of the church and its sacraments.[56] In particular, the diversity in baptismal theology highlights more than any other issue the great variety in evangelicalism. Since evangelicalism is a multiformed phenomenon, any comparison of its baptismal theology with Orthodoxy must be done on a community-by-community basis. Traditional differences remain over the validity of infant baptism and the efficacy of the sacrament. For the Orthodox, baptism is the sacrament of initiation into the kingdom of God and the life of the Church.[57] Some evangelical traditions of the Reformation (such as Lutherans and Anglicans) would agree, but others (such as the Anabaptists) would not. Likewise, the eucharistic theology of the Orthodox Church affirms a "real presence" of Christ in the elements, without offering a detailed explanation of how this is so. Vital to this discussion is the recognition by leading Orthodox scholars, such as Bishop Kallistos Ware, that God is not confined to the sacraments to bring about new life in Christ.[58]

The finest introduction to monastic spirituality is by Roberta Bondi, *To Love As God Loves* (Philadelphia: Fortress, 1987). See also the classic by Vladimir Lossky, *The Mystical Theology of the Eastern Church* (Crestwood, N.Y.: St. Vladimir's Seminary Press, 1976). Lossky, however, has overstressed the apophatic character of Orthodox theology at the expense of the predominantly cataphatic assertions of Scripture. The book also fails to reflect a tension that exists within the patristic tradition itself concerning the place of apophaticism in theology. See also the work by a monk of the Eastern Church, *Orthodox Spirituality: An Outline of the Orthodox Ascetical and Mystical Tradition*, 2nd ed. (Crestwood, N.Y.: St. Vladimir's Seminary Press, 1978), which is useful but in need of critical refinement; Tomas Spidlik, *The Spirituality of the Christian East* (Kalamazoo, Mich.: Cistercian, 1986), which is highly technical.

[56]One of the best Orthodox ecclesiologists of our time has produced a work that only a few evangelicals have begun to read: John Zizioulas, *Being as Communion* (New York: St. Vladimir's Seminary Press, 1985). See the important response by Miroslav Volf, "Catholicity of the Local Church," *The Jurist* 52 (1992): 525-45; and *After Our Likeness* (Grand Rapids: Eerdmans, 1997).

[57]This is based on a theory of original sin that denies inherited "guilt." For a comparison of Augustine's view with that of the Greek Church Fathers see Bradley Nassif, "Toward a 'Catholic' Understanding of St. Augustine's View of Original Sin," *Union Seminary Quarterly Review* 29, no. 4 (1984): 287-99. Except for infant baptism, G. R. Beasley-Murray's *Baptism in the New Testament* (London: Macmillan, 1962) provides a close equivalent to Orthodox baptismal theology. As always, see Meyendorff, *Byzantine Theology*, pp. 192-95.

[58]Once it has been completed, the Orthodox response to the *Baptism, Eucharist and Ministry* document

Additionally, Orthodox and evangelicals differ over their conceptions of "tradition." Further work is needed to clarify what each means by this word. Modern evangelicals have not developed a theology of tradition. Historically, they have restricted their definition to include as valid only that which is found in the Bible. While some cultural contexts more than others necessitate the raising of the level of historical consciousness among evangelicals, the content of tradition remains an open question. How much of past Christian tradition has continuing relevance for the present? Clearly there exists an evangelical *paradosis* that goes back to the Reformers, who were not against tradition itself but only the abuses of it. Yet how much of early and medieval church history should be appropriated remains an open question. While some evangelicals strongly wish to claim the Church Fathers as part of their theological heritage, aspects of patristic teaching cannot be accepted because of its perceived lack of conformity with the Bible (which is true for Orthodoxy as well, for that matter). Also, for the Orthodox, tradition includes not just the reception of truths but a living connection with the past through the bond of the Holy Spirit in the Church. Hence the Lord himself through the church is the final criterion of tradition.[59]

Moreover, the use of icons in Christian worship requires future exploration. Those of a Puritan iconoclastic persuasion simply cannot be reconciled with the Orthodox conception of icons, as developed particularly in eighth- and ninth-century Byzantium. Evangelicals should be reminded that the same Byzantine Orthodox Church which produced the Council of Chalcedon (A.D. 451) also drew out from that Council the Christological implications for the justification of the Seventh Ecumenical Council (A.D. 878).

In conclusion, as evangelical students venture forth in this exciting field of theological inquiry, they would do well to consider it a sacred calling. Though the Bible remains the major source for systematic theology, Millard Erickson has reminded us that God may enlighten our comprehension of him through illumination from sources beyond the Scriptures.[60] The best preparation for this task is the prayerful union of mind and heart—a union eloquently expressed by a famous fourth-century monk, Evagrius Ponticus: "If you are a theologian, you will pray

---

of the World Council of Churches will provide evangelicals with an official, universally agreed-upon statement with which to interact. See also John Erickson, "The Local Churches and Catholicity: An Orthodox Perspective," in *The Jurist* 52 (1992): 490-508. "The Church is a eucharistic organism," he says, "because the Church is a baptismal organism," p. 505. Also Metropolitan Maximos of Pittsburgh, "Some Preliminary Notions of 'Baptismal Ecclesiology': Baptism and Eucharist, Constitutive of the Church as Communion," unpublished paper, 1997; and Kallistos (Timothy) Ware, "Church and Eucharist, Communion and Intercommunion," *Sobornost* 7, no. 7 (1978): 550-67.

[59]A striking similarity with this view can be found in George Eldon Ladd, *A Theology of the New Testament* (Grand Rapids: Eerdmans, 1974), pp. 390-91.

[60]Millard J. Erickson, *Christian Theology*, 3 vols. (Grand Rapids: Baker Book House, 1986), 1:66-79.

truly. And if you pray truly, you are a theologian."

Resources for Additional Study

Breck, John. *The Power of the Word in the Worshipping Church*. New York: St. Vladimir's Press, 1986.

Clendenin, Daniel. *Eastern Orthodox Christianity: A Western Perspective*. Grand Rapids: Baker, 1994.

————. *Eastern Orthodox Theology: A Contemporary Reader*. Grand Rapids: Baker, 1994.

Dockery, David S. *Biblical Interpretation Then and Now: Contemporary Hermeneutics in the Light of the Early Church*. Grand Rapids: Baker, 1992.

Florovsky, Georges. *The Collected Works*. Vols. 1-5. Belmont, Mass.: Nordland, 1972-1979.

————. *The Collected Works*. Vols. 6-14. Belmont, Mass.: Notable & Academic Books, 1979-.

Meyendorff, John. *Byzantine Theology: Historical Trends and Doctrinal Themes*. 2nd ed. New York: Fordham University Press, 1981.

————. *The Orthodox Church*. 4th ed. New York: St. Vladimir's Press, 1996.

Nassif, Bradley, ed. *New Perspectives on Historical Theology: Essays in Memory of John Meyendorff*. Foreword by Henry Chadwick. Grand Rapids: Eerdmans, 1996.

Stamoolis, James. *Eastern Orthodox Mission Theology*. Maryknoll, N.Y.: Orbis, 1986.

Ware, Timothy (Kallistos). *The Orthodox Church*. 3rd rev. ed. New York: Penguin, 1993.

Zizioulas, John. *Being as Communion*. New York: St. Vladimir's Seminary Press, 1985.

Chapter 7

New Dimensions in Reformation Theology

Marvin Anderson

••••••••••••••••••••••••••

The future of history vis-à-vis any epoch pivots around the questions
of how best to know. This grand passion is a struggle of memory against forgetting.[1]

HAVING BANISHED HUBRIS FROM THE CANONS OF KNOWLEDGE, WE must not succumb to Lethe, trading arrogance for oblivion. "The experience of remembering underpins the belief that the past existed and hence makes possible, even imperative, an effort to reconstruct what happened."[2] What we forget is very real indeed.

This essay describes in short compass what can be remembered of a particular place and time for the sake of the future. The place was Europe and the time was one of dynamic consequences. Reformation Europe continues to be the subject of careful investigation and the source of new dimensions of human activity, central to which is a radically simplified religious life that placed the laity and the clergy on an equal footing in the eyes of God. Confidence in their vocation under God drove these early modern persons to the farthest reaches of the planet and to consider the heavens in all their immensity. They worried not only about how to go to heaven but also how the heavens go! The consequences of such confidence still work themselves out in the present.[3]

---

[1]Joyce Appleby, Lynn Hunt and Margaret Jacob, *Telling the Truth About History* (New York: Norton, 1994), p. 270.
[2]Ibid.
[3]Stephen Ozment, *Protestants: The Birth of a Revolution* (New York: Doubleday, 1992), p. 217.

The "long sixteenth century" in Italy runs from 1450 to 1650 and is determined by economic history that charts a slow recovery from population loss and economic crisis caused by the 1348 plague.[4] Another perspective is to measure these decades from early Erasmus (1501) to the end of the Thirty Years' War (1648). In this scenario the humanist agenda coalesces with the confessional struggle to restore the map of Europe. From Cracow to Cambridge and from Scotland to Muscovy this period arrests the attention of these willing to listen to the questions raised by the material evidence of the past. Topics that readily come to mind touch both on the theological core of this confessional age and on its social realities. Among them are popular belief, the alien existence of Turks without and Jews within and the status of the clergy. These topics readily come to mind, each with its own set of parameters. Current analysis of questions that emerge from the social reality of this age of Renaissance can and do reverse cherished memories. The Columbian Quincentenary celebration met resistance from modern residents of Hispanic America. In similar fashion the Annales School of French historiography and the economic and/or social focus of recent study seeks to describe a truly comparative history. Canonical, long-term deterministic theologies have been discarded for interrogation of subject matter to determine its internal logic.[5] The older political and religious focus of Von Ranke or past Luther scholars is passé.

This chapter introduces readers to only three of twenty-five central subjects, any group of which well illustrate the dynamic vision of this Renaissance world of Michelangelo and Machiavelli, of Tatian and Teresa of Ávila, of Calvin and Copernicus, of Luther and Loyola. New dimensions in Reformation studies can put the reader in touch with the driving force of Western culture, whose agenda is set by those fifteen decades, whether it is the Enlightenment's endorsement of reason or Newtonian science, Darwinian inquiry or the post-Newtonian world of Niels Bohr, particle physics and black holes à la Stephen Hawking.

Three approaches to our theme, new dimensions in Reformation studies, come first of all from the stimulating essay of Heiko Oberman titled "One Epoch—Three Reformations,"[6] then from the selection of printed sources included in the Lutheran Brotherhood Reformation Research Library microfilm collection and finally from

---

[4]John A. Marino, "The Italian States in the 'Long Sixteenth Century,' " in *Handbook of European History, 1400-1600: Late Middle Ages, Renaissance and Reformation*, ed. Thomas A. Brady Jr., Heiko A. Oberman and James D. Tracy, vol. 1, *Structures and Assertions* (Leiden: Brill, 1994), pp. 331-35.

[5]Ibid., p. 356. Typical of the new approach is the exploration of pamphlet literature or *flugschriften*. See Robert W. Scribner, *For the Sake of Simple Folk: Popular Propaganda for the German Reformation*, 2nd ed. (Oxford: Clarendon, 1994). An exciting use of such literature is found in Mark U. Edwards Jr., *Printing, Propaganda and Martin Luther* (Berkeley: University of California Press, 1994).

[6]Heiko A. Oberman, "One Epoch—Three Reformations," in *The Reformation: Roots and Ramifications* (Edinburgh: T & T Clark; Grand Rapids: Eerdmans, 1994), pp. 201-20.

a perusal of topics in the _Oxford Encyclopedia of the Reformation._[7] In Professor Oberman's stimulating essay, the thirty thousand volumes in the Lutheran Brotherhood Reformation Research Library filmed thus far in European libraries and the 2,080 pages of the _Oxford Encyclopedia,_ one can sense the exciting vistas that this European phenomenon called the Reformation provides.

The _Oxford Encyclopedia of the Reformation_ includes nine articles on popular religion, one on the Jews and another on anti-Semitism. It contains separate entries on the Ottoman Empire, the clergy, pamphlets, printing and refugees. The theological core of the Reformation era under discussion is well covered in articles on justification, Scripture, synods, disputations and various confessions or controversies.

Visits to European libraries indicate the enormous quantity of printed sources that survive for the 1500s alone. Extrapolation from current incomplete bibliographies such as the _Index Aureliensis_ project as many as 261,000 sixteenth-century surviving titles in print. It is hard to imagine what questions future scholars will address once these 31,320,000 pages of print can be searched with modern technology.

It is time to sample the wealth of information on our three topics to illustrate new trends in research of this epoch. Popular religion, aliens within/aliens without and clerical status will suffice for this purpose.

Popular Belief

Social realities of everyday life establish the matrices for comprehending sixteenth-century life. For example, in the tenth century a squirrel could have traveled from Paris to Moscow, jumping from tree to tree without ever touching ground. Vast forested stretches of northern Europe were inhabited in the popular imagination by the little folk. The theology of ghosts indicates that the popular mentality was indeed conditioned by the cultural context of its society.[8] To drive a stake through the heart of a suicide victim remained a legal requirement in England until 1823. Otherwise the dead person's ghost would not rest quietly.[9]

Woe to the unscriven souls whose unrepented sins were not forgiven at the moment of death, for Satan would carry them off. Satan could possess a person forcibly. In his role as tempter, luring sinners into the torments of hell, the devil practiced _Teufelsgespenst._ Such trickery was not overcome by the Reformation, which in many ways may have rendered its followers more defenseless than before

---

[7]Stephen Chasteen, project editor, Academic Reference Department, Oxford University Press. Letter to author, January 6, 1995.

[8]"Ghosts and Fairies," in _Religion and the Decline of Magic,_ by Keith Thomas (New York: Scribner's, 1971), pp. 587, 595.

[9]Ibid., p. 595.

due to its abolition of traditional ritual.[10] Central European belief that the dead came back to seek a companion from the world of the living lasted into the twentieth century. Scribner observes that rituals of separation from the dead were not weakened by the abolition of purgatory.[11] People's relationships with the dead after their act of dying remained significant. Regular points of contact between these folk encompassed boundaries such as crossroads, where the supernatural could enter this world.[12]

Sacramentalism holds that the sacred can be present and can be experienced through the material world. Magic, however, has "inner-worldly" effects. In the twentieth century the inner-worldly has been split off from the otherworldly, the latter being relegated to the fringe of understanding at best. Official religion tends to observe reality this way and in Reformation ideologies attacks the notion of a sacramental world. This was perhaps the most important mental shift, since it denied that the supernatural world could be known through the power of the natural. "This left, in its most radical applications, no space for sacred time, persons, places or things, only an inner-worldly realm of purely human action in which acts of piety had no transcendental efficacy."[13]

This limiting of the inner space of persons does not abate the persistence of popular magic. Reorientation of ordinary belief is a longer-term prospect than teleological theologians can imagine. As reformers reoriented cognitive belief around the official expression of sacral space, they all too frequently emptied the lives of ordinary people who were confused about the power of the gospel. A new paradigm did not alter the popular understanding of supernatural power. Of such are the empty lives of early modern persons.

Another component of popular religion was uncovered by the Inquisition. The most extreme penalties handed out by some inquisitors were not against those accused of crimes of sorcery *(maleficium)* but of magic. Techniques that were designed to induce amatory response were classified as *maleficia ad amorem*. These charms were held to subvert free will in order to coerce sin. Catholic theology was especially sensitive to attacks on free will by predestinarian Protestantism and thus eager to maintain the sinner's primary responsibility for succumbing to love charms.[14]

---

[10]Robert W. Scribner, "Elements of Popular Belief," in *Handbook of European History, 1400-1600*, 1:237. Compare the Book of Common Prayer (1549): Confirmation (response to Lord's Prayer): "What desirest thou of God in this prayer? . . . that he will keep us from all sin and wickedness, and from our ghostly enemy . . ."

[11]Ibid., p. 238.

[12]See Philippe Ariès, *The Hour of Our Death* (London: 1981), and Piero Camporesi, *The Fear of Hell: Images of Damnation and Salvation in Early Modern Europe* (University Park: Pennsylvania State University Press, 1991).

[13]Scribner, "Elements of Popular Belief," p. 253.

[14]M. O'Neil, "Magical Healing, Love Magic and the Inquisition in Late Sixteenth Century Modena," in *Inquisition and Society in Early Modern Europe*, ed. S. Haliczer (Totowa, N.J.: Barnes & Noble, 1987), p. 98.

Investigations at Modena pursued what they considered to be socially inappropriate liaisons. Those of lower status in society held out hopes of sudden transformation of their economic circumstances by use of such charms. Here principles of social hierarchy combined with inquisitorial method to discourage amorously ambitious inferiors.[15] A common procedure was to take a shoelace belonging to the desired person to Mass. When the priest turned to the congregation to say "Dominus Vobiscum," a knot was to be tied in the shoelace to the words, "I am not tying you, string, but the heart of you, N.N., so that you can go to no one but me."[16] Formulas were substituted for the priestly words in order to divert their efficacy to magical ends.

Lutheran theologians utilized popular interest in astrology to communicate their message. There are close links between astrological prophecy and apocalyptic concerns in Lutheranism.[17] Annual *practica,* or almanacs, contained predictions for everything from the weather to impending disaster. From Johann Lichtenberger's *Prognostica* (1482), copied in large measure from a Paduan professor who in turn defended an Arab writer, to the predictions of Johann Carion, such wide-ranging pronouncements on a pessimistic secular future fit in well with Martin Luther's sense of crisis and Philipp Melanchthon's penchant for consulting astral phenomena.

Luther published his own edition of Lichtenberger at Wittenberg in 1527, distinguishing between true prophecy of the Holy Spirit and false prophecy inspired by Satan. Nonetheless, held Luther, astrology is not to be scorned, since God himself warns and threatens the godless.[18] Melanchthon, however, was more enthusiastic about such matters. Barnes points to both the Hellenistic strain in his thought and the free action of God.[19] As the century progressed, these *practica* became a form of preaching in which Acts 7 was cited that Moses was a mathematician learned in the wisdom of the Egyptians.[20]

Such *practica,* usually a small quarto booklet appended to the yearly almanac, appeared in at least 1,940 known copies between 1480 and 1630, and the total is quite possibly 50 percent higher. The standard form began with a preface on astrology itself as an ancient and beneficial art, followed by chapters in no fixed order on "ruling" planets for the new year, weather for each lunar quarter, the outlook

---

[15]Ibid., p. 99.

[16]Ibid., p. 102.

[17]Robin Bruce Barnes, "Apocalyptic Astrology," in *Prophecy and Gnosis: Apocalypticism in the Wake of the Lutheran Reformation* (Stanford, Calif.: Stanford University Press, 1988), pp. 141-81.

[18]Ibid., pp. 146-47. Compare Calvin's warning in his *Advertissement contre l'astrologie judicaire* of 1549. This has been edited by Olivier Millet (Geneva, 1985) and translated by Mary Potter in *Calvin Theological Journal* 18 (1983): 157-89.

[19]Ibid., p. 148. See also Clyde Manschrek, *Melanchthon: The Quiet Reformer* (Nashville: Abingdon, 1958), pp. 102-12.

[20]Ibid., p. 151. See also pages 165-68, "The Preaching of the Stars."

for good, for sickness and health, for war and peace, and the prospects for various lands and social classes.[21] The clergy had good reason to be concerned about their role, given the penchant to integrate such prognostication with popular belief in astral control of human experience. Calvin's treatise on judicial astrology is reminiscent not only of the European fascination with secondary causation (God being the primary source) but also the necessity to explore in fresh ways questions of providence, predestination and human freedom.

Popular religion is a new dimension in Reformation studies in which social anthropology and social reality challenge the historian to explore these facets of everyday reality.[22] The human dimension of this confessional age challenges theologians to consider once again not only the dark night of the soul à la John of the Cross but also the reality contained in the ancient Cornish prayer:

From Ghoulies
And Ghosties
And long-legged Beasties
And things that go bump
In the night,
Good Lord,
Deliver Us.[23]

Aliens Within, Aliens Without

Aliens within: Jewish presence. The year 1492 marked the expulsion of Jews from Spain and their alienation from ancient customs through their forced conversion. It marked stage two of a gradual exclusion of the Jews from western Europe, beginning in 1290 with their expulsion from England. Many Jews in Spain became Christians to save their lives; these were known as *conversos* or "new Christians" and numbered over one hundred thousand. On September 27, 1480, the Catholic monarchs appointed the first inquisitors for Seville, where the initial auto-da-fé was held the following February 6 in this hotbed of Judaizers. The Spanish Inquisition was structured with an inquisitor general as a means of solidifying royal control and excluding papal control. Between 1484 and 1530 some 91.6 percent of the Valencia Inquisition's victims were *conversos*.[24]

Robert Bonfil observes that the Jews were the only group without political power

---

[21]Robin Bruce Barnes, "Hope and Despair in Sixteenth-Century German Almanacs," in *The Reformation in Germany and Europe: Interpretations and Issues,* ed. Hans R. Guggisberg, Gottfried G. Krode and Hans Füglister (Gütersloh: Gütersloher Verlagshaus, 1993), p. 441.

[22]Hans-Christopher Rublack, "Reformation und Moderne, Soziologische, theologische und historische Ansichten," in *Reformation in Germany and Europe,* pp. 17-38.

[23]*The Oxford Dictionary of Quotations,* 2nd ed.(London: Oxford University Press, 1954), p. 6.

[24]John Lynch, *Spain (1516-1598): From Nation State to World Empire* (Oxford, U.K.: Blackwell, 1991), pp. 33 n. 28, 209.

to whom Christians "accorded the right of theoretical and practical dissent."[25] A radical change was brought about by the "new Christians" and their impact on both Jewish and Christian identity. Thus the year 1492 was reversed almost precisely around the year 1500.[26]

Christian negative attitudes toward Jews matured at this time even as Jewish learning left its mark on Christian biblical scholarship via the Soncino Press from 1488.[27] It was the Brescia edition of the Hebrew Bible in its two parts of 1492 and 1494 that Luther used to prepare his Old Testament German translation. Thus 1492 marks another kind of milestone of Jewish influence on Christian Old Testament studies.

The Christian ritual murder accusation against the Jews was a painful episode in Jewish-Christian relationships. At Trent the sermons of Bernardino Feltre claimed that "Jews drink the blood of Christians at Eastertide,"[28] an antisacrament that was a confirmation of the diabolical nature of the Jews. The entire Jewish community at Trent was exterminated in 1475. The Trent affair was the first time that anti-Jewish myths were spread by the newly invented printing press.

The end of coexistence came at Venice when the first ghetto was instituted. Following the discriminatory decisions of the Fourth Lateran Council (1215), Pope Paul IV segregated Jews into separate neighborhoods. Confinement in these neighborhoods required Jews to wear a yellow sign as a badge of infamy, to calculate months as thirty days long, to dispense of all real estate and so on.

The role of Portuguese *conversos* paradoxically led to a reversal in Christians' attitude toward Jews and opened a phase of reintegration in western Europe.[29] In 1497 Jews endured forced conversions in Portugal[30] and as a result of the Portuguese Inquisition established themselves in western European countries. In Italy they were able to return to Judaism by joining already existing Jewish communities.[31] These were merchants with strong business ties who were allowed to occupy mercantile positions instead of serving as usurers at the margin of society. Sometimes the unhelpful label *Marrano* was applied to the *conversos*.

---

[25]Robert Bonfil, "Aliens Within: The Jews and Anti-Judaism," in *Structures and Assertions*, 1:263.

[26]Ibid., p. 267. Compare Heiko Oberman, *The Roots of Antisemitism in the Age of Renaissance and Reformation* (Philadelphia: Fortress, 1984). For the March 31, 1492, edict of expulsion, see Jane S. Gerber, *The Jews of Spain: A History of the Sephardic Experience* (New York: Free Press, 1994), pp. 285-89; 115-44.

[27]"Soncino," in *Encyclopedia Judaica*, vol. 15 (New York: Macmillan, 1971), cols. 140-42, and Gilbert Dahan, "L'exégèse juive de la Bible," in *Le temps des Reformes et la Bible*, by Guy Bedouelle and Bernard Roussel (Paris: Editions Beauchesne, 1984), pp. 401-25, esp. 421-23: "L'utilisation des auteurs juifs dans l'exégèse chrétienne."

[28]Bonfil, "Aliens Within," p. 272. See Ronnie Po-Chia Hsia, *The Myth of Ritual Murder: Jews and Magic in Reformation Germany* (New Haven, Conn.: Yale University Press, 1988).

[29]Ibid., p. 292.

[30]Maria José Pimenta Tavarez, *Os judeus em Portugal no seculo XV,* 2 vols. (Lisbon, 1982-1984).

[31]Bonfil, "Aliens Within," pp. 292-93.

New dimensions of Reformation study were opened by the information that national identity as Portuguese or Spanish bound new Christian and old Christian more firmly than did religious loyalty. Bonfil points to a confraternity in Amsterdam modeled on the *Hebra de casar horphaos* of Venice, where dowries were awarded to poor girls from the nacao in preference to a girl from the confraternity itself who was Jewish.[32] The contribution of the *conversos* to restructuring perceptions of Jewish identity is enormous. What theologians need to explore are communities in which free choice of religious expression is possible. As Bonfil puts it, such experiences "produced a total restructuring of Christians' and Jews' awareness of one another."[33]

Aliens without: Ottoman Turks. Ottoman power grew in the fourteenth century, crushing a Christian army of Crusaders at Nicopolis in 1396. In 1402 Timur shattered Ottoman lands, with the result that Ottoman dynastic struggle preoccupied these raiders of Christian Europe. At court children from Christian vassal families were "hosted," that is, held hostage. One such hostage who spent many years in Murad II's palace became the famous Vlad the Impaler. This son of Vlad Dracula, ruler of Wallachia (1436-1446), entered vampire legend as Count Dracula.[34]

These aliens from without left an indelible mark on Reformation Europe from the fall of Constantinople (1453) to the successful defense of Vienna in 1683. Classical Ottoman civilization expanded from 1400 to 1600, granting to Christians in their territories what were known as *timars*. Revenues were assigned from an area called a timar in exchange for military obligations to provide troops and equipment when called to join the sultan's army.

Ottoman power grew in the reigns of Bayezid II, Selim I (1512-1520) and Süleyman (1520-1566). Reformation scholars are familiar with Bayezid's brother Jem, taken hostage by the Knights Templar in 1482 and the object of intense negotiations until his death in 1495. Selim employed artillery that he tested in the Crimea, blasting rival cavalry armies in 1514 and again in 1516-1517. This, along with the janissary system of forced converts of captive lands, "made the Ottoman state the superpower of the entire eastern Mediterranean region."[35] The political reality of the alien Turk from without enabled the Protestant reform to survive the attacks of Catholic princes.

Süleyman in ten of his thirteen campaigns sought to checkmate the Habsburg hegemony in Spain and at Vienna. He took Belgrade in 1521 and in 1526 crushed the Hungarians on the plain of Mohacs. The campaigns of 1529 and 1532 moved

---

[32]Ibid., p. 294.
[33]Ibid., p. 296.
[34]Cemal Kafadar, "The Ottomans and Europe," in *Structures and Assertions*, 1:593.
[35]Ibid., p. 608. On the subject of weaponry, see J. R. Hale, *War and Society in Renaissance Europe, 1450-1620* (Baltimore: Johns Hopkins University Press, 1985), pp. 46-74.

huge numbers of troops across vast spaces. Süleyman failed to take Vienna and was unable to draw the imperial army into the field. Much of Hungary lay under Ottoman control for 150 years, although clearly there were limits to Ottoman expansion. Later conquest of Cyprus in 1570 and a naval defeat at Lepanto led to further victories at a staggering cost. Decline set in around 1600, when the Turkish armies camped about Vienna in 1683.

What did the Ottoman and European worlds have in common, apart from shared discourse to shared rhythms that jointly form the early modern world?[36] Kafadar points to a complex of traditions such as shared medical knowledge from Galen, an intellectual world steeped in Greek learning and a monetary economy. He is helpful in pointing to fissures for both the Ottoman and the Europeans in the religious realm. The Ottoman legacy is neither Balkan yoke nor Jewish utopia.[37]

Two aspects of this period from 1453 to 1683 are intriguing. French alliances after 1525 with Turkish forces helped to prevent the extermination of Protestantism by preventing the Habsburgs from seizing control of western Europe. As De Lamar Jensen demonstrates, French foreign policy had precisely this effect.[38] The primary purpose for its continuation after 1559 was commercial participation in Levantine trade.

More controversial is the essay by Sir Geoffrey Elton in the Owen Chadwick festschrift.[39] Elton asserts that Europe's "identity as a continent derived from external wants, from the reaction to such events, and from the development of practices and ideas original to the region."[40] In this view the traditional view of the rise of Europe as linked to the cooperative effects of the Renaissance, Reformation and Reconnaissance becomes episodic at best. The emergence of the real Europe is a temporary phenomenon that gained general acceptance only in the eighteenth century. The facts of Europe must be defined by nongeographical criteria within which exist many communities, political and otherwise.[41]

As the center of gravity moved away from the Mediterranean, new and unprecedented entities arose, such as the internally secure nation-state, a capitalist economy and a world of ideas dominated by natural science and the study of history. Since the Reformation shaped Europe in so many ways, its disappearance in the period from 1685 to 1870 marks the end of that temporary phenomenon known as

---

[36]Ibid., pp. 620-21.
[37]Ibid., pp. 624.
[38]De Lamar Jensen, "The Ottoman Turks in Sixteenth Century French Diplomacy," *Sixteenth Century Journal* 16 (1985): 451-70. See also Michael Heath, "Unlikely Alliance: Valois and Ottomans," *Renaissance Studies* 3 (1989): 307-8.
[39]Geoffrey R. Elton, "Europe and the Reformation," in *History, Society and the Churches*, ed. Derek Beales and Geoffrey Best (Cambridge: Cambridge University Press, 1985), pp. 89-104.
[40]Ibid., p. 97.
[41]Ibid., p. 90. See Denys Hay, *Europe: The Emergence of an Idea*, 2nd ed. (Edinburgh: University Press, 1968).

Europe.[42] As the decline of Turkish dominance helped to create Europe as a concept, so the advance of contemporary Asia into the western part of Europe contributes to its demise.[43]

More positive views of the Turkish presence in Europe come from the ambassador for the archduke (later emperor) Ferdinand. While he was in Istanbul, he wrote four letters containing observations to an old friend. "No value is attached to anything but personal merit," he wrote, while contrasting the land that preferred horses as a means of transport to that of camels.[44] The Turks succeed in all that they attempt because good qualities are gifts to be developed by training, constant toil and zeal. "Our method is very different," wrote Ogier Ghiselin de Busbecq, "there is no room for merit, but everything depends on birth . . ."[45]

The lengthening shadow of Ottoman conquest fell across the Balkans, overwhelmed Hungary and menaced Vienna. Failing to capture Malta in 1565, Süleyman turned the North. One hundred thousand troops attacked the Hungarian fortress of Szigeth, with the seventy-two-year-old sultan taking the field in person. The huge naval battle at Lepanto pitted 270 Turkish ships against the Christians' 208. Superior firepower at close range (1,800 guns to 750) sank some 70 Ottoman ships. "There was a crucifix on every deck, and the Christians knelt at mass in gleaming armor before battle was joined."[46] The biggest battle of the sixteenth century saw fifteen thousand Christians perish along with thirty thousand Turks. One hundred thirteen Ottoman galleys were sunk and 117 were captured.[47]

The Ottoman campaign lasted from March to October. Organizational and logistical considerations came to the fore as the empire's borders lengthened to some nine thousand miles. Ultimately, as Mackenney observes, Christian maritime power expanded to outflank the mighty Ottoman Empire.[48]

Financial crises stemming from cheap American silver (1580) and inflation, which changed the system of taxation, shook the empire. In the time of Süleyman general revenue was 537 million aspers, the equivalent of 10 million gold pieces. In 1653 revenue was 507 million aspers, now worth only 4.2 million gold pieces. After 1591 the treasury experienced a growing deficit.[49]

---

[42]Ibid., pp. 97, 104.

[43]Ibid., p. 104. Elton seems to include Russia in this category in his comments about Russian novelists and the aftermath of two world wars.

[44]Richard Mackenney, *Sixteenth Century Europe: Expansion and Conflict* (New York: St. Martin's, 1993), p. 249.

[45]Ibid.

[46]Ibid., p. 261.

[47]Ibid., p. 262.

[48]Ibid., p. 264.

[49]V. J. Perry, "The Ottoman Empire, 1566-1617," in *The New Cambridge Modern History*, vol. 3, *The Counter-Reformation and Price Revolution, 1559-1610*, ed. R. B. Wernham (Cambridge: Cambridge University Press, 1968), pp. 370-72. See also *Cambridge History of Islam* (Cambridge: Cambridge

Jan III Sobieski was acclaimed Polish king in 1674, having annihilated an entire Ottoman army at Chocin.[50] He was married to the sensational Marie-Casimire de la Grange d'Arquien, known as Marysienka. Their marriage was a brilliant partnership in love, war and politics. Sobieski, who was preoccupied with the terror of the Turk, belonged to a class of nobility, as did Tomasz Zamoyski (1594-1638), whose vast estates and Oriental interests led him to be fluent in Turkish, Tartar, Arabic and Persian.[51]

In 1683 the Turks invaded Vienna. They laid siege in the middle of July with 140,000 men. The Polish relief force assembled at Cracow with 26,000 men. The combined relief force of 74,000 hauled their artillery across a pontoon bridge spanning the raging Danube. At 5:30 p.m. on September 12, Sobieski galloped through the sultan's camp. Panic and slaughter were on every hand.[52] He wrote to his beloved Marysienka that the enemy fled in confusion. "There is enough powder and ammunition alone for a million men."[53]

Sobieski sent the Ottoman green standard to the pope with the terse message "Veni, vidi, Deus vinxit" (I came, I saw, God conquered). Europe was saved from the Turk.[54] Davies tells of Czar Nicholas I of Russia, who in 1828 came to Warsaw to be crowned king of Poland. Thinking of his own costly Turkish wars, he looked up at the statue of Sobiesksi in Azienki Park and said, "There is the other fool who wasted his time fighting the Turks."[55]

Aliens within and aliens without summarize the historical experiences of Europeans at this time. Reformers viewed themselves as citizens in an alien country, looking for a city whose builder and maker was God. They were sojourners and exiles for whom a fresh reading of Scripture became a comforting message from their distant and eternal home. John Calvin refers to God himself as a fugitive who accompanied the children of Israel night and day on their flight from Egypt.[56]

Heiko Oberman describes the Reformation as one epoch with three reformations. The theological core from that time has been banished by some historians who focus on their concern on groups rather than individuals, marking a shift in interest "from treatises to tax roles," blocking "all access to a period when God and the Devil, not banks and bombs, were Great Powers."[57]

University Press, 1970), 1:324.
[50]Norman Davies, *God's Playground: A History of Poland,* vol. 1, *The Origins to 1795* (New York: Columbia University Press, 1982), p. 474.
[51]Ibid., p. 477.
[52]Ibid., p. 483.
[53]Ibid., p. 484.
[54]Ibid., p. 486.
[55]Ibid., p. 491.
[56]Heiko A. Oberman, "Initia Calvini: The Matrix of Calvin's Reformation," in *Calvinus Sacrae Scripture Professor,* by Wilhelm Neuser (Grand Rapids: Eerdmans, 1994), p. 153.
[57]Ibid., p. 205.

The first reformation was the powerful conciliar movement still alive in French experience of popular sovereignty during the sixteenth century. The second was the emancipation of the urban bourgeoisie and the establishment of the urban elites. Zurich comes to mind here. The third was the infiltration of civic councils by urban concerns. The variation on this third option is the armory that city hall furnished to the Reformation, which was that of the refugees.[58] After 1548 the urban reformation was succeeded by that of the refugees. Oberman points out that with the Zurich defeat at Kappel in 1531 the deportees could no longer view exile as God's rejection of his chosen people. Now the Reformed in exile had a new understanding of the Jews, for they shared their homelessness.[59] This also became the experience of the clergy.

Clerical Status

The eve of the Reformation was thick with clerical privilege and anticlerical sentiment. Life was all too comfortable for the clergy, whose neglect of their pastoral duties sparked outcry after outcry, including references to Ezekiel 34, where the Old Testament prophet speaks woes against the shepherds of Israel who only take care of themselves alone and thus will be held accountable for neglecting the flock (vv. 2, 10). Reginald Pole, cardinal of England, chose this for his homily at the Council of Trent, excoriating those who neglected their pastoral duties.[60] Woodcuts depict the sheepfold with Martin Luther and Jan Hus as true shepherds guarding the flock from within.

Recent discussion of anticlericalism points to its pervasive negative tone from the late Middle Ages through the confessional age.[61] This phenomenon is indisputable, although Robert Scribner notes that the historian's problem is how to evaluate its significance for the Reformation.[62] German Reformation pamphlets indicate that central to these concerns was the function of the Word of God.[63] Drawing on some four hundred such printed sources, Rublack classifies criticism of the clergy in terms of three main issues:

1. attitude of the clergy toward worldly goods and power
2. clergy lifestyle

---

[58]Ibid., p. 214.

[59]Ibid., p. 219. See also Frederick A. Norwood, *Strangers and Exiles: A History of Religious Refugees* (Nashville: Abingdon, 1969).

[60]Dermot Fenlon, *Heresy and Obedience in Tridentine Italy: Cardinal Pole and the Counter-Reformation* (Cambridge: Cambridge University Press, 1972), pp. 119-20.

[61]Peter A. Dykema and Heiko A. Oberman, eds., *Anticlericalism in Late Medieval and Early Modern Europe* (Leiden: Brill, 1993).

[62]Ibid., pp. 149-50.

[63]Hans-Christoph Rublack, "Anticlericalism in German Reformation Pamphlets," in Dykema and Oberman, *Anticlericalism*, p. 462.

3. their understanding of the clerical office[64]

From Jan Hus's treatise on simony to Erasmus's *Praise of Folly* and Simon Fish's *Supplication of Beggars,* the clergy were subjected to severe criticism. Hus defines simony as heresy in deed, while Erasmus castigates clerical stupidity. Fish reveals the evils that a lewd and unproductive clergy spread in Tudor society.[65] Another chorus of protest comes from women writers of this period who believed that the clergy misunderstood the nature of women on the basis of sheer prejudice and misreading of the Bible.[66] Marguerite of Navarre's *Heptameron* cataloged the ways in which men mistreated women. Two of these seventy-two stories refer to pious priests, while seventeen focus on sinful clerics and immoral priests.[67] Marie Dentiere, former abbess in Picardy who converted to evangelical faith, married a pastor and lived in Geneva just prior to 1536. In her 1559 *Very Useful Letter . . . Sent to the Queen of Navarre* Marie directs her anticlericalism against the Reformed pastors called to replace Calvin during his exile. A brief section titled "A Defense for Women" points to the graces that God gave to some good women. This is a special case of anticlericalism and exposes the injustice that women suffered at the hands of clergy during this period.[68]

How did the clergy react to the ongoing critique of their roles? Many changed their clerical behavior. Satire became confrontation, as in the case of John Calvin. Seminaries established by the Council of Trent and staffed by the Jesuits were restructured. Each response invites reflection. Finally, Protestants educated leaders in their newly established universities, setting a long-term agenda for the faithful servant.[69]

Calvin pressed his friend Bernard Roussel to abandon the Roman system of benefice, since it was revenue derived from the sacrilege of the Mass, whether by proxy or in absentia.[70] "There is not a single coin that is not besmirched with theft, or sacrilege, or piracy."[71] Roussel had been with the early French Reformers and

---

[64]Ibid., p. 463.

[65]Matthew Spinka, ed., *Advocates of Reform from Wyclif to Erasmus* (Philadelphia: Westminster, 1953), pp. 196-278. Erika Rummel, ed., *The Erasmus Reader* (Toronto: University of Toronto Press, 1990), pp. 155-68. A. G. Dickens and Dorothy Carr, eds., *The Reformation in England to the Accession of Elizabeth I* (London: Edward Arnold, 1987), pp. 6-19.

[66]Jane Dempsey Douglas, "A Report on Anticlericalism in Three French Women Writers, 1404-1549," in *Anticlericalism in Late Medieval and Early Modern Europe,* p. 243.

[67]Ibid., p. 250.

[68]Ibid., pp. 253-56.

[69]Three works come to mind. See Andrew Pettegrew, ed., *The Reformation of the Parishes* (Manchester: Manchester University Press, 1993); Rosemary O'Day, *The English Clergy: The Emergence and Consolidation of a Profession, 1558-1642* (Leicester, U.K.: Leicester University Press, 1979); David Hall, *The Faithful Shepherd* (New York: Norton, 1972).

[70]Carlos M. N. Eire, "Antisacerdotalism and the Young Calvin," in *Anticlericalism in Late Medieval and Early Modern Europe,* p. 598.

[71]Ibid., p. 599.

had the king's sister Marguerite of Navarre for his patron. Calvin in his letter of 1537 asked his friend, who had become bishop of Oleron, to avoid compromise. This letter is a stinging indictment of clerical abuse, which offends God because its worship is impious and offends one's neighbor because it mistreats the laity.[72]

At Geneva Calvin participated in an anticlerical revolution. For example, in 1535 Geneva had 245 Catholic clergy recruited from the city and diocese of Geneva; all were citizens and constituted a social elite. Twenty Protestant clergy replaced these 245 Catholic clerics, most of whom were from France and none of whom were citizens.[73] This is a social revolution with enormous consequences. Finally in 1559 the academy at Geneva was organized. Though doctors were specified on Calvin's return to Geneva in 1541, there was an eighteen-year delay in implementation. Here pastors were prepared for service primarily in France.

It is of interest that the Genevan curriculum develops with the adding of specialist chairs. Secular rulers desired the study of law as well as theology. Preparation came with a heavy dose of classical learning. Latin was the language of instruction. Not all future contingencies were met in the course of study. Between 1559 and 1620 a total of 2,674 students are known to have attended, 729 of whom became ministers.[74] Lack of academic ability could rule out candidates, and a weak voice could disqualify graduates from placement.[75]

The 1559 Genevan academy statutes were heavily exegesis-oriented, consisting primarily of commentary on the Old and New Testaments. Starting from 1587 with Beza and confirmed in 1620 at the Reformed French synod of Alès, *loci communes* were given over to a professor who taught them separately from Old and New Testament. Thus the teaching of theology made dogmatics the privileged science rather than the biblical exegesis courses so characteristic of the first two decades of the young Genevan academy. If indeed the early period contributed to making pastors into polemicists, the second "stimulated in the Reformed Churches of France a taste for controversy . . . clearly shown during the quarrel provoked by the theses of Moise Amyraut on Hypothetical Universalism."[76]

The statutes of the Genevan academy deserve careful scrutiny, for in addition to Latin, Greek and Hebrew they provided for the teaching of philosophy and theology. Calvin came to be seen as the author of these statutes, which were adopted

---

[72]Ibid., p. 591.

[73]Robert Kingdon, "Calvin and the Government of Geneva," in *Calvinus Ecclesiae Genevensis Custos*, ed. Wilhelm Neuser (Frankfurt am Main: Verlag Peter Lang, 1984), pp. 49-67.

[74]Karin Maag, "Education and Training for the Calvinist Ministry: The Academy of Geneva, 1559-1620," in Pettegrew, *Reformation of the Parishes*, p. 144.

[75]Ibid., pp. 140, 142. See also Leopold Schümmer, "Le ministère pastoral dans L'Institution Chrétienne de Calvin," *La Revue Réformée* 45 (1994-1995): 9-47.

[76]Richard Stauffer, "Calvinism and the Universities," in *University and Reformation*, ed. Leif Grane (Leiden: Brill, 1981), p. 90.

by the city council in May 1559.[77] As a student progressed through the seven classes of the secondary level *(schola privata)*, French, Latin and Greek were stressed. The classical component included Cicero's *Amicitia,* Terence and a Latin catechism in the fourth class, as well as study in Greek of Lucian's *Dialogues on Death* and Aesop's *Fables* in the second class.[78] The first class read logic, using the manuals of John Sturm and Conrad Neobar or Philip Melanchthon.[79] The university *(schola publica)* assigned the teaching of Aristotle's *Ethics* and *Politics* to the professor of Greek and Cicero's *Rhetoric* to the arts professor.[80]

Olivier Fatio demonstrates that between 1583 and 1595 a precise definition of theology as found in Lambert Daneau's *Compendium* constituted a new methodology. Segregating sacred doctrine from sacred Scripture was not a concern of Calvin, Melanchthon, Martyr, Hyperius or Musculus.[81] Apparently Daneau interacted with Zanchi, who in 1591 presented a definition of theology that was oriented around a double knowledge of God (1) as he is in himself and in his nature *(in se ipso et in sua natura)* or (2) as he is outside himself and in his effects *(extra se et in suis effectis)*. *In se* presents God in two ways, as essence (unity and trinity) or attributes (simplicity, immensity, eternity, omnipotence).[82] Daneau's reflection did not lead to full imitation of this scholastic content, as Fatio more recently argues:

> He remained, nevertheless, more reserved than Zanchi with regard to metaphysics. . . . Zanchi began his own doctrine of God with definitions in the light of which he understood Scripture. . . . Daneau, on the other hand, presented a less speculative theology in spite of its method and rationalizing character. He made a point of beginning with Scripture.[83]

The shift to *elenchi,* such as that of François Turretin, would be a more subtle process as fresh loci that focused on the nature and attributes of God replaced the exegetical

---

[77]Ibid., p. 80.

[78]Henri Meylan, "Collèges et Académies protestantes en France au XVIᵉ siècle," in *D'Erasme A Théodore De Bèze* (Genève: Librairie Droz, 1976), p. 193. Luther cites Aesop in his 1520 *On Christian Freedom* and prepared an edition of Aesop's fables for the schools. Thomas More translated Lucian. See the introduction to vol. 3, pt. 1, of the Yale edition, *Translations of Lucian* (New Haven, Conn.: Yale University Press, 1974), especially pp. xli-lv. Aesop was printed at Geneva in 1594 (Latin), 1596 (French) and 1598 (French). See Paul Chaix, Alain Dufour and Gustave Moeckli, *Les livres imprimés à Genève de 1550 à 1600* (Genève: Librairie Droz, 1966). Calvin read and annotated his copy of Lucian in 1545.

[79]Irena Backus, "L'Enseignement de la Logique à L'Académie de Genève entre 1559 et 1565," *Revue de Théologie et de Philosophie* 111 (1979): 154-55.

[80]Meylan, "Collèges et académies protestantes en France au XVIᵉ siècle," p. 193. Regarding the Lutheran side, see Carl S. Meyer, "Melanchthon's Visitation Articles of 1528," *Journal of Ecclesiastical History* 23 (1972): 309-22.

[81]Olivier Fatio, *Méthode et théologie: Lambert Daneau et les débuts de la scholastique réformee* (Genève: Librairie Droz, 1965), pp. 150-53.

[82]Ibid., p. 152.

[83]"Lambert Daneau," in *Shapers of Religious Traditions in Germany, Switzerland and Poland, 1560-1600,* ed. Jill Raitt (New Haven, Conn.: Yale University Press, 1981), p. 116.

ones of Vermigli. Zanchi himself denied that this theological interest in the nature of God came from Vermigli. Beza cannot be faulted for this transition when the content of the loci that he preferred is examined. That preference with its polemical context is qualitatively different from the controversy raised by the penchant for dialectical speculation about the nature and attributes of God, which Richard Stauffer finds so characteristic of Geneva after 1620.[84] As Beardslee puts it,

> Speculative logic had triumphed over the soteriological insight of the Reformation . . . in which he [Turretin] separates predestination from soteriology . . . a doctrine which . . . is introduced even before the doctrine of creation. . . . He obscures it for practical religion.[85]

The teaching of dogmatics from these fresh loci, now viewed as *elenchi*, not only stimulated controversy but also lowered the linguistic competence of theology students in Greek and Hebrew,[86] thereby severing the links with exegesis that Vermigli and Beza had been careful to maintain. In Vermigli's case, the use of historical and legal arguments were also mitigating factors against construction of dogmatic systems, against which Melanchthon and Calvin (contra Socinus) cautioned.[87] François Turretin, for example, first discussed the essence of God and his attributes, then the Trinity, then the decrees of God and finally predestination. The knowledge of God was not any longer the starting point, as it was for Calvin. When Richard Muller defends Turretin's codification of Reformed dogma, which describes as both "the God who truly is and his self-revelation,"[88] he defends a trend in Reformed dogmatics that departed from the exegetical tradition practiced by Beza.[89]

In the end, what motivated the preparation of preachers at Geneva was the significance of the biblical languages, the rhetorical concern with topics derived from Scripture itself and the use of Aristotelian metaphysics to clarify the dogmatic agenda. What rescued the Genevan academicians from speculative theology, preoccupied as it is with questions about the nature of God as he is in himself, was Calvin's own comment on Hilary of Poitiers,

---

[84]Stauffer, "Calvinism and the Universities," p. 90.

[85]See John W. Beardslee III, ed. and trans., *Reformed Dogmatics* (New York: Oxford University Press, 1965), pp. 18-19.

[86]Ibid., p. 91.

[87]Marvin Anderson, "Royal Idolatry: Peter Martyr and the Reformed Tradition," *Archiv für Reformationsgeschichte* 69 (1978): 183-85; Robert M. Kingdon, "The Function of Law in the Political Thought of Peter Martyr Vermigli," in *Reformation Perennis: Essays on Calvin and the Reformation in Honor of Ford Lewis Battles*, ed. B. A. Gerrish (Pittsburgh: Pickwick, 1981), pp. 159-72.

[88]Richard A. Muller, "Scholasticism Protestant and Catholic: Francis Turretin on the Object and Principles of Theology," *Church History* 55 (1986): 205.

[89]Pierre Fraenkel, *De l'écriture a la dispute: Le cas de l'Académie de Genève sous Théodore de Bèze* (Lausaunne: Revue de Théologie et de Philosophe, 1977), pp. 33-34. See Marvin Anderson, "Theodore Beza: Savant or Scholastic?" *Theologische Zeitschrift* 43 (1987): 320-32.

we ought to play the philosopher soberly and with great moderation; let us use great caution that neither our thoughts nor our speech go beyond the limits to which the Word of God itself extends. . . . How can the mind by its own leading come to search out God's essence when it cannot even get to its own? Let us then willingly leave to God the knowledge of himself. For, as Hilary says, he is the one fit to witness to himself, and is not known except through himself. But we shall be "leaving it to him" if we conceive him to be as he reveals himself to us, without inquiring about him elsewhere than from his Word. . . . And let us not take it into our heads either to seek our God anywhere else than in his Sacred Word, or to think anything about him that is not prompted by his Word, or to speak anything that is not taken from that Word.[90]

Though Daneau and Zanchi were tempted to shift the focus from Scripture to metaphysical speculation about God, that "fall" did not occur in the first six decades of the Genevan academy.

The Catholic response to their pastoral crisis took several forms, one of which was seminary legislation at Trent and later the Jesuit *Ratio Studiorum*. The latter was an educational experience forged in the necessity to recover large territories of Europe where Protestantism had made inroads. It endorsed the success of Protestant clerical education.[91] In all, the Jesuits controlled more than five hundred colleges and seminaries between 1615 and 1645, totaling some two hundred thousand students.[92] By teaching, preaching and writing the Jesuits prepared the movement to counter Wittenburg, Zurich and Geneva in classrooms such as those in the enormous Clementinum in Prague, now the state library of the Czech Republic.

Observations

This essay illustrates the current dynamic status of Reformation studies in three areas: popular religion, aliens within and without, and clerical status. It is obvious that social and intellectual historians are at odds with each other as each discipline seeks to assign preliminary significance to the undifferentiated mass of human activity in this long century that we call the Reformation.[93]

A search for new printed sources, particularly in central Europe, turns up many

[90]Calvin *Institutes of the Christian Religion* 1.13.21. Compare Charles Partee, "Calvin's Central Dogma Again," *Sixteenth Century Journal* 18 (1987): 191-99.

[91]Twenty-third session, Council of Trent, July 1563. Purity of life, detachment from the world, spiritual formation toward ecclesiastical service and the capacity to fulfill sacerdotal functions are the primary goals. See Oskar Garsten, "Educational System of the Jesuit Order," in *Rome and the Counter-Reformation in Scandinavia: Jesuit Educational Strategy, 1553-1622* (Leiden: Brill, 1992), pp. 40-65.

[92]Ibid., pp. 64-65.

[93]See Stephen Ozment, *Protestants*, pp. xiv, 1-7, 218-19.

volumes of this period not located in Western libraries.[94] My own work on Peter Martyr Vermigli has uncovered copies of his printed works in dozens of libraries.[95] Marc Bloc, the great medievalist, wrote (*Annals* 5.5.8-9) that the important thing is not to enumerate but to ponder.[96] So must we all ponder the insights of these early modern pioneers in the realm of creation and of the Spirit.

Bibliography is still the vestibule of the sciences. The future of Reformation studies lies in exploration of the printed texts that have survived the ravages of time and the savagery of human activity. Together with the archival documentation of manuscript collections, fresh vistas will emerge from the theological core and social context of the confessional age (1483-1648).

Central to much of inquiry is a return to the sources of Christian reflection in canonical Scripture of the Old and New Testaments. This discovery was put in poetic fashion by Alexander Pushkin in *The Prophet*.

> He laid his finger on my eyes:
> His touch lay soft as slumber lies,
> And like an eagle's, his crag shaken,
> Did my prophetic eyes awaken.
> Upon the wastes, a lifeless clod,
> I lay, and heard the voice of God:
> "Arise, oh, prophet, watch and hearken,
> And with my Will thy soul engird
> Roam the gray seas, the rooks that darken,
> And burn men's hearts with this, my Words."[97]

In Martin Luther's *Small Catechism* (1529) there is a table of duties for various classes of persons. It sums them all up at the end: Christians in general are to love their neighbors as themselves (Rom 13:9) and are to make intercession for all persons (1 Tim 2:1). Luther concludes with the phrase:

> Let each his lesson learn with care
> And all household well will fare.[98]

This is indeed the purpose of Reform for all time, that persons would love their

---

[94] *Catalogus Librorum Sedecimo Saeculo Impressorum, Qui in Bibliotheca Nationali Hungariae Széchényianna Asservanter*, vols. 1-3 (1990). This work contains 15,268 separate entries for 12,989 titles. Four thousand of these *are not* in Western libraries.

[95] John Patrick Donnelly, Robert M. Kingdon and Marvin W. Anderson, eds., *A Bibliography of the Works of Peter Martyr Vermigli* (Kirksville, Mo.: Sixteenth Century Journal Publishers, 1990). See unique Czech copy on pp. 80-81 and the German on pp. 70-71.

[96] Cited in Lewis W. Spitz, *The Protestant Reformation, 1517-1559* (San Francisco: Harper & Row, 1985), p. 385.

[97] Avrahm Yarmolinsky, ed., *The Poems, Prose and Plays of Alexander Pushkin* (New York: Random House, 1936), pp. 61-62.

[98] Mark A. Noll, ed., *Confessions and Catechisms of the Reformation* (Grand Rapids: Baker, 1991), p. 80.

neighbors as they do God and themselves.

Resources for Additional Study

Barnes, Robin Bruce. "Hope and Despair in Sixteenth-Century German Almanacs." In *The Reformation in Germany and Europe: Interpretations and Issues.* Edited by Hans R. Guggisberg, Gottfried G. Krode and Hans Füglister. Gütersloh, Germany: Gütersloher Verlagshaus, 1993.

Gerrish, B. A., ed. *Reformation Perennis: Essays on Calvin and the Reformation in Honor of Ford Lewis Battles.* Pittsburgh: Pickwick, 1981.

Noll, Mark A., ed. *Confessions and Catechisms of the Reformation.* Grand Rapids: Baker, 1991.

Ozment, Stephen. *Protestants: The Birth of a Revolution.* New York: Doubleday, 1992.

Scribner, Robert W. *For the Sake of Simple Folk: Popular Propaganda for the German Reformation.* Oxford: Clarendon, 1994.

Chapter 8

New Dimensions in Baptist Theology

Timothy George

••••••••••••••••••••••••••••

S EVERAL YEARS AGO WILL D. CAMPBELL PUBLISHED A FASCINATING novel titled *The Glad River*. The chief character is a man named Doops Momber. His real name was Claudy Momber, but everybody calls him Doops because Claudy sounds too much like a girl's name. He grew up among the Baptists of Mississippi, attended the revivals, the hayrides and the Sunday-school wiener roasts, but somehow he never got baptized. Later when he is inducted into the army, his sergeant asks, "You a Protestant or a Catholic?" Doops does not answer for a moment. Then he says, "I guess I'm neither. I'm neither Catholic nor Protestant. I never joined. But all my people are Baptist." "But there's a P on your dog tag. Why not a C?" "They asked me what I was and I told them the same thing I told you. And the guy stamped a P on it." "Why do you suppose they did that?" the sergeant asks. "Well," says Doops, "I guess in America you have to be something."[1]

The confusion Doops encounters about his religious identity is symptomatic of many other Baptist Christians who, unlike Doops, have indeed taken the plunge but who have no more solid understanding than he about what that means in a postdenominational age of generic religion and dog-tag Christianity. Several years ago I published an essay titled "The Renewal of Baptist Theology," which began with the following lamentation.

There is a crisis in Baptist life today which cannot be resolved by bigger budgets, better programs, or more sophisticated systems of data processing and mass

---

[1]Will D. Campbell, *The Glad River* (New York: Holt, Rinehart & Winston, 1982), p. 107.

communication. It is a crisis of identity rooted in a fundamental theological failure of nerve. The two major diseases of the contemporary church are spiritual amnesia (we have forgotten who we are) and ecclesiastical myopia (whoever we are, we are glad we are not like "them"). While these maladies are not unique to the people of God called Baptists, they are perhaps most glaringly present among us.[2]

This article is a sequel to that earlier essay. First of all, I want to point out some of the difficulties in speaking about the theological identity of Baptists. Then, in the heart of the paper, I will present a mosaic for the renewal of Baptist theology by identifying five major components for such an agenda.

Diversity and Adversity

The first problem in sorting out the theological identity of Baptists is the sheer diversity of the movement. From the beginning of the Baptist experiment in seventeenth-century England, General (Arminian) and Particular (Calvinistic) Baptists developed diverse, even mutually incompatible, paradigms for what it meant to be a Baptist. The Particulars, who were better educated, better organized and more successful than the Generals, forged alliances with other mainstream Dissenting bodies denying that they were in any way guilty of "those heterodoxies and fundamental errors" that had been unfairly attributed to them.[3] The Generals, on the other hand, were drawn into the orbit of that "swarm of sectaries and schismatics," as John Taylor put it, which included Levellers, Ranters, Seekers, Quakers and, at the fag end of the Puritan movement, the mysterious Family of Love. It was, as Christopher Hill has called it, a world turned upside down. An anonymous rhymester may well have had the General Baptists in mind when he penned these lines in 1641: "When women preach and cobblers pray, the fiends in hell make holiday."[4]

The diversification of the Baptist tradition, which began in England, was accelerated in America, where the great fact of national life was the frontier—a seemingly endless expanse of space that offered limitless opportunities for escaping the past. "If you and yours don't agree with me and mine, you can pack your Scofield Bible in your hip pocket and start your own church!" And so they did. And the line stretches from Roger Williams, who left Massachusetts to practice soul-liberty in Rhode Island, to Brigham Young, who carried the Mormons to Utah, to Jim Jones in California and David Koresh in Waco. The frontier was always there.

As for the Baptists, one only has to skim through Mead's *Handbook of Denominations* to appreciate the bewildering variety. Among many others, there are

---

[2]Timothy George and David S. Dockery, eds., *Baptist Theologians* (Nashville: Broadman, 1990), p. 13.
[3]William L. Lumpkin, ed., *Baptist Confessions of Faith* (Valley Forge, Penn.: Judson, 1959), p. 244.
[4]Michael Watts, *The Dissenters* (Oxford: Clarendon, 1978), p. 83.

American Baptists, Southern Baptists, National Baptists, United Baptists, Conservative Baptists, General Association of Regular Baptists (GARB), Free Will Baptists, Landmark Baptists, Duck River and Kindred Associations of Baptists, Six Principle Baptists, Primitive Baptists, Seventh Day Baptists, Two-Seed-in-the-Spirit Predestinarian Baptists and the National Baptist Evangelical Life and Soul-Saving Assembly of the USA, Inc.! That's a lot of Baptists! How do you talk about theological identity amid that kind of variety?

There's a second factor we also need to consider—not only *diversity* within the tradition but *adversity* from the environing culture. While Baptists in America, especially in the South, have long been accustomed to the accoutrements of an established religion, we began as a small, persecuted sect. Long after the 1689 Act of Toleration granted statutory freedom of worship, Baptists, along with other Nonconformists in England, suffered harassment, discrimination and ridicule. One critic labeled them as "miscreants begat in rebellion, born in sedition, and nursed in faction."[5] The struggles for religious liberty continued for Baptists in America, where Obadiah Holmes was publicly beaten on the streets of Danvers, Massachusetts, and John Leland was clapped up in a Virginia jail.

An example of the low esteem in which Baptist folk were held in the early nineteenth century was recorded by David Benedict, who traveled by horseback through all seventeen states of the new nation collecting historical information and impressions about the Baptists. One person, "a very honest and candid old lady," gave Benedict the following impression she had formed of the Baptists:

> There was a company of them in the back part of our town, and an outlandish set of people they certainly were. . . . You could hardly find one among them but what was deformed in some way or other. Some of them were hare-lipped, others were bleary-eyed, or hump-backed, or bow-legged, or clump-footed; hardly any of them looked like other people. But they were all strong for plunging, and let their poor ignorant children run wild, and never had the seal of the covenant put on them.[6]

Despite diversity within and adversity without, by mid-nineteenth century Baptists in America had developed a remarkable unity of purpose and vision, a theological consensus that even cut across the seismic fault line produced by slavery and the Civil War. Thus Francis Wayland, a Northern Baptist, could write:

> I do not believe that any denomination of Christians exists, which, for so long a period as the Baptist, have maintained so invariably the truth of their early confessions. . . . The theological tenets of the Baptists, both in England and America, may be briefly stated as follows: they are emphatically the doctrines of

---

[5]Henry Sacheverell, *The Perils of False Brethren* (London, 1709), p. 36.
[6]David Benedict, *Fifty Years Among the Baptists* (New York: Sheldon, 1860), pp. 93-94.

the Reformation, and they have been held with singular unanimity and consistency.

Thus despite countless splits and some doctrinal defections (for example, the lapse of certain Baptists into universalism), there emerged among Baptists in late nineteenth-, early twentieth-century America what might be called an orthodox Baptist consensus, represented in the North by Augustus H. Strong, in the South by E. Y. Mullins.

One knew instinctively when the bounds of this consensus had been transgressed. Thus in the controversy surrounding the forced departure of Crawford Howell Toy from the Baptist Seminary at Louisville in 1879, both Toy himself and the colleagues who bade him a tearful adieu were all aware, as Toy himself put it, that he "no longer stood where most of his brethren did."[7]

Erosion of Theological Consensus

The history of the Baptist movement in the twentieth century can be written largely as the story of a theological consensus that obtained in most places but eroded with the fundamentalist-modernist disputes. The Baptist apologetic made a two-part response to the dispute, which was not really adequate to deal with the challenge at hand. The first part was an appeal to "Baptist distinctives," an effort that was fueled by old-fashioned denominational braggadocio, as seen in the book *Baptist Why and Why Not* published by the Southern Baptist Sunday School Board in 1900. Chapter titles include "Why Baptist and Not Methodist," "Why Baptist and Not Episcopalian," "Why Immersion and Not Sprinkling," "Why Close Communion and Not Open Communion" and so on.[8]

Further emphasis on Baptist distinctives such as the separation of church and state, the nonsacramental character of the ordinances and the noncreedal character of our confessions appeared as a litany of negative constraints rather than a positive exposition of an essential doctrinal core. Indeed, for some Baptists, these so-called distinctives, often interpreted in a attenuated, reductionistic form, became the essence of the Baptist tradition itself.

This consensus was further eroded by what may be called the privatization of Baptist theology. Historically, Baptist life was shaped by strong communitarian features. The congregation was not merely an aggregate of like-minded individuals but a body of baptized believers. Baptists were never doctrinal anarchists who boasted of their "right" to believe in anything they wanted to. Instead of flaunting their Christian freedom in this way, Baptists used it to produce and publish *confessions* of faith, as a means both of declaring their own faith to the world and of

---

[7]See George H. Shiver, ed., *American Religious Heretics* (Nashville: Abingdon, 1966), pp. 56-88.
[8]James M. Frost, *Baptist Why and Why Not* (Nashville: Sunday School Board, 1900).

guarding the theological integrity of their own fellowship.[9] Nor did Baptists want their young children "to think for themselves," as the liberal cliché has it, but instead to be thoroughly grounded in the faith once for all delivered to the saints. Thus they developed Baptist *catechisms* and used them in both home and church to instruct their children in the rudiments of Christian theology.

The communitarian character of Baptist life, exemplified by covenants, confessions and catechisms, was undermined by the privatization of Baptist theology and the rising tide of modern rugged individualism that swept through American culture in the early twentieth century. It should be noted that this movement influenced Baptists at both ends of the religious spectrum. Liberal Baptists followed the theological trajectory of Schleiermacher and Ritschl into revisionist models of theology that denied, in some cases, the most fundamental truths of the gospel.[10] At the other extreme, anti-intellectual pietism and emotion-laden revivalism pitted theology against piety, soul religion against reflective faith, thus producing a schizophrenic split between sound doctrine and holy living. Although Billy Sunday belonged to another denomination, many Baptists could resonate with his assertion that he did not know any more about theology than a jackrabbit knew about Ping-Pong!

What are the benchmarks for shaping Baptist theological identity for such a time as this? Rather than put forth subtle speculations or a new methodology, I propose that we look again at five classic principles drawn from the wider Baptist heritage. These five affirmations form a cluster of convictions that have seen us through turbulent storms in the past. They are worthy anchors for us to cast into the sea of postmodernity as we seek not merely to weather the storm but to sail with confidence into the future God has prepared for us.

Identity Markers

Orthodox convictions. In 1994 the Southern Baptist Convention unanimously adopted a resolution acknowledging that "Southern Baptists have historically

---

[9]See the classic statement by James P. Boyce in his "Three Changes in Theological Institutions," in *James Petigru Boyce: Selected Writings*, ed. Timothy George (Nashville: Broadman, 1989), pp. 48-59.

[10]Thus by the end of his life in 1921, A. H. Strong, a moderate throughout his career, had sided with the fundamentalists in their dispute with modernism. Lamenting "some common theological trends of our time," Strong warned that "under the influence of Ritchl and his Kantian relativism, many of our teachers and preachers have swung off into a practical denial of Christ's deity and of His atonement. We seem upon the verge of a second Unitarian defection, that will break up churches and compel secessions, in a worse manner than did that of Channing and Ware a century ago. American Christianity recovered from that disaster only by vigorously asserting the authority of Christ and the inspiration of the Scriptures.... Without a revival of this faith our churches will become secularized, mission enterprise will die out, and the candlestick will be removed out of its place as it was with the seven churches of Asia, and as it has been with the apostate churches of New England." *Systematic Theology* (Valley Forge, Penn.: Judson, 1907), p. ix.

confessed with all true Christians everywhere belief in the Triune God, Father, Son, and Holy Spirit, the full deity and perfect humanity of Jesus Christ, His virgin birth His sinless life, His substitutionary atonement for sins, His resurrection from the dead, His exaltation to the right hand of God, and His triumphal return; and we recognize that born again believers in the Lord Jesus Christ may be found in all Christain denominations." The recognition of common Christian convictions shared by Baptists and other believers has led the Baptist World Alliance to sponsor interconfessional discussions and dialogues with both Roman Catholics and Protestants of several denominational traditions.

Baptists are orthodox Christians who stand in continuity with the dogmatic consensus of the early church on matters such as the scope of Holy Scripture (canon), the doctrine of God (Trinity) and the person and work of Jesus Christ (Christology). Leon McBeth is correct when he observes that Baptists have "often used confessions not to proclaim 'Baptist distinctives' but instead to show how similar Baptists were to other orthodox Christians."[11] Thus the "Orthodox Confession" of 1678 incorporated (article 38) the Apostles', Nicene and Athanasian creeds, declaring that all three "ought thoroughly to be received, and believed. For we believe, that they may be proved, by most undoubted authority of Holy Scripture and are necessary to be understood of all Christians."[12] Reflecting this same impulse, the Baptists who gathered in London for the inaugural meeting of the Baptist World Alliance in 1905 stood in that assembly and recited in unison the Apostles' Creed.

Fundamentalism arose in the early part of the twentieth century as a protest against the concessions and denials of liberal theologians on such cardinal tenets as the virgin birth of Christ, the inerrancy of the Bible, penal substitutionary atonement and so on. This was a valid and necessary protest, and we should be grateful for those worthy forebears who stood with courage and conviction on these matters. However, the problem with fundamentalism as a theological movement was its tendency toward reductionism—not what it affirmed but what it left out.

In recent years the inspiration and authority of the Bible have again assumed a major role in Baptist polemics, especially within the Southern Baptist Convention. From the drafting of the "Baptist Faith and Message" in 1963 through the adoption of the "Presidential Theological Study Committee Report" in 1994, Southern Baptists have repeatedly affirmed their confidence in the inerrancy, or the total truthfulness, of Holy Scripture. As the latter report declares, "What the Bible says, God says; what the Bible says happened, really happened; every miracle, every event, in every book of the Old and New Testaments is altogether true and trustworthy."

---

[11]H. Leon McBeth, *The Baptist Heritage* (Nashville: Broadman, 1987), p. 68.
[12]W. L. Lumpkin, ed., *Baptist Confessions of Faith* (Valley Forge, Penn.: Judson, 1959), p. 326.

In more recent years, however, the SBC has found it necessary to address other pressing doctrinal issues such as the being of God and the importance of using biblical language to address God (over against certain models of contemporary feminism) and the belief in Jesus Christ as sole and sufficient Savior (over against universalism and soteriological pluralism). Millard Erickson has been a pioneer among Baptist theologians in writing with wisdom and depth on the classic theme of Christology, especially in his magisterial study *The Word Became Flesh*. All Baptists need to cultivate a holistic orthodoxy, based on a high view of the Scriptures and congruent with the trinitarian and christological consensus of the early church. Only in this way will we avoid the dangers of rigid reductionism on the one hand and liberal revisionism on the other.

Evangelical heritage. Baptists are evangelical Christians who affirm with Martin Luther and John Calvin both the formal and the material principles of the Reformation: Scripture alone and justification by faith alone. In setting forth these twin peaks of evangelical faith, the Reformers were not introducing new doctrines or novel ideas. They argued like this: If the doctrine of the Trinity really presents us with the true God of creation and of redemption; if Jesus Christ really is what we confess him to be, that is, God from God, Light from Light, very God from very God; and if original sin is as pervasive and debilitating as we believe it to be, then the doctrine of justification by faith alone is the only faithful interpretation of the New Testament promise of forgiveness, pardon and new life in Christ. While not agreeing with everything Luther or Calvin taught, Baptists claim the heritage of the Reformation as their own. We gladly identify ourselves with other evangelical believers who are "not ashamed of the gospel of Christ: for it is the power of God unto salvation" for all who believe (Rom 1:16 KJV).

The word *evangelical* has myriad other meanings as well, and Baptists in North America can rightly claim at least two of them. First, we are heirs of the evangelical awakening that swept across the eighteenth century, producing Pietism in Germany, Methodism in England and the First Great Awakening in the American colonies. Many features of Baptist life resonate deeply with this mighty moving of the Spirit of God: our evangelistic witness and missionary vision, our historic emphasis on disciplined church life and godly living, our commitment to a regenerate church membership and Spirit-filled worship, our refusal to divorce the personal and social dimensions of the gospel.

More recently, the word *evangelical* has been associated with the postfundamentalist resurgence among Bible-believing Christians in North America. Significantly, the two most formative shapers of this movement are (Southern) Baptists: Billy Graham and Carl F. H. Henry. Far more important than wearing the evangelical label is the substance of the word in the three senses outlined here. Baptists of North America can and should rightly lay claim to the doctrinal legacy of the Reformation, the missionary and evangelistic impulse of the Great Awakening and a transdenominational fellowship of Bible-believing Christians with whom we share a common commitment to the Word of God and the task of world evangelization. Perhaps no theologian has better negotiated the Baptist-evangelical worlds than Millard Erickson. He has taught in several Baptist denominational settings, and his textbook on Christian theology has become a classic in numerous evangelical seminaries.

Reformed perspective. Despite a persistent Arminian strain within Baptist life, for much of our history most Baptists have adhered faithfully to the doctrines of grace as set forth in Pauline-Augustinian-Reformed theology. David Benedict, following his extensive tour of Baptist churches throughout America in the early nineteenth century, gave the following summary of the Baptist theology he encountered: "Take this denomination at large, I believe the following will be found a pretty correct statement of their views of doctrine. They hold that man in his natural condition is entirely depraved and sinful; but unless he is born again—changed by grace—or made alive unto God—he cannot be fitted for the communion of saints on earth, nor the enjoyment of God in heaven; that where God hath begun a good work, he will carry it on to the end; that there is an election of grace—an effectual calling, etc., and that the happiness of the righteous and the misery of the wicked will both be eternal."[13]

In 1856 James Petigru Boyce set forth his plan for Southern Baptists' first theological seminary. He warned against the twin errors of Campbellism and Arminianism, the distinctive principles of which "have been ingrafted upon many of our churches: and even some of our ministry have not hesitated publicly to avow them."[14]

As late as 1905, F. H. Kerfoot, Boyce's successor as professor of systematic theology at Southern Seminary, could still say, "Nearly all Baptists believe what are usually termed the 'doctrines of grace.' "[15] E. Y. Mullins, who disliked the labels "Calvinist" and "Arminian," sought to transcend the controversy altogether. While retaining most of the content of traditional Calvinist soteriology, he gave it a new casting by restating it in terms of his distinctive theology of experience. A. H. Strong played a similar role among Northern Baptists during this same era.

For some, the evangelical Calvinism of earlier Baptist generations has been eclipsed by a truncated hyper-Calvinism with its anti-missionary, antievangelistic emphases. Many other factors have also contributed to the blurring of this part of the Reformation heritage that has shaped Baptist identity: the routinization of

---

[13]David Benedict, *A General History of the Baptist Denomination in America* (Boston: Lincoln & Edmands, 1813), 2:456.

[14]George, *James Petigru Boyce*, p. 33.

[15]Quoted, Thomas J. Nettles, *By His Grace and for His Glory* (Grand Rapids: Baker, 1986), p. 50.

revivalism, the growth of pragmatism as a denominational strategy, an attenuated doctrine of the Holy Spirit, and a general theological laxity that has resulted in doctrinal apathy. While seeking to restate traditional themes in fresh, contemporary ways, Baptists would do well to connect again with the ideas that informed the theology of such great heroes of the past as John Bunyan, Roger Williams, Andrew Fuller, Adoniram Judson, Luther Rice and Charles Haddon Spurgeon.

I rejoice in the growing awareness of Reformed theology among many Baptists today. I know of nothing that has happened in the history of salvation since the days of Fuller, Carey and Spurgeon that would render their understanding of God's grace obsolete in the modern world. To the contrary, a renewed commitment to the sovereignty of God in salvation, worship that centers on the glory of God rather than the entertainment of the audience, and a perspective on history and culture that sees Jesus Christ as Lord of time and eternity—all of this can only result in the building up of the body of Christ.

At the same time, it is imperative for Reformed Baptists to guard against the real dangers of hyper-Calvinism, which emphasizes divine sovereignty to the exclusion of human responsibility and denies that the offer of the gospel is to be extended to all peoples everywhere. And as we call on our fellow Baptist brothers and sisters to return to the rock from which we were hewn, we must learn to live in gracious equipoise with those who don't ring all five bells quite the way we do! In this regard we do well to heed the following statement by the great missionary statesman Luther Rice: "How absurd it is, therefore, to contend against the doctrine of election, or decrees, or divine sovereignty. Let us not, however, become bitter against those who view this matter in a different light, nor treat them in a supercilious manner; rather let us be gentle toward all men. For who has made us to differ from what we once were? Who has removed the scales from our eyes?"[16]

Baptist distinctives. While Baptists owe much to the great doctrinal legacy of the mainline Reformers, our ecclesiology most closely approximates the Anabaptist ideal in its emphasis on the church as an intentional community composed of regenerated and baptized believers who are bound to one another and their Lord by a solemn covenant. One of the most important contributions that Baptists have made to the wider life of the church is the recovery of the early church practice of baptism as an adult rite of initiation signifying a committed participation in the life, death and resurrection of Jesus Christ. In many contemporary Baptist settings, however, baptism is in danger of being divorced from the context of the decisive life commitment. This unfortunate development is reflected both in the liturgical placement of baptism in the worship service—often tacked on at the end as a kind

---

[16]James B. Taylor, *Memoir of Rev. Luther Rice, One of the First American Missionaries to the East* (Baltimore: Armstrong & Berry, 1840), pp. 332-33.

of afterthought—and in the proper age and preparation of baptismal candidates. This situation muffles the historic Baptist protest against infant baptism, a protest that insisted on the intrinsic connection between biblical baptism and repentance and faith.[17]

We must also guard against a minimalist understanding of the Lord's Supper that reduces this vital ordinance to an empty ritual detached from the spiritual life of believers. Several years ago I experienced a powerful service of the Lord's Supper at the First Baptist Church of Dallas, Texas. During a Sunday-morning service that great congregation was asked to kneel and prayerfully receive the elements while the meaning of the ordinance was carefully explained from the Scriptures. In this kind of setting the experience of worship is a transforming encounter with the living Christ. We need not fall prey to the lure of sacramentalism or the false doctrine of transubstantiation to reclaim the historic Baptist understanding of the Lord's Supper, which has nowhere been better described than in the Second London Confession of 1689: "Worthy receivers, outwardly partaking of the visible elements in this ordinance, do then also inwardly by faith, really and indeed, yet not carnally and corporally, but spiritually receive, and feed upon Christ crucified and all the benefits of His death: the Body and Blood of Christ, being then not corporally, or carnally, but spiritually present to the faith of believers, in that ordinance, as the elements themselves are to the outward senses."

Confessional context. As Baptists seek to be faithful shapers of the future under the lordship of Jesus Christ, we would do well to remember and reclaim the confessional character of our common Christian commitment. Baptists are not a creedal people. We regard no humanly devised statement as being equal to the Bible. Nor do we believe that the state has any authority to impose religious beliefs on its subjects. However, Baptists have historically approved and circulated confessions of faith for a threefold purpose: as an expression of our religious liberty, as a statement of our theological convictions and as a witness of the truths we hold in sacred trust. Our confessions are always accountable to Holy Scripture and are revisable in the light of that divine revelation.

Just as a confession declares what we believe, so a church covenant declares how we live. It sets forth in practical terms the ideal of the Christian life: a living faith working by love leading to holiness. The congregation's covenant also outlines that process of mutual admonition and responsibility through which fellow believers engage to "watch over" one another in encouragement, correction and prayer.

Finally, catechesis is concerned with passing on the faith intact to the rising generation. This responsibility is shared jointly by parents and pastors. May God

---

[17]See Timothy George, "The Reformed Doctrine of Believers' Baptism," *Interpretation* 47 (1993): 242-54.

give us again Baptist families and Baptist churches who will take seriously the awesome responsibility of indoctrinating our children in the things of God.

Conclusion

In his commentary on Daniel (9:25), John Calvin compared the work of God among his ancient people with the challenge of Calvin's own day: "God still wishes in these days to build his spiritual temple amidst the anxieties of the times. The faithful must still hold the trowel in one hand and the sword in the other, because the building of the church must still be combined with many struggles." That struggle continues today not against enemies of flesh and blood but against principalities and powers, against lethargy and laziness, against defection and darkness on every hand. Yet God does continue to build the church amid the anxieties of the times. For nearly four centuries God has blessed and used the people of God called Baptists in ways that future historians will record as remarkable beyond belief. As we remember and give thanks for the mighty acts of God in days gone by, let us press forward in the earnest expectation that the Lord "hath yet more truth and light to break forth out of His Holy Word." Above all, let us never forget that it is "not by might, nor by power, but by my Spirit, saith the Lord."

Chapter 9

New Dimensions in American Evangelical Theology

The Mainstreaming of Evangelical Theological Education

Timothy P. Weber

....

E VANGELICALS WERE LATECOMERS TO THE WORLD OF ACCREDITED theological education, but in the past three decades they have become a significant part of the Association of Theological Schools (ATS) in the United States and Canada. In 1994 the 223 institutions affiliated with ATS could be divided into three parts: 89 mainline Protestant (40 percent),[1] 79 evangelical (35 percent), and 57 Roman Catholic (25 percent).[2] (See appendix one for a listing of evangelical schools.) Though evangelical institutions make up only a third of ATS member schools, they enroll slightly over half of all the students.[3]

---

[1]Classifying schools can be tricky. For reasons that will become clear, I have designated seven schools sponsored by mainline Protestants as evangelical: three American Baptist (Central, Northern and Eastern), two Anglican/Episcopal (Wycliffe College and Trinity Episcopal School for Ministry), one Presbyterian (University of Dubuque Theological Seminary) and one Reformed (Western Theological Seminary).

[2]Most of the basic statistical information for this study comes from the following: Directory, *Bulletin 41*, pt. 4 (Pittsburgh: Association of Theological Schools, 1995); Membership List, *Bulletin 41*, pt. 7 (Pittsburgh: Association of Theological Schools, 1994); *Fact Book on Theological Education: For the Academic Year 1993-1994* (Pittsburgh: Association of Theological Schools, 1994); *1993 Theological Faculty Survey of the Center for the Study of Theological Education, Auburn Theological Seminary*. Some data from materials published by the Association of Theological Schools have been tabulated by the Auburn Center and are used in this report. Special thanks to Barbara Wheeler of Auburn Theological Seminary, who provided crucial data for the study and then helped me interpret it properly.

[3]"Slightly over half" refers to the figures for total head count (63,425): evangelical, 51 percent; mainline

If current trends continue, evangelicals will probably play an even larger role in ATS in the future. At present, evangelicalism is the growing edge of North American theological education. Of eleven "candidates for accredited membership" in ATS, eight are evangelical.[4] Of these schools five were founded decades ago and are only now seeking accreditation. The other three were started in the mid-1980s.

Evangelicals are still in the seminary-building business. Thanks to the controversy at their convention, Southern Baptists have started six new seminaries since 1990.[5] Popular evangelical magazines like *Christianity Today* and *Moody Monthly* carry advertisements for other new schools. It remains to be seen how many of these institutions will survive, but contemporary evangelicalism has enough vitality to attempt such ambitious undertakings. Mainline Protestants, on the other hand, suffer from shrinking memberships and financial resources. Catholics have a shortage of priests and those with priestly vocations. For them, starting new schools seems out of the question.

The accreditation of evangelical theological education, which is what we mean by "mainstreaming," has received little scholarly attention.[6] The purpose of this study is rather simple. Using the latest research available, it will examine the rise of accredited evangelical institutions by answering three basic questions: What is an evangelical theological school? Where did the evangelical schools in ATS come from? How do they compare with other schools in the ATS?

Identifying Evangelical Theological Schools

Asking these questions leads to the debate over the meaning of the term *evangelical,* which has been raging since the so-called evangelical renaissance of the 1970s. Historically, *evangelical* has been applied to a number of religious groups from a variety of Christian traditions. Theological differences among evangelicals complicate any effort to define the movement or the schools that serve it. According to a few scholars, such diversity makes the label *evangelical* meaningless. Donald Dayton, for example, calls it "an essentially contested concept" that even its defenders cannot define and suggests that it be discarded. But most scholars still think that

---

Protestant, 38 percent; Catholic, 11 percent. The figures for FTE (46,363) are only slightly different: evangelical, 48 percent; mainline Protestant, 40 percent; Catholic, 12 percent.

[4]The remainder consists of two mainline Protestant institutions and one Roman Catholic. Of the twenty-three "associate member" schools, which are taking the first steps toward full accreditation, twelve are evangelical, six are mainline Protestant and five are Roman Catholic.

[5]Of the six, only one is freestanding (Baptist Theological Seminary at Richmond). The rest are university- or college-based divinity schools (Wake Forest, Gardner-Webb, Hardin-Simmons, Baylor and Mercer). Wake Forest and Mercer are scheduled to open in the fall of 1996; the other four have already opened. Truett Theological Seminary at Baylor has identified itself as an evangelical school; the identities of the others are not yet clear.

[6]See, for example, "A Bibliography of Theological Education," *Theological Education* 30, no. 2 (1994): 89-98, which includes very little that is directed at evangelical theological education.

all evangelicals, despite their differences, bear a certain "family resemblance."[7]

Defining "evangelical." Although this study cannot resolve evangelicalism's definition problems, it needs a working definition of the term. George Marsden observes that the term *evangelical* has been used in three ways.[8] First and most broadly, *evangelical* is a conceptual category that applies to all who adhere to certain foundational beliefs: the inspiration and final authority of the Bible, eternal salvation only through faith in Christ, a serious commitment to evangelism and missions, the necessity of personal conversion and a spiritually transformed life. Most evangelicals arrive at these convictions through the Protestant Reformation. Others say they come to them more directly, by restoring or returning to the apostolic teachings of the Bible.

Second, *evangelical* is a label applied to a broadly based but quite diverse historical movement made up of many different denominations with similar roots and tendencies. This revivalistic, popular or democratic evangelicalism includes all groups shaped by the revivals of the eighteenth and nineteenth centuries, the various attempts to reproduce New Testament Christianity, and a democratic or even populist religious ethos. A mosaic of denominationally distinct evangelicals (Methodists, black Christians, Southern Baptists, holiness groups, Pentecostals, restorationists and the like) went their own way institutionally and theologically but over time developed similar styles of hymnody, personal piety, evangelistic techniques and worship. Sometimes this kind of evangelicalism accommodated itself to American culture by stressing individualism and following popular intellectual fashions. Occasionally it took a more countercultural stance.

Third, and most narrowly, *evangelical* refers to a self-conscious transdenominational community. In the early 1800s, transdenominational or coalition evangelicalism took shape as an "assemblage of independent agencies and their supporters, plus some denominationally-sponsored seminaries and colleges which support[ed] such parachurch institutions."[9] The "evangelical united front" of voluntary religious and political agencies set out to Christianize America. By the end of the century the network included cooperative revivals, missionary, educational and publication societies, and a string of colleges and Bible institutes in which evangelicals from many traditions worked together and derived their primary (though not exclusive) identity.

---

[7] For a good example of the difficulty in finding a generic definition of the word *evangelical*, see Donald W. Dayton and Robert K. Johnston, eds., *The Variety of American Evangelicalism* (Knoxville: University of Tennessee Press, 1991).

[8] Most of what follows is taken from three sources: George Marsden, "Introduction: The Evangelical Denomination," in *Evangelicalism and Modern America*, ed. George Marsden (Grand Rapids: Eerdmans, 1984), pp. vii-xiv; George M. Marsden, *Understanding Fundamentalism and Evangelicalism* (Grand Rapids: Eerdmans, 1991); George M. Marsden, *Reforming Fundamentalism: Fuller Seminary and the New Evangelicalism* (Grand Rapids: Eerdmans, 1987).

[9] Marsden, "Introduction," p. xii.

These three kinds of evangelicals responded differently to the rise of theological liberalism in the early twentieth century.[10] Many who had been influenced by dispensationalism organized a militant and separatistic fundamentalist movement to stem the modernist tide. By the 1930s, a large part of the transdenominational coalition had assumed this oppositional style. After World War II, however, a group of second-generation fundamentalists called for a "new evangelicalism" to reverse what they considered the needless marginalization of traditional faith. They felt they could better capture America for Christ by rejecting the old fundamentalism's combativeness and cautiously (and sometimes selectively) entering the world of modern scholarship. In time the fundamentalist and new evangelical wings of the coalition pulled apart. Militant fundamentalists condemned evangelical leaders like Billy Graham, the symbolic head of the new movement, for being too cooperative and compromising. Eventually many who had eagerly participated in the early reform of fundamentalism worried about how civil and scholarly the new evangelicalism should be. Since the 1970s, "card-carrying evangelicals" (as Marsden calls the new evangelical coalition) have battled each other over the cognitive limits of their movement and the nature of "true" evangelicalism.[11]

All seventy-nine of the schools on our list can be identified as evangelical in one of the three ways (conceptual, historical or transdenominational). Some institutions are clearly conceptual (for example, Missouri Synod Lutheran, Mennonite and "old school" Reformed). They have broadly defined evangelical beliefs, but for ethnic, cultural, theological or "churchly" reasons they have never fully identified with either the revivalistic evangelical movement or the transdenominational coalition.[12] Others reflect variations within popular evangelicalism (for example, Nazarene, Southern Baptist, restorationist, Pentecostal and so on). They have common roots in nineteenth-century revivalism and have felt the influence of post-World War II "card-carrying" evangelicals. Yet they remain fiercely denominational (even sectar-

---

[10]Some historians have argued that the American evangelical response to modernity was much more complicated than the prevailing "two-party paradigm" in American religious historiography allows. Despite the widespread practice of understanding American religious history in terms of opposing groups (for example, public vs. private, fundamentalist vs. modernist, conservative vs. liberal, evangelical vs. mainline), twentieth-century American evangelical religion was much more complicated, with many evangelicals occupying a middle position between extremes. See Douglas Jacobsen and William Vance Trollinger Jr., "Historiography of American Protestantism: The Two-Party Paradigm and Beyond," *Fides et Historia* 25 (Fall 1993): 4-15.

[11]Timothy P. Weber, "Fundamentalism Twice Removed: The Emergence and Shape of Progressive Evangelicalism," in *New Dimensions in American Religious History*, ed. Jay P. Dolan and James P. Wind (Grand Rapids: Eerdmans, 1993), pp. 261-87.

[12]In fact, Old School Presbyterians aggressively opposed most forms of populist evangelicalism during the nineteenth century. It is therefore ironic that their scholastic approach to theology came to dominate so much of twentieth-century fundamentalism and "new evangelicalism." Resistance to the "presbyterian paradigm" (Dayton) underlies much of the current controversy over evangelical identity.

ian) and work hard to maintain their own identities. Still other schools function primarily within the transdenominational coalition. Most of these institutions are interdenominational, but some have denominational connections. In other words, while all of the schools on our list can be defined as evangelical, they do not represent the same brand of evangelicalism.

Denominational and theological identities. No matter how hard the term *evangelical* is to define, many people in theological education today still want to apply it to themselves. Thus one answer to the question, What is an evangelical theological school? is to examine the particular institutions that claim to be evangelical.

This approach also has its difficulties. To do it justice requires following evangelical schools over time through their individual histories, which goes far beyond the scope of this modest study. However, examining the catalogs of evangelical institutions provides basic but important information about what the term means in specific settings. After all, school catalogs are informational and marketing documents. In addition to containing course descriptions and degree requirements, they project a certain public image in hopes of attracting a particular clientele.

What does reading academic catalogs tell us about the identity of these schools? At first glance, it seems that evangelical theological education is mostly *denominational*. Nearly three out of four evangelical institutions (57 of 79) are directly tied to forty-one different denominations.[13] (See appendix two for a list of denominations sponsoring evangelical schools.)

Ever since its emergence in the First Great Awakening,[14] evangelical religion has contained both unifying and divisive elements. The powerful experience of the new birth, from which developed a distinctive understanding of the Christian life, often (but not always) broke down theological and denominational barriers.[15] Evangelicals in the nineteenth and twentieth centuries fought (sometimes bitterly) across denominational boundaries over issues of biblical interpretation, the nature of the church and its sacraments, the operation of the Holy Spirit in the believer's life, the usefulness of formal creeds, the role of women in the church and the relationship between divine sovereignty and human freedom. Not surprisingly, most evangelical schools today still retain these denominational divisions. Some schools are owned—and more or less operated—by their sponsoring bodies, while others maintain less structured and more complicated denominational relationships.

---

[13]Evangelical schools are *much less denominational* than those of the mainline Protestants. While 72 percent (57 of 79) of evangelical institutions are denominational, the figure for mainline Protestant schools is 81 percent (72 of 89).

[14]Harry S. Stout, *The Divine Dramatist: George Whitefield and the Rise of Modern Evangelicalism* (Grand Rapids: Eerdmans, 1991).

[15]For a study of how evangelicals forged new alliances and disrupted old ones, see Nathan O. Hatch, *The Democratization of American Christianity* (New Haven, Conn.: Yale University Press, 1989).

Here is the most obvious source of evangelical diversity. Very few schools market themselves as *merely evangelical*. Most position themselves within a particular evangelical tradition. For example, while the Assemblies of God Theological Seminary calls itself evangelical, its primary identity is Pentecostal: "The commitment to the Pentecostal dimension of Christianity is what distinguishes the Assemblies of God from other groups within Evangelical Christianity." Thus "Pentecostal distinctives are central to each of [AGTS's] degrees and course offerings."[16] Eastern Baptist Theological Seminary was founded in 1925 to conserve "the great historic evangelical beliefs" within a well-defined Northern (now American) Baptist framework. Emmanuel School of Religion "is committed to the lordship of Jesus Christ, to the authority of Scripture, and to the vision of Christian unity and faithfulness expressed in the work of such thinkers as Thomas and Alexander Campbell and Barton W. Stone."

The Reformed Presbyterian Theological Seminary is loyal to the inerrant Scriptures and the Westminster Standards. The Mennonite Brethren Biblical Seminary is "an evangelical, Anabaptist educational institution." Nazarene Theological Seminary "is committed to the Wesleyan-Arminian theological tradition, grounded on faith in Christ and on Scripture as understood within that tradition, with special emphasis on the doctrine of entire sanctification, which leads to holiness of heart and life." Trinity Episcopal School for Ministry affirms that the truths of "God's Word written . . . have been faithfully transmitted in the Apostles' and Nicene Creeds, faithfully interpreted in the 39 Articles of the Anglican Reformation and given liturgical expression in the Book of Common Prayer." Concordia Seminary believes that "the Book of Concord is a true and unadulterated statement and exposition of the Word of God." In other words, most institutions on our list are evangelical in distinctive and sometimes quite different ways.

To understand this aspect of evangelical theological education, it is best to think in terms of *denominational or theological families*, not just specific denominations. A careful culling of the list of seventy-nine evangelical schools suggests that all but a few can be identified with nine denominational or theological traditions: Anabaptist-Pietist (8), Anglican-Episcopalian (3), Baptist (19), Lutheran (4), Pentecostal-charismatic (4), Presbyterian-Reformed (11), restorationist (4) and Wesleyan-holiness (10). If we designate premillennial as a separate theological tradition, we can include an additional ten institutions that do not fit into any of the other categories. Thus we can account for 92 percent of evangelical schools. Only six schools remain "unaligned," though without too much difficulty we can place four of them in other categories. (See appendix three for evangelical schools according

---

[16]In this paragraph and throughout the article, unless otherwise cited, the quotation comes from the school's catalog.

to their denominational/theological families.)

Such groupings may suggest that evangelical schools exist in rather discrete or separate enclaves. To some extent, this is true. These institutions are not interchangeable just because they are labeled evangelical. Students attracted to Nazarene or Asbury or Alliance *because* they are holiness schools would never think of applying to Westminster or Reformed or Erskine. As a rule, evangelical restorationists do not attend Missouri Synod Lutheran schools like Concordia, no matter how "evangelical" they may be in relation to other Lutheran seminaries. And fundamentalist Baptists who believe that the timing of the rapture is a theological issue of first importance will avoid any school not committed to dispensational premillennialism. Thus a school's advertised identity attracts some potential students and repels others.

Nevertheless, many evangelicals tend to overlook such identity markers. While some schools are remarkably homogeneous (in Southern Baptist seminaries all faculty and over 90 percent of students are from the Southern Baptist Convention), others are remarkably diverse. Nearly all evangelical schools—whatever their family ties—welcome students from other denominations. At Northern Baptist, for example, nearly two-thirds (65 percent) of the students are not American Baptists.[17] At Trinity Evangelical Divinity School, only 13 percent of the students are from the Evangelical Free Church, with the rest coming from 122 other church groups.[18] Of course, such diversity is expected in the unaligned or nondenominational schools. Rather typical is Columbia Biblical Seminary, which draws students from twenty-two different denominations. Students and faculty at Fuller Seminary represent 108 different groups (Presbyterians, nondenominational and Pentecostal/charismatics being the three largest). Clearly, most schools are no more *merely denominational* than they are *merely evangelical.*

Evangelical theological institutions come from a wide range of Christian traditions. Though all of them share certain basic theological convictions and many come from denominations with similar histories, not all of them are part of the transdenominational coalition of "card-carrying" evangelicals. While many outsiders have a hard time telling evangelicals apart, insiders recognize that evangelical religion has its own separate territories with well-marked borders. Yet many other evangelicals do not view denominational connections as being decisive or important. While boundaries do exist, a large number of evangelicals act as if they did not.

The Origins of Accredited Evangelical Theological Education
The detailed history of evangelical theological education has never been writ-

---

[17]While 35 percent are American Baptist, another 22 percent belong to other Baptist denominations. By contrast, at Denver Conservative Baptist Seminary, which calls itself "an evangelical seminary in the Baptist tradition," only 30 percent of the students are Baptists of any kind.

[18]Timothy C. Morgan, "Re-engineering the Seminary," *Christianity Today,* October 24, 1995, p. 75.

ten.[19] Nearly all of the theological institutions founded by Protestants in the nineteenth century were evangelical in one of the three ways described above. They were of various kinds and qualities. Many were rather informal, nondegree-granting institutions. Some were training schools for Christian workers where laypersons and aspiring clergy with or without college degrees could receive a practical education in a variety of religious subjects. Some schools started out as Bible institutes or as Bible departments in undergraduate colleges, then progressed over time to graduate-level status.[20] A few schools serving immigrant churches began as "foreign language departments" in established seminaries before striking out on their own. Others were started from scratch to serve the needs of a particular denomination or a theological party within a denomination. Still others were offshoots of existing evangelical institutions no longer considered suitable.

The revolution in evangelical theological education. Many, but not all, of these nineteenth-century institutions were caught up in the revolution in American higher education after the Civil War.[21] Some theological schools, especially those with ties to the newer universities, wanted to attain academic respectability in their own right.[22] With the quest for higher academic standards invariably came an openness to the latest critical scholarship of the Bible, theology and church history as well as an interest in comparative religions and the emerging social sciences. In short, rising scholarly aspirations often resulted in new and more complicated theological identities.[23]

In the 1880s and 1890s, the theological dividing lines within schools and denominations were anything but clear. The evangelical tradition was still strong, but in some places it was undergoing modifications in light of the new learning. In a few schools conservatives put more liberal faculty members on trial for heresy, but in most institutions the differences between conservatives and liberals were not always so obvious.

By World War I, however, the differences were plain to everybody, although some liberals still valued the evangelical label and refused to surrender it to more

---

[19]Good histories have been written about parts of it, to be sure: Glenn T. Miller, *Piety and Intellect: The Aims and Purposes of Ante-bellum Theological Education* (Atlanta: Scholars Press, 1990); James W. Fraser, *Schooling the Preachers: The Development of Protestant Theological Education in the United States, 1740-1875* (Lanham, Md.: University Press of America, 1988).

[20]Virginia Lieson Brereton, *Training God's Army: The American Bible School, 1880-1940* (Bloomington: Indiana University Press, 1990).

[21]George M. Marsden, *The Soul of the American University: From Protestant Establishment to Established Unbelief* (New York: Oxford University Press, 1994); George M. Marsden and Bradley J. Longfield, eds., *The Secularization of the Academy* (New York: Oxford University Press, 1992).

[22]Conrad Cherry, *Hurrying Toward Zion: Universities, Divinity Schools and American Protestantism* (Bloomington: Indiana University Press, 1995).

[23]William Hutchison, *The Modernist Impulse in American Protestantism* (New York: Oxford University Press, 1982).

conservative Protestants. For example, at the height of the fundamentalist-modernist controversy in the 1920s, leading liberals like Shailer Mathews, Harry Emerson Fosdick and Henry Sloane Coffin insisted that they were evangelicals too. "Modernist" schools like the University of Chicago Divinity School, Union Theological Seminary in New York and Yale Divinity School continued to offer a full slate of courses in missions and evangelism.[24]

Most of the seventy-nine evangelical schools currently in ATS were founded in the twentieth century. Why did evangelicals build their own schools? In general, they established them for the same reasons that motivated the pioneers of theological education in the early nineteenth century: existing schools were not teaching the right theology, schools were too far away to meet local needs, and small denominations wanted a theological school to call their own.[25]

While a number of twentieth-century evangelical institutions fell into the last category, schools founded by small denominations that wanted their own seminary, most of those established after World War I were protest schools. Probably more than anything else, theological controversy was the fertilizer for growing new institutions. As destructive as the fundamentalist-modernist controversy was to the peace of the churches, it created a strong school-building impulse. Conservative Presbyterians started Westminster because the General Assembly reorganized Princeton along more inclusive lines; fundamentalists founded Eastern Baptist because they believed that existing denominational seminaries in the East were too liberal; some evangelical Methodists organized Wesley Biblical Seminary because in their view no other institution in the Deep South adequately promoted evangelical Wesleyan convictions. Evangelicals started new schools when they decided that existing schools were no longer sufficiently evangelical. But sometimes evangelicals founded new schools because they were unable to resolve theological or interpersonal disputes within their own institutions. For example, from Princeton came Westminster, from Westminster came Covenant, and from Covenant came Biblical.[26]

As evangelicalism itself diversified, new schools staked out new territory. In 1947 "reforming fundamentalists" founded Fuller Theological Seminary to promote the agenda of the more moderate "new evangelicalism," though at times the lines between the old fundamentalism and the new evangelicalism were hard to locate in the seminary's early days.[27] Colorado Conservative Baptists organized Denver

---

[24]One suspects that the content of such courses was much different from that being taught in more traditional institutions; but the fact that liberal schools still taught them demonstrates how deep their evangelical roots went. See Robert L. Kelly, *Theological Education in America: A Study of 161 Theological Schools in the United States and Canada* (New York: George Doran, 1924), pp. 425-29.

[25]For an analysis of early-nineteenth-century theological education, see Miller, *Piety and Intellect.*

[26]See Harold J. Ockenga, "From Fundamentalism, Through New Evangelicalism, to Evangelicalism," in *Evangelical Roots*, ed. Kenneth Kantzer (Nashville: Thomas Nelson, 1978), p. 42.

[27]Marsden, *Reforming Fundamentalism.*

Seminary in 1950 and positioned it between Northern Baptist liberals and separatistic fundamentalists. According to an old promotional blurb, "Here is no unanchored liberalism—freedom to think without commitment. Here is no encrusted dogmatism—commitment without freedom to think. Here is a vibrant evangelicalism—commitment with freedom to think within the limits laid down in Scripture." Southern Baptist "moderates," many of whom could easily qualify as evangelicals in other contexts, have started six new schools since 1990 because in their view Southern Baptist Convention seminaries had moved too far to the theological and political right. Regent College in Vancouver was founded to promote lay ministry and spiritual formation, emphases early supporters believed were neglected in other evangelical institutions.

Seeking accreditation. Why did evangelical schools want to be accredited? At first, few seemed all that interested—or qualified. In the mid-1930s thirty-eight "elite" theological schools formed an accrediting agency for institutions that offered authentic graduate-level instruction. Though most of the charter schools accredited in 1938 by what was then called the American Association of Theological Schools would have considered themselves connected in some way to the evangelical tradition, only one of them, the Southern Baptist Theological Seminary, makes the list of seventy-nine evangelical institutions today. The remaining thirty-seven schools were already what we now call mainline Protestant.

For many schools, the road to accreditation was long and hard. While some evangelicals (Anglican, Reformed and Lutheran) have long-standing intellectual traditions, others (Anabaptist, pietist, Baptist, holiness, Pentecostal) have emphasized Christian living over the life of the mind.[28] Likewise, some revivalist evangelicals have wondered why God-called ministers need any formal theological education at all or have considered Bible institute training more than adequate. In other cases theological separatism kept evangelicals sequestered behind the high walls of the fundamentalist subculture.

Eventually most evangelical schools wanted to be accredited. Reasons varied and each institution had its own story to tell. But in general, evangelicals wanted the respect that came with accredited degrees. A number of market forces pushed evangelical schools in this direction. As their educational levels rose after World War II and more evangelicals entered the professions, it was only natural for laypeople to expect higher educational standards of their ministers, who for their own reasons wanted to be seen as professionals. Thus a broad-based process of professionalization nudged schools toward seeking accreditation.

In order to renew the mainline churches, which was a goal of the new evangelical

---

[28]For a forceful critique of evangelical intellectual life, see Mark A. Noll, *The Scandal of the Evangelical Mind* (Grand Rapids: Eerdmans, 1994).

program, aspiring reformers needed comparable academic credentials. As more evangelicals pursued doctor's degrees in religion in the forties and fifties,[29] they quickly discovered how difficult it was to get into good graduate schools without an accredited seminary degree. In short, if evangelicals were going to play in the larger academic and religious game, their schools needed to be recognized by the educational establishment. Students clearly wanted accredited degrees. Schools that demurred had a hard time competing with institutions that advertised their new accredited status.

Fundamental to the mainstreaming of evangelical theological education, then, was evangelicals' changing view of themselves, particularly in relation to the broader culture. After decades of feeling marginalized in their own society, many evangelicals longed for a more respected role in American life.[30] Sometimes they used their improving economic status to wedge their way into the dominant culture or, as in the last decade or two, they resorted to politics. At other times the point of entry was education. When evangelicals finally understood that being accredited was a recognition of educational quality and not a sign of theological compromise, they were able to overcome even those barriers erected by theological separatism in schools like Talbot, Multnomah, Biblical, Liberty and Dallas.

Thus the accrediting of evangelical schools marks the mainstreaming of evangelical theological education. In its first twenty years, ATS grew to seventy-five accredited schools, including sixty-three mainline Protestant and twelve evangelical.[31] The real turning point for evangelical schools in ATS came in the 1960s, when the number of evangelical institutions doubled to twenty-four and Roman Catholics began joining the ATS for the first time.[32] The list of accredited evangelical schools has grown steadily ever since, at about twice the rate of mainline Protestants. Evangelicals added twelve new schools in the 1970s, ten in the 1980s, and in the first half of the 1990s eleven more (plus eight candidates for accreditation and twelve associate members). In other words, of the fifty-nine fully accredited evangelical schools, 81 percent were admitted after 1960, in contrast to 100 percent of the

---

[29]It was not uncommon in the early days of the new evangelical movement for scholars to earn *two* doctorates, one from an unaccredited evangelical school and another from an accredited university or divinity school. This attempt to find respectability in two different worlds can be seen among faculty at places as different as Fuller and Dallas during the 1950s and 1960s. The double doctorates have declined, though a few evangelicals still expend the effort.

[30]James Davison Hunter, *American Evangelicalism: Conservative Religion and the Quandary of Modernity* (New Brunswick, N.J.: Rutgers University Press, 1983).

[31]Mainline Protestant growth in ATS was as follows: thirty-seven in the 1930s, fifteen in the 1940s, nine in the 1950s, seven in the 1960s, seven in the 1970s, six in the 1980s, and none fully accredited so far in the 1990s (although there are two candidates for accreditation and six associate member schools).

[32]Five Roman Catholic schools were accredited in the 1960s, thirty-three in the 1970s, nine in the 1980s and four so far in the 1990s (plus one candidate for accreditation and five associate members).

Catholic schools and only 31 percent of mainline Protestant schools.[33] (See appendix four for a listing of when evangelical schools became accredited.)

Of the seventy-nine evangelical schools, eleven are in Canada and sixty-eight are in the United States. Of the Canadian schools, four are in the western provinces,[34] three in the central provinces[35] and four in the eastern provinces.[36] In the United States the heaviest concentration is located east of the Mississippi River. There are twelve evangelical schools in the East,[37] twenty-two in the Middle West,[38] seventeen in the South,[39] five in the Southwest,[40] one in the Mountain States[41] and eleven in the West.[42]

ATS has changed substantially over the last three decades. With the influx of evangelical and Roman Catholic institutions, the demographics of the association have shifted. At present, evangelical and Roman Catholic schools together make up 60 percent of ATS-affiliated institutions and have 62 percent of the students. Mainline Protestant schools, which dominated ATS for its first forty years, now make up only 40 percent of member schools and 38 percent of the students.

Comparing Evangelical Schools with Other ATS Schools

One way to understand evangelical theological schools is to compare them to other ATS institutions in four areas: ethos, enrollments, faculty and governance.

Ethos. Like individuals, educational institutions have their own personalities. Every school has an ethos, or corporate culture, consisting of how it understands its past, the way it does things educationally and administratively, its complex web of internal and external relationships, and the expectations and assumptions (published and unpublished) that govern personal and group behavior. An institution's

---

[33]It is also instructive to compare how long it took schools from the three groups to achieve full accreditation once they joined ATS. The average mainline Protestant school affiliated with ATS in 1948 and received full accreditation in 1961. For evangelical schools, the averages are 1968 and 1973; for Catholics, 1970 and 1975. This means that the typical evangelical and Catholic schools were accredited only five years after joining ATS, while it took the average mainline Protestant school thirteen years. These differences are mostly due to the aggressive advocacy of ATS's executive director Jesse Ziegler during the sixties. See Jesse H. Ziegler, *ATS Through Two Decades: Reflections on Theological Education, 1960-1980* (Vandalia, Ohio: privately printed, 1984).

[34]Two in British Columbia and one in Alberta.

[35]Two in Saskatchewan and one in Manitoba.

[36]Three in Ontario and one in Nova Scotia.

[37]One in Massachusetts, one in New York, nine in Pennsylvania and one in Maryland.

[38]Three in Ohio, three in Michigan, three in Indiana, four in Illinois, one in Iowa, one in Minnesota, one in South Dakota and six in Missouri.

[39]Three in Virginia, two in North Carolina, two in South Carolina, two in Kentucky, four in Tennessee, one in Alabama, two in Mississippi and one in Louisiana.

[40]Four in Texas and one in Oklahoma.

[41]Colorado.

[42]Eight in California and three in Oregon.

ethos is also shaped by the larger religious culture in which it is located.

As we have already seen, American evangelical religion is made up of many distinct denominational/theological families. Each has its own history, list of heroes and heroines, special code language, and even insider jokes and stories that outsiders do not know or fully understand. Therefore, for a variety of historical and theological reasons, the campus ethos at Oral Roberts differs from the one at Calvin or Eastern Mennonite or Golden Gate Baptist. Even within the same denominational family, there may be many significant regional differences, as a comparison of Northern and Southern Baptists, Methodists and Presbyterians will attest.[43]

Nevertheless, these distinctive family groups are part of a much larger extended family culture, over two hundred years in the making, that enables one kind of evangelical to recognize another.[44] Most evangelicals tend to pray the same way, sing the same songs, care about the same things and describe their religious lives in the same terms. In addition to the many "local dialects" spoken in particular family groups, there is a lingua franca among evangelicals that allows communication between families. One learns to "speak evangelical" by living in the evangelical popular culture—by listening to evangelical preaching, attending Bible studies and prayer groups, participating in a parachurch organization, listening to Christian music, singing hymns and choruses, tuning in to evangelical radio and television programs, patronizing a Christian bookstore—or attending an evangelical school.[45] This popular culture exists to support and perpetuate evangelical religious life: repentance, personal commitment to Jesus Christ as Lord and Savior, prayer, witnessing, Bible reading, fellowship, occasional bouts of guilt, and the personal awareness of having one's sins forgiven and being a child of God. Though these elements may be packaged differently from one evangelical family to another,[46]

---

[43]For example, when I moved from Denver Conservative Baptist Seminary to Southern Baptist Theological Seminary in Louisville, I discovered that leaders or popular authors in one place were virtually unknown in the other. See Timothy P. Weber, "Evangelicalism North and South," *Review and Expositor* 92 (Summer 1995): 299-317.

[44]Barbara G. Wheeler, "You Who Were Far Off: Religious Divisions and the Role of Religious Research," H. Paul Douglass Lecture, Religious Research Association, 1995.

[45]See, for example, Grant Wacker, "Searching for Norman Rockwell: Popular Evangelicalism in Contemporary America," in *The Evangelical Tradition in America*, ed. Leonard I. Sweet (Macon, Ga.: Mercer University Press, 1984), pp. 289-315; Nathan Hatch, "Evangelicalism as a Democratic Movement," in *Evangelicalism and Modern America*, ed. George Marsden (Grand Rapids: Eerdmans, 1984), pp. 71-82; Patricia Klein et al., *Growing Up Born Again: A Whimsical Look at the Blessings and Tribulations of Growing Up Born Again* (Old Tappan, N.J.: Power Books, 1987); Quentin J. Schultze, ed., *American Evangelicals and the Mass Media* (Grand Rapids: Zondervan, 1990); R. Laurence Moore, *Selling God: American Religion in the Marketplace* (New York: Oxford University Press, 1994), esp. pp. 238-65.

[46]To examine how the evangelical culture is expressed in specific groups, see Nancy Ammerman, *Bible Believers: Fundamentalists in the Modern World* (New Brunswick, N.J.: Rutgers University Press, 1987); Randall Balmer, *Mine Eyes Have Seen the Glory: A Journey into the Evangelical Sub-culture in America*

together they constitute a generic evangelical ethos.[47]

What does examining the catalogs of evangelical schools tell us about their ethos? For one thing, evangelicals put a lot of stress on doctrine. Two-thirds of the evangelical institutions in ATS print some kind of doctrinal statement in their academic catalogs. Some are brief: North Park's "credal basis" consists of two items—new life in Christ and the Bible as the authoritative Word of God. Others are much longer: Dallas's doctrinal statement is five pages long, double columns. Many schools are committed to the doctrinal standards of their supporting denominations, while others have statements of their own devising. Schools without a published statement usually recount their histories in such a way that no one can miss the institution's doctrinal orientation.

Evangelical schools take these theological statements quite seriously. Certain institutions allow faculty some flexibility within the standards, but others require faculty to affirm them "without mental reservation." At Westminster, for example, at the time of their election, faculty pledge that they "believe the Scriptures of the Old and New Testaments to be the Word of God, the only infallible rule of faith and practice," and that they subscribe to the Westminster Confession of Faith. At Eastern Baptist, all administrators and professors affirm annually the seminary's doctrinal Basis, though non-Baptists are exempt from the statements on baptism and the nature of the church. Even Fuller, probably the most progressive evangelical school, requires that "the ultimate positions of faculty members not be at variance with the basic theological stance of the community as set forth in the Statement of Faith and other official statements."

Why are evangelical schools so concerned about stating their theology and then sticking to it? There are probably two reasons, one epistemological and one historical. Evangelicals believe that the Christian faith has a definable content. The Bible is God's self-disclosure and is meant to be understood and believed. Thus spelling out clearly what the Bible teaches is one way of affirming its authority and honoring the Christian tradition. Similarly, many evangelicals have painful memories of "losing" institutions because their theological identities were allowed to change over time. When they founded their own schools, most evangelicals insisted that doctrinal boundaries be clearly drawn and strenuously monitored.

What characterizes these doctrinal statements? Though all evangelicals are

---

(New York: Oxford University Press, 1989); Kathleen C. Boone, *The Bible Tells Them So: The Discourse of Protestant Fundamentalism* (Albany: State University Press of New York Press, 1988); Alan Peshkin, *God's Choice: The Total World of a Fundamentalist Christian School* (Chicago: University of Chicago Press, 1986).

[47]Stephen Land's observations about Pentecostal spirituality also apply to the entire evangelical movement: religious movements consist of three dimensions—doctrine (orthodoxy), behavior (orthopraxy), and piety or passion (orthopathy). See Stephen J. Land, *Pentecostal Spirituality: A Passion for the Kingdom* (Sheffield, U.K.: Sheffield Academic Press, 1993).

committed to biblical authority, their attitudes toward *theological orthodoxy* vary widely. From the movement's inception, some evangelicals have fiercely defended orthodoxy, while others have viewed it as the refuge of dead and abusive religion.[48] In nineteenth-century Presbyterianism, for instance, Old School evangelicals frequently charged New School evangelicals with heresy because in promoting revivals they departed from the details of creedal Calvinism.[49] In more recent times, defenders of Reformed orthodoxy continue to polemicize against other evangelicals—fundamentalists, dispensationalists, Arminians, Pentecostals and charismatics—for not living up to their intellectual and orthodox standards.[50] In both past and present, one group of evangelicals has wielded orthodoxy as a club against other groups.

Where do such competing views of orthodoxy come from? Some evangelicals identify with the magisterial Reformation's emphasis on correct doctrine. Others prefer the radical Reformation's stress on discipleship or pietism's repudiation of "dead orthodoxy" and insistence on conversion or restorationism's rejection of any doctrinal formula not explicitly found in the Bible.

These competing perspectives help to explain why some evangelicals always seem to start with doctrine and eventually get around to experience, while others start with experience and eventually get around to doctrine. Nevertheless, no matter where they begin, both groups end up in pretty much the same place. All evangelicals more or less affirm the *doctrinal content* of historic Christianity—as seen through their particular "family" lenses. In this sense they are much closer to Roman Catholic institutions than to most mainline Protestant institutions, where requiring faculty to subscribe to confessions or well-defined traditions is uncommon.[51]

Though their doctrinal statements are generally similar, it must be noted that all evangelical schools exist along a theological spectrum. There is an evangelical left, center and right based on attitudes toward critical scholarship, openness to new ideas, willingness to allow some dissent, relationships with other religious traditions, and stance on various social and political issues. As a result, many evangelical schools call themselves separatist, conservative, orthodox, progressive or ecumenical (even

---

[48]Hatch, *The Democratization of American Christianity.*

[49]For an example of an "orthodox and Reformed" reading of evangelical history, see Iain H. Murray, *Revival and Revivalism: The Making and Marring of American Evangelicalism, 1750-1858* (Edinburgh: The Banner of Truth Trust, 1994).

[50]See especially David Wells, *No Place for Truth: Or, Whatever Happened to Evangelical Theology?* (Grand Rapids: Eerdmans, 1993), then compare another Reformed theologian's plea for a "hermeneutic of charity" in Richard Mouw, *Consulting the Faithful: What Christian Intellectuals Can Learn from Popular Religion* (Grand Rapids: Eerdmans, 1994).

[51]For an intriguing analysis of how fundamentalism compares with historic Christian orthodoxy, see Jaroslav Pelikan, "Fundamentalism and/or Orthodoxy: Toward an Understanding of the Fundamentalist Phenomenon," in *The Fundamentalist Phenomenon*, ed. Norman J. Cohen (Grand Rapids: Eerdmans, 1990), pp. 3-21.

mainline) to indicate their ethos. To a large extent, where a school positions itself along the spectrum determines what kind of corporate culture it has and what kind of students it hopes to attract.

One of the most striking things about these doctrinal statements is their stress on biblical inspiration and authority. Evangelicals, it is safe to say, like to think they are more biblical than everyone else. While others appear to question the Bible's authority or historical reliability, evangelicals stay loyal to the book even when they cannot agree on what it teaches. The motto of Ashland Theological Seminary captures this kind of ultimate allegiance characteristic of evangelical schools: "The Bible, the whole Bible, and nothing but the Bible." Evangelicals claim to make "the Word" the center of their concerns.

Not all evangelical schools, however, articulate their doctrine of Scripture in exactly the same way. Even after the intense and well-publicized "battle for the Bible" during the 1970s, when many argued that all *real* evangelicals believed in biblical inerrancy, not all evangelical schools—or denominational/family traditions—used inerrancy language in their doctrinal statements. Typical of most that do is the statement of Alliance Theological Seminary: "The Old and New Testaments, inerrant as originally given, were verbally inspired by God and are a complete revelation of His will for the salvation of man. They constitute the divine and only rule of Christian faith and practice."

But other evangelical schools make no mention of the inerrancy of the original autographs. Northern Baptist's statement of faith is rather simple: "The Bible is the revealed Word of God, given by the Holy Spirit through chosen men, and so is fully inspired, authoritative, and the sufficient rule of faith and practice for the believer." Though the precise language may vary, all evangelicals maintain a high view of biblical authority and inspiration. What they believe about Scripture is well summarized in the basis of agreement of the Associated Canadian Theological Schools (a consortium of Baptist and Evangelical Free Church schools in British Columbia): "Whatever terms are used, whether 'infallible' as in the 16th century, or 'verbal' and 'plenary' as in the 19th century, or 'inerrant' now, what has been meant has always been exactly the same, the Holy Scriptures alone are fully authoritative and fully trustworthy as the very Word of God written."

Evangelical schools as a whole seek to regulate the personal behavior of their students in ways that are unheard of in mainline Protestant and Catholic schools. Just under half of the academic catalogs of ATS-affiliated evangelical schools contain statements about personal conduct. Many others refer readers to student handbooks for such standards. Given their emphasis on conversion as the real starting point of the Christian life, evangelicals believe that born-again persons should live transformed lives: thus the concern for "Christian lifestyles" and codes of behavior. When they get specific, as most of them do, the standards almost always forbid tobacco, alcohol, illegal drugs and illicit sex. Sometimes the codes get quite explicit about the latter: all premarital, extramarital and homosexual sex is condemned. Some schools also seek to regulate certain amusements like dancing and gambling and suggest caution in choosing movies, theater, television and music. A few institutions publish rather detailed dress codes to insure appropriate attire in the classroom, library, cafeteria and other public places on campus.[52]

The existence of such behavior codes may strike many people as quaint holdovers from nineteenth-century revivalist culture. Nothing comparable is found in mainline Protestant or Roman Catholic institutions, though they too have their own highly prescriptive—but rarely published—behavioral or attitudinal expectations. Most evangelical schools maintain such codes out of conviction or for the sake of their supporting constituencies. Of course, publishing dress and behavior codes is one thing and enforcing them is another. Many evangelical institutions increasingly find acting *in loco parentis* difficult when students in the 1990s are so much older than they used to be—and live off campus. Furthermore, a recent study indicates that evangelical students view such matters quite differently than their parents did and may not be conforming to traditional evangelical mores.[53]

In the future more evangelical schools will probably take Biblical Theological Seminary's approach. Though its commitments to premillennialism, the Westminster Confession and theological separatism make it one of the most conservative schools in the ATS, Biblical has decided to take another approach: "Students are expected to dress and conduct themselves as befits servants of Christ. Students are also adults who should have internalized biblical standards of behavior before reaching seminary. Biblical does not therefore delimit proper behavior for students or staff."[54]

Finally, perusal of academic catalogs reveals that most evangelical schools demonstrate some entrepreneurial spirit, which is expressed through strange blends of innovation and tradition. Unlike many mainline Protestant seminaries with long-standing ties to universities or other educational establishments, a large segment of evangelical schools have histories of institutional independence that allowed them freedom to do things their own way. As a result, evangelical schools

---

[52]It is important to note the variations within evangelicalism on certain behavioral issues. Some churches with European roots (for example, Missouri Synod Lutherans and Christian Reformed) have few scruples about the moderate use of alcohol, and some evangelicals in tobacco-growing regions of the South see nothing wrong with smoking.

[53]See James Davison Hunter, *Evangelicalism: The Coming Generation* (Chicago: University of Chicago Press, 1987), pp. 50-75. Hunter surveyed students in sixteen evangelical institutions of higher learning (including seven seminaries) and found, among other things, that behavior patterns among evangelical young people are much different from those of their parents.

[54]This "progressive" approach may reflect the legal liability that schools assume when they declare their intention to regulate the behavior of their students.

can sometimes appear to outsiders as overly experimental or even quirky. While they teach something like "that old-time religion," they are quick to start new specialized degree programs, build extension centers hundreds of miles from home base and use the latest electronic delivery systems.[55] This is because most evangelicals like to think and act in missional terms, which leads to a pragmatic and entrepreneurial approach. Of course, many evangelical schools are innovative because they have to be. With small endowments and little support from small sponsoring denominations, many institutions rely almost totally on tuition and gift income. Unless they constantly locate new student markets, most schools will not survive.[56]

Enrollment. Evangelical schools tend to be larger than mainline Protestant and Catholic institutions. According to FTEs, the average evangelical school enrolls 314 students, the average mainline Protestant school 200, and the average Catholic school 107.[57] According to total head count, evangelicals average 452, mainline Protestants 260 and Catholics 143.

According to table 1 (below),[58] not all evangelical schools are huge. Though the largest ATS institutions are all evangelical (four over 1,000 in FTE, six over 1,000 in total headcount), most evangelical schools are not nearly as large. Almost half have FTEs of under 150 students; and 85 percent have FTEs under 500. According to the figures for total head count, 29 percent of evangelical schools have fewer than 150 students; and 74 percent have fewer than 500.

Number of Students	Total Headcount		FTE	
	Schools	%	Schools	%
1-75	4	5%	17	22%
76-150	20	25%	22	28%
151-300	26	33%	13	16%
301-500	9	11%	15	19%
501-1000	14	18%	8	10%
1000+	6*	8%	4**	5%

*Southwestern Baptist (3,458), Fuller (2,968), Southern Baptist (1,921), Trinity Evangelical Divinity School (1,710), Dallas (1221) and New Orleans Baptist (1,102).
**Southwestern Baptist (2,569), Fuller (2,080), Trinity Evangelical Divinity School (1,510), Southern Baptist (1,335).

Table 1. Enrollments in evangelical schools (1993)

[55] Robert W. Ferris, *Renewal in Theological Education: Strategies for Change* (Wheaton, Ill.: Billy Graham Center, 1990).
[56] Evangelical schools are also starting to feel pressure from some of the megachurches, which are experimenting with their own church-based theological education.
[57] Based on the figures available in the ATS directory for 1993-1994.
[58] Figures are based on the ATS directory for 1994-1995, published as *Bulletin 41*, pt. 4.

Faculty. Comparing faculties also reveals some important differences. In 1993, the average evangelical school employed 15.2 full-time faculty, the average mainline Protestant 12.6 and the average Catholic 11.2, which translates into full-time faculty to student ratios of 1:20.6 in evangelical schools, 1:15.8 in mainline Protestant and 1:9.5 in Catholic.

Evangelical institutions allocate their faculty differently from other schools. When all ATS faculty are broken down according to teaching fields (see table 2), the differences between evangelical, mainline Protestant and Catholic schools are revealing. Evangelicals employ a higher percentage of biblical specialists and a much larger contingent of teachers in the practical fields, where students are taught to use the Bible in teaching, preaching, evangelism and missions.

	Mainline	Evangelical	Catholic
Bible	22.9%	27.0%	18.3%
Theology	12.3	11.1	24.7
Ethics	7.2	2.2	11.5
History	13.3	8.9	8.9
Practics	26.5	36.6	20.3
Education	4.8	8.2	1.7
Human science	2.8	.6	.1
Religion	3.0	.2	.7
Formation	1.0	1.0	4.9
Area studies	.8	.7	.4
Arts	3.3	.5	6.8
Tools	1.5	1.5	.7
Other	.6	1.4	.7

Table 2.   Allocation of faculty by teaching fields (by percentages)

There are a few surprises as well. For example, why do evangelicals, who put so much emphasis on *behavior,* have so few ethicists on their faculties? Possibly evangelicals assume that by stressing biblical authority (the rule of faith and *practice*), such issues are covered as a matter of course. Or perhaps as theological schools began adding ethics professors to their faculties (roughly 1925 to 1945), evangelicals were out of the educational mainstream.

During the 1980s ATS encouraged member schools to consider the importance of diversity in hiring new faculty. How, then, do schools compare in terms of age, race and gender? As of 1992, the average age of faculty serving in ATS member schools was 51.7 years. The difference between the three groups was as follows: faculty in evangelical schools, 51.64 years; mainline Protestant, 52.34; and Catholic, 50.63. Though these figures seem fairly close, the differences are important for purposes of faculty retirement and replacement.

According to a 1991 study of all faculty in ATS (table 3), evangelical schools are, on average, slightly more racially diverse in their faculties than Catholic schools, but considerably less diverse than mainline Protestant institutions.

	Asian	Black	Hispanic	Indian	White
Evangelical	1.5	1.9	1.4	.1	94.9
Mainline	2.2	9.0	1.7	.2	86.4
Catholic	.9	.9	2.5	—	95.7
ATS averages	1.7	4.7	1.8	.1	91.5

Table 3. The racial makeup of faculties in ATS member schools (by percentages)

Schools differ most remarkably on the presence of women faculty. Mainline Protestant schools employ the greatest number of women (21 percent). Somewhat surprising is the fact that Roman Catholics have a higher percentage of women faculty than evangelicals. Despite the Catholic tradition of an exclusively male priesthood, women make up 18 percent of faculty members in Catholic institutions. In evangelical schools, the figure is only 8 percent, with almost all women faculty teaching in the "practical" fields of Christian education, counseling, music and the like. Very few women teach Bible, theology or church history in evangelical institutions.

Why is this so? Like Roman Catholics, evangelicals seem conflicted over gender. Although Roman Catholics restrict the priesthood to men, women religious have played an indispensable role in the Catholic educational system. Since most evangelicals are "low church," there is no sacramental function reserved for men. Therefore teaching and preaching doctrine become the most authoritative roles in ministry, the ones that many evangelicals think that women must be excluded from.

Ever since their movement emerged, evangelicals have disagreed on the public role of women in teaching and preaching. During the nineteenth century, the most sacramental, liturgical and "orderly" evangelical traditions were not open to women in public ministry. Others permitted them to preach or teach but not serve as pastors. In time some traditions removed all restrictions on women's participation. As a general rule, the more revivalistic and Spirit-oriented traditions were more open to women in public ministry.

At the beginning of the twentieth century, a number of evangelical denominations and educational institutions actually championed expanding ministerial roles for women. For example, some denominations and parachurch groups authorized women to serve as evangelists, home and foreign missionaries, Bible teachers, pastor's assistants and even ordained ministers. Women taught in many of the Bible schools founded to train lay workers. Such advocacy and opportunity diminished rapidly after the rise of fundamentalism, which understood the Bible in more restrictive ways. What was fairly common in the early part of the century—women functioning in various public ministries—became virtually unknown in many evangelical circles by World War II.[59] Since the mid-1970s, evangelicals have been polarized by gender questions. Evangelical egalitarians encourage the inclusion of women at all levels of religious life, while evangelical traditionalists seek to keep women out of pastoral and, sometimes, other kinds of leadership roles.[60]

The full range of views is represented in evangelical theological education. In order to maintain traditional gender models (and, in some cases, to comply with church law), a few schools restrict the access of women students to certain parts of the curriculum. These restrictions range from not allowing women to take homiletics classes to excluding them completely from the M.Div. degree program.[61] Other schools, also in keeping with their historic traditions, maintain an open and even supportive approach to women with pastoral callings.[62]

Probably most evangelical institutions are located somewhere between these two positions, largely because their faculties cannot agree on what the Bible teaches on this issue. Many steer a middle course: while they want to encourage women to follow their callings, they do not want to be seen as promoting women's ordination or women pastors, two topics that remain extremely controversial in many circles. For example, a number of schools acknowledge that Bible believers do not agree on gender questions, admit women into all degree programs, then decline to take a position on women in the pastorate, leaving the matter to the individual conscience or to churches to decide.[63]

Where does such institutional ambivalence leave women students who feel called to pastoral or some other form of religious leadership? In many places where faculties agree to disagree, women get mixed messages: while they are welcome to enroll and they have access to the entire curriculum, they sometimes hear professors and fellow students say that what they are doing is expressly forbidden in the Bible, which is about the worst thing that one evangelical can say about another. Of course,

---

[59]See Donald Dayton, *Discovering an Evangelical Heritage* (New York: Harper & Row, 1976); Janet Hassey, *No Time for Silence: Evangelical Women in Public Ministry at the Turn of the Century* (Grand Rapids: Zondervan, 1986); Margaret Bendroth, *Fundamentalism and Gender, 1875 to the Present* (New Haven, Conn.: Yale University Press, 1993); Betty A. DeBerg, *Ungodly Women: Gender and the First Wave of American Fundamentalism* (Minneapolis: Fortress, 1990).

[60]For the range of evangelical views on this subject, see Bonnidell Clouse and Robert G. Clouse, eds., *Women in Ministry: Four Views* (Downers Grove, Ill.: InterVarsity Press, 1989).

[61]Such schools are invariably Reformed or fundamentalist in tradition.

[62]This is typically the case at Wesleyan, holiness, Pentecostal, pietistic and "progressive" evangelical institutions.

[63]This is the stance of many Free Church seminaries, where the autonomy of the local church is valued. Most, but not all, Baptist schools take this approach (for example, Denver Conservative Baptist Seminary and Bethel Theological Seminary). On the other hand, while Southern Baptist Theological Seminary admits women to all degree programs, since 1995 it has hired as new faculty only those who oppose women serving as pastors.

not all women students at evangelical seminaries aspire to the pastorate. Most women in evangelical schools, who make up a quarter to a third of the students in many of them, pursue the M.A. degree, not the M.Div.

How do faculties in evangelical and mainline Protestant schools compare in their academic training?[64] A 1991 survey asked all ATS professors where they had earned their doctorates (including both Ph.D./Th.D. and D.Min.). When the results were tabulated, faculties in mainline Protestant schools listed 197 different institutions, while those in evangelical schools listed 174. The two lists are quite similar overall; but when one compares them in terms of schools most attended, major differences emerge. Table 4 lists each group's top ten institutions according to the number of graduates and the percentage of total faculty from that institution who are teaching in ATS schools.

Mainline Protestant	Evangelical
1.Chicago (104, 8.5%)	Southwestern Baptist (97, 9.5%)
2. Yale (94, 7.7%)	Southern Baptist (94, 9.2%)
3. Harvard U., Div. Sch. (74, 7.1%)	Fuller (49, 4.8%)
4. Princeton Sem. (71, 5.8%)	New Orleans Baptist (36, 3.5%)
5. Union (N.Y.) (65, 5.3%)	Dallas (35, 3.4%)
6. Boston (46, 3.8%)	Princeton Sem. (25, 2.4%)
7. Duke (42, 3.4%)	Harvard U., Div. Sch. (20, 2.0%)
8. Columbia U. (37, 3.0%)	Aberdeen (19, 1.9%)
9. Vanderbilt (37, 3.0%)	Concordia (16, 1.6%)
10. Claremont (30, 2.5%)	Emory (16, 1.6%)

Table 4. Institutions where faculty earned doctorates

At first glance, the lists do not seem to have much in common. Only two of the mainline Protestant "top ten" show up on the evangelical list (Princeton and Harvard). To be sure, evangelical schools have faculty with degrees from all the schools on the mainline list, but in substantially smaller numbers. While 49 percent (600 persons) of all the faculty in mainline Protestant schools graduated from the ten institutions named above, only 11 percent (112 persons) of evangelical faculty earned doctorates from the same institutions.

Furthermore, the evangelical list suggests that faculty members tend to stay close to home for doctoral work: six of their top ten are evangelical institutions.[65] If we examine the entire list of 174 schools, we find that 38 percent of those teaching in evangelical schools earned their highest degree at an evangelical institution. But

---

[64]Because the Catholic educational system for doctoral education is so different from the others, we will compare only mainline Protestant and evangelical faculties.

[65]Those figures seem even more significant in light of the fact that there are only twelve evangelical schools that grant the research doctorate (with thirty-three offering the D.Min.), in contrast to twenty-four mainline Protestant institutions offering the research doctorate (sixty, the D.Min).

that statistic may be a bit misleading: of the 385 people with "evangelical" doctorates, 235 earned them at Southern Baptist seminaries. Since the vast majority of people with Southern Baptist doctorates teach at one of the six Southern Baptist Convention seminaries, that leaves only 150 other persons (15 percent) who studied for their doctorate at non-Southern Baptist evangelical institutions. In fact, more evangelical faculty earned doctorates at mainline Protestant institutions (177, or 18 percent) than received them at the non-Southern Baptist evangelical schools. By contrast, only 2 percent of those teaching at mainline Protestant schools earned their doctorates at evangelical institutions.[66]

Faculty members at evangelical schools earned about as many European doctorates as their mainline Protestant counterparts.[67] Nevertheless, the evangelicals greatly preferred English and Scottish schools over German and Swiss ones, by a six-to-one margin.[68] Mainline Protestants preferred the English and Scottish universities only slightly.[69]

Such statistics indicate that the faculties of evangelical schools are not nearly as parochial as many have assumed. Since World War II, evangelicals have sought academic respectability by attending the same institutions that mainline Protestants attend. As a result, there is considerable diversity on evangelical faculties.[70] Because so many evangelicals have studied in mainline schools or at the same universities attended by their faculties, there is some evidence to support the claim often heard in evangelical circles that evangelicals understand mainline Protestantism much more than mainline Protestants understand evangelicalism.

Governance. Though governance structures are not always visible to the casual observer, they are crucial in determining the character and identity of institutions. There is no typical governance structure for evangelical schools. Included in the seventy-nine institutions are independent, freestanding, denominationally controlled and university- or college-related theological schools. The latter configuration seems to be making a comeback among evangelicals. Of the six new Southern Baptist schools, only one is not connected to an undergraduate college or university.[71] Some

---

[66]The 2 percent translates to twenty-one degrees that were earned at nine different evangelical institutions, but most of these degrees were from just two schools: seven from Fuller and seven from Southern Baptist.

[67]The actual statistics are as follows: for evangelicals, 125 faculty (12.5 percent) with degrees from twenty-four European institutions; for mainline Protestants, 124 faculty (10.3 percent) with degrees from forty schools.

[68]Ninety-two evangelical faculty (9.1 percent) graduated from thirteen schools in the British Isles, while only fourteen (1.4 percent) graduated from six German and Swiss universities.

[69]Fifty-nine (4.9 percent) of the faculty in mainline Protestant schools graduated from fourteen English and Scottish universities, while forty-five (4 percent) graduated from German and Swiss schools.

[70]Some schools still like to hire their own doctoral graduates: institutions like Dallas Seminary and the Southern Baptist Seminary have only recently begun to change this practice.

[71]See note 5.

older freestanding institutions (for example, Trinity Evangelical Divinity School and Western Evangelical Seminary) have recently become part of new university configurations.

Here again, there are some significant variations between evangelical, mainline Protestant and Catholic schools. Table 5 shows that evangelical institutions are less likely than the others to have boards that are concerned with their business alone. Only two-thirds of the boards governing evangelical theological schools are solely responsible for them, as opposed to three-quarters of the mainline Protestant schools and four-fifths of the Catholic institutions. One-third of the evangelical governing boards are also responsible for other institutions connected to the theological school.

	Evangelical	Mainline	Catholic
For theological school only	65	75	82
For college/seminary combination	25	8	6
For university complex	9	15	8

Table 5. Types of governing boards (by percentage)

Likewise, boards of evangelical theological schools are more likely to have members elected by the sponsoring denomination than by the board itself. Less than half (44 percent) of those on evangelical governing boards are elected by fellow board members, while 48 percent are elected and 7 percent appointed by the denomination. In contrast, 54 percent of mainline board members are elected by the boards themselves. Thirty percent are elected or appointed by the sponsoring church bodies. (The remainder of mainline board members are ex-officio from the school's administration or elected by members of the school community.)

In comparison to the mainline institutions, very few evangelical or Catholic theological schools include any faculty, alumni or students on their governing boards, which is one way for boards to become more inclusive of the school's many constituencies. As table 6 indicates, the practice has not been especially widespread on mainline Protestant boards either, but it does occur more frequently there.[72]

Most of the time, the makeup of governing boards and the method used to elect board members hardly seem momentous. But they can become vitally important under some circumstances. Since 1990 the most public controversies involving ATS member schools have occurred in evangelical institutions whose entire trustee board is directly elected by the sponsoring church body. Since the Southern Baptist Convention underwent a conservative resurgence in the 1980s, the redirection of

---

[72]It must be noted that many governance differences have historical explanations and are not directly tied to distinctive evangelical, mainline Protestant or Roman Catholic approaches to theological education.

	Mainline	Evangelical	Catholic
Faculty serve on board	28	7	10
Alumni serve on board	37	9	0
Students serve on board	29	9	8

Table 6. Boards with faculty, alumni and students (by percentage)

the seminaries along more conservative lines has become a high denominational priority. As a result, board trustees have moved aggressively to fulfill the Southern Baptist Convention's mandate, sometimes according to the ATS commission on accrediting without paying close enough attention to their own stated rules. The limits of academic freedom and the nature of denominational loyalty come under special scrutiny during times of rapid change. One thing is abundantly clear: no matter how they are elected, governing boards possess the power to define an institution's values and direction.

Conclusion

Evangelical institutions are different from other kinds of theological schools. Their desire for accredited status, their membership in ATS and their association with schools that are different from them have all played a part in shaping evangelical theological education in the last thirty or forty years.

Has it been worth it? What did "going mainstream" actually do for evangelical schools? These are questions worth pondering and studying in more detail. What is certain is that on account of accrediting standards, evangelical schools have had to beef up their faculties, add books to their libraries and become much more intentional about conducting business and reaching institutional goals. In order to meet accrediting standards, some evangelical schools had to spend years of strenuous effort. Others (for example, the International School of Theology) were created *de novo* with ATS standards in mind. Perhaps evangelical schools in ATS look so much alike because they have all had to conform to the same accrediting standards.

What impact has the growing evangelical presence made on ATS? Since the 1960s, when they began joining the association in large numbers, evangelicals have become increasingly visible. There have been four evangelical presidents: Olin Binkley of Southeastern Baptist (1962-1964), David Hubbard of Fuller (1974-1976), Russell Dilday of Southwestern Baptist (1988-1990) and Robert Cooley of Gordon-Conwell (1991-1994). Evangelicals have also served in other official capacities, including membership on the executive committee and the commission on accrediting. They have contributed regularly to the ATS journal, *Theological Education,* have gone out as visiting team members and have served on special task forces as well as on standing and ad hoc committees. Evangelicals were full participants in the recent redevelopment of ATS accrediting standards, which reflect their concerns in ways that the original standards did not. Since 1990 Daniel Aleshire, formerly of Southern Baptist Seminary, has served as ATS associate director for accrediting. Nevertheless, many evangelicals believe that they are still significantly underrepresented within ATS structures, especially those having to do with theological scholarship.

Accreditation remains an important value for evangelicals, as the number of evangelical schools seeking full membership in ATS indicates. Those schools already in the association seem pleased to stay there. Sometimes being in the mainstream has not been easy. Though they belong to the same organization, there remain enormous differences between evangelical, mainline Protestant and Roman Catholic theological institutions. Evangelical schools have occasionally been at odds with other ATS-member institutions over some of their entrepreneurial efforts or their definition and practice of academic freedom. Some evangelicals feel they need to remain on the lookout against ATS actions that might compromise their theological independence. As already mentioned, a few evangelical schools have been disciplined by ATS for not following their own declared principles and procedures during times of rapid institutional change. All in all, however, evangelicals seem to have found a home in the mainstream of theological education. Becoming accredited not only brought evangelical schools academic recognition but actually made them better institutions in the process—all without sacrificing their evangelical identities.

Appendix 1: Evangelical Theological Schools in ATS

1. Acadia Divinity College
2. Alliance Theological Seminary
3. Anderson University School of Theology
4. Asbury Theological Seminary
5. Ashland Theological Seminary
6. Assemblies of God Theological Seminary
7. Associated Canadian Theological Schools of Trinity Western University
8. Associated Mennonite Biblical Seminary
9. Azusa Pacific University C. P. Haggard Graduate School of Theology
10. Baptist Missionary Association Theological Seminary
11. Beeson Divinity School
12. Bethel Theological Seminary
13. Biblical Theological Seminary
14. Briercrest Biblical Seminary
15. Calvin Theological Seminary
16. Canadian Theological Seminary

17. Capital Bible Seminary
18. Central Baptist Theological Seminary
19. Church of God Theological Seminary
20. Cincinnati Bible Seminary
21. Columbia Biblical Seminary
22. Concordia Lutheran Seminary (Alberta)
23. Concordia Lutheran Theological Seminary (Ont.)
24. Concordia Seminary (Mo.)
25. Concordia Theological Seminary (Ind.)
26. (Conservative Baptist) Seminary of the East
27. Covenant Theological Seminary
28. Dallas Theological Seminary
29. Denver Conservative Baptist Seminary
30. Eastern Baptist Theological Seminary
31. Eastern Mennonite Seminary
32. Edmonton Baptist Seminary
33. Emmanuel School of Religion
34. Erskine Theological Seminary
35. Evangelical School of Theology
36. Fuller Theological Seminary
37. Golden Gate Baptist Theological Seminary
38. Gordon-Conwell Theological Seminary
39. Harding University Graduate School of Religion
40. Houston Graduate School of Theology
41. International School of Theology
42. Liberty Baptist Theological Seminary
43. Lincoln Christian Seminary
44. Logos Evangelical Seminary
45. Memphis Theological Seminary
46. Mennonite Brethren Biblical Seminary
47. Midwestern Baptist Theological Seminary
48. Moravian Theological Seminary
49. Multnomah Biblical Seminary
50. Nazarene Theological Seminary
51. New Orleans Baptist Theological Seminary
52. North American Baptist Seminary
53. North Park Theological Seminary
54. Northern Baptist Theological Seminary
55. Ontario Theological Seminary
56. Oral Roberts University School of Theology

57. Philadelphia Theological Seminary
58. Providence Seminary
59. Reformed Presbyterian Theological Seminary
60. Reformed Theological Seminary
61. Regent College
62. Regent University School of Divinity
63. Seventh-day Adventist Theological Seminary
64. Shaw Divinity School
65. Southeastern Baptist Theological Seminary
66. Southern Baptist Theological Seminary
67. Southwestern Baptist Theological Seminary
68. Talbot School of Theology
69. Trinity Episcopal School for Ministry
70. Trinity Evangelical Divinity School
71. University of Dubuque Theological Seminary
72. Wesley Biblical Seminary
73. Western (Conservative Baptist) Seminary
74. Western Evangelical Seminary
75. Western Theological Seminary
76. Westminster Theological Seminary
77. Westminster Theological Seminary in California
78. Winebrenner Theological Seminary
79. Wycliffe College

Appendix 2: Denominations Sponsoring Evangelical Schools

1. Anglican Church of Canada
   Wycliffe College
2. American Baptist Churches in the USA
   Central Baptist Theological Seminary
   Eastern Baptist Theological Seminary
   Northern Baptist Theological Seminary
3. Assemblies of God
   Assemblies of God Theological Seminary
4. Associate Reformed Presbyterian Church
   Erskine Theological Seminary
5. Baptist Convention of Ontario and Quebec
   Acadia Divinity School
6. Baptist General Conference
   Associated Canadian Theological Schools
   Bethel Theological Seminary

7. Baptist Missionary Association of America
   Baptist Missionary Association Theological Seminary
8. Brethren Church (Ashland, Ohio)
   Ashland Theological Seminary
9. Christian and Missionary Alliance
   Alliance Theological Seminary
   Canadian Theological Seminary
10. Christian Churches and Churches of Christ
    Cincinnati Bible Seminary
    Emmanuel School of Religion
    Harding University Graduate School of Religion
    Lincoln Christian Seminary
11. Christian Reformed Church
    Calvin Theological Seminary
12. Church of God (Anderson, Ind.)
    Anderson University School of Theology
13. Church of God (Cleveland, Tenn.)
    Church of God School of Theology
14. Churches of God, General Conference
    Winebrenner Theological Seminary
15. Church of the Nazarene
    Nazarene Theological Seminary
16. Conservative Baptist Association of America
    (Conservative Baptist) Seminary of the East
    Denver Conservative Baptist Seminary
    Western (Conservative Baptist) Seminary
17. Cumberland Presbyterian Church
    Memphis Theological Seminary
18. Episcopal Church
    Trinity Episcopal School for Ministry
19. Evangelical Congregational Church
    Evangelical School of Theology
20. Evangelical Covenant Church
    North Park Theological Seminary
21. Evangelical Formosan Church
    Logos Evangelical Seminary
22. Evangelical Free Church of America
    Trinity Evangelical Divinity School
23. Evangelical Free Church of Canada
    Associated Canadian Theological Schools

24. Fellowship of Evangelical Baptist Churches in Canada
    Associated Canadian Theological Schools
25. Friends, Religious Society of
    Houston Graduate School of Theology
26. General Baptist State Convention, N.C.
    Shaw Divinity School
27. General Conference Mennonite Church
    Associated Mennonite Biblical Seminary
28. Independent Baptist
    Liberty Baptist Theological Seminary
29. Lutheran Church—Canada
    Concordia Lutheran Seminary
    Concordia Lutheran Theological Seminary
30. Lutheran Church, Missouri Synod
    Concordia Seminary (Mo.)
    Concordia Theological Seminary (Ind.)
31. Mennonite Brethren Church in North America
    Mennonite Brethren Biblical Seminary
32. Mennonite Church
    Associated Mennonite Biblical Seminary
    Eastern Mennonite Seminary
33. Moravian Church in America
    Moravian Theological Seminary
34. North American Baptist Conference
    Edmonton Baptist Seminary
    North American Baptist Seminary
35. Presbyterian Church (U.S.A.)
    University of Dubuque Theological Seminary
36. Presbyterian Church in America
    Covenant Theological Seminary
37. Reformed Church in America
    Western Theological Seminary
38. Reformed Episcopal Church
    Philadelphia Theological Seminary
39. Reformed Presbyterian Church
    Reformed Presbyterian Theological Seminary
40. Seventh-day Adventist Church
    Seventh-day Adventist Theological Seminary
41. Southern Baptist Convention
    Golden Gate Baptist Theological Seminary

Midwestern Baptist Theological Seminary
New Orleans Baptist Theological Seminary
Southeastern Baptist Theological Seminary
Southern Baptist Theological Seminary
Southwestern Baptist Theological Seminary

Appendix 3: Evangelical Schools According to Their Denominational/ Theological Families

Anabaptist-Pietist (8-10 percent)
Ashland Theological Seminary
**Associated Canadian Theological Schools[1]
Associated Mennonite Biblical Seminary
Eastern Mennonite Seminary
Mennonite Brethren Biblical Seminary
Moravian Theological Seminary
North Park Theological Seminary
Winebrenner Theological Seminary
Anglican-Episcopal (3-4 percent)
Philadelphia Theological Seminary
Trinity Episcopal School for Ministry
Wycliffe College
Baptist (19-24 percent)
Acadia Divinity College
**Baptist Missionary Association Theological Seminary
Bethel Theological Seminary
Central Baptist Theological Seminary
**Conservative Baptist Seminary of the East
**Denver Conservative Baptist Seminary
Eastern Baptist Theological Seminary
Edmonton Baptist Seminary
Golden Gate Baptist Theological Seminary
**Liberty Baptist Seminary
Midwestern Baptist Theological Seminary
New Orleans Baptist Theological Seminary
North American Baptist Seminary
Northern Baptist Theological Seminary
Shaw Divinity School

_____

[1]ACTS is a consortium of three "believers' church" seminaries: Canadian Baptist Seminary (Baptist General Conference), Northwest Baptist Seminary (Fellowship of Evangelical Baptist Churches in Canada) and Trinity Western Seminary (Evangelical Free Church of Canada).

Southeastern Baptist Theological Seminary
Southern Baptist Theological Seminary
Southwestern Baptist Theological Seminary
**Western (Conservative Baptist) Seminary
Lutheran (4-5 percent)
Concordia Lutheran Seminary (Alberta)
Concordia Lutheran Theological Seminary (Ont.)
Concordia Seminary (Mo.)
Concordia Theological Seminary (Ind.)
Pentecostal-Charismatic (4-5 percent)
**Assemblies of God Theological Seminary
**Church of God School of Theology
*Oral Roberts University School of Theology
*/**Regent University School of Divinity
Presbyterian-Reformed (11-14 percent)
*/**Biblical Theological Seminary
Calvin Theological Seminary
Covenant Theological Seminary
Erskine Theological Seminary
Memphis Theological Seminary
Reformed Presbyterian Theological Seminary
Reformed Theological Seminary
University of Dubuque Theological Seminary
Western Theological Seminary
*Westminster Theological Seminary
*Westminster Theological Seminary in California
Restorationist (4-5 percent)
Cincinnati Bible Seminary
Emmanuel School of Religion
Harding Graduate School of Religion
Lincoln Christian Seminary
Wesleyan-Holiness (10-13 percent)
**Alliance Theological Seminary
Anderson University School of Theology
*Asbury Theological Seminary
*Azusa Pacific University Graduate School of Theology
**Canadian Theological Seminary
Evangelical School of Theology
Houston Graduate School of Theology
Nazarene Theological Seminary

*Wesley Biblical Seminary
*Western Evangelical Seminary
Premillennial (schools not already listed above) (10-13 percent)[2]
*Briercrest Biblical Seminary
*Capital Bible Seminary
*Columbia Biblical Seminary
*Dallas Theological Seminary
*International School of Theology
*Multnomah Biblical Seminary
*Providence Seminary
Seventh-day Adventist Theological Seminary
*Talbot School of Theology
Trinity Evangelical Divinity School[3]
Nonaligned (6-8 percent)[4]
*Beeson Divinity School
*Fuller Theological Seminary
*Gordon-Conwell Theological Seminary
Logos Evangelical Seminary[5]
*Ontario Theological Seminary
*Regent College

*Nondenominational, interdenominational or independent schools
**Schools with denominational/theological identities that are also premillennial

Appendix 4: When Evangelical Schools Received ATS Accreditation
The 1930s (1-2 percent)
Southern Baptist Theological Seminary (1938)
The 1940s (5-8 percent)
Western Theological Seminary (1940)
Asbury Theological Seminary (1944)[6]
Calvin Theological Seminary (1944)

---

[2]Counting those listed under denominational headings, there are twenty-two premillennial schools, or 28 percent of the total. Most of the schools would identify with dispensational premillennialism. Seventh-day Adventist Theological Seminary teaches historicist premillennialism.
[3]Though Trinity Evangelical Divinity School is owned by the Evangelical Free Church of America, a denomination with roots in Scandinavian pietism, it functions more like a nondenominational seminary.
[4]Without too much forcing, Beeson could be classified as a Baptist school and Fuller, Gordon-Conwell and Regent College as Presbyterian-Reformed institutions.
[5]Logos is a denominational seminary affiliated with the Formosan Evangelical Church.
[6]Asbury lost its accreditation in 1954 but had it reinstated in 1960.

University of Dubuque Theological Seminary (1944)
Southwestern Baptist Theological Seminary (1944)
The 1950s (6-10 percent)
Eastern Baptist Theological Seminary (1954)
Moravian Theological Seminary (1954)
New Orleans Baptist Theological Seminary (1954)
Fuller Theological Seminary (1957)
Associate Mennonite Biblical Seminary (1958)
Southeastern Baptist Theological Seminary (1958)
The 1960s (12-20 percent)
Central Baptist Theological Seminary (1962)
Golden Gate Baptist Theological Seminary (1962)
Concordia Seminary (Mo.) (1963)
North Park Theological Seminary (1963)
Gordon-Conwell Theological Seminary (1964)
Midwestern Baptist Theological Seminary (1964)
Anderson University School of Theology (1965)
Bethel Theological Seminary (1966)
North American Baptist Seminary (1968)
Concordia Theological Seminary (Ind.) (1968)
Northern Baptist Theological Seminary (1968)
Ashland Theological Seminary (1969)
The 1970s (10-17 percent)
Denver Conservative Baptist Seminary (1970)
Nazarene Theological Seminary (1970)
Seventh-day Adventist Theological Seminary (1970)
Trinity Evangelical Divinity School (1973)
Memphis Theological Seminary (1973)
Western Evangelical Seminary (1974)
Mennonite Brethren Biblical Seminary (1977)
Reformed Theological Seminary (1977)
Talbot School of Theology (1978)
Wycliffe College (1978)
The 1980s (14-24 percent)
Oral Roberts University School of Theology (1980)
Erskine Theological Seminary (1981)
Emmanuel School of Religion (1981)
Covenant Theological Seminary (1983)
Acadia Divinity College (1984)
Columbia Biblical Seminary (1985)

Regent College (British Columbia) (1985)
Trinity Episcopal School for Ministry (1985)
Eastern Mennonite Seminary (1986)
Westminster Theological Seminary (1986)
Evangelical Theological Seminary (1987)
Canadian Theological Seminary (1989)
Church of God School of Theology (1989)
Ontario Theological Seminary (1989)

The 1990s (11–19 percent)

Alliance Theological Seminary (1990)
Azusa Pacific University Graduate School of Theology (1990)
Lincoln Christian Seminary (1991)
Wesley Biblical Seminary (1991)
Winebrenner Theological Seminary (1991)
Assemblies of God Theological Seminary (1992)
Providence Seminary (1992)
Regent University School of Divinity (1992)
Dallas Theological Seminary (1993)
International School of Theology (1994)
Reformed Presbyterian Theological Seminary (1994)

Candidates for Accredited Membership

Associated Canadian Theological Schools
Beeson Divinity School
Biblical Theological Seminary
Edmonton Baptist Seminary
Houston Graduate School of Theology
Multnomah Biblical Seminary
Shaw Divinity School
Western (Conservative Baptist) Seminary

Associate Members

Baptist Missionary Association Theological Seminary
Briercrest Biblical Seminary
Capital Bible Seminary
Cincinnati Bible Seminary
Concordia Lutheran Seminary (Alberta)
Concordia Lutheran Theological Seminary (Ont.)
Conservative Baptist Seminary of the East
Harding Graduate School of Religion
Liberty Baptist Theological Seminary
Logos Evangelical Seminary

Philadelphia Theological Seminary
Westminster Theological Seminary in California

Chapter 10

New Dimensions in Pentecostal/Charismatic Theology

J. Rodman Williams

....

I AM HAPPY TO HAVE AN OPPORTUNITY TO CONTRIBUTE TO A FESTSCHRIFT honoring Millard Erickson. For a number of years in teaching systematic theology, I have made use of his *Christian Theology, Readings in Christian Theology* and *Contemporary Options in Eschatology*. Both his style and his substance have been invariably pleasing and helpful. So many thanks! I am indeed grateful.

My best contribution to this festschrift, I believe, is to treat the subject of new dimensions in Pentecostal/charismatic theology from a biblical/theological/existential perspective. For over thirty of my thirty-five years of teaching systematic theology, I have participated in the Pentecostal/charismatic renewal. As a theologian, I have found "new dimensions" to open up in this renewal movement. What I write in this article will doubtless be found controversial by many. However, I invite the reader's careful attention as I seek to be as straightforward and direct as possible. In many ways, this essay is a simple Bible study.

The word *Pentecostal* is often used to refer to a movement in the late nineteenth and early twentieth centuries that resulted in the formation of a number of Pentecostal denominations such as the Pentecostal Holiness Church, the Church of God (Cleveland, Tennessee), the Assemblies of God, the Church of God in Christ and the Church of the Foursquare Gospel. The term *charismatic* is applied to a similar movement arising in the latter half of the twentieth century in Protestant churches such as the Episcopal, Presbyterian and Lutheran churches, and later in the Roman Catholic Church.

The term *classical Pentecostal* refers to early Pentecostal churches, the term *neo-Pentecostal*, or *charismatic*, refers to the movement within Protestant churches, and *charismatic* (occurring alone) is used in regard to the Roman Catholic Church.[1] The term *Pentecostal/charismatic* may be used to refer to common distinctives in this basically unitary movement.[2]

The Pentecostal/charismatic movement contains two basic distinctives: (1) Pentecost is viewed as a continuing event, and (2) spiritual gifts are said to be valid for today. Because of space limitations, I will discuss only the first of these.

Let us begin with the biblical record of Pentecost in Acts 2. The chapter contains two parts: first, the Spirit's coming with the result that the disciples of Jesus were filled with the Holy Spirit and spoke in other tongues (vv. 1-21), and second, the preaching of the gospel with thousands being saved (vv. 22-41). Charismatics, along with other evangelicals, lay strong emphasis on the ongoing proclamation of the saving message. In that sense what happened at Pentecost surely continues. But charismatics further affirm that the Pentecostal filling (v. 4) continues to take place. Moreover, they claim that this event has been confirmed in their own lives and experience. There has been a personal engagement of the Spirit's coming and filling accompanied by speaking in tongues.[3] Because of this engagement, charismatics hold, there is a deeper understanding of the primary Pentecostal event.[4]

Long before Pentecost the Scriptures record the Spirit's coming on individuals to enable them to fulfill certain tasks—for example, an artisan for the building of the tabernacle (Ex 31:3), a judge or a king for the ruling of Israel (Judg 3:10; 1 Sam 16:13), a prophet for the speaking of God's word (Mic 3:8). At times the Spirit came mightily upon a person for the performing of prodigious feats (Judg 14:6), sometimes prophesying day and night (1 Sam 19:24) and sometimes even carrying a person bodily from one place to another (1 Kings 18:12).

Nowhere in the Old Testament is the Spirit said to be given to the people as a whole; however, the hope is held out that this will someday occur. Moses expressed a deep yearning that all God's people might be prophets ("Would that all the LORD's people were prophets, that the LORD would put His Spirit upon them!" Num 11:29 NASB),[5] and Joel prophesied that the time will come when God will pour out the Spirit on all humankind (Joel 2:28).

In the New Testament there is a kind of step-by-step unfolding of fulfillment.

---

[1]See, for example, H. V. Synan, *In the Latter Days: The Outpouring of the Holy Spirit in the Twentieth Century* (Ann Arbor, Mich.: Servant, 1984), p. ix.

[2]I will be using the term *charismatic* in this article partly for the sake of brevity and also as appropriate terminology for one standing within the Reformed tradition.

[3]Some charismatics would say "*often* accompanied by speaking in tongues."

[4]References to Pentecost hereafter will relate to this primary event.

[5]The NASB is used here and throughout unless otherwise noted.

First, certain persons, prior to Jesus' ministry, continued the Old Testament line of individuals occasionally anointed by the Holy Spirit (Lk 1:41-42, 67-68; 2:25-32), those upon whom the divine Spirit came for prophetic utterance. Second, John the Baptist is said to "be filled with the Holy Spirit even from birth" (Luke 1:15 NIV) for the lifelong purpose of preparing the way for Christ. John moved "in the spirit and power of Elijah" (Lk 1:17), and the divine fervor set fires of repentance burning in the hearts and lives of those who heard him. Third, Jesus received the anointing of God's Spirit when he was baptized in the Jordan (Lk 3:22; 4:1), and the Spirit is said to "come down and remain" (John 1:33 NIV), thus a continuing endowment. According to one account, just following Jesus' baptism, the Holy Spirit "immediately drove him out into the wilderness" (Mark 1:12 RSV), thus the picture of a divine energy that mightily propels and directs. Thereafter Jesus began his prophetic ministry with the words, "The Spirit of the LORD is upon Me, because He anointed Me to preach the gospel" (Lk 4:18). At one point Jesus declared that the "heavenly Father [would] give the Holy Spirit to those who ask Him" (Lk 11:13).[6] Toward the end of Jesus' ministry he spoke of the coming power of the Spirit with which the disciples will later be endowed (Lk 24:49).

Pentecost was therefore the climax to which preceding events pointed. It was an outpouring of the Holy Spirit upon the community of faith long ago prophesied by Joel: "This is what was spoken of through the prophet Joel . . . I will pour forth of My Spirit upon all mankind" (Acts 2:16-17). Pentecost was also a baptism with the Holy Spirit. Jesus had said, "You shall be baptized with the Holy Spirit not many days from now" (1:5). Further, the Pentecostal event, as had nothing before, related to the exalted and glorified Christ: In Peter's words, "He [Christ] has poured forth this which you both see and hear" (2:33). This event occurred to the disciples of Jesus, to those who believed in him, with a Spirit filling of such intensity that the disciples began speaking in other tongues. Thereby they were declaring "the wonderful works of God" (2:11 KJV). This was evidently done with such exuberance that some mockingly said that the disciples were drunk: "full of new wine" (v. 13 KJV).[7] The purpose of this outpouring was power for ministry: "You shall receive power when the Holy Spirit has come upon you; and you shall be My witnesses both in Jerusalem, and in all Judea and Samaria, and even to the remotest part of the earth" (1:8). Pentecost was both a climactic and a future-oriented event.

Now we come back to the charismatic testimony, namely, that they too have shared in the Pentecostal event. Of course, the original Pentecost historically has happened. The claim, rather, is that Pentecost has basically recurred in their lives in that they too have been filled with the Spirit, have spoken in other tongues and

---

[6]The parallel passage in Matthew 7:11, instead of "the Holy Spirit," reads "good things" (KJV), *agatha*.
[7]F. F. Bruce refers to this as "words spoken by the disciples in their divine ecstasy," *The Book of the Acts*, New International Commentary on the New Testament (Grand Rapids: Eerdmans, 1988), p. 52.

been given fresh power for witness in word and in deed.

But does the biblical text suggest continuation of the primary Pentecostal event? First, we observe some words of Peter spoken on the Day of Pentecost about the promise of the Spirit. Peter had finished his message, which consisted of two parts: the first an explanation that what had just happened to him and the other gathered disciples was the fulfillment of Joel's promise (Acts 2:14-21) and the second the proclamation of the death and resurrection of Christ (vv. 22-36). Then Peter declared, "Repent, and let each of you be baptized in the name of Jesus Christ for the forgiveness of your sins; and you shall receive the gift of the Holy Spirit. For the promise is for you and your children, and for all who are far off, as many as the Lord our God shall call to Himself" (vv. 38-39).

The word *promise* refers to "the promise of the Holy Spirit," for Peter shortly before had spoken about Christ thus: "Having been exalted to the right hand of God, and having received from the Father the promise of the Holy Spirit, He has poured forth this which you both see and hear" (v. 33). Thus the promise of the gift of the Spirit is not the promise of salvation (which relates to repentance and baptism) but the promise of the same Spirit of power that the disciples had received.[8] Further, according to Peter, the promise will reach out to those "far off" in both time and space,[9] to all whom God "calls to Himself," that is, to salvation. Thus while the event of the Spirit at Pentecost in Jerusalem was a first, historically, it was only the beginning of the fulfillment of God's promise: the gift of the Spirit would continue through the generations.[10]

The second reason for viewing the coming of the Spirit at Pentecost as a continuing event is the further record in the book of Acts. Particularly outstanding is the narrative in Acts 10 and 11 about the centurion Cornelius, his relatives and his friends in Caesarea. While Peter was preaching the gospel, they also experienced an outpouring of the Holy Spirit accompanied likewise by speaking in tongues: "The gift of the Holy Spirit had been poured out upon the Gentiles also. For they [Peter and those with him] were hearing them speaking with tongues and exalting God" (10:45-46). Peter later emphasized that this event of the Spirit was identical

---

[8]William Neil describes the gift of the Spirit as the "gift of the new power which Peter's audience has seen at work in the Pentecostal experience of the Apostles and Peter's associates," *The Acts of the Apostles*, New Century Bible Commentary (Grand Rapids: Eerdmans, 1981), p. 79. Eduard Schweizer writes that in Acts "salvation . . . is never ascribed to the Spirit. According to Ac. 2:38 the Spirit is imparted to those who are already converted and baptized," in *Theological Dictionary of the New Testament* (Grand Rapids: Eerdmans, 1968), 6:412. Kirsopp Lake states that in the various Acts passages that deal with the gift of the Spirit "there is no suggestion of regeneration by the Spirit, or of the view that salvation depends on it." *Beginnings of Christianity, The Acts of the Apostles*, ed. Frederick J. Foakes-Jackson and Kirsopp Lake, vol. 5 (Grand Rapids: Baker, 1979), p. 109.

[9]"Far off" is a translation of *eis makran. Makran* is used of "both place and time." TDNT, 4:372.

[10]"Acts 2:39 probably refers to future generations." See "μακράν" in Bauer, Arndt, Gingrich and Danker, *Greek-English Lexicon of the New Testament* (Chicago: University of Chicago Press, 1979), p. 487.

with what had happened to himself and others at Pentecost. Seeking to justify his action of preaching to the Gentiles, Peter declared, "As I began to speak, the Holy Spirit fell upon them, just as He did upon us at the beginning. . . . If God therefore gave to them the same gift as He gave to us after believing[11] in the Lord Jesus Christ, who was I that I could stand in God's way?" (11:15, 17). The Pentecostal event of the Spirit had occurred again.

Under the impact of the Holy Spirit the Gentiles likewise spoke in tongues. Since the gift of the Spirit was the same as "at the beginning," the tongues must likewise have been the same in essence. Since at the original Pentecost the disciples were speaking "the wonderful works of God" in tongues and in Caesarea were "speaking with tongues and exalting God," they both were undoubtedly a speaking of praise to God.[12]

Other Acts accounts likewise depict Pentecost as a continuing event. In Samaria Philip had preached the gospel with the result that many "believed Philip" and were baptized (8:12). Peter and John some days later "came down [from Jerusalem] and prayed for them, that they might receive the Holy Spirit" (vv. 15-16). Thereafter the apostles' hands were laid and the Spirit "was bestowed" (v. 18). The words following about Simon the magician seem to imply that the Samaritans then spoke in tongues.[13] In Ephesus Paul led some twelve men to faith in Christ—"to believe in Him" (19:4)—and baptized them. Thereafter "when Paul had laid his hands upon them, the Holy Spirit came on them, and they began speaking with tongues and prophesying" (v. 6).

Thus we see that Pentecost was a continuing event. The promise of the Spirit

---

[11]"After believing." The NASB translation of the Greek aorist participle *pisteusasin* expresses antecedent action. NIV and KJV read "who believed." J. D. G. Dunn states that "the aorist participle does in fact usually express antecedent action" (*Baptism in the Holy Spirit* [Philadelphia: Westminster, 1970], p. 159). According to Ernest DeWitt Burton, "The aorist participle is most frequently used of an action antecedent in time to the action of the principal verb" (*Syntax of the Moods and Tenses in New Testament Greek* [Chicago: University of Chicago Press, 1898], p. 63. The aorist participle may also express coincident action. If so, the translation above would read (as in the RSV) "when we believed." Dunn continues that "it is the context, not the grammatical form, which determines this." I would urge that the context here clearly points to antecedent action (as in NASB, NIV and KJV).

[12]I. Howard Marshall writes: "Just as the Jewish believers had received the Spirit and praised God in other tongues on the day of Pentecost, so now these Gentiles received the identical gift of God." *The Acts of the Apostles*, Tyndale New Testament Commentary (Grand Rapids: Eerdmans, 1980), p. 194.

[13]Simon the magician seeing *(idon)* that "the Spirit was bestowed through the laying on of the apostles' hands" (v. 18). Both the word structure and context suggest tongues. Regarding word structure, A. T. Robertson states that "the participle *[idon]* shows plainly that those who received the gift of the Holy Spirit spoke with tongues" (*Word Pictures in the New Testament* [Nashville: Broadman, 1930-1933], 3:107). Concerning context F. F. Bruce states that "the context leaves us in no doubt that their [the Samaritans'] reception of the Spirit was attended by external manifestations such as had marked His descent on the earliest disciples at Pentecost" *(The Book of the Acts*, p. 181). See my *Renewal Theology*, vol. 2, *Salvation, the Holy Spirit and Christian Living* (Grand Rapids: Zondervan, 1990), p. 210, n. 5, for other quotations.

was proclaimed by Peter as given to all generations, and in demonstration there was an ever widening circle of fulfillment in the book of Acts. Since no limits have been set, the promise surely continues in our time.

Charismatic experience must stand wholly under the biblical norm. If that is the case, I am convinced there will be vindication. There is abundant biblical data regarding the giving of the Spirit. First, the Spirit was given for enablement. In the Old Testament the Spirit brought additional wisdom and power for fulfilling certain tasks. The Spirit came upon Jesus to enable the fulfillment of his ministry. The disciples at Pentecost upon whom the Spirit was poured out were enabled thereby to carry forward the mission of the gospel. The texts in Acts further imply that the Samaritans, Caesareans and Ephesians by the gift of the Spirit were included in the ever enlarging circle of those called likewise to be witnesses of Christ.

Second, the Spirit was not given for either salvation or sanctification. This is obviously the case in the line of anointings through John the Baptist and was surely true for Jesus, who needed neither salvation nor sanctification. The disciples at Pentecost were already believers when the Spirit was poured out. The Samaritans had come to faith and baptism before the Spirit was bestowed.[14] Like the Ephesians, they received the Holy Spirit thereafter with the laying on of hands. Although the Holy Spirit was outpoured while Peter was preaching the gospel to the Caesareans, the context suggests that it was for the further outreach of the gospel.[15] Acts has little to say about the activity of the Holy Spirit in the occurrence of salvation because the focus of the book is on the role of the Holy Spirit in the outreach of the gospel and the empowering of its messengers.[16] This is a marked difference, for example, from the letters of Paul in which much attention is given to the Holy

---

[14]Thus says Calvin, "Luke is not speaking here [in regard to the Spirit's bestowal—Acts 8:18] about the general grace of the Spirit, by which God regenerates us to be His own 'sons' " (*New Testament Commentaries: The Acts of the Apostles 1-13*, trans. J. W. Fraser and W. J. G. McDonald [Grand Rapids: Eerdmans, 1965], p. 236). F. F. Bruce writes, "The prior operation of the Spirit in regeneration is not in view here" (*The Book of the Acts*, p. 188, n. 34).

[15]According to R. R. Williams, "Throughout Acts, the Holy Spirit is thought of as the means whereby Christians receive power to witness to Christ and His resurrection" (*The Acts of the Apostles* [London: SCM Press, 1953], p. 36). This would surely include the Caesareans. In connection with the Caesareans, R. C. H. Lenski writes, "This falling of the Holy Spirit upon people . . . is entirely separate from the Spirit's reception by faith for salvation" (*The Acts of the Apostles* [Minneapolis: Augsburg, 1961], p. 431).

[16]In I. H. Marshall's words, "Acts is a book about mission. It is not unfair to take 1.8 as a summary of its contents: 'You shall be my witnesses in Jerusalem and in all Judea and Samaria and to the end of the earth.' The purpose of the Christian church was to bear witness" (*The Acts of the Apostles*, p. 25). Basic to this mission and witness is the need for empowerment. Thus I would add that the "contents" of Acts also include the first part of 1:8: "You shall receive power when the Holy Spirit has come upon you." Since, as Marshall says, "the purpose of the Christian church was to bear witness," the primary matter is enabling power. Acts again and again portrays how the power was received. This emphasis is vital to an understanding of the book of Acts. It is both a book about mission *and* the empowerment of the gospel messengers at certain critical points.

Spirit's activity in the Christian life.

Third, there is an ongoing concern in Acts that believers receive (the gift of) the Holy Spirit. Although God sovereignly poured out his Spirit in Jerusalem and Caesarea without a human medium, Peter and John in Samaria and Paul in Ephesus laid hands for the reception of the Holy Spirit. Paul's concern is particularly shown in that he earlier asked the Ephesians, "Did you receive the Holy Spirit when you believed?"[17] (Acts 19:2). Paul's question implies the possibility that believers might not yet have received the Holy Spirit (recall, for example, the Samaritans). Since it turns out that the Ephesians' knowledge of the Holy Spirit was lacking and that they had only known the baptism of John, Paul led them to faith in Christ and afterward laid hands on them to receive the Holy Spirit. Believing was primary, but receiving was also important.

Fourth, it is apparent in the book of Acts that the gift of the Holy Spirit occurred both subsequent to and coincident with initial faith. In regard to subsequence, the Holy Spirit "filled" some hundred and twenty waiting believers, fell upon the Samaritans some time after they had believed and been baptized, and came upon the Ephesians following their faith, baptism and laying on of hands. In regard to coincidence, the Holy Spirit was poured out upon the Caesareans while Peter was proclaiming salvation in Christ. In light particularly of the incidents of subsequence, the important matter is both the nonidentity of salvation and the coming of the Spirit. Often there was an interval between the two events.

Fifth, speaking in tongues is specifically said to have occurred in Jerusalem, Caesarea and Ephesus. It is also implied (as noted) in Samaria. Thus speaking in tongues, according to Acts, may be called the normal or usual accompaniment of receiving the Pentecostal gift of the Spirit. Moreover, it also is apparent that tongues was both the primary activity and the initial evidence of the reception of the Spirit.[18] In each case the first thing that happened was speaking in tongues—tongues and preaching (Jerusalem), tongues and exalting God (Caesarea), tongues and prophesying (Ephesus). In regard to initial evidence, the clearest statement regards the Caesareans. Just after the words "the gift of the Holy Spirit had been poured out on the Gentiles also," the text adds, "for they were hearing them speaking with tongues and exalting God" (Acts 10:45-46).[19]

---

[17]KJV reads, "Have ye received the Holy Spirit since ye believed?" NIV, while translating as NASB does above, has a footnote to "when" as "after." Again, this is an instance of an aorist participle, namely, *pisteusantes* (recall *pisteusasin* in Acts 11:17). Even if the aorist participle in this case expresses coincident action, the sense is still the same, implying the possibility of a believing prior to reception of the Holy Spirit.

[18]J. D. G. Dunn writes, "It is a fair assumption that for Luke 'the Samaritan' Pentecost, like the first Christian Pentecost [that is, in Jerusalem], was marked by ecstatic glossolalia. If so, then the fact is that *in every case* [italics Dunn's] where Luke describes the giving of the Spirit it is accompanied and 'evidenced' by glossolalia" (*Jesus and the Spirit* [London: SCM Press, 1975], p. 189).

[19]Dunn adds, "The corollary is then not without force that Luke intended to portray 'speaking in tongues'

Sixth, prayer and sometimes laying on of hands often provided the context for the Holy Spirit to be received. Jesus himself was praying immediately prior to the Spirit's coming on him: "While He was praying, heaven was opened, and the Holy Spirit descended upon Him" (Lk 3:21-22). The disciples in Jerusalem prior to Pentecost were "continually devoting themselves to prayer" (Acts 1:14); the centurion in Caesarea before the outpouring of the Holy Spirit was one who "prayed to God continually" (10:2); Peter and John "came down and prayed for them [the Samaritans]" and afterward "began laying their hands on them, and they were receiving the Holy Spirit" (8:15, 17); "Paul laid his hands upon them [the Ephesians]" (19:6). In regard to prayer, this may point to asking for the gift of the Holy Spirit in accordance with Jesus' words: "If you . . . know how to give good gifts to your children, how much more shall your heavenly Father give the Holy Spirit to those who ask Him?" (Lk 11:13).

In some evangelical circles objection is raised not so much from an exegetical base as from the use of Acts as a guideline for contemporary experience. For example, one writer's view is that Acts is a transitional book "from law to grace" and thus "the transitions [Jerusalem, Caesarea and so on] it records are never to be repeated."[20] Another somewhat similar viewpoint is that since Acts is historical narrative and the Epistles didactic material, "the revelation of the purposes of God should be sought primarily in its *didactic* rather than its *descriptive* parts. . . . What is described as having happened to others is not necessarily intended for us."[21] Such viewpoints as "transitional" and "descriptive" only avoid the necessity of coming to terms with Acts and its own particular importance for us in our time.

Persons of charismatic experience find such attitudes about Acts very strange. Unlike those who stand at a distance from the Acts narratives, charismatics feel much at home. They claim that the promise of the gift of the Holy Spirit has been actualized[22] in their own lives. Often it has occurred, they say, against the background of much prayer and sometimes the laying on of hands: thus was the gift received. The usual testimony adds that they too have spoken in tongues and have thereby glorified God. In most cases they were already believers, and they claim that the gift of the Holy Spirit further equipped them for ministering the gospel. For charismatics, the Holy Spirit has engaged them personally in such a way as to

---

as 'the initial evidence' of the outpouring of the Holy Spirit" (ibid., pp. 189-90). Ernst Haenchen states, "The Spirit makes itself known in Acts by the gift of speaking in tongues" (*The Acts of the Apostles* [Oxford: Basil Blackwell, 1971], p. 304).

[20]John F. MacArthur Jr., *Charismatic Chaos* (Grand Rapids: Zondervan, 1992), p. 172.

[21]John R. W. Stott in *Baptism and Fullness* (Downers Grove, Ill.: InterVarsity Press, 1976), p. 15.

[22]In the Roman Catholic charismatic renewal the word *actualized* (or *actualization*) is often used in a sacramental context as referring to "an actualization of graces objectively conferred" in the sacraments of initiation (baptism, confirmation). See, for example, *Christian Initiation and Baptism in the Holy Spirit: Evidence from the First Eight Centuries,* by Kilian McDonnell and George Montague (Col-

give vital understanding of and resonance with the biblical record.

Incidentally, I sometimes wonder about noncharismatic critics. What can they really say to the millions of Christians who claim a continuing Pentecost in their lives? Are they all misguided? Are they guilty of distorting the Scriptures? What about the testimony to a speaking in tongues that again and again accompanies their experience? Are they all deluded? Is it possible that charismatics are on a genuine biblical track that has been confirmed in their lives? Could it be that many critics are not really able to cope with basic charismatic issues because of a *lack of experience* in their own lives?

Perhaps a word of personal testimony is in order. Prior to my own charismatic experience (in 1965) I was quite negative about the whole matter. I did sense among many charismatics a certain vitality and enthusiasm, but was it (whatever it was they had) biblical? Soon two passages of Scripture began to stand out for me: Acts 2:39 and Luke 11:13. In the former (as earlier noted) Peter declared that the gift of the Holy Spirit would be available to all generations thereafter. What was that gift? For a time I identified it with salvation,[23] but my exegesis led me to question this interpretation. The gift of the Holy Spirit seemed to refer to what Peter and the other disciples had been promised and received, and that was hardly salvation. Even if it was a distinct promise to those who believed, did not the gift come automatically along with salvation? Had I not already received this gift with my salvation? Reading with more determination than ever, and noting that the gift often occurred to believers and that prayer was frequently the context, I wondered all the more. Incidentally, the matter of speaking in tongues was totally beyond my comprehension.

What turned the tide for me was Luke 11:13, Jesus' words about the gift of the Holy Spirit: "If you . . . know how to give good gifts to your children, how much more shall your heavenly Father give the Holy Spirit to those who ask Him?" Ah, there was the same promise of the gift of the Spirit to God's children, but with all emphasis (vv. 9-10) on *asking* for the gift—indeed asking, seeking, knocking. Continuing prayer! This made me reflect on Jesus' own praying prior to the Holy Spirit's descent on him, the disciples' constantly devoting themselves to prayer before they received the promised gift, the Roman centurion who prayed continually to God prior to the Spirit's being poured out—on and on. God, the heavenly Father,

---

legeville, Minn.: Liturgical Press, 1990), for such a sacramental actualization view (pp. 83-88). The gift of the Holy Spirit viewed as sacramentally bestowed is actualized in charismatic experience.

[23]As do some exegetes, for example, Dunn and Bruce. Dunn writes, "The gift of the Spirit . . . is the gift of saving grace by which one enters into Christian experience and life" (*Baptism in the Holy Spirit*, p. 226). Bruce states, "The gift of the Spirit may comprehend a variety of gifts of the Spirit, but first and foremost 'the saving benefits of Christ's word as applied to the believer by the Spirit' " (*The Book of the Acts*, p. 71). Recall, however, earlier quotations from William Neil, Eduard Schweizer and Kirsopp Lake, with which I agree.

sovereignly gives, but not without the sincere praying of his children.[24]

So not quite knowing what to expect, I entered into earnest prayer for the gift of the Holy Spirit. Then suddenly it happened—the coming of a personal presence and power that led me immediately to praise and glorify God. Ordinary language no longer sufficing, I was soon speaking in another language as the exaltation of God went on and on. It seemed like Pentecost all over again—as if I were with the early disciples declaring the "wonderful works of God." As a result of this experience I found myself more fully endowed to bear witness to God's truth.

Against the background of the scriptural record I am convinced that the charismatic experience of many has confirmed and illuminated the biblical text. There has been the engagement of the Spirit of such a kind as to make the Acts narratives vividly contemporaneous. It has—and this is critical—happened with untold numbers of people.

It may be objected that the biblical basis for this point has been restricted to the Lukan material: the Gospel of Luke and the book of Acts. This has been done in part because I am convinced that theological reflection, exegetical study and personal experience have not sufficiently come to terms with Luke's distinctive charismatic emphases.[25] Especially is this true of the book of Acts.

By no means do I intend to suggest a canon within the canon: Lukan theology and experience over against the rest of the New Testament. Indeed, *all* the biblical record is needed for a fully rounded picture of truth. However, it is a fact that in Luke-Acts—particularly Acts—is to be found the scriptural data relating to the empowering of the gospel witness in various stages. Paul, however, writes to churches already founded by that witness (especially by Paul himself[26]), and so he focuses on the way of Christian living. None of the New Testament letters are as missionary-oriented as Acts. Nor is Luke concerned about such pneumatological matters as life in the Spirit, sanctification, the inner assurance of the Spirit and so on. It is apparent that we need Luke *and* Paul for both the missiological and ecclesiological New Testament emphases.

It is important to recognize two basic operations of the Holy Spirit: the Spirit

---

[24]In the Heidelberg Catechism one of the questions (116) is "Why is prayer necessary for Christians?" Then follows the striking answer: "Because it is the chief part of the gratitude which God requires of us, and because *God will give his grace and Holy Spirit only to those who sincerely beseech him in prayer without ceasing,* and who thank him for these gifts" (italics added).

[25]See, however, Roger Stronstad, *The Charismatic Theology of St. Luke* (Peabody, Mass.: Hendrickson, 1984). Clark Pinnock in the foreword writes, "The meaning of this book is that the walls must come down between Pentecostals and evangelicals. If canonical Luke has a charismatic theology as Stronstad proves, we cannot consider Pentecostalism to be a kind of aberration born of experiential excesses but a 20th century revival of New Testament theology and religion" (pp. vii-viii).

[26]Paul refers to "the power of the Spirit," the empowered witness by which he proclaimed the gospel "in the power of signs and wonders, in the power of the Spirit; so that from Jerusalem and round about as far as Illyricum I have fully preached the gospel of Christ" (Rom 15:19).

upon (or *on*) persons for outward witness and the Spirit *within* (or *in*) people for inner character. As earlier noted, there is an Old Testament line—we may call it "charismatic"—that extends all the way to the ministry of Jesus ("the Spirit of the Lord is *upon* me") and reaches a zenith at Pentecost (where Jesus' words—"the Holy Spirit will come *upon* you"—were fulfilled) in such measure as to be an outpouring. It continues beyond Pentecost to other communities of Christians (for example, Ephesus, where "the Holy Spirit came *on*" the twelve disciples).

In Acts, however, there is no reference to any interior work of the Spirit. The New Testament letters deal largely with the Spirit within—for example, "the Holy Spirit who lives *in* us" (2 Tim 1:14). By the Spirit within we are no longer "in the flesh" ("you are not in the flesh . . . if indeed the Spirit of the Lord dwells *in* you," Rom 8:9), the same "Spirit who indwells" will someday give life to our mortal bodies (v. 11); by the Spirit we may put "to death the deeds of the body" (v. 13)—on and on. Also to be noted is the fruit of the indwelling Spirit, namely, "love, joy, peace, patience, kindness, goodness, faithfulness, gentleness, self-control" (Gal 5:22). Truly, "the Spirit *upon*" and "the Spirit *within*" are both vital operations of the Holy Spirit.

What charismatics attest is a distinctive operation of the Holy Spirit, "the Spirit upon," which is not to be identified with "the Spirit within." It is the coming of the Holy Spirit upon people of faith with such explosive force as to cause a breaking forth in pneumatic speech and in powerful expression of the gospel. This operation of the Spirit is not to be assumed because the Spirit is already at work within a community or person; it is rather a unique operation that presupposes saving faith.

Charismatics, it should be added, do not claim that their Pentecostal experience makes them the only ones who are able to bear witness to the gospel. All true believers by virtue of the Spirit's indwelling reality can surely and effectively attest to the gospel. Pentecost represents an additional infusion of power that makes still more effective the witness in word and deed.[27] It is a filling with the same Spirit who dwells within.

Nor does the event of Pentecost create a superior class of Christians. All believers

---

[27]Dwight L. Moody, a century ago, testified to this additional infusion of power. After many years of preaching, Moody related how two women would say to him regularly, "*You* need the power of the Holy Spirit." Reflecting on their words, Moody stated, "I need the power! Why, I thought I had power [because] I had the largest congregation in Chicago and there were many conversions." Soon though, the two godly women were praying with Moody, and "they poured out their hearts in prayer that I might receive the filling of the Holy Spirit. There came a great hunger into my soul. . . . I began to cry out as I never did before. I really felt that I did not want to live if I could not have this power for service." Then "one day, in the city of New York—oh, what a day!—I cannot describe it, I seldom refer to it; it is almost too sacred an experience to name." After this, says Moody, "I went to preaching again. The sermons were not different; I did not present any new truths, and yet hundreds were converted. I would not now be placed back before that blessed experience if you should give me all the world" (W. R. Moody, *The Life of D. L. Moody* [Westwood, N.J.: Barbour, 1985], pp. 146-47, 149). Moody was surely a precursor of those in our time who are being filled with the Holy Spirit and are finding a fresh power for witness.

by grace stand on the same level. Thus Pentecost is not a "second work of grace," for all have received "grace upon grace" (Jn 1:16). Rather, Pentecost is a release of "power from on high" (Lk 24:49) that enables believers to be more effective witnesses to the gospel. Unlike the grace of salvation, which is self-oriented, the Pentecostal experience is wholly other-directed. Pentecost is not for salvation but for service. It is *not* a graduation to a superspirituality but a release of power for the missionary challenge.

Since the Pentecostal gift—the gift of the Holy Spirit—is promised, it is a continuing blessing. To review briefly: Jesus declared that the heavenly Father would give the Holy Spirit to those who ask for it, and Peter proclaimed that the gift of the Holy Spirit is promised to all generations. In the former case the wording and context imply that the promise is to believers (those who can call God "Father"). In the latter, the promise is made to all whom God "calls to himself." In both cases the promise is essentially the same.

The gift of the Holy Spirit is wholly for ministry. The background of Jesus' words is the need for bread to minister to another. In the preceding account the man who is told to ask, seek and knock is calling for bread to pass on to someone else (see Lk 11:5-12). Similarly, Jesus speaks of the promise of the Father to baptize in the Holy Spirit for the purpose of ministering the gospel. The gift is not for personal blessing (although this surely occurs) but for ministry to the needs of others.

The practical question concerns how the promised gift of the Holy Spirit is to be received. To repeat a point made earlier: there is nothing automatic about the reception of the gift. Recall Paul's question for the Ephesians, "Did you receive the Holy Spirit when you believed?" This unmistakably implies that faith is not necessarily accompanied by reception of the gift of the Spirit. This may occur later. The issue becomes one of how reception occurs.

We have already stressed the importance of two things: prayer and the laying on of hands. Prayer refers to earnest, believing prayer asking God for the gift of the Holy Spirit. This is not earning something through effort—it is a gift to be received—but it is in an atmosphere of believing prayer that the gift is bestowed.

Laying on hands for the gift of the Holy Spirit may also prove helpful. Hands may be the outward channel through which the gift is received. Even as water baptism relates to forgiveness of sin, so does the laying on of hands relate to the bestowal of the Holy Spirit.[28] Hands laid on the believer vividly symbolize the

---

[28]For churches that practice confirmation, this may be an appropriate occasion for the reception of the empowering gift. According to the Episcopal Book of Common Prayer the bishop is to lay hands upon each confirmand and pray, "Strengthen, O Lord, your servant _____ with your Holy Spirit; empower him for your service; and sustain him all the days of his life." Observe the emphasis on empowering. The Roman Catholic Church views confirmation as a sacrament and declares that "the effect of the sacrament of confirmation is the full outpouring of the Holy Spirit as once granted the apostles on the

coming of the Holy Spirit on a person. However, hands no more than water baptism guarantee the reception of the spiritual reality.

In regard to speaking in tongues—often a stumbling block—we need to understand that such speech is a normal expression of being filled with the Holy Spirit. The fullness of the Spirit's presence brings forth fullness of praise.[29] Or, to put it a bit differently, the penetration of the Spirit can be of such potency as to go deeper than ordinary speech can express. Resulting tongues are an overflow of the Holy Spirit's dynamic presence and power; such is transcendent praise. While tongues should never be forced (which is an impossibility), they may be expected. Further, against the background of such overflowing praise, the "wonderful works of God" are all the more powerfully proclaimed.

Now a final word, particularly to evangelicals. The stress on regeneration remains central. We must continue to proclaim the necessity of new birth through Christ. Surely the Holy Spirit makes new birth possible: "born of the Spirit" (Jn 3:6). We must continue to make every effort to proclaim the good news. This is precisely where an additional work of the Spirit comes in, namely, for the empowering of the witness. "Born of the Spirit" needs to be supplemented by "filled with the Holy Spirit" (Acts 2:4). Evangelicals who strongly emphasize the proclamation of the gospel message should all the more be concerned about the special work of the Spirit to empower the messenger.

Charismatic theology is actually evangelical theology in extension.

Resources for Additional Study

Berkhof, H. *The Doctrine of the Holy Spirit.* Richmond, Va.: John Knox, 1964.

Cox, H. *Fire from Heaven: The Rise of Pentecostal Spirituality and the Reshaping of Religion in the Twenty-first Century.* Reading, Mass.: Addison-Wesley, 1995.

Ervin, H. M. *Spirit Baptism: A Biblical Investigation.* Peabody, Mass.: Hendrickson, 1987.

Lindsell, H. *The Holy Spirit in the Latter Days.* Nashville: Thomas Nelson, 1983.

Lloyd-Jones, M. *Joy Unspeakable: Power and Renewal in the Holy Spirit.* Wheaton, Ill.: Harold Shaw, 1984.

McGee, Gary B., ed. *Initial Evidence.* Peabody, Mass.: Hendrickson, 1991.

Menzies, R. F. *Empowered for Witness: The Spirit in Luke-Acts.* Sheffield, U.K.: Sheffield Academic Press, 1994.

Rea, John. *The Holy Spirit in the Bible.* Lake Mary, Fla.: Creation House, 1990.

Stronstad, Roger. *The Charismatic Theology of St. Luke.* Peabody, Mass.: Hendrickson, 1984.

Williams, J. R. *Renewal Theology.* Vol. 2, *Salvation, the Holy Spirit and Christian Living.* Grand Rapids: Zondervan, 1990.

---

day of Pentecost" (*Catechism of the Catholic Church*, p. 1302).

[29]Paul writes in Ephesians 5:18-19: "Be filled with the Spirit, speaking to one another in psalms and hymns and spiritual songs." The filling with the Spirit brings forth praise, including spiritual songs that may refer, as J. D. G. Dunn says, to "spontaneous singing in tongues" (*Jesus and the Spirit*, p. 239). Here indeed is fullness of praise.

Chapter 11

New Dimensions in Theological Method

Clark H. Pinnock

••••••••••••••••••••••••••••••

THEOLOGICAL METHODOLOGY IS IMPORTANT BECAUSE EVERY THEOLO-gian follows a method, whether consciously or unconsciously. Like cooks, theologians utilize ingredients in a certain manner. They follow procedures, appeal to sources, place them in order, weigh their importance and so on. Method underlies all that they do and affects all that they say. It usually holds the key to the system or school of thought. Though abstract and metatheological, method is not remote from vital concerns, since understanding it can result in better work and can help the community test for truth.[1]

But methodology must not be assigned exaggerated importance either. Theology (like art) can be done spontaneously without any thought about method. Theology is ordinarily written first and analyzed as to method afterward. Often the issue is only raised when it is in trouble. Do painters go through a checklist of criteria for good art every time they mix the paint? Do cyclists reflect on how they maintain balance before they set out? Of course they don't. Cooks, painters, cyclists and theologians work naturally, out of their expertise, mostly unconscious of method. Too much thinking about method spoils creativity.[2]

G. C. Berkouwer never explained his method, but everyone agrees that he did

---

[1]Insightful after many years is John B. Cobb, *Living Options in Protestant Theology: A Survey of Methods* (Philadelphia: Westminster, 1962).

[2]My own method has been recently subject to study by David G. Guretzki, "The Theological Method of Clark H. Pinnock" (master's thesis, Briercrest Biblical Seminary, 1995).

good work. Perhaps he did not find time to set forth his method—he failed to complete his set of projected volumes of dogmatics as it is. Though he must have had a method, he got on with his work, leaving to others the task of explicating his procedures. This is typical of theologians—most of whom work on specific issues without pausing to discuss method. This may be due to modesty, besides having better things to do. Discussing one's method would appear a little egotistical, as if the focus of one's work were oneself.[3]

Understanding method may promote a better understanding of theology and thus may improve contributions that are made to it. Questions of method are unavoidable when eyebrows are raised. When a theologian makes a surprising proposal, people naturally wonder how it was arrived at. How was it that Aquinas felt free to use Aristotle so liberally? Was it right for Turretin to try to legitimate theological assertions as scientists do? Method becomes especially important when changes are occurring, when theology is not just business as usual.[4]

In the twentieth century, this topic is front and center, which may indicate that theology is in trouble. Theologians have been provoked to explain their methods by the willingness of the other sciences to explain theirs. They are shamed when the often naive way they do theology is compared to the sophisticated ways science is done. But method is also front and center today because theological claims to truth are widely challenged and the situation is so pluralistic. One can only ask how it got so confused. The nature of God is more important than theological method certainly; but epistemological and methodological issues can be important too, since how we know God and even our understanding of God can rest on the method being employed.[5]

Evangelical Method

Theologians are evangelical (according to my definition) if they network with people in that movement. Although there is some family resemblance and a shared historical heritage, *evangelical* is basically a sociological term today. It refers to a loose community, its institutions and networking, involving seminaries and colleges, magazines and journals, luminaries and evangelists, missionary and parachurch organizations and so on. An evangelical theologian is one who (like Millard

---

[3]Regarding Berkouwer, J. C. De Moor, *Towards a Biblically Theological Method: A Structural Analysis and a Further Elaboration of G. C. Berkouwer's Hermeneutic-Dogmatic Method* (Kampen: Kok, 1980). The ponderous title hints at the often abstract nature of method.

[4]David Tracy distinguishes five basic methods in contemporary theology in *Blessed Rage for Order: The New Pluralism in Theology* (New York: Seabury, 1975). For background to method, see J. J. Mueller, *What Are They Saying About Theological Method?* (New York: Paulist, 1984).

[5]Tom Oden protests making method too central, but sometimes there is not much freedom to choose: Thomas C. Oden, *The Living God: Systematic Theology* (San Francisco: Harper & Row, 1987), 1:319.

Erickson himself) identifies with this Protestant, postfundamentalist and antiliberal movement that has flourished in North America since World War II. They are called evangelicals because a group of conservative Protestants rooted in fundamentalism took the name to describe themselves (in 1943, at the founding of the National Association of Evangelicals), and it stuck. Theologically and ecclesiastically, the movement is very diverse. An evangelical theologian may be Baptist, Presbyterian, Wesleyan, Pentecostal, Anglican, Lutheran, dispensationalist and so on. This does not make it easy to identify their theological method, if there is one.

A list of contemporary evangelical theologians (besides Erickson) would include Carl Henry, John Stott, Donald Bloesch, Stan Grenz, Jim Packer, Alister McGrath, Charles Ryrie, Tom Oden, Nancy Murphey, H. I. Lederle, David Wells, Richard Lints, John Frame, Bruce Demarest, John Gerstner, Wayne Grudem and others. Because the group is a sociological network, there are other theologians who are similar to them doctrinally but cannot be called evangelical. For example, Oden and Bloesch are called evangelical because they network with the movement; Geoffrey Wainwright and Robert Jenson are not called evangelical because they do not. Too bad, because evangelical theology would be richer if they did.[6]

Given this technicolor coalition, is there an evangelical theological method? Since evangelicals do not think much about method, it's hard to say. Most of them do theology without thinking about how. Probably a number do not view method as a complicated business. They know instinctively that it involves exegesis and collation. What is there to discuss aside from the inspiration and interpretation of the Bible? In that case, their thinking about method would be located in books about inspiration and in the prolegomena of the systematic theologies. There remains a lacuna of formal studies on evangelical theological method.[7]

Typically, evangelical method is of the *sola scriptura* variety familiar in conservative Protestantism, which David Tracy calls orthodoxy. It represents the formal principle of the Reformation in which the Bible is the *norma normans, non normata*—the norm that cannot be corrected by other sources. This method accepts as its ultimate criterion an unreserved fidelity to the sacred authority of the Bible alone. It does not admit that modern claims to truth can have substantial relevance for theology. It is not impressed by counterclaims to positions derived biblically and does not grant such claims cognitive status if they are found contrary to the Bible.

---

[6]A useful introduction to evangelical theology is contained in the thirty-three essays in Walter A. Elwell, ed., *Handbook of Evangelical Theologians* (Grand Rapids: Baker, 1993).

[7]The lacuna is noted by Richard Lints, *The Fabric of Theology: A Prolegomenon to Evangelical Theology* (Grand Rapids: Eerdmans, 1993), p. 9. Some examples are John D. Woodbridge and Thomas E. McComiskey, *Doing Theology in Today's World: Essays in Honor of Kenneth S. Kantzer* (Grand Rapids: Zondervan, 1991); Robert K. Johnston, *Evangelicals at an Impasse: Biblical Authority in Practice* (Atlanta: John Knox, 1979); and Robert K. Johnston, ed., *The Use of the Bible in Theology: Evangelical Options* (Atlanta: John Knox, 1985).

The method is strongly oriented toward the Bible as its source of doctrine. It does not aim at novelty and prides itself in abstaining from it. Evangelicals scorn liberals for drawing too heavily on culture and experience for their ideas and seek to avoid doing so in their own work. Theology for evangelicals is the task of articulating the content of revelation mediated in the Scriptures. For this reason biblical criticism poses a threat to them, lest it undermine the authority of the Bible. It is naive about the role played by other sources, such as tradition and reason, without (however) actually denying it.[8]

In my discussion of areas of growth in evangelical thinking about theological method, I want to distinguish the *sola scriptura* method in the two forms in which it appears among evangelicals: namely, the form of simple biblicism and the form of philosophical biblicism. First, by the term *simple biblicism* I refer to a trust in the Bible without reservation, to the delight evangelicals experience from meditating on Scripture and submitting to it. They feel immense gratitude for this means of grace that the Spirit has bestowed on the church to equip it. Scripture is a gift of the Spirit, and evangelicals want to be open to all that God says in this text. Scripture for them is the tangible sacrament of the Word of God nourishing them like milk and honey. Not a theory about the Bible, simple biblicism is the basic instinct that the Bible is supremely profitable and transforming, alive with God's breath. Without being free of every difficulty, the Bible nevertheless bears effective witness to Jesus Christ.

Simple biblicism trusts the Bible without reservation, letting it teach and shape us, not picking and choosing what to accept in it. As such, it is not sectarian but has a broad appeal, not only among Protestant but in Catholic traditions as well, which value the apostolic canon. Being simple, it is open to growth in understanding even of method. It wants to know as much as possible about what it means to depend on the Bible and how truth may be extracted and applied. Although committed without reservation to the Bible, it has an open attitude when it comes to learning what the Bible says, even about itself. Although wanting a reasonable faith, simple biblicism is not overly anxious about erecting rational foundations in the modern sense. It reflects a postmodern lack of anxiety about such foundations and is content with soft rather than hard rational supports.[9]

---

[8]The method is explained by Clark H. Pinnock, *Biblical Revelation: The Foundation of Christian Theology* (Chicago: Moody Press, 1971), chap. 3, and is evaluated by Avery Dulles, *Models of Revelation* (New York: Doubleday, 1983), pp. 37-41. Hans Küng holds to *sola scriptura* too but gives biblical criticism more room than do evangelicals: Catherine M. LaCugna, *The Theological Methodology of Hans Küng* (Chico, Calif.: Scholars Press, 1982), chap. 2. Mark Noll traces the struggle over biblical criticism among evangelicals in *Between Faith and Criticism: Evangelicals, Scholarship and the Bible in America* (San Francisco: Harper & Row, 1986).

[9]Stanley J. Grenz is a postmodern, soft-rational, simple biblicist type of theologian who does not discuss inspiration until page 494. See for yourself in *Theology for the People of God* (Nashville: Broadman & Holman, 1994), pp. 494-527.

Second, there is a philosophical biblicism, sometimes existing in combination with simple biblicism. My own early book (for example) *Biblical Revelation: The Foundation of Christian Theology* reveals both a simple and a philosophical biblicism. On the one hand, it breathes the warm love of the Bible that is typical of simple biblicism. On the other hand, as the subtitle indicates, it is concerned about strong, rational foundations. The book argues that we need verifiable revelational data with which (if we had it) we could speak with absolute certainty to the world. Such verified propositions (if we had them) would provide an Archimedian point outside the human situation, which would save us and all humankind from relativism. The book seeks to prove empirically that the Bible claims to be a book of timeless divine oracles and is (in effect) the philosophical golden grail. In arguing in this fashion, the book continues the rationalist tradition of B. B. Warfield and old Princeton Seminary.

Such biblicism is designed to achieve rational security, appealing to those who thirst for the modern type of rational certainty. As Carl Henry puts it, if the Bible were viewed as the axiom in a system of rational truth, we could appeal to it as a propositional authority and be able to do theology that is not culturally conditioned, as theology otherwise is. Henry writes: "God's revelation is rational communication conveyed in intelligible ideas and meaningful words, that is, in conceptual-verbal form." There is appeal in this for those who wish to escape uncertainty.[10]

Comparing the biblicisms, the simple version is more open to what the Bible actually contains than the philosophical version, since the latter requires a Bible that fits into an ideological agenda but the former does not. Philosophical biblicism is more easily threatened by what exegesis might turn up and requires a more elaborate theory of truthfulness to fit the requirements. A test for the presence of philosophical biblicism in evangelical systematic theology is the length of the prolegomenon. It takes Stanley Grenz 30 pages and Millard Erickson 259 pages to get to the doctrine of God, which goes to show that if you want rational foundations, you cannot expect to be brief. It requires one to discuss a whole range of topics about the Bible that are not discussed in the Bible but are still crucial for the agenda of philosophical biblicism.[11]

Both biblicisms, however, are oriented toward propositional revelation, and both look for doctrinal content. But philosophical biblicism is more adamant in its

---

[10]Carl F. H. Henry, *God, Revelation and Authority*, vol. 3, *God Who Speaks and Shows* (Waco, Tex.: Word, 1979), p. 248.

[11]Wayne Grudem (for example) has to discuss the Bible as the Word of God (not a biblical appellation for it), the contents of the canon (not given in Scripture), the authority and inerrancy of the Bible (neither term is biblical when used in this way) and so on. It is just not easy to get theology started when philosophical biblicism is the method: *Systematic Theology: An Introduction to Biblical Doctrine* (Grand Rapids: Zondervan, 1994), pp. 47-138.

version of propositionalism. It maintains that revelation is given in the form of words with clear content that enable us to know God's plan. Each proposition of the Bible amounts to a divine assertion, and theology exists to organize these assertions as a botanist might collect specimens of plants. Good theology according to this ideal is a correct summarization of biblical truth. Truth is thought to be unchanging and capable of being stated in timeless and culture-free ways. Theology aims at a set of universally valid propositions. The method is reminiscent of Catholic Neo-Scholasticism, except that the latter has advantages. Catholic method can appeal to tradition and the teaching office where the Bible is unclear, but philosophical biblicism cannot do so openly. Evangelicals do rely on tradition, as is apparent in the fact that none doubt the creeds, but they dare not call attention to it lest the appearance of the *sola scriptura* principle be questioned.[12]

The method, whether simple or philosophical, is a kind of biblicism, and it highlights biblical summarization. It wants to bring biblical teaching together in a systematic fashion. Grudem's systematic theology is subtitled *An Introduction to Biblical Doctrine* because he wants us to think that its content is a biblical summary and that any intellectual moves are biblically justified. It quaintly suggests that the book is nothing more than what Scripture plainly teaches on various topics. It suggests that the author just collected relevant biblical passages and summarized them. He just picked up the truths of the Bible and set them forth without any contextual influences worth mentioning. It is intended to yield a theology that is timeless and culture-free, a theology from nowhere for everyone. It does not want attention drawn to the fact that the influence of high Calvinism is everywhere evident in his exegesis. It does not want to make an issue of the fact that the author adheres to a tradition and that his work vindicates specific conservative (and in Grudem's case also charismatic) beliefs. Grudem would not want us to think that he is reading into the Bible, a complex book, ideas coming from his own setting and community.

Although capable of subtlety, evangelical theology is not often subtle, because it is written for a popular movement rather than the academy. Laity may not want subtlety, and leaders who wield power often want the theology to be simple and stark. They tend not to favor theology with mysterious, paradoxical and experiential elements. Because of this context, even theologians who know that theology is subtle may not want to give that impression.

The distinction between simple and philosophical biblicism roughly corresponds to the distinction between modern and postmodern theology. Simple biblicists, like postmoderns, do not see such a need for rational foundations in the modern sense.

---

[12]I discuss the similarity between some evangelicals and Catholics in *Tracking the Maze: Finding Our Way Through Modern Theology from an Evangelical Perspective* (San Francisco: Harper & Row, 1990), chap. 2.

It's not that they do not value reasons for faith; they are just satisfied with more modest reasoning. They operate more consciously out of a faith community and take their stand in a pluralistic world from it. They do not pretend to have a universal perspective. In contrast, philosophical biblicists do believe in objective, absolute truth "out there," which can be viewed objectively from "nowhere." For them, the fact that we are socially located is not a matter of great moment nor that thinking can be and ought to be free of bias. They are reluctant to admit that *what* we see is influenced by our historical location. In a day when many think that the objectivity ideal is impossible, philosophical biblicists hold to it. Ironically, evangelicals may turn out to be the last modernists.[13]

New Dimensions in Evangelical Method

The fundamental principle of evangelical method is not changing. Evangelicals continue to insist on complete fidelity to the apostolic (biblical) traditions. Theology must be congruent with the Word of God as mediated by the Scriptures. In this they stand with the whole church, east and west, confessing the Nicene Creed and the apostolicity of the church. They insist that the writings of the New Testament are the original and fundamental testimony to Jesus Christ, valid for all time, and that this unique witness cannot be replaced by later testimony. As the Formula of Concord declares, "Holy Scripture alone is acknowledged as the judge, norm, and rule, according to which as by the only touchstone, all doctrines are to be examined and judged, as to whether they be godly or ungodly, true or false" (Epitome of the Articles).

What *is* open to change and growth in understanding is the many and varied ways in which God speaks in Scripture and in the way theology listens. Many are awakening to the fact that more is involved in grounding their work in the Bible than in appealing to it as a flat rule. And because their commitment to the Bible is less encumbered by philosophical presuppositions, simple biblicists are more open to what it means to do really biblically grounded theology. Let us focus on two issues.

First, evangelicals are learning, as John Goldingay writes, "that scripture is characterized by the richness of a living reality, almost like a person who needs to be understood from different angles and in different roles if that person is to be understood at all."[14] The Bible presents a complex and multifaceted claim, as we

---

[13]For background to a growing rift between modern and postmodern evangelicals, see Timothy R. Phillips and Dennis L. Okholm, eds., *Christian Apologetics in the Postmodern World* (Downers Grove, Ill.: InterVarsity Press, 1995). Of particular interest and delight, "There's No Such Thing as Objective Truth, and It's a Good Thing Too" by Philip D. Kenneson, pp. 155-70.

[14]John Goldingay, *Models for Scripture* (Grand Rapids: Eerdmans, 1994), p. 18. James D. G. Dunn makes the point in "The Authority of Scripture According to the Scripture," in *The Living Word* (London: SCM Press, 1987), chap. 5.

know from observing the New Testament's use of the Old. It does not stop with the literal meaning of texts but delves into the tendencies and canonical context as well. There is richness in the Bible, and there must be flexibility in our use of it. Evangelicals are learning to use the Bible biblically.

The fact is that Scripture cannot be reduced to a single category. Large sections are narrative, prophecy and instruction, while other parts mediate experiences of God that are like our own. The Bible seldom talks about its "authority," and it says nothing at all about its "inerrancy." Laying down the law is not a dominant feature of the Bible, and errorlessness (whatever that means) is not a stated concern of the writers. We are starting to face the fact that some of our traditions have been built up deductively, not inductively from the Bible, and that there is a gap between the way Scripture speaks of itself and the way we have spoken.

Roman concepts of authority have skewed the discussion by pushing us in the direction of legal and literalist categories. Our vaunted doctrine of Scripture was not founded solely on exegesis but was framed partially in response to historical factors. This is not a terrible problem—it means we are like other mortals. A problem would arise if we became prisoners of the picture we created and refused to grow beyond it.

I am hopeful about simple biblicists because they are open in principle to accepting the situation. Because of their openness, they are able to see (for example) that in Scripture, terms like *authority, inspiration* and *inerrancy* are little used to describe the Bible. They can see that biblical data has been stretched to make room for these categories and would welcome fresh thinking. In my case, what was presented in *The Scripture Principle* was a scaled-down theory of inspiration and a more nuanced model of authority than the one I learned from Warfield, who had exaggerated these categories for reasons of the systematic picture he favored. Evangelicals are learning not to force the Bible onto a Procrustean bed of extra-scriptural assumptions about authority and perfection but to let it speak as it wants to. Our biblical scholars, who are less imprisoned by ideology and more open to the actual text, will keep the pressure on for growth.[15]

The second issue on which evangelicals are experiencing growth lies in the area of procedures of method. They are seeing that there are a number of tests for truth to apply when theology seeks to make assertions. This is a major issue for a method that likes to talk about being *sola scriptura*. The new realization is that the Bible is *alone* in the sense of being the sole infallible norm but not *alone* in the way it functions as such. Beyond the Bible are other factors that come into play when we assess meaning. It would not be true to say that evangelicals have not realized this before. Tradition (for example) funds their loyalty to Scripture and creedal

---

[15]Clark H. Pinnock, *The Scripture Principle* (San Francisco: Harper & Row, 1984).

orthodoxy, and reason plays a central role in their apologetics. They give the impression that they have a one-source method, but in reality they have always used several sources. What is new is their willingness to acknowledge it and then reflect on it.[16]

First, there is the role of tradition and proper respect for the mind of the church in our understanding of the Bible. The Reformers viewed interpretation as a corporate exercise. *Sola scriptura* did not mean for them that an individual could bypass the sense of the faithful church. Anyone knows that any heretic can quote the Bible to support any position. Evangelicals are learning that although Scripture is primary, tradition is also an important source of insight. Its value shows up in other ways too. Members of the community may well say of a position they suspect, "But that won't preach." Calvin himself wondered whether his doctrine of double predestination was right, since it would make admonitions meaningless and deprive people of hope (*Institutes* 3.23.13). His hesitancy has been widely felt ever since, and the doctrine has nearly disappeared (thankfully).

Second, there is the role of reason, which can help theology speak coherently and consistently. It pressures theology to crosscheck its assertions with reality to see if they agree with the relevant data. Davis Young, for example, is pressing the issue with respect to Noah's flood. He reasons that if general revelation as discerned by geologists fails to support the hypothesis of a universal flood, exegetes should look for a better way to read the text of Genesis. The implication is that extrabiblical data can illumine the text and can guide us in its interpretation. Howard Van Till is pressing the issue with regard to evolution. He says we should not ignore the light of general revelation as discerned by science when it can help us interpret the Bible. Both science and the Bible should be taken seriously. Not doing so is one of the failings of evangelical thinking, according to Mark Noll.[17]

Third, there is the factor of culture and setting. Though we have tried to ignore it, the Word of God is heard within real-life contexts. We come to the text with questions, and the answers that we find depend somewhat on who we are and where we are. A Masai notices different things in the stories of Genesis than does an American. We notice different things in Mark from one reading to the next as our circumstances change. There is a reader horizon as well as a textual horizon when it comes to hermeneutics. Of course, this dimension must not be allowed to take

---

[16]A groundbreaking book is by Donald A. D. Thorson, *The Wesleyan Quadrilateral: Scripture, Tradition, Reason and Experience as a Model of Evangelical Theology* (Grand Rapids: Zondervan, 1990).

[17]Davis Young, *The Biblical Flood: A Case Study of the Church's Response to Extra-biblical Evidence* (Grand Rapids: Eerdmans, 1995); Howard Van Till, *The Fourth Day: What the Bible and the Heavens Are Telling Us About the Creation* (Grand Rapids: Eerdmans, 1986); Mark A. Noll, *The Scandal of the Evangelical Mind* (Grand Rapids: Eerdmans, 1994), chap. 7. Bernard Ramm made this point a generation ago, but it has not sunk in: *The Christian View of Science and Scripture* (London: Paternoster, 1955).

over. A fresh interpretation must also be a valid interpretation capable of being tested. But lying behind the richness of interpretation is God's desire that the Bible should be heard in a timely way by every hearer. God does not want theology to become irrelevant and sidestep its responsibility to speak a crucial word. It is a temptation for theologians to stick with original meaning and not take risks discerning the mind of the Spirit for this moment. God's Word is a timely witness, not a timeless abstraction, and theology ought to be listening to what the Spirit is saying to the churches (Rev 2:7).[18]

Evangelicals are learning to work more self-consciously with a fuller pattern of sources in their theological method. Theologians such as Fackre, Oden, McGrath, Lints and Grenz—less influenced by the heritage of fundamentalism than some others—already work this way and set a good example. The result of a fuller method is the enrichment of theology. It makes theology more catholic and less parochial, more comprehensible and less strident, more timely and less irrelevant.

I am frankly more optimistic about simple biblicists making course corrections in the light of these dynamics than the philosophical biblicists. This is because the latter carry much heavier presuppositional baggage than the former. The rational system of propositionalism makes them less able to change and adopt needed corrections. Thinking that they possess timeless divine propositions, thinking in either/or terms—either our absolutes or complete relativism—such thinking is not easily altered by pointing to fresh considerations.

Philosophical biblicists may be empirically or rationally oriented. The difference has to do with whether they validate the Scripture principle by historical evidences (for example, a christological apologetic) as John Montgomery does or by pure logic (for example, it is a basic assumption of logical thought) as Carl Henry does. It is easier for the philosophical biblicist who is empirically oriented to accept change, because the facts may appear subtler and more surprising than they did at first. The door is always open, to seeing a different pattern in the data. It is harder for a philosophical biblicist who is rationalistically oriented to be so open, because facts (in this way of thinking) do not exist outside the system and thus cannot exercise a reforming influence on it. It is harder for reality to get through to such a person, perhaps even impossible. I have a vivid memory of my wife, having listened to Gordon Clark (Carl Henry's mentor), challenging him to say if he knew whether his own wife existed and if so how he knew. A rational system such as his is impervious to falsification by appealing to data and therefore is impervious to reform and growth.

Nevertheless, it should impress philosophical biblicists that the Bible does not see itself as their system sees it. That way of thinking, though it exalts the Bible, is

---

[18]On the reader horizon, Anthony C. Thiselton, *New Horizons in Hermeneutics* (Grand Rapids: Zondervan, 1992) and Grant R. Osborne, *The Hermeneutical Spiral: A Comprehensive Introduction to Biblical Interpretation* (Downers Grove, Ill.: InterVarsity Press, 1991), appendices 1-2.

not actually biblical. For all the bravado, it is not a scripturally grounded system and does not use the Bible appropriately. Philosophical biblicism has problems with the Bible, which does not make the subtle claim to inerrancy that it requires, does not look like a rational axiom and does not deliver propositional revelation in the amounts required. Furthermore, the rational ideal that it espouses is beyond our reach and is unnecessary anyhow. It would be better, as Roger Olson says, for us to do our work in postmodern ways.[19]

A Method of Engagement

As their thinking matures and their method grows in quality, evangelical theology will be in a better position to do good work in a good cause. An "evangelical" method must be evangelistic as well. More than some others, evangelicals with a heart for missions will want to do theology not for themselves but for a broken world. They will want their method to deploy the truth of God effectively for the sake of the nations, because they know that the purpose is not to feed our own appetites but to become all things to all people in order to win them (1 Cor 9:19-23). Pursuing the truth in theology is not a selfish endeavor—the aim is to present truth to outsiders with a view toward their embracing it. Theology is not for our eyes only but for all eyes to see.[20]

The method that we need is a bipolar one: a method that is faithful to the Word of God but also crucial and timely, faithful to the Bible and not afraid of engagement. Evangelicals are growing toward a method that is neither correlational nor confrontational but a genuine engagement. They are developing a method that mediates between the horizons of the Bible and modern life.

First, the criterion and norm would be the undiminished Christian message attested in the Scriptures. It would proclaim in no uncertain terms that Jesus Christ is Lord and his name above every name. It would proclaim the Word of God and the good news of the gospel of Jesus Christ. It would not allow "correlation" in the sense of the blending of insights from the Bible and other sources on an equal basis.[21]

---

[19]Roger E. Olson, "Whales and Elephants: Both God's Creatures, but Can They Meet? Evangelicals and Liberals in Dialogue," *Pro Ecclesia* 4 (1995): 165-89, and "Postconservative Evangelicals Greet the Postmodern Age," *The Christian Century*, May 3, 1995, pp. 480-83.

[20]Wolfhart Pannenberg is strengthening the resolve of evangelicals to forsake the ghetto and pursue truth in public: *An Introduction to Systematic Theology* (Grand Rapids: Eerdmans, 1991). The first-fruits of his influence is seen in Stanley J. Grenz and Roger E. Olson, who dedicated a book to him: *Twentieth-Century Theology: God and the World in a Transitional Age* (Downers Grove, Ill.: InterVarsity Press, 1992). One volume of the Erickson trilogy was dedicated to Pannenberg also.

[21]We respect the fears of Donald G. Bloesch in this regard: *A Theology of Word and Spirit: Authority and Method in Theology* (Downers Grove, Ill.: InterVarsity Press, 1992), pp. 259-62. Bloesch is our evangelical Karl Barth. But evangelicals are not Barthian, and they will wonder why the relation between the truth of special revelation and the truth of general revelation must always clash (pp. 262-64). Bloesch offers a recipe for doing theology behind the barricades. Evangelicals, because of their respect for reason and general revelation, will modify what he says, as they should.

Second, the goal would be cruciality and timeliness. Evangelicals want the truth of the gospel to make contact with the present-day world of human experience in all its ambivalence and changeableness. We do not want to stand defensively apart from other people. Rather, we want to make the intelligibility of faith and doctrine apparent. There are risks to take as we reach out to and confront competing truth claims, but this is what we are called to do. The test of our theology is not only how strongly we have maintained traditional convictions but also how well we have responded to the issues of the day.[22]

Resources for Additional Study

Bloesch, Donald G. *A Theology of Word and Spirit: Authority and Method in Theology*. Downers Grove, Ill.: InterVarsity Press, 1992.

Cobb, John B. *Living Options in Protestant Theology: A Survey of Methods*. Philadelphia: Westminster, 1962.

Goldingay, John. *Models for Scripture*. Grand Rapids: Eerdmans, 1994.

Johnston, Robert K. *Evangelicals at an Impasse: Biblical Authority in Practice*. Atlanta: John Knox, 1979.

Johnston, Robert K., ed. *The Use of the Bible in Theology: Evangelical Options*. Atlanta: John Knox, 1985.

Küng, Hans. *Theology for the Third Millennium: An Ecumenical View*. New York: Doubleday, 1988.

LaCugna, Catherine M. *The Theological Method of Hans Küng*. Chico, Calif.: Scholars Press, 1982.

Lints, Richard *The Fabric of Theology: A Prolegomenon to Evangelical Theology*. Grand Rapids: Eerdmans, 1993.

Mueller, J. J. *What Are They Saying About Theological Method?* New York: Paulist, 1984.

Thiselton, Anthony C. *New Horizons in Hermeneutics*. Grand Rapids: Zondervan, 1992.

Thorson, Donald A. D. *The Wesleyan Quadrilateral: Scripture, Tradition, Reason and Experience*. Grand Rapids: Zondervan, 1990.

Tracy, David. *Blessed Rage for Order: The New Pluralism in Theology*. New York: Seabury, 1975.

---

[22]Evangelicals can learn from Hans Küng's reflections on his bipolar method expounded late in his career: *Theology for the Third Millennium: An Ecumenical View* (New York: Doubleday, 1988).

Chapter 12

New Dimensions
in Scripture

Louis Igou Hodges

••••••••••••••••••••••••••••

T HE WESTERN WORLD IS CURRENTLY IN THE THROES OF AN AUTHORITY
crisis so severe that it leaves virtually no aspect of life or thought unscathed. An
antiauthoritarian mindset has resulted as authority has been relocated, from above
to sources below. The modern mood, which characteristically rejects the epistemological intrusion of the supernatural dimension, is accordingly transient, relative and
shifting, vowing allegiance only to itself.[1]

At the storm center is the crucial issue of biblical authority. Twentieth-century
theologians commonly deny the existence of revealed truth; in fact, by the tenets of
postmodernism any rational theology is impossible.[2] Therefore Edward Farley and
Peter C. Hodgson can declare, "The house of authority has collapsed, despite the
fact that many people still try to live in it."[3] It is evident, however, historically, that

---

[1]Carl F. H. Henry, *The Christian Mindset in a Secular Society: Promoting Evangelical Renewal and National
Righteousness* (Portland: Multnomah, 1981), p. 81, cited in David F. Wells, "Word and World: Biblical
Authority and the Quandary of Modernity," in *Evangelical Affirmations*, ed. Kenneth S. Kantzer and
Carl F. H. Henry (Grand Rapids: Zondervan, 1990), p. 169. See also Carl F. H. Henry, "The Authority
of the Bible," in *The Origin of the Bible*, ed. Philip Wesley Comfort (Wheaton, Ill.: Tyndale House,
1992), p. 13; William E. Hull, "Response" (to Clark Pinnock, "What Is Biblical Inerrancy?"), in *The
Proceedings of the Conference on Biblical Inerrancy, 1987* (Nashville: Broadman, 1987), p. 85; D. A.
Carson, "Recent Developments in the Doctrine of Scripture," in *Hermeneutics, Authority and Canon*,
ed. D. A. Carson and John D. Woodbridge (Grand Rapids: Baker, 1986), pp. 8, 46.
[2]Henry, "Authority of the Bible," pp. 16-17; Alister McGrath and David Wenham, "Evangelicalism
and Biblical Authority," in *Evangelical Anglicans: Their Role and Influence in the Church Today*, ed. R. T.
France and A. E. McGrath (London: S.P.C.K, 1993), p. 26.
[3]Edward Farley and Peter C. Hodgson, "Scripture and Tradition," in *Christian Theology: An Introduction to
Its Traditions and Tasks*, ed. Peter C. Hodgson and Robert H. King (Philadelphia: Fortress, 1982), p. 50.

all efforts to preserve faith in the Creator and Redeemer, untethered to the divinely inspired Word, fail. Rejecting the truth content of supernatural revelation results in an elusive and unsustainable subjectivism that robs faith of any objective authority. It leaves an empty, illusionary controlling center of mysticism that is incompetent to deal in any decisive manner with the epistemological, moral and theological case loads of the contemporary context.[4] It comes as no surprise that in this milieu there is a decline in both biblical literalism and the recognition of the authority of Scripture, even in supposedly evangelical churches.[5]

Although the word *evangelical* has been used by four centuries of theologians, today it refers to the branch of the Christian church that adheres firmly to several basic convictions, the principal one being that Scripture is the inspired Word of God that serves as the infallible guide for both knowledge of God and Christian living. This formal (or formative) principle of the Reformation constitutes the watershed issue that divides evangelicalism from all other Protestant movements. It means that Scripture defines the center of gravity and is the central determining and legitimating resource for all true evangelical thought and theology.[6]

Recently this strong tenet and its corollary of inerrancy have come under attack by thinkers who consider themselves evangelicals. The result has been a degree of fragmentation and considerable ink lashing between the different sides.[7]

The issues raised are of great consequence. Because the doctrine of Scripture is fundamental to all others, involving both an ontology and an epistemology, it may be rightly stated that the matter of biblical authority is one of the most important issues facing the Christian church today.[8] Furthermore, since the Christian depends on Scripture for the knowledge of God, the authority and interpretation of God's written revelation are, practically speaking, as important to the individual believer as God is. It is noteworthy that theological deviations characteristically are caused by either the neglect of biblical truth or an improper

---

[4]Henry, "Authority of the Bible, " p. 25; H. D. McDonald, "The Bible in Twentieth-Century British Theology," in *Challenges to Inerrancy: A Theological Response*, ed. Gordon Lewis and Bruce Demarest (Chicago: Moody Press, 1984), p. 108; Wells, "Word and World," p. 170.

[5]Carson, "Recent Developments," pp. 47-48; Millard J. Erickson, *Where Is Theology Going? Issues and Perspectives on the Future of Theology* (Grand Rapids: Baker, 1994), p. 89.

[6]Alister McGrath, *Evangelicalism and the Future of Christianity* (Downers Grove, Ill.: InterVarsity Press, 1995), pp. 19, 55; Kenneth S. Kantzer, "Unity in Diversity in Evangelical Faith," in *The Evangelicals: What They Believe, Who They Are, Where They Are Going*, ed. David F. Wells and John D. Woodbridge (Nashville: Abingdon, 1975), p. 39; McGrath and Wenham, "Evangelicalism and Biblical Authority," p. 27.

[7]Carson, "Recent Developments," pp. 6-10.

[8]Donald Guthrie, "Biblical Authority and New Testament Scholarship," in *Vox Evangelica XVI*, ed. Harold H. Rowdon (Exeter, U.K.: Paternoster, 1986), p. 7; Erickson, *Where Is Theology Going?* p. 91; J. I. Packer, "Encountering Present-Day Views of Scripture," in *The Foundation of Biblical Authority*, ed. James Montgomery Boice (Grand Rapids: Zondervan, 1978), p. 61.

interpretation of the text.[9] Therefore all other lesser or supposed authorities must be tested and authenticated by holy Scripture. The Christian frame of thought and value structure must be governed by God's self-revelation. Ultimate control by anything or anyone else is an intolerable and destructive slavery.[10]

The Consensus Position

The issues under debate in no way nullify the strong agreement on certain givens regarding Scripture that undergird contemporary evangelicalism. All affirm the total inclusive authority of Scripture as the inspired Word of God, which must serve as the foundation for all knowledge. Because of the ontological and moral gap between God and humankind, true knowledge of God is accessible only by revelation and saving knowledge only by special revelation. To find truth and its applications to the ultimate questions of life, evangelicals necessarily turn to the Scriptures. God's written revelation takes priority over all other authorities and ways of thinking. Serious theology can be constructed only on the foundation of belief in Scripture as a definitive disclosure of transcendent, eternal truth.

Scripture has been given in order to bring human beings into a right standing with God through a personal relationship with Jesus Christ as Lord and Savior. It also provides the instruction by which Christ extends his lordship, enabling believers to seek God's glory in all things.[11] Additionally it is in Jesus Christ, both its primary subject and its interpretive key, that the overarching unity of Scripture is to be found.[12]

Issuing from the divine origin of Scripture is its supreme authority. Bernard Ramm has defined authority as "that right or power to command action or compliance, or to determine belief or custom, expecting obedience from those under authority, and in turn giving responsible account for the claim or right to power."[13] Scripture is the norm or rule that is itself above rule.[14] The authority of the written Word allows evangelicals to address contemporary culture with an objectivity that guards against both relativism and subjectivism.

Despite unanimity on these core concepts, there are notable differences in stance

---

[9]David S. Dockery, *Christian Scripture: An Evangelical Perspective on Inspiration, Authority and Interpretation* (Nashville: Broadman & Holman, 1995), p. 151.

[10]McGrath and Wenham, "Evangelicalism and Biblical Authority," p. 24; Gordon D. Fee, "Issues in Evangelical Hermeneutics: Hermeneutics and the Nature of Scripture," *Crux* 26, no. 2 (June 1990): 23.

[11]Kenneth Kantzer, "Inerrancy and the Humanity and Divinity of the Bible," in *Proceedings*, p. 154; Dockery, *Christian Scripture*, p. 40.

[12]Dockery, *Christian Scripture*, p. 25.

[13]Bernard Ramm, *The Pattern of Religious Authority* (Grand Rapids: Eerdmans, 1957), p. 10.

[14]Anthony N. S. Lane, "*Sola Scriptura?* Making Sense of a Post-Reformation Slogan," in *A Pathway into the Holy Scripture*, ed. Philip E. Satterthwaite and David F. Wright (Grand Rapids: Eerdmans, 1994), p. 324.

regarding the infallibility and inerrancy of Scripture within evangelicalism. While including six general varieties of evangelicals in his taxonomy,[15] Gabriel Fackre discerns three views of inerrancy and infallibility. Under the former (inerrancy refers to the position that the Bible is without error in all that it affirms) he sees (1) a conservative view (transmissive inerrancy) that pays little more than lip service to the role of the human authors, minimizes critical inquiry, practices grammatical-historical interpretation and gives great attention to harmonization, (2) a moderate view (trajectory inerrancy) that devotes some attention to the historical and literary aspects of the biblical writings, assigns a modest role to critical scholarship, allows for ancient Near Eastern figures of speech and an imprecision in numbering (by modern standards) and understands the infallibility of Scripture to refer to doctrine and morals, so that mistakes in transmission are possible on peripheral matters such as science and history, and (3) a liberal view (intentional inerrancy) that stresses authorial intention, viewed as flawless and discovered through the guarded probing of the literary form of the text and historical circumstances by means of critical scholarship.

Under the category of infallibility (those who believe that there are mistakes in the autographs, but these do not affect adversely the purposes of God in giving Scripture) Fackre observes (1) a conservative position (unitive infallibility), in which the Bible is not perceived as a textbook of secular matters but as the gospel of Christ for sinful persons—hence the defense of the evangelical faith does not require positing errorless autographs, (2) a moderate position (essential infallibility), which sees in the Bible the substance of Christian life and thought (that is, the most essential doctrines) through which the text (with its lack of uniformity) must be read, selected and interpreted, and (3) a liberal view (Christocentric infallibility), which, while assuming a propositional base, selects, interprets and even rejects a given text (for example, Paul's view of women) by the standard of Jesus Christ.[16]

In a similar analysis, which focuses more particularly on the way in which the doctrine of inerrancy is articulated within evangelical circles, David Dockery identifies nine different positions:

1. Mechanical dictation, which virtually ignores or denies the role of the human authors[17]

2. Absolute inerrancy, which denies dictation but affirms the accuracy of the Bible in all matters while taking neither the human nor the historical aspects with great seriousness

---

[15](1) Fundamentalism, (2) old evangelicals, (3) new evangelicals, (4) peace and justice evangelicals, (5) charismatic evangelicals and (6) ecumenical evangelicals. Gabriel Fackre, "Evangelical Hermeneutics: Commonality and Diversity," *Interpretation* 43, no. 2 (April 1989): 118-19.

[16]Ibid., pp. 121-26.

[17]In recent days only a few, the "super-fundamentalists," have actually held to mechanical dictation. See Kantzer, "Inerrancy and the Humanity and Divinity of the Bible," pp. 154, 161 (n. 14). The problem of semantics emerges in the interpretation of statements made by these occasional and rare writers.

3. Critical inerrancy, which understands the Bible to be accurate in all that it affirms to that degree of precision intended by each individual author and makes cautious use of critical methodologies in interpretation

4. Limited inerrancy, which holds that the Bible is inerrant only in matters having to do with faith and practice, salvation and matters that can be empirically verified

5. Qualified inerrancy, which by faith confesses that the Bible is inerrant and makes an effort to take seriously both its human and divine qualities

6. Nuanced inerrancy, which recognizes the various types of literature in the Bible and sees inspiration as tailored to the different genre; takes seriously both the human and the divine elements

7. Functional inerrancy, which affirms that the Bible is inerrant in its purpose of bringing people to salvation and Christian growth

8. Inerrancy is irrelevant, which neither affirms nor denies inerrancy, which is viewed as adiaphorous

9. Biblical authority, which recognizes that the Bible is authoritative only as it brings persons into a personal encounter with God; verbal inspiration is denied; errors are present but inconsequential[18]

Most discussions of inerrancy, however, do not operate in terms of such technical nuances. Usually two or three poles are in view. Harold O. J. Brown speaks of three groups: (1) the group represented by the International Council on Biblical Inerrancy, which considers inerrancy to be a watershed issue of the historical Christian faith, (2) those who hold to inerrancy but insist that the unity of believers is of more fundamental importance and (3) a group, represented by Jack Rogers, who argue that inerrancy is a later doctrine formulated by scholastic Calvinists and is not the historic position of the church.[19]

We will now examine a number of contemporary trends in theology as related to the doctrine of Scripture.

The Doctrine of Scripture

Interestingly, those in each of the major camps use many of the same theological blocks in constructing their bibliologies. The starting point for the evangelical view of Scripture is the doctrine of inspiration. Its origin in a transcendent source gives to the Bible a derived authority from God that is living, unchanging and demanding and possesses the power to relativize all other thought.[20] Biblical authors affirm in absolute terms that God has made himself known in a way that

---

[18]David S. Dockery, "Variations in Inerrancy," *SBC Today* (May 1986): 10-11; cited in J. Terry Young, "The Relationship Between Biblical Inerrancy and Biblical Authority," in *Proceedings*, p. 406.

[19]Harold O. J. Brown, "The Inerrancy and Infallibility of the Bible," in *The Origin of the Bible*, ed. Philip Wesley Comfort (Wheaton, Ill.: Tyndale House, 1992), p. 40.

[20]Wells, "Word and World," p. 171; Young, "Biblical Inerrancy and Biblical Authority," pp. 394-99.

is cognitive, rational and meaningful. The only barriers they recognize in the process of revelation are moral and spiritual, not philosophical or linguistic. Through the unavoidable use of propositional revelation, Scripture is given to bring human beings to a personal knowledge of God. Propositional revelation and personal revelation are complementary, not antithetical or contradictory.[21]

When rightly understood, the doctrine of inspiration means that there is a dual authorship to holy Scripture (2 Pet 1:20-21). Divine thoughts are clothed in human language. This union is often illustrated by the helpful, though admittedly limited, analogy of the hypostatic union.[22] It is in the attempt to articulate precisely the relationship between the divine Author and the human writers, while avoiding both an ebionitic concept (loss of the divine side) and a docetic view (denial of the human side), that tensions continue to emerge.[23] On the one hand the apostle speaks of all Scripture (particularly the Old Testament, and to the New Testament by analogy) as *theopneustos* (God-breathed); it is the product of the powerful, creative breath of God's Spirit (2 Tim 3:16).[24] The manner in which the Spirit worked in the biblical writers is not specified and remains a mystery. But the Spirit brooded over each writer, working concursively through all the many processes involved in bringing each book of the canon to its final form, including reflection, feeling, worshiping and responding to crises. In all the research, selection, composition and editing, the Spirit checked false impressions and prevented the inclusion of erroneous matters, so that Scripture is the completely trustworthy word of the living God.

On the other hand there are countless indications of the historical contexts and processes of human life in which the different books were produced. Evangelicals do not deny the humanity of Scripture and its implications, as is often charged.

---

[21]McDonald, "The Bible in Twentieth-Century British Theology," p. 110; Dockery, *Christian Scripture,* pp. 22-23; Kevin Vanhoozer, "God's Mighty Speech-Acts: The Doctrine of Scripture Today," in *A Pathway into Holy Scripture,* p. 178; Henry, "The Authority of the Bible," p. 19.

[22]Kantzer, "Inerrancy and the Humanity and Divinity of the Bible," p. 161, n. 21; Dockery, *Christian Scripture,* p. 38; John Gerstner, "A Protestant View of Biblical Authority," in *Scripture in the Jewish and Christian Traditions: Authority, Interpretation, Relevance,* ed. Frederick E. Greenspahn (Nashville: Abingdon, 1982), p. 54; Harold O. J. Brown, "The Arian Connection: Presuppositions of Errancy," in *Challenges to Inerrancy: A Theological Response,* ed. Gordon Lewis and Bruce Demarest (Chicago: Moody Press, 1984), p. 391; B. B. Warfield, "The Divine and the Human in the Bible," in *Selected Shorter Writings,* ed. John E. Meeter, (Nutley, N.J.: Presbyterian & Reformed, 1970, 1973), 2:547.

[23]Dockery, *Christian Scripture,* pp. 37-38, 66; H. Edwin Young, "Response" (to J. I. Packer, "Inerrancy and the Divinity and the Humanity of the Bible"), in *Proceedings,* p. 150; Kantzer, "Inerrancy and the Humanity and Divinity of the Bible," p. 159. J. I. Packer refers to the human authors as being only secondary and in one sense as having contributed nothing. J. I. Packer, "The Inspiration of the Bible," in *The Origin of the Bible,* ed. Philip Wesley Comfort (Wheaton, Ill.: Tyndale House, 1992), pp. 31, 33.

[24]B. B. Warfield, "The Biblical Idea of Inspiration," in *The Inspiration and Authority of the Bible,* ed. Samuel G. Craig (Philadelphia: Presbyterian & Reformed, 1967), pp. 132-33.

What they deny is (1) that humanness necessarily involves error and (2) that the omnipotent, omniscient God is unable to work concursively through the spontaneous, free and creative literary exercises of divinely prepared men in such a way that what they wrote as his spokesmen was absolute truth. Inspiration includes all of the essential characteristics of normal literary composition.[25]

Behind the tensions regarding the divine and human elements in Scripture are two different methodologies. Inerrantists work deductively from the self-teaching of Scripture regarding its nature and authority, as well as the attributes of its divine author, and interpret the phenomena associated with human authorship in the light of Scripture's own claims. This method begins with certain theological assumptions and arranges the human phenomena within that grid. Non-inerrantists, however, begin with their exegetical and historical understanding of the phenomena and work inductively toward a view of the nature of Scripture, even if it requires modifications of its self-teaching.[26] While perceptive inerrantists realize that an adequate doctrine of inspiration and biblical authority must take into account both the self-teaching of Scripture and the phenomena (a method called abduction, adduction or retroduction),[27] God's explanatory voice must be heard first and must be given functional control over the interpretation and ordering of the human phenomena.[28] The choice made between the two methodologies is of momentous importance because the answer to the question (inerrancy or errancy) is determined by the approach employed. Deductivists, who begin with the express claims of Scripture, inevitably end with a high view of its authority, and inductivists, who begin with the phenomena, conclude with a correspondingly lower view.[29]

---

[25]Carson, "Recent Developments," pp. 23, 28; Brown, "The Arian Connection: Presuppositions of Errancy," pp. 390, 400; J. I. Packer, "The Inspiration of the Bible," p. 35; Dockery, *Christian Scripture*, pp. 42, 68; Young, "Response" (to J. I. Packer), in *Proceedings*, p. 149; Kenneth Kantzer, "Inerrancy and the Humanity and Divinity of the Bible," pp. 153, 158.

[26]Fee, "Issues in Evangelical Hermeneutics," p. 25; H. M. Vroom, "Contemporary Questions Concerning the *Sola Scriptura*," *Reformed World* 39, no. 1 (March 1986): 458; T. Jerry Young, "The Relationship Between Biblical Inerrancy and Biblical Authority," in *Proceedings*, p. 404. Erickson illustrates the two methodologies employed by applying the two different starting points to the question of whether or not Jesus was sinless. The starting point determines the answer. Millard J. Erickson, *Christian Theology* (Grand Rapids: Baker, 1983-85), 1:208.

[27]Paul D. Feinberg, "The Meaning of Inerrancy," in *Inerrancy*, ed. Norman L. Geisler (Grand Rapids: Zondervan, 1979), pp. 270-76; Carson, "Recent Developments," p. 25; Bruce Corley, "Biblical Teaching on Inspiration and Inerrancy," in *Proceedings*, p. 450.

[28]Dockery, *Christian Scripture*, p. 56, n. 11; Millard J. Erickson, "Problem Areas Related to Biblical Inerrancy," in *Proceedings*, p. 175; Young, "Response" (to J. I. Packer), " in *Proceedings*, p. 148.

[29]Warfield, *The Inspiration and Authority of the Bible*, pp. 202-225; Hywel Jones, *The Doctrine of Scripture Today: Trends in Evangelical Thinking* (London: British Evangelical Council, 1969), p. 17. For a third approach, see William L. Hendricks, "The Difference Between Substance (Matter) and Form in

The self-teaching of Scripture is anchored securely in several facts. First, as biblical writers proclaim "thus saith the Lord," they operate in an atmosphere where inerrancy is assumed, holding God's people accountable for the message that is conveyed.[30] There is no indication that any biblical author ever questioned the truthfulness of another inspired writer in any specific detail. Absolute certainty and finality prevail about what is written.

Second is the witness of Jesus Christ to the authority and reliability of the Old Testament. He believed in its recorded history (Mk 12:26; Lk 11:31-32), miracles (Jn 3:14; Lk 4:25-27), prophecies (Mt 13:14; 24:15), ethical standards (Mt 19:3-5; Mk 10:18-19), inspiration (Mk 12:36) and eternal duration (Mt 5:17; Lk 16:17). He used the very words of specific texts as the foundation for theological pronouncements (Mt 22:31-32).[31] The unequivocal confidence placed by Jesus Christ in the Scriptures is the ultimate argument for the evangelical view of the Bible. From it springs an irrefutable case for the unconditional authority of the written Word, despite feeble attempts at weakening it by arguments from the kenosis, from a supposed accommodation to first-century thought forms, or from supposed literary emendations to the Gospel accounts.[32] Acceptance of the lordship of Jesus Christ necessitates the methodological commitment to his view of the infallible authority of Scripture.[33]

That lordship is mediated in turn by means of the biblical documents through which he is revealed exclusively and definitely. There is therefore an organic and essential connection between Christ and the Scriptures. Christ is honored when people receive the Old Testament as he did and the inspired, normative witness to him given through his commissioned apostles. The authority of Christ is blended with the authority of Scripture, and no wedge must be driven between the living Word and the written Word.[34] Evangelicals do not practice bibliolatry, but they

---

Relationship to Biblical Inerrancy," in Proceedings, p. 486.

[30]Brown, "The Inerrancy and Infallibility of the Bible," pp. 43-44.

[31]Wayne A. Grudem, "Scripture's Self-Attestation and the Problem of Formulating a Doctrine of Scripture," in *Scripture and Truth*, ed. D. A. Carson and John D. Woodbridge (Grand Rapids: Zondervan, 1983), pp. 19-59; Robert P. Lightner, *The Savior and the Scriptures* (Philadelphia: Presbyterian & Reformed, 1966); John Wenham, *Christ and the Bible* (Downers Grove, Ill.: InterVarsity Press, 1972).

[32]See Gerstner, "A Protestant View of Biblical Authority," p. 47; McDonald, "The Bible in Twentieth-Century British Theology," pp. 101-4.

[33]Gerstner, "Protestant View of Biblical Authority," p. 47; Kantzer, "Unity and Diversity in Evangelical Faith," p. 45; H. Edwin Young, "Response" (to Kenneth Kantzer, "Inerrancy and the Humanity and Divinity of the Bible"), in *Proceedings*, p. 172; Packer, "Inerrancy and the Divinity and the Humanity of the Bible," p. 138. Because the evangelical view is tied to the lordship of Christ, it is not proved by a circular argument. See Gerstner, "Protestant View," pp. 54-58; Kantzer, "Unity and Diversity in Evangelical Faith," p. 45.

[34]McGrath and Wenham, "Evangelicalism and Biblical Authority," pp. 23, 27; McDonald, "The Bible in Twentieth-Century British Theology," pp. 106-7, 113; Vanhoozer, "God's Mighty Speech-Acts," p. 179.

have great reverence for the book through which they come to know the Lord whom they worship. Horatius Bonar observed perceptively that exclusive regard for the written Word leads to rationalism, while exclusive regard for the person of Christ leads to mysticism.[35]

Third is the nature of God. Devout minds cannot begin to imagine the word of a perfect God—who is omniscient, holy, loving, who is the standard of all truth—being in error and therefore subject to correction by finite minds. Because God is faithful and true, the reader of holy Scripture will not be led astray.

Fourth is the powerful and all-encompassing providence by which God "works all things after the counsel of His own will" (Eph 1:11 NASB). God from the beginning has exercised full control over the range of possibilities of expression within every language, has overseen the most minute details in personal lives, has controlled even the remote ancestry of biblical writers to bring each to the exact point of working concursively through their spontaneous literary activity, and has supernaturally preserved each canonical writer from error in penning the biblical books.[36]

Fifth, inerrancy is in keeping with the historical, orthodox position of the church. Despite attempts to demonstrate the contrary,[37] belief in the absolute truthfulness of Scripture has been the standard belief of the church, whether presupposed, implied or stated, until the rise of modern criticism. Never in its history has the church held to the authority of a fallible word.[38]

The careful weighing of these five facts leads consistent evangelicals[39] to classify inerrancy as a proper inference or, even more strongly, an entailment from the biblical doctrine of inspiration.[40] An erroneous Bible would have neither force nor

---

[35]Horatius Bonar, *Catechisms of the Scottish Reformation* (London: James Nisbit, 1866), pp. xiv-xv.

[36]Vern S. Poythress, "Adequacy of Language and Accommodation," in *Hermeneutics, Inerrancy and the Bible,* ed. Earl D. Radmacher and Robert D. Preus (Grand Rapids: Zondervan, 1984), p. 352; Millard J. Erickson, "Immanence, Transcendence and the Doctrine of Scripture," in *The Living and Active Word of God: Studies in Honor of Samuel J. Schultz,* ed. Morris Inch and Ronald Youngblood (Winona Lake, Ind.: Eisenbrauns, 1983), p. 203; Kantzer, "Inerrancy and the Humanity and Divinity of the Bible," p. 156. Any denial that God can speak inerrantly through human writers is a denial of the biblical doctrine of providence.

[37]See Jack B. Rogers and Donald K. McKim, *The Authority and Interpretation of the Bible: An Historical Approach* (San Francisco: Harper & Row, 1979). Rogers and McKim are well refuted by John D. Woodbridge, *Biblical Authority: A Critique of the Rogers/McKim Proposal* (Grand Rapids: Zondervan, 1982).

[38]Brown, "The Arian Connection," pp. 395, 400; Roger Nicole, "The Inspiration and Authority of Scripture: J. D. G. Dunn Versus B. B. Warfield," *Churchman* 97, no. 3 (1983): 199; L. R. Bush III, "Evangelism and Biblical Authority," in *Evangelism in the Twenty-first Century,* ed. Thom S. Rainer (Wheaton, Ill.: Harold Shaw, 1989), p. 106; Guthrie, "Biblical Authority and New Testament Scholarship," p. 8; Vanhoozer, "God's Mighty Speech-Acts," p. 144; John D. Woodbridge, "Is Biblical Inerrancy a Fundamentalist Doctrine?" *Bibliotheca Sacra* 142, no. 568 (October/December 1985): 299.

[39]Kenneth Kantzer, "Parameters of Biblical Inerrancy," in *Proceedings,* p. 119, n. 1.

[40]Robert Preus, "The Inerrancy of Scripture," in *Proceedings,* p. 49; Nicole, "Inspiration and Authority of Scripture," p. 202; J. I. Packer, "Problem Areas Related to Biblical Inerrancy," in *Proceedings,* p. 205.

authority because its every statement would be subject to the potential correction and countermanding of finite and imperfect minds. Thus human opinion and personal preference would usurp the ultimate place of authority.[41] Inspiration guarantees the truthfulness of everything which is affirmed within holy Scripture. Although, technically speaking, infallibility has to do with the function of Scripture and inerrancy has to do with its nature, the terms have come to be used synonymously except by those like Stephen Davis who arbitrarily confine "infallibility" to matters of faith and practice and "inerrancy" to all matters that are affirmed.[42] Inerrancy means that in its autographs the Bible, when properly interpreted, is true in all that it affirms to the degree that each author intended to be precise.[43] It contains "neither errors of act (material errors) nor internal contradictions (formal errors)."[44] Therefore "what the biblical writer really *says* or really *means* or really *affirms* is always true."[45] Existing texts correspond so closely to the original that for all practical purposes they may be regarded as inerrant, as well as good translations from those texts.[46]

Inerrancy thus applies to all statements in Scripture that have scientific or cosmological implications, although it is obvious that biblical writers do not employ twentieth-century scientific vocabulary and that the primary purpose of the Bible is theological and moral, not scientific. Likewise all historical statements and references are true when judged by the standards of accuracy employed at the time of their composition. This doctrine of inerrancy rules out spurious claims to authority on the part of canonical writers. This comprehensive view of inerrancy is required by a number of realities: (1) the Bible itself recognizes no distinction

---

[41]Wells, "Word and World," p. 165; Nicole, "Inspiration and Authority of Scripture," p. 203; J. Barton Payne, "Hermeneutics as a Cloak for the Denial of Scripture," *Bulletin of the Evangelical Theological Society* 3, no. 4 (Fall 1960): 98-99; J. I. Packer, "Inerrancy and the Divinity and the Humanity of the Bible," p. 137; Millard J. Erickson, "Problem Areas Related to Biblical Inerrancy," in *Proceedings*, p. 180.

[42]Stephen T. Davis, *The Debate About the Bible: Inerrancy Versus Infallibility* (Philadelphia: Westminster, 1977).

[43]Feinberg, "Meaning of Inerrancy," p. 294; Dockery, *Christian Scripture*, p. 264.

[44]Brown, "The Arian Connection," p. 38.

[45]Kenneth Kantzer, "Parameters of Biblical Inerrancy," p. 121, n. 8. Biblical writers operate with a correspondence view of truth: truth is that which conforms to reality, in opposition to lies, deceit or errors. A view of truth that is only personal or intentional does not represent the biblical teaching. See Roger Nicole, "The Biblical Concept of Truth," in *Scripture and Truth*, ed. D. A. Carson and John D. Woodbridge (Grand Rapids: Zondervan, 1983), p. 293; Norman L. Geisler, "The Concept of Truth in the Contemporary Inerrancy Debate," in *The Living and Active Word of God: Studies in Honor of Samuel J. Schultz*, ed. Morris Inch and Ronald Youngblood (Winona Lake, Ind.: Eisenbrauns, 1983), pp. 233-36; John S. Feinberg, "Truth: Relationship of Theories of Truth to Hermeneutics," in *Hermeneutics, Inerrancy and the Bible*, ed. Earl D. Radmacher and Robert D. Preus (Grand Rapids: Zondervan, 1984), pp. 18, 40; Preus, "The Inerrancy of Scripture," p. 49.

[46]Brown, "The Arian Connection," p. 385; Brown, "The Inerrancy and Infallibility of the Bible," pp. 41-42.

between matters of faith and practice on the one hand and historical and scientific matters on the other; (2) the immutability and perpetual establishment of the written Word implies total reliability and truthfulness;[47] (3) for Paul, untruthful statements would not be profitable for holy purposes (2 Tim 3:15).[48]

Attached to this understanding of inerrancy are important advantages and implications. It provides for both the layperson and the scholar the assurance of a trustworthy standard and bequeathes to the scholar the absolutely essential epistemological base for a consistent prolegomenalogical method. It assures the diligent reader that when Scripture is properly interpreted, the voice of God Almighty will be heard and his will known.[49] On the other hand the doctrine imposes on every believer the necessity of daily reading Scripture and submitting to the voice of the living God that it articulates. Since the Holy Spirit is never self-contradictory, all alleged manifestations of the Spirit must be tested by Scripture.[50] Implied also within inerrancy is the clarity of Scripture, which excludes study restricted to a scholarly hierarchy, and a unity throughout the book and testaments that encompasses diversity without contradiction.[51]

Presupposed in the definition of inerrancy are a number of qualifications. While some well-intentioned writers accuse inerrantists at this point of suicide by a thousand qualifications, these boundaries are merely dictates of common sense that are applied to the study of all serious literature. Though the doctrine of full inerrancy may involve difficulties, they are far fewer than the ones generated by any alternative.[52] First, inerrancy does not require a verbal exactness or perfection in literary style that would deny the true nature of language as used in the Bible.[53] Second, each biblical writer must be understood in the light of his particular culture, time, standard of precision and linguistic patterns. When this fact is recognized, many alleged contradictions begin to disappear.[54] Third, proper

---

[47] Grudem, "Scripture's Self-Attestation," p. 49.

[48] Ibid.; J. I. Packer, "The Inspiration of the Bible," p. 30.

[49] Millard J. Erickson, "Implications of Biblical Inerrancy for the Christian Mission," in *Proceedings*, p. 227.

[50] Lane, "*Sola Scriptura?*" pp. 309-10.

[51] Fred H. Klooster, "The Role of the Holy Spirit in the Hermeneutic Process: The Relationship of the Spirit's Illumination to Biblical Interpretation," in *Hermeneutics, Inerrancy and the Bible*, ed. Earl D. Radmacher and Robert D. Preus (Grand Rapids: Zondervan, 1984), p. 465; Robert T. Sandin, "The Clarity of Scripture," in *The Living and Active Word of God*, p. 244; Carl R. Trueman, "Pathway to Reformation: Tyndale and the Importance of the Scriptures," in *A Pathway Into Holy Scripture*, p. 18; Dockery, *Christian Scripture*, pp. 40, 47.

[52] Brown, "The Inerrancy and Infallibility of the Bible," p. 45.

[53] Kantzer, "Parameters of Biblical Inerrancy," p. 114.

[54] J. I. Packer, "Problem Areas Related to Biblical Inerrancy," in *Proceedings*, p. 208. Peter Davids suggests that the ancient reader would never have raised the type of questions that are brought up for discussion by modern scholars. Peter H. Davids, "Authority, Hermeneutics and Criticism," in *New Testament Criticism and Interpretation*, ed. David Alan Black and David S. Dockery (Grand Rapids: Zondervan, 1991), p. 27.

hermeneutics must be employed so that no author is made to say something that he never intended. His qualifications, phenomenological (as opposed to scientific) standpoint, organizational method, citation procedure, individual grammatical-syntactical style and overall purpose must be taken into account in the study of the text.[55] Fourth, there is a major difference between a proven error and a difficulty. At this late date in history not all the information is always available to do the historical, cultural or linguistic reconstruction that would solve every problem. The doctrine of inerrancy, however, means that if all the necessary data were available, no contradictions would remain.

This view of inerrancy has prompted evangelicals to attempt to harmonize texts in which there are apparent contradictions. There are many instances where harmonization arises quite naturally and is appropriate when the Bible is treated as a friend and is given the benefit of the doubt because of its self-teaching.[56] However, when an attempt at reconciliation seems forced, desperate or glib, it is better to admit that insufficient data is present and to store it in a mental icebox, believing that when and if all necessary data are available, a solution will become evident.[57] While intellectual integrity and honest scholarship require that each problem be faced seriously, inerrantists do not hinge their commitment to the full authority of Scripture on the ability to resolve every potential difficulty.[58]

At the opposite pole, within evangelicalism, is another view of biblical authority which is quite different in substance from the view of complete inerrancy. A number of contemporary scholars see the locus of authority not in its content, which must be identified with revelation, but in its capacity to bring about acts of salvation,

---

[55]In recent years many scholars have espoused narrative theology, which is easily translated into different cultures. But it must be remembered that the Bible speaks in the imperative mood as well as the indicative. The narrative concept must not be allowed to dilute the authority of Scripture. See Erickson, *Where Is Theology Going?* pp. 101-2; Erickson, "Problem Areas Related to Biblical Inerrancy," p. 182.

[56]D. A. Carson perceptively notes that "the difficulties raised by the biblical phenomena are on the whole a good deal less intractable than is sometimes suggested." Carson, "Recent Developments," p. 23.

[57]Davids, "Authority, Hermeneutics and Criticism," p. 30; D. A. Carson, "Redaction Criticism: On the Legitimacy and Illegitimacy of a Literary Tool," in *Scripture and Truth,* p. 139; Examples of excess in the attempt at harmonization include positing six crowings of the cock at the time of Peter's denial and suggesting more than three denials by Peter. See Dockery, *Christian Scripture,* p. 74; Craig L. Blomberg, "The Legitimacy and Limits of Harmonization," in *Hermeneutics, Authority and Canon,* ed. D. A. Carson and John D. Woodbridge (Grand Rapids; Zondervan, 1986), p. 148; Pinnock, "Parameters of Biblical Inerrancy," p. 100.

[58]Kantzer, "Parameters of Biblical Inerrancy," p. 118; Davids, "Authority, Hermeneutics and Criticism," p. 31; Nicole, "The Inspiration and Authority of Scripture," p. 211. There are times when a writer probably assumed knowledge on the part of his audience, knowledge that would have prevented the appearance of a contradiction, but that knowledge has not been preserved for us. See Blomberg, "Legitimacy and Limits," p. 142. In regard to doctrinal matters it must be noted that truth communicated from an infinite mind to finite minds would present difficulties for those with human, earthbound limitations. See Kantzer, "Parameters of Biblical Inerrancy," p. 117.

liberation, forgiveness, and pledges of love. In this functional view the stress is placed on a supposed internal authority that dynamically affects the community of faith.[59] Graeme Garrett writes:

> The "inspiration" of scripture, therefore, needs to be understood dynamically not statically. Inspiration is not some intrinsic feature of the biblical text that can be isolated and examined as one might, say, the style or form of the text. It is rather the mysterious unity of power and meaning which marks the operation of the text within the life of the community of faith.[60]

David Kelsey even suggests that the doctrine of Scripture ought properly to be subsumed under ecclesiology rather than revelation.[61]

Within this perspective, sometimes called the Amsterdam School, are a number of features. There is a transfer of authority from the cognitive and propositional nature of Scripture, in Barthian tones, to its functional purpose, with the result that inerrancy is superfluous (as well as distasteful), and the text itself is no longer considered the locus of meaning.[62] The authority of Scripture is not viewed as exercised in the giving of information, but in bringing about wholeness and personal renewal, remaking the thoughts, intentions, imaginations and rememberings of men and women.[63] Furthermore, since Scripture is observed from the standpoint of the phenomena, there is a greater use of and respect for critical methodologies, such as form criticism and redaction criticism in interpretation and exegesis. The Bible is approached in terms of its developmental process, and its authors are assumed to have incorporated nonrevelational or "secular" sources with their inherent imperfections.[64] Accompanying this view of Scripture are charges that those who believe in full inerrancy are engaging in bibliolatry and hold to a docetic view of Scripture that borders on heresy.[65]

Inerrantists contend that the case for a modified concept of inerrancy is untenable on a number of grounds. First, it is not the historic teaching of the church but

---

[59]Farley and Hodgson, "Scripture and Tradition," p. 53; Anthony C. Thiselton, "Authority and Hermeneutics: Some Proposals for a More Creative Agenda," in *A Pathway into the Holy Scripture*, 110, 116; William R. Barr, "Scripture as Word of the Living God," *Lexington Theological Quarterly* 22, no. 3 (July 1987): 79; Henry, "The Authority of the Bible," 24.

[60]Graeme Garrett, "Scripture, Inspiration and the Word of God," *Pacifica* 6 (1993): 92.

[61]David H. Kelsey, *The Uses of Scripture in Recent Theology* (Philadelphia: Fortress, 1975), cited in Vanhoozer, "God's Mighty Speech-Acts," p. 162.

[62]Henry, "The Authority of the Bible," p. 23; Brown, "The Inerrancy and Infallibility of the Bible," p. 39; Wells, "Word and World," p. 158; Erickson, "Immanence, Transcendence and the Doctrine of Scripture," p. 199.

[63]N. T. Wright, "How Can the Bible Be Authoritative?" *Vox Evangelica XXI*, ed. Harold H. Rowdon (Exeter, U.K.: Paternoster, 1989), p. 30; Barr, "Scripture as Word of the Living God," pp. 81, 83.

[64]Erickson, "Immanence, Transcendence and the Doctrine of Scripture," pp. 199-202.

[65]John Lewis, "Response" (to Kenneth Kantzer, "Parameters of Biblical Inerrancy"), in *Proceedings*, p. 130; James D. G. Dunn, *The Living Word* (London: SCM Press, 1987), p. 106.

is closer to the conservative neo-orthodoxy of Karl Barth. Second, by their methodology errantists must put Scripture through another sifting process altogether, as fallible minds must determine what is divine or soteriological and what is not. Third, the view constitutes a de facto denial of God's providence, which asserts the ability of the omnipotent, omniscient Creator to bring about his will even among sinful human beings.[66] Fourth, it confuses the once-for-all work of the Spirit in inspiration with his continuing ministry of illumination. Fifth, this view can provide no consistent epistemological explanation for why lives ought to be transformed by a dynamic Scripture.[67] Sixth, there are many historical examples of the long-term destructive spiral that often results in denominations and institutions that embrace lesser views than full inerrancy.[68]

The Canon

A crucial doctrine underpinning the authority of Scripture is that of the canon. The entire process involving the formation and reception of the canonical writings is difficult and is a matter that merits more careful study and elucidation on the part of evangelicals. There is, however, important agreement on a number of aspects. The acceptance by both Jesus and the apostles of the common Jewish canon of their day cements the boundaries of the Old Testament. The number of books that are accepted in the New Testament is determined by the literary production of those unique first-century witnesses (the apostles) to whom Jesus promised the special ministry of the Holy Spirit in recalling and interpreting his person and his mission. The basic principle of canonicity for both testaments is divine inspiration. Certainly God guided the church in the recognition of that inspiration, but the church added no new status to the books that it collected and preserved. Canonicity was implicit from the final production of each inspired book. Furthermore, with the death of the authorized first-century witnesses, the canon must be regarded as forever closed until the parousia.

When evangelicals speak of the canon, they have in view all of the inspired writings. The *sola scriptura* principle implies *tota scriptura*. No hermeneutical principle is allowed that isolates a canon within a canon. Such a procedure destroys the foundation of the Christian faith and mocks the supernatural Author of holy Scripture.[69]

---

[66]Carson, "Recent Developments," p. 15; Henry, "The Authority of the Bible," p. 23; Nicole, "The Inspiration and Authority of Scripture," p. 212; Brown, "The Inerrancy and Infallibility of the Bible," p. 46; Kantzer, "Parameters of Biblical Inerrancy," pp. 122-23, n. 22. The loss of the full sovereignty of God is certainly evident in the writings of Clark Pinnock. See Vanhoozer, "God's Mighty Speech-Acts," p. 166.

[67]Henry, "The Authority of the Bible," p. 24.

[68]Brown, "The Inerrancy and Infallibility of the Bible," p. 46; Nicole, "The Inspiration and Authority of Scripture," p. 212. Dockery warns that this "slippery slope" argument must be used with care. Dockery, *Christian Scripture*, p. 66.

[69]Bruce Waltke, "Historical Grammatical Problems," in *Hermeneutics, Inerrancy and the Bible*, ed. Earl

The Role of the Holy Spirit

The objective, inspired Word must be complemented and completed by the subjective ministry of the Holy Spirit within the individual. To be sure, the Spirit never makes the Bible into something that it has never been before, but there is a sense in which interpretation transcends the grammatical-historical level. True understanding requires the illuminating work of the original divine Breather of holy Scripture, since perspicuity is not *ex opere operato*.[70]

It is by virtue of the internal witness of the Spirit that a believer acknowledges the inherent authority of Scripture. The instrument employed is the written Word and the response produced is faith and assurance. This witness means that Scripture may rightly be described as self-authenticating *(anapodeiktos)*. The text is supreme over the interpreter, needing an interpretation but not a normative interpretation.[71]

Hermeneutics and Exegesis

A careful interpretation of Scripture is demanded by a commitment to its full authority. It is impossible to live under the authority of a Scripture that is not properly understood.[72] It is also possible to deny the authority of the Bible, which is confessed doctrinally, by the use of faulty hermeneutical principles, whether intentionally or unintentionally.

Godly scholars who revere Scripture have therefore agreed on a number of principles, based on common sense and the nature of language,[73] which serve to expose the original author's intended meaning. Hermeneutics naturally leads into exegesis, in which the meaning of words, phrases, idioms and other expressions in particular texts are studied in terms of how these segments of language were employed in the literary world of the author and how he contoured them for his

D. Radmacher and Robert D. Preus (Grand Rapids: Zondervan, 1984), p. 82; Klooster, "Role of the Holy Spirit in the Hermeneutic Process," p. 467; Roger Nicole, "The Inspiration and Authority of Scripture: J. D. G. Dunn Versus B. B. Warfield" (continued), *Churchman* 98, no. 3 (1984): 199. Erickson notes that the selective utilization of Scripture texts shifts the basis of authority from the content of the message to the internal condition of the hearer. Erickson, *Where Is Theology Going?* pp. 95-96.

[70]Klooster, "Role of the Holy Spirit in the Hermeneutic Process," pp. 452, 464; Kantzer, "Inerrancy and the Humanity and Divinity of the Bible," pp. 157-58; Dockery, *Christian Scripture*, p. 159; Trueman, "Pathway to Reformation," p. 25.

[71]Klooster, "Role of the Holy Spirit in the Hermeneutic Process," pp. 457-58; Brown, "The Arian Connection," p. 399; Sandin, "Clarity of Scripture," pp. 241-43; McGrath, *Evangelicalism and the Future*, p. 61; McGrath and Wenham, "Evangelicalism and Biblical Authority," p. 34; Preus, "Inerrancy of Scripture," p. 55; Lane, *"Sola Scriptura?"* p. 326.

[72]Robert K. Johnston, "Biblical Authority and Hermeneutics: The Growing Evangelical Dialogue," *Southwestern Journal of Theology* 34, no. 2 (Spring 1992): 22, 27; Dockery, *Christian Scripture*, p. 166.

[73]See such texts on hermeneutics as Milton S. Terry, *Biblical Hermeneutics: A Treatise on the Interpretation of the Old and New Testaments* (1890; reprint, Grand Rapids: Zondervan, 1964); A. Berkeley Mickelsen, *Interpreting the Bible* (Grand Rapids: Eerdmans, 1963); J. Robertson McQuilkin, *Understanding and Applying the Bible*, rev. ed. (Chicago: Moody Press, 1992).

own unique purposes. Maintaining the priority of exegesis provides safety from relativism and superficial or erroneous readings of the text.[74]

It is imperative that all interpretation be carried out under the authority of the Scripture itself. It has long been held within the Reformed tradition that the only infallible rule of interpretation is Scripture itself; thus Scripture is its own best interpreter. While reason, tradition and Christian experience may provide assistance, Scripture alone is normative. This principle is usually extended to the joint principles of the analogy of faith, by which obscure texts are interpreted in the light of clearer passages, and the rule of faith (a useful principle but capable of parochial abuse), by which no single text may be interpreted in a way that is contrary to the teaching of the Bible as a whole (often understood as that which is summarized in a particular confession).[75]

Proper interpretation will also have a number of important characteristics. It will be theocentric and doxological, showing the attributes of God in their awe-inspiring splendor. It will be dialogical, as God through Scripture is addressed and in turn addresses the readers or hearers, resulting in their sanctification and edification.[76] It will be open in that there will be a readiness for the presuppositions, preunderstanding and worldview of the interpreter to be reshaped by biblical revelation.

Another important characteristic of worthy interpretation is the focus on the intended meaning of the original author. Authorial intentionality, as expressed in the language of the text, determines the meaning that God desires to communicate. Therefore there is no authentic meaning that was not part of the original intention of the author as expressed verbally and linguistically in the text, though there are limitless applications of that meaning (the "significance" of E. D. Hirsch). To add meaning to the text is to deny biblical authority and to open the door to myriad forms of unbridled subjectivism.[77]

---

[74]Richard N. Longenecker, "On Reading a New Testament Letter—Devotionally, Homiletically, Academically," *Themelios* 20, no. 1 (October 1994): 7; Harvie M. Conn, "Normativity, Relevance and Relativism," in *Inerrancy and Hermeneutic: A Tradition, a Challenge, a Debate,* ed. Harvie M. Conn (Grand Rapids: Baker, 1988), p. 198.

[75]Sandin, "Clarity of Scripture," pp. 243, 253; Waltke, "Historical Grammatical Problems," p. 124; Thomas A. Noble, "Scripture and Experience," in *A Pathway into the Holy Scripture,* p. 293. On the danger of finding authority in experience, as in pietism, see George C. Fuller and Samuel T. Logan Jr., "Bible Authority: When Christians Do Not Agree," in *Inerrancy and Hermeneutic: A Tradition, a Challenge, a Debate,* pp. 248-50.

[76]Conn, "Normativity, Relevance and Relativism," p. 194; Packer, "Problem Areas Related to Biblical Inerrancy," p. 209.

[77]Wells, "Word and World," pp. 161-62; Carson, "Recent Developments," 140; Conn, "Normativity," p. 206; Sandin, "Clarity of Scripture," p. 252; Dockery, *Christian Scripture,* pp. 55, 157, 161; Nicole, "The Inspiration and Authority of Scripture" (continued), p. 22; Robert W. Yarbrough, "Retreating Authority: Evangelical-Liberal Rapprochement?" *Christian Scholar's Review* 19, no. 2 (1990): 158; Robert L. Cate, "The Importance and Problem of Distinguishing Between Biblical Authority and Biblical Interpretation," in *Proceedings,* p. 387. Wells cites James Hunter, who notes that there is a new

An area of difficulty in interpretation is the separation in the Bible of that which applies only to the culture of the original authors and that which is normative for all time. There are areas in this regard where there is no consensus among evangelicals—for example, the role of women in the ministry of the church. However, a number of guidelines are appropriate. It is imperative that twentieth-century culture be interpreted by the Bible, not the Bible by modern culture. Robertson McQuilkin argues strongly that the Bible itself must be allowed to distinguish between teaching that is permanent and universal and teaching that is limited.[78] The serious aberrations from traditional orthodoxy that are evident in movements such as liberation theology, feminist theology, gay theology and black theology (where theology is done from below, based on a given context) demonstrate clearly the hazard of allowing any contemporary context or crisis to set the agenda. Scripture must never be forced into a preordered agenda; rather, it must set and control the agenda.

In contrast to the hermeneutical framework within which most evangelicals operate is the interpretational milieu of modern theology. The actual use of Scripture in writers such as Dilthey, Heidegger, Bultmann and Gadamer is fundamentally antithetical to the historic principles of *sola scriptura* and *claritas scripturae*.[79] Many of the specialized "genitive theologies" show great exegetical ingenuity in making Scripture support their own causes, even if violence is done to the overall teaching of biblical revelation. Even some evangelicals fall prey to the temptation of making the Bible into a nose of wax when concepts of sin, divine wrath and eternal punishment for the wicked are abandoned and notions of the prosperity gospel, self-realization and possibility thinking are espoused.[80]

A fundamental plank in most nonevangelical hermeneutics is the divorce of meaning from the biblical text as it was originally delivered. Critical theories seek meaning not in the text itself but in their creative reconstruction of the history and development behind the text. Academic circles commonly demand that text and meaning be disengaged and refuse to allow any authoritative use of the text.[81] For writers like Paul Ricoeur, the text has an autonomy that allows it to speak freely in

---

generation of evangelicals who are disengaging the text from meaning and deriving the meaning from internal, private intuition—in neo-orthodox fashion. See Wells, "Word and World," p. 165.

[78]J. Robertson McQuilkin, "Problems of Normativeness in Scripture: Cultural Versus Permanent," in *Hermeneutics, Inerrancy and the Bible*, ed. Earl D. Radmacher and Robert D. Preus (Grand Rapids: Zondervan, 1984), p. 230.

[79]Sandin, "Clarity of Scripture," p. 237; Farley and Hodgson, "Scripture and Tradition," p. 51.

[80]Farley and Hodgson, "Scripture and Tradition," p. 51; Lane, *"Sola Scriptura?"* p. 315; Sandin, "Clarity of Scripture," p. 237; Carson, "Recent Developments," p. 47; John S. Feinberg, "Truth, Meaning and Inerrancy in Contemporary Evangelical Thought," *Journal of the Evangelical Theological Society* 26, no.1 (March 1983): 30.

[81]Wells, "Word and World," pp. 159, 161, 169.

changing situations, irrespective of the author's intentions.[82] Likewise, members of the structuralist and poststructuralist camps insist that authorial intent is irrelevant and that truth itself is incoherent. According to the reader-response theory, meaning is not something that inheres as fixed within texts but is created or modified by the subjective response of the reader.[83]

Evangelicals see grave dangers in separating the text from meaning. Not only has it given rise to a multitude of theologies that are conspicuously incompatible with one another, but it allows a hermeneutical irresponsibility, eisegesis on the part of the interpreter, since the meaning intended by the writer is nondeterminative and ultimately of no consequence, and a corresponding textual selectiveness that finally ends in futility. It also destroys the doctrine of perspicuity and in principle destroys the nature and basis of preaching in the worship of the church.[84]

The Use of Higher Critical Methodologies

Alongside the debate concerning hermeneutics is an intense disagreement among evangelicals over the legitimacy or role of critical methodologies in the study of holy Scripture. The urgency and necessity of textual (or lower) criticism, in which every effort is made by the use of both internal and external evidence to determine the original Hebrew, Aramaic and Greek texts of the Bible, is unquestioned. However, those methodologies classified under higher criticism are suspect. Included are (1) historical criticism in which historical narratives are studied to determine what actually happened, what is described or what is alluded to in a given passage, (2) source criticism in which the sources thought to be employed by a given writer are investigated, (3) form criticism, in which the forms of biblical passages are carefully analyzed to determine if they belong to an identifiable group, usually with a view toward reconstruction of the oral traditions which are projected to have lain behind the written records, and (4) redaction criticism, which seeks to discover the theological nuances of a given writer through the study of the various techniques involved in the literary formation and development of the text in terms of both the written and oral traditions, especially about Jesus. D. A. Carson notes that despite these technical distinctions, methodologically, source criticism, form criticism and redaction criticism collapse into one procedure that is commonly called "redaction

---

[82]Paul Ricoeur, *Philosophical Hermeneutics and Theological Hermeneutics: Ideology, Utopia and Faith* (Berkeley: Center for Hermeneutical Studies, 1976), p. 5, cited in Sandin, "Clarity of Scripture," p. 240.

[83]Bernard P. Robinson, "Biblical Authority: Is It Time for Another Paradigm Shift?" *Scripture Bulletin* 18 (February 1988): 37-38.

[84]Wells, "Word and World," pp. 157, 162, 172; Carson, "Recent Developments," p. 42; Dockery, *Christian Scripture,* p. 161; Payne, "Hermeneutics as a Cloak," p. 96; Nicole, "Inspiration and Authority of Scripture" (continued), p. 202; Feinberg, "Truth: Relationship of Theories of Truth to Hermeneutics," p. 40.

criticism."[85]

There are three different schools of thought concerning the use of this method in evangelical circles. More than one evangelical has articulated a real animosity toward the use of the higher critical methodology.[86] Others point out harmful features that necessitate its being used with reservation and caution.[87] A third group highlights the positive benefits associated with the careful use of critical methodology. They insist that a total disavowal would be to treat the Bible as less than human, less than historical and less than literature. Anything that clarifies the author's intentions within his original cultural context, providing a better understanding of background, date and the author himself, is desirable. Furthermore, critical interaction can reveal the blind spots and shortcomings of one's own theology, correcting preunderstandings and allowing for a fuller entry into the Bible's culture and the theological framework of each biblical writer.[88]

In the discussion of the use of the critical methodology, a number of serious reservations emerge from discerning evangelicals. The foremost concerns the antisupernaturalism, with its attendant denial of divine revelation and inspiration, which is often wedded presuppositionally to the method and results in a surrender of biblical authority and trustworthiness to the ever-fluctuating and omniprovisional opinions of the critics.[89] Associated with this bias is the imposition of a modern secular worldview that judges the biblical material on the basis of a transient and provisional understanding of reality, especially one incapable of being ordered from the outside by a transcendent God. Methodologically there is also objection to pitting history against theology as though they were incompatible.[90] Nowhere in the Bible is there any evidence of the utilization of the kinds of presuppositions employed by critical methodologists.[91]

In the use of this method evangelicals find especially troubling the shift in authority from the inspired text to the human scholar. Some writers warn of the

---

[85]Carson, "Redaction Criticism," p. 122.

[86]Preus, "The Inerrancy of Scripture," p. 57; John Warwick Montgomery, "Why Has God Incarnate Suddenly Become Mythical?" in *Perspectives in Evangelical Theology*, ed. Kenneth Kantzer and Stanley Gundry (Grand Rapids: Baker, 1979), pp. 57-65.

[87]Erickson, "Immanence, Transcendence and the Doctrine of Scripture," pp. 200-201; Alan F. Johnson, "The Historical-Critical Method: Egyptian God or Pagan Precipice?" *Journal of the Evangelical Theological Society* 26, no. 1 (March 1983): 10.

[88]Davids, "Authority, Hermeneutics and Criticism," pp. 25-26, 31, 33; Carson, "Redaction Criticism: On the Legitimacy and Illegitimacy of a Literary Tool," 140-41; Waltke, "Historical Grammatical Problems," p. 77; Johnson, "The Historical-Critical Method," p. 7; Dockery, *Christian Scripture*, pp. 50, 139, 167; Kantzer, "Parameters of Biblical Inerrancy," p. 122.

[89]Carl F. H. Henry, *God, Revelation and Authority*, 6 vols. (Waco, Tex.: Word, 1979), 4:393; Henry, "The Authority of the Bible," p. 20.

[90]McGrath and Wenham, "Evangelicalism and Biblical Authority," pp. 31-32; Carson, "Redaction Criticism: On the Legitimacy and Illegitimacy of a Literary Tool," p. 126.

[91]Paige Patterson, "Response" (to Clark Pinnock, "What Is Biblical Inerrancy?"), in *Proceedings*, p. 91.

danger of the exaltation of a priest-scholar class who alone, in functional denial of the priesthood of all believers, can declare what in Scripture is from God and what is merely human.[92] Both scholars and laypersons must come as listeners and learners before the same book as its servants, not its masters. All biblical study must be conducted in the context of a worshipful listening to the Spirit.[93]

Related to this reservation is the realization that the critical study of Scripture cannot locate or elevate new material to the same level of authority as Scripture itself. It is the sacred books in their canonical form that constitute the inspired Word of God, not the human sources from which material may have been taken and not the historically reconstructed experiences or context, either real or imaginary.[94]

With these qualifications in mind, many evangelicals have attempted to use critical methods as an end toward understanding the text without sacrificing the divine authority and complete inerrancy of Scripture. Carl F. H. Henry has suggested ten guidelines for a proper use of historical criticism. They include setting apart the supernatural, the miraculous and the objective factuality of biblical events from the subjective judgment of the critics; the requirement that the historian come under the claims of supernatural revelation; and the necessity that biblical events be interpreted by the inspired record.[95] In this light Alan F. Johnson in his presidential address to the Evangelical Theological Society (1982) concluded,

> The challenge of the hour calls Christian scholars to careful discrimination, scrupulous criticism of our personal presuppositions and methodologies, humility in the face of our limited knowledge, and patient, loving, yet penetrating analysis of the attempts of our colleagues to bring historical criticism to the aid of a believing interpretation of the Biblical material.[96]

New Dimensions: Guidelines for Further Study

These differences in regard to the use of critical methods do not negate the strength and vitality of evangelicalism. As doubts about the credibility of critical methodology continue to mount, the emptiness of nonevangelical theology becomes more

---

[92]Guthrie, "Biblical Authority and New Testament Scholarship," p. 8; Young, "Response" (to J. I. Packer), in *Proceedings*, p. 147; Millard Erickson, "Problem Areas Related to Biblical Inerrancy," in *Proceedings*, p. 183; Eckhard Schnabel, "History, Theology and the Biblical Canon: An Introduction to Basic Issues," *Themelios* 20, no. 2 (January 1995): 21.

[93]E. Earle Ellis, "Historical-Literary Criticism—After Two Hundred Years: Origins, Aberrations, Contributions, Limitations," in *Proceedings*, p. 418.

[94]Davids, "Authority, Hermeneutics and Criticism," pp. 28, 30-31; Wright, "How Can the Bible Be Authoritative?" p. 12; Guthrie, "Biblical Authority and New Testament Scholarship," p. 19; Farley and Hodgson, "Scripture and Tradition," p. 53; Waltke, "Historical Grammatical Problems," p. 91.

[95]McGrath and Wenham, "Evangelicalism and Biblical Authority," p. 31; Henry, *God, Revelation and Authority*, 4:403.

[96]Johnson, "The Historical-Critical Method," p. 14.

apparent, and the need for an objective, certain authority becomes more pressing, evangelicals ought to be in a unique place for leadership and influence as the world heads into the twenty-first century. There are, however, a number of issues that need to be addressed lest this witness be clouded.

First, Christian fellowship on a personal level must be maintained between inerrantists and errantists. Biblical authority is essential to the *bene esse* (well-being) of a believer's faith, but not its *esse* (existence). Therefore the Christian integrity of those with whom one disagrees should not be repudiated. Treating one another in Christian love will help prevent the doctrine of inerrancy, held as a watershed issue, from becoming the occasion of bloodshed.[97] Evangelicals need to learn the difference between fellowship on a personal level and fellowship on an institutional level. The inerrantist ought to be able to appreciate and communicate lovingly with noninerrantists even when it may be impossible for formal institutional sanction to be extended (that is, for the other to be a coworker in the same school, church or missionary activity). The Holy Spirit does not bless and work within an atmosphere of bitterness and ill will. Likewise errantists should not look intellectually in a condescending manner on inerrantists with whom they disagree.

Second, a greater degree of humility is in order. One's own fallible interpretations and applications must not be fused with the infallible Word, since only God is the possessor of all the truth. Greater tolerance and understanding on a personal level are needed in the discussion of the authority of Scripture, to prevent evangelicalism from splitting into mutually suspicious splinter groups.[98] The line must not be crossed between contending for the faith and being contentious about the faith.[99] Great effort needs to be expended in listening to and attempting to understand each other instead of reacting toward one another.[100] The biblical injunction "Let everyone be quick to hear, slow to speak and slow to anger"(Jas 1:19 NASB) may mean that evangelicals ought to spend more time airing differences privately and seeking areas of commonality instead of enthusiastically denouncing fellow believers before a watching Christless world. It may be found that some differences are more semantic than real. This change of mood can be enhanced in two ways. On

---

[97]Kantzer, "Unity and Diversity in Evangelical Faith," pp. 54, 66; Guthrie, "Biblical Authority and New Testament Scholarship," p. 11; Pinnock, "What Is Biblical Inerrancy?" in *Proceedings*, p. 79; Erickson, "Problem Areas Related to Biblical Inerrancy," p. 189; Fuller and Logan, "Bible Authority," pp. 244, 251.

[98]Kenneth S. Kantzer, "Problems Inerrancy Doesn't Solve" (editorial), *Christianity Today* 31, no. 3 (February 1987): 15; Vroom, "Contemporary Questions," p. 466; McGrath, *Evangelicalism and the Future*, pp. 146, 189. Kantzer states that "a growing tendency toward unity at the center is discernible in evangelicalism." Kantzer, "Unity and Diversity in Evangelical Faith," p. 57.

[99]D. A. Carson and John D. Woodbridge, eds., preface to *Scripture and Truth*, p. 9.

[100]T. Terry Young, "The Relationship Between Biblical Inerrancy and Biblical Authority," in *Proceedings*, p. 409. F. F. Bruce wrote of his desire to be an unhyphenated evangelical. F. F. Bruce, *Answers to Questions* (Exeter, U.K.: Paternoster, 1972), p. 204.

the one hand the training of scholars for academic positions ought to include the whole-life experience of being nurtured and mentored within the Christian church rather than just the rigorous intellectual discipline (including the development of critical capacities) of new converts who have been brought to faith through parachurch ministries. On the other hand administrators might well question the validity of a "publish or perish" agenda that occasions premature and unwise statements being put into permanent form. A scholar's true worth ought to be determined by more factors than the number of pages to his or her supposed credit.

Third, Scripture should be used appropriately. It must never be treated as a lifeless, legalistic code but as an instrument that brings the faithful reader into the mystery of God's presence. Its primary purpose is to bring human beings into a right relationship with God through the finished work of Jesus Christ. Richard Longenecker suggests that believers need to cultivate three different ways of reading and studying the Bible: devotionally (seeking spiritual direction and edification), homiletically (setting out the message of a book clearly, indicating its relevance for the hearer and applying its principles to contemporary life) and academically (leading all Christians into deeper understandings of Scripture and greater appreciations of their faith).[101] This threefold study of Scripture ought to result in the writing of exegetical commentaries of the highest quality and a deeper, more penetrating exposition of the text from evangelical pulpits.[102]

Fourth, an evangelical perspective on tradition needs to be thoughtfully formulated. To be sure, no tradition should ever be raised to the level of Scripture; even the most cherished doctrinal statement must be regarded as a subordinate standard. However, it is impossible to brush aside two thousand years of reflection, debate and digestion by the great teachers of the church and to approach Scripture with a mind that is empty of everything ever learned and taught by the church. A proper respect for tradition is in order not only because it is the vehicle through which values are transmitted from one generation to another but also because there is more to the interpretation of Scripture than any single mind can discern. Rigorous biblical study done within the believing community protects the individual from idiosyncrasies and excesses, and an acquaintance with the Spirit-led reflection of the past warns of heresies to be avoided and suggests workable, time-tested models for difficult doctrines. Right regard for tradition will help forge a solution to the unsolved dilemma at the heart of Protestantism: the balance between the freedom of the individual to possess and to interpret the Scriptures apart from coercion by a fallible and potentially corrupt church and the necessity of maintaining a fixed doctrinal

---

[101]Longenecker, "On Reading a New Testament Letter," pp. 5-6.

[102]See Millard J. Erickson, "Implications of Biblical Inerrancy for the Christian Mission," in *Proceedings*, p. 223.

expression of truth.[103]

Fifth, attempts need to be made to bridge the great gulf between scholarly study and the level of understanding of the Bible among laypersons. The subtleties encompassed within the discussion of the inerrancy question, for one example, are beyond the grasp of the average person in the pew.[104] In order to overcome this problem, evangelical scholars need to exercise a servant role in seeking to inform and to build up the body of Christ. This end might be achieved through publication of more midlevel, semipopular works by knowledgeable scholars, which are informed by technical research but aimed at increasing the comprehension of the Christian masses.[105] New ways of furthering the depth of understanding among the laity need also to be explored.

Sixth, some areas of evangelical scholarship merit finer tuning. More thought needs to be devoted to the nature, limits and proper place of harmonization of apparent discrepancies, and creative possibilities need to be explored in the light of the biblical culture and the realities of human speech and interpersonal relations. Likewise the extent and limitations of qualifications to inerrancy need to be addressed thoroughly with due respect to the nature of language and the external and internal motions involved in the research and writing process. These objectives will certainly require the articulation of a statement that maintains forcefully and accurately both the divine and the human qualities of holy Scripture, thus integrating its natural and supernatural elements. For the human element to be given its due regard, more careful analysis will need to be invested in delineating the usefulness and appropriate limitations of the higher critical methodologies, especially the boundaries beyond which a given scholar may no longer legitimately claim to be an evangelical.[106]

Seventh, evangelicals must articulate historic orthodoxy in terms that are intelligible to the changing world of the twenty-first century. These changes include an emerging influence from the Third World; the inevitable intellectual, moral and spiritual bankruptcy of both liberal theology and secular humanism, which is evident in the ascendancy of postmodernism; and the arrival of the electronic age.

---

[103]Nicole, "Inspiration and Authority of Scripture" (continued), p. 24; McGrath and Wenham, "Evangelicalism and Biblical Authority," pp. 28-30; Wells, "Word and World," p. 155; Trueman, "Pathway to Reformation," p. 17; Lane, *"Sola Scriptura?"* pp. 310, 322.

[104]Ted G. Jelen, "Biblical Literalism and Inerrancy: Does the Difference Make a Difference?" *Sociological Analysis* 49, no. 4 (Winter 1989): 423, 427.

[105]Erickson, *Where Is Theology Going?* p. 92; Klooster, "Role of the Holy Spirit in the Hermeneutic Process," p. 469; Jelen, "Biblical Literalism and Inerrancy," pp. 423, 427; Craig L. Blomberg, "Critical Issues in New Testament Studies for Evangelicals Today," in *A Pathway Into the Holy Scripture,* pp. 78-79; Patterson, "Response" (to Clark Pinnock), in *Proceedings,* p. 91.

[106]Carson, "Recent Developments"; Johnson, "The Historical-Critical Method," p. 14; Dockery, *Christian Scripture,* p. 69; Erickson, *Where Is Theology Going?* pp. 104-5; Nicole, "The Inspiration and Authority of Scripture" (continued), p. 210.

Evangelicalism must remain distinct from the surrounding culture while providing at the same time the divinely given and therefore perpetually relevant alternative to it. In a world where the electronic text and the information explosion give the impression that any word is fluid, incomplete, expandable, provisional and nonauthoritative, there is correspondingly a marked decline in reading and a shift to visual phenomena. Thus the Bible must be set apart from all other texts in its uniqueness (the reality behind terms like *revelation* and *inspiration* will have to be emphasized), and new ways of reading Scripture, tailored to the contemporary world, need to be explored. The church will also need to find innovative ways of conveying biblical content that are based on its truthfulness as God's Word, not merely on the impressiveness of the presentation.[107]

Summary

As it faces the new century, the evangelical church needs to relate, in a sensitive yet dynamic way, the heritage of the past to the realities of the present. This will involve instilling a new appreciation for doctrine and a proclamation of the great doctrines of the faith, including the inspiration and authority of Scripture. Objective realities will need to be put forth as the basis of authority shifts toward personal experience.[108] In its teaching a balance must be sought between commitment to truth on the one side and the practice of love on the other (Eph 4:15) so that neither is compromised and God dishonored in the process.

Alongside the articulation of the doctrine of Scripture there must be an unreserved trust in its truth and a new dedication to learn and to obey its teachings. A lack of application belies the confession of belief in its authority.[109] A commitment to the full authority of Scripture will also mean greater reserve in seeking and assessing results according to the canons of the behavioral sciences. All methodologies must be brought under the scrutinizing light of holy Scripture.

The effects of belief in the unadulterated authority of Scripture will be evident in a number of important areas, the first being the ministry of preaching. Ministers who must preach from a fallible document are in a pitiable position; since they have no sure word, they must attempt to reinforce their own idiosyncratic thoughts and ideas or those of someone else, rather than those of God. Christian audiences begin to feel insecure in this atmosphere, while non-Christian critics discern that behind the rhetoric and pulpit eloquence there is nothing more substantial than cotton candy. The preacher who holds to an inerrant authority will first come under its authority personally,

---

[107]Phil Mullins, "Sacred Text in an Electronic Age," *Biblical Theology Bulletin* 20, no. 3 (Fall 1990): 101-5; Erickson, *Where Is Theology Going?* pp. 98-100; McGrath, *Evangelicalism and the Future*, p. 129.

[108]McGrath, *Evangelicalism and the Future*, pp. 108, 112; Erickson, *Where Is Theology Going?* p. 97.

[109]Carson, "Recent Developments," p. 48; McGrath, *Evangelicalism and the Future*, p. 71; Packer, "Implications of Biblical Inerrancy for the Christian Mission," in *Proceedings*, p. 246.

acknowledging an individual indebtedness to divine grace. Then the preacher speaks forth the message of God in the text to the audience (expository preaching) and makes biblical substance, not personal style or charisma, the focus of worship and personal commitment. Thus the doctrine of inerrancy gives to the preacher the boldness to preach with authority truths that may not be popular or comfort producing but are founded on the objective declarations of an omniscient God.[110]

It is in the authoritative Word that the foundational truths are also found that mandate the evangelistic proclamation of the gospel worldwide. An inerrant Bible guarantees that the Great Commission is Christ's will for the church, a command that requires the faithful participation of every believer. It provides both the conviction and the assurance of the need for evangelism and the motivation for sacrificial involvement. The absolute, normative authority of Scripture means that all of its truths must be accurately expressed in the native thought forms and idioms of each language group (contextualization) without subjective selectivity, change of substance or distortion by any means, including the missionary's own worldview.[111]

Related to preaching is the church's counseling ministry. Scholars and practitioners have struggled with the integration of biblical truth and the conclusions drawn from the social sciences. While insights from the secular sources may well be employed by the Christian counselor (general revelation means that all truth is ultimately from God no matter what may be its source), Scripture in its total teaching, not just in selected passages, must exercise the ultimate authority over sources that are provisional, human and potentially fallible. Certainly truth from both sources will be ultimately complementary, but in the state of imperfect psychological knowledge and less-than-perfect biblical interpretation, counselors may well have to deal with apparent contradictions. Furthermore the counselor's hope for effecting personality and character modification must be in the power of the Holy Spirit, working through properly applied principles of a well-interpreted Bible. The counselor, learned in principles from the social sciences, should have the greatest skill in applying biblical principles tactfully and appropriately to specific problem areas that are commonly studied in the secular data. It is essential that the counselor look to the Bible not merely as another source of data but as the binding revelation of God for humankind.[112]

---

[110]Carson, "Recent Developments," p. 46; Erickson, "Implications of Biblical Inerrancy for the Christian Mission," pp. 228-29, 235; Packer, "Implications of Biblical Inerrancy for the Christian Mission," p. 249; Joe H. Cothen, "The Relationship Between Views of the Bible and Missions and Evangelism," in *Proceedings*, p. 497; Schnabel, "History, Theology and the Biblical Canon," p. 21; Bush, "Evangelism and Biblical Authority," pp. 107-8, 110.

[111]Timothy Lenchak, "The Bible and Intercultural Communication," *Missiology: An International Review* 22, no.4 (October 1994): 459; Erickson, *Where Is Theology Going?* p. 107; Carson, "Recent Developments," pp. 42-43; McQuilkin, "Problems of Normativeness in Scripture," p. 224.

[112]Lawrence J. Crabb Jr., "Biblical Authority and Christian Psychology," *Journal of Psychology and Theology*

A final area to be noted is the matter of ethics. Inerrancy provides the conviction for believers to speak out on the great moral issues confronting society. It provides a trustworthy revelation of a God whose moral nature is the ultimate foundation for all morality and whose law is the revealed foundation. It is important that the will of God be made known in matters such as sexuality, the sanctity of life, care for the poor and starving, divorce and mass destruction. The Bible must never be used to sanction wicked practices such as slavery or personal revenge. While it is true that all evangelicals may not reach the same conclusions on particular matters (for example, capital punishment), the fact of an inerrant and trustworthy word from God provides a basis for further study and consensus seeking so that the church can speak unitedly and powerfully to a surrounding world lost in darkness.[113]

Resources for Additional Study

Carson, D. A., and John D. Woodbridge, eds. *Hermeneutics, Authority and Canon*. Grand Rapids: Zondervan, 1986.

──────. *Scripture and Truth*. Grand Rapids: Zondervan, 1983.

Comfort, Philip Wesley, ed. *The Origin of the Bible*. Wheaton, Ill.: Tyndale House, 1992.

Conn, Harvie M., ed. *Inerrancy and Hermeneutics: A Tradition, a Challenge, a Debate*. Grand Rapids: Baker, 1988.

Dockery, David S. *Christian Scripture: An Evangelical Perspective on Inspiration, Authority and Interpretation*. Nashville: Broadman & Holman, 1995.

Geisler, Norman L., ed. *Inerrancy*. Grand Rapids: Zondervan, 1979.

Henry, Carl F. H. *God, Revelation, and Authority*. 6 vols. Waco, Tex.: Word, 1976-1983.

Pinnock, Clark H. *Biblical Revelation: The Foundation of Christian Theology*. Chicago: Moody Press, 1971.

The Proceedings of the Conference on Biblical Inerrancy 1987. Nashville: Broadman, 1987.

Radmacher, Earl D., and Robert D. Preus, eds. *Hermeneutics, Inerrancy and the Bible*. Grand Rapids: Zondervan, 1984.

Satterthwaite, Philip E., and David F. Wright, eds. *A Pathway into the Holy Scripture*. Grand Rapids: Eerdmans, 1994.

Warfield, Benjamin B. *The Inspiration and Authority of the Bible*. Edited by Samuel G. Craig. Philadelphia: Presbyterian & Reformed, 1967.

9, no. 4 (Winter 1981): 305-7, 310-11; Edward E. Hindson, "The Inerrancy Debate and the Use of Scripture in Counseling," *Grace Theological Journal* 3, no. 2 (1982): 213, 215-16, 218; Erickson, *Where Is Theology Going?* p. 103; Packer, "Implications of Biblical Inerrancy for the Christian Mission," p. 249; J. Robertson McQuilkin, "The Behavioral Sciences Under the Authority of Scripture," *Journal of the Evangelical Theological Society* 20, no. 1 (March 1977): 31-43. Compare Larry Crabb, "Conversations: Putting an End to Christian Psychology," *Christianity Today* 29, no. 9 (August 1995): 16-17.

[113]Robert S. Alley, "The Morality of God and the Morals of Inerrancy: Some Thoughts on Justice, Compassion, Peace and Freedom," in *Biblical v. Secular Ethics: The Conflict*, ed. R. Joseph Hoffmann and Gerald A. Larue (Buffalo, N.Y.: Prometheus Books, 1988), pp. 132, 134-35; John R. Wilch, "The Use and Misuse of Scripture in Ethics," *Consensus* 11, no. 3 (1985): 18; I. Howard Marshall, "Using the Bible in Ethics," in *Essays in Evangelical Social Ethics*, ed. David F. Wright (Greenwood, S.C.: Attic Press, n.d.), pp. 40-51; Erickson, "Implications of Biblical Inerrancy for the Christian Mission," p. 233.

Chapter 13

New Dimensions in the Doctrine of God

John S. Feinberg

·····························

THE PHILOSOPHY OF IMMANUEL KANT, ESPECIALLY TWO OF KANT'S claims, casts a long shadow over the last few centuries of Western philosophy and theology. Philosophers and theologians have wrestled with the implications of his Copernican revolution in philosophy, but it is his claim to have put an end to metaphysics that theologians have found especially troublesome. Both of these doctrines and their implications continue to have significance for contemporary discussions about God.

Before Copernicus and the revolution that he inaugurated, the earth was believed to be the center of the universe, and the sun was thought to revolve around it. However, through experiments and calculations, Copernicus came to see things differently. He realized that the sun is the center of the universe and that the earth revolves around the sun. This discovery brought about a revolutionary change in perspective.

Similarly, Kant's epistemology gave birth to what is known as the Copernican revolution in philosophy. Prior to Kant, philosophers believed that the mind is fundamentally passive in acquiring knowledge. Sensory stimuli from the world bombard the senses, and a representation of the world is mirrored in the mind of the knower. By the time of Kant, it was agreed that human sensory perceptors might distort the representation of the world, but fundamentally, a person could know accurately through sense perception what the world is like. Kant's revolutionary claim was that in the relation of knowing the mind of the knowing subject is active as well as the object of knowledge. The mind operates on the sensory data received from the external world, just as the world impacts the mind. Neither is passive.

One result of this change in perspective was Kant's distinction between the thing-in-itself and the thing-for-us. Since the mind is active in the knowing relationship, Kant saw that it is impossible for anyone to observe an object just as it is in itself. We only have access to things as they appear to us, and, of course, how they appear depends not only on how our senses function but also on how our mind structures the sensory data from the world to make a judgment about what is being perceived. Contrary to the pre-Kantian notion that we see things just as they are in themselves, Kant saw that one implication of his Copernican revolution was that the knower's subjective involvement in the knowing process makes it impossible for anyone to know things as they are in themselves.

In the twentieth century in particular, we have seen these doctrines taken to their logical extreme. Philosophers have argued that not only is the mind active in the knowing process but it brings a lot of "baggage" with it to the knowing relation. Past experiences and beliefs shape our concepts of things, and our conceptual framework dramatically influences our perception of the world. Thus all observation and all thought are theory-laden. But if that is so, how can we ever be sure that what we think about our world is true? And if such issues cast serious doubts about our ability to know correctly what the physical world is like, they cast equally grave doubts about the possibility of accurate knowledge of more abstract items of knowledge, such as concepts and worldviews. In light of these implications of Kantian epistemology, how can one religion claim to know that its God is the true God as opposed to any other religion's God? In fact, given Kant's claims and their implications for the subjectivity of all knowledge, how can any theist prove a case against an atheist? These issues are very important in contemporary discussion about God.

Kant's second claim, to put an end to metaphysics, has been equally significant for theologians and philosophers after him. Again, the doctrine stems from Kant's epistemology. In his *Critique of Pure Reason,* Kant begins by placing himself broadly within the tradition of empiricism. He writes,

> There can be no doubt that all our knowledge begins with experience. For how should our faculty of knowledge be awakened into action did not objects affecting our senses partly of themselves produce representations, partly arouse the activity of our understanding to compare these representations, and, by combining or separating them, work up the raw material of the sensible impressions into that knowledge of objects which is entitled experience? In the order of time, therefore, we have no knowledge antecedent to experience, and with experience all our knowledge begins.[1]

---

[1]Immanuel Kant, *The Critique of Pure Reason,* trans. Norman Kemp Smith (New York: St. Martin's, 1965), p. 41. Kant goes on to clarify (pp. 41-42) that though all knowledge begins with experience, that does not mean it all arises out of experience. What Kant calls our faculty of knowledge is also involved. Here we see from the very outset of the *Critique* Kant's wedding of the empiricist and rationalist traditions.

If all knowledge begins with experience, and Kant clearly means sense experience, then things that are beyond our sense experience are beyond our knowledge. On the basis of this idea, Kant introduced a further distinction. Objects of experience (sense experience) are in what Kant called the phenomenal realm, the realm of appearances. Objects beyond sense experience are in another realm, the noumenal realm. Given Kant's distinction between the thing-in-itself and the thing-for-us, the thing-in-itself is a noumenon. He also put into this category such things as the immortal soul, the world in its entirety and God. According to Kant, things in the noumenal realm are not demonstrable or knowable.[2]

The implications for metaphysics are clear and significant. If only things in the phenomenal realm can be objects of knowledge, and if God is a noumenon, then God is not an object of knowledge. But if God is not an object of knowledge because there is no empirical way to know God or to demonstrate anything about God, it is clear why and how this puts an end to traditional metaphysics. In his *Critique of Practical Reason* Kant invoked the concept of God to ensure the moral governance of a world in which virtue is crowned with happiness. But that is all that can be said about God. He is removed from the realm of demonstration, knowability and meaningful discourse.

Although philosophers and theologians have not agreed with everything Kant said, they have taken seriously his challenge about the possibility of doing metaphysics when the subject matter is nonempirical. In one way or another, theologians have responded to this Kantian and empiricist challenge.

What have been the main reactions within evangelicalism and outside evangelicalism to these two Kantian doctrines? As to evangelicalism, broadly speaking, several main reactions are noteworthy. Typically, evangelicals adopt what has become known as the modern (or Enlightenment) notion of rationality. This concept of rationality says that one does not have a right to believe something unless it is supported by sufficient argument and evidence. How much is sufficient? According to classic foundationalism, a belief has sufficient support if it is supported by evidences that are supported (inferred) ultimately from beliefs that are properly basic. A properly basic belief is a belief that is self-evident, evident to the senses or incorrigible.[3]

Incorporating this notion of rationality, evangelicals commonly accept Kant's basic empiricist stance but argue that there are empirical data that allow us to support theistic belief (and perhaps even prove it true). A long tradition of thinkers

---

[2]See ibid., pp. 269-72, for the doctrine that a noumenon is not an object of knowledge, and pp. 267-68 to show that the thing-in-itself is part of this noumenal realm.

[3]See Alvin Plantinga, "Reason and Belief in God," in *Faith and Rationality*, ed. Alvin Plantinga and Nicholas Wolterstorff (Notre Dame, Ind.: Notre Dame Press, 1983), and Kelly Clark's explication of Plantinga's views in *Return to Reason* (Grand Rapids: Eerdmans, 1990).

has believed that it is possible by rational and evidential argumentation to demonstrate God's existence and many other key tenets of evangelical theism.

A second evangelical response to Kant's concerns, which also incorporates the modern notion of rationality, argues that metaphysics as it relates specifically to God is revealed. The content of our theology is an object of knowledge not because it is empirical but because it is revealed by God. Hence we can know that the claims of theology are true. In addition, there are empirical data that support revealed truth, and one can use such data to build a strong, cumulative, probabilistic case for matters like God's existence.

As to the question of objectivity and subjectivity in our knowledge, both of these evangelical positions would likely claim that despite the knower's coming to the acquisition of knowledge with his or her conceptual framework, it is still possible to see the world correctly and to know the truth about matters of fact. Hence there is no need to be skeptical about the truth of one's beliefs, and one can convince others that one's views are correct.

A third broadly evangelical response to Kant's concerns holds that Christian metaphysical beliefs are revealed, but since God has revealed them in his Word, we have a right to say they are matters of knowledge. This response differs from the second response, however, by arguing that it is not necessary to support such views evidentially. This general reaction to Kant's concerns may be slightly nuanced in various ways. The approach known as Reformed epistemology rejects the Enlightenment concept of rationality and says that while theistic belief can be supported by evidence, certain beliefs, such as belief in God's existence, are properly basic for many believers and thus need not be supported by argument and evidence for believers to be within their epistemic rights and to be rational in their belief.[4]

Cornelius Van Til demonstrates another approach to this third option. Van Til believed not only that we do not have to demonstrate evidentially the truth of Christianity to nonbelievers but that we cannot do so. His point was not that Christian metaphysics is nonempirical and thus not open to empirical confirmation. Rather, Van Til took very seriously the claim that we can see things only from our point of view, and he noted that the nonbeliever's point of view is tainted by sin. Because of this, nonbelievers will never be persuaded by reason and argument. Likewise, believers' mindset is controlled by their relation to God through Jesus Christ. Subjectivity covers the worldview of both believer and nonbeliever. Hence, in the case of the unbeliever, appeal to argument and evidence lead nowhere. The only appropriate methodology for Christian apologists is Van Til's presuppositional

---

[4]Here I am thinking of Plantinga. Of course, I must add that Plantinga is very clear that he rejects what he calls the Enlightenment concept of rationality and the classical foundationalism he believes goes with it. He substitutes a different concept of rationality. For details see Plantinga, "Reason and Belief in God."

method. Believers should use it and let the Holy Spirit persuade nonbelievers that their views are inconsistent and that Christian theism alone is consistent. Van Til's views take seriously biblical teaching on the noetic effects of sin and link with that doctrine the implications of Kant's Copernican revolution for the issue of objectivity and subjectivity of human knowledge.[5]

When we move beyond evangelical theology, we find a variety of responses to Kant's doctrines. I want to sketch the general contours of four such reactions. Some who agree with Kant's Copernican revolution believe that the element of subjectivity in the knowing process does *not* make it impossible for us to know the world aright. I am thinking of those philosophers at the end of the nineteenth and the start of the twentieth centuries who adopted a positivistic view of science. One of the hallmarks of this positivism was a rigorous espousal of empiricism. Positivists reasoned that our language should be purged of anything that could not be empirically verified or falsified. Since God was not empirically observable in any way, talk of God should be removed. The most radical forms of positivism claimed that more than language about the nonempirical must be removed. It was claimed that if a proposition was neither empirically verifiable nor falsifiable, the thing(s) of which it spoke were nonexistent. On this view, just as Kant had said, traditional metaphysics was impossible. But, unlike Kant, positivism did not invoke God as a principle of practical reason. Proponents of this view, accepting Kant's principles, reasoned that there is no God.

A second nonevangelical response to Kant also agrees with Kant's Copernican revolution and with his comments about empiricism. However, these thinkers claim that because subjectivity colors the knowing process and because most religions are difficult, if not impossible, to support convincingly by empirical evidence, we are not in a position to know which religion is the true religion. Nonetheless, these thinkers do not jettison belief in God. Rather, they encourage each individual to find an individual paradigm for understanding God and God's relation to the world. Since that understanding will be theory-laden, there is no way to establish it or any other concept of God as the correct one. Hence everyone should be open to dialogue with adherents of other

---

[5]This must not be misunderstood. I am not saying that Van Til consciously adopted Kant's teaching. Rather, my point is that philosophers since Kant have taken seriously the teaching that the mind is not passive in the knowing process. To one degree or another, this accepted belief is taken to imply that the mind either can or cannot know things correctly in light of its being influenced by past experiences and beliefs. Van Til, implicitly accepting the view that the mind is active in the knowing process, argues on the basis of Scripture that sin has affected the mind's ability to understand truth. Whether or not Van Til is appealing consciously to Kant's Copernican revolution, my point is that a pre-Kantian view of the mind as essentially passive would not fit with this biblical teaching. But the Kantian view and its application to the mind's ability to know the world accurately fits with Van Til's claims about sin's effects on the mind's ability to understand spiritual truth.

religions, and all should adopt a stance of tolerance in a religiously pluralistic world.

In the early twentieth century, a third response to Kant adopted his Copernican revolution and agreed that there is no way to demonstrate the truth of traditional metaphysical beliefs. Nonetheless, holders of this position wanted to maintain a concept of God that was not far from the traditional evangelical notion. They claimed that there is a way to confirm belief in God, but it is not an empirical, cognitive way. Rather, God's existence and God's demands can be known by means of some nonverbal encounter. This encounter is beyond reason and evidence. For someone who has had this experience, no reason or evidence is necessary to prove God's existence, nor could rational argument or empirical evidence unsettle that belief. Hence neo-orthodoxy took Kant's principles seriously but claimed to find a way around the implications of those Kantian doctrines in order to maintain theistic belief.

A fourth reaction to Kant has been gaining wide acceptance outside of evangelicalism within the latter part of the twentieth century. This perspective accepts the Copernican revolution and its basic implications for subjectivity in the knowing process. Moreover, it agrees that traditional metaphysics is impossible in light of the demands of empiricism. However, accepting the empiricist challenge, proponents of this approach argue that we can do metaphysics, but it must be empirically based. The result is an empirically based naturalistic account of God known as process theism. Typically, process thinkers believe that they can confirm their empirical account of God through observation of the world. Many admit, however, that enough subjectivity enters the knowing process that the best we can do is get an approximation to the truth about the world. In light of those facts and in the spirit of tolerance, some of these thinkers propose openness to other religions and their perspectives. Some who hold this view believe it possible to show that their underlying empirical process metaphysics can fit and can be incorporated into the various narratives about God and God's relation to the world found in religions other than Christianity.

This lengthy prolegomena to my essay has set the stage for a proper understanding of the current and future scene with respect to discussions within theology proper. Both evangelicals and nonevangelicals have taken Kant's principles very seriously. Moreover, the literature produced by both camps contains certain central core issues that continue to be the subject of debate and discussion. These core issues serve as "umbrella issues" for a series of other questions under discussion within each camp. Evangelicals are being forced to deal with the core issues under discussion in both evangelical and nonevangelical camps. One common denominator in all of this is process theology. One reason it is so attractive is that it apparently takes Kant's principles seriously without throwing out metaphysics altogether and without throwing out all talk of God.

In this chapter, I focus on two core theological issues, one from the evangelical camp and another from the nonevangelical camp. I believe that they raise a series of issues that will likely remain under discussion for some years to come. As I lay out these issues, it will become evident that process theism is a common denominator and that evangelicals must face the challenge of process theology within their own camp as well as engage in the discussions going on among nonevangelicals that surround process theism and its implications. The shadow of Kantian thinking looms large over all of this.

Basics of Process Theism

In *Religion in the Making* Alfred North Whitehead wrote that "Christianity has always been a religion seeking a metaphysic."[6] He meant that since the Bible records God's revelation and humanity's responses, it mainly records religious experiences without clearly enunciating a general explanation of reality. While Scripture surely presupposes a certain worldview, it is true that no metaphysic is explicitly stated in Scripture. Throughout the centuries theologians and philosophers have produced various understandings of reality for communicating the Christian message to their own day. Whitehead purported to do the same for our day. His system, most thoroughly expounded in *Process and Reality* (1929), was not merely an attempt to set forth a secular understanding of the nature of reality, for the principles of his system were intended to cover all of reality, including God. Hence he ended *Process and Reality* with a chapter on God and the world.

Many influences have led to process theism, not the least of which is Kantian epistemology and its implications for metaphysics outlined above.[7] In addition, process theology relies heavily on attacking classical Christian theism as inadequate. Process theists claim that traditional theism is deficient in that some of its fundamental notions present a perception of God that is both logically incoherent and morally repugnant. Traditional theism is said to hark back to the metaphysics of Plato and Aristotle. They recognize two types of reality: the present world of becoming, time, change and real relations, and another "world of timeless, changeless, and unrelated being, which is alone 'real' in the full sense of the word and so alone worthy of the epithet 'divine.' "[8] When these ideas were tied together in traditional theism to God and the world, it meant that God is timeless, immutable, unrelated to the world and unaffected by what happens in it (impassible). It also meant that God was the totally transcendent absolute with whom one could have

---

[6]Alfred N. Whitehead, *Religion in the Making* (New York: Macmillan, 1926), p. 50.
[7]For details of the scientific, religious/theological and philosophical backdrops of process theism, see my "Process Theology," *Evangelical Review of Theology* 14, no. 4 (October 1990): 291-334.
[8]Schubert Ogden, "Toward a New Theism," in *Process Philosophy and Christian Thought*, ed. Delwin Brown, Ralph James and Gene Reeves (Indianapolis: Bobbs-Merrill, 1971), p. 179.

no relation and that if the real is not in this world but in the other world, what goes on in this world is really insignificant.[9]

None of this sits well with process theologians. If God dare not interact in the world so as to enter into real relations with his creatures because that might cause change in God (and God as immutable cannot change in any way), then the God of traditional theism is really irrelevant to modern humanity. Central in all of this is a rejection of the classical notion of divine impassibility, which is a logical corollary to God's immutability. If God cannot change, then surely God cannot feel emotions like compassion, since that would constitute a change in God. Charles Hartshorne cites Anselm's statement to the effect that God is passionless and does not feel compassion toward humanity, though God is able to express compassion in terms of human experience. That is, God can comfort us to show us compassion, but God cannot actually feel that compassion.[10] Hartshorne remarks:

> Anselm's God can give us everything, everything except the right to believe that there is one who, with infinitely subtle and appropriate sensitivity, rejoices in all our joys and sorrows in all our sorrows. But this benefit which Anselm will not allow God to bestow upon us is the supreme benefit which God and only God could give us.[11]

If God is unaffected by what we do and if our world is not the real world, then nothing we ever do or suffer ultimately makes any difference to God, and nothing that happens in this world is of significance.[12] Identifying the chief aim of humankind as glorifying God is meaningless, for God as absolute is beyond our power to contribute to God's greatness.[13] Likewise, we cannot speak meaningfully of serving God, for, as Hartshorne claims, "if God can be indebted to no one, can receive value from no one, then to speak of serving him is to indulge in equivocation."[14]

Process theists point out that Scripture portrays God otherwise. God changes his mind (for example, deciding not to destroy Nineveh), enters relationships with people (for example, God makes covenants with Abraham and David) and shows emotions like anger and compassion. Likewise, if God cannot enter time because that would involve the potential for change and for entering into relationships, then God is locked out of the world. But Scripture indicates otherwise. Finally, if what happens here is really insignificant, then why the biblical emphasis on God's actions to redeem fallen humanity and a fallen world? Scripture and common sense alike

---

[9]Ibid., pp. 179-80.
[10]Charles Hartshorne, *The Divine Relativity* (New Haven, Conn.: Yale University Press, 1948), p. 54—Hartshorne citing Anselm.
[11]Ibid.
[12]Schubert Ogden, *The Reality of God* (New York: Harper & Row, 1963), p. 51.
[13]Hartshorne, *The Divine Relativity*, p. 58.
[14]Ibid.

suggest that what goes on in this world is very significant, not only to us but to God.

A final complaint is that the God of classical theism is typically portrayed as a God of power and force, an absolute sovereign who determines and accomplishes his will in the world regardless of what people think. The God of traditional theism, according to process thinkers, is like a monarchical tyrant who sometimes resorts to force. This removes any sense of human freedom and in essence portrays God as a "cosmic bully."[15] Such a God, by destroying freedom, can hardly hold people morally accountable for what they do, and yet we are told that he does. A God who acts in this way is utterly repugnant, and it is utter lunacy to think that moderns can believe in, let alone love as a Father, such a deity. Process theists insist that such a conception of God must go.

Major Concepts in Process Theology

Reality as process, becoming. According to process thinkers, the ultimate real actualities are actual entities, but they are not static objects. Everything is in the process of becoming, and as such it is also in the process of perishing (that is, its previous states slip from subjective immediacy). As events in process, three things are true of all actual entities. They are the objective results of the events out of which they arose, and they reflect the qualities of those prior events. Nonetheless they are "subjects," distinct centers of feeling, which are combinations of their constituent parts and data. As each actual entity at each stage perishes, it perishes from subjective immediacy and is swallowed up in the following events. As such, they become permanent givens in the data of history that influence new events as they come to be.[16]

Process thinkers constantly remind us that theirs is a metaphysic of events and becoming, not a metaphysic of being and substance.[17] In arguing for a metaphysic of becoming rather than a metaphysic of being and substance, process thinkers are not rejecting being altogether. Their point is that we must not think of a world of beings which *qua* beings are static, unmovable, unchangeable. That kind of substance metaphysic is what they reject. Atomic theory, let alone common sense, shows us that everything is dynamic and in a process of motion, even the most solid piece of matter.[18]

---

[15]See on this point, for example, Norman Pittenger, "Understanding the World and the Faith," *Theology* 90 (1987): 183. See also David Basinger, "Human Coercion: A Fly in the Process Ointment?" *Process Studies* 15 (1986).

[16]John Hayward, "Process Thought and Liberal Religion," *American Journal of Theology and Philosophy* 6 (May/September 1985): 118.

[17]Pittenger, "Understanding the World and the Faith," p. 182. See also Hartshorne's detailed explanation of the problems with a philosophy of substance in "The Development of Process Philosophy," in *Process Theology*, ed. Ewert H. Cousins (New York: Newman, 1971).

[18]Hartshorne, "Development of Process Theology," pp. 61-62.

One final note on reality as becoming. This analysis may be thought to refer only to animate beings. On the contrary, it refers to all actual entities, from the smallest blip of existence to the highest level of being. Whatever is true of actual entities is true of them all. Hence process thinkers all subscribe to Whitehead's dictum that "God is not to be treated as an exception to all metaphysical principles, invoked to save their collapse. He is their chief exemplification."[19]

The process God. Process thinkers uniformly affirm that God, like all actual entities, is dipolar or bipolar. God has a primordial nature (conceptual pole) and a consequent nature (physical pole). God's primordial nature is permanent and unchanging. It is the envisagement of the realm of possibilities, the eternal objects, but this has been understood in various ways even by Whitehead. Whitehead's basic metaphysical assumptions demand that the same principles relevant to God apply to all other actual entities. Hence, just as God envisages eternal objects, so must all other actual entities. Each actual entity prehends its own possibilities and also the entire realm of all possibilities. In God's case, of course, the two are coterminous, whereas for other actual entities they are not. Of course, God does not merely know the possibilities, but God organizes them with respect to their relative value as well as their possible joint actualization in any given occasion.[20] Some process thinkers portray God's primordial nature as nothing more than the ordering of the eternal objects, getting them ready for ingression into the world.[21]

In *Process and Reality*, Whitehead makes God's relation to the eternal objects significantly different from what he perceived in *Religion in the Making*. In *Process and Reality* he claims that since everything must be somewhere (that is, it must be some actual entity), this must be true of the general potentiality of the universe. The "somewhere" for eternal objects is the nontemporal actual entity (Whitehead's designation for God). That is, the primordial mind of God *is* the eternal objects. According to this view, God does not create the eternal objects. Even though God orders and evaluates them, they are basically equivalent to God's primordial nature.[22]

God's consequent nature, God's physical pole, is changing and impermanent. Moreover, it is concrete. If God were nothing but primordial, God would be pure possibility apart from any reality. God must have a concrete, physical pole to

---

[19]Alfred N. Whitehead, *Process and Reality* (New York: Macmillan, 1929), p. 521.

[20]Daniel Day Williams, "How Does God Act?" in *Process and Divinity*, ed. William Reese and Eugene Freeman (Lasalle, Ill.: Open Court, 1964), p. 171.

[21]See, for example, Williams's description of God's primordial nature as the "envisagement of the realm of possibility" and the order which characterizes the world so that it can be one determinate world and yet that primordial nature is something actual, for "there is a definite *structure* [italics mine] of possibility which characterizes every existing reality" (p. 171).

[22]John Cobb, "A Whiteheadian Doctrine of God," in *Process Philosophy and Christian Thought*, ed. Delwin Brown, Ralph James and Gene Reeves (Indianapolis: Bobbs-Merrill, 1971), p. 230.

complete the vision of the possibilities. That concrete pole is God's consequent nature, and in essence, the consequent nature is the world. According to Whitehead, God's consequent nature results from physical prehensions of actual entities. How many? All of them, but that means the world! Hence process thinkers often refer to the world as God's body. For process thinkers, God's being and that of the world interpenetrate one another. Since the world is changing and developing, so is God, and changes in the world enrich God's being.[23]

God, then, is dipolar, a unity composed of a synthesis of physical and mental pole. In so being, God is like all other actual entities. Reality is bipolar. In response to the God of traditional Christian theism, process theism's dipolar God is personal, mutable and passible. Hartshorne's treatment of these issues is representative. Early in *The Divine Relativity* Hartshorne argues that the process God is a personal God. What is crucial, however, is to see his definition of *personal.* For Hartshorne, to be personal means to be related.[24] Throughout *The Divine Relativity* Hartshorne's main thesis is that God, of all beings, is supremely related, or "surrelative."[25] Of course, since God's being interpenetrates the being of all else, God is definitely the supremely relative being.

As to immutability, from the description of God's consequent nature it is clear that the process God is mutable. Though traditional theism sees this as a defect, Hartshorne argues to the contrary. He claims that mutability has typically been rejected because it is assumed that if God changed, he would have to change for better or for worse. If for worse, God would be unworthy of admiration, but if for better, then in what sense could we speak of God as perfect, lacking nothing, as we typically do?[26] Hartshorne dismisses the idea that God could possibly change for the worse, because he does not believe it can be proved that there is ever more sorrow than joy in the world. Hence there would always be a net increment of value accruing to God at any moment. As to the objection about apparent imperfection if God changes for the better, Hartshorne answers, "My reply is that, as we are here using the term, perfect means completely worthy of admiration and respect, and so the question becomes, is such complete admirableness infringed by the possibility of enrichment in total value? I say it is not."[27]

It also follows from the preceding that God is not unaffected by the world. God experiences our sufferings and joys with us as we experience them.[28] What we think and do affects God, and that means, among other things, that we are able to enhance

---

[23]See Pittenger, "Understanding the World and the Faith," p. 184, as exemplary of this notion.
[24]Hartshorne, *Divine Relativity,* pp. vii-viii.
[25]Ibid., p. vii and throughout the work.
[26]Ibid., pp. 45-46.
[27]Ibid., p. 46.
[28]Ibid., pp. 42-59. See also Ogden, *Reality of God,* pp. 44-70.

and enrich God, to add value to God's being by our actions.[29] Hartshorne states that true religion is serving God. But serving God is not merely admiring or obeying God. It is contributing and conferring benefit to God that he would otherwise lack.[30]

If God is as immanent in the world as process thought perceives him to be, it would appear that the process God is very active. A closer look at the system, however, shows this not to be so. God as creator is denied, and miracles in the sense of divine interventions in the natural order to suspend it are denied as vestiges of a mythological vision of reality. And God's action in Christ is really quite passive.

What, then, can and does God do? Daniel Day Williams reminds us that God exercises causality in the world but always in relation to beings that have their own measure of causal self-determination as they interact with others.[31] What this ultimately amounts to for process thinkers is that whatever God does, God will not infringe on the freedom of other actual entities. God is omnipotent in the sense of having the ability to do anything that is doable, but controlling the activities of free, self-determining beings is not something that can be done.

How, then, does God act? In his primordial nature God acts "by presenting to the creatures the unity, the richness, and the limits of possibility as ordered by his vision."[32] In essence, God acts in his primordial nature not by acting but by being. God supplies for each actual occasion its initial subjective aim. God presents the possibilities for becoming; but even if God has a preference among them for the specific actual entity, process thinkers quickly note, it is up to the individual entity to decide which of the possible aims to actualize. God will not limit the freedom of others. As to God's consequent nature, when one recognizes that the world is itself God's body but is composed of multitudes of actual entities that are themselves becoming (and God cannot limit their freedom), in effect God's action really is their action. Consequently, as Daniel Williams explains, God's consequent nature acts by being prehended—felt by creatures.[33]

Does God do anything unilaterally in the world? According to Williams, we must ultimately remain agnostic about that matter, for there is no way to separate God's act from involvement in the activities of the world. Williams says that

> to assign any particular historical event to God's specific action in the world is
> to risk ultimate judgment on our assertions. Faith leads us to take that risk. We
> say God sent his Holy Spirit at Pentecost. He spoke to Jeremiah, he heals
> diseases, he will send the Lord again. But all such assertions in so far as they

---

[29]Ibid., p. 133.
[30]Charles Hartshorne, "The Dipolar Conception of Deity," *Review of Metaphysics* 21 (1967): 274.
[31]Williams, "How Does God Act?" p. 170.
[32]Ibid., p. 171.
[33]Ibid., p. 176.

conceivably refer to historical events require us to acknowledge the limits of our sight and our knowledge. In specific assertions about what God is doing now, or precisely how he has acted, and how he will act, we surely can be mistaken.[34]

Evangelicalism and God, Time, and Eternity

I critique process theism elsewhere.[35] My intent here is to present it as a system that both responds to Kantian claims about epistemology and metaphysics and serves as the backdrop for two contemporary discussions (one within and one outside of evangelicalism) about God.

Evangelical discussions about God cover many issues. The Trinity is a perennial topic. Discussions about creation continue to occupy much attention, especially as evangelicals grapple with various ways of accommodating their thinking both to Genesis and to science. In addition, as long as there are differences of opinion about the relation of divine sovereignty to human free will, there will be plenty of grist for the evangelical theological mill. And these issues are important.

I believe, however, that anyone working within theology proper must engage in discussions about God's relation to time and eternity as we move toward the next millennium. I believe this is and will be a watershed issue for evangelical theism in the upcoming years. Those who hold the traditional view that God is atemporally eternal must not only meet the challenge of the many biblical, theological and philosophical arguments against that view but also answer process theism's complaint that the atemporal, totally immutable, absolutely sovereign and thoroughly remote God of traditional theism is utterly irrelevant to the religious needs of men and women today. On the other hand, those who believe that God is temporal are bucking tradition and a long line of arguments supporting that tradition. They must also show, since a temporal and mutable God is one of the hallmarks of process theology, how they can hold to a temporal God without capitulating to process theism.

Let me sketch some of the debate surrounding this issue. As I do so, it will become clear that this issue is actually an umbrella for a series of issues within the doctrine of God. While the doctrine of divine eternity is a comfort to the religious, it is also a very important doctrine from the standpoint of an overall theological system. The most fundamental question about divine eternity is what it means. Is eternity timelessness or is it never-ending existence within time? Eternity also raises significant questions through its implications for other doctrines. If God is time-

---

[34]Ibid., p. 180. Though the process God heretofore presented may sound identical to pantheism, process thinkers vehemently deny this. Two of the clearest explanations of why this is not so come from Hartshorne and Ogden. See Schubert Ogden, *Reality of God*, p. 61ff., and Hartshorne, *Divine Relativity*, p. 88.

[35]See my "Process Theology."

lessly eternal, can he act within time? If God is timelessly eternal, must he also be totally immutable? On the other hand, if God is temporal, isn't his life as fleeting as ours after all? If God is in time, doesn't he become so enmeshed in time and change that our concept of God becomes that of process theology?

The notion of atemporal, or timeless, eternity has a long tradition in Christian thought. It was held by such theologians as Augustine, Boethius, Anselm and Aquinas. It is clearly the more complex of the two notions of eternity.[36]

Nelson Pike provides a helpful explanation of atemporal eternity. Something that is timelessly eternal has two closely related characteristics: it lacks temporal extension and it lacks temporal location.[37] To say that something lacks temporal extension means that it lacks temporal duration. World history extends through time both backward and forward. We can speak of successive moments in the history of the world. Something that is timeless has no temporal spread or succession whatsoever. As Pike says of God's timeless eternity, "It is not just that the life of God lacks temporal limits: the point is that it has no temporal spread at all."[38] This does not mean that God's life has not endured forever but that it has endured atemporally. As to the meaning of atemporal duration, Stump and Kretzmann begin to explain it in terms of the idea of a moment. "The temporal present is a durationless instant, a present that cannot be extended conceptually without falling apart entirely into past and future intervals. The eternal present, on the other hand, is by definition an infinitely extended, pastless, futureless duration."[39] In other words, take that *temporally* durationless moment and extend it indefinitely, and you have the idea of atemporal duration.

To speak of temporal location is to speak of a particular time when something exists. But this involves more than assigning a date to events and more than being able to identify "now" by some reading on the clock and calendar. It also involves being able to say of something or someone that it existed or happened "before" or "after" something else. In other words, it involves locating one's position at a specific point on the continuum of time. Something that is timelessly eternal also lacks temporal location. It does not exist now or later, before or after. This is not so because it is nonexistent. Nor is it so because it exists simultaneous to all times. It is so because it is outside all contact with time. As for God's timeless eternity, God may perceive of all times at once, but that does not mean that God is temporally located at all or any of them. In summing up these two elements of timelessness, Pike

---

[36]In *The Consolation of Philosophy* 5.6 we find Boethius's classic definition that "eternity, then, is the complete possession all at once of illimitable life."

[37]Nelson Pike, *God and Timelessness* (New York: Schocken, 1970), p. 7.

[38]Ibid.

[39]Eleonore Stump and Norman Kretzmann, "Eternity," in *The Concept of God*, ed. Thomas Morris (Oxford: Oxford University Press, 1987), p. 225.

explains, "The point seems to be that God is not to be qualified by temporal predicates of any kind—neither time-extension predicates (such as, e.g., 'six years old') nor time-location predicates (such as, e.g., 'before Columbus')."[40]

Temporal eternity is a much simpler concept. Some philosophers refer to it as sempiternity. Others simply refer to God as temporally eternal by saying that God is everlasting. The fundamental notion of sempiternity is existence at all times. God's existence extends endlessly backward and forward from our point in time. God never had a beginning, and God will not cease to exist. As Morris explains, sempiternity is a "*temporal* notion, a conception of God's eternity in terms of time: God's existence is temporally infinite in duration, unbounded in the past and future. On this conception, there is in the life of God a past, present and future, as in the life of his creatures. But unlike any of his creatures, God is everlasting, and necessarily so."[41]

Arguments for Timeless Eternity

Many arguments are used to support timeless eternity. This section describes several of the major ones.

Timelessness: a logical derivation from other doctrines. Proponents of atemporal eternity often claim that it is logically derived from other doctrines that theists must hold. If so, then it seems the doctrine of divine atemporal eternity is an essential Christian doctrine. There are several ways to derive timeless eternity from other doctrines, and I offer a way that is as clear as any.

In his *Monologium* Anselm argued that a perfect being (greatest conceivable being) could not be perfect unless it were simple. From simplicity, Anselm moves to God as unlimited and eventually to God's timelessness.

Let us look more closely at this derivation. First, must a most perfect being also be simple? Anselm begins the *Monologium* by arguing that things having their goodness through something else (that is, they are contingent) are not supremely good. Only that which has its qualities through itself is supremely good.[42] By the end of chapter four, Anselm has reasoned that there can be only one such being and it is what it is through itself. In the following chapters (5-14) Anselm argues that everything else exists through the creation of this supreme being. Everything depends on it for existence, but it depends only on itself. In chapter sixteen we see the crucial turn in the argument. Anselm discusses what it is for God to be just.

---

[40]Pike, *God and Timelessness*, p. 8.

[41]Thomas Morris, *Our Idea of God* (Downers Grove, Ill.: InterVarsity Press, 1991), p. 120. For further discussion of whether a sempiternal being can be a necessary being, see William Kneale, "Time and Eternity in Theology," *Proceedings of the Aristotelian Society* 61 (1960-61): 101-7.

[42]Anselm, "Monologium," in *St. Anselm: Basic Writings*, trans. S. N. Deane (La Salle, Ill.: Open Court, 1968), chap. 1, p. 40.

Any attribute would do to make Anselm's point, but he happens to pick justice. At issue is whether justice or justness is a property independent of God's nature or is not independent of it. Anselm argues for the latter position:

It seems, then, that by *participation* in this quality, that is, justness, the supremely good Substance is called just. But, if this is so, it is just through another, and not through itself. But this is contrary to the truth already established, that it is good, or great, or whatever it is at all, through itself and not through another. So, if it is not just, except through justness, and cannot be just, except through itself, what can be more clear than that this Nature is itself justness? And, when it is said to be just through justness, it is the same as saying that it is just through itself.[43]

This introduces the crucial concept, simplicity, and explains why it is necessary. To say that justness or any other attribute is separate from God's nature means that God participates in that attribute. But that seems to say that there must be parts to God's nature. On the other hand, to say that God's nature is justness and so on, means that God's nature is identical to each of these attributes, and if God's nature is identical to each of them, they are identical to each other. This is clearly the notion of divine simplicity.

Note why Anselm believes God must be simple. To say that an attribute is separate from God's nature as an abstract entity is to say that God depends on it in some way for existence. Anselm has already argued that the supremely perfect being exists through itself, not through anything else. To depend for its existence on something else is to deny that it depends for its existence only on itself. To deny that is to deny that it is the most supreme being. But what is this notion of depending for one's existence only on oneself? This is the attribute of aseity.

Now the logical derivation becomes clear. It is not from perfection per se to simplicity and then to eternity. Rather, it is from perfection to aseity, from aseity to simplicity, and then from simplicity to eternity.[44] From simplicity, the entailment may go one of two ways. Simplicity may be taken to imply immutability and immutability to imply eternity, or simplicity may be seen as implying eternity, and eternity as implying immutability. I shall explain the entailment from simplicity to eternity, for it is more typical and, I think, in many respects clearer.

Why must a simple being be timeless? William Mann explains:

The Doctrine of Divine Simplicity (DDS) maintains that God has no "parts" or components whatsoever. He has no properties, neither essential nor accidental. He has no spatial extension. Nor does he have any temporal extension: there is no division of his life into past or future stages, for that would imply temporal

---

[43]Ibid., chap. 16, p. 65.

[44]For clarification of the move from aseity to simplicity in Anselm, see his "Monologium," pp. 66-67. For a clear exposition of the move from perfection to aseity to simplicity, see Alvin Plantinga, *Does God Have a Nature?* (Milwaukee, Wis.: Marquette University Press, 1980), pp. 32-33.

compositeness. The DDS in turn is motivated by the consideration that God is a perfect being, and that *qua* perfect, he must be independent from all other things for his being the being he is, and he must be sovereign over all other things. If God himself were composite, then he would be dependent upon his components for his being what he is, whereas they would not be dependent upon him for their being what they are.[45]

Here we have a clear statement of the relation between aseity and simplicity and simplicity and timelessness. The rationale is clear. To be simple is to have no parts. To be temporal is to have successive stages in one's life, but that is parts. A timeless being has no temporal stages in its existence, so a simple being must be timeless.

Immutability necessitates timeless eternity. Another argument for timeless eternity can be made on the basis of immutability alone. If God is unchangeable, there is no change in God's being, purposes or will. If God had a beginning or could go out of existence, God would not be immutable as to his being. Moreover, even if God always existed but did so in successive stages so that what God was or what God knew differed from one point in his existence to another point in his existence, God would not be immutable. One could speak of God's being at point t and then at point $t + 1$ and so on. That seems to involve change. At $t + 1$ God would exist in a different state of affairs, that is, the state of affairs of existing at $t + 1$ rather than existing at t, even though everything else about God would remain unchanged.

It should be clear, from the perspective of atemporal eternity, that the kinds of change envisioned are changes that rule out immutability. Moreover, the kind of succession envisioned must be temporal succession. Otherwise it is hard to see the difference between state of affairs t and $t + 1$. But if succession in God rules out immutability, and if the only kind of succession in the imagined case that makes sense is temporal succession, then an immutable God must also be timeless.[46]

Nature of time necessitates a timeless God. Some argue that in light of the nature of time, it is impossible for God to be in time. Time as we know it is physical or clock time. Such time is a function of the relation and movement of our planet to the sun. Any other time within our universe would also be a measure of the relation of physical objects in the universe to one another. Moreover, relativity theory tells us that there is no absolute time across the universe, so it is hard to speak of a given moment as being simultaneous across the universe.

If this is the nature of time, then God cannot be in time. God is not a physical object, and God cannot be physically present at any point in the universe. Theolo-

---

[45]William E. Mann, "Simplicity and Immutability in God," in *The Concept of God*, ed. Thomas Morris (Oxford: Oxford University Press), p. 255. See also Mann, pp. 256-57, for an explanation of the move from simplicity to eternity and from eternity to immutability.

[46]Stephen Charnock, *The Existence and Attributes of God* (Minneapolis: Klock & Klock, 1977), p. 81. See also Morris, *Our Idea of God*, p. 127.

gians and philosophers usually say that God transcends all spatial locations. In light of the nature of time and the nature of God, it really does not make sense to speak of God as existing in time.[47]

There is another angle to this nature of time argument as well. If God exists forever temporally, we have a problem on our hands. It is one thing to claim that God operates within our physical time but really is not subject to physical time. But if God is a temporal being, then even before creating anything God must have been temporal. But what could that temporality amount to? It surely cannot be temporality in the sense of physical, clock time, for no physical objects existed before God created. What would it mean to say God was temporal before creation? Of course, there is no such problem with an atemporal God. If it makes sense at all to say that God is outside of time, then it makes sense regardless of whether we are talking of God before creation, during this age or even during the eternal state.

Timelessness and the foreknowledge/free will problem. This argument will appeal only to those who hold some form of indeterministic free will. Christian theists typically claim that God knows what will occur in the future. But if God really knows what will happen, how can it fail to occur? It is not that God's knowledge causes it to happen but only that if God knows something will occur, it cannot fail to do so. But how can there be such guarantees if indeterministic free will operates in our world?

Indeterminists have acknowledged this problem and have offered various solutions to it. The Boethian approach appeals to divine timeless eternity. Boethius claimed that God knows all things that will happen in our future, so divine foreknowledge is upheld. However, as timelessly eternal, God knows them as present. In that respect Boethius believed that God really cannot be said to know the future, for all events are timelessly present before him. However, this does not remove from God's knowledge anything that theists traditionally say God knows. On the other hand, Boethius believed that since God knows what he knows as present rather than as future, questions about the necessity of the future need not arise. Because there is genuine contingency to the future, human freedom is safeguarded.

The Boethian strategy for handling the freedom/foreknowledge problem is the only approach that appeals to God's timelessness and even necessitates God's timelessness. For those who accept it, the Boethian resolution also offers a strong argument in favor of timeless eternity, since the Boethian solution presupposes timeless eternity.[48]

---

[47]Morris, *Our Idea of God*, p. 125. See also pp. 12 and 125-26 for possible temporalist responses to this line of argument.

[48]A similar problem arises concerning God's foreknowledge of God's own actions and freedom. For discussion of this issue with a possible atemporalist resolution, see Brian Leftow, *Time and Eternity* (Ithaca, N.Y.: Cornell University Press, 1991), p. 282.

Temporal God leads to process theism. According to this argument, the notion of a timeless God is a safeguard against adopting views about God that are objectionable. This in itself is not proof that God is timeless. It only notes potential negative implications of believing in a temporal God. A God who is temporal is in some sense mutable. If God is mutable, then God is probably not impassible. God can really experience emotions, and perhaps even suffers with us as we suffer. Moreover, if God is temporal and mutable, the doctrine of divine simplicity must be abandoned. In addition, if God is in time, it can be argued that God cannot know all of time at once but must know it successively as it occurs. And, as argued, if one is an indeterminist, it is hard to see how God can know the future. Temporalist indeterminists cannot solve the freedom/foreknowledge problem by appeal to the Boethian strategy. Their options are the Molinist strategy, the Ockhamist strategy or the view that God does not know the future. Many indeterminists are convinced that only denying divine foreknowledge of the future solves the problem. Of course, adopting such a view may mean rejecting divine omniscience or redefining omniscience as knowledge of all that can be known and then stating that the future is not something to be known. In either case, something traditional theists have affirmed, that God knows the future, is given up.

All of these divine attributes as understood by traditional theism seem in jeopardy if divine timelessness goes. But if so, the picture of God that begins to emerge is the process concept. If, however, the process God is objectionable, then we shouldn't hold it and shouldn't hold views about God that seem to lead inevitably to that view. This argument for timelessness, then, says that adopting the view of God as timeless is a safeguard against slipping into process theology. Those who reject process views and want to hold to a temporal God must explain how one can espouse sempiternity and avoid succumbing to process theism. Not being able to do so constitutes one more reason to embrace timeless eternity.

Arguments Against Timeless Eternity

Although many arguments favor timeless eternity, the notion has many problems as well. This section identifies some of the most frequently voiced complaints against the notion.

Timelessness and God as a person. Some temporalists complain that a timeless being could not be a person.[49] This is so, the argument goes, because a timeless being could not do various activities that a person typically does. Richard Coburn makes the point as forcefully as any when he writes:

Surely it is a necessary condition of anything's being a person that it should be

---

[49]For a related argument that a timeless God could not be understood as living, see Kneale, "Time and Eternity in Theology," p. 99.

capable (logically) of, among other things, doing at least some of the following: remembering, anticipating, reflecting, deliberating, deciding, intending, and acting intentionally. To see that this is so, one need only ask oneself whether anything which necessarily lacked all of the capabilities noted would, under any conceivable circumstances, count as a person. But now an eternal being would necessarily lack all of these capacities inasmuch as their exercise by a being clearly requires that the being exist in time. After all, reflection and deliberation takes time; deciding typically occurs at some time—and in any case it always makes sense to ask, 'When did you (he, they, etc.) decide?'; remembering is impossible unless the being doing the remembering has a past; and so on. Hence, an eternal being, it would seem, could not be a person.[50]

To these activities Sturch adds that a timeless being apparently could not speak, write a letter, smile, grimace or weep, be affected by any other being (since being affected is a change, and as atemporal, it is immutable) or respond to anything, since responses come after their stimuli, and there is no before or after for a timeless God.[51]

Divine eternity and divine action. Whether God qualifies as a person to a large extent depends on whether God can act. Scripture portrays God as doing any number of things in our world. God creates the universe, parts the Red Sea, leads the children of Israel out of Egypt, becomes incarnate, raises Christ from the dead, strikes sinners like Ananias and Sapphira dead, answers prayer and, according to Nebuchadnezzar (Dan 4:34-35), is involved in the rise and fall of empires and kingdoms. The difficulty for atemporal eternity seems to be at least threefold. Such actions take time to do. For God to do these actions seems to involve God in acts that have a beginning, a middle and an end (impossible for an atemporal God for whom there are no successive stages). Moreover, such actions occur at specific points in time and to do them at the appropriate time seems to necessitate that God, when he acts, has temporal location.[52] Finally, in order to act at certain times in our history, God must know exactly what time it is in our history, and yet as atemporal, all events are present to him. God knows the successive order of events in human history. He

---

[50]Robert Coburn, "Professor Malcolm on God," *Australasian Journal of Philosophy* 40-41 (1962-1963): 155. See also Pike, *God and Timelessness*, pp. 122-23. For an interesting discussion of these issues from the perspective of one who thinks God, though timeless, could do some of these activities, see R. L. Sturch, "The Problem of Divine Eternity," *Religious Studies* 10 (1974), and Paul Helm, *Eternal God* (Oxford: Clarendon, 1988), pp. 59-63.

[51]Sturch, "Problem of Divine Eternity," pp. 489-90.

[52]Pike, *God and Timelessness*, p. 118, sees the problem of temporal location (not so much temporal duration) as the inconsistency with timelessness. However, it also seems that if God acts in time, God's actions partake of the nature of time, and many acts in time take time to do (they have a beginning, middle and end—there is temporal succession in them). Hence if God does these sorts of actions, there is change in God's states, which is impossible for an immutable and atemporal being.

just cannot know that it is now time in our world for event t, and then at *t* + 1 know that it is *t* + 1 in our world. For God to know such things would mean that God's knowledge changes as our world is changing, but that is impossible for an atemporal being.

If this line of argument about divine action is correct, it appears that an atemporal God is locked out of the world. But that is surely contrary to Scripture and an unwelcome position for traditional Christian theism.[53] This is a significant argument, and atemporalists have attempted several ways of handling it. Stump and Kretzmann's answer is representative of the response given by many atemporalists. They believe it is wrong to claim that an eternal entity cannot act in time because this fails to recognize an important distinction. It is one thing to act (1) "in such a way that the action itself can be located in time" and another to act (2) "in such a way that the effect of the action can be located in time."[54] For temporal creatures like us, the distinction is not one that makes a difference, but it does matter for an atemporal being, since (1) is impossible for an atemporal being. However, none of this argues against (2) in regard to an atemporal being. Stump and Kretzmann's answer is that God acts outside of time and yet, given God's omnipotence, can make his actions have effects in time at just the right time.[55]

This account of God's acts raises several questions. Does God do these acts sequentially, or is it only the effects that are sequential? Atemporalists answer that the latter is the case. God does not accomplish various effects in our world by separate exercises of his own agency. God does everything in one timeless act. This may cause Calvinists no reason for pause, but Arminian indeterminists who have questions about God's knowledge of our future may well wonder how God, before creating the world, can act and react to human (indeterministically) free actions done after God created.

There is another problem. Given that God is atemporal and immutable, God had better not at one timeless point of his existence do these acts and then stop doing them. If God were to do so, that would not only necessitate some sort of temporal sequence but would also destroy immutability in the strong sense the atemporalist uses. The only way to avoid this problem seems to be that God's one timeless act is an act he is always doing. It never begins and never ends.

There is another problem for God's acting in our world, and it is whether as atemporal God can know what time it is now in our world. I shall explain that problem below. But beyond all of these problems is a fundamental question. The atemporalist can say that God does all actions timelessly and continuously and is

---

[53]For an explanation of the absurdity involved in imagining that a timeless being can act timelessly, see Pike, *God and Timelessness,* pp. 104-5.

[54]Stump and Kretzmann, "Eternity," p. 241.

[55]Ibid.

able to make those actions have just the right results in our world at the right time. But the temporalist asks what that really means and how it could be true. Given the lack of clarity of such notions, the temporalist is dubious about the accuracy of such claims.

Divine eternity and divine simplicity. We have seen that atemporal eternity can be logically derived from a set of God's perfections. Divine simplicity is very important in the derivation. One way to reject this argument is to deny that simplicity entails atemporal eternity. Another is to agree to the entailment but reject divine simplicity.

Temporalists invariably choose the latter strategy. In fact, many theists, apart from the temporal/atemporal eternity issue, reject the doctrine of divine simplicity. I offer some of the reasons for rejecting divine simplicity. An initial objection is that theologians who hold it offer no biblical passages that say God is simple. If one holds the doctrine on biblical grounds, one must argue it inferentially from other divine attributes that Scripture does teach. Louis Berkhof holds the doctrine, but his admission about its biblical backing is most revealing:

> The simplicity of God follows from some of His other perfections; from His self-existence, which excludes the idea that something preceded Him, as in the case of compounds; and from His immutability, which could not be predicated of His nature, if it were made up of parts. This perfection was disputed during the Middle Ages, and was denied by the Socinians and Arminians. *Scripture does not explicitly assert it, but implies it where it speaks of God as righteousness, truth, wisdom, light, life, love, and so on, and thus indicates that each of these properties, because of their absolute perfection, is identical with His being.*[56] (italics mine)

The italicized material is a classic example of question begging and of being misled by surface grammar. Berkhof assumes that because there are biblical passages that speak of God as righteousness and truth, for example, such language makes the metaphysical point that God's being is these attributes. However, Berkhof forgets that there are also biblical passages that refer to God as righteous (rather than righteousness) and true and faithful (rather than as truth). If we look solely at the surface grammar of these passages, we can make a case against and for simplicity along the lines of the argument Berkhof has used. But since there are two types of passages, it is simply question begging to appeal only to the one kind and argue that its surface grammar tells us that the Bible teaches simplicity.

In addition, Berkhof's line of argument assumes that the biblical writer is trying to teach something about the way the attribute named relates to God's very being. But this is just question begging. It is dubious that the biblical writer is trying to say anything more than that God has the attribute named. There surely needs to be further evidence in the text that the author means to say that the attribute named

---

[56]Louis Berkhof, *Systematic Theology* (Grand Rapids: Eerdmans, 1939), p. 62.

either is equal to God's being or is only a part of God's being. Berkhof can only be right that the author is implying by statements that God is righteousness and truth that God is simple, if indeed it has been shown already that God is simple. But as Berkhof admits, there are no Scriptures that explicitly say this about God. So concluding that these verses imply divine simplicity is clearly question begging.

There are other problems with the doctrine of divine simplicity. Plantinga raises objections which seem quite compelling, and I note the main ones. First, if God is identical with each of his properties (as is required with property simplicity), then each of his properties is identical with each of his properties. But then God has only one property, and that doesn't square with the belief that God has a series of distinct properties (justice, love, omnipotence and so on).[57]

Second, if God is identical with each of his properties, then since those properties are each properties, God must be nothing more than a property. But "no property could have created the world; no property could be omniscient, or indeed, know anything at all. If God is a property, then he isn't a person but a mere abstract object; he has no knowledge, awareness, power, love or life."[58]

So far we have talked only of properties that are typically associated with God, like omnipotence and love. God has these properties essentially; that is, without them there is no God. But God also has a lot of accidental properties that do not per se refer to God's very being but are true of him.[59] For example, God has the property of having created Adam, the property of knowing that Adam sinned and the property of being thought of by me as I write this sentence. There are many other such properties that relate to God, but surely they are not essential to God's very being. The problem is deeper than whether all of God's properties are essential or whether some are accidental. The problem is that given the doctrine of simplicity with its property identity thesis, God is not only identical with his mercy, love and power, but God is also identical with these other properties, and they are identical with one another. It is hard to see how such properties can be identical with one another and hard to see why one would hold a view that makes God *identical with* purely accidental properties.[60]

---

[57]Plantinga, *Does God Have a Nature?* p. 47.

[58]Ibid. For further discussion of the problems of divine simplicity, as well as its relation to aseity, see Plantinga. For a defense of the doctrine of divine simplicity see William Mann, "Divine Simplicity," *Religious Studies* 18 (1981): 451-71.

[59]Brian Leftow, "The Roots of Eternity," *Religious Studies* 24 (1988): 198-99, says that such attributes are not really to the point because "a simple being is identical only with its real or intrinsic attributes, for only having a distinct real, intrinsic attribute would entail involving real, intrinsic complexity" (p. 199). However, Plantinga is careful to note that he is using the term *property* in the broad sense in which it is used in contemporary discussions. But it also seems that the point of dependence on one's attributes (intrinsic or extrinsic) is still the point that generates the urge to hold simplicity. Hence it is appropriate for Plantinga to raise these sorts of attributes.

[60]I am basing this discussion on Plantinga's argumentation on pp. 40-44. For an interesting discussion of

These problems with simplicity are good reasons to reject it. But if it is rejected, there is no way for it to serve as an argument for atemporal eternity. This does not mean temporalism is correct; only that it cannot be rejected on the grounds of any argument that appeals to divine simplicity.

Divine eternity and divine immutability. Earlier we saw that divine immutability and atemporal eternity seem to go together and argue for one another and that there is a logical entailment between the two. If there is no way to refute this claim, temporalists are in trouble.

There are at least three ways temporalists may address this issue. They may deny that God is immutable. This is the typical approach of process theologians. A second strategy maintains that God is immutable in the sense that atemporalists claim, but it argues that there is no logical entailment between atemporal eternity and that notion of immutability. This strategy is of only limited value, for if one defines the doctrines as atemporalists traditionally have, it is very hard to break the entailment. Third, the temporalist may argue that the traditional strong sense of immutability atemporalists have held is not the only possible way to define it and remain true to Scripture. Immutability needs a more nuanced definition, and once such a definition is given, one can see that it is consistent with a temporal God and with the aspects of divine immutability that Christian theists have been most concerned to preserve.

The third strategy seems most promising, though space does not permit pursuing it.[61] Scripture clearly teaches that God does not change. Passages such as Psalm 102:24-27, Malachi 3:6[62] and Hebrews 1:10-12 say God does not change. On the other hand, various passages show God involved in different sorts of changes. Some passages speak of the Lord changing his mind (Ex 32:14; Judg 2:18; 1 Sam 15:35; Ps 106:45; Jer 26:19; Amos 7:3,6; Jon 3:10). Other passages portray God as caring for his people and intervening on their behalf. And other passages describe God as regretting something (for example, Gen 6:6). Moreover, God's wrath is directed against the unrighteous (Rom 1:17), and yet when sinners repent, God forgives them (1 Jn 1:9).

How can we make sense of this? My suggestion is that there are many ways a

---

another problem involving divine simplicity, see William Hasker, "Simplicity and Freedom: A Response to Stump and Kretzmann," *Faith and Philosophy* 3 (April 1986).

[61]See my forthcoming book on the doctrine of God, in which I elaborate this notion of immutability.

[62]Nicholas Wolterstorff, "God Everlasting," in *God and the Good,* ed. Clifton Orlebe and Lewis Smedes (Grand Rapids: Eerdmans, 1975), pp. 201-2, argues that these are the only two passages in Scripture that say that God does not change. But he claims that they are typically taken out of context to assert ontological changelessness in God, whereas the passages don't say that. The Malachi passage, for example, only teaches God's faithfulness, not ontological immutability. In context, the Psalm 102 passage teaches that God's years have no end, not that God is ontologically immutable. Regardless of the technical points of exegesis, theologians have traditionally cited such verses to teach immutability, and that is my only point here.

being might change,[63] but orthodox Christianity has maintained that God had better not change, at least in being (including attributes), purposes and will. God can, however, change his relationships without changing either his being, purposes or will. Does this notion of immutability fit the concept of a sempiternal God? I believe it does. Biblical language about divine change is consistent with a sempiternal God. It does not give any reason to demand that God change being, purposes or will. This, of course, does not prove that temporal eternity is correct. It only refutes the atemporalist's claim that holding divine immutability necessitates holding atemporal eternity.

Divine omniscience and timeless eternity. Though this issue potentially raises several issues, I shall focus only on the question of whether God knows what time it is now in human history and hence knows the truth about indexical propositions that include the word *now*.[64] In order for God's reaction to our action actually to occur in our history, God must know what time it is from our perspective in order to guarantee that the action God does timelessly has its effect on us at the time in our world when it is supposed to do so. But how can a God outside of time know exactly what time it is in our world?

There is no question that a timeless being can know the whole plan of history and can know the relation of one event to another (that one is before or after the other, for example). Those who believe God has decreed all things, of course, would expect God to know every event of history and in the right order. Those who do not believe God has decreed all things but still believe God just somehow knows everything that happens in human history would also agree that a timeless being knows the whole of history and knows it in its right sequence. Moreover, in knowing

---

[63]For a full discussion of this issue, see my forthcoming books on the doctrine of God and on the subject of God, time and eternity.

[64]The other major issue surrounding omniscience, the problem of freedom and foreknowledge, was presented with atemporalist arguments. For those who want to pursue further the issue of freedom and foreknowledge, let me suggest some contemporary literature: Marilyn Adams, "Is the Existence of God a 'Hard' Fact?" *The Philosophical Review* 76 (1967); Robert Adams, "Middle Knowledge and the Problem of Evil," *American Philosophical Quarterly* 14 (1977); William L. Craig, *The Only Wise God* (Grand Rapids: Baker, 1987); John M. Fischer, "Freedom and Foreknowledge," *The Philosophical Review* 92 (January 1983); Alfred J. Freddoso, "Accidental Necessity and Logical Determinism," *The Journal of Philosophy* 80 (May 1983); Helm, *Eternal God*, pp. 95-170; Anthony Kenny, *The God of the Philosophers* (Oxford: Clarendon, 1979), chap. 5; Brian Leftow, "Eternity and Simultaneity," *Faith and Philosophy* 8 (April 1991): 148-51, 172-75; Brian Leftow, *Time and Eternity* (Ithaca, N.Y.: Cornell University Press, 1991), chap. 11; Brian Leftow, "Timelessness and Foreknowledge," *Philosophical Studies* 63 (1991); William Mann, "Simplicity and Immutability in God," pp. 262-64; Morris, *Our Idea of God*, p. 129; Nelson Pike, "Divine Omniscience and Voluntary Action," in *Philosophy of Religion*, ed. Steven M. Cahn (New York: Harper & Row, 1970); Pike, *God and Timelessness*, pp. 53-86, 174-75; Alvin Plantinga, "On Ockham's Way Out," *Faith and Philosophy* 3 (July 1986); Bruce Reichenbach, "Omniscience and Deliberation," *International Journal for Philosophy of Religion* 16 (1984); John S. Feinberg, *The Many Faces of Evil* (Grand Rapids: Zondervan, 1994), chap. 4.

the whole plan of history, God also knows that the point in history at which I write this sentence is 8:46 a.m. central standard time on November 24, 1995.

Despite an atemporal God's knowing such things about the present, there are many things an atemporal God cannot know that are happening in our world. God can know the date and time when I would write this sentence, but God cannot know that this very moment is that date and time. For God to know what time it is now would mean that with each new moment of our time, there would be changes in God's knowledge that occur with the passage of our time. Hence some of what God would know would instantiate a temporal sequence for him (that is, at one moment, God would know it was time t on earth and after that God would know it was $t+1$ on earth). This would rule out immutability in the atemporalist's strong sense, for there would be changes in God's knowledge. The dilemma for the atemporalist is rather clear: (1) either God does know what time it is for us in the way outlined, but then God is a temporal being and apparently mutable, or (2) God remains atemporal and immutable but does not know what time it is in our world. If one opts for the first horn of the dilemma, atemporalism is lost. If one opts for the second horn (as atemporalists usually do), God does not know what time it is in our world as the events of our world are occurring. If God doesn't know that, how can God get his reactions to us to occur in our world at the right time?[65] How can God be said to be omniscient, since God does not know something that is knowable? As Robert Coburn explains:

> If a being is omniscient, then presumably it follows that this being knows everything which (logically) can be known. But it is easy to see that an eternal being could not know everything which (logically) can be known, and this is because some of the facts which (logically) can be known, are knowable only by temporal beings, by beings who occupy some position (or some positions) in time. Consider, for example, the fact that the day which is now elapsing (I write this on May 12, 1962) is May 12, 1962; or more simply, that today is May 12, 1962. Clearly to know this fact is tantamount to knowing one's temporal position, and being oriented in time. But if this is true, then a necessary condition of knowing this fact, it would seem, is having some position in time concerning which there are truths of the type indicated to be known. To see the matter in another light, assume that the idea of a non-temporal knower makes sense. Then ask, could such a knower know, e.g., that today is May 12, 1962? The obvious answer, I submit, is that it could only if it could use temporal indicator words. For otherwise, it could not express and *a fortiori* could not entertain a truth such as the above. But a necessary condition of being able to use temporal indicator

---

[65]For presentations of this line of argument, see Wolterstorff, "God Everlasting," p. 197, Hasker, "Concerning the Intelligibility of 'God Is Timeless,' " *New Scholasticism* 57 (Spring 1983): 182ff., and Morris, *Our Idea of God*, pp. 132-33.

words is being an occupant of time. Hence, God's alleged eternity is logically incompatible with his alleged omniscience.[66]

As Norman Kretzmann says, "Thus the familiar account of omniscience regarding contingent events is drastically incomplete. An omniscient being must know not only the entire scheme of contingent events from beginning to end at once, but also *at what stage of realization that scheme now is.*"[67]

Temporalists, of course, can handle the problem of divine omniscience and knowledge of temporal indexical propositions. The temporalist can hold that God knows the truth about all temporal indexicals about the present and the past. Which indexical propositions are about the present and which are about the past is constantly changing because of the passage of time, but this does not mean God either forgets anything or learns something, and this sort of change does not prove that God lacks immutability in person, purposes and will. As to temporal indexicals about the future, their truth is not knowable by anyone, so it is no deficiency that God does not know what is impossible to know.

I trust that the preceding discussion of the God, time and eternity question shows its significance for evangelicalism. It involves an understanding of many of the divine attributes, divine action and the freedom and foreknowledge question. This is why it is an "umbrella issue." For this reason alone (not to speak of the challenge that process theism presents to traditional theism in regard to these issues), evangelicals must attend to this issue.

Nonevangelicals, Postmodernity and Religious Pluralism

When we move beyond the scope of evangelical theology, we find a postmodern mindset capturing the day. *Postmodernism* refers to a number of different views in a number of different fields. There are philosophical, political, theological, social and ecological views, for example, that go by this label. *Postmodernism* also refers to certain concepts of rationality. Some postmodern notions are ideas all of us might applaud, whereas others seem detrimental to traditional evangelical thinking. Postmodernism has generated a variety of contemporary views, each with its own perspective on the nature of God. Moreover, the postmodern mindset typically urges tolerance of and openness to other world religions.

To understand postmodernism, we must identify what it is reacting to. The answer is the modern mindset. In a broad sense, "the modern age" refers to the

---

[66]Robert Coburn, "Professor Malcolm on God," *Australasian Journal of Philosophy* (August 1963): 155-56, cited in Pike, *God and Timelessness*, pp. 88-89. See also Arthur Prior, "The Formalities of Omniscience," *Philosophy* (1962), as quoted in Kenny, *The God of the Philosophers*, p. 39.

[67]Norman Kretzmann, "Omniscience and Immutability," in *Philosophy of Religion*, ed. Steven M. Cahn (New York: Harper & Row, 1970), p. 95. For various attempts to respond to this problem, see Leftow, *Time and Eternity*, pp. 321-34, and Hector-Neri Castaneda, "Omniscience and Indexical Reference," *The Journal of Philosophy* 64 (April 1967): 203.

period begun by Galileo, Descartes and Newton, a period that continued with the nineteenth-century rationalism and scientism that are still influential today. In a narrower sense, the modern period was a period of artistic and cultural activity in the early twentieth century.[68] The modern mentality is broadly characterized by a deterministic model of reality ("Newtonian science") that is used to interpret phenomena ranging from physics to sociology, psychology and religion.[69]

According to the modern mindset, it is possible to have a rational, objective approach to reality. This approach tried to get at reality through the natural and social sciences.[70] Modern theologies work against the backdrop of this modern worldview. The basic epistemological doctrine of the modern world is sensate empiricism, according to which knowledge of the world beyond ourselves comes exclusively through sense perception. Given this assumption, there can be no knowledge of values. All moral and aesthetic values must be considered arbitrary preferences. Likewise, there can be no genuine religious experience in the sense of a direct experience of God. Belief in God is therefore entirely groundless or at best rooted in an inference from our sensory knowledge of the world.[71] According to this epistemology, it is possible through empirical observation objectively to know what is true about the world (as long as the discussion addresses things in the world). Hence it is possible to talk of truth as a correspondence between our language and the world.

From this epistemology stems the Enlightenment, or modern, concept of what it means to be rational. The Enlightenment conception of rationality holds that maintaining a belief is only rational when it rests on the basis of sufficient evidence, arguments or reasons. But what counts as *sufficient evidence?* Classic foundationalists reply that belief has sufficient support when it is supported by evidences that are supported (inferred) ultimately from beliefs that are properly basic. A properly basic belief is a belief that is either self-evident, evident to the senses or incorrigible.[72]

The basic ontological doctrine of modernity is the mechanistic doctrine of nature, according to which the physical world is composed of inanimate, insentient atoms that interact by deterministic impact. This mechanistic view of nature allows for two possible worldviews, which are the two worldviews of the modern period. In the dualistic version, the human self or soul is regarded as being above nature and as being the only locus of value in the world. Dualistic modernism therefore

---

[68]William Beardslee, "Christ in the Postmodern Age: Reflections Inspired by Jean-François Lyotard," in *Varieties of Postmodern Theology*, ed. David Griffin, William Beardslee and Joe Holland (Albany: State University of New York Press, 1989), p. 63.

[69]Ibid., p. 64.

[70]David Griffin, introduction to *Varieties of Postmodern Theology*, pp. 1-2.

[71]David Griffin, "Postmodern Theology as Liberation Theology: A Response to Harvey Cox," in *Varieties of Postmodern Theology*, p. 85.

[72]See Plantinga, "Reason and Belief in God," and Clark, *Return to Reason.*

leads to alienation, anthropocentrism and intellectual fragmentation in the form of a radical split between the sciences and the humanities. This dualism is unintelligible apart from supernaturalism, because a supernatural deity is needed to explain the interaction of sentient mind and insentient matter.

Because of the difficulties inherent in it, dualistic modernity has increasingly given way to modern materialism, which entails determinism, reductionism, atheism and nihilism. When combined with the sensate empiricism that it implies, this worldview entails positivism—the view that the only truth we can know is that which comes through the natural sciences. Religion, theology, ethics and metaphysics can deliver no additional truths, according to this perspective. We can reasonably believe only the worldview provided by the natural sciences, and in that worldview there is no God, no freedom and no meaning to the distinction between good and evil.[73] "The modern world freed technology, politics, economics, and culture from nearly every restraint."[74] The modern world has produced an increasingly powerful and destructive technology. Critics of modernity claim that the modern world is building a scientific deathtrap for humanity and nature, which became evident in the twentieth century with the two world wars and the nuclear age that followed.

The increasing secularization of society gradually shut out from public life the awe and power of the religious. Autonomous science and technology are the religion of the public realm, while individual pietism is the religion of the private realm.[75] "Thus, we see the negative climax of the modern scientific promise of freedom and progress: ever more destructive wars, threats of nuclear annihilation, genocide, totalitarianism, ecological poisoning, erosion of community, marginalization of the poor, and public suppression of religious Mystery. What emerged in the eighteenth century as a bold dream converts itself dialectically in the late twentieth century into a frightening nightmare. This is the cultural end of the modern world."[76]

Early modern theologies tried to accommodate themselves to the modern worldview by reducing theology's content (often by demythologizing it) in order to reach a universal theology that represented the essence of all religions (eighteenth-century deism is an example). Late modern theologies returned to particularity rather than striving for universality and thereby gave up their claim to provide a basis for public policy in an increasingly pluralistic society. In addition, late modern theology appealed to criteria of validation other than the public criteria used in science and science-based philosophy, such as self-consistency and factual adequacy. Instead it appealed to truth as subjectivity or contrasted the perspective (language-

---

[73]Griffin, "Postmodern Theology as Liberation Theology," pp. 85-86. See also Joe Holland, "The Postmodern Paradigm and Contemporary Catholicism," in *Varieties of Postmodern Theology*, p. 10.
[74]Holland, "The Postmodern Paradigm," p. 11.
[75]Ibid., p. 15.
[76]Ibid., p. 12.

game) of objective science with that of religion or appealed to a revelation to a particular community that allowed people to speak "from faith to faith." In all of these cases, however, they conceded the arena of public discourse to the modern worldview. In so doing, they avoided the demands of public verification. Late modern theology sought to articulate biblical faith in a context in which people's faith, religion or piety was generally assumed to be a private matter without relevance to public policy.[77]

One pervasive feature of modern theology, according to critics, has been a separation of systematic theology from theological ethics, especially social ethics. It became abstract and thereby seemed irrelevant to the social evils of the time— racism, sexism, social and economic injustice, imperialism, war, nuclearism and ecological destruction—which stand contrary to the will of God as portrayed in the theology. Separating theology from ethics has had the effect of sanctioning the status quo. Hence, according to critics, when German theologians of the 1930s and 1940s explicated the Christian faith with no negative reference to Nazism, they implied that the politics of the Nazis were not antithetical to it.[78]

Postmodern theological responses to modernity. The major tenets of modernity have been rejected in one way or another by postmodernists. This is not to say, however, that postmodernists agree about what should replace these central ideas. As Griffin, Beardslee and Holland show, there have been four different types of theological response to modernity. These responses suggest the general mindset (theological and otherwise) of postmodernity. In this section I want to describe three of the four briefly and then focus on the one with the most optimistic outlook, one that incorporates process theology.

The most radical postmodern theology is deconstructionist or eliminative postmodernism. "Philosophical postmodernism is inspired variously by pragmatism, physicalism, Ludwig Wittgenstein, Martin Heidegger, and Jacques Derrida and other recent French thinkers. . . . It overcomes the modern worldview through an anti-worldview: it deconstructs or eliminates the ingredients necessary for a worldview, such as God, self, purpose, meaning, a real world, and truth as correspondence. While motivated in some cases by the ethical concern to forestall totalitarian systems, this type of postmodern thought issues in relativism, even nihilism."[79]

This type of postmodern philosophy believes that an objective approach to the facts of experience proves, paradoxically, that an objective approach is not possible and that this realization undermines the modern worldview along with

---

[77]Griffin, introduction to *Varieties of Postmodern Theology*, p. 2.
[78]Griffin, "Postmodern Theology as Liberation Theology," pp. 81-82.
[79]David Griffin, "Introduction to SUNY Series in Constructive Postmodern Thought," in *Varieties of Postmodern Theology*, p. xii.

every other worldview. It believes that we are moving into a postmodern age in which this relativistic outlook will increasingly undermine the modern world-view.[80]

A keynote of this position is a need to exercise tolerance toward all people and all viewpoints. Since absolute truth is impossible to attain and since it is impossible to demonstrate one position as preferable over another, there is no room for excluding anyone or any position from the dialogue table. Likewise, this general approach argues (following the later philosophy of Wittgenstein) that our social (and so on) norms are all conventional (they cannot be proved right by reason or empiricism) and they reflect the societies in which those norms were chosen. Anyone is a product of his or her linguistic community and the language games of that society. Typically societies have been dominated by males and by traditional religious beliefs. We have inherited the basic mindset of these cultures, but we need to see that these foundational ideas that we have are theory laden, not theory independent. We must, then, deconstruct our basic ideas of men and women and their relations to one another in societies, identify societal notions that were generated by the underlying male-dominated, traditional-religion-dominated mindset, and do away with such ideas. Doing so frees us from such biased views and opens us to dialogue with all people and all viewpoints.[81]

A second kind of postmodern theology is liberationist postmodernism, as represented by Harvey Cox and Cornel West. Unlike other postmodern theologies, Cox's does not discuss whether an objective analysis of the facts of experience undermines the modern worldview. "But he does argue that theologians should not be constrained by the cultural mind-set that has been shaped by this worldview. The primary concern of a postmodern theology, in Cox's view, is to be liberationist, and for this purpose it can build most effectively upon the premodern piety of the religious communities. While Cox's theology is clearly postmodern in seeking to overcome the privatization of faith, it retains late modern theology's rejection of the need for theology to be self-consistent and adequate to the various facts of experience."[82]

Unlike modern theology's emphasis on totalitarian control that tends to legiti-mize totalitarian governments and economic systems (capitalist and socialist) oppressive to many people who live under them, liberation theologies reject such systems and opt for freeing the oppressed. Instead of separating theology from

---

[80]Griffin, introduction to *Varieties of Postmodern Theology*, pp. 3-4.
[81]For two examples of a deconstructive postmodern theology, see Mark C. Taylor, *Erring: A Postmodern A/theology*, (Chicago: Univ. of Chicago Press, 1984), and Jean-François Lyotard, *The Postmodern Condition: A Report on Knowledge* (Minneapolis: Univ. of Minnesota Press, 1984). For a response to Taylor and Lyotard, see David Griffin, "Postmodern Theology and A/Theology: A Response to Mark C. Taylor," and Beardslee, "Christ in the Postmodern Age," in *Varieties of Postmodern Theology*.
[82]Griffin, introduction to *Varieties of Postmodern Theology*, pp. 4-5.

ethics, as is often done in modern theologies, liberation theologies opt for doing theology as praxis and thereby deliberately wed social ethics to theology.

David Griffin calls a third kind of postmodernist theology "restorationist or conservative postmodernism" and cites Pope John Paul II as one of its key proponents. Like conservative postmodernism in general, it grows out of classical resistance, most often religious, to modernity. Conservative postmodernists see their critique of modernity vindicated by the modern breakdown and the postmodern breakthrough. Tending toward a cyclical rather than a linear view of history, they are naturally drawn to a return to classical roots. They are appalled by the appeal to primal roots, which they see as pagan. But the conservative consciousness does more than look for a return to classical forms. Only if it is truly open to new possibilities, along with the continuity of tradition and the authority of structure, does it warrant the name *postmodern*. The new possibilities must embrace something beyond either the classical or the modern imagination—for example, John Paul II's imaging of a new global human solidarity and his ecological concern for the fate of the earth.[83]

A fourth kind of postmodern theology Griffin labels constructive or revisionary postmodernism. According to Griffin, this approach does not reject the modern worldview by rejecting the possibility of worldviews altogether. Rather, it constructs a postmodern worldview by revising modern and traditional concepts. Revisionary postmordernism offers a new unity of scientific, ethical, aesthetic and religious intuitions. "It rejects not science as such but only that scientism in which the data of the modern natural sciences are alone allowed to contribute to the construction of our worldview. . . . Going beyond the modern world will involve transcending its individualism, anthropocentrism, patriarchy, mechanization, economism, consumerism, nationalism, and militarism. Constructive postmodern thought provides support for the ecology, peace, feminist, and other emancipatory movements of our time, while stressing that the inclusive emancipation must be from modernity itself."[84]

Griffin's constructive postmodernism is worthy of specific attention.[85] Griffin claims that perhaps the most basic difference between deconstructive and constructive postmodernism involves their respective attitudes about theory and practice. The former

> follows Hume's precedent in rejecting from theory all those commonsense beliefs that are in conflict with modern premises. Hume did not stop believing in causality as real influence and in an actual world which existed independently

---

[83]See Joe Holland, "The Cultural Vision of Pope John Paul II: Toward a Conservative/Liberal Postmodern Dialogue," in *Varieties of Postmodern Theology*, pp. 109-10.

[84]"Griffin, "Introduction to SUNY Series," pp. xii-xiii.

[85]As seen in Griffin, "Postmodern Theology and A/Theology: A Response to Mark C. Taylor," and Griffin, "Liberation Theology and Postmodern Philosophy: A Response to Cornel West," in *Varieties of Postmodern Theology*.

of his perception. But because these beliefs could not be justified by his philosophic theory, given its premises, he relegated them to the status of "practice." Whitehead, by contrast, said that we should appeal to practice not to *supplement* our philosophic theory but to *revise* it. The rule for philosophic theory is that "we must bow to those presumptions, which, in despite of criticism, we still employ for the regulation of our lives." Philosophy should be "the search for the coherence of such presumptions." Metaphysics should be empirical primarily in the sense of including and reconciling these various notions.[86]

As already noted, two key dogmas of modernity are its epistemological belief in sensate empiricism and its ontological belief that the fundamental existents of the world are devoid of spontaneity or the power of self-movement (mechanistic view of nature). Griffin refers to this second view as the nonanimistic view of nature or nonanimism. He claims that this second tenet was derived from supernaturalistic theism with its belief in divine omnipotence. As to sensate empiricism, it too arose in a supernaturalistic context. What could be known of the world was known through sense perception. Any knowledge that was unavailable through sense perception would be provided by divine revelation of some sort. As modernism moved into its later period (eighteenth century through twentieth century), God was left out. People began adopting materialism with respect to the mind. Knowledge about good and evil and God was thought to be simply groundless and unconfirmable. The epistemological result was solipsism.[87]

Griffin's revisionary postmodernism has a different answer. It does not accept nihilistic deconstructionism, but it does not return to a supernatural God either. I quote his answer at length to demonstrate how thoroughly it relies on process theology. Griffin writes:

> In contrast with the nonanimism of modernity, Whiteheadian postmodernism develops a neoanimistic view in which all actual individuals embody a principle of spontaneity. The ultimate or absolute reality, which is embodied in all actual individuals, is *creativity*. Creativity eternally oscillates between two modes. In one mode, creativity is self-determination, final causation, or "concrescence," in which an individual becomes concrete by creating itself out of others. Through the embodiment of creativity in this mode, every individual is partly *causa sui*. As soon as this act of self-creation is completed, creativity swings over into its other mode, which is other-creation, efficient causation, or "transition." ... The actual world is comprised entirely of creative events and the societies they form. The human mind or soul is a society composed of a series of high-level creative events; the human body is a society composed of a vast number of lower-level

---

[86] Griffin, "Postmodern Theology and A/Theology," p. 40.
[87] Ibid., pp. 41-42.

creative events of various levels. This perspective thereby contains no mind-body problem of how a soul exercising final causation can interact with bodily substances exercising only efficient causation. Mind and body are both composed of events exercising both kinds of causation. This perspective likewise contains no problem of how an experiencing mind can interact with nonexperiencing physical atoms. It is part and parcel of this neoanimistic viewpoint to regard all creative events as "occasions of experience." Whereas the dualism of first-stage modernity treated human experience as virtually supernatural, revisionary postmodernism "refuses to place human experience outside nature." Because some level of experience is attributed to all actual individuals whatsoever, the avoidance of dualism does not require the assumption that the mind or soul is strictly identical with the body (or brain). The mind or soul can be thought of as a series of occasions of experience, each of which unifies the manifold experiences of the body (and the remainder of the past world) into a central experience of enjoyment and purpose. This doctrine avoids the substantial, isolated self of early modernity. ... there is no underlying, enduring, unchanging subject of change for which relations to changing events are merely accidental. The things that endure, such as minds and molecules, "are not the completely real things." The completely real individuals do not *endure*, they *occur*. They are occasions of experience, which arise out of their relations to prior occasions of experience and include them in their own constitutions. This view is in fact so relational as to insist that the whole past is included in each occasion of experience: "Each atom is a system of all things." This view radically undermines the early modern independent self which had no kinship with nature, and no essential relations to nature or other selves.[88]

As to the other doctrine of modernity, sensate empiricism, revisionary postmodernism based on Whiteheadian philosophy has a different answer. Revisionary postmodernism rejects the tacit identification of perception with sense perception. Whitehead saw sense perception as a high-level derivative form of perception. It stems from a primordial type of perception, called *prehension*, that humans share with all other individuals. "This doctrine, that human beings share nonsensory perception with all other individuals, is simply the epistemological side of the ontological doctrine that all individuals are 'occasions of experience' which arise out of their relations to (their prehensions of) previous individuals."[89]

Belief in these two types of perception supports moral and value judgments. As Griffin explains,

One of the reasons for the modern denial of cognitive status to moral beliefs ... has been the conviction that moral beliefs could not be rooted in perception.

---

[88]Ibid., pp. 42-43.
[89]Ibid., p. 45.

Sensory perception, of course, gives us information only about physical things, not nonphysical things such as values. If all genuine perception is sensory, moral beliefs must therefore have been fabricated out of nothing (or rather, out of ideological interests and the will to power). As we have seen, however, even those who hold this view cannot avoid presuppositions about good and evil.... Revisionary postmodernism helps us avoid such self-contradictions by pointing to the nonsensory mode of perception through which we learn all sorts of truths, such as those about an actual world, causal efficacy, and the distinction between past, present, and future. We can therefore, without an *ad hoc* notion of special "moral faculty," speak in terms of a direct intuition or perception of moral values.[90]

Where is God in all of this? Griffin says that revisionary postmodernism agrees with deconstructive postmodernism that the supernatural God of premodern and early modern theology cannot be believed in. But it does not eliminate God altogether. Rather, it opts for a God who is naturalistic, not supernaturalistic. What we get is the adoption of Whitehead's process God. In supernatural theism, all power and creativity belong to God alone. In naturalistic theism, these belong inherently to the world of finite existents as well as God.[91] Griffin further explains how such a God allows us to escape moral relativism[92] and how this God allows us to speak about "the truth" of things.[93] But he notes that this God does not know the truth about the future, nor can we.[94]

This is clearly an empirical understanding of reality and of God. As such, it takes Kantian epistemology seriously without adopting Kant's conclusions about metaphysics altogether. Whether this form of postmodern theology wins the day remains to be seen. However, it vividly illustrates why process theology is likely to occupy much attention among nonevangelical theologians in upcoming years. Because evangelical theologians long to dialogue with those outside their camp and because a major issue under discussion among evangelicals (God, time and eternity) also involves process theism, I anticipate that process theology will be a major subject of discussion within evangelicalism as well. Even though evangelicals and nonevangelicals may have differing interests and agendas in regard to process theism, let us hope that evangelicals will seize the opportunity that this common interest in process thought affords them to engage nonevangelical theologians in discussions that will prove profitable in moving nonevangelicals toward evangelicalism without evangelicals abandoning their foundational beliefs about God in favor of process beliefs.

---

[90]Ibid., pp. 47-48.
[91]Ibid., pp. 48-49.
[92]Ibid., pp. 49-50.
[93]Ibid., p. 50. In his further article on Cornel West and liberation theology, Griffin takes up again the issue of truth as correspondence. See David Griffin, "Liberation Theology and Postmodern Philosophy: A Response to Cornel West," in *Varieties of Postmodern Theology*, pp. 133-41.
[94]Ibid.

Chapter 14

New Dimensions in the Study of Angels & Demons

Robert V. Rakestraw

••••••••••••••••••••••••••••••

ANYONE UNAWARE OF THE ATTENTION GIVEN TO ANGELS AND DEMONS in recent years would have to be either a hermit or a recent arrival from another planet. What is especially notable about this surge of interest is that not only Christians but also those outside the church have been swept up by the phenomenon. While there is a cyclical pattern of interest in certain theological topics *within* the Christian world, there is not usually, due to the peculiar subject matter, a corresponding interest in current Christian issues from the general public. What interest there is focuses mostly on the significance of the topic as a news item, as with creation versus evolution, the relationship between healing and prayer, and the Jesus Seminar.

The recent explosion of interest in angels and demons, however, has a broad existential quality to it that attracts people of widely diverse religious interests.[1] This

---

[1]Front-page cover stories on angels appeared in the December 27, 1993, issues of both *Time* and *Newsweek*. Some noteworthy popular-level books on angels and angelic appearances include two books by Sophy Burnham: *A Book of Angels* and *Angel Letters* (New York: Ballantine, 1990 and 1991 respectively); Douglas Connelly, *Angels Around Us* (Downers Grove, Ill.: InterVarsity Press, 1994); Duane A. Garrett, *Angels and the New Spirituality* (Nashville: Broadman & Holman, 1995); two books by Karen Goldman: *The Angel Book: A Handbook for Aspiring Angels* and *Angel Voices* (New York: Simon & Schuster, 1993 and 1994 respectively); Robert J. Grant, *Are We Listening to the Angels?* (Virginia Beach: A.R.E. Press, 1994); Timothy Jones, *Celebration of Angels* (Nashville: Thomas Nelson, 1994); Peter J. Kreeft, *Angels and Demons* (San Francisco: Ignatius, 1995); Terry Law, *The Truth About Angels* (Orlando, Fla.: Creation House, 1994); Geddes MacGregor, *Angels: Ministers of Grace* (New York:

is particularly true of the attention given to good angels but is also relevant to the concern many have with the demonic side of reality, whether in the discussion of multiple personalities, the nature of human evil (as, for example, in M. Scott Peck's *People of the Lie*[2]) or the grip evil forces have on our deteriorating inner cities and even on some of our formerly respected institutions and professions (such as government, education and the legal profession).

Because of the attention angels and the demonic are receiving in both Christian circles and the wider society, pastors, educators and other Christian leaders need to devote substantial time and energy to this customarily peripheral category of systematic theology. We need both a refresher course in biblical angelology and demonology and an update on some of the most helpful and/or provocative thinking in these areas from those who work within the framework of Scripture and Christian tradition. If we are to benefit those who desire some sanity in the midst of a bewildering sea of voices, we cannot consign this area of study to writers and popularizers not grounded on solid biblical and theological foundations. God's people deserve to have the best minds working on this topic (which Karl Barth called "the most remarkable and difficult of all" spheres of dogmatics[3]) as well as other current theological concerns.

My approach in this essay will be first to indicate briefly some recent thinking on the subject of angelology and demonology in general, then present one contemporary author who discusses holy angels, highlight some contributions in the area of Satan and evil spirits, and conclude with some suggestions for further study and evangelical engagement. While this is primarily a descriptive rather than a constructive essay, I will include some critique and some directions for further study.

Good and Evil Spirits

In his *Christian Theology*, Millard Erickson devotes a chapter to good and evil angels, noting that even with the great amount of attention given to demonology and demon possession and the growing interest in good angels, "there has not been a balanced inquiry into the nature and activity of angels, both the good and the evil."[4] He is obviously thinking of something more in-depth than the volume by C. Fred Dickason, *Angels: Elect and Evil*, which has served as a generally helpful popular introduction to the subject.[5] After briefly surveying the doctrine, Erickson presents

---

Paragon House, 1988); and Marilynn C. Webber and William D. Webber, *A Rustle of Angels* (Grand Rapids: Zondervan, 1994).

[2]M. Scott Peck, *People of the Lie* (New York: Simon & Schuster, 1983).

[3]Karl Barth, *Church Dogmatics*, ed. G. W. Bromiley and T. F. Torrance (Edinburgh: T & T Clark, 1960), 3:369.

[4]Millard J. Erickson, *Christian Theology* (Grand Rapids: Baker, 1985), 3:437.

[5]C. Fred Dickason, *Angels: Elect and Evil* (Chicago: Moody Press, 1975).

the biblical teaching on good angels. "They evidently grow in knowledge by observing human actions and hearing of human repentance (Lk 12:8; 15:10; 1 Cor 4:9; Eph 3:10)."[6] Angels are immaterial beings. "Physical manifestations recorded in Scripture must be regarded as appearances assumed for the occasion (angelophanies)."[7] Concerning guardian angels, Erickson concludes that there is insufficient evidence for the idea that each person (or at least each believer) has a specific angelic guardian in this life.[8]

In his discussion of evil angels he considers briefly and then discards three modern approaches: the demythologizing effort of Bultmann, the depersonalizing approach of Tillich and the dynamic nothingness view of Barth.[9] In accord with recent scholarship, he refrains from using Isaiah 14:12-17 and Ezekiel 28:1-19 as references to the original state and fall of Satan. Surprisingly, he makes no mention of these texts.[10] He sees demons as fallen angels and understands 2 Peter 2:4 and Jude 6 as speaking of their fall.[11] On the question of demonization, Erickson notes wisely that the biblical writers did not attribute all illness to demon possession. "Nor was epilepsy mistaken for demon possession. We read in Matthew 17:15-18 that Jesus cast out a demon from an epileptic, but in Matthew 4:24 epileptics (as well as paralytics) are distinguished from demoniacs." When Jesus did cast out demons, he did it without pronouncing an elaborate formula. He simply commanded them to come out. While Erickson advises us to be alert to the possibility of demon possession, he cautions us against thinking that this is the primary manifestation of the forces of evil today. "In actuality, Satan, the great deceiver, may be encouraging interest in demon possession in hopes that Christians will become careless about other more subtle forms of influence by the powers of evil."[12] Overall, Erickson's discussion of angels, while brief, is a balanced and biblically based overview of the main issues.

A topic sometimes discussed under the category of angels and demons is the New Testament teaching on "the powers."[13] The scholarship of Walter Wink has

---

[6]Erickson, *Christian Theology*, p. 441.

[7]Ibid., p. 439.

[8]Ibid., p. 445.

[9]Ibid., pp. 446-47.

[10]I say "surprisingly" because some study Bibles and contemporary writers who relate Isaiah 14 and Ezekiel 28 to the fall of Satan continue to influence numerous preachers and lay Christians. Those who see Satan's fall in one or both of these texts include Michael Green, *I Believe in Satan's Downfall* (Grand Rapids: Eerdmans, 1981), pp. 36-41 (now published, without revision, as *Exposing the Prince of Darkness* [Ann Arbor, Mich.: Servant, 1991]), and Dickason, *Angels*, pp. 127-37. Arguing against the view of Green and Dickason is Sydney H. T. Page, *Powers of Evil: A Biblical Study of Satan and Demons* (Grand Rapids: Baker, 1995), pp. 37-42.

[11]Erickson, *Christian Theology*, pp. 447-48.

[12]Ibid., pp. 449-50.

[13]Sometimes the Pauline concept of "the powers" is discussed under the category of the demonic. Erickson, however, covers this topic under his study of sin, specifically the social dimension of sin (*Christian Theology*, pp. 648-52). In his discussion of the powers Erickson follows Hendrikus Berkhof,

been particularly influential in recent discussions of this theme. His three-part work *Naming the Powers, Unmasking the Powers* and *Engaging the Powers* combines scriptural exegesis, social and psychological analysis, historical research and personal insights in a valuable assessment of the benevolent and malevolent forces at work in society.[14] Wink's thesis undergirding all three volumes is that "the New Testament's 'principalities and powers' is a generic category referring to the determining forces of physical, psychic, and social existence. These powers usually consist of an outer manifestation and an inner spirituality or interiority. Power must become incarnate, institutionalized or systemic in order to be effective. It has a dual aspect possessing both an outer, visible form (constitutions, judges, police, leaders, office complexes), and an inner, invisible spirit that provides it legitimacy, compliance, credibility, and clout."[15]

While Wink does not believe in the real, independent existence of personal angels, demons and Satan, his extensive study of the Scriptures dealing with these topics and the principalities and powers is valuable in provoking us to think more deeply and through some different lenses than we have customarily done as evangelicals. Gabriel Fackre notes that "Wink's insights have enabled clergy better to understand peculiar forces alive in the church as institution, the 'angels' of the congregations in which we live and work."[16]

Fackre's comment refers to Wink's view of the "angels" of the churches in Revelation 2—3, which he sees as something other than human messengers, bishops or pastors. "Everywhere else that the term 'angel' appears in the Apocalypse, it unambiguously refers to *heavenly* messengers." The angels of the seven churches are some sort of spiritual guardians. Yet "the angel is not something separate from the congregation, but must somehow represent it as a totality." According to Wink, "the fact that the angel is actually addressed suggests that it is more than a mere personification of the church, but the actual spirituality of the congregation as a single entity. The angel would then exist in, with, and under the material expressions of the church's life as its interiority. As the corporate personality or felt sense of the whole, the angel of the church would have no separate existence apart from the

Christ and the Powers (Scottsdale, Penn.: Herald, 1962), and John Howard Yoder, *The Politics of Jesus* (Grand Rapids: Eerdmans, 1972), pp. 140-62, in seeing the powers not as angels or demons but as "created realities which give an order to society and are capable of having either a constructive or detrimental effect" (p. 649). Erickson writes, "It is difficult to determine whether Paul thought of these powers as being in any way personal, but it is clear that he did not identify them with angels" (p. 649). However, elsewhere in his *Christian Theology* he speaks of the angels' great power being taught in Scripture, in part, by "the titles assigned to at least some of them—principalities, powers, authorities, dominions, thrones" (p. 441).

[14]Walter Wink, *Naming the Powers* (Philadelphia: Fortress, 1984); *Unmasking the Powers* (Philadelphia: Fortress, 1986); and *Engaging the Powers* (Minneapolis: Fortress, 1992).

[15]Wink, *Unmasking the Powers*, p. 4.

[16]Gabriel Fackre, "Angels Heard and Demons Seen," *Theology Today* 51 (1994): 355.

people." Wink notes, however, that the converse is equally true, for "the people would have no unity apart from the angel. Angel and people are the inner and outer aspects of one and the same reality. The people incarnate or embody the angelic spirit; the angel distills the invisible essence of their totality as a group. The angel and the congregation come into being together and, if such is their destiny, pass out of existence together. The one cannot exist without the other."[17]

Wink goes on to say that "the angel of a church becomes demonic when the congregation turns its back on the specific tasks set before it by God and makes some other goal its idol."[18] Such an insight has been helpful to some working in local churches. One of Wink's colleagues commented about service in an earlier ministry: "I didn't understand about the angel, so in trying to foster institutional change I attacked individuals. I thought they were evil people because they were doing evil things. That merely created such an unpleasant situation that I had to resign to get out of it. I didn't realize that I was up against the angel of the institution."[19] Wink's discussion of the angels of the nations and the angels of nature are similarly provocative. His insights justify the time invested in studying his trilogy, even for evangelicals who do not accept his definitions of angels and demons. Discovering and understanding the "spirit" of a corporate entity—whether it be a local church, a mission society, or a neighborhood composed mostly of one ethnic group—is essential for all who live or work with that group.[20]

Holy Angels

Lawrence Osborn offers us a stimulating discussion of good angels, exploring the potential role of angelology in contemporary orthodox theology.[21] His article, a revision of the 1993 Tyndale Christian Doctrine Lecture, presents angels in terms of both their function and their being. He suggests several practical benefits of a sound angelology, noting that angels have never been a major element in evangelical theology. They have rather received little more than the bare affirmation of their existence. Osborn states that changing times warrant a change in this attitude. Christians living under modernism were to some extent wise to avoid stressing

---

[17]Wink, *Unmasking the Powers*, p. 70.

[18]Ibid., p. 78.

[19]Ibid., p. 79.

[20]Some evangelicals who have interacted with Wink are Clinton E. Arnold, *Ephesians: Power and Magic* (Cambridge: Cambridge University Press, 1989), pp. 47-51, 129-32, 189-92; Clinton E. Arnold, *Powers of Darkness* (Downers Grove, Ill.: InterVarsity Press, 1992), pp. 198-201; Fackre, "Angels Heard and Demons Seen," pp. 354-58; Garrett, *Angels and the New Spirituality*, pp. 206-15; Page, *Powers of Evil*, pp. 126, 240-46; Nigel Wright, *The Satan Syndrome* (Grand Rapids: Zondervan, 1990), pp. 143-44. A good summary of the first two volumes of Wink, as well as of some of his other writings, is in Thomas H. McAlpine, *Facing the Powers* (Monrovia, Calif.: MARC, 1991), pp. 17-25.

[21]Lawrence Osborn, "Entertaining Angels: Their Place in Contemporary Theology," *Tyndale Bulletin* 45 (1994): 273-96.

angelology, lest the gospel be considered premodern, precritical or superstitious. However, he writes, times are changing. Because of the weakening and possibly imminent demise of modernity, there has emerged a dramatic resurgence of interest in spirituality and a renewed popular interest in angels. "Angels figure far more extensively in New Age thought than they have done in Christianity over the last two or three centuries."[22] Even in Christian circles, due in part to the supernatural thrillers of Frank Peretti,[23] angelology has become a prominent feature of popular Christianity. Christian theologians must no longer avoid the topic.

In his article, Osborn presents a very useful ten-page overview and critique of Barth's contribution to angelology. He rightly points out that Barth's extensive account of angels is virtually unique in contemporary Protestant theology.[24] Among other points, Osborn first highlights and then critiques Barth's position on the question of angelic being versus function. He observes that according to Barth, there is no scriptural basis for any definition or exposition of angels in terms of their being. Therefore we should focus on the adjective *ministering*, not the noun *spirits* in Hebrews 1:14. Osborn disagrees with Barth that the biblical view of angels is an entirely functional one. According to Osborn, in addition to the obvious fact that Hebrews 1:14 must mean something when it designates angels as "spirits," we should follow the lead offered by Barth himself in seeking to understand angels by trying to understand heaven. Asking how we are to express the otherness of heaven and hence of angels, Osborn states that the invisible (to us) dimension of heaven is as real as the visible dimensions of God's created order. Philosopher of science Karl Popper, for example, often speaks of a third world, "an objective but non-physical dimension of reality in which resides all actual and possible objective knowledge."[25] If heaven can be said to be the inwardness of creation, as Walter Wink has suggested, it may be more immanent than transcendent. Osborn disagrees with Clinton Arnold, who has criticized this view of heaven as tantamount to a psychologization of angels and demons.[26] Defending Wink and to some extent Carl Jung (on whom Wink admittedly leans), Osborn notes that Jung's archetypes—those common features of humanity's collective unconscious—are not mere projections or personifications. They have actual existence and "are the real inhabitants of this domain which he calls the collective unconscious."[27] Osborn does not accept the view of Arnold and others that the interpretation of angelic entities as the inwardness of

---

[22]Ibid., p. 274.
[23]Frank Peretti, *This Present Darkness* and *Piercing the Darkness* (Westchester, Ill.: Crossway, 1986 and 1989 respectively).
[24]See Barth, *Church Dogmatics*, 3:369-531.
[25]Osborn, "Entertaining Angels," p. 289.
[26]Arnold, *Powers of Darkness*, pp. 194-205.
[27]Osborn, "Entertaining Angels," p. 291.

created structures is a denial of their actual existence. In fact, according to Osborn, "the criticism of inwardness as a metaphor for heaven may, in fact, amount to an assimilation of Christianity to the world-view of Modernity. Arnold takes for granted that the domain of the psyche (and, by extension, the inwardness of creation) is private and subjective, less real than the domain of physical phenomena. . . . However, this denial of the reality of the subjective is an integral part of the dichotomy between public and private, which is a hallmark of Modernity."[28]

Continuing his critique of Barth, Osborn takes issue with Barth's identification of the ministry of angels with praise and witness. There is, says Osborn, "too much emphasis on the divine-human axis within Barth's theology" and "even within this narrow focus, there is too much emphasis on the divine pole. Barth's insistence on divine sovereignty reduces human and angel alike to a state of overawed impotence." Barth's exclusive emphasis on praise and witness thus "seriously underplays the power which biblical accounts appear to vest in such beings."[29] Osborn recognizes Barth's admission that angels are also the agents of providence and the bearers of the mystery of creation. Yet he feels that the overall thrust of Barth's angelology is to reduce the angels to an entirely peripheral role. Osborn's point seems to be valid, both in his critique of Barth and in his understanding of the biblical view of angelic service to humanity.

In his concluding section, "The Relevance of Angels," Osborn makes several helpful observations. I will mention only one—the apologetic significance of angels. Osborn refers to theologians' earlier dismissal of angelology as futile speculation with no practical significance for the Christian life or mission. He recognizes that there may have been, on the part of some, a commendable apologetic desire behind this: "to avoid putting unnecessary stumbling blocks in the way of predominantly secular materialist audiences." However, the cost of such a move is high. "If the world does not possess a depth dimension, an openness to God, deism is a more satisfactory way of understanding the God-world relation than traditional theism."[30] The European values study has revealed a marked swing away from materialism during the 1980s. New Agers, for example, do not regard angels as the stuff of speculation. "On the contrary, their fascination with angels is driven by a very practical desire for a wholeness which integrates physical, psychological and spiritual realities. . . . That fascination and that desire are potentially important bridge points between Christians and New Agers."[31] Such

---

[28]Ibid., p. 292.
[29]Ibid., pp. 284-85.
[30]Ibid., p. 293, n. 52.
[31]Ibid., pp. 293-94. Two other stimulating essays I would like to have interacted with in this discussion of good angels include Thomas F. Torrance, "The Spiritual Relevance of Angels," in *Alive to God: Studies*

a suggestion merits not only further discussion but also specific application in our service for Christ.

Satan and the Demonic

Nearly half a century ago, James Stewart wrote about the banishment of the demonic from serious study of the natural world, the world of the mind and soul, and the world of Christian theology. In his view this had a deleterious effect on several areas of theological thought. Christian anthropology suffered, for example, because the sense of a cosmic battle played out on the stage of world events, as well as in the inner life, had disappeared. "We have lost Paul fighting with wild beasts at Ephesus, and Luther flinging his ink-pot at the devil."[32] The doctrine of the atonement suffered the most, however. With the theologians of Stewart's day stressing mainly or solely the revelatory aspect of Christ's death, the New Testament themes of triumph over the demonic and redemption from moral evil were not taken seriously. Stewart insists that "however we may interpret it, we must recognise that here we are dealing, not with some unessential apocalyptic scaffolding, but with the very substance of faith."[33] Since Stewart's day theologians have developed a more multifaceted theology of the atonement and over the past fifteen or twenty years have devoted serious interest to demonic and cosmic warfare as integral components of the Christian gospel.

In the 1970s few serious studies of demonology and spiritual warfare were available.[34] Today, however, the situation is quite different. A number of biblical scholars, theologians, missiologists and pastors have begun to address the issues raised by Stewart intentionally and thoroughly. While these writings vary in depth of scholarship, intended readership and theological presuppositions, they demonstrate the seriousness with which the demonic world is being studied in evangelical circles. Not all of the popular handbooks are geared to the sensational.[35] Some are

---

in *Spirituality*, ed. J. I. Packer and Loren Wilkinson (Downers Grove, Ill.: InterVarsity Press, 1992), pp. 122-39, and Stephen R. L. Clark, "Where Have All the Angels Gone?" *Religious Studies* 28 (1992): 221-34.

[32] James S. Stewart, "On a Neglected Emphasis in New Testament Theology," *Scottish Journal of Theology* 4 (1951): 293.

[33] Ibid., p. 300.

[34] Worthy of note from an earlier generation are three books by Merrill F. Unger: *Biblical Demonology* (Wheaton, Ill.: Scripture Press, 1957); *Demons in the World Today* (Wheaton, Ill.: Tyndale, 1976); and *What Demons Can Do to Saints* (Chicago: Moody Press, 1977); as well as John W. Montgomery, ed., *Demon Possession* (Minneapolis: Bethany Fellowship, 1973).

[35] The sensational approach to spiritual warfare is seen in Rebecca Brown, *He Came to Set the Captives Free* (Chino, Calif.: Chick Publications, 1986). For example, Brown takes the references to evil beasts and wild beasts in Leviticus 26:6, 22 to refer to "vampires and werewolves" [sic] of legend. She emphasizes that these creatures actually exist (she describes her encounter with a "werewolf") and are produced when demons inhabit humans (pp. 223-30). "The demons bring about the physical changes

worthy of careful study because they have been hammered out on the anvil of Scripture study and experience by wise and seasoned Christians.[36] Even if we cannot accept every aspect of their theology and methodology, we can learn much from them. It is easy to discard casually the ideas and approaches of those who work frequently with demonized persons or in geographical regions that are highly resistant to the gospel when we merely read about them from the comfort of our desk or easy chair. It is another matter to be at the altar or in the counseling room when the demonic presence makes itself known. In this section on Satan and the demonic, I will limit myself to consideration of the controversial spiritual warfare movement.[37]

---

in the person's body that change them into animal-like shapes and also give them super-human strength and characteristics" (pp. 223-24). "Evil beasts" of Titus 1:12 and "brute beasts" of Jude 10 refer to these creatures.

Brown also teaches that spiritual warfare involves peoples' spiritual bodies, not their physical bodies (pp. 177-88). "Our spirit bodies can move, think and talk just the same as our physical bodies." She states that we will rarely be conscious that our spirit bodies are standing "in the gap" (based on Ezek 22:30) for someone, and she admits that "the concept of our spirits being separated and geographically away from our physical body is strange and difficult to accept" (pp. 182-83).

Another sensational book (that has sold hundreds of thousands of copies) is by Frank and Ida Mae Hammond, *Pigs in the Parlor: A Practical Guide to Deliverance* (Kirkwood, Mo.: Impact, 1973). The Hammonds write that because owls and frogs are classified among the creatures mentioned in Deuteronomy 14:7-19 as being unclean and abominable, "they are types of demon spirits" (p. 142). The authors, addressing Christians who desire victory in their lives, ask, "Does everyone need deliverance?" They reply, "Personally, I have not found any exceptions" (p. 12). For a critique of *Pigs in the Parlor,* see Wright, *The Satan Syndrome,* pp. 105-7. Wright also analyzes other questionable approaches to demonology (pp. 99-130). Other highly valuable critiques of popular (but not always biblical and/or judicious) materials on demonology and spiritual warfare are Garrett, *Angels and the New Spirituality,* Page, *Powers of Evil,* and David Powlison, *Power Encounters: Reclaiming Spiritual Warfare* (Grand Rapids: Baker, 1995).

[36]While I do not endorse everything in these books, I believe some wise counsel from experienced leaders is found in Green, *I Believe in Satan's Downfall;* Charles H. Kraft, *Defeating Dark Angels: Breaking Demonic Oppression in the Believer's Life* (Ann Arbor, Mich.: Servant, 1992); Francis MacNutt, *Deliverance from Evil Spirits: A Practical Manual* (Grand Rapids: Baker, 1995); Ed Murphy, *The Handbook for Spiritual Warfare,* rev. ed. (Nashville: Thomas Nelson, 1996); Timothy M. Warner, *Spiritual Warfare* (Wheaton, Ill.: Crossway, 1991); and Thomas B. White, *The Believer's Guide to Spiritual Warfare* (Ann Arbor, Mich.: Servant, 1990).

[37]The following summary of events leading to the Fuller Seminary academic symposium is taken from C. Peter Wagner and F. Douglas Pennoyer, eds., *Wrestling with Dark Angels: Toward a Deeper Understanding of the Supernatural Forces in Spiritual Warfare* (Ventura, Calif.: Regal, 1990), pp. 5-9. I will not be able in this essay to deal with some authors whose writings and approaches have become quite influential in the spiritual warfare movement, such as Neil T. Anderson, *The Bondage Breaker* (Eugene, Ore.: Harvest House, 1990), C. Fred Dickason, *Demon Possession and the Christian* (Chicago: Moody Press, 1987), and the bestselling spiritual warfare novels by Frank Peretti. Some evaluative remarks on these materials include Charles Hummel, *Fire in the Fireplace,* 2nd ed. (Downers Grove, Ill.: InterVarsity Press, 1993), pp. 193-95 (on Anderson); William Sailer, review of *Demon Possession* by Fred Dickason, *Evangelical Journal* 7 (1989): 83-86; and J. Lanier Burns, review of *This Present Darkness* by Frank Peretti, *Bibliotheca Sacra* 147 (1990): 240-42.

In December 1988, a meeting of evangelicals, Pentecostals and charismatics was convened by the Fuller Seminary School of World Mission. Known as the "Academic Symposium on Power Evangelism," the conference brought together forty scholars from Christian institutions in the United States and Canada. The term *power evangelism* was chosen as the theme partly because it was the title of a book by John Wimber, an adjunct faculty member at Fuller Seminary. Along with C. Peter Wagner he taught the highly controversial MC510 course on signs and wonders from 1982 to 1985. The academic symposium was convened because of a growing awareness among academicians that curricula in some Bible colleges and seminaries were not adequately dealing with the issues raised by the new emphasis on power ministries.

Those who participated in the symposium were chiefly faculty members from schools that had begun to experiment with power-oriented teaching. Of the forty participants, seven represented classical Pentecostal/charismatic institutions, four represented Wimber's Vineyard movement, and twenty-nine came from traditional evangelical institutions. Participants in the symposium included Neil Anderson of Biola University/Talbot School of Theology; Walter Bodine and Jack Deere, two professors who had recently left the faculty of Dallas Theological Seminary; Peter Davids of Regent College; Wayne Grudem and Timothy Warner of Trinity Evangelical Divinity School; F. Douglas Pennoyer of Seattle Pacific University; British psychologist Elizabeth Moberly; Vineyard founder John Wimber; and twelve persons from the Fuller Seminary School of World Mission, including Charles Kraft and C. Peter Wagner.

Wagner and Pennoyer edited a collection of the papers and responses delivered at the symposium, giving it the title *Wrestling with Dark Angels: Toward a Deeper Understanding of the Supernatural Forces in Spiritual Warfare.*[38] The volume includes articles such as "Power Evangelism," by Wimber; "Territorial Spirits," by Wagner; "Finding Freedom in Christ," by Anderson; "Sickness and Suffering in the New Testament," by Davids; and Kraft's response to Pennoyer's essay, "Collective Captivity" (the idea that "demons working through individuals can control the society to some extent and actively use the system to prevent the gospel light from penetrating into members' lives").[39] Overall, the volume is a good introduction to some of the key thinkers and concepts in the current spiritual warfare movement.

In his chapter Wagner proposes the following hypothesis concerning territorial spirits (admittedly tentative, due to the newness of this area of research): "Satan delegates high ranking members of the hierarchy of evil spirits to control nations, regions, cities, tribes, people groups, neighborhoods, and other significant social

---

[38]See previous note.
[39]Wagner and Pennoyer, eds., *Wrestling with Dark Angels*, p. 250.

networks of human beings throughout the world. Their major assignment is to prevent God from being glorified in their territory, which they do through directing the activity of lower ranking demons."[40] He agrees with Warner that "Satan does indeed assign a demon or corps of demons to every geopolitical unit in the world."[41] He supports this view with Scriptures such as 2 Corinthians 4:3-4, Ephesians 6:12, Matthew 12:28-29, Deuteronomy 32:8, Daniel 10:10-21, 2 Kings 17:30-31 and Acts 13:6-12.[42] Wagner's remarks on these passages are so brief, however, that we must look elsewhere for a developed defense of the territorial spirits view. Two books that make a better case for the concept are Wagner's edited collection *Engaging the Enemy: How to Fight and Defeat Territorial Spirits*[43] and a volume edited by Charles Kraft, *Behind Enemy Lines: An Advanced Guide to Spiritual Warfare.*[44] While neither book, unfortunately, contains a detailed study of the relevant biblical passages, each offers some help in understanding the strategic warfare/territorial spirits view.[45] Wagner describes three levels of spiritual warfare: (1) ground level, which is commonly known as deliverance, or casting demons out of individuals; (2) occult level, which confronts witchcraft, Satanism and the like; and (3) strategic level, or cosmic level spiritual warfare, which deals with territorial spirits.[46] In a chapter of *Behind Enemy Lines,* Wagner answers the "twenty-one questions" he is most frequently asked about strategic-level spiritual warfare.[47] Here Wagner gives a biblically attuned and generally balanced apology for the position. He firmly but graciously defends the practice of proactively coming against the principalities that hold a specific region or people group in spiritual captivity. Once the "strong man" (Mt 12:29) is bound, the captives are set free. He argues that some notoriously

---

[40]C. Peter Wagner, "Territorial Spirits," in *Wrestling with Dark Angels,* ed. Wagner and Pennoyer, p. 77.

[41]Wagner, "Territorial Spirits," p. 74.

[42]Ibid., pp. 75-80.

[43]C. Peter Wagner, ed., *Engaging the Enemy* (Ventura, Calif.: Regal, 1991).

[44]Charles H. Kraft, ed., *Behind Enemy Lines* (Ann Arbor, Mich.: Servant, 1994).

[45]See Vernon J. Sterk, "Territorial Spirits and Evangelization in Hostile Environments," in *Engaging the Enemy,* ed. Wagner, pp. 151-54, and Charles H. Kraft, "Spiritual Power: Principles and Observations," in *Behind Enemy Lines,* ed. Kraft, pp. 31-62.

[46]Wagner, "Twenty-one Questions," in *Behind Enemy Lines,* ed. Kraft, p. 127.

[47]Ibid., pp. 123-47. References to "spiritual mapping" are sprinkled throughout *Behind Enemy Lines.* Spiritual mapping is a new evangelistic strategy based on "extensive research into the demographics and history of a geographic region in an effort to understand its personality and specific problems. This research is then used to develop effective prayer and evangelism strategies. Some practitioners ... emphasize discerning the name of a 'territorial spirit' and praying specifically against that spirit" (Doug Trouten, "Charting Spiritual Realities," *Minnesota Christian Chronicle,* October 26, 1995, p. 10). A case for the strategy is presented in C. Peter Wagner, ed., *Breaking Strongholds in Your City* (Ventura, Calif.: Regal, 1993). For critiques of spiritual mapping and warfare praying, see G. Breshears, "The Body of Christ: Prophet, Priest, or King?" *Journal of the Evangelical Theological Society* 37 (1994): 13-16, and two articles in *Evangelical Missions Quarterly* 31 (1995): Mike Wakely, "A Critical Look at a New 'Key' to Evangelization" (pp. 152-62), and Tai M. Yip, "Spiritual Mapping: Another Approach" (pp. 166-70).

resistant regions yield to gospel truth in a measure not previously seen from conventional evangelistic strategies.

Some evangelicals object to the spiritual warfare emphasis of Wagner and Kraft, and their criticisms should be taken seriously.[48] Both sides argue, at times, from silence. Objectors frequently state that there is no biblical exhortation or example directing us toward strategic level spiritual warfare. Conflict with demons in Scripture is at the personal level only. Defenders of strategic warfare reply that there is no biblical teaching opposing cosmic warfare strategies. In fact, they find support for the concept in such passages as Luke 10:19 ("I have given you authority . . . to overcome all the power of the enemy") and Matthew 16:18-19 (where "the keys of the kingdom" for binding and loosing are given to Peter for the tearing down of the gates of Hades as Christ builds his church).[49] Perhaps the best approach is one that is both/and rather than either/or. In some cases the confrontational approach may be necessary and wise, while in other situations (probably most situations) the best course is to proclaim boldly the good news and to deal with evil spirits as they emerge in the heat of the battle.

The final author I will consider is Gregory A. Boyd, who is completing a two-volume study on Satan and spiritual warfare from a rather unusual standpoint—theodicy.[50] He argues that the intellectual problem of evil arises from a worldview in which evil is not expected. Suffering is not expected in paradise but *is* expected in a state of war. The logical "problem of evil" disappears for us when we accept the warfare worldview of the Bible. The Gospels, for example, portray the fundamental mission of Jesus as advancing the kingdom of God by vanquishing the kingdom of Satan. Jesus saw suffering people primarily as victims of Satan. Sickness and demonization are not necessarily people's fault but are casualties of war. All evil, directly or indirectly, goes back to "the god of this age."

Paul and other New Testament authors understood the main significance of Jesus' death to be victory over Satan and the demonic powers that serve Satan. While the early church proclaimed and developed this worldview, some of the church fathers, especially Augustine, began to appropriate significant elements of Hellenistic philosophy that were alien to the biblical tradition. God came to be seen as timeless, noncontingent, changeless and unrelated to the world. This view of God, when combined with an understanding of God's sovereignty as "control," swallows up the warfare worldview. Everything that happens follows a divine blueprint,

---

[48]See, for example, David Powlison, *Power Encounters.*

[49]Wagner, "Twenty-one Questions," pp. 132-34.

[50]Boyd's volumes are *God at War* (Downers Grove, Ill: InterVarsity Press, 1997) and *Satan and the Problem of Evil* (InterVarsity Press, forthcoming). This sketch of Boyd's view is based on a summary he gave me as well as on the paper he presented at the Wheaton Theology Conference in 1994, "The Centrality of Satan in a Postmodern Theodicy: An Evangelical, Postmodern Reflection on Evil."

drawn up by the One who sovereignly orchestrates both good and evil for his purposes.

According to Boyd, the intellectual problem of evil now emerges in full force and appears to be unsolvable. Even if we accept the idea of spiritual forces fighting in the heavenlies, we cannot understand why God, who is all-good and all-powerful, wills such a cosmic war in the first place. We begin to address the personal problem of evil by speaking of the "good" that comes to us through suffering. Or we think of it as punishment. We lose the sense of urgency that accompanies those who engage in warfare, and instead of seeing our prayers and actions as having major significance for the cause of the war, we tend to retreat from the battle and pray "Thy will be done" without a full recognition of our part in the advancement of God's kingdom on earth.

Boyd's work argues that Satan and demons are real, personal beings engaged in a cosmic war against humanity. While the outcome of the war is certain (the victory was assured at Calvary), there is an openness to the future, genuine freedom to accept our responsibilities in this world, and very real power at our disposal to bless and curse others. We have power over the evil one and his forces, but we need to learn how to wield that power. We will suffer some losses and lose some battles in the process of learning. Boyd goes on to explain how such a warfare theodicy is theologically and philosophically superior to all other options and how this warfare worldview can be plausibly articulated in our postmodern culture.

In his lay-oriented apologetic work *Letters from a Skeptic*, Boyd presents in brief, popular form what he develops more thoroughly in his two-volume work. Speaking of God's omniscience and creaturely freedom, Boyd contends that while God knows with certainty many things that will happen in the future (such as events determined either by present circumstances or by God's own will), he "can't foreknow the good or bad decisions of the people He creates until He creates those people and they, in turn, create their decisions." If God loves the creatures he brings into existence, he must give them genuine freedom. Love requires freedom. Because God created out of love and created free beings, "there are risks in creation, even for God."[51] Thus we may speak of the "openness" of God and of the future. When God's good creatures choose not to love, there arise not only human sin and the evils that attend it but also "natural evil": famines, earthquakes, tornadoes, AIDS and the like. While some natural evils are due either to the limitations of the natural order (for example, drowning) or to the deeds of evil persons (for example, many famines), some are attributable to the cosmic forces of evil: Satan and the demons. These evil forces are waging war on a cosmic scale against God and everything that is good. "In the Christian view, then, the earth has been literally sieged by a power outside itself.

---

[51]Gregory A. Boyd and Edward K. Boyd, *Letters from a Skeptic* (Wheaton, Ill.: Victor, 1994), pp. 30, 33.

There is a power of pure evil which now affects everything and everybody on the earth.... And thus the entire cosmos ... is in a state of chaos (Rom 8)."[52] Boyd acknowledges that the Bible is silent on exactly how demonic forces tamper with the natural order, but he holds that the concept is biblical.[53] The earth is a battlefield. "And on battlefields ... all sorts of terrible things happen.... In the end, we are all more or less casualties of war." Boyd claims that this view of rational creatures (human, angelic and demonic) as genuinely free, God as a loving risk-taker, the future as open and unknown in some respects, and the earth as a battlefield is the only position that makes sense of evil, whether "moral" or "natural," if we hold to the existence of an all-loving and all-powerful God.[54] God is sovereign, but he exercises his sovereignty and providence not so much by control or meticulous intervention in persons' lives as by granting, to those who seek him, spiritual power to wage war and overcome the evil one. The outcome is sure because of Calvary.

While Boyd's warfare theme will find enthusiastic acceptance by many evangelicals, especially those with a more Arminian theological approach, the view of God and the future as open will not be welcomed as readily. Some are even speaking of an "evangelical megashift" in describing the openness of God position espoused by Boyd and others.[55] Boyd will argue, however, that his warfare theodicy is much more biblical than the meticulous providence view and makes sense only with a view of the future as genuinely open. Some (I include myself here), however, will want to hold to the themes of conflict and victory, yet without sacrificing the foreknowledge of God in the more traditional understandings (whether Calvinist or Arminian).

It will be interesting to follow the debate. Whatever the outcome, Boyd's project will surely draw attention to the warfare that pervades our existence as individuals, families, the community, the church and the world at large. Because there is much in the Scriptures to support a cosmic warfare theme and because, as Stewart noted, this is "the very substance of faith," it will be unfortunate if the debate over some

---

[52]Ibid., p. 36.

[53]Boyd writes, "I am not suggesting that every (or any) particular incident of 'natural' evil can be directly explained by reference to a particular demonic activity (though such cannot be ruled out *a priori*), only that the general state of disarray in our world can be accounted for by the demonic warfare we are caught up in. Nor am I suggesting that reference to the demonic can carry the full weight of explanation for such disasters. Some reference to the possible loss of innate powers over nature that humans lost (and demonic powers gained?) in the fall, and some reference to the incompossible qualities of a morally neutral environment which benefit humanity in some situations but necessarily harm us in others, are also needed to give a full account of 'natural' evil" ("The Centrality of Satan," p. 16, n. 7). Page observes that by attributing natural evil to Satan and his angels we may be helping to preserve belief in the goodness of God (*Powers of Evil*, p. 268).

[54]Boyd and Boyd, *Letters from a Skeptic*, pp. 36-37.

[55]See Gabriel Fackre, "An Evangelical Megashift? The Promise and Peril of an 'Open' View of God," *The Christian Century*, May 3, 1995, pp. 484-87; Roger Olson et al., "Has God Been Held Hostage by Philosophy?" *Christianity Today*, January 9, 1995, pp. 30-34.

theological issues (particularly the open view of God) becomes so heated that it obscures and draws attention away from the task of the church militant. Such an outcome would grant another victory to the enemy and might even be part of his plan.

Where to Go from Here

While the topic of angels and demons has never attracted a great amount of attention from past or present evangelical scholars, it is a significant category of biblical truth. The biblical texts on the spirit world are part of the "all Scripture" that is useful for teaching, rebuking, correcting and training in righteousness (2 Tim 3:16). Fortunately, there are some worthwhile resources for additional study of the topics in this essay. [56] Yet more work needs to be done. As evangelicals move into the twenty-first century, we need to recognize and accept several challenges. Perhaps the greatest (and most exciting) opportunity is that raised by Osborn when he speaks of the apologetic significance of angels. There is a need for high-quality articles and books for the popular, non-Christian market that will attract attention to the gospel of Christ. There is also a need for books on Satan and demons.

In this postmodern, New Age era, those who attract and draw people to their body of beliefs and believers are those who show how their religious concepts answer the personal quests and thought forms of spirituality seekers. Angels, Satan and

---

[56]Some suggested readings for further study are the following articles in Joel B. Green, Scot McKnight and I. Howard Marshall, eds., *Dictionary of Jesus and the Gospels* (Downers Grove, Ill.: InterVarsity Press, 1992), "Angels, Archangels," "Demons and Exorcism," "Principalities and Powers," "Satan, Devil." Related topics are found in Gerald F. Hawthorne, Ralph P. Martin and Daniel G. Reid, eds., *Dictionary of Paul and His Letters* (Downers Grove, Ill.: InterVarsity Press, 1993). Wayne Grudem, *Systematic Theology* (Grand Rapids: Zondervan, 1994), includes useful chapters on "Angels" and "Satan and Demons." The latter chapter is refreshingly different for a systematics text in that it grapples with issues of spiritual warfare, deliverance and demonization in Christians.

Victor Knowles has written a 440-page volume titled *What the Bible Says About Angels and Demons* (Joplin, Mo.: College Press, 1986) that is thorough and easy to understand, while interacting with more academic works. A small, sensible, biblically geared layperson's guide to good angels is Connelly's *Angels Around Us*. The contribution of Page, *Powers of Evil*, is perhaps the best overall work on Satan and demons since the publication of Merrill Unger's *Biblical Demonology* in 1952. One well-known theologian (who had not yet seen Page's book) told me that he regards Green's *I Believe in Satan's Downfall* as the most helpful treatment of Satan and demons. I have used Green and the volume edited by Montgomery, *Demon Possession*, as texts in my seminary elective course on demonology. Both have served well to introduce and integrate the biblical and practical dimensions of the topic. An older but still valuable work is *Occult Bondage and Deliverance* by Kurt Koch and Alfred Lechler. The subtitle indicates the approach: *Advice for Counseling the Sick, the Troubled and the Occultly Oppressed* (Grand Rapids: Kregel, 1970). A more recent manual (one that a very successful pastor friend considers the best of the deliverance-ministry lot) is Kraft's *Defeating Dark Angels*.

Finally, on the principalities and powers, in addition to Arnold's *Powers of Darkness* and his more scholarly *Ephesians: Power and Magic*, there is the fine forty-page essay by P. T. O'Brien, "Principalities and Powers: Opponents of the Church," in *Biblical Interpretation and the Church*, ed. D. A. Carson (Nashville: Thomas Nelson, 1984), pp. 110-50.

demons are not excess baggage in Christian belief; they are *necessary* components of a holistic worldview. Evangelical Christianity is in a unique position with its teachings on these topics to evangelize those seeking spiritual reality.

Another challenge facing us is to produce works on the warfare themes of Scripture that are both scholarly and useful in ministry. Whichever way we lean in the debate, we all, as evangelicals, acknowledge the major biblical emphasis on the conflict between God and Satan. All three levels of spiritual warfare mentioned by Wagner need careful study and analysis, especially by scholars sensitive to both exegetical/theological concerns and empirical data from respected pastors, missionaries and others on the front lines of evangelistic, counseling and discipleship ministries. Scholars who can be open-minded and objective while investigating all aspects of the question will contribute immensely to the clarification and application of biblical warfare teachings. Other challenges before us include further consideration of the nature of structural/institutional evil and more complete and more accurate documentation of purported encounters with angelic and demonic forces.[57]

Is there an evangelical consensus on the theme of angels and demons? Concerning good angels, we can answer yes. It is true that Osborn disagrees with Arnold concerning the inwardness of heaven and the angelic realm, noting that this approach to heaven (coupled with a defense of Wink on this point) "has been subjected to severe criticism from certain evangelical quarters."[58] But this is not a serious topic of debate among evangelicals. Similarly, the controversy over whether or not the principalities and powers are personal angelic and demonic beings, while beneficial for clarifying and understanding these key Pauline concepts, is not on the front burner of evangelical scholarship. More serious disagreement exists in the category of spiritual warfare, and the issue of strategic-level warfare is just one area of controversy. Space considerations exclude an analysis of the major debate over deliverance theories and methods, but there are helpful materials that get to the heart of the issues.[59]

Even though evangelicals are divided on some matters, we agree on several key aspects of ministry. First, God's people are involved in a cosmic war, and the hosts of heaven and hell are serving their respective lords, either helping or hindering us. We should not be surprised by either intense opposition or gracious assistance in the battle. However, we need to avoid becoming preoccupied with either aspect of the spirit world, and we may not always be able to identify precisely when and how these forces are active among us. Second, God's people should be able to minister effectively to those oppressed by the devil, when such persons are evident in our

---

[57]Some values and dangers of studying the demonic are presented in Page, *Powers of Evil*, pp. 267-70.
[58]Osborn, "Entertaining Angels," p. 290.
[59]See, for example, Powlison, *Power Encounters*, and Wright, *The Satan Syndrome*.

midst. Jesus Christ came to destroy the works of the devil (1 Jn 3:8). Third, in all of our ministries, whether consciously engaged with the spirit world or not, we must seek our strength and wisdom from God through prayer and the Scriptures, in partnership with wise and godly believers. Fourth, ultimately our attention must be directed to the King of kings and Lord of lords, not angels, demons, past successes and failures, or theories and techniques of deliverance. Whatever we do in service for Christ's kingdom, we do for the glory of God, with our eyes on him.

Chapter 15

New Dimensions
in Humankind & Sin

David L. Smith

....

I T HAS BEEN MORE THAN TWO DECADES SINCE KARL MENNINGER PENNED his lament on the loss of virtually any concept of sin in contemporary society.[1] And in the interim not much has changed. The majority of people today view themselves as autonomous, not responsible to any higher power. They have no idea that they need to submit to God or that they may fall short of God's standard.

Among theologians, however, the doctrine of humankind and sin is alive and well. Theologians are exploring many intriguing directions in an effort to make the doctrine more relevant to the present age, three of which are explored in this essay: (1) models for explaining sin, (2) the transmission of sin and (3) the humanity of Christ and original sin.

Models for Explaining Sin

A doctrine of sin requires an explanatory model. One model depicts sin in terms of the highest good in view. Robert Brow asserts that the highest good may be discovered "by asking the question, 'If you succeeded perfectly in what you are trying to do, what would count as perfect success?' Sin then becomes what prevents the person from attaining that goal."[2] For Christians, the highest good is eternal joy in the presence of God. They have various models to explain this goal and the nature of the sin that keeps them from attaining it. But increasingly, evangelicals are

---

[1]Karl Menninger, *Whatever Became of Sin?* (New York: Hawthorne, 1973).
[2]Robert Brow, "Sin," in List CETA-L, January 26, 1995, available from
  CETA-L@UOTTAWA.BITNET.

questioning the traditional model in deference to one that they find more in keeping with their view of God's nature.

The traditional model. The traditional explanation of sin is closely tied to justice or righteousness. The early patristic theologians saw justice in terms of covenantal theology as set forth in the Old Testament (for example, Deut 16:20; Is 56:1). This justice was set in a relational context. If God's people obeyed, God would bless them; if they disobeyed, God would punish them.[3] This view is reflected by Irenaeus, who declared that God is a Judge who sends both righteous and unrighteous to a fitting place.[4] Tertullian avowed that God's justice will prevail and will be dispensed to all people according to their just deserts.[5]

When the Christian church was established as the official religion of the Roman Empire, a fundamental shift in thinking took place. The relational/covenantal conception of justice changed to a forensic one. John Driver explains it aptly:

> Instead of holding to the concept of biblical covenant law, the paradigm for understanding juridical metaphors became the Roman concept of law which was not only distributive but predominantly retributive. Law, rather than primarily reflecting God's intention for right relationships within the community of grace, became a system of just reward and equivalent retribution.[6]

Driver blames this change, in large measure, on an overwhelming sense of guilt introduced into the Western church by Augustine.[7] Brow concurs with Driver, citing the Augustinian paradigm of sinners as criminals declared guilty by an impassive judge who condemns them to death. Christ was viewed as the One who paid the penalty for sinners, allowing them to go free.[8]

The forensic model reached its acme in the Middle Ages with Anselm's theology. He held it intolerable that one of God's creatures should sin and not be punished; such a failure would be a violation of supreme justice.[9] Because the sinner cannot possibly recompense God's fractured justice, God must bring it about through Christ, whom God sent to represent humanity.[10] Anselm set out the court of law model in its most forthright substitutionary form: in his death on Calvary Christ took the sinner's place.

---

[3]David L. Smith, *With Willful Intent: A Theology of Sin* (Wheaton, Ill.: Victor/BridgePoint Books, 1994), p. 188.

[4]Irenaeus *Against Heresies* 3.25.2, in *The Ante-Nicene Fathers*, ed. Alexander Roberts and James Donaldson (Grand Rapids: Eerdmans, 1951), 1:459.

[5]Tertullian *Against Marcion* 11, in *The Ante-Nicene Fathers*, 3:307.

[6]John Driver, *Understanding the Atonement for the Mission of the Church* (Scottsdale, Penn.: Herald, 1986), p. 332.

[7]Ibid., p. 33.

[8]Robert Brow, "Evangelical Megashift," *Christianity Today*, February 19, 1990, p. 12.

[9]Anselm of Canterbury, *Why God Became Man*, trans. Joseph M. Colleran (Albany, N.Y.: Magi, 1969), 1:13.

[10]Ibid., 2:6.

The Protestant Reformers were Augustinian in their theology of sin. They accepted Anselm's court of law paradigm. John Calvin is representative of the view, defining sin as "rebellion against the will of God, . . . a violation of the law, upon which God's judgment is pronounced without exception."[11] The major difference between classical Catholicism and Reformation Protestantism was that the former counted Christ's substitution for the sinner on the basis of submission to the Catholic Church, whereas the latter based this redemption in an act of faith. The Protestant version of the model has been carried into twentieth-century evangelicalism.

A new model. Many modern evangelicals prefer to downplay the wrath of God in favor of the love of God. Accordingly, they have thrown out the courtroom model and have embraced a family model that is centered in Jesus' parable of the prodigal son (Lk 15:11). Sin is saying to God, "Father, I don't want to do things your way anymore; I want to take my own path in life." The sinner "goes off into a far country" and spends life in riotous living (Lk 15:13). And so there is a great rupture between Father and child. But the Father waits patiently for the child's return and eagerly welcomes the wandering one home. When the child returns to the Father's open arms, there is great revelry. Such is the biblical picture of God's desire to be reunited with his sinful children.

Brow advises us that the "new model theology" has invested many of the key terms of Scripture with new understanding. Hell is not a juridical sentence but a freely made choice. Faith is not a particular decision but a continuous looking in the right direction (toward Christ). Instead of a judge in a Roman courtroom, an Israelite judge (as in the book of Judges) is fighting for the freedom and peace of the people. God's wrath does not connote angry condemnation but the bad consequences that God—just like any loving parent—determines in response to wrong or negative behavior. "Instead of a stockade for the saved, or an agency to save souls, the church is viewed as a royal priesthood functioning to make known the love of God, to say 'your sins are forgiven' as Jesus did."[12]

Younger evangelicals wonder whether God is really "obsessed with staging a cosmic war crimes trial of the original sin of humans made in his image."[13] Indeed, since Augustine's views about sex and marriage approached the demonic, should we accept his doctrine of original sin? "The Augustinian law court forensic model of sin has also become uncongenial to the new breed of evangelical parents, who assume that God cannot be less loving than they are."[14]

Some observations. The divergence in models for explaining sin reveals differences

---

[11]John Calvin, *Institutes of the Christian Religion*, trans. Ford L. Battles, ed. John T. McNeill, 2 vols., Library of Christian Classics 20-21 (Philadelphia: Westminster, 1977), 1:423.
[12]Brow, "Evangelical Megashift," p. 14.
[13]Brow, "Sin."
[14]Ibid.

in evangelical theological thinking. Differences in thought ultimately lead to differences in practice. Whether the reason for mission activity is viewed as an effort to save souls from hell (traditional) or as an effort to obey the Great Commission to make disciples (new thinking) has a significant effect on how evangelism is done. Thinking of God as the Judge of the whole earth who is waiting to toss hapless sinners into eternal torment (traditional) or as the ideal loving Father who seeks reconciliation with his erring children (new thinking) drastically affects a pastor's sermon. Such a paradigm shift spells a shift in a wide variety of areas.

The Transmission of Sin

The doctrine of original sin has been discussed since New Testament times, and many questions have arisen regarding Adam's legacy to his posterity. Some are as old as the church itself; others are more contemporary, posed in the light of modern ideas and concerns.

Historical background. Two strains of thought appeared early in the life of the church and have persisted to the present. The first suggests that Adam's sin destroyed (for him and for his posterity) a special relationship with God, thus making our first parents and their descendants weak and susceptible to sin. The second implies that all human beings have inherited not only Adam's proclivity to sin but also his guilt, and they stand before God condemned to eternal death.

From at least the second century, the Greek fathers held that the chief inheritance that Adam bequeathed to his posterity because of his sin was mortality. They also stressed that his progeny lost the special bond with God that people enjoyed before the Fall. Tatian (A.D. 110-172) believed that because the special relationship with God was fractured, humankind was left open to demonic assault and so to sin.[15] Gregory of Nyssa (330-394) taught that Adam's sin was a historical act that resulted in the weakening of human nature and the dulling of perception.[16] Thus Adam's descendants are prone to sin. John of Antioch (347-407) asserted that the Fall destroyed human intimacy with God and brought mortality to humankind, which, in turn, caused Adam's descendants to be inclined to sin.[17]

The Western fathers agreed that human beings are inclined toward sin. But they argued that Adam's guilt was a part of the human lot. Such a view was apparent as early as the third century. Tertullian (160-220) was a traducian: because every soul is the result of parental procreation, every soul has its nature in Adam.[18] Augustine

---

[15]Tatian *Address of Tatian to the Greeks,* in *The Ante-Nicene Fathers,* 2:71.
[16]F. R. Tennant, *The Sources of the Doctrine of the Fall and Original Sin* (New York: Shocken, 1968), p. 323. Compare Gregory of Nyssa, *Catechetical Orations,* in *The Nicene and Post-Nicene Fathers of the Church,* 2nd ser. (Grand Rapids: Eerdmans, 1951), 5:482-83.
[17]John Chrysostom *Epistle to the Romans,* Homily 10, in *The Nicene and Post-Nicene Fathers,* 11:402.
[18]Tertullian *A Treatise on the Soul* 28, in *The Nicene and Post-Nicene Fathers,* 3:220.

of Hippo (354-430) asserted that all human beings have inherited Adam's guilt; even infants (should they die unbaptized) are condemned to eternal separation from God. Augustine held that a human soul is contaminated by the sexual act that creates it. Sin is transmitted from father to child in the male semen. Out of all of Adam's race, only Jesus was sinless, for only Mary was impregnated without human semen.[19]

The dichotomy in view continued through the Middle Ages, with Thomas Aquinas taking the Augustinian position and Duns Scotus the Greek view. Luther and Calvin were Augustinian in theology, whereas Zwingli took a more Greek view. John Calvin (1509-1564) did not elaborate on how Adam's transgression and guilt are extended to all of humankind, but it was ordained by God—so he claimed—that humanity should inherit a depraved nature and its condemnation.[20] James Arminius (1560-1609) disagreed with Calvin's theology of sin, arguing that God "has entered into a covenant of grace with Adam, and with the whole of his posterity with him."[21] It is not until human beings break that covenant by personally sinning that they incur Adam's guilt.

Twentieth-century evangelical theologians have continued the dualism. E. Y. Mullins asserted that Christ's death is efficacious for original sin in all humans (1 Cor 15:22). People "are not condemned therefore for hereditary or original sin. They are condemned only for their own sins."[22] J. O. Buswell Jr. saw Adam as the "federal" head of the race, and so "we are in Adam and individually guilty and corrupt sinners."[23] Millard Erickson has held that because of Adam's sin all humans have inherited a flawed nature, guilt and divine condemnation. But that guilt is not imputed until a person has willfully embraced the depraved nature in a rebellious act.[24]

A biblical analysis. Much of the impetus for a doctrine of original guilt came from Augustine of Hippo. Unfortunately, a Latin mistranslation of Romans 5:12 formed the basis for his views. It changed the statement "because all sinned" to "in whom all sinned." Thus Augustine concluded that "it is manifest that in Adam all sin, so to speak, en masse."[25] But correctly translated, the passage includes no mention or even suggestion of inherited guilt. Rather, it declares that death has come to all

---

[19]Augustine *On Forgiveness of Sin and Baptism* 3.15, in *The Nicene and Post-Nicene Fathers,* 5:74.

[20]Calvin, *Institutes,* 1:249.

[21]"Apology," in *The Writings of James Arminius,* trans. James Nichols, ed. W. R. Bagnall (Grand Rapids: Baker, 1956), 1:318.

[22]Edgar Y. Mullins, *The Christian Religion in Its Doctrinal Expression* (Philadelphia: Judson, 1917), p. 302.

[23]J. O. Buswell Jr., "The Nature and Origin of Sin," in *Basic Christian Doctrines,* ed. Carl F. H. Henry (Grand Rapids: Baker, 1971), p. 105.

[24]Millard J. Erickson, *Christian Theology* (Grand Rapids: Baker, 1985), 2:638-39.

[25]Augustine, as quoted by D. Parker, "Original Sin: A Study in Evangelical Theory," *Evangelical Quarterly* 61 (1989): 53.

humans "because all have sinned." The text does *not* say that all have sinned in Adam.[26]

We must also take into account Ezekiel 18:20, which asserts that the soul that sins is the one that will die. The prophet specifically states that the son will not share his father's guilt, or vice versa. Clearly, the idea of inherited guilt is not a biblical one.

How *is* sin transmitted? The Bible tells us that every soul is guilty before God because of its own transgression. What role does Adam's sin play in the sin of his posterity? His disobedience allowed sin to establish a staging area within the human heart. As a result, all have contracted the "virus" of sin. That virus may be seen as a state of sin characterized by overwhelming tendencies that eventuate in transgression.

Elsewhere I speculate that Augustine may have been right about the transmission of original sin (not guilt) in the sense that it occurs through procreation.[27] It is well known that many aspects of personality are transmitted biologically. In addition, certain tendencies toward depression and alcoholism can also be inherited.[28] Is it not reasonable, therefore, to suppose that a tendency toward sin may also be inherited?

Moreover, not only are tendencies toward sinning transmitted from parent to child but also tendencies toward specific sins. Psychiatric studies of adopted children show disorders in children that are present in the natural parents but not in the adoptive ones.[29] The common use of genograms (a tracing of character and personality flaws through a family tree) in counseling suggests a similar notion. Scripture hints at such tendencies. Cain murdered Abel and unleashed a succession of violent, murderous generations. David had a problem with concupiscence, as did some of his descendants. His son Solomon was involved in idolatry, a sin that ensnared many following generations.

Even a casual observation of human behavior demonstrates that sin is frequently transmitted from one generation to the next by parental modeling. It is a truism that children inherit the worst traits of their parents. Much of this occurs when children imitate their parents' language and behavior. A father blasphemes continually, and before long his young son is blaspheming too. A mother complains incessantly, and before long her daughter does the same. It comes as no surprise

---

[26]For an exegesis of Romans 5:12, see Smith, *With Willful Intent*, pp. 290-95.

[27]Ibid., p. 369.

[28]Janice Keller Phelps and Alan E. Nourse, *The Hidden Addiction and How to Get Free* (Boston: Little, Brown, 1986), p. 87. But compare Ted Peters, *Sin: Radical Evil in Soul and Society* (Grand Rapids: Eerdmans, 1994), pp. 294-327.

[29]See *DSM-IV: Diagnostic and Statistical Manual of Mental Disorders*, 4th ed. (Washington: American Psychiatric Association, 1994), pp. 89, 283.

that many juvenile alcoholics begin drinking liquor that they find at home.

But sin can be transmitted in many ways. Tatian taught that Adam's sin broke the special bond humans enjoyed with God, thus opening them to demonic assault. Recent studies on Satan and the demonic have provided both biblical and experiential evidence of ancestral or familial demons. Parents who participate in the occult or the demonic predispose their children (even those who are believers) to demonization by the same spirits.[30] While most evangelicals hold that believers cannot be fully possessed by demons, they may be deceived or oppressed by demons. Or they may engage in behavior that invites demonic invasion. Someone has said, "While perhaps you cannot as a Christian be possessed by a demon, you can't stop it from whispering in your ear." Nor would it be inconceivable that familial demons encouraged tendencies toward specific sins.

Another force that fosters the transmission of sin from one person to another is institutional or societal. According to Emil Brunner, evil contaminates society, spreading from one person to the next, even affecting people against their volition. It also taints institutions and generates more evil, which then reinfects the lives of individual human beings.[31] Ted Peters warns that "[sin] emerges from a network of human relations."[32] Liberation theologian Gustavo Gutiérrez agrees that sin pervades societal structures and issues in the abuse and enslavement of others.[33] Not all of these theologians identify themselves as evangelicals, but we need to listen to what they are saying. Much of the laxity in contemporary moral standards, for example, may be traced to societal views, which inevitably issue in individual sin. Sins such as racism and nationalism find their roots in societal and institutional evils.

Some observations. The transmission of sin is an ancient issue, but it remains an important one. That sin can be transmitted in a variety of ways contributes to its insidious nature.

Individual sins seem to recur in successive generations. Given the apparent resurgence in demonic activity today, churches may want to consider reinstating the ancient practice of having new believers verbally renounce the world, the flesh and the devil before they are baptized. Pastors and teachers should pay attention to a solid, biblically based theology of Satan and demons in their teaching. A discipling program comparable to Neil Anderson's Steps to Freedom in Christ is also useful.[34] Given that specific sins seem to recur in successive generations, parents should be

---

[30]See C. Fred Dickason, *Demon Possession and the Christian: A New Perspective* (Westchester, Ill.: Crossway, 1987), pp. 162-63.

[31]Emil Brunner, *The Doctrine of Creation and Redemption,* trans. Olive Wyon, vol. 2, *Dogmatics* (Philadelphia: Westminster, 1952), p. 96.

[32]Peters, *Sin,* p. 80.

[33]Gustavo Gutiérrez, *The Truth Shall Make You Free: Confrontations,* trans. Matthew J. O'Connell (Maryknoll, N.Y.: Orbis, 1990), p. 137.

[34]See Neil T. Anderson, *The Bondage Breaker* (Eugene, Ore.: Harvest House, 1993), pp. 185-214.

counseled to warn their children about moral weaknesses in the family fabric. For example, if lust has been a family difficulty over several generations, parents should alert their children to the problem and take whatever preventive measures are possible. These sins can and do crop up in Christian homes. Given the dimensions of institutional sin, evangelical Christians need to become more proactive within secular society (a fine model is provided by the Mennonite Central Committee, but I would like to see activity in political areas as well). Christians are supposed to be the salt of society, bringing healing and opposing corruption. But evangelicals have accomplished little in this area of life.

The Human Nature of Jesus

A third area of development in the doctrine of humankind and sin concerns the human nature of Jesus Christ. The creeds assert that he is fully God but fully man. The book of Hebrews (4:15) states that Jesus was "tempted in every way, just as we are—yet was without sin." Since Jesus is the second Adam and the representative of humankind, his humanity is of major significance to us. The question of whether or not Jesus possessed the Adamic nature continues to be debated.[35]

Background. A sophisticated doctrine of the person of Christ began with the anti-Gnostic fathers. Tertullian, for example, declared Jesus to be two substances "conjoined in One Person—Jesus, God and Man."[36] While asserting that Christ was human in the same way every other person is human, Tertullian was loath to allow that Jesus' flesh was sinful in nature. How it occurred is a mystery, but "in making it His own, He made it sinless."[37]

The ecumenical councils of the fourth and fifth centuries debated the person of Christ but concentrated largely on how the man Jesus was also divine God. Augustine's understanding was typical of the majority view: in Christ two substances or natures constitute a single person. Because of his uniqueness as the God-Man, it was impossible for the man Jesus to sin *(non posse peccare)*.[38]

Scholasticism modified the traditional Western view somewhat. Abelard, for example, accepted the idea of two natures in one person, but he explained Christ as a man assumed by the Word. This man never acted out of a desire to please himself but did only what would please God *(posse non peccare)*. Thus Abelard located the union of deity and humanity in the sphere of the human will.[39]

---

[35] I use the term *Adamic nature* rather than *sin nature* (which is probably more common) because the book of Hebrews insists that Jesus was without sin.

[36] Tertullian *Against Praxeas* 27, in *The Ante-Nicene Fathers*, 3:624.

[37] Tertullian *On the Flesh of Christ* 17, in *The Ante-Nicene Fathers*, 3:536.

[38] Reinhold Seeburg, *The History of Doctrines*, trans. Charles E. Hay (Grand Rapids: Baker, 1977), 1:258-59.

[39] Ibid., 2:64-65.

Reformed theologians basically maintained traditional views here. Luther held that the man Jesus was completely under the guidance of his divine nature *(non posse peccare)*.[40] Calvin cited many texts that assert Christ's humanity (for example, Rom 1:3; 8:3) and then declared that in spite of such assertions Jesus was nonetheless born without original sin by special sanctification of the Holy Spirit *(non posse peccare)*.[41]

Schleiermacher emphasized the humanity of Jesus but noted that he was "distinguished from all by the potency of his God-consciousness, which was a veritable existence of God in him."[42] He saw nothing contradictory in claiming that Jesus was as human as any person but was also sinless. Sin, Schleiermacher maintained, is a very tiny part of the nature of humanity. Thus Christ was a person in whom God-consciousness was perfected *(posse non peccare)*.[43]

Many twentieth-century theologians began to move away from the *non posse peccare* position, holding that Jesus' humanity involved an Adamic (that is, post-Fall) nature. Karl Barth believed that Jesus had a fallen human nature. But because Jesus is the revelation of God in the world, "it is necessary that He should be a man in quite a different way from all other men."[44] Although Jesus was human, because he was "God with us," he did not sin. Paul Tillich rejected the term *the sinlessness of Jesus,* preferring to aver that Christ—like all human beings—possessed finite freedom but—unlike other humans—was not estranged from the ground of his being. He did, however, assert that in Jesus' temptations there existed the real possibility of defeat *(posse non peccare)*.[45]

Wolfhart Pannenberg agrees with Tillich, stating that "Jesus' sinlessness is not an incapability for evil that belongs naturally to his humanity but results only from his entire process of life." Indeed, to suggest that Jesus was truly human but had no post-Fall nature "contradicts not only the anthropological radicality of sin but also the testimony of the New Testament and of early Christian theology that the Son of God assumed sinful flesh and in sinful flesh itself overcame sin."[46] John Macquarrie refuses to insulate Christ from the universal fact of human sin because to do so would deny that he was fully and truly human. Macquarrie rejects the view of *non posse peccare* because if Jesus could not really be tempted, then he was not

---

[40]Ibid., 2:305.

[41]Calvin, *Institutes*, 1:478-81.

[42]Friedrich Schleiermacher, *On Religion: Speeches to Its Cultured Despisers* (San Francisco: Harper & Row, 1958), p. 385.

[43]Ibid.

[44]Karl Barth, *Church Dogmatics*, 4.1, in *Church Dogmatics: A Selection*, trans. and ed. G. W. Bromiley (New York: Harper & Row, 1961), p. 112.

[45]Paul Tillich, *Systematic Theology* (Chicago: University of Chicago Press, 1957), 2:126-27.

[46]Wolfhart Pannenberg, *Jesus—God and Man*, trans. Lewis L. Wilkins and Duane A. Priebe (Philadelphia: Westminster, 1968), p. 362.

actually human and the temptations were really deceptions.[47]

Contemporary evangelicals espouse a more conservative view, almost halting between the two poles. Most reject any idea of a post-Fall Adamic nature.[48] Yet they seem to be somewhat uneasy with any suggestion that Jesus did not share completely the humanity of Adam's children. Consequently, they devise interesting arguments to attempt to circumvent such a thought.[49]

A proposal. It is easy to see why those who hold to the Augustinian (or Reformed) view of original guilt reject any idea of Jesus having a post-Fall Adamic nature, since he would then be condemned along with all of humankind. But this position experiences difficulty interpreting such passages as Luke 3:23, Romans 1:3, 8:3, Hebrews 2:17, 4:15, and many others that assert Jesus' full humanity.

But let us suppose (given the argument above) that what is transmitted from generation to generation is not guilt but rather the propensity to sin. Jesus, then, was born into the world with that same desire to sin that fills every human being (yet without any guilt). But Jesus depended wholeheartedly on the Holy Spirit and lived his life to please the Father. He was able to sin (just as we are) and felt the pull of sin (just as we do). But Jesus chose not to give in to sin (as all who are Spirit-filled may do). According to Trevor Hart, "On the one hand we can say that Jesus' moral life was fully human; yet on the other hand that his goodness was the very work of God himself, as, indeed, it is in all Christians when it occurs."[50]

What a great Savior we have (far greater, indeed, than one who could not sin)! Hebrews 4:15-16 explains how Jesus can sympathize with us as we wrestle with sin. He knows how it feels to be tempted with a burning desire to commit some sin and thus functions as a realistic model for us in winning the victory over sin. As Jesus overcame temptation through the power of the Spirit and the Word, so can we overcome.

Some observations. Such a view has profound implications for ministry. Jesus would not be seen as someone far above the ordinary person but as a brother who also encountered wrong desire and the terrible attraction it has for us, someone who wrestled with temptation and can show us how to overcome it. Evangelists can present Jesus as a truly compassionate Savior who knows how terrible sin is and yet understands its attractiveness, since he had to deal with it in much the same way that we do.

---

[47]John Macquarrie, *Jesus Christ in Modern Thought* (London: SCM Press, 1990), p. 397.
[48]So Stanley Grenz, *Theology for the Community of God* (Nashville: Broadman & Holman, 1994), p. 360, and Millard Erickson, *The Word Became Flesh* (Grand Rapids: Baker, 1991), p. 562.
[49]Ibid. Compare Wayne Grudem, *Systematic Theology* (Grand Rapids: Zondervan, 1994), pp. 537-39.
[50]Trevor A. Hart, "Sinlessness and Moral Responsibility: A Problem in Christology," *Scottish Journal of Theology* 48 (1995): 51.

Conclusions
The theology of humankind and sin needs further exploration by evangelical theologians. Regarding the first area (models for explaining sin), it seems evident that while the forensic model is deficient, the family model is also lacking in some respects and could use further development. It may be that some other model, one that would combine aspects of the latter with the classic covenantal view, would be preferable. The transmission of sin (particularly as it may apply to specific sins) is an intriguing field that is vital to ministry. There is considerable need here for experts in many fields (theology, medicine, sociology, counseling, psychology and so on) to work together to develop a coherent, biblically centered theology.

The nature of Jesus' humanity also needs continuing exploration, especially in light of teachings in the book of Hebrews. What does it mean to be human? Is it really possible to be tempted as all other humans are tempted but not have a post-Fall Adamic nature (in other words, does the propensity to sin play a vital role in human temptation)? A reexamination of the underpinnings of the doctrine of original sin (although there will never be agreement this side of heaven!) could prove helpful in finding some answers to the following questions: Are the Greek or Latin fathers correct in regard to guilt and bondage to sin? Can a biblical case be made for original guilt in a straightforward interpretation of Scripture *(sensus literalis),* that is, without reading Augustine and Calvin into the interpretation? Would the human desire to sin (albeit without sinning) prevent Jesus from being the Savior?

The doctrine of humankind and sin needs to be kept in the forefront of practical theology and needs to be made as relevant as possible to the person in the pew (and, for that matter, to the person in the street).

Resources for Additional Study
The following recent books provide help in working through a modern theology of humankind and sin.

Anderson, Neil T. *The Bondage Breaker.* Eugene, Ore.: Harvest House, 1993.

Boer, Harry R. *An Ember Still Glowing: Humankind as the Image of God.* Grand Rapids: Eerdmans, 1990.

Dickason, C. Fred. *Demon Possession and the Christian: A New Perspective.* Westchester, Ill.: Crossway, 1987.

Erickson, Millard J. *The Word Became Flesh.* Grand Rapids: Baker, 1991.

Hoekema, Anthony A. *Created in God's Image.* Grand Rapids: Eerdmans, 1986.

Hughes, Philip E. *The True Image: The Origin and Destiny of Man in Christ.* Grand Rapids: Eerdmans, 1989.

Macquarrie, John. *Jesus Christ in Modern Thought.* London: SCM Press, 1990.

Peters, Ted. *Sin: Radical Evil in Soul and Society.* Grand Rapids: Eerdmans, 1994.

Plantinga, Cornelius, Jr. *Not the Way It's Supposed to Be: A Breviary of Sin.* Grand Rapids: Eerdmans, 1995.

Pruyser, Paul W., ed. *Changing Views of the Human Condition.* Macon, Ga.: Mercer University

Press, 1987.

Ramm, Bernard. *Offense to Reason: The Theology of Sin.* San Francisco: Harper & Row, 1985.

Smith, David L. *With Willful Intent: A Theology of Sin.* Wheaton, Ill.: Victor/BridgePoint Books, 1994.

Chapter 16

New Dimensions in Christology

Carl F. H. Henry

••••••••••••••••••••••••••••

I F MIDCENTURY THEOLOGICAL OBSERVERS COULD PROTEST THAT EVAN-
gelicals amid their evangelistic priorities largely neglected Christology as an area of
doctrinal inquiry and research, that complaint no longer has validity. Evangelicals
in recent decades have contributed significantly to the investigation and study of
christological concerns, and they have been engaged at the frontiers of dialogue.

The Radicalization of Christology

This larger involvement in Christology has been provoked in part by the pluraliza-
tion and radicalization of this realm of theological interest. The dominance of
professional societies by higher critical views of Scripture reinforced the modernist
differentiation of the Christ of faith from the supposedly real historical Jesus. The
critical process of Scripture selection and rejection results inevitably in extremely
divergent views. Simultaneously, rival reconstructions of the presumably authentic
Jesus multiplied. Not all of those supposedly "real" Jesuses can be genuine; many
can only be viewed even by one or another critical scholar as inventive mythology.

Never before in its history has the professing church issued as pervasive a flood
of essays and books aiming to deluge confidence in the Christ of the New
Testament. Much of this speculation proceeds from churchmen who receive hand-
some salaries to interpret the Christian essentials to the world.

Rudolf Bultmann (1884-1976) insisted from the early 1940s onward that the
Gospels in their entirety were essentially a literary myth. Their significance, he held,
lay not in their ontological or historical factuality about Jesus of Nazareth but in

their supposed testimony to an existential experience that is available through our obedient response to a divine confrontation of the will.

The growing defection from orthodoxy was clearly visible, not only on the Continent but in Britain as well. Prominent churchmen, notably John Hick and Maurice Wiles, joined in *The Myth of God Incarnate* (1977), edited by Hick, to dismiss the orthodox doctrine of divine incarnation in Jesus as fictional. Some deviant scholars reduced Jesus to a reformer seeking to purify orthodox Pharisaism, or to a disillusioned herald of the imminent end of the world, or to a misguided Zealot or a magician dabbling in secret rites or to some other role that forfeited cognitive and practical continuity with the supernatural Savior portrayed by the New Testament. *The Identity of Jesus of Nazareth*, by this present writer, describes more than a score of conflicting critical portrayals of Jesus.[1]

The French-born New Testament scholar Oscar Cullmann (1902-) emerged as a vigorous opponent of Bultmannian existentialism. Pursuing an inductive approach to the biblical testimony, Cullmann insisted that God's self-disclosure and salvific activity are historical rather than existential and that the life, death and resurrection of Jesus Christ make up the midpoint of salvation history.[2] Although Cullmann fell short of thorough evangelical orthodoxy, he aggressively challenged for a generation both modernist historicism and neo-orthodox existentialism. He spoke for many who hold that responsible scholarship allows Scripture to speak for itself without the interpreter's arbitrary imposition of critical presuppositions.

The revival of evangelical interest in Christology was not stimulated only by critical misrepresentations of Jesus. Evangelical scholars increasingly pursued Christology under the pressure of fidelity to the biblical witness and in quest of a truly scriptural portrayal of Jesus. A recurring interest in biblical and systematic theology, and in New Testament studies especially, prompted closer investigation of the scriptural narrative.

Few doctrinal problems were more pressing than that of the two natures of Christ in one person: how could Jesus of Nazareth at one and the same time be thoroughly divine and thoroughly human? Idealist and quasi-pantheist theologians at the beginning of the century often looked in the direction of kenotic theory—the belief that God emptied himself of certain divine features in the incarnation. But if God set aside divine attributes in the incarnation, could Jesus Christ any longer be said to be truly divine? Some conservative scholars held that Jesus Christ set aside the independent utilization of divine attributes so that in his incarnate redemptive mission he possessed but did not exercise divine perfections other than with the Father's consent. Yet the question arises, Did the incarnate Christ ever exercise

---

[1]Carl F. H. Henry, *The Identity of Jesus of Nazareth* (Nashville: Broadman, 1992).
[2]See Oscar Cullmann, *Salvation in History* (Philadelphia: Westminster, 1967).

divine attributes independently of the Godhead? A more likely alternative, proposed by the present writer, is that the incarnate Son set aside the coordinate exercise of divine attributes for their subordinate exercise.

The classical affirmation of the Council of Chalcedon (A.D. 451) declared Jesus Christ to be

> at once complete in Godhead and complete in manhood, truly God and truly man . . . of one substance with the Father as regards his Godhead . . . and at the same time of one substance with us as regards his manhood, like us in all respects, apart from sin . . . recognized in two natures, without confusion, without change, without division, without separation . . . the characteristics of each nature being preserved and coming together to form one person and subsistence.[3]

Modernists typically denied that Jesus is God ontologically, affirming instead that he is God functionally. Hence they did not move beyond anthropology and humanism. They contended that by following Jesus' example of uncompromising obedience to the Father one can be delivered from inner personality tensions and discord to a unified selfhood correlated with life's supreme values. Humanists stripped away the underlying modernist confidence in the existence of a personal God and held that whatever integrates the divided self functions as divine.

It is true that some scholars who insisted on the divinity of Christ held that the New Testament speaks of Christ functionally, not ontologically. They did not on that account necessarily deny that Christ's essential divinity is a presupposition of his moral union with the Father. But numerous idealistic philosophers earlier in this century defined Christ's essential divinity in terms of his unbroken ethical obedience to the Father only. But uncompromised moral obedience is what the Creator expected of Adam, and it is what God has ultimately in view for all believers.

Cullmann so emphasized the functional agency of Christ in the New Testament that he obscured, though not intentionally, the passages that speak of Christ's ontological significance. The claim that the New Testament depicts Jesus as only functionally divine has been disputed by I. Howard Marshall, Richard N. Longenecker, R. T. France and others. Longenecker stresses that ontological conceptions underlie the depiction of Jesus' functional role even if the Christology of the early Jewish Christians was primarily functional.[4] Evangelical scholars have consistently emphasized that ontological Christology is the presupposition of functional Christology.

Millard J. Erickson comments that while the theological writing of Paul was "explicitly ontological" and "the Christology of the Fathers at the councils and

---

[3]"The Definition of Chalcedon," in *Documents of the Christian Church*, ed. Henry Bettenson (New York: Oxford University Press, 1967), p. 51.
[4]Richard N. Longenecker, *The Christology of Early Jewish Christianity* (Naperville, Ill.: Allenson, 1970), p. 155.

especially Chalcedon even more so . . . this was not something foreign to the first believers' understanding of those ideas."[5]

The volume *The Myth of God Incarnate* imposed the category of myth on the doctrine that Jesus is the incarnation of an eternally existing being. Scholars who held that Jesus was simply a pious Jew ascribed the supposed evolution of incarnation doctrine to a variety of contributory factors: a speculative refinement of Old Testament representations of divine wisdom as personal, pagan notions of mythological gods coming to fraternize with humans, or the dying-and-rising divinities of the mystery religions. According to these approaches there is no historical basis for orthodox Christology. Modernists were specially eager to strip away any metaphysical claims from the apostle Paul's view, since undisputed Pauline letters reach back to the earliest Christian decades.

The High Claim for Jesus

Study of the relevant New Testament texts illuminates one issue—the application to Jesus of the term *theos*. Murray J. Harris emphasizes that *theos* is the one christological title that is primarily ontological and unequivocally asserts the deity of Christ.[6] John 1 and John 20:28 clearly and indisputably apply *theos* to Jesus. Beyond that, Harris lists 2 Peter 1:1, Hebrews 1:8 and Titus 2:13 as "highly probable" and Romans 9:5 and John 1:18 as "probable."

Harris emphasizes that even had the early church never explicitly applied to Jesus the title *theos*, his deity would still be apparent from the depiction of Jesus as the object of human worship, his creatorial agency, his forgiveness of sins and final judgment of persons and nations, his possession of divine attributes, ascription to him of titles used of Yahweh in the Old Testament, and the association of saving faith and divine blessing with him.

J. D. G. Dunn contends that the high claim for Jesus was a product of ecclesial evolution and lacks a basis in the Gospel accounts of the days of his flesh. The line of christological evolution leads progressively in early Christianity, he holds, from an initial affirmation of Jesus' eschatological and/or resurrection sonships, to the claim of divine transcendence also in his death, and in his early ministry and life as well, and subsequently in his birth also, until finally a claim was made for his divine personal existence.[7]

Dunn postulates that the New Testament embodies two strands of belief. In one

---

[5]Millard J. Erickson, "Christology from an Evangelical Perspective," *Review and Expositor* 88, no. 4 (Fall 1991): 390.

[6]See Murray J. Harris, *Jesus as God: The New Testament Use of "Theos" in Reference to Jesus* (Grand Rapids: Baker, 1992).

[7]See James D. G. Dunn, *Christology in the Making: An Inquiry into the Origins of the Doctrine of the Incarnation* (London: SCM Press, 1980).

Jesus depicts himself as the Son of God (not necessarily implying preexistence). In the other Jesus supremely manifests God's creative wisdom (not personal). John allegedly merged these conceptions into the novel doctrine of the incarnation of a preexisting personal divine being. Dunn argues, that is, that John blended the philosophical notion of an impersonal preexisting Logos principle with the theological concept of divine sonship, thereby to fashion the portrayal of Jesus as a divinely preexistent person who becomes man for our salvation. Dunn contends that Christian orthodoxy emerged from this Johannine insight, but instead of rejecting it as illegitimate, Dunn considers the inference legitimate.

Dunn's effort to support his theory on biblical grounds has been widely challenged. His misrepresentation of the incarnate Son as a person "independent" of God encourages the unjustifiable charge that John compromises monotheism. Moreover, Dunn inexcusably dilutes the sense of Colossians 1:15-20 to strip it of even a functional Christology.

Contemporary Critical Methods

The Anglican New Testament scholar and mediating evangelical C. F. D. Moule (1908-), while disdainful of both destructive biblical criticism and systematic theology, taught students nonetheless to use contemporary critical methods to espouse conservative theological perspectives. Author of many books, he emphasized in *The Origin of Christology* the difference between a developmental view of New Testament Christology and an evolutionary view of it.[8]

The evolutionary approach, championed by modernist scholars, rejects miraculous supernaturalism and holds that New Testament references to Jesus as a preexistent divine Redeemer are a speculative elaboration of religious perspectives not really rooted in biblical history. The developmental approach, by contrast, holds that from the person and teaching of Jesus contained in the New Testament there gradually developed more theologically sophisticated formulations of what was already implicit in the biblical data. The unfolding New Testament Christology, Moule contends, articulates what Jesus and his followers had in principle affirmed from the outset. Moule insists that the substance of the main christological titles—Son of Man, Son of God, Christ, the Lord—was already present in the thought and teaching of Jesus, and that Jesus' claims are not merely functional but ontological as well.

Moule confronts the modernist theory that the primitive Palestinian community regarded Jesus at best as merely a devout rabbi for whom, as for others, death was final. The impact of Hellenistic religion transformed this estimate by elevating Jesus to the status of "the divine Lord of a Savior-cult." With an eye on the Aramaic

---

[8]C. F. D. Moule, *The Origin of Christology* (Cambridge: Cambridge University Press, 1977).

phrase *marana tha* ("even so come Lord Jesus") in the earliest Pauline literature (1 Cor 16:22), Moule comments that "one does not call on a dead rabbi to come."

I. H. Marshall[9] and Martin Hengel[10] reject, as do all evangelical scholars, the theory that the early church's Christology breaks decisively with Jesus' own claims. Hengel considers Jesus' impact on his early disciples to be the basis of subsequent doctrinal development. The New Testament works out the theological implications of their worship of Jesus.

It would be futile for Jesus' followers to claim deity on his behalf if in fact Jesus himself nowhere made the claim either explicitly or implicitly. Evangelicals grant, says Erickson, that Jesus never overtly affirmed his deity. Yet they share Peter Stuhlmacher's warning that to rest claims about Jesus only on apostolic interpretation runs great risks. With Reginald Fuller they emphasize that a direct line of continuity exists between Jesus' self-understanding and the early church's christological understanding of him. Erickson considers decisive for Jesus' divinity his use of the *amen*, which implies the universal validity of his teaching, and his use of *abba*, attesting his special intimacy with the Father.[11] So too his emphatic use of "I say to you" signified divine authority, and his direct forgiveness of sins is unthinkable apart from it.

As critical theories of Scripture multiplied, the divergent appraisals of Jesus and his significance became ever more extreme and radical. Critical interpreters set aside more and more of the biblical data and substitute their own creative alternatives, however far-fetched they may seem, even to their colleagues.

Critical Distortions

D. A. Carson has emphasized how imperative it is for Christians living in a pluralistic society to address prevalent distortions of the biblical portrait of Jesus. Long before the current fad of postmodernism, he notes, nonevangelical theologians practiced what essentially anticipated recent deconstructionism. By picking and choosing among the texts and then interpreting them outside their authorial context, they assured the freedom to construct a wholly novel Christology. This procedure did not seek to vindicate a universally valid view of Jesus. Instead, it was a stimulus to ever more "creative" interpretation increasingly distanced from authorial intent and scriptural legitimation.[12]

In 1992 Australian feminist Barbara Thiering's *Jesus the Man: A New Interpre-*

---

[9]I. Howard Marshall, *The Origins of New Testament Christology* (Downers Grove, Ill.: InterVarsity Press, 1976).

[10]Martin Hengel, *The Son of God: The Origin of Christology and the History of Jewish-Hellenistic Religion* (Philadelphia: Fortress, 1976).

[11]Erickson, "Christology from an Evangelical Perspective," p. 386.

[12]See D. A. Carson, *The Gagging of God: Christianity and Pluralism at the End of the Twentieth Century* (Grand Rapids: Zondervan, 1994).

tation from the Dead Sea Scrolls appeared, assuring us that Jesus was married and, after fathering three children, was subsequently divorced and remarried.[13] The same year British journalist A. N. Wilson's *Jesus* appeared, following fast on his earlier disavowal of Christianity.[14] Then came American Episcopal bishop John Spong's *Born of a Woman: A Bishop Rethinks the Birth of Jesus,* which traces the oppression of women to the New Testament doctrine of the virgin birth of Jesus. Spong informs us that Jesus was probably married to Mary Magdalene.[15] As if that were not enough, Gore Vidal's maverick novel *Live from Golgotha* added to the distortion of Christian belief at about the same time.[16]

The publication of such works prompted Oxford tutor and chaplain N. T. Wright of Worchester College to give a series of addresses, issued in paperback as *Who Was Jesus?* and then a larger volume titled *Jesus and the Victory of God.*[17] While Wright sounds no call to a fully reliable Bible, he nonetheless insists that the desperately needed alternative to endless modern misstatements of Jesus' person and significance lies in a recovery of the Gospels "as historical, as well as theological and faith-based, documents."[18] Although that does not say all that needs to be said, it might perchance encourage some critics to contemplate the possibility that the claim for Jesus—that God was active and not only in him but *as* him—is true. Wright argues that radical contemporary views offer us not a historically factual Jesus whom we must resist in the name of New Testament faith but an imaginary Jesus whom we ought to "resist in the name of serious history."[19]

A radical attitude toward Scripture is evident in newly emerging views of Jesus that capture media attention and are often publicized without evangelical comment or countercriticism. Thiering's earlier book *The Qumran Origins of the Christian Church* ignores the fact that no serious scholar has found any clear reference to Christianity in the Dead Sea Scrolls.[20] Thiering ventures to depict the Gospels as code language relating the interrelationship of Qumran and Jesus. A reviewer is excusably tempted to think that only a victim of hallucinations could promote the wild scenarios Thiering offers us: Jesus was extinguished at Qumran, drugged and then buried in a cave with Judas Iscariot and Simon Magus the sorcerer. Simon administered (as an antidote) the spices

---

[13]See Barbara Thiering, *Jesus the Man: A New Interpretation from the Dead Sea Scrolls* (Sydney: Theological Explorations, 1992).

[14]See A. N. Wilson, *Jesus* (London: Sinclair-Stevenson, 1992).

[15]See John Spong, *Born of a Woman: A Bishop Rethinks the Birth of Jesus* (San Francisco: HarperSanFrancisco, 1992).

[16]Gore Vidal, *Live from Golgotha* (New York: Random House, 1992).

[17]N. T. Wright, *Who Was Jesus?* (Grand Rapids: Eerdmans, 1992); N. T. Wright, *Following Jesus: Biblical Reflections on Christian Discipleship* (Grand Rapids: Eerdmans, 1994).

[18]Wright, *Who Was Jesus?* p. 96.

[19]Ibid., p. 18.

[20]Barbara Thiering, *The Qumran Origins of the Christian Church* (Sydney: Theological Explorations, 1983).

the grief-stricken women had placed in the tombs. Jesus revived and gave the impression of being resurrected from death. Jesus died—we are assured—in the A.D. 60s, after joining Peter and Paul in missionary journeys.

The current phenomenon of postmodernism, which denies objective truth and meaning, does not self-evidently proceed from a specific denial of a high view of the Bible. Rather, it builds on philosophical deconstructionism and the new hermeneutic to emphasize the interpreter's creative liberty to understand and reshape the text to suit personal preferences. Samara Schneiders professes to regard the Bible "as scripture, that is, as the word of God that is inspired, revelatory, authoritative and normative for the Church." Yet Schneiders finds in the account of Jesus' conversation with the woman at the well in John 4 the possibility "that she was not a whore whom Jesus converted but a potential spouse whom he invited to intimacy."[21] But she concludes that the account really has no historical basis and reflects "a reading back into the public ministry of Jesus the Johannine community's postresurrection experience of the Samaritan mission and the influence of the Samaritan converts within the community of the fourth gospel."[22]

It is remarkable that scholars who so readily discard historical elements of the Gospels also simultaneously and confidently project historical alternatives of their own at a distance of two millennia, scarcely aware of the self-referential consequences of their relativizing of historical phenomena. In his study *Literary Criticism and the Gospels: The Theoretical Challenge,* Stephen D. Moore cleverly observes that more recent critical theories simply treat Bultmann as Bultmann treated the Gospels—that is, they demythologize him. Bultmann concluded that one could affirm of Jesus virtually nothing of historical certainty but that he lived and died. Consequently, Bultmann channeled Christian interest into the Christ of faith. But during the last three decades, Moore stresses, "the historical Jesus . . . has made an impressive recovery from the beatings inflicted on him by earlier scholarship."[23]

Along with Moule, evangelical scholars insist that the constructive development of Christology takes place only within the New Testament and not in the post-apostolic era. They regard Chalcedon as simply a more explicit and philosophically articulate statement of what is implicit in the inspired Scriptures.

The Chalcedonian Definition

Controversy over Chalcedon does not in our time focus as much on the nuances of Greek philosophical terms such as *hypostasis, physis* and *ousia* but rather, as France

---

[21]Samara Schneiders, *The Revelatory Text: Interpreting the New Testament as Sacred Scripture* (San Francisco: HarperSanFrancisco, 1991), p. 194.

[22]Ibid., p. 186.

[23]Stephen D. Moore, *Literary Criticism and the Gospels: The Theoretical Challenge* (New Haven, Conn.: Yale University Press, 1989), p. 173.

notes, on whether Jesus can legitimately be depicted as "divine" and in what sense.[24] Geoffrey W. Bromiley comments that "the present century has witnessed a new and welcome interest in the Chalcedonian definition, not as a metaphysical formulation, but as a basic and almost doxological confession."[25]

Does the development of the orthodox view as stated by Chalcedon reflect, as E. L. Mascall contends, a theoretical supplementation by the postapostolic church?[26] Donald Bloesch thinks that through the witness of the Spirit the Chalcedonian doctrine of the two natures communicates infallible truth that must be "taken seriously as a normative statement of the church's faith," while at the same time it imperfectly reflects the divine mystery of God in Christ and is not to be considered "faultless or undeceiving."[27] To reconcile the nuances here would seem to call for something less demanding than logic.

The connection of recent expositions with the classic creeds becomes a significant issue. This is particularly so for frontier Catholic writers. It is curious to find Michael J. Perry, in an essay titled "The Authority of Text, Tradition and Reason: A Theory of Constitutional 'Interpretation,' " going out of his way to comment, "In my tradition, which is Roman Catholic, the work of 'the best and the brightest' of contemporary Scripture scholars and theologians makes no theistic presuppositions."[28]

Edward C. F. A. Schillebeeckx frequently uses traditional terms which, in modern context, stand nonetheless in ambiguous relationships to Chalcedonian orthodoxy.[29] Colin Gunton insists that "it is very difficult to maintain a real connection with earlier ages unless we can at least in some way affirm their words as our words."[30] The Vatican expressed disapproval over Schillebeeckx's writings and the writings of Hans Küng that devalued the Roman Church's absolute formulations of dogma. Karl Rahner (1904-1984), with Schillebeeckx, sought a modern restatement of what Chalcedon meant by asserting that Jesus Christ was "true God and true man." He was also put under a Vatican ban on publication for

[24]R. T. France, "Christology," in *New Twentieth Century Encyclopedia of Religious Knowledge*, ed. J. D. Douglas (Grand Rapids: Baker, 1991), p. 183.

[25]Geoffrey W. Bromiley, "Christology," in *International Standard Bible Encyclopedia*, ed. G. W. Bromiley (Grand Rapids: Eerdmans, 1979), 1:665.

[26]E. L. Mascall, *Jesus: Who He Is—and How We Know Him* (New York: Longmans, Green, 1985).

[27]Donald G. Bloesch, *A Theology of Word and Spirit* (Downers Grove, Ill.: InterVarsity Press, 1992), p. 122.

[28]Michael J. Perry, "The Authority of Text, Tradition and Reason: A Theory of Constitutional Interpretation," in *Natural Rights and Natural Law*, ed. Robert F. Davidow (Fairfax, Va.: George Mason University Press, 1986), p. 186.

[29]See Edward Schillebeeckx, *Jesus: An Experiment in Christology* (London: Collins, 1979); Edward Schillebeeckx, *Christ: The Experience of Jesus as Lord* (New York: Crossroad, 1981).

[30]Colin Gunton, *Yesterday and Today: A Study in Continuities in Christology* (Grand Rapids: Eerdmans, 1983), p. 5.

a time. Rahner defended a theory of *kenosis,* or divine self-emptying, in the incarnation.

Evangelical Christians have insisted on the ontological divinity of Jesus and in the main have also approved the Chalcedonian definition. "Those who reject the Formula of Chalcedon," writes Christopher Butler, have "almost without exception" discarded essential Christianity as well.[31] Modernist theologians and philosophers like Hegel, Schleiermacher and Ritschl were hostile to classic Christology and promoted instead a unitary divine-human nature as a preferred alternative. Modernists were prone to define Jesus' oneness with God in terms of the Nazarene's undeviating moral obedience to the Father and sought to escape ontological affirmations. But perfect moral obedience is what God desired even from Adam. It is what God desires from all humankind, without implying that divinity is within everyone's grasp.

As in earlier generations among conservative scholars like B. B. Warfield and J. Gresham Machen, endorsement of Chalcedon runs through the evangelical mainstream as we face a new century and millennium. George Carey insists that the definition encapsulates the church's continuing confession of Jesus as both human and divine.[32]

France cautions, however, that "popular Christian devotion, based on Chalcedonian orthodoxy, has almost inevitably tended toward a sort of docetism which refuses to take Jesus' humanity seriously."[33] But that assuredly has not been the intention of evangelical scholars, who remain firmly committed to the "two natures, one person" formula. Klaas Runia sets the declaration approvingly over against inadequate modern variations by Wolfhart Pannenberg and others.

Aloys Grillmeier emphasizes the continuity of Chalcedon with apostolic teaching, contrary to those who, like C. Norman Kraus, reject Chalcedon for supposedly "shifting the focus of theological meaning from its original New Testament intention."[34] Harold O. J. Brown emphasizes that Chalcedon did not "project a view of Christ other than the Christ of the New Testament."[35] Erickson writes that the Chalcedonian formula "preserved the genuineness and completeness of both the divine and the human natures, their distinctives and yet the unity of the person."[36]

---

[31]Christopher Butler, "Jesus and Later Orthodoxy," in *The Truth of God Incarnate,* ed. Michael Green (Grand Rapids: Eerdmans, 1977), p. 97.

[32]George Carey, *God Incarnate: Meeting the Contemporary Challenges to a Classic Christian Doctrine* (Downers Grove, Ill.: InterVarsity Press, 1976), p. 5.

[33]France, *Christology,* p. 184.

[34]Aloys Grillmeier, *Jesus Christ Our Lord* (Scottsdale, Penn.: Herald, 1987), p. 59.

[35]Harold O. J. Brown, *Heresies: The Image of Christ in the Mirror of Heresy and Orthodoxy from the Apostles to the Present* (Garden City, N.Y.: Doubleday, 1984), p. 194.

[36]Erickson, "Christology from an Evangelical Perspective," p. 390.

Dutch theologian Klaas Runia,[37] French theologian Henri Blocher[38] and British theologian H. Dermott McDonald[39] all insist that we must not say less than Chalcedon did. Bernard Ramm also approves Chalcedonian Christology.[40] Stephen T. Davis and Rebecca D. Pentz, likewise, argue for the retention of the formulation.[41]

Harold O. J. Brown points out that christological study has made no substantial progress since Chalcedon and that the postulation of kenotic Christology must be seen as regressive.[42] David Wells illustrates the divergence and confusion of recent christological thought by the contrasting approaches of Barth, Pittenger and Schillebeeckx. He attributes this fluidity to a questioning of the normativity of Scripture and the mislocation of theological meaning in the interpreter rather than in the text.[43]

So diverse are the portraits of Jesus put forward by contemporary scholars that Jarislov Pelikan's account of images of Jesus through the ages almost pales into unimpressiveness.[44] Anyone who is tempted to opt for one of the many current portrayals is simply settling for one of many strands of conflicting tradition. Étienne Trocmé, in *Jesus as Seen by His Contemporaries*, finds it "difficult to imagine where so many eminent scholars derive the certainty with which they defend these contradictory theses."[45] To recover the authentic Jesus, Trocmé proposes another approach, comparing Jesus' attitude or response to the several views people had of him. This procedure yields four or five different portraits. Jesus viewed himself very differently from what can be inferred regarding his "origin" or prevalent cultural patterns. Moreover, his "extraordinary zest," the novelty and boldness of his teaching, the "absolute nature of his appeal" and his call to action reflect an "exceptional personality with almost unlimited talents."[46] Jesus accepted these sometimes or somewhat conflicting reactions, we are told, in the larger context of "a very high authority."

Having said this, Trocmé avers that Jesus is a mystery that requires of us "an intuitive and necessarily imperfect solution." He sees no hope of unraveling the mystery because, as Trocmé alleges, this diversity existed in pregospel tradition and

---

[37]Klaas Runia, *The Present-Day Christological Debate* (Downers Grove, Ill.: InterVarsity Press, 1984).

[38]Henri Blocher, *Christologie* (Vaux-sur-Seine: Faculté de Theologie Evangelique, 1987).

[39]H. Dermott McDonald, "Christ's Two Natures: The Significance of Chalcedon Today," *Christianity Today*, September 26, 1976, pp. 12-14.

[40]Bernard Ramm, *An Evangelical Christology—Ecumenic and Historic* (Nashville: Thomas Nelson, 1985).

[41]Stephen T. Davis and Rebecca D. Pentz, *Encountering Jesus: A Debate on Christology* (Atlanta: John Knox, 1988).

[42]Brown, *Heresies*, p. 193.

[43]David Wells, *The Person of Christ* (Westchester, Ill.: Crossway, 1984).

[44]Jarislov Pelikan, *Jesus Through the Centuries: His Place in the History of Culture* (New Haven, Conn.: Yale University Press, 1986).

[45]Étienne Trocmé, *Jesus As Seen by His Contemporaries* (Philadelphia: Westminster, 1978), p. 122.

[46]Ibid., p. 124.

is reflected in "the groping efforts of the evangelists and theologians in the first century."[47] "The mystery of Jesus is that he is and remains the object whom everyone contemplates, but never becomes a possession owned by anyone, even his disciples."[48] Indeed, "the unbeliever may also be in contact with him." Instead of rising above the exasperating diversity of contemporary portrayals of Jesus, therefore, Trocmé seems only to supplement them by another unsure and elusive addition.

With good reason Erickson comments that while contemporary evangelicalism seeks "to preserve the same theological values that the Chalcedonian fathers prized in their day, problems are present which incarnational Christology did not face in earlier times."[49] Erickson lists as making theological construction more difficult the higher critical devaluation of Scripture, problems attending the messianic self-consciousness of Jesus, the comparatively few texts in which Jesus is expressly declared to be divine and the laboriousness of translating the philosophical categories of Chalcedon into contemporary equivalents, especially those championed by process theologians. In addition, he notes "the logical problem" involved with insisting that Jesus was both fully divine and human, the sociological problem adduced by champions of liberation theology or feminist theology or black theology who find these incompatible with a "white, western, male" redeemer.

Despite the imposing litany of complaints he compiled, Erickson stresses that the theological landscape has been altered in recent decades in a way that advantages evangelical Christianity. Earlier datings for New Testament writings have overtaken long-entrenched modernist theories, so that the critical approach is far from secure in its claim that the high view of Christ reflects the pagan Hellenistic milieu rather than Palestinian Christianity. The reliability of the biblical accounts has been promoted not only by archaeological findings but to some extent also by the rise of canonical theology with its repudiation of the documentary theory (that behind the present narratives there exist older, more reliable sources that the biblical writers allegedly mythologized). Radical Bultmannian form criticism correlated with existential theology has had its half-day. The value attached even to John's Gospel as a historical source in the aftermath of discovery of the Dead Sea Scrolls is an indicator of the turning tide.

The British Catholic historian Paul Johnson declares that since

the low-water mark in the historicity of the Judeo-Christian tradition—which he places in the forepart of the 20th century—the tide of faith driven by the force of historical and archaeological scholarship has been flowing back again . . . Those who continued to deny the historicity of the Pentateuch were forced back onto the defensive and obliged to insist, with logical absurdity, on higher,

---

[47]Ibid., p. 125.
[48]Ibid., p. 126.
[49]Erickson, "Christology from an Evangelical Perspective," p. 380.

or rather totally different, standards of proof for Old Testament assertions as opposed to those in purely secular records. . . . The late 19th/early 20th century notion that the New Testament was a collection of late and highly imaginative records can no longer be seriously held.[50]
Johnson emphasized that the historicity of Jesus is much better authenticated than many secular figures of antiquity whose existence no one has ever presumed to question. Johnson does indeed concede that the vindication of historical records does not in and of itself "prove" that Jesus was and is God, or that the incarnation actually occurred, although it places all of this in a plausible context.

The Reliability of the Biblical Narratives

Erickson, by contrast, asserts that quite apart from the doctrine of the divine inspiration of the Bible, the Scriptures offer "sufficient demonstrably authentic and reliable material to construct an incarnational Christology" with "a reasonable degree of probability."[51] That may, of course, be a tall order, since no exegesis takes place without some assumptions about reliability and its ground. The same Scriptures that affirm the supernaturalness of Jesus teach that divine inspiration is a quality of the text. Unregenerate human beings tends to be most distortive in dealing with the Word of God. When the subject is human salvation and destiny, no details can be dismissed as irrelevant. Jesus himself commits us to a wholly reliable Scripture. If the text is to be approached on the assumption of intrinsic trustworthiness only where its claims can be verified on other grounds, then the credibility of much of the narratives would seem to remain in doubt. The history of Christianity clearly attests that where the reliability of the Bible is questioned, rival portraits of Christ soon emerge. More than that, the risen Lord rules his church by the Spirit through the Scriptures as his authoritative word.

Erickson would no doubt grant all this and contend for the essential reliability of the text, as did F. F. Bruce (1910-1990) in England, George E. Ladd (1911-1982) in the United States and R. K. Harrison in Canada.

Bringing assumptions to bear on the question of the reliability or unreliability of the biblical narratives can be inferred by a comparison and contrast of the entries for Jesus in major encyclopedias, which are usually thought to express the normative view. In his discussion of the reliability of Luke, Mircea Eliade gives an ambiguous verdict that can lead in alternative directions: "In writing history Luke took his standards at least partly from the conventions of time. Yet the practice of Greek, Jewish and Roman historians, even if freer than that of their modern counterparts, nevertheless maintained some fidelity to sources and

---

[50]Paul Johnson, lecture given in Dallas, Texas, 1992.
[51]Erickson, "Christianity from an Evangelical Perspective," p. 385.

fact."[52] Consider Rowan A. Greer's aggressively negative article on Jesus in the international edition of another encyclopedia:

> Christian definitions of Jesus as Saviour gradually moved beyond regarding him as the Messiah and ended by understanding him to be the incarnation of God's eternally begotten Son.[53]

Greer continues:

> Matthew and Luke claim that Jesus was conceived and born supernaturally. . . . For three reasons this claim is problematic. First, it is made only by Matthew and Luke and cannot be found elsewhere in the New Testament. Second, the genealogies in Matthew 1 and Luke 3 may be construed to imply that Jesus' descent from David originally was traced through Joseph. Finally, references to Jesus having brothers and sisters, while not necessarily excluding his virgin birth, might argue against Mary's perpetual virginity. . . . The virgin birth cannot be demonstrated historically. . . . The concern that lies behind the claim of Matthew and Luke is really theological. Jesus' birth was miraculous in the sense that it took place because of God's unique purpose. Thus the historian cannot refute the theological meaning of the doctrine of Christ's virgin birth. . . . It is impossible to treat the Gospel accounts [of Jesus' resurrection] as accurate reports of what happened. As with the birth narratives, we probably must conclude that the factual basis of the narratives is irrecoverable.[54]

Here arguments are adduced that would be met with strenuous counterargument, even by a first-year divinity student. The verdict that the narratives are of unsure historical reliability is not a conclusion reached by meticulous study of the records but rather is a presupposition that the interpreter holds as he approaches the narrative.

In contrast to critical assumptions that the biblical narratives are nonhistorical in their significance and that the theological priorities of the accounts require dismissing historical considerations as irrelevant, the distinguished historian Kenneth S. Latourette takes a notably different stance:

> No other life lived on this planet has so widely and deeply affected mankind. That becomes the more remarkable when account is taken of the brevity of that life and of its public career, of the lack of care given by Jesus to the perpetuation of his influence, and of the seeming weakness and frustration of a brief venture that appeared to end on a Roman Cross. Here is a feature of the human record which puzzles the historian, but which to the Christian is central in that record.[55]

---

[52]Mircea Eliade, "Luke," in *The Encyclopedia of Religion* (New York: Macmillan, 1987), 8:16.

[53]Rowan A. Greer, "Jesus Christ," in *The Encyclopedia Americana* (Danbury, Conn.: Grolier, 1990), 16:38.

[54]Ibid., 16:40-41.

[55]Kenneth Scott Latourette, "Jesus Christ," in *Colliers Encyclopedia* (New York: Macmillan Educational, 1992), 13:559.

Some modern critical theories still reflect the philosopher David Hume's skeptical view of miracles, claiming that it is always more reasonable to reject testimony to the miraculous than to accept it, a view somewhat chastened by the era of quantum physics as against a wholly determinate mechanistic universe. But Ronald Nash reduces Hume's assault on miracles to an a priori objection. Miracles, he stresses, pose no threat to science or to whatever laws science postulates to explain natural phenomena. Nash probes the question of what miracles must be factual if Christianity is true, and he focuses on two: the incarnation of God in Christ and the resurrection of Jesus.[56] The apostle Paul does not hedge the claim for Jesus' resurrection but declares the historicity of the resurrection to be necessary to the truth of Christianity and to the validity of Christian belief (1 Cor 15:12-19).

The distinguished literary critic C. S. Lewis (1898-1963) contests the claim that people in biblical times believed in miracles because they were ignorant of the laws of nature. In fact, says Lewis, they knew certain laws very well. Joseph knew what led to a woman's conceiving a baby. When he learned of Mary's pregnancy, he wanted to put her away. At first he assumed that she had conceived "naturally." He subsequently accepted the Christian belief that a miracle had occurred. He would not have recognized it for what it was, except for some awareness of the laws of nature.[57]

Lewis writes of the depth and sanity of Jesus' moral teachings, usually accepted even by those who opposed him, and yet of their contrast with "the quiet appalling nature of this man's theological remarks."[58] Jesus told others they were sinners without even remotely speaking in such terms of himself. He forgave the sins even of those who presumably had not offended him. His claim to be God was the most shocking statement ever uttered by human lips. He so equated himself with the living God that pious Jews sought to kill him. Accept him as God you must, or reject him as a madman, a fool or something worse, remarks Lewis.[59] Reducing the accounts to legend and denying Jesus' historical existence runs counter to all the principles on which literary historians insist. He was not simply a good man, for he claimed to be God. Jesus was and is for Christians not simply human or even simply Godlike, but fully God and man. Here one recalls Lewis's reminder that the miracles of the Bible climaxed by "the grand miracle" signal the inbreaking of a new and glorious day. The miracles, he comments,

are the first fruits of that cosmic summer which is presently coming on. Christ

---

[56]See Ronald Nash, "Faith and Reason," in *Searching for a Rational Faith* (Grand Rapids: Zondervan, 1988).

[57]C. S. Lewis, *God in the Dock: Essays on Theology and Ethics* (Grand Rapids: Eerdmans, 1970), pp. 26, 72, 100.

[58]Ibid., pp. 156-57.

[59]C. S. Lewis, *The Case for Christianity* (New York: Macmillan, 1943), p. 440.

has risen, and so we shall rise. . . . To be sure, it feels wintry enough still; but often in the very early spring it feels like that. Two thousand years are only a day or two by this scale. A man really ought to say, "The Resurrection happened two thousand years ago" in the same spirit in which he says, "I saw a crocus yesterday." Because we knew what is coming behind the crocus . . . it remains with us . . . to die in this winter, or to go into that spring and that summer.[60]

Doctrine "from Above" Versus Doctrine "from Below"

Recent Christology is divided over whether doctrinal construction should proceed "from above" or "from below." Although the contrasting terms *from above* and *from below* were employed by Luther, they were revived to widespread contemporary use largely through Pannenberg's books.[61] Critics of Chalcedon often complain that its exponents begin with the premise that Christ is divine, that is, the eternal second person of the Trinity, and then seek within this framework to expound the earthly life and work of Jesus.

Pannenberg insists that Christology must rise from the data of the Jesus of history, in contrast to the view of Bultmann and others who dismissed history as irrelevant to faith. Pannenberg focuses on the resurrection as the main key to Christology, since it reflects a divine dimension in the life of Jesus.

By contrast, almost all distinctively modern Christology begins "from below." Focusing on the human reality of Jesus, it expounds the essential humanity of the Nazarene in terms applicable to all human beings. Consequently, the term *divinity* is applied to Jesus only in ambiguous ways, as illustrated by the view of John A. T. Robinson.[62] Gunton has noted that such Christologies are prone to portray Christ as a superman of sorts, whose extra features distinguish him from the rest of us. At the same time they portray him as distinctively less than the divine Christ of Christian orthodoxy.[63] The inevitable outcome is that the incarnation becomes mythological.

For Pannenberg, however, belief in divine incarnation in Christ is an appropriate conclusion, with the result that Christology "from below" does not exclude the divinity of Jesus Christ. Yet Thomas Oden remarks pointedly that theologians run counter to the classical Christian exegetes when, like Harnack, Bultmann, Tillich and Pannenberg, they discuss the work of Christ ahead of the person of Christ. Only after establishing the identity of the Nazarene can they speak properly and adequately about his work. Efforts to develop a Christology from below, through

---

[60]Lewis, *God in the Dock*, p. 87.
[61]See Wolfhart Pannenberg, *Revelation as History* (New York: Macmillan, 1968); Wolfhart Pannenberg, *Jesus: God and Man* (Philadelphia: Westminster, 1968).
[62]John A. T. Robinson, *The Human Face of God* (Philadelphia: Westminster, 1973).
[63]Gunton, *Yesterday and Today*.

history, Oden remarks, "are due to be succeeded by a recovery of classic Christological exegesis on its own terms, unintimidated by modernity."[64]

Evangelicals accordingly reject process philosophy as the context in which to expound Christology, since its view that the world is as necessary to God as God is to the world runs counter to the Christian doctrine of creation, and its implications for the two-nature theory are destructive in that the incarnation is viewed as the culmination of a process whereby Christ emerges from humanity.

Perhaps no contemporary evangelical has stated more succinctly yet comprehensively the enduring testimony of Chalcedon than has Geoffrey W. Bromiley:

> The humanity of Christ is not a limiting factor which demands either a restriction or a spasmodic and paradoxical manifestation of the divine attributes, but a specific form in which the true and living God can and does bring all His attributes to expression, achieving a unity of person, a communion of natures, and a communication of attributes, graces and operations, without any distortion of humanity on the one side, or on the other any forfeiture of deity, whether within the Godhead or in the human form.[65]

The Chalcedonian definition, as we have noted, has gained new visibility through several developments that propel it once again into the forefront of theological interest. The charge leveled by secular philosophers that the one person/two natures doctrine is illogical, on the ground that divine being and human beings presumably have mutually exclusive properties, continues to evoke refutation. Thomas V. Morris contends that as incarnate, the one person Jesus Christ had two minds and ranges of consciousness, the one canopying the other. He insists that a "two minds" view is not incompatible with Christ's personal unity.[66]

Gordon Clark regards Chalcedon's greatest weakness as its failure to define terms.[67] He considers a substance philosophy, to which Thomism is devoted, a handicap to the retention of the term *person*. Even Athanasius, he notes, considered "the substance of God" to be merely a circuitous way of referring to God without any implication of an underlying element to which attributes are added. Clark would discard the notion of *substance* and clarify the term *person*. He defines *person* as a composite of truths, more exactly, or propositions: "a person is the propositions he thinks."[68]

That definition does not, he hastens to add, reduce the Godhead to "one Person."

---

[64]Thomas Oden, *The Word of Life*, vol. 2 of *Systematic Theology* (San Francisco, Harper & Row, 1989), p. 533.
[65]Bromiley, "Christology," p. 666.
[66]See Thomas V. Morris, *The Logic of God Incarnate* (Ithaca, N.Y.: Cornell University Press, 1986); Thomas V. Morris, "The Metaphysical of God Incarnate," in *Incarnation, Trinity and Atonement*, ed. Ronald Feinstra and Cornelius Plantinga (Notre Dame, Ind.: University of Notre Dame Press, 1989).
[67]Gordon Clark, *The Incarnation* (Jefferson, Md.: Trinity Foundation, 1988), p. 15.
[68]Ibid., p. 55.

Although the three persons are omniscient, they do not all know/experience the same truths. The Father cannot say, "I walked the Emmaus Way"; the Spirit cannot say, "I begat the Son"; and only the Son can say, "I was incarnated." Some critics of Clark's view claim that he gives no example of statements that could not be made by the man Jesus. But surely the man Jesus cannot say, "I sent the Son into the world."

The Son remains a divine person, yet we must not—Clark insists—declare the human nature impersonal. In the cry of desolation God forsook a person, not merely a nature. The New Testament does not hesitate to speak of Jesus as a man.

The Chalcedonian definition precipitated the first major and enduring division in Eastern Christendom. Nestorianism held that Jesus was a human person. Although he aggressively opposed all heretics, Nestorius was himself condemned by ecclesiastical authorities as a heretic who allegedly split the God-man into two distinct persons. Nestorius stressed that Jesus Christ was truly a man and that in their union in Jesus the divine and human natures are unaltered and distinct. He emphasized that Jesus lived a truly human life involving growth, temptation and suffering—which presupposes that the human nature was not fused into the divine. Nestorius ranged the two natures side by side in a union that was little more than moral. The Nestorians were charged with implying that the two natures were in effect two loosely united persons.

Yet there can be no doubt that Jesus was born as a person and suffered as a person. Does the affirmation that Jesus was the God-man then require that Jesus was a divine person and a human person? The ambiguity, Clark holds, is due to a failure to define personhood.

Such issues indicate that the theological task facing evangelical Christians includes serious study and careful exposition of both the teaching of the Bible and the intention of Chalcedon. The classic definition has often been portrayed as the climax of christological investigation. We conclude with Oskar Skarsaune that Chalcedon can be considered the prelude to a new phase in the christological controversy as well as the conclusion of an earlier one.

Chapter 17

New Dimensions in Salvation

Alister E. McGrath

....

I T IS A GREAT PLEASURE TO PAY TRIBUTE TO MILLARD J. ERICKSON, WHO has done so much to consolidate and develop evangelical confidence and maturity, particularly in the field of systematic theology.[1] In what follows, I propose to explore new dimensions in an evangelical approach to the doctrine of salvation. But why explore "new dimensions"? Why not rest content with traditional evangelical approaches, which have proved so satisfactory in the past? Are we not, in effect if not in intention, commending the abandonment of traditional evangelical approaches—approaches that have been defended vigorously and persuasively by the very scholar honored in this volume? Clearly, this is not the case. I am convinced that we do need to explore new dimensions in evangelical thought. It has expanded into new areas, leading to new challenges and opportunities and to new developments in our own context that force new issues onto our agenda—issues to which we must respond if we are to ensure that evangelicalism maintains its engagement with the world.

As evangelicalism has been forced to confront new challenges, it has developed its thinking on a number of issues, including the doctrine of salvation. Yet this

---

[1]On aspects of evangelical expansion and identity, see Millard J. Erickson, *The Evangelical Mind and Heart* (Grand Rapids: Baker, 1993), pp. 13-14; D. F. Wells and J. D. Woodbridge, eds., *The Evangelicals* (Nashville: Abingdon, 1975); D. G. Bloesch, *The Essentials of Evangelical Theology*, 2 vols. (San Francisco: Harper & Row, 1978-1979); David Dockery, ed., *Are Southern Baptists Evangelicals?* (Nashville: Broadman, 1993); Alister E. McGrath, *Evangelicalism and the Future of Christianity* (Downers Grove, Ill.: InterVarsity Press, 1995).

development is not about change. It is about applying the gospel to new situations; it is about meeting challenges not envisaged by our forebears. The gospel has not changed. But evangelicals are thinking through its implications for situations unknown to earlier generations of their peers and are allowing the full richness and relevance of the eternal gospel to make an impact on the diverse situations and cultures of our world. In this essay I explore two developments that are of major significance to evangelical thinking in regard to the doctrine of salvation: (1) the expansion of evangelicalism in Asia and Africa and (2) the growth of religious pluralism in the West. Each development demands a response, which this essay attempts to articulate.

Evangelical Expansion in Asia and Africa

Since World War II evangelicalism has expanded rapidly, particularly in Asia and Africa. Traditional evangelical approaches to many issues, including the articulation of the Christian understanding of salvation, have often been significantly influenced by a Western (and, more specifically, a North American) context. Evangelicals have often inadvertently clothed the *evangel* in Western dress, using Western concepts and values to articulate the gospel in non-Western contexts. Many in Asia and Africa have responded that Western evangelicals require them to accept Western ideas and values before they can accept the gospel! One "new dimension" that is urgently required in evangelical thinking on salvation, as well as in other issues, is the identification of core gospel truths and values in order to eliminate ideas and values that are simply responses to the Western context in which evangelicalism developed during its formative phase. As evangelicalism becomes a global phenomenon, it must ensure that nothing human is placed in the path of God's saving grace.

David F. Wells, one of evangelicalism's most significant and respected contemporary exponents, identifies the task of evangelical theology as follows:

> It is the task of theology, then, to discover what God has said in and through Scripture and to clothe that in a conceptuality which is native to our own age. Scripture, at its *terminus a quo*, needs to be de-contextualized in order to grasp its transcultural content, and it needs to be re-contextualized in order that its content may be meshed with the cognitive assumptions and social patterns of our own time.[2]

There is much wisdom in this approach. Wells encourages us to take the trouble to apply the central themes of Scripture to our own situations, whatever they may be. The diversity of cultural and social situations leads to a corresponding diversity of

---

[2]David F. Wells, "The Nature and Function of Theology," in *The Use of the Bible in Theology: Evangelical Options*, ed. R. K. Johnson (Atlanta: John Knox, 1985), p. 177.

applications of the gospel, without in any way calling into question the unity of that gospel. We cannot export a prepackaged interpretation and application of Scripture to other contexts. What John Calvin had to say about the application of the gospel in the sixteenth-century city of Geneva cannot be uncritically applied to twenty-first century tribes in eastern Uganda. We must establish the particular significance of the gospel to each and every context we encounter, not just assume that what works fine in Wheaton, Illinois, will do just as well in Kampala.

The first major new direction is valuing our evangelical past while recognizing that it cannot be exported uncritically and in a prepackaged form to the new frontiers of evangelical expansion.[3] There must be a constant willingness to ask, What does God's salvation mean for these people in this context?

Space constraints prevent me from indicating in detail how this can be done. However, a single case study can serve to indicate the sort of approach that needs to be explored. In analyzing the significance of Jesus in Ghana, Ghanaian theologian Kofi Appiah-Kubi[4] notes the importance of deliverance and healing in African culture in this region. Although many Westerners regard the idea of deliverance from evil spirits or malevolent ancestors as superstition, such forces are a real and important aspect of life in a rural Ghanaian context. As Appiah-Kubi points out, the gospel engages these questions directly and dramatically, demonstrating and proclaiming the manner in which Jesus Christ triumphs and gains the victory over such evil forces. Yet most Westerners would regard such an approach as unsophisticated or superstitious.

Western evangelicalism has tended to neglect such aspects of the gospel. Perhaps as evangelical expansion continues in non-Western regions, those of us who are Westerners will discover more of the richness of the gospel from those who know its relevance and power in non-Western situations. This important historical development can help us recover the biblical understanding of salvation in all its fullness. We err when we regard past Western articulations and contextualizations of salvation as adequate for the global evangelical community.

The Rise of Religious Pluralism

The rise of religious pluralism in the West has raised new challenges for evangelicalism.[5] John Hick is a noted exponent of prescriptive pluralism, which insists that

---

[3]For a significant exploration of this point from an evangelical perspective, see Harvie M. Conn, *Eternal Word and Changing Worlds* (Grand Rapids: Zondervan, 1984). More broadly, see Robert J. Schreiter, *Constructing Local Theologies* (Maryknoll, N.Y.: Orbis, 1985).

[4]Kofi Appiah-Kubi, "Christology," in *African and Asian Contributions to Contemporary Theology*, ed. J. Mbiti (Geneva: Ecumenical Institute, 1976), pp. 55-65.

[5]See Alister E. McGrath, "The Challenge of Pluralism for the Contemporary Christian Church," *Journal of the Evangelical Theological Society* 35 (1992): 361-73; Alister E. McGrath, "The Christian Church's Response to Pluralism," *Journal of the Evangelical Theological Society* 35 (1992): 487-501.

all religions are saying the same thing, irrespective of their apparent differences. In an important study Hick has argued that there is a common core structure to all religions, which "are fundamentally alike in exhibiting a soteriological structure. That is to say, they are all concerned with salvation/liberation/enlightenment/fulfilment."[6] This suggestion has been seized upon by many liberal thinkers who are anxious to undermine the distinctiveness of Christianity. One of the central tasks of evangelicalism must therefore be to defend and articulate the distinctiveness of the Christian understanding of salvation—indeed, more than that: the *uniqueness* of the Christian understanding both of salvation and of the Savior.

The Christian notion of salvation is complex and highly nuanced. To articulate the various aspects of salvation, the New Testament uses images drawn from personal relationships, physical healing, legal transactions and ethical transformation. Yet however salvation is to be understood, it is grounded in the life, death and resurrection of Jesus Christ.[7] In affirming the uniqueness of the Christian idea of salvation, three controlling considerations must be acknowledged.

The Christian God is unique. The Christian tradition bears witness to a particular understanding of God. It cannot be merged into the various concepts of divinity found in other religions. To allow that non-Christian religions may know something of God is not to say that their knowledge is consistent with Christianity or that every aspect of the Christian understanding of God is found in other religions. We are talking about "points of contact" and occasional convergences, not identity or even fundamental consistent agreement. There was a period when there was some sympathy for the idea that mutual understanding among the world's religions would be enhanced if Christians accepted a kind of "Copernican revolution" in which they stopped regarding Jesus Christ as of central importance and started focusing their attention on God. Being God-centered, we were assured, would be more helpful than being Christ-centered.

The attraction of this model has diminished substantially as both the relative poverty of its intellectual foundations and its practical consequences have become increasingly clear. Hick once argued that all religions should be seen as planets orbiting the sun.[8] But Raimundo Panikkar, writing from an Indian perspective, criticizes this notion, arguing for a total displacement of "God" or "the absolute" from such a center. Instead, each religion is to be viewed as a galaxy in its own right, turning reciprocally around other such galaxies.[9]

---

[6]John Hick, *The Second Christianity* (London: SCM Press, 1983), p. 86.

[7]See Alister E. McGrath, "Christology and Soteriology: A Response to Wolfhart Pannenberg's Critique of the Soteriological Approach to Christology," *Theologische Zeitschrift* 42 (1986): 222-36.

[8]John Hick, *God and the Universe of Faiths* (London: Macmillan, 1973), pp. 120-32.

[9]Raimundo Panikkar, "The Jordan, the Tiber and the Ganges," in *The Myth of Christian Uniqueness,* ed. J. Hick and P. Knitter (Maryknoll, N.Y.: Orbis, 1988), p. 109.

An incarnational Christology is now seen as a serious barrier to interreligious understanding only in the sense that the Qur'an is also a barrier. Both are integral to the faiths in question. To eliminate them would be to alter the faiths radically, assisting interfaith reconciliation at the cost of destroying the distinctiveness of the religions in question. By what authority does the pluralist take an abusive approach that does violence to the integrity of these systems? In the seminars of academe, this may amount to nothing more than just another hypothetical possibility. But in the real world, we must learn to live with conflicts between such defining and distinctive characteristics of faiths and not insist on smoothing them over. Religions are not putty to be molded by pluralist ideologues but are living realities that demand respect and honor.

Traditional Christian theology strongly resists the homogenizing agenda of religious pluralists, not least on account of its high Christology.[10] The suggestion that all religions are more or less talking about vaguely the same God finds itself in difficulty in relation to two essentially Christian doctrines—the Incarnation and the Trinity. For example, if God is Christlike, as the doctrine of the divinity of Christ affirms in uncompromising terms, then the historical figure of Jesus, along with the witness to him in Scripture, becomes of foundational importance to Christianity. Such distinctive doctrines are embarrassing to those who wish to debunk what they term the "myth of Christian uniqueness," who then proceed to demand that Christianity abandon doctrines such as the Incarnation that imply a high profile of identification between Jesus Christ and God in favor of various "degree Christologies," which are more amenable to the reductionist program of liberalism. In much the same way, the idea that God is in any sense disclosed or defined christologically is set to one side on account of its theologically momentous implications for the identity and significance of Jesus Christ, which liberal pluralism finds an embarrassment. Let us turn to consider pluralistic objections to the Incarnation and the Trinity.

First, the idea of the Incarnation is rejected, often dismissively, as a myth.[11] Thus Hick and his collaborators reject the doctrine of the Incarnation on various logical and commonsense counts while failing to deal with the question of why Christians developed this doctrine in the first place.[12] There is an underlying agenda to this dismissal of Jesus' incarnation, a central part of which is the elimination of the sheer *distinctiveness* of Christianity. A sharp distinction is thus drawn between the historical person of Jesus Christ and the principles that he is alleged to represent.

---

[10]The same point applies to Islam, which strongly resists attempts to homogenize or relativize the teaching of the Qur'an.

[11]Perhaps most notably in John Hick, ed., *The Myth of God Incarnate* (London: SCM Press, 1977).

[12]See Alister E. McGrath, "Resurrection and Incarnation: The Foundations of the Christian Faith," in *Different Gospels*, ed. A. Walker (London: Hodder & Stoughton, 1988), pp. 79-96.

Paul Knitter is but one of a small galaxy of pluralist writers concerned to drive a wedge between the "Jesus event" (unique to Christianity) and the "Christ principle" (accessible to all religious traditions and expressed in their own distinctive but equally valid ways).

It is fair (and necessary) to inquire about the pressure for such developments, since a hidden pluralist agenda appears to govern the outcome of this christological assault—a point made in a highly perceptive critique of Hick's incarnational views from the pen of Wolfhart Pannenberg. "Hick's proposal of religious pluralism as an option of authentically Christian theology hinges on the condition of a prior demolition of the traditional doctrine of the incarnation." Hick, Pannenberg notes, assumes that this demolition has already taken place and chides him for his excessive selectivity—not to mention his lack of familiarity with recent German theology—in drawing such a conclusion.[13]

It is highly significant that the pluralist agenda forces its advocates to adopt heretical views of Christ in order to meet its needs. In an effort to fit Jesus into the "great religious teachers of humanity" category, the Ebionite heresy has been revived in the guise of political correctness. Jesus is one of the religious options available by the great human teachers of religion. He is "one of the lads," to use a Yorkshire phrase.

Second, the idea has been dismissed that God is made known through Christ. Captivated by the image of a "Copernican revolution" (probably one of the most overworked and misleading phrases in recent writings in this field), pluralists demand that Christians move away from a discussion of Christ to a discussion of God, yet failing to recognize that the "God of the Christians" (Tertullian) might be rather different from other divinities and that the doctrine of the Trinity spells out the nature of that distinction. The loose and vague talk about "God" or "Reality" found in much pluralist writing is not a result of theological sloppiness or confusion. It is a considered response to the recognition that for Christians to talk about the Trinity is to speak about a specific God (not just "deity" in general), who has chosen to make himself known in a highly particular manner in and through Jesus Christ. It is a deliberate rejection of authentically and distinctively Christian insights into God in order to suggest that Christianity, to rework a phrase of the English deist writer Matthew Tindal (1656-1733), is simply the republication of the religion of nature.[14]

Yet human religious history shows that natural human ideas of the number,

---

[13]Wolfhart Pannenberg, "Religious Pluralism and Conflicting Truth Claims," in *Christian Uniqueness Reconsidered*, ed. G. D'Costa (Maryknoll, N.Y.: Orbis, 1990), p. 100.
[14]Tindal's chief work is titled *Christianity as Old as Creation, or the Gospel a Republication of the Religion of Nature* (1730). See Peter A. Byrne, *Natural Religion and the Religion of Nature* (London: Routledge, 1989).

nature and character of the gods are notoriously vague and muddled. The Christian emphasis is on the need to worship not gods in general (Israel's strictures against Canaanite religion being especially important here) but a God who has chosen to make himself known. As Robert Jenson has persuasively argued, the doctrine of the Trinity is an attempt to spell out the identity of this God and to avoid confusion with rival claimants to this title.[15] The doctrine of the Trinity defines and defends the particularity and distinctiveness, and ultimately the *uniqueness,* of the "God of the Christians." The New Testament gives a further twist to this development through its language about "the God and Father of our Lord Jesus Christ," locating the identity of God in the actions and passions of Jesus Christ. To put it bluntly, for Christians, God is christologically disclosed.[16]

This point is of considerable importance. Most Western religious pluralists appear to work with a concept of God that is shaped by the Christian tradition, whether this is openly acknowledged or not. For example, pluralists often appeal to the notion of a gracious and loving God. Yet this is a distinctively Christian notion of God, which is ultimately grounded and substantiated in Jesus Christ. There is no such thing as a "tradition-independent notion of God." Even Kant's idea of God, allegedly purely rational in character and hence independent of culture, is actually ethnocentric. It has been deeply shaped by implicit Christian assumptions that were an ingrained part of Kant's social matrix. As Gavin D'Costa has pointed out, John Hick's concept of God, which plays such a significant role in his pluralist worldview, has been decisively shaped (whether or not he is prepared to admit this) by christological considerations. "How credibly," he asks, "can Hick expound a doctrine of God's universal salvific will if he does not ground this crucial truth in the revelation of God in Christ, thereby bringing Christology back onto center stage?"[17]

Pluralists have driven a wedge between God and Jesus Christ, as if Christians were obliged to choose between one or the other. As the pendulum swings toward a theocentric approach (on the assumption that the "god" in question is common to all religious traditions), the Christology of the religious pluralists becomes reduced to something of negligible proportions. Only the lowest possible Christology within the Christian tradition is deemed to be worthy of acceptance in the modern period (looking away from the awkward fact that this Christology was rejected as heretical by the early church). If the pluralists have some infallible source of knowledge about the nature and purposes of God apart from Christ, then what is the point of the gospel? And what kind of God is it who can be known apart from Christ? Are we talking about the God and Father of our Lord Jesus Christ

---

[15]Robert Jenson, *The Triune Identity* (Philadelphia: Fortress, 1982), pp. 1-20.

[16]For an excellent defense of this point, see Millard J. Erickson, *The Word Became Flesh: A Contemporary Incarnational Christology* (Grand Rapids: Baker, 1991).

[17]Gavin D'Costa, *John Hick's Theology of Religions* (New York: University Press of America, 1987), p. 103.

(1 Pet 1:3) at all or about some different deity? An idea of God can be allowed as "Christian" only if it is subjected to the standard of God's self-disclosure through Jesus Christ, as is made known to us through Scripture.

What is the relevance of this point to our theme? Salvation, in the Christian understanding of the notion, involves an altered relation with God, whether this is understood personally, substantially, morally or legally. But which God are we talking about? Old Testament writers were quite clear that salvation, as they understood it, was not about a new relationship with any of the gods of Canaan, Philistia or Assyria, but with the one and only covenant God of Israel, whom they knew by the distinguishing personal name "the LORD" (Hebrew *yhwh*). For Christianity, the notion of salvation explicitly includes and centers on a relationship, inaugurated in time but to be consummated beyond time, with none other than the God and Father of our Lord Jesus Christ (1 Pet 1:3). We are thus dealing with a highly particularized notion of salvation.

Jesus Christ is the unique Savior. For Christians, salvation is a possibility only on account of Jesus Christ. The early Christians had no hesitation in using the term *savior* (Greek *sōtēr*) to refer to Jesus Christ, despite the fact that this term was already widely used within the complex and diverse religious context in which the gospel first emerged. For the New Testament writers, Jesus was the only Savior of humanity. On the basis of the evidence available to the New Testament writers, this conclusion seemed entirely proper and necessary. The evidence concerning Jesus needed to be interpreted in this direction and was thus interpreted.

This does not, however, mean that the first Christians thought that Jesus as *sōtēr* offers the same *sōtēria* as others who bore this title before him. In classical Greek religion, Poseidon and the Dioskouroi were all acclaimed as *sōtēres*;[18] yet the "salvation" in question appears to have been conceived in terms of a temporal deliverance from a present threat rather than a notion of eternal salvation.

The New Testament thus affirms the *particularity* of the redemptive act of God in Jesus Christ.[19] The early Christian tradition, basing itself on the New Testament, reaffirmed this particularity. While allowing that God's revelation went far beyond Jesus Christ (in that God made himself known to varying degrees through such means as the natural order of creation, human conscience and civilization), the general knowledge of God was not understood to entail universal salvation. John Calvin stated the various styles of knowledge of God available to humanity when he drew his celebrated distinction between a "knowledge of God the creator" and

---

[18]See Walter Burkert, *Greek Religion* (Oxford: Blackwell, 1975), pp. 137, 213, and references.
[19]See Lesslie Newbigin, *The Finality of Christ* (Richmond, Va.: John Knox, 1969); Clark H. Pinnock, *A Wideness in God's Mercy: The Finality of Jesus Christ in a World of Religions* (Grand Rapids: Zondervan, 1992), pp. 49-80.

a "knowledge of God the redeemer."[20] The same general principle is maintained in Lutheran dogmatics and is often expressed in terms of the distinction between *Deus absconditus* and *Deus revelatus*. As Carl Braaten points out, the Lutheran tradition recognizes a twofold structure within the revelation of God: the hidden God of creation and law *(Deus absconditus)* and the revealed God of covenant and gospel *(Deus revelatus)*.[21]

We have already touched on the importance of Jesus Christ in relation to the Christian understanding of God and the pluralist tendency that ends up, as Harvard theologian Harvey Cox puts it, "soft-pedaling the figure of Jesus himself." For Cox—regarded as a radical theologian in the 1960s—the most appropriate way for Christians to engage in meaningful interfaith dialogue is to begin recognizing that "Jesus is, in some ways, the *most* particularistic element of Christianity."[22] Cox here recognizes the need to begin from something concrete and historical instead of some abstract symbol. For Christians, this particularistic element is Jesus Christ. Christian theology, Christian spirituality and above all Christian worship are strongly Christ-focused.

The New Testament, which endorses and legitimates this Christocentrism, does not merely regard Jesus Christ as *expressive* of a divine salvation that may be made available in other forms. He is clearly understood as *constitutive* of that salvation. In the Christian tradition, Jesus is viewed as more than *rasul* ("the sent one," to use the fundamental Muslim definition of the sequence of prophets culminating in Muhammad). He is seen as the one who establishes as much as the one who is sent—a prophet and a savior. Pluralists have a number of options here, from declaring that the New Testament is simply mistaken on this point (which precludes a serious claim to be Christian) to suggesting that the New Testament affirmations may be true for Christians but have no binding force in this respect *extra muros ecclesiae* (outside the bounds of the church).[23] Yet the New Testament clearly regards Jesus Christ as, at least potentially, the Savior of the world, not simply of Christians, thus pointing to the strongly universal character of his saving work.

The Christian understanding of salvation is unique. Christianity possesses a unique conception of salvation. Its understanding of what salvation comprises distinguishes it from every other religion. In part, this reflects the strongly christological dimension of the Christian understanding of salvation—that believers are united with

[20]See Edward A. Dowey, *The Knowledge of God in Calvin's Theology* (New York: Columbia University Press, 1952).

[21]Carl E. Braaten, "Christ Is God's Final, Not the Only Revelation," in *No Other Gospel! Christianity Among the World's Religions* (Minneapolis: Fortress, 1992), pp. 65-82; quote on p. 68.

[22]Harvey Cox, *Many Mansions* (Boston: Beacon, 1988), pp. 5, 6.

[23]For a survey and a criticism of these options, see Pinnock, *A Wideness in God's Mercy,* pp. 64-74.

Christ.[24] This distinctive emphasis on the implication of Jesus Christ in the nature of salvation sets Christianity apart from other faiths, much to the irritation of those committed to a pluralist agenda.

The notion of salvation varies considerably from one religion to another. In the native religions of West Africa in particular, for example, there is often no discernible transcendent element associated with their notions of salvation. A certain laziness in dealing with English translations of the religious writings of other faiths, especially those originating in India and China, has given rise to the assumption that all religions share common ideas of salvation. In fact, the English term *salvation* is often used to translate Sanskrit or Chinese terms with connotations and associations quite distinct from the Christian concept. These divergences are masked by the process of translation, which often suggests a degree of convergence that is absent in reality. So important are these points that they will be explored in more detail.

These divergent concepts of salvation are conceived in such radically different ways and are understood to be attained in such different manners that only someone who was doggedly determined, as a matter of principle, to treat them as aspects of the same greater whole would have sufficient intellectual flexibility to do so. Do Christianity and Satanism really share the same understanding of salvation? My Satanist acquaintances certainly do not think so. In fact, Satanists accept that there is a God, but they choose to worship God's antithesis. This dualism hardly bodes well for a pluralist theory of the religions and emphasizes the dogmatic nature of the pluralist agenda.

But someone who does not insist that all religions are basically the same might reasonably suggest that far from offering different ways of achieving and conceptualizing salvation, they offer different salvations altogether. The Rastafarian vision of a paradise in which blacks are served by menial whites, the Homeric notion of Tartaros, the old Norse concept of Valhalla, the Buddhist vision of nirvana, the Christian hope of resurrection to eternal life—all are obviously different. How can all the routes to salvation be equally valid when the goals to be reached in such different ways are quite unrelated?

Christian conceptions of salvation focus on the establishment of a relationship between God (in the Christian sense of the term) and his people and use a variety of images to articulate its various aspects. Underlying these convergent images of salvation is the common theme of "salvation in and through Christ." Salvation is a possibility only on account of the life, death and resurrection of Jesus Christ, and that salvation is shaped in his likeness. Joseph A. Di Noia comments that when Christians attempt to explain what the word *salvation* includes,

---

[24]A point stressed by Millard J. Erickson, *Christian Theology* (Grand Rapids: Baker, 1986), 3:953.

we find ourselves talking about the triune God; the incarnation, passion, death and resurrection of Jesus Christ; grace, sin and justification; transfiguration and divinization; faith, hope and charity; the commandments and the moral virtues; and many other characteristically Christian things as well. We should not be surprised if, in trying to answer a cognate question, a member of another religious tradition, say a Buddhist, should also become very specific about Nirvana and all that bears on its attainment. We should not be surprised, furthermore, if the descriptions of salvation and Nirvana do not coincide. . . . Salvation has a specific content for Christians. It entails an interpersonal communion, made possible by Christ, between human persons and the Father, Son and Holy Spirit. At least at first sight, this seems to be something very different from what Buddhists can be supposed to be seeking when they follow the Excellent Eightfold Path that leads them on the way to realizing enlightenment and the extinction of self in Nirvana. At least on the face of things, what Buddhists mean by "Nirvana" and what Christians mean by "salvation" do not seem to coincide.[25]

Pluralist writers, anxious to defend the idea that the world's religions share a common understanding of salvation, occasionally point to Hindu "kitten salvation" as evidence that the notion of grace is not distinctively Christian. This suggestion needs to be subjected to critical examination. The distinction between kitten salvation and "monkey salvation" within the *bhakti marga* tradition of Hinduism rests on the observation that tiger cubs are carried by the tigress whereas baby monkeys have to hang on to their mothers. The idea of kitten salvation, specific to this form of Hinduism, is often appealed to as an indication of the "convergence" of the religions over the grace of God.

Yet the situation is not as simple as this analysis might suggest. The concept is not found in any of the foundational documents of Hinduism, dating from the Vedic period (2000-600 B.C., in which a synthesis between the polytheistic sacrificial religion of the Aryans and the pantheistic monism of the Upanishads took place) or the pantheistic period (600 B.C.-A.D. 300). It emerged during the Puranic period (A.D. 300-A.D. 1200), during which Syrian forms of Christianity became established in the southern regions of India, and is especially associated with the medieval writer Sri Ramanuja (1050-1137).[26] The assumption that kitten salvation points to an inherent similarity between Hindusim and Christianity is dangerously simplistic; it might equally well illustrate the well-known tendency of some Hindu writers to

---

[25]J. A. Di Noia, O.P., "Christian Universalism: The Nonexclusive Particularity of Salvation in Christ," in *Either/Or: The Gospel or Neopaganism*, ed. C. E. Braaten and R. W. Jenson (Grand Rapids: Eerdmans, 1995), pp. 36-47.

[26]The best study remains J. B. Carman, *The Theology of Ramanuja* (New Haven, Conn.: Yale University Press, 1974).

borrow ideas from Christianity.[27] Similarities may reflect the kind of borrowing associated with the strongly syncretistic tendencies of some forms of Hinduism; they need not reflect fundamental convergence.

The distinctively Christian understanding of salvation can also be articulated at a more philosophical level, drawing on some of the insights found, for example, in the writings of Ludwig Wittgenstein, who stresses the need to establish the context in which words are used.[28] For Wittgenstein, the *Lebensform* ("form of living") within which a word was used was of decisive importance in establishing the meaning of that word. The Christian lebensform is thus of controlling importance in understanding what the Christian concept of salvation implies, presupposes and expresses. The Christian notion of salvation is used in the context of a community that worships and adores Christ, grounds its entire hope in his saving work and looks forward to final union with him on the last day.

This point seems to be appreciated by pluralist writer Paul Knitter. Noting that "all knowledge is theory-laden," Knitter concludes that "each religion is speaking within its own language-game."[29] This use of a Wittgensteinian concept clearly indicates an awareness of the need to identify the use of words in "language-games" to ascertain their specific meaning *within the tradition that employs them.* The word *salvation* is clearly a case in point. Its use and associations within the Christian tradition, especially in worship, point to a distinctive understanding of what the Christian faith is understood to confer on believers, its ultimate basis and the manner in which this comes about.[30]

If the term *salvation* is understood to mean "some benefit conferred on or achieved by members of a community, whether individually or corporately," all religions offer salvation. All (and by no means only) religions offer *something*. However, this is such a general statement that it is devoid of significant theological value. All religions, along with political theories such as Marxism and psychotherapeutic schools such as Rogerian therapy—may be legitimately considered salvific.[31] The statement "all religions offer salvation" is thus potentially little more than a

---

[27]The nineteenth-century writer Ramohun Roy is a case in point. See the useful material assembled by Dermot Killingley, *Ramohun Roy in Hindu and Christian Tradition* (Newcastle-upon-Tyne: Grevatt & Grevatt, 1993).

[28]A theme explored with considerable skill in Fergus Kerr, *Theology After Wittgenstein* (Oxford: Blackwell, 1988).

[29]Paul Knitter, in *The Myth of Christian Uniqueness,* ed. J. Hick and P. Knitter (Maryknoll, N.Y.: Orbis, 1988), p. 183.

[30]Such a conclusion is defended, although for different reasons, in Joseph-Augustine Di Noia, *The Diversity of Religions: A Christian Perspective* (Washington, D.C.: Catholic University of America Press, 1992).

[31]Note especially the subtitle of the significant study of E. Brooks Holifield, *A History of Pastoral Care in America: From Salvation to Self-Realization* (Nashville: Abingdon, 1983). See also Philip Rieff, *The Triumph of the Therapeutic* (Chicago: University of Chicago Press, 1967).

tautology. Only by using the most violent of means can all religions be said to offer the same "salvation." Respect for the integrity of the world's religions demands that salvation be particularized, which is to say that the distinctive morphology of a religion's understanding of salvation (including its basis, its mode of conveyance and appropriation, and its inherent nature) must be respected, not coercively homogenized to suit the needs of some particular pressure group within the academy.

Conclusion

My concern in this paper has been to map out an agenda that evangelicals in the next generation must address. Assuming that this essay will primarily be read by persons in Western contexts, I wish to suggest that our agenda has both external and internal aspects. Externally, we must ensure that traditional Western ways of conceptualizing and articulating the New Testament proclamation of salvation in Christ do not become a barrier to persons in non-Western cultures who wish to discover the wonder of Christ and his saving gospel. It is improper to demand or suppose that Scripture must be interpreted in Asia or Africa in the light of and on the basis of Western ideas; each culture must be permitted to engage with and be transformed by Scripture.

Internally, we must address the issues raised by pluralism within Western culture; more specifically, we must challenge the lazy assumption, common to the superficial discussion of such issues that has become characteristic of Western liberalism, that "all religions are the same" and the conclusion drawn from this—that all religions are saying more or less the same thing. Evangelicals must insist that the *uniqueness* of the Christian conception of the basis, nature and mode of procurement of salvation be recognized as a matter of integrity. The Christian understanding of salvation is unique. The Christian gospel is unique. The Christian Savior is unique. As we "strive to give a coherent statement of the doctrines of the Christian faith, based primarily upon the Scriptures, placed in the context of cultures in general,"[32] we can rest assured that as we seek to engage with new cultural contexts—whether through expansion into new cultures or through changes in existing cultures—we can continue to affirm, proclaim and defend that same eternal gospel.

---

[32]Erickson, *Christian Theology*, 1:21.

Chapter 18

New Dimensions in the Holy Spirit

Roger Nicole

················

WE OFTEN HEAR OR READ THAT THE TWENTIETH CENTURY HAS BEEN the century of the Holy Spirit. This assertion is arrogant as well as false. Who would want to say that the Holy Spirit, mentioned by name more than 230 times in the New Testament, was not strongly operative in the first century? Who would deny the Spirit's presence in the sixteenth-century Reformation? Who would ignore the Spirit's role in the Great Awakening and in the nineteenth-century surge of missions and of revival? It is myopic indeed to imagine that the Spirit of God remained hidden until the twentieth century. Truly God's Spirit has been active in the creation of the world (Gen 1:1) and will remain active in this world until the great consummation (Rom 8:11).

Historical Overview

Some people mean merely to say that an intensive study of the Holy Spirit has not been done until the twentieth century. This is also false. The abundance of biblical references to the Holy Spirit (more than 330) implies that God's people who possessed the Bible did in fact pay attention to this topic. In the fourth century the Christian church had to struggle not only against Arianism but also against Macedonianism, which denied the deity of the Holy Spirit. Basil of Caesarea (330-379) wrote a treatise on the Holy Spirit. It is notable also that the Christian church never accepted a view of the Godhead in two persons. It traded a monolithic Jewish concept for a trinitarian view of one God in three persons (for example, Mt 28:19; 2 Cor 13:13; 1 Pet 1:2). Both the Apostles' Creed (early eighth century) and the Nicene Creed (325) have a trinitarian structure. At Constantinople (381) the article on the Holy Spirit was developed more fully than in Nicaea and in a very appropriate way.

The question of the procession of the Holy Spirit—from the Father and the Son, as acknowledged in the West and as stipulated at the Council of Toledo (589), or from the Father through the Son, as generally held in the East—occupied theologians in both areas. The difference escalated into the Great Schism between East and West (1054), which prevails to this day.

During the Reformation the form of the Holy Spirit's revelation through tradition was intensely discussed. Certain left-wing bodies (for example, the Anabaptists) asserted that the Spirit's revelation continues to this day through personal disclosures made by the Spirit to individuals. John Calvin in his *Institutes of the Christian Religion* (1559) devotes one long chapter to the doctrine of the Trinity but two books (3-4), or forty-five chapters, to the work of the Holy Spirit in the individual and the community.

The seventeenth century saw the publication of three works of considerable size and depth. Thomas Goodwin (1600-1680) left nineteen manuscripts, which were published posthumously by his son under the title *The Work of the Holy Ghost in our Salvation.* This is volume six in the modern twelve-volume edition of Goodwin's *Works.*

Perhaps even more notable is the great work of John Owen (1616-1683), who published in 1674 *Pneumatologia or a Discourse Concerning the Holy Spirit,* reprinted in Goold's edition of Owen's *Works* as volume three (1862; 647 pages). To this he added *The Reasons of Faith* (1677), *The Causes, Ways and Means of Understanding the Work of God* (1678) and *The Work of the Holy Spirit in Prayer* (1682). Two additional manuscripts were published posthumously in 1693: *The Work of the Holy Spirit as a Comforter* and *As He Is the Author of Spiritual Gifts.* These five treatises have been reproduced together in volume four of Goold's edition (1862; 520 pages). This is probably the most extensive work ever produced on the subject. In it Owen complains of the lack of published materials on the subject: "I know not any who ever went before me in this design of representing the whole economy of the Holy Spirit with all His adjuncts, operations and effects" (p. 7).

J. G. Walch in his *Bibliotheca Theologica Selecta* (1758) lists some twenty-five authors who dealt with this subject, many of whom had written before Owen published his work. None of these even remotely approximates the range or size of Owen's two volumes. The well-known Arminian theologian John Goodwin (born 1594) produced in 1670 a massive volume, *"Pleroma Pneumatikon": A Being Filled with the Holy Spirit.* This was volume ten of Nichol's series (Edinburgh: James Nichol, 1867). John Flavel (1623-1691) in his *Method of Grace* deals with "the Holy Spirit: applying to the souls of men the eternal redemption."

In the nineteenth century the works of two of the foremost and soundest Scottish theologians were published. In 1856 James Buchanan (1804-1870) published *The Office and Work of the Holy Spirit.* He deals with the work of the Spirit in conversion and after conversion. The book covers some of the materials discussed by Owen, whom Buchanan knew, but has few quotations except those from the Scripture. It includes an interesting discussion of illustrative examples of conversion, mostly from the Scripture itself.

George Smeaton (1814-1889) delivered the Ninth Cunningham Lectures on *The Doctrine of the Holy Spirit* (Edinburgh: T & T Clark, 1889). This work, highly praised by Warfield, includes a chapter on the history of the doctrine. Anyone who asserts that the doctrine of the Holy Spirit has received close attention only in the twentieth century needs to review Smeaton's work.

The catalog of the library of the Princeton Theological Seminary for 1886 indicates that the seminary's holdings included the books named above and seven works published in the eighteenth century (written by Daunt, Hurrion, Knight, Lampe, Ridley, Serle and Warburton) and fourteen more dating from the nineteenth century (written by Arthur, Carne, Goode, Hare, Heber, Kahnis, Kelly, Moberly, Morgan, Parker, Stowell, Walker and Winston, as well as an anonymous work, *Operations of the Spirit of God*).

J. F. Hurst's *Literature of Theology* (pp. 451-53) lists twenty-seven additional works (written by Bristol, Burton, Clemance, Cumming, Dewar, Dixon, Dunn, Faber, Hewlett, Lowry, Manning, Moule, Murray, Norton, Pratt, Quick, Redford, Reeve, Sartorius, Selby, Shirley, Short, Smith, Stone, Thompson, Webb and Wirgman), a number of which were published between 1886 and 1900.

In 1888 Abraham Kuyper (1837-1920) gathered in three volumes a series of articles that had appeared in the weekly *De Heraut. Het Werk van den Heiligen Geest* is a massive treatment of more than nine hundred pages. Kuyper praises the work of John Owen and lists seventy-four of his works in English, together with the data for seventeen of them in Dutch translation. Kuyper also mentions the titles of other works on the Holy Spirit that appeared between 1599 and 1735, a number of which were listed by Walch. He also names three works from the nineteenth century but deems them inadequate for the amplitude of the subject. Like Owen, Kuyper complains about the paucity of literature on this subject.

Kuyper's first volume deals with the Holy Spirit's work in creation, inspiration of Scripture and Christ's incarnation. The second volume deals with sin and grace in the work of salvation in its beginning. The third volume gives extensive developments on sanctification, love and prayer. Kuyper correlates the various aspects of the Holy Spirit's work as well as the different elements in the work of salvation. His grasp of Scripture is magnificent. Some of Kuyper's idiosyncrasies, like justification from eternity, also show up from time to time.

This work was published in English in 1900 and has been reprinted many times. An introductory note by B. B. Warfield expresses high praise for Kuyper: "It is no small gain to survey the whole field of the work of the Holy Spirit in its organic unity under the guidance of so fertile, so systematic and so practical a mind" (p. xxvii). Warfield calls attention to a number of works in English not noted by Kuyper and to several later works written in French, Dutch and German. He adverts particularly to the work of K. A. Kahnis, who had started a comprehensive work in 1847 but never proceeded beyond the first volume, even though he lived another forty-one years (1814-1888) with a productive writing career. As Kuyper had given a list of Owen's works, so Warfield subjoined a list of Kuyper's works up to 1900.

The end of the nineteenth century saw a strong emphasis on the Holy Spirit. We note A. J. Gordon (1836-1895), who wrote *The Holy Spirit in Missions* (New York: Revell, 1893) and *The Ministry of the Holy Spirit* (New York: Revell, 1895); A. B. Simpson (1844-1919), *The Holy Spirit*, 2 vols. (New York: Alliance Publishing, 1895); Handley C. G. Moule (1841-1920), *Veni Creator* (London: Hodder & Stoughton, 1890); G. Campbell Morgan (1863-1945), *The Spirit of God* (New York: Revell, 1900). These men and their associates sparked a renewal of spirituality and zeal for missions that were very beneficial in the life of the church. In that same period Wilhelm Kölling published his *Pneumatologie* (Gütersloh: Bertelsmann, 1894) and K. F. Nösgen (1835-1913), his *Geschichte der Lehre vom Heiligen Geist* (Gütersloh: Bertelsmann, 1899) and *Das Wesen und Wirken des Heiligen Geistes* (Berlin: Trowitzsch, 1905-1907).

The Holy Spirit was the subject of important presentations in the first half of the twentieth century. Notable among them is the work of H. B. Swete (1835-1917). After authoring two brief volumes, Swete initiated a massive historical study, *The Holy Spirit in the New Testament* (1909) and *The Holy Spirit in the Ancient Church* (1916). The work was continued by H. Watkin-Jones, *The Holy Spirit in the Medieval Church* (1922) and *The Holy Spirit from Arminius to Wesley* (1929). In the same vein G. Nuttall wrote *The Holy Spirit in Puritan Faith and Experience* (1946). Some extensive symposia were published: B. H. Streeter, ed., *The Spirit* (1925), and *De Heilige Geest* by conservative Reformed scholars belonging to Kuyper's denomination (1949). A great number of one-volume publications were issued, including works by C. K. Barrett, G. S. Hendry, R. B. Hoyle, Regin Prenter, H. W. Robinson, E. F. Scott, W. H. G. Thomas, H. P. van Dusen and J. F. Walvoord. The fifth part of Karl Barth's *Church Dogmatics*, which he did not have time to put into print, was to be devoted to the application of salvation by the Holy Spirit.

Recent Trends: Pentecostalism

And so we come to the second half of the twentieth century. This period has been marked by a renewal of interest in the work of the Holy Spirit. Among the factors prompting this are the recrudescence of charismatic gifts and a considerable return to the solid biblical understanding of the Puritan theologians.

The church has experienced charismatic phenomena throughout its history. But these movements were at best marginal at the beginning of the twentieth century, Pentecostalism remaining marginal until the 1940s. This was due to several factors. Pentecostals were highly critical, even contemptuous, of people and churches that were not charismatic. They often recruited their members from other churches instead of evangelizing unconverted people. They often considered theological study as inimical to true spirituality. They emphasized miraculous healing to the point of denying the concrete reality of sickness and death. But the ability to speak in tongues proved to be an unreliable indicator of true spirituality: some manifestly Spirit-filled people did not speak in tongues, while some notable tongues-speakers proved to be scandalous sinners.

But these shortcomings, while not disappearing completely, became greatly attenuated, starting in the 1930s. By 1950 the Pentecostal movement had a membership in the millions in the United States, with important contingents in many other nations, notably Sweden. They also could rejoice in a flourishing mission enterprise. Substantial books presenting the Pentecostal point of view were published, notably Carl Burmback's *What Meaneth This?* (1947), Myer Pearlman's *The Heavenly Gift* (1935) and Ernest Williams's three-volume *Systematic Theology* (1953).

One volume that has received particularly wide acclaim is Frederick Dale Bruner, *A Theology of the Holy Spirit: The Pentecostal Experience and the New Testament Witness* (Grand Rapids: Eerdmans, 1970). This work begins with a factual description of the Pentecostal experience and proceeds to an elaborate study of Scripture, principally in Acts and the epistles to the Corinthians (from which it claims support for Pentecostal distinctives), nineteen pages of documents and finally an impressive bibliography of thirty-five pages.

Another work of considerable influence was written by the Anglican J. D. G. Dunn, *Baptism in the Holy Spirit* (London: SCM Press, 1970). His analysis of the New Testament led him to the conclusion that the possession (or baptism) of the Holy Spirit is the distinguishing feature of conversion and that it is often manifested by supernatural gifts such as glossolalia. He faults Pentecostals for associating this gift with a "second experience" and faults traditional churches for representing water baptism as the agent of regeneration or as representing conversion as a response to gospel preaching and baptism as a mere symbol without operative power. He writes, "Faith demands baptism as its expression; Baptism demands faith for its validity. The gift of the Spirit presupposes faith as its condition. Faith is shown to be genuine only by the gift of the Spirit" (p. 228).

This very bold approach did not find universal agreement, but it saved Pentecostalism from being dismissed as a largely emotional movement without intellectual substance or proper biblical foundation. Increasingly Pentecostals, as well as movements that emphasize faith healing, acknowledge that people who are spiritually healthy may experience physical sickness and that recourse to medical treatment is not improper.

Surely death is but the most aggravated form of illness, and yet from the time of Pentecost not a single Christian has managed to avoid it. The sickness and death that afflict everyone would amount to an immense defeat for the whole Christian church if the atoning work of Christ had in fact secured physical health in this life for all believers. Similarly, while many Pentecostals recognize speaking in tongues as the sign that accompanies the baptism of the Holy Spirit, others do not feel constrained to view as spiritually deficient those who do not experience glossolalia.

The Pentecostal movement in the United States has grown from around one million members in 1950 to more than ten million in 1995. Figures in the *World Almanac* 1995 indicate that one Pentecostal group, the Church of God in Christ, with 5.5 million members, is now the fourth largest Protestant denomination, after the Southern Baptists, the United Methodists and the National Baptist Convention U.S.A. Missions statistics are even more spectacular: Patrick Johnstone in *Operation World* (Grand Rapids: Zondervan, 1993) estimates that in 1995 Pentecostals in the world may well number 150 million out of a total of some 400 million evangelicals.

For more than fifty years some Pentecostal groups have participated in the fellowship and work of certain parachurch movements. The Assemblies of God was active in the National Association of Evangelicals, which was founded in 1944. T. Roswell Flower was the second president, following Harold John Ockenga. They have also participated in notable numbers in the Evangelical Theological Society. They have supported joint crusades of evangelization, as, for instance, the Billy Graham campaigns.

Two volumes dealing with the history and meaning of the movement are particularly helpful: J. T. Nichol, *Pentecostalism* (New York: Harper & Row, 1966), an excellent presentation with nine pages of bibliography, and Walter J. Hollenweger, *The Pentecostals* (Peabody, Mass.: Hendrickson, 1988). *The Pentecostals* is a translation of a German work published in 1969, itself a condensation of a ten-volume typewritten work. It is massive in scope and depth: twenty chapters are devoted to the history and development of the Pentecostal movement in various countries of the world, and twelve chapters contain a discussion of Pentecostal beliefs and practice. Notes (2,523 of them) are included at the end of each chapter. An appendix contains nine official declarations of faith. A bibliography of works in fifteen languages occupies thirty-four pages, and the index, fourteen pages. This is an encyclopedic work, indispensable to anyone who wishes to gain a good understanding of the history and doctrine of the Pentecostals.

The charismatic movement has not been confined to the Pentecostal denominations, gaining a footing in many churches, including the Roman Catholic Church. This is remarkable because the distribution of gifts did not follow a hierarchical pattern: a layperson may speak in tongues as well as a bishop! Cardinal Suenens of Belgium is probably the highest-ranking supporter of a movement that has considerable momentum and tends to overcome clerical and sacramental emphases. (See Kilian McDonnell, *Charismatic Renewal and the Churches* [New York: Seabury, 1976].)

A notably constructive approach to the charismatic movement is presented by J. I. Packer in "Theological Reflections on the Charismatic Movement." The article appeared in 1980 in two issues of *The Churchman* and was later expanded into *Keep in Step with the Spirit* (Old Tappan, N.J.: Fleming H. Revell, 1984). The whole volume, which deals with perfectionism as well as the charismatic movement, is an evenhanded study of the Holy Spirit. Portions of *A Quest for Holiness* (Wheaton, Ill.: Crossway Books, 1990) and *Rediscovering Holiness* (Ann Arbor, Mich.: Servant, 1991) by the same author are valuable contributions to the study of the Holy Spirit's work.

Between 1988 and 1992 J. Rodman Williams published a three-volume work entitled *Renewal Theology: Systematic Theology from a Charismatic Perspective* (Grand Rapids: Zondervan). This represents 1,473 pages in two columns and is a major synthesis of a theological outlook from a charismatic perspective. The author is well acquainted with Christian doctrine and holds a doctorate from Columbia University. Williams's treatment of the person and work of the Holy Spirit occupies the major part of the second volume (pp. 139-409). Williams had written other works on the Holy Spirit, but this is the most comprehensive and integrated in the structure of the Christian organism of truth.

From 1966 to 1996, many works appeared on the Holy Spirit or certain aspects of the Spirit's work. Systematic theologies have included this topic in their general presentations of the Christian faith, for example, Jürgen Moltmann (1926-), *The Spirit of Life* (Minneapolis: Fortress, 1992). The third volume of W. Pannenberg's (1928-) *Systematic Theology* relates to this topic. Other significant authors include Thomas Oden, whose third volume of systematic theology is titled *Life in the Spirit* (San Francisco: Harper, 1992); Rousas Rushdoony, *Systematic Theology*, 2 vols. (Valecito, Calif.: Ross House, 1994), and Robert Reymond, whose major work on systematic theology is soon to appear. Baptist authors have been outstanding in this field, notably Thomas Finger (2 vols., 1985-1989), J. Leo Garrett (2 vols., 1990-1995), Stanley J. Grenz (1 vol., 1995), Wayne Grudem (1 vol., 1995) and Gordon Lewis and Bruce Demarest (3 vols., 1987-1995). In this category we would of course name Millard J. Erickson, to whom this festschrift is dedicated, who dealt with the doctrine of the Holy Spirit in the third volume of his *Christian Theology* (Grand

Rapids: Baker, 1983-1985). Inasmuch as he has subsequently devoted a large volume to the doctrine of the Incarnation, *The Word Became Flesh* (Grand Rapids: Baker, 1991), I close this essay with congratulations and the hope that he may produce a work of similar magnitude on the doctrine of the Holy Spirit.

Postscript
The Holy Spirit (Downers Grove, Ill.: InterVarsity Press, 1997), a volume by Sinclair Ferguson, has appeared since this article was prepared, and I take pleasure in commending it. This is a very able exposition of the orthodox Reformed understanding. It contains a well-informed, lucid presentation of Ferguson's views and discusses alternative positions.

I need to mention also Gordon Fee's massive volume *God's Empowering Presence: The Holy Spirit in the Epistles of Paul* (Peabody, Mass.: Hendrickson, 1994). In this volume of nearly one thousand pages after a searching exegesis of 164 passages, Fee offers a synthesis of 117 pages, a select bibliography and some copious indexes.

Chapter 19

New Dimensions in Church

Boyd Hunt

....

F OR THE MOST PART, DISCUSSIONS OF THE CHURCH HAVE BEEN VERY much alive in the twentieth century,[1] stimulated first by the influence of the ecumenical movement, and then by the post-World War II multidimensional church renewal movement.[2] The voluminous literature on the subject has not given rise to any broad consensus regarding the nature, purpose and organization of the church. Change, innovation and experimentation are more the rule than the exception, which means that diligent effort to rethink the biblical foundations of the doctrine of the church remains a top priority on the theological agenda. In summarizing emerging dimensions in the ongoing effort to rethink the doctrine of the church,[3] the present study considers the following topics: biblical resources, the

---

[1]There have, of course, been pockets of neglect. For instance, Hordern observes that liberals in general had little concept of the church, since the necessity for churches was considered a practical concern, not a theological one. William E. Hordern, *A Layman's Guide to Protestant Theology,* rev. ed. (New York: Macmillan, 1968), p. 109.

   Hudson, under the heading of "Every Man's Hat His Own Church," describes shifting patterns of church order among twentieth-century American Baptists, who regarded churches as free to improvise on a pragmatic basis, quite divorced from biblical considerations. W. S. Hudson, ed., *Baptist Concepts of the Church* (Philadelphia: Judson, 1959), pp. 213-18.

[2]Patterson provides an extensive compilation of passages from the best in church renewal literature from 1952 to 1970. Bob E. Patterson, *The Stirring Giant: Renewal Forces at Work in the Modern Church* (Waco, Tex.: Word, 1971).

[3]By *new dimensions* is meant constructive insights that take cognizance of the present and yet build on the foundation of past American evangelical achievements, especially in the area of systematic theology.

multifaceted main idea of the church, the nature and mission of the church, the form of the church and the church's need for continual renewal.

Biblical Resources

Biblical teaching regarding the church includes (1) the gradual unfolding of the church idea and (2) terms that are used for the church. Most of the New Testament uses of the term *church* occur in Acts and the Epistles, so questions arise concerning the church idea in other parts of the Bible, namely, the Old Testament and the Gospels. The inestimable importance of the Old Testament is that the New Testament idea of the church is deeply rooted in the Hebrew Scriptures. According to the Old Testament, Israel is God's people, chosen not only to privilege but also to mission. The prophets looked forward to a coming great day of the Lord and a new covenant, creating the new people of God in the last days (Jer 31:31-34). Yet this Old Testament teaching, significant as it is, remained incomplete. The New Testament idea of the people of God far transcends the ethnic (Jewish), political (nation kingdom) and cultic (temple sacrifices, priestly rituals, holy days) limitations associated with the Old Testament idea of God's people.

With the coming of Jesus the new and revolutionary concept of the people of God promised in the Old Testament broke into history. Since Jesus seldom used the word *ekklēsia,* the common New Testament term for the church, some modern interpreters have questioned whether the church was actually in his intention.[4] The word *ekklēsia* occurs only three times in the Synoptic Gospels (Mt 16:18; 18:17 [twice]) and, surprisingly, not at all in John. But the idea of the church is everywhere in Jesus' teaching. He called into being a new, kingdom-of-God kind of people of God; he trained disciples; he established the practices of baptism and the Lord's Supper; he promised the Holy Spirit to guide his followers; and after his resurrection he charged his new community with the astounding global task represented by the Great Commission.[5]

The key term *ekklēsia* (from which we derive our word *ecclesiology,* the doctrine of the church), in secular Greek literature as well as in the Septuagint (the Greek translation of the Old Testament), referred to an assembly of gathered persons.

---

[4]For an earlier statement of the modern situation, see R. Newton Flew, *Jesus and His Church,* 2nd ed. (London: Epworth, 1943). More recently, with the discovery of the Dead Sea Scrolls, has come a wider acceptance of the authenticity of Jesus' use of *ekklēsia.* See Edmund P. Clowney, "The Biblical Doctrine of the Church," in *The Church in the Bible and the World,* ed. D. A. Carson (Grand Rapids: Baker, 1987), p. 16.

[5]This is not to say that prior to the resurrection and Pentecost Jesus' followers clearly understood his intention regarding the church. In fact, as late as the Jerusalem Council (Acts 15) the early Christians were still debating the necessity of circumcision for Gentile converts. Not until the ministry of Paul did the separation begin to take shape between gospel-rejecting Judaism and Christianity, together with a recognition of the identity of the church as the people of the new covenant of the last days as predicted in the Old Testament.

Employing the term in a political, nonreligious sense, the Greeks used it of an assembly of citizens of a Greek city-state who were summoned to carry on state business. Interestingly, this secular use does occur in the New Testament. Luke uses it to describe a riot of Ephesian citizens who were angered by the adverse economic effects that Paul's preaching had on the city's idol-making trade. Three times in the passage *ekklēsia* refers to this unauthorized assembly of pagan rioters (Acts 19:32,39,41). Ordinarily, however, the New Testament uses *ekklēsia* to refer to an assembly of believers.

Even though the New Testament characteristically used *ekklēsia* to refer to an assembly of believers,[6] the King James Version mysteriously translated it with the etymologically ambiguous term *church*, not *assembly*. This confusing translation obscured the notion of a gathered assembly and facilitated the shift in meaning from an assembly of God's people (the *ekklēsia* of God, 1 Cor 1:1) to the far different idea of the church that had developed in Christian history, namely, the notion of a hierarchical, clergy-centered institution.

Yet *ekklēsia* is by no means the only word used to refer to the church.[7] Terms and images abound, yet three expressions have proved to be especially significant: "the people of God" (1 Pet 2:9-10), "the body of Christ,"[8] whether referring to the local church (1 Cor 12:27) or to the church in general (Eph 1:22-23; 5:25), and "the temple of the Holy Spirit" (Phil 2:1; Eph 2:21-22). The extensiveness of the discussions of these trinitarian images witnesses to the wealth of the biblical resources regarding the nature of the church.

The Multifaceted Main Idea of the Church

If we are biblical when we think church, we think corporately—we think people. The focus of the church is on people, on *God's people*, on a living organism, not on a building, an organization or a place. As the Christian life represents the individual aspect of Christian experience, the church represents its corporate dimension.[9]

---

[6]F. J. A. Hort, *The Christian Ekklēsia* (London: Macmillan, 1897). A classic discussion of the uses of *ekklēsia* in the New Testament.

[7]Minear treats ninety-six biblical images for the church. Paul S. Minear, *Images of the Church in the New Testament* (Philadelphia: Westminster, 1960); also *The Interpreter's Dictionary of the Bible*, s.v. "Church, Idea of."

[8]This image, with its focus on the concept of one body with many members, vividly expresses the corporate nature of the church. Wrapped up in the figure is the wonder of the new oneness of humanity that God is creating redemptively through the gospel of Christ—the miracle of a new society, a new race, a new kingdom, a new Jerusalem, and (remembering the cosmic dimension of redemption) a new heaven and a new earth!

[9]Understanding the relation between these two dimensions is highly important, especially for evangelicals who insist that the individual facet of redemption takes a certain logical priority over the corporate aspect simply because in the New Testament an initial, personal, redemptive relation with Christ precedes church membership. Those who practice infant baptism usually discuss the church *before* the

Just as God in the beginning created human life with corporate as well as individual dimensions, so it is with Christian experience, but in an even profounder sense. Scripture is emphatic in teaching that God pursues his redemptive purposes by working through groups as well as individuals. The risen Christ appeared to, gave the Great Commission to and poured out his Spirit on *gathered* believers. The church, as the assembling of the saints (the word *saints* always occurs in the plural in the New Testament), is so essential that one sure way to make shipwreck of the Christian life is for believers to neglect coming together (Heb 10:24-25). God's people have only to think of the inestimable contribution other believers have made to their well-being through Bible translations, hymns, Bible commentaries and books such as *Pilgrim's Progress* to begin to recognize their immeasurable indebtedness to other believers.

Key aspects of the multifaceted nature of the main church idea take the shape of "dynamic polarities," or poles in complementary tension (both/and) rather than in opposing relation (either/or). For instance, Scripture pictures the church as *both* divine *and* human as well as *both* general *and* particular.[10]

As divine and human, the church is both a spiritual organism, created without spot or blemish by God's Spirit (Eph 5:27), and an earthly organization composed of redeemed but imperfect persons. The mystery of the church is that while it is God's creation with amazing Spirit-imparted powers of inner renewal, it is also an organization of fallible persons, persons whose relationships are marred by factions and quarreling and persons who often lack serious commitment to Christ.[11]

Christian life, thus viewing the church as the realm of redemption. See J. Robert Nelson, *The Realm of Redemption* (London: Epworth, 1951). Those who practice believer's baptism usually discuss the church *after* the Christian life, thus viewing the church as a fellowship of believers. See Ernest A. Payne, *The Fellowship of Believers* (London: Carey Kingsgate, 1952).

[10]Compare Garrett's list of eight "complementarities." See James Leo Garrett Jr., *Systematic Theology*, (Grand Rapids: Eerdmans, 1995), 2:481.

[11]The distinction between the divine and human aspects of the church sheds considerable light on an understanding of the church's mystery. It helps to explain why some who observe the church in today's world remain hopeful for its future, but others despair. Those who think of the church's human aspect are prone to speak of its waning cultural influence. In the church-despairing 1960s, for instance, Guthrie titled his chapter on the church "Living or Dead," reflecting his concern that the church was in dire trouble. S. C. Guthrie, *Christian Doctrine* (Atlanta: Knox, 1968). Those who are serious about the church's divine aspect tend to be more hopeful regarding its future. See, for instance, Dean M. Kelley, *Why Conservative Churches Are Growing: A Study in Sociology of Religion* (New York: Harper, 1972).

The distinction also helps to explain how the church can be a mixed body embracing not only believers but also unbelievers or those who join the church without a personal conversion experience (Mt 7:15-23), as well as why no outward organization can ever be immediately identified with the one, ideal church of God. God's Word stands forever in judgment over imperfect historical entities. C. C. Morrison observes that the church is the only organization that keeps on saying week after week, year after year, age after age, "We have left undone those things we ought to have done, and we have done those things we ought not to have done." Quoted by Robert M. Brown, *The Spirit of Protestantism* (New York: Oxford Unversity Press, 1961), p. 99.

As general and particular, "the church" refers to the people of God in a general sense, addressing either God's people everywhere through all time (Mt 16:18; 1 Cor 15:9; Eph 5:25) or God's people in a general region (Acts 8:1; 9:31). Ordinarily, however, the New Testament uses the term to speak of a specific congregation or a number of specific congregations, assembled or unassembled (Rom 16:16; 1 Cor 1:2; 11:16; 2 Thess 1:4).[12]

The Nature and Mission of the Church

Discussions of the nature and mission of the church often revolve around the four classical marks of the church according to the Constantinople Creed (451; popularly known as the Nicene Creed): the church is one, holy, catholic and apostolic. Until Reformation times these marks were interpreted in terms of a clerical (priestly), dogmatic, sacramental union of church and state institutionalism. Luther and Calvin reinterpreted them and added two distinctively Protestant marks: the pure preaching of the Word of God and the correct administration of baptism and the Lord's Supper (two ordinances versus the seven sacraments of medieval Catholicism). Shirley Guthrie, a Presbyterian, faults the Reformation revision on the ground that it does not take seriously the church's mission. His point is that an overly exclusive emphasis on the Protestant marks involves assuming that the church's primary function is simply to care for itself.[13] The Reformation revision might also be faulted for centering on the clergy and omitting the crucial concept of the ministry of the laity. So, in spite of the wide use of the traditional marks in discussions of the nature and mission of the church, the following restatement focuses on four recent concerns. The church is viewed as a redemptive reality, as an eschatological community, as called to holistic ministry/mission and as indispensable to the furthering of God's purpose in history.

First, the church is a redemptive reality.[14] The centrality of the redemptive motif to biblical thought is evident in the fact that the heart of the Bible is its witness to

---

[12]Unfortunately, instead of recognizing that the general and particular aspects of the church are a dynamic polarity and are thus inseparable, people sometimes oppose the two ideas to one another as though they were incompatible. Yet, in God's sight, the local church is always the representative (for better or for worse) of the general church in a particular place. In 1 Corinthians 1:2 Paul cannot think of the church at Corinth without at the same time thinking of all believers everywhere. Mind-boggling as the concept may be, in the language of the last book of the New Testament, even the least and lowliest congregation is fashioned by God's Spirit to serve as a golden lampstand in a sin-darkened world (Rev 1:12-20; compare Mt 5:14).

[13]Shirley C. Guthrie, *Christian Doctrine*, rev. ed. (Louisville, Ky.: Westminster/John Knox, 1994), pp. 363-64.

[14]Philip Yancey, suggesting that the notion of redemption has grown "fusty," nevertheless argues for its centrality. Speaking of a trilogy of ideas—the goodness of creation, the fallenness of creation and the redemption of creation—he contends that moderns err on the side of either goodness or fallenness rather than completing the cycle by seeing the world through the lens of redemption. See "The Good, the Bad, the Redeemed," *Christianity Today*, September 11, 1995, p. 96.

Christ. Only in Christ is the glory of God in all its fullness revealed (Jn 1:1-14). This is the basis for the slogan that the Bible is a book of redemption, and it is that or nothing else. Terms such as *glory, kingdom* and *covenant* do not stand alone in the biblical view but are adequately understood only in a christocentric and redemptive context.[15] To create, God but speaks and the worlds are called into being. But when God redeems, in the person of his Son, he mounts a cross, dies and rises again. Only on the cross is the divine omnipotence supremely revealed. The almighty God breaks the shackles of sin through a cross and a resurrection. Consequently, to say that the church is a redemptive reality is to charge it with the consummate presence and power of the sovereign, triune God.

To say that the church is a redemptive reality is to stress that it is the sign and agent of the kingdom of God in history. The kingdom of God is preeminently redemptive in nature. Its power is the redemptive power of the crucified and risen Christ—spiritual power, the power of the Holy Spirit—not military might, political expertise, intellectual genius or cultural achievement. Its power is the way of the cross, the way of indefatigable spiritual and moral power, never a shallow triumphalism.[16]

Finally, to say that the church is a redemptive reality is to stress that it is by definition a *voluntary* people of God.[17] Trust in Christ cannot be coerced. To be redemptive, that is, to be Christian, faith must be free, free from beginning to end, free to reflect the Spirit's vitality as a spring of water welling up (Jn 4:14; 2 Cor 3:17). Such spontaneity is a benchmark of "amazing grace." It was the mark of Jesus' sonship, "who for the joy set before him endured the cross" (Heb 12:2).

Second, the church is an eschatological community,[18] which is implicit in the

---

[15]John Walvoord, Charles Ryrie, Robert Saucy, Ken Barker, John Feinberg and others think of redemption as reductive or as too anthropocentric (forgetting its cosmic aspect?). Barker holds that most statements of a theological center are too limited (for example, promise or covenant), too broad (for example, God) or too anthropocentric (for example, redemption). Kenneth L. Barker, "The Scope and Center of Old and New Testament Theology and Hope," in *Dispensationalism, Israel and the Church*, ed. Craig A. Blaising and Darrell L. Bock (Grand Rapids: Zondervan, 1992), pp. 305-6.

[16]Boyd Hunt, *Redeemed! Eschatological Redemption and the Kingdom of God*, pt. 2, *The Kingdom Present* (Broadman & Holman, 1993), pp. 65-133, esp. pp. 78-83.

[17]Marty speaks of the American stress on voluntary Christianity as the most dramatic shift in power style on the Christian scene in our time. Over against catholicization he speaks of baptistification and concludes that for the moment, baptistification is the more aggressive in American Christianity. See Martin E. Marty, "Baptistification Takes Over," *Christianity Today*, September 2, 1983, pp. 33-36.

[18]*Eschatology* comes from two Greek words: *eschata*, "last things," and *logos*, "doctrine," the doctrine of the last things. Last things can refer to (1) the chronologically future things yet to break into human history, or, in addition to this, to (2) the part of present experience and history that abides, that is ultimate.

Grenz strongly affirms that the church is an *eschatological* community. While he holds that eschatology includes a reference to future events, he especially stresses that it provides insight into God's call to find meaning and purpose in the present. Stanley J. Grenz, *Theology for the Community of God* (Nashville: Broadman & Holman, 1994), esp. chaps. 17, 24.

basic truth that the church is a redemptive community. All of God's redemptive work, since it represents the inbreaking of the eternal (the last things) into the temporal, inevitably involves an eschatological dimension.[19] It is helpful, then, to speak of three aspects of eschatological redemption. Old Testament redemption is eschatological as the *promise* of last things. Redemption at Christ's first coming is eschatological as the *initial* inbreaking into history of the last things, the inauguration of the long-promised kingdom of God, of which the church is the sign and the agent. And finally, redemption at Christ's second coming is eschatological as the *consummation* of God's redemptive kingdom purpose in Christ, including the church in glory.

Notice, however, that the Old Testament prophets did not clearly distinguish between Christ's *two* comings, thus failing to anticipate specifically the present extended missionary interim between the two comings with its resulting long delay of the final consummation. Consequently, the three stages of eschatological redemption can be viewed as basically two: the Old Testament promise and the New Testament fulfillment, with the understanding that the New Testament fulfillment unfolds in two stages corresponding to the two comings of Christ.[20]

The significance of the eschatological dimension for an understanding of the nature and mission of the church is that it underscores the polar nature of present interim. That is, the present is both a time of unparalleled spiritual *abundance* through Christ[21] and a time of ongoing (even on occasion intensified) *conflict* between the powers of good and the powers of evil. To neglect this eschatological tension between abundance and conflict is to close the door to any adequate view of what God is doing in the world through the church. On the one hand, God continues to achieve startling victories through his people, advances that literally alter the course of history, such as the Protestant Reformation, the Evangelical Revival in England, the Great Awakening in America and the modern missions movement. On the other hand, frightful outbreaks of superhuman evil repeatedly erupt to turn the course of history backward and downward for a time. The final

---

[19]Ladd stops short of this conclusion. Instead, he distinguishes between the kingdom present as *historical* and the kingdom consummated (after the second coming) as *eschatological*. This conclusion involves a diminished appreciation of *the eschatological abundance/conflict tension* characteristic of God's redemptive work in the present, so that Ladd tends to underplay the abundance aspect of the present eschatological tension. George Eldon Ladd, "The Kingdom of God," in *Dreams, Visions and Oracles*, ed. Carl E. Armerding and W. Ward Gasque (Grand Rapids: Eerdmans, 1977), p. 141.

[20]Cullmann's analogy for the two-stage New Testament fulfillment of the Old Testament promise is the famous D-Day/V-Day analogy drawn from World War II and the Normandy landing. Although the Normandy landing represented a decisive victory for the Allies, the war raged on, delaying V-Day. Oscar Cullmann, *Christ and Time*, trans. Floyd V. Filson (Philadelphia: Westminster, 1950), p. 84.

[21]Koenig especially argues that the New Testament was written by and for people who felt themselves extraordinarily gifted by God through the Christ-Pentecost events. John Koenig, *Charismata: God's Gifts for God's People* (Philadelphia: Westminster, 1978), p. 48.

end is not yet. Always the church points beyond itself to Christ. Its perfection is in him.

Such kingdom vision, to be sure, is not easily maintained. The story of evangelicals in the first part of the twentieth century was at times the story of the loss of the vibrant eighteenth- and nineteenth-century kingdom vision reflected in the awakenings and missionary advances of the period. Snyder laments the fact that after 1890 social gospelers secularized kingdom vision and conservatives spiritualized it by emphasizing the inward and individual to the neglect of the outward and cultural. But he also contends that since World War II there have been encouraging signs of an evangelical recovery of kingdom vision.[22] This, however, is to anticipate the emphasis of the next section.

Third, the church is called to holistic ministry/mission.[23] Each word in the phrase *holistic ministry/mission* is highly significant. *Ministry* can be used as a verb or a noun. *To minister* is to serve God and others selflessly for Christ's sake,[24] which, as the doctrine of the priesthood every believer holds, is the primary calling of every believer.[25] In the nominal and ecclesiastical sense, ministry refers to *the* ministry—the office and work of the clergy.

"The Son of Man," Jesus insisted, "did not come to be ministered unto, but to minister" (see Mk 10:45). So it is with all who would be his disciples. Not only is their singular mission to minister, but Christ himself is their model for ministry.[26] To this end they are called to minister and are richly gifted for ministry by the Holy Spirit.[27] Such ministry involves the minister's total lifestyle. Ministry actions are

---

[22]Howard A. Snyder, *The Community of the King* (Downers Grove, Ill.: InterVarsity Press, 1977), pp. 21-31.

[23]*Wholistic* is sometimes spelled *holistic*. *Wholistic* emphasizes the relation of the term to the word *whole*. Stott, for instance, views the Christian mission in terms of the whole world, the whole gospel, the whole mission and the whole church. He might have included the whole person and the whole creation. John R. W. Stott, "The Biblical Scope of the Christian Mission," *Christianity Today*, January 4, 1980, p. 34.

[24]Fisher Humphreys and Philip Wise, *A Dictionary of Doctrinal Terms* (Nashville: Broadman, 1983), pp. 71-72.

[25]Though clearly presented in Scripture, the doctrine of the priesthood of every believer has come into its own mainly with the church renewal movement since World War II. The association of the doctrine with the Reformation misses the fact that the doctrine relates to ecclesiology (all believers are ministers) as well as to soteriology (all believers may approach God directly). As Snyder observes, the Reformers missed the ecclesiological idea. Howard A. Snyder, *The Problem of Wineskins: Church Structure in a Technological Age* (Downers Grove, Ill.: InterVarsity Press, 1975), p. 196, n. 20. See also Shirley C. Guthrie, *Christian Doctrine*, rev. ed. (Louisville, Ky.: Westminster/ John Knox, 1994), p. 365.

[26]Erickson points out that ministry relates especially to the church's character, not just to what it does. He cites two character attributes as being especially crucial for ministry in today's changing world: willingness to serve and adaptability. Millard J. Erickson, *Christian Theology* (Grand Rapids: Baker, 1985), 3:1067-68.

[27]An invaluable study of spiritual gifts in the church, based on the author's doctoral research at Cambridge, is Kenneth S. Hemphill, *Spiritual Gifts: Empowering the New Testament Church* (Nashville: Broadman, 1988).

not separately compartmentalized "religious" actions. They are potentially any of the actions that make up the daily lives of believers (Rom 12:1).

Ministry and mission are inseparably intertwined. No believer ministers long without a vital sense of calling and mission. And the claim to mission without ministry is idolatry. Mission is purpose, calling, task. To stress the mission of the church is to recognize that God creates his people for a task. People and purpose belong together in the church; the church exists for task as well as privilege. This is what the claim that *the church is mission* is meant to say. God's people are on mission every hour of every day.[28]

To view the church as mission is to remember that the church is the sign of the kingdom of God, the great redemptive God movement, not a mere ecclesiastical institution. The church's goal is not to build itself up but to reach out to the world in redemptive concern.

Viewed holistically, the church's *ministry* includes each of the church's essential functions: worship, nurture, evangelism and service.[29] The church's *mission* is as wide as the "all things" in Paul's assertion that God's kingdom redemptive goal is to sum up *all things* in Christ (Col 1:20; Rev 21:5). This is a breathtaking comprehensiveness that includes all of life's God-created dimensions: religious, individual, social, economic, political, cultural and cosmic.[30] "Whether you eat or drink or whatever you do," says Paul, "do it all for the glory of God" (1 Cor 10:31). Again and again believers discover new zeal in their Christian calling when they realize that their daily work is meant to be God's work and that their daily walk is itself the arena of obedience to God.[31]

The church is called to holistic ministry/mission. But who receives the call? Since the church is God's people, the mission of the church is the mission of all believers. Over against the stifling, widespread practice of active clergy/passive laity, the biblical truth is that all of God's people are called to be God's ministers. No greater challenge faces the church today than the call to close the gap between what the Bible teaches and what churches practice regarding the

---

[28]As important as Wagner's emphasis on mission as evangelism is, surely he unduly limits the idea of mission when he excludes worship, nurture and other things Christians do in obedience to God from the church's mission. How can what is done in obedience to God be other than mission? Yet his volume represents one of the ablest presentations of the wholistic emphasis. C. Peter Wagner, *Church Growth and the Whole Gospel* (San Francisco: Harper & Row, 1981), p. 93.

[29]See Boyd Hunt, *Redeemed! Eschatological Redemption and the Kingdom of God* (Nashville: Broadman & Holman, 1993), pp. 197-98 (esp. p. 197, n. 29), pp. 224-26; also pp. 102-6, on the relation of evangelism and service.

[30]The Southern Baptists' Faith and Message Statement (1963) employs a fine phrase that is rooted in nineteenth-century usage, "the great *objects* of the kingdom of God" (art. 14). The term *objects* refers to goals or ends. Articles 11-17 summarize the comprehensiveness of the objects: evangelism and missions, education, stewardship, cooperation, the social order, peace and war, religious liberty.

[31]Edwin Walhout, "The Liberal-Fundamentalist Debate," *Christianity Today*, March 1, 1963, p. 520.

holistic ministry/mission of all of God's people.[32]

A fourth and final characteristic of the church's nature and purpose is that the church is indispensable to the furthering of God's redemptive purpose in history. Attempts today to have Christianity without churches fly in the face of the fact that the idea of churchless Christianity is foreign to the Bible.[33] Human existence as created by God is inescapably corporate as well as individual, so that for God to work through persons is for God to work through groups, small and large, as well as through individuals. To say that the church is indispensable is simply to affirm that the God of the Bible chooses to work through human instruments in furthering his purposes.[34]

The Form of the Church

To fulfill their mission, churches require structure and order. The Bible provides few explicit details in reference to church structures,[35] but what it does give, however, turns out to be far more helpful. Church structures change as doors of opportunity around them open and close. Therefore churches need guiding principles that with the Spirit's help can be applied in a variety of situations. Instead of dictating fixed rules, God gifts people with the Word and the Spirit and permits them to discover new structures appropriate to their changing needs. How else could the redemptive purpose of growing responsible church persons be achieved? Furthermore, biblical principles provide invaluable guards against the waste generated by too hasty experimentation.

Three New Testament principles to guide churches in developing changing

---

[32]See the discussion of leadership/laity ministry roles below.

[33]Trueblood's statement that a churchless Christianity is not intrinsically absurd (since ancient Greeks and Romans, who were avidly religious, possessed nothing even similar to a church) needs to be understood in light of his claim in the same passage that the church, instead of being something added incidentally, was absolutely intrinsic to Christianity from its beginning. D. Elton Trueblood, *The Future of the Christian* (New York: Harper, 1971), pp. 20-21.

[34]To say that the church is indispensable is not, of course, to say that joining a church always involves in practice an initial conversion experience. But it is to assert their close relation. Compare the relation of faith and works. James is adamant: faith without works is dead (Jas 2:26).

Far from being wholly optional, as though a believer could flourish in the Christian life without it, church participation is similar to "a forced option" like breathing. In a sense breathing is optional—you do not have to breathe! But the alternative is, to say the least, costly!

Bloesch surely did not mean to be taken seriously when he wrote that Christ does not really need the church, that he may choose instead to work directly. Of course, that Christ could so choose is not the question. The problem is the lack of evidence that the gospel is ever spread apart from God's use of human agency. Donald G. Bloesch, *Crumbling Foundations* (Grand Rapids: Eerdmans, 1984), p. 126.

[35]Even with reference to such basic matters as deacons and pastors, the New Testament makes no direct reference to the noun *deacon* until Philippians 1:1, and no direct reference to *pastor, bishop* or *elder* until Acts 11:30.

church forms, principles that reflect the central christological-redemptive theme of Scripture, are (1) *the Christological principle:* Jesus Christ is Lord of the church, (2) *the organic principle:* church forms grow out of the church's nature, and (3) *the voluntary principle:* order and freedom complement each other in the church. The christological principle is the strongest argument for congregational polity: because Christ is the Lord of the church, congregations must be free to go to him directly without any necessary interposition of hierarchical structures such as bishops and synods. The organic principle requires that the church's redemptive and spiritual nature take precedence over organizational concerns: programs exist for people, not the reverse. The voluntary principle says that personal freedom is to be exercised in an orderly and responsible manner, neither neglecting the principles nor stifling the leading of God's Spirit.

The decisive New Testament grouping of God's people is the local church.[36] God's people group in various ways, and every gathering in Jesus' name has something of a "churchly" nature.[37] As invaluable as each grouping can be in its own setting, in the long run the well-being of the kingdom of God in the world is inextricably linked to the well-being of local churches.[38]

Local churches are accessible, meeting where their members live; they meet every Lord's Day when this is at all practicable; they often bridge gaps between generations, races, economies and cultures, providing a diversity not afforded by small groups[39] as well as structures that are more personal and more flexible than general bodies, which extend over large areas and assemble less frequently. For these and other reasons local churches offer the most effective setting for the implementation of the church's four basic functions, for the meaningful observance of the ordinances of baptism and the Lord's Supper, and for the exercise of church discipline.

---

[36] A local church is a group of God's people established after the New Testament pattern that thrives and replicates.

For the megachurch idea, see Millard J. Erickson, *Where Is Theology Going?* (Grand Rapids: Baker, 1994), pp. 42-51.

[37] While their "churchly" nature helps to explain the vitality of some parachurch groups, their lack of identity as local churches helps to explain their frequent temporariness and their usual limited, single-ministry focus.

[38] After noting the neglect of the local church by the lay academy movement that flourished in Europe after World War II, Edge asks how they hoped to make any continuing impact on the world without a base from which the people of God could invade the world, a place of continuing fellowship where those who are "coming alive" can be taught and equipped. Findley B. Edge, *The Greening of the Church* (Waco, Tex.: Word, 1971), pp. 17-18.

[39] In recent years interest in the role of small groups has burgeoned into a small-group movement. See Findley B. Edge, *The Greening of the Church* (Waco, Tex.: Word, 1971).

With reference to the Sunday school's use of small groups, some writers are severely critical of the Sunday school (see Edge, *Greening,* pp. 44, 126, 162), although others speak most favorably of it (see Lavonn D. Brown, *The Life of the Church,* Layman's Library of Christian Doctrine 13 [Nashville: Broadman, 1987], pp. 26, 147.

The local church suggests the New Testament affinity for a congregational form of church polity. Although it is often said that the New Testament reflects no particular type of church polity, Erickson is nearer the truth when he concludes that the congregational form of church government most nearly fulfills the principles laid down in the New Testament.[40] Supporting Erickson's conclusion is the biblical focus on such matters as the local use of *ekklēsia,* the priesthood of every believer, the direct access of every believer (and congregation) to God, the importance of each member of the body and the ministry of the laity as the foundational ministry of the church.

The importance of the local church is also implicit in the view of the church as a theological democracy. The church is a democracy under Christ, meaning that in the church the lordship of Christ confronts the self-interest of believers. Furthermore, the practice of congregationalism in the New Testament leaves room for the exercise of leadership roles and spiritual gifts as well as for collaborative efforts among congregations. Along with a sense of congregational autonomy goes a keen sense of congregational interdependence.

Second, in summarizing a theology of church form, the matters of leadership and laity ministry roles are crucial. Kenneth Hemphill, in an illuminating chapter titled "An Early Look at Ministry Structure," considers 1 Thessalonians 5:12-22. He finds significance in this passage since it is from one of Paul's earliest letters and it addresses the critical *ongoing aspect* of leadership roles in the local church.[41] Paul is concerned that members of the community recognize leaders who labor selflessly in their midst and thus are worthy of esteem. Exegetes such as Hemphill, without denying the presence of some development, see set-apart leaders as essential to the structure of New Testament congregations from the beginning, over against critics who claim that the Pastoral Epistles are second-century documents reflecting an official episcopal type of ministry structure that evolved from an earlier informal, charismatic type. How could there have been any effective building "on the foundation of the apostles and prophets, with Christ Jesus himself as the chief cornerstone" (Eph 2:20; compare Acts 2:42) without gifted leaders?

New Testament leadership roles reflect both an unfolding pattern and a notable flexibility. With regard to pattern, leadership roles are both general and local. General roles include apostles, prophets, evangelists and teachers. Local roles include especially pastors and deacons. In regard to flexibility in leadership roles, the New Testament pictures types of roles and freedom to modify these types rather than rigid, unchanging functions. Just as general leadership roles overlap, with no unvarying lines clearly separating the activities of apostles, prophets, evangelists and

---

[40]Millard J. Erickson, *Christian Theology* (Grand Rapids: Baker, 1985), 3:1086.

[41]Kenneth S. Hemphill, *Spiritual Gifts: Empowering the New Testament Church* (Nashville: Broadman, 1988), pp. 18, 25-30.

teachers from one another, so also local leadership roles remain open to change as new needs arise. This recognition of apostle-type and pastor-type roles not only facilitates understanding the emergence of new leadership roles in New Testament churches but also legitimizes the further development of new roles today.[42]

The pattern and flexibility that pertain to leadership roles apply also to ordination practices. As a setting apart, ordination involves a public commitment both on the part of the one ordained and on the part of those who do the ordaining. Because not all leadership roles involve the same degree of public commitment, congregational practices of ordination inevitably vary.[43] The primary concern, as in all congregational practices, is that everything be done in a fitting and orderly way (1 Cor 14:40).

The ministry role of the laity has been thoroughly examined in recent discussions of the church and its ministry.[44] Following World War II, church renewal leaders suddenly awakened to the extent to which secularism had penetrated modern culture. They began to realize how insulated from society the churches had become. They recognized that if churches were to penetrate the world as first-century churches penetrated it, laypersons would need to abandon their spectator role and become aggressively involved in witness to the marketplace. Thus pastors would need to become enablers of the laity in ministry (Eph 4:12).

For more than forty years now this doctrine of the ministry of the laity has been widely proclaimed. Recognizing, however, that proclamation is not practice, Edge says that we are in danger of talking the ministry of the laity to death.[45] Nonetheless he is aware that there have been significant breakthroughs. Laity in greater numbers have become involved in ministry, and reports of creative new ways of ministry continue to multiply. Undeniably, these successes amount to something of a revolution in the churches' understanding of their ministry.

A third topic in summarizing a theology of church structure is the need to structure the church's basic functions of worship, nurture, evangelism and service.[46] These functions embrace the total life of God's people. They gather and they scatter. As they gather, they worship and are nurtured; as they scatter, they evangelize and

---

[42]Humphreys, addressing the issue of the appropriateness today of ministerial roles not existing in New Testament times, argues effectively for legitimate development. Fisher Humphreys, "Ordination and the Church," in *The People of God*, ed. Paul Basden and David S. Dockery (Nashville: Broadman, 1991), p. 293.

[43]Humphreys refers to a variety of concepts related to setting leaders apart, such as ordained, installed, licensed, inducted, inaugurated, investiture, appointed, commissioned, graduated and certified. Fisher Humphreys, "Ordination in the Church," in *The People of God: Essays on the Believers' Church*, ed. Paul Basden and David S. Dockery (Nashville: Broadman, 1991), p. 296.

[44]See the final paragraph in the above discussion of the church's calling to wholistic ministry/mission.

[45]Findley B. Edge, *The Doctrine of the Laity* (Nashville: Convention, 1985), p. 10.

[46]See note 29.

serve. Again, the church is always on mission.

The basic functions do not change. They were the functions of the New Testament churches, and they will be the functions of the churches that exist when Christ returns. To be sure, as cultures change, the functions require new forms in order to maintain effective expression.[47] Yet congregations remain under a biblical mandate to maximize every effort to actualize each of the functions in their life and work.

The church's primary function is to worship (Mt 22:37). Everything God's people are called to be and to do grows out of their worship—their right relation to God, to others, to self and to the material order. If worship is not what it ought to be, the other functions cannot be adequately sustained. Without worship God's people soon grow weary in well doing. And since people's personal relation to God in redemption takes logical priority over material and temporal needs, evangelism exercises a certain priority over service (Mt 16:26).[48]

Although it is possible in these ways to speak of priorities among the functions, *none of the functions is expendable or secondary in importance.* When God's people, majoring on their God-given functions, are convinced that the church's business is God's business, their spirit and attitude improve markedly. But when a church neglects its basic purposes and focuses instead on worldly standards of success, as evidenced by an inordinate concern with budgets, buildings and bodies, its people become disenchanted, easily succumbing to the tragic delusion that the church is nonessential.

Fourth, a theology of church form includes evaluating the legitimacy of denominational divisions. American churches today find themselves in a time of transition as they reassess the future of denominations.[49] Some writers condemn denominationalism as sinful,[50] but others recognize that oneness in Christ can be compatible with responsible denominational existence and cite several reasons.

First, denominational diversity can provide a valuable system of checks and balances among God's people that would not be possible in a one-church situation.[51]

---

[47]Seeking to avoid renewal efforts that are no more than shallow emotional responses to new situations, Young suggests a number of helpful guiding principles. Doyle L. Young, *New Life for Your Church: A Renewal Handbook for Pastors* (Grand Rapids: Baker, 1989).

[48]The *logical* priority of evangelism over service is not necessarily a *chronological* priority. Feeding a starving person, for example, takes chronological priority over withholding food until efforts in personal evangelism have been pursued.

[49]Erickson attributes a perceived decline in denominationalism today in part to society's trend toward decentralization, including a stress on decision making at the local level and the individualism of baby boomers. Millard J. Erickson, *Where Is Theology Going?* (Grand Rapids: Baker, 1994), pp. 34, 42.

[50]Guthrie calls for churches to acknowledge the sinfulness of their denominational divisions. Shirley C. Guthrie, *Christian Doctrine*, rev. ed. (Louisville, Ky.: Westminster/John Knox, 1994), p. 361.

[51]For instance, see Martin E. Marty, "The Frightful, Beneficial Mess of American Religion," *The Christian Century*, December 14, 1988, pp. 1150-52. Marty concludes, "Two cheers, at least, for our frightful mess."

Where, for instance, would Christendom in general be today without the insights of peace-loving Quakers? While Christian unity is from God, so is Christian diversity. Second, denominational differences are often substantive. For instance, the Baptist insistence on religious liberty, which was once an occasion for persecution, is now generally affirmed by churches in the United States. Third, Christianity appears to thrive more where there is a diversity of denominations than where there is a single prevailing church.[52] To acknowledge that Christianity has experienced its greatest expansion in the last four hundred years, the era of greatest denominational fragmentation, is not to place a premium on division at the expense of unity but simply to recognize the importance of both diversity and unity. Fourth, the oneness of believers in Christ is something far more basic than anything that can be achieved by merging significantly differing denominational identities. Neither interdenominationalism nor nondenominationalism gives any evidence of providing a surer path to spiritual vitality and maturity than accountable denominationalism.

For reasons such as these, few serious Christians today are anxious for denominational divisions to disappear. At the same time many voices are being raised in gratitude for every indication of decreasing acrimony and increasing civility in discussions of denominational differences.

A fifth, a theology of church form includes the theme of religious liberty. Vital to the church as a redemptive reality is the voluntary nature of Christian response. When it is applied to church-state relations, this voluntariness translates into the revolutionary idea of a free church in a free state, or the doctrine of religious liberty.[53] Especially sensitive in contemporary discussions of church/state relations are issues pertaining to the nature of American civil religion, such as prayer in public schools, the legislation of personal morality and the idea of America as a Christian nation. As difficult to implement as religious liberty is in such situations, the voluntary principle at its heart insists that values must be freely appropriated if they are to be significant. Meaning cannot be coerced. Liberty of conscience, therefore, is a supremely superior social value simply because without it other values cannot be *freely* appropriated.

Observing that separation into denominations is often as beneficicial as it is inevitable, Trueblood contends that membership in a worthy tradition is the most powerful single stimulus in Christian behavior. D. Elton Trueblood, *Foundations for Reconstruction* (New York: Harper, 1946), pp. 53-55, 57.

[52]John Macquarrie, *Christian Unity and Christian Diversity* (Philadelphia: Westminster, 1975), pp. 16-17.

[53]Underscoring the fact that the Bible does not absolutize the separation of church and state, Estep speaks of their *institutional* separation. William R. Estep Jr., "Church and State," in *The People of God: Essays on the Believers' Church,* ed. Paul A. Basden and David S. Dockery (Nashville: Broadman, 1991), p. 274.

A key consideration is that both church and state are ordained by God and are answerable to God. The idea of a free church in a free state is simply a recognition of the fact that religious liberty inescapably involves civil liberty; without civil liberty there can be no religious liberty.

The Church's Need for Continuing Renewal

The subject of renewal has dominated discussions of the doctrine of the church since World War II. It is also the church's foremost perennial need, since today's renewed church may well become tomorrow's defeated, discouraged church. It represents an ongoing necessity, not something that can be achieved once and for all. Continuing renewal is the impossible possibility that makes church life forever challenging and exciting.

Continuing renewal is costly. It is not triumphalism.

Continuing renewal is the work of the Holy Spirit. *Can these dead bones live? The wind blows where it wills. You hear the sound, but you cannot tell from whence it comes or whither it goes. The water that I give becomes a spring of water welling up to eternal life.*

Continuing renewal is more overflow than ought. It is the spontaneity of the left hand not knowing what the right hand is doing. It refuses to count the cost.

Continuing renewal is full of promise and hope. It says there is always a way—always a way through the valleys of darkness and discouragement, always a way to keep on keeping on.

Chapter 20

New Dimensions
in Eschatology

Bruce A. Ware

·····························

$\mathbf{M}$Y FIRST ACQUAINTANCE WITH MILLARD J. ERICKSON CAME THROUGH
a text I read as a young, groping seminary student, *Contemporary Options in
Eschatology*.[1] It gave me my first glimpse into the writings of a man whose life and
work I have long admired, writings that are notable for their clarity, fairness,
thoroughness and scholarly competence. Since the subject of eschatology provided
my first exposure to Erickson's work, I find it fitting to contribute to this festschrift
an examination of the evangelical doctrine of eschatology at the end of the second
millennium since our Lord's first coming, specifically, (1) the ever-widening evangelical commitment to what is commonly referred to as "inaugurated eschatology"
and (2) the strenuous and controversial dialogue among evangelicals over the destiny
of the unsaved, particularly the unsaved unevangelized.

Any understanding of contemporary evangelical eschatology must recognize the
central place of inaugurated eschatology. Few concepts in eschatology in recent years
have been more influential to the whole scope of eschatological thinking than this
one. The widespread acceptance of inaugurated eschatology as a theological framework has contributed significantly to renewed discussions between covenant and
dispensational theologians that are characterized more by positive and constructive
engagement and less by the sharp and entrenched disagreement of a previous era.

Inaugurated eschatology involves two interrelated questions: (1) Is knowledge

---

[1]Millard J. Erickson, *Contemporary Options in Eschatology: A Study of the Millennium* (Grand Rapids:
Baker, 1977).

of the gospel of Christ and, hence, conscious faith in Christ necessary for salvation? and (2) What is the ultimate destiny of all the unsaved, whether or not they have heard the gospel of salvation through faith in Christ? The traditional doctrine of the eternal conscious punishment of the unsaved is being questioned and has been abandoned by some. This important topic has sparked a great deal of current interest.

I have selected these two broad areas because they represent two contrasting kinds of issues. Evangelicals have tended to come together on the subject of inaugurated eschatology, but they seem to be witnessing increasing polarization on the subject of the destiny of the unevangelized. Why? It seems to me that fundamental methodological issues account for both the agreement on the first issue and the disagreement on the second issue. Thus the reader is encouraged to consider not only the issues discussed in the following pages but also the question of what is behind the movement toward greater agreement on the one hand and greater disagreement on the other.

Inaugurated Eschatology

George Eldon Ladd must be credited with developing and defending the concept of inaugurated eschatology within an evangelical theological community that gave him sharply contrasting reviews.[2] Although Ladd is a premillennialist, he received his strongest support from members of the amillennial community, whose commitment to covenant theology allowed them to embrace more readily the notion of the one unified kingdom of God, present now in part while awaiting complete fulfillment in the age to come. If there is one covenant of grace spanning the history of fallen and redeemed humankind, it stands to reason that God's kingdom or rule, while always and only one unified kingdom, may be manifest in various partial expressions leading up to its ultimate eschatological realization.

Ladd's sharpest criticism came from some of his premillennial colleagues, whose dispensational commitments render it highly problematic to conceive of the *one* kingdom of God present now while its prophesied political, national, geographical and soteriological dimensions seem absent and hence unfulfilled. Given a dispensational framework, in which God administers his relations with his people appropriate to the dispensation in which they live, talk of the presence of the kingdom, which kingdom has as its focus Messiah's physical and earthly reign over the redeemed nation of Israel, seems inappropriate and clearly at odds with a literal understanding of such messianic prophecy.

For Ladd and his followers, inaugurated eschatology, or "the presence of the

---

[2]For example, George Eldon Ladd, *Crucial Questions About the Kingdom of God* (Grand Rapids: Eerdmans, 1952); *The Presence of the Future* (Grand Rapids: Eerdmans, 1974); *A Theology of the New Testament* (Grand Rapids: Eerdmans, 1974).

future,"[3] is derived from New Testament teaching on the simultaneous present and future aspects of the kingdom of God. Jesus, for example, rebuked the unbelieving Pharisees (Mt 12) for rejecting him as a satanically empowered exorcist, reasoning that "if I drive out demons by the Spirit of God, then the kingdom of God has come upon you" (Mt 12:28). Clearly Jesus is making the audacious claim that the long-awaited kingdom of God's righteousness, justice, peace and victory over all sin and evil is here, and it is here in Jesus—the Spirit-anointed Messiah.

But Jesus understood the presence of the kingdom to be partial, not whole. As Jesus stood to read in the synagogue of his hometown, Nazareth, on the sabbath, the scroll of Isaiah was handed him. He found Isaiah 61:1-2 and read, then announcing that "today this scripture is fulfilled in your hearing" (Lk 4:21). What Jesus did *not* quote and what was *not*, by implication, fulfilled as yet is also significant. Jesus read through the statement "to proclaim the year of the LORD's favor" but stopped short of reading the following phrase, "and the day of vengeance of our God." It seems clear, then, that Jesus saw his coming as the fulfillment part of what was promised in the Old Testament regarding the future coming kingdom of God, while implying that certain other aspects awaited future fulfillment. Jesus came to save the world, not judge it (Jn 3:17). Nevertheless, all judgment has been given to the Son to be exercised in an hour yet to come (Jn 5:22-29). Jesus' incarnation, life, teachings, miracles, death and resurrection all proclaim that this is the favorable year of the Lord's gracious salvation. The day of God's vengeance awaits Christ's return. The kingdom of future glory and power both is here and is yet to come.

Second, when Jesus is asked by disciples of John the Baptist, imprisoned for rebuking Herod (see Mt 14:3-5), whether he is in fact the long-awaited Messiah, Jesus responds, "Go back and report to John what you hear and see: The blind receive sight, the lame walk, those who have leprosy are cured, the deaf hear, the dead are raised, and the good news is preached to the poor" (Mt 11:4-5). John, the righteous forerunner of Messiah, certainly expected the true Messiah to accomplish what numerous Old Testament prophecies had announced—peace for God's people, the end of evil's tyranny and God's triumph over corruption, injustice and sin of every kind (for example, Is 42:1-4, Ezek 37:24-28 and especially Mal 3:1-6, where John's own role as the messenger announcing the Lord's coming is followed by a description of the Lord as a refiner's fire and a fuller's soap). Given these promises and their clear connection with the coming of Messiah, John is puzzled over whether Jesus is this Messiah. John sits in prison wondering about the justice, the peace, the righteous refining of society and the triumph of God over sin and evil.

Jesus responds to John's query by stringing together several other Old Testament

---

[3]See, for example, Ladd, *The Presence of the Future.*

promises also connected with Messiah's coming—the blind see, the deaf hear, the dead are raised. How is this a response to John's question? Is it not that Jesus implicitly instructs John to distinguish different aspects of promised kingdom reality, some of which are fulfilled now (hence, Jesus is truly God's Messiah), and some of which, by implication, await future fulfillment? If so, Jesus teaches us all through his response to John that the nature of God's kingdom is one in which its promised future power and glory are both here in part while they await complete and final fulfillment.

The force of this conception of inaugurated eschatology became increasingly apparent to those in the broad evangelical community, including dispensationalists who at first rejected it. The particular problem faced by dispensationalism arises from its commitment to maintaining a sharp distinction between Israel and the church. Kingdom promises made to Israel cannot be fulfilled, even in partial and preliminary ways, in the church. As dispensationalists began to give serious consideration to ways in which promises made to Israel might have their fulfillment both in this (church) age and in the one to come, they realized that a literal fulfillment of those promises to Israel might be maintained. The future restored Israel remains the ultimate target toward which they are directed, yet God mercifully widens the scope of the recipients of the promise to include those of the faith of Abraham (those who believe in Christ) who receive certain of the benefits of these promises in an inaugurated fashion.

Shifts have occurred within dispensationalism in order to accommodate an inaugurated eschatology.[4] The earlier dispensational commitment to a sharp distinction between Israel and the church had led to a two new-covenants theory. Since the new covenant of Jeremiah 31 was explicitly made with Israel (Jer 31:31) and since the church was not Israel, the church's new covenant, spoken of in 2 Corinthians 3 and Hebrews 6-8, must refer to a different new covenant. Faced with serious exegetical objections to their view, dispensationalists sought to reformulate their understanding both of the new covenant and of the broader question of Israel's relation to the church.

The model of covenant theology, in which the promises to Israel are absorbed by the church, remained unacceptable. Dispensationalists' commitment to a literal hermeneutic required them to allow Old Testament promises made to Israel to be what a plain and normal reading of them would suggest—promises of covenant blessings to the ethnic and national people of Israel, in their land and ruled by their Messiah in an age of peace and justice. How could they honor the intended

---

[4]For an extended discussion of a modified dispensational treatment of the new covenant, see Bruce A. Ware, "The New Covenant and the People(s) of God," in *Dispensationalism, Israel and the Church: The Search for Definition,* ed. Craig A. Blaising and Darrell L. Bock (Grand Rapids: Zondervan, 1992), pp. 68-97.

meanings of those kingdom promises to Israel under the new covenant and also honor the New Testament application of that kingdom and its new covenant to the church? Inaugurated eschatology steps into the breach with a new, modified version of dispensationalism commonly known as "progressive dispensationalism."[5] It avoids the either/or approaches of earlier covenant and dispensational theologies that *either* the church in this age fulfills the kingdom and covenant promises made to Israel (as proposed by covenant theology) *or* that the restored millennial nation of Israel—not the church—fulfills those same promises (as proposed by dispensational theology). Those promises are fulfilled *both* in the church *and* in a future restored Israel. The new covenant applies rightly to the church even as it awaits its full and final realization in the nation of Israel, which God will yet save and over which the Messiah will yet reign. The kingdom has come, yet it awaits coming; the new covenant has been inaugurated, yet it awaits its complete fulfillment, particularly with the nation of Israel with which it was made.

This shift in dispensational eschatology, particularly in relation to Israel and the church, has resulted in a closer and more congenial discussion with covenant theologians, most of whom share a commitment to inaugurated eschatology. Disagreements remain, to be sure. The issue of whether we should expect a future for national, ethnic Israel in their land, saved by God in a great national conversion with Christ the Messiah reigning over Israel and the nations from his throne in Jerusalem—on this there is still disagreement. But what is heartening is that a basic eschatological framework established by inaugurated eschatology is now widely shared by these two theological traditions. Our disagreements have more to do with the specific manner in which aspects of the already and not yet find their fulfillment than with fundamentally different schemes of eschatology viewed more holistically.

Destiny of the Unevangelized

The issue of the destiny of the unevangelized is one of the most significant and difficult facing evangelicalism at the close of the twentieth century. The rise of religious pluralism and a corresponding tolerance toward divergent theological and religious perspectives put pressure on evangelicalism to reexamine its position on the destiny of those who stand apart from saving grace and, in particular, outside a knowledge of the gospel of salvation by faith through the death and resurrection of Jesus Christ. The question of the destiny of the unevangelized actually involves many issues, which may be expressed in terms of two questions: (1) Is knowledge of the gospel of Christ, as well as conscious faith in Jesus Christ, necessary for salvation? and (2) What destiny do the unsaved face? In particular, what is the

---

[5]See especially Craig A. Blaising and Darrell L. Bock, *Progressive Dispensationalism* (Wheaton, Ill.: Victor Books, 1993), and Robert L. Saucy, *The Case for Progressive Dispensationalism: The Interface Between Dispensational and Non-dispensational Theology* (Grand Rapids: Zondervan, 1993).

destiny of the unsaved unevangelized?

Is knowledge of and faith in the gospel of Jesus Christ necessary for salvation? This question is eliciting a major and growing response within evangelicalism as it seeks to sort out its commitment to the supremacy of Christ in a global religious community. This issue involves two separate questions. First, Is Jesus Christ the eternal Son of God who became incarnate in order that by his death and resurrection *alone* sinners might be saved and reconciled to their Creator God? The second question concerns the application of the benefits of Christ's saving work to the lives of individual sinful humans: Is knowledge of the gospel of Christ's death and resurrection followed by saving faith in Christ alone necessary for salvation?

Three main positions offer answers to these two questions.[6] Pluralism, as represented most notably by John Hick,[7] answers no to both. Jesus Christ, along with other major world religious figures, presents finite and human insight into the common quest for God. All paths lead to the same destination, and the path through Christ is simply one among many. Thus knowledge of and faith in the gospel of Christ are not necessary for salvation. Various religious traditions present equally valid but culturally relative religious truth, and salvation may come through many different paths.

Inclusivism, as represented by evangelicals such as J. N. D. Anderson, John Sanders and Clark Pinnock,[8] answer yes to the first question and no to the second. These evangelicals are wholly committed to the traditional Christian conviction that Jesus is the only Savior, that the salvation of any and all who are saved is based solely on the redeeming work of Christ through his death and resurrection. But when asked whether people must hear and believe in the gospel of Jesus Christ to be saved, inclusivists argue that some people may be saved apart from knowledge

---

[6]Some very fine works describing and assessing these views are being produced by evangelicals, for example, Harold A. Netland, *Dissonant Voices: Religious Pluralism and the Question of Truth* (Grand Rapids: Eerdmans, 1991); Daniel B. Clendenin, *Many Gods, Many Lords: Christianity Encounters World Religions* (Grand Rapids: Baker, 1995); Dennis L. Okholm and Timothy R. Phillips, eds., *More Than One Way? Four Views on Salvation in a Pluralistic World* (Grand Rapids: Zondervan, 1995); John Sanders, ed., *What About Those Who Have Never Heard? Three Views on the Destiny of the Unevangelized* (Downers Grove, Ill.: InterVarsity Press, 1995); Millard J. Erickson, *How Shall They Be Saved? The Destiny of Those Who Do Not Hear of Jesus* (Grand Rapids: Baker, forthcoming).

[7]For example, John Hick, *Disputed Questions in Theology and the Philosophy of Religion* (New Haven, Conn.: Yale University Press, 1993); John Hick, *Problems of Religious Pluralism* (New York: St. Martin's, 1985); John Hick, *God Has Many Names* (London: Macmillan, 1980); John Hick, "A Pluralist View," in *More Than One Way?* pp. 27-59; John Hick and Paul Knitter, eds., *The Myth of Christian Uniqueness* (Maryknoll, N.Y.: Orbis, 1987).

[8]For example, J. N. D. Anderson, *Christianity and World Religions* (Downers Grove, Ill.: InterVarsity Press, 1984); John Sanders, *No Other Name: An Investigation into the Destiny of the Unevangelized* (Grand Rapids: Eerdmans, 1992); Clark Pinnock, *A Wideness in God's Mercy: The Finality of Jesus Christ in a World of Religions* (Grand Rapids: Zondervan, 1992); Clark Pinnock, "An Inclusivist View," in *More Than One Way?* pp. 93-123.

of the gospel through revelation of God's grace and love mediated through his creation or in some cases through other religions. Millard Erickson has taken a position on this issue that places him most closely to the inclusivist view. He holds that God *may* save some apart from knowledge of the Christian gospel, yet he is doubtful that many (perhaps none) will be so saved.[9] At the other end of the spectrum, Clark Pinnock is very hopeful that the wideness of God's mercy will be extended to many who have never heard of Christ but will be saved, nonetheless, by this unknown to them but sole Savior of sinful humans.

Exclusivism, as represented by evangelicals such as Ronald Nash, John Piper, Douglas Geivett and Gary Phillips,[10] answer yes to both questions. They agree with the inclusivists that Christ's atoning work is the only basis for salvation. But contrary to both inclusivism and pluralism, they hold that sinners may receive the benefits of that atoning death only by knowing and consciously believing in Christ, who died and was raised for their salvation. This view is offensive both to the broader pluralistic communities of faiths (in ways inclusivism escapes) and to many evangelicals who consider the implications of this view intolerable (over half of the world's population have not heard of Christ and thus are without hope). Nevertheless, exclusivists are persuaded that Scripture itself, rightly understood, requires this admittedly difficult position. Proposing that salvation may be gained any way other than through conscious faith in Christ is dangerously misleading and morally intolerable. People's well-being is not served by abandoning the truth, even when that truth seems harsh.

For evangelicals, the ultimate question is simply, What does Scripture teach regarding the salvation and destiny of the unevangelized? Evangelicals from Martin Luther on have accepted and defended the clear teaching of Scripture, despite the consequences. Evangelicals need to recommit themselves to earnest endeavors to understand what God has revealed on this question. When we differ, may we all resolve to continue searching the Scriptures in order to discern their true teaching. Clearly, additional exegetical work and theological reflection must be done on many key passages that relate directly to this issue. May the search continue, and may the evangelical movement display its heartfelt commitment to the principle of *sola scriptura*.

Second, what destiny do the unsaved face? In particular, what is the destiny of

---

[9]Millard J. Erickson, "Hope for Those Who Haven't Heard? Yes, But ..." *Evangelical Missions Quarterly* 11 (April 1975): 122-26; and *Christian Theology* (Grand Rapids: Baker, 1983), 1:172-73.

[10]For example, Ronald H. Nash, *Is Jesus the Only Savior?* (Grand Rapids: Zondervan, 1994); John Piper, *Let the Nations Be Glad! The Supremacy of God in Missions* (Grand Rapids: Baker, 1993), esp. chap. 4; Alister E. McGrath, "A Particularist View: A Post-Enlightenment Approach," in *More Than One Way?* pp. 149-80; R. Douglas Geivett and W. Gary Phillips, "A Particularist View: An Evidentialist Approach," in *More Than One Way?* pp. 211-45.

the unsaved unevangelized? This question has likewise elicited much recent discussion,[11] and it is apparent that variations of three main positions are being increasingly solidified. First, the traditional[12] evangelical view is being reasserted and defended despite its unpopularity among its critics. According to this view, all unsaved people, whether or not they have had opportunity to hear the gospel, are guilty before their Creator God, whose existence, character and moral will have been made known in creation and conscience. They face the certainty of God's wrath, God's judgment and eternal, conscious separation from God.[13] Theologians over the centuries have freely admitted the difficulty of this doctrine of hell as a place of everlasting, personal, conscious torment.

As unpopular as this doctrine is, church theologians have remained convinced that, in the end, it reflects clear biblical teaching. Our Lord himself clearly taught that hell consists of eternal, conscious punishment. Two factors need to be kept in mind as evangelical thinkers propose other views. First, the traditional view has been maintained over the centuries despite adverse cultural pressure, not to mention deep personal and spiritual agonizing. Its continuance as the dominant view of the church represents a strength of conviction that must be respected. When a difficult doctrine which receives severe criticism and even ridicule is nonetheless maintained over the centuries, we need to consider the cost and commitment demonstrated by those who have advanced it. Second, the final and only ultimately persuasive basis for the church's doctrine of hell as a place of eternal, conscious torment is its conviction that this represents the best and only fully defensible understanding of the biblical text. Other views, if they are to gain serious hearings among evangelicals, must deal primarily with Scripture's teaching on this subject.

---

[11]Some helpful anthologies and interactive volumes have been produced in recent years, including William V. Crockett, ed., *Four Views on Hell* (Grand Rapids: Zondervan, 1992); William V. Crockett and James G. Sigountos, eds., *Through No Fault of Their Own? The Fate of Those Who Have Never Heard* (Grand Rapids: Baker, 1991); Nigel M. de S. Cameron, ed., *Universalism and the Doctrine of Hell* (Grand Rapids: Baker, 1992); John Sanders, ed., *What About Those Who Have Never Heard?* In addition, Millard Erickson has recently published a three-part series of articles on the destiny of the unevangelized, taken from his W. H. Griffith Thomas Lectures at Dallas Theological Seminary, February 1994: Millard Erickson, "The Fate of Those Who Never Hear," *Bibliotheca Sacra* 152 (January/March 1995): 3-15; "Is There Opportunity for Salvation After Death?" *Bibliotheca Sacra* 152 (April/June 1995): 131-44; "Is Hell Forever?" *Bibliotheca Sacra* 152 (July/September 1995): 259-72. Erickson's forthcoming book on this subject offers extended discussion of the issues presented in these articles. See Millard J. Erickson, *How Shall They Be Saved?*

[12]As Harold O. J. Brown has shown, this view clearly is the traditional and dominant view of Christian theologians from the early church to the modern period. See his "Will the Lost Suffer Forever?" *Criswell Theological Review* 4, no. 2 (1990): 261-78.

[13]For example, Ajith Fernando, *Crucial Questions About Hell* (Wheaton, Ill.: Crossway, 1991); Larry Dixon, *The Other Side of the Good News: Confronting the Contemporary Challenges to Jesus' Teaching on Hell* (Wheaton, Ill.: Victor, 1992); John Blanchard, *Whatever Happened to Hell?* (Durham, U.K.: Evangelical Press, 1993).

The church's doctrine of hell has strong and convincing biblical support, strong enough to withstand the social and cultural pressures noted above. Contemporary evangelicals need to arrive at conclusions that are based on the text of Scripture, whether or not they are acceptable to any human culture.

A second view, held by several British[14] and North American[15] evangelicals, asserts that God will extinguish the lives of the unsaved in the final judgment. In the words of Edward Fudge's influential defense of this position, the divine judgment directed at the unregenerate is a "fire that consumes" their very lives. Although some advocates of this position favor the term *annihilationism* and others *conditional immortality*,[16] all agree that the unsaved cease to exist as a result of God's judgment.

While advocates of this position provide much exposition of biblical texts, their fundamental drive stems from an aversion to the possibility of an eternal hell as a place of everlasting, conscious torment. John Stott prefaces his biblical rationale for annihilationism with "Well, emotionally, I find the concept [of eternal, conscious torment] intolerable and do not understand how people can live with it without either cauterising their feelings or cracking under the strain."[17] Granted, Stott urges readers not to follow their emotions but to go where Scripture leads them. Another advocate of annihilationism, Clark Pinnock, writes:

> Let me say at the outset that I consider the concept of hell as endless torment in body and mind an outrageous doctrine, a theological and moral enormity, a bad doctrine of the tradition which needs to be changed. How can Christians possibly project a deity of such cruelty and vindictiveness whose ways include

---

[14]Most notably John R. W. Stott with David L. Edwards, *Evangelical Essentials: A Liberal-Evangelical Dialogue* (Downers Grove, Ill.: InterVarsity Press, 1988); Stephen Travis, *Christian Hope and the Future* (Downers Grove, Ill.: InterVarsity Press, 1980); Stephen Travis, *I Believe in the Second Coming of Jesus* (Grand Rapids: Eerdmans, 1982); Philip Edgcumbe Hughes, *The True Image: The Origin and Destiny of Man in Christ* (Grand Rapids: Eerdmans, 1989); John W. Wenham, *The Goodness of God* (Downers Grove, Ill.: InterVarsity Press, 1974).

[15]Most notably Edward W. Fudge, *The Fire That Consumes: The Biblical Case for Conditional Immortality*, rev. ed. (Carlisle, U.K.: Paternoster, 1994); Clark Pinnock, "The Destruction of the Finally Impenitent," *Criswell Theological Review* 4, no. 2 (1990): 243-59; Clark Pinnock, "The Conditional View," in *Four Views of Hell*, pp. 135-66.

[16]Although annihilationism and conditional immortality propose the same basic outcome for the unsaved (extinction), they do so for different reasons. Annihilationism holds that human beings, by God's created design, are immortal beings. The judgment that comes upon the unsaved consists, finally, in bringing to an end the existence of those who otherwise would have lived on eternally. Conditional immortality holds, as the term itself suggests, that eternal life (that is, immortality) is a gift of God, conditioned on the reception of salvation offered in Christ. On this view, humans by nature are mortal beings, and the gift of supernaturally endowed immortality is given only to believers. The judgment, then, consists in the outpouring of divine wrath upon the unsaved that ends their existence. For an expression of the same basic distinction of these views, see Stott (with Edwards), *Evangelical Essentials*, p. 316.

[17]Stott (with Edwards), *Evangelical Essentials*, p. 314.

inflicting everlasting torture upon his creatures, however sinful they may have been? Surely a God who would do such a thing is more nearly like Satan than like God, at least by any ordinary moral standards, and by the gospel itself.[18]
It seems undeniable that moral judgments regarding the fairness of eternal, conscious torment as punishment for sins committed in a temporal and finite context form the framework within which Scripture is interpreted and from which acceptable conclusions are drawn. As evangelicals, annihilationists affirm their commitment to Scripture as the only final and ultimate authority for faith and practice in the Christian church. Yet on emotional and moral grounds (Pinnock's "ordinary moral standards") they enter the discussion already having concluded the moral impossibility of the view that the greatest part of the church has held to be the most responsible and only fully defensible biblical view. The challenge for evangelicals is to negotiate how we will discuss our differences. What common appeal to scriptural teaching can be made when interpretations long advanced by Christian thinkers are dismissed a priori? This is one of several theological issues dividing evangelicals in which a prior moral posture taken by an advocacy group precludes a particular proposal, even a view long held by the church. Thus the discussion never has a chance to begin.

A third view on the destiny of the unsaved, with particular emphasis on the unsaved unevangelized, is sometimes called the postmortem evangelism (PME) view, or, as Gabriel Fackre prefers, the divine perseverance view.[19] This view maintains the traditional exclusivist view that Jesus' death and resurrection is the only basis for salvation and that only through faith in Christ can anyone be saved.[20] Vast numbers of people, however, never hear about Christ in this life, and many who do never understand accurately the gospel of salvation by Christ's atoning work. In the light of this, PME advocates argue, it would seem clear that God, in fairness and compassion toward lost sinners, will provide for them a postmortem presentation of the gospel ("eschatological evangelism"), giving every person opportunity to

---

[18]Pinnock, "The Destruction of the Finally Impenitent," pp. 246-47.

[19]Gabriel Fackre, "Divine Perseverance," in Sanders, ed., *What About Those Who Have Never Heard? Three Views on the Destiny of the Unevangelized,* pp. 71-95. See also Donald Bloesch, *Essentials of Evangelical Theology* (San Francisco: Harper & Row, 1978) 2:211-34; Donald Bloesch, "Descent into Hell (Hades)," in *Evangelical Dictionary of Theology,* ed. Walter Elwell (Grand Rapids: Baker, 1984), pp. 313-15; Stephen T. Davis, "Universalism, Hell and the Fate of the Ignorant," *Modern Theology* 6 (January 1990): 173-86; Stephen T. Davis, *Risen Indeed: Making Sense of the Resurrection* (Grand Rapids: Eerdmans, 1993).

[20]Not all advocates of PME embrace exclusivism on this point. A notable exception is Clark Pinnock, who holds both to inclusivism (salvation is possible for people, through God's revelation in creation and to some extent through other world religions, apart from conscious knowledge of and faith in Christ) and to postmortem evangelism (all those for whom the gospel was not clearly apprehended will be presented the gospel of Christ after death and before the final judgment). See Pinnock, *A Wideness in God's Mercy.*

turn to Christ and be saved prior to the final judgment. Biblical support for this view is given primarily from 1 Peter 3:19-4:6, plus Ephesians 4:8-9 and John 5:25.

Interestingly, both advocates and critics of the PME view admit that this section in 1 Peter is a difficult Scripture to interpret. Even so, the 1 Peter text provides the strongest support for this, given their reading of it. This being the case, is the PME view first and foremost commended by the strength of the clear teaching of Scripture? What compels its advocates to propose and defend it? As with the annihilationist proposal, moral concerns seem to drive the PME view. Though scriptural evidence is offered for the PME view, the strength of this evidence is not what supports the adoption of the view. Rather, its advocates have already precluded the possibility that the traditional view may be correct, and thus some other position must be true and needs to be proposed. The Bible is then invoked and conclusions are drawn. To the extent that prior convictions of what may or may not be true (or morally acceptable) are permitted, to that extent we run the risk of supplanting biblical authority and replacing it with some moral authority independent of the text, controlling both our interpretation of that text and the theological positions we advance.

As evangelical theological reflection and debate continue on this urgent and critical issue of the destiny of the unevangelized, there is a growing need to reexamine the presuppositions from which we interpret Scripture and develop our positions. As Rudolf Bultmann made unforgettably clear, there is no such thing as presuppositionless exegesis or theological formulation. Evangelicals have come to agree with Bultmann on this point without reservation. However, where we have clearly differed with Bultmann is over the proper use of the presuppositions of the contemporary era or of any particular culture as the filter through which the Bible is understood and its teachings are accepted or rejected. Part of the evangelical heritage stemming from the Reformation cry *sola scriptura* is a commitment not only to consider the Bible our supreme authority for faith and practice but also to commit ourselves to reshaping our presuppositions to reflect increasingly those of the Scriptures themselves, a commitment to try to understand the text as it was intended to be understood and to apply it afresh to our contemporary settings.

It is possible to continue affirming biblical authority while approaching Scripture with presuppositions shaped not by the text of Scripture but by the values and moral commitments of our cultures. The result, then, is deceptive. It has the appearance of being based on biblical teaching, but in fact what has guided both the biblical interpretation and the theological conclusion is the set of culturally formed presuppositions through which these investigations and deliberations have taken place. Apart from the importance of the issue of the destiny of the unsaved in itself, it seems to this writer that the more foundational issue of the presuppositions governing our theological formulation raised by our disagreements here is one that must be faced and addressed with great intentionality if we as evangelicals are going to move on together, despite our differences. It is one thing to differ on interpretations and overarching theological positions when we agree in principle on the methodology by which we all proceed and to which we all submit. But when the differences involve methodology itself, hope for a unity that transcends our disagreements slackens.

Conclusion

These two stimulating and challenging areas of eschatological discussion among evangelicals illustrate both the promise and the difficulty of our task. When we are able to set aside primary commitments to our systems and allow seriously for the possibility that Scripture must correct what we have long thought must be true, there is hope of coming closer together as evangelical Christians and theologians. All sides in the debate must be willing to challenge the presuppositions and commitments of their views in order to look afresh at the text of Scripture. The fact that dispensationalists and covenant theologians are in constructive dialogue today is strong testimony to the power of Scripture, as ministered by the Holy Spirit, to reshape our minds, hearts and theological commitments.

If the first issue illustrates the promise of evangelical dialogue, the second manifests one of our main areas of challenge. We must come to terms with what we are bringing to the table as we discuss among ourselves and look to Scripture for guidance. Surely, we all agree, no one can (or should) shed his or her cultural perspective. But what do we do with the values and moral commitments that make up our thinking, especially when these stand in conflict with the tradition of the church and its understanding of biblical teaching? Yes, the tradition may be wrong. But where moral bases are adduced that reject the tradition out of hand, a defense of those moral bases must be given and the case for them must be shown to be the Bible's own perspective. Nothing less will be compelling for evangelical theology. May God grant evangelical theologians the grace to remain faithful to the inerrant Word in the face of strong cultural pressures to compromise. Wherever this requires change in our systems and wherever this demands the fortitude to stand firm, may God's Word lead us to our conclusions.

Chapter 21

New Dimensions in Church & Culture

God in European Society & the End of the Twentieth Century

Wolfhart Pannenberg
Translated by Mark Railey

....

EUROPEAN CHRISTIANITY AT THE END OF THE TWENTIETH CENTURY finds itself in a situation that differs dramatically from the situation at the beginning of the century. Despite the many countercurrents swirling around the turn of the century, the Christian foundation for society, at least in the public's eye, remained solidly anchored in Western culture. People anticipated that the new century would include a complete and global missionary diffusion of Christianity blended with Western civilization. Contrary to their hopes, the Europe of today has become a mission field for other religions. In European cultural consciousness, Christianity is a thing of the past. Few Europeans expect a future society based on a foundation of Christian belief, and yet they continue to expect Christians to contribute toward a philanthropic and benevolent moral. Clearly, Europeans are not concerned with the condition of the Christian faith.

Faith and Culture

What is the reason for the increasing distance between Christian faith and public culture? This question is not easy to answer. Both of the great wars of the century, especially World War I, have undoubtedly played an important role in this distancing. After World War II, particularly in Germany, there arose a temporarily renewed interest in the Christian foundation of our cultural tradition. Since the end of the sixties, however, a renewed and deepened sense of alienation from Christianity has displaced that earlier interest.

The years of the Second Vatican Council and the period immediately following were probably both a zenith and a turning point for society. It was a period of intensive expectation, not only for the renewal of Roman Catholicism but also for changes throughout Christendom, particularly the impending sectarian division and the renaissance of its cultural meaning. In the seventies these expectations within the public consciousness led to disappointment in that nothing seemed to change in relation to the church. Demands for cultural-political change stepped into the foreground, particularly an emancipation from perceived definitive Christian values. Since then, the national media seem to have focused greatly on perceived pretenses within the churches. They find neither the Christian faith nor Christian theology as being of national interest. This seems unfair and works against the interests of the cultural identity of our Western society. Those concerned with the future of Western culture should take a stronger interest in Christianity. Furthermore, it is essential that the church promote a future perspective for Christianity in its relationship to Western culture.

In many Western societies a functional shift has occurred in the principle of the neutrality of the state in regard to differences of religious opinion. Historically the constitutional principle of state neutrality vis-à-vis the diverse religious communities corresponded to the religious freedom of the individuals in the communities. From this a different question has emerged: How does the political order of a society respond to religious expression in a cultural tradition that is dependent on cultural and political order? If the neutrality of the state in regard to religious questions changes, even if it is just the issue of religious expression within the individual cultural situation, then this changes the meaning of the neutrality principle and would lead to society's becoming detached from the dominant culture's religious roots. Such a position toward the neutrality of the state in religious questions could be an expression of uncertainty concerning the security of culture and societal systems. According to Talcott Parsons, the founder of the sociological systems theory, the societal system, including the political order, depends on the cultural system, and again this has its roots in religion.

The individual citizen's strong inner sense of commitment to societal and political standards emerges from his cultural foundation within the societal system and ultimately from his religious roots. This means that the political order is not at all neutral and may oppose the dominant culture with its religious expression. The decisive value of a society and its legal system is contained within its roots. The neutrality of the state, vis-à-vis the religious sources and the religious expression of the particular culture, therefore can have in a sense only one option for detaching society from its sources, and that option is to support a *different* religious foundation in society.

Multicultural Challenges

In recent years the perception has emerged that the society of the future will be a multicultural one. I consider the term *multicultural society* to be misleading in the sense that a multicultural society suggests a multiplicity of cultural foundations within a single societal system. Throughout history more or less tolerant cultures have emerged alongside intolerant ones, and they continue to emerge. Societies that allow room for different cultures enable them to participate in societal life. The amount of participation is determined by the societal system on which the entire leading culture is dependent. The foundation as such is not multicultural. Otherwise, the unity of the societal system could not be grounded in it.

As tolerant societies receive individuals from different cultures, tolerance with respect to the care of their cultural traditions and religious expressions is empowered. In this regard, tolerance is different from the neutrality of the societal system vis-à-vis differences of religion. Tolerance accepts differences in the way people conduct themselves. Tolerance creates excellent cultures. With respect to its cultural grounding, a societal system's determinative rule decides how much room tolerance will give. This means that tolerance permits variations in conduct within its framework. This idea must be respected. What this means for the question of the religious neutrality of the state becomes clear when participants of unpopular sects or religions come into conflict with society's legal system. At this point the religious neutrality of every state inevitably ends.

Challenges of this sort are coming to the fore with the increasing number of Muslims residing in European countries. Since for orthodox Islam, no difference exists between the laws of the state and the laws of religion, life in a Western constitutional state brings with it restrictions on the Muslim's religious freedom. Living in the way of sharia leads to conflicts with the legal system of the secular state. It is clear to many constitutional lawyers that the legal system of Western democracies largely has its foundation in the Christian cultural tradition. The separation of church and state does not involve a complete separation but allows for the independence of the secular state with its legal processes. The churches or even the plurality of religious communities represent the primary outworking of the specific Christian expression in cultural consciousness. For other religions, however, this legal principle for a societal system is less effective.

The distinction between church and state in the definitive Christian cultural tradition has its foundation in a Christian eschatological awareness that realizes the ultimate form of human society in justice and peace, which is anticipated in the future kingdom of God and therefore is not held as really occurring in the present social order. The secularism of the state is the sole temporary order for the socialization of the individual, an order that remains basically improvement deficient and yet capable of improvement for the individual who does not transgress its demands and so becomes an embodiment of the societal determination of humanity. This idea, along with the Christian understanding of the secularism of governmental regulations given the incompleteness of the legal process and the consciousness of this incompleteness, is a condition for a free society. Such a distinctly secular state, however, does not carry its legitimation within itself. If that were the case, then the distinction between state and religion would be nonexistent. For example, a state religion could be founded on a concern for human rights, and tendencies to move in this direction are clearly present. Such tendencies, however, endanger the validity of human rights themselves. Human rights are historically rooted in the provisional right of the individual to be protected from being dominated by the state. They are unable, therefore, to justify governmental regulation. As political authority is justified, the expression of human rights reveals mainly the provisional nature of the societal order.

It is thus self-evident that the modern pluralistic society is more dependent on Christian preconditions than a "multicultural" society. Social stability and permanence require the modern society to express outwardly its awareness of Christian preconditions—its cultural basis—because society cannot legitimate itself without changing its fundamental character. The modern pluralistic society that orders itself as a secular democracy exposes itself to considerable imperilments, which result in a chronic legitimation deficit. This legitimation deficit is a consequence of the removal of society's Christian basis, through which the difference between church and state and the present political order has its justification and therefore also its legitimation.

The Church and Secular Society

The continued granting of independence to and justification for the social order by society's definitive Christian roots confronts the church with a question: What is the church's relationship to the secular society and its political order? A couple of significant points, through which are manifested the increasing detaching of the Christian expression in tradition through the last decades, may be presented out of the perspective that in Germany in the last decades social changes have occurred in certain ways.

First, the public school system continues to provide information about Christianity and its importance for Western culture, specifically German national culture. A religion lesson that is regulated by the churches cannot sufficiently facilitate knowledge about the Christian foundation of our culture. Society should have an independent interest in facilitating knowledge about the foundations of its leading cultural tradition. Knowledge about the role Christianity has played in this cultural tradition should not be limited to individual religious confessions, for this knowledge is not irrelevant for those confessions to which none of the Christian churches belong. As such knowledge needs to be transmitted within the cultural tradition, so also with the religious confession to which the maturing individual is personally bound. The failure of the facilitation of rudimentary foundational knowledge about Christianity and its importance for our culture has spread ignorance concerning these topics. Such ignorance when bound to the climate of emancipation easily creates within Western societies prejudices against Christianity.

Second, legislation in regard to marriage and family and deviant forms of sexual behavior has promoted separation between the values of society and the Christian tradition. Germany changed its divorce procedure, replacing the determination of the guilt of one or the other (or both) partners with a morally neutral principle of "no fault" as justification for the breakup of the marriage. As the public began to openly sanction annulment, moral disapproval dissolved. In time pornography, homosexuality and abortion came to be accepted. Today cohabitation has the same status as marriage, even for homosexuals. The sense of the importance of marriage as a standard for fellowship between genders is in decline. And marriage as a definitive relationship for rearing future generations is also in decline. This trend has particularly great repercussions for the church and its relationship to the state and society because according to the separation of state and religious education, the family has become the locus of religious socialization. Christianity's social impact will deteriorate as the family disintegrates, since the Christian understanding of marriage is rooted in it.

Third, the deteriorating status of Christian values in our cultural tradition is apparent in the acceptance of abortion, with its lowered regard for the sanctity of human life. The same problem surfaces with the deregulation of euthanasia, as an individual apparently incapable of making a decision would be placed under the authority of a family member or a doctor in regard to life-and-death decisions.

Christianity views the individual as made in the image of God. This view supports the sanctity of human life. To what extent can Christian churches in a secular Western society continue to promote Christianity's traditional view of the individual? To the extent that the churches and the social order share a common foundation in the Christian heritage. If this common foundation fades, the churches must be renewed. A Christian lifestyle is the best witness to an alienated society— for we are strangers in a strange land. As in ancient Rome, Christians pray for the preservation of law and peace in this world. They also concern themselves with building a positive relationship with society as well as with the renewal of the mission to an unbelieving world.

The process of European unification has presented a challenge to the churches, particularly the Roman Catholic Church. This challenge can be met only as Christian churches practice ecumenical cooperation among uniting nations. The political unification of Europe must include an understanding of the common cultural heritage, since it requires external economic collaboration and a new consciousness that is not offended by the differences between national cultures. The unification of Europe can find its foundation within the consciousness of the peoples of Europe only when prejudice regarding diversity of expression is wiped out. This common European national cultural heritage is conclusively established within Christianity. The ancient roots of our cultural tradition have been conveyed within European national cultures through the Christian formation of conscious-ness. The variations of their national cultures require Europeans to address their common cultural heritage when they unite through the bond of Christian tradition.

How Christianity can serve as a unifying force is admittedly not obvious in light of the existence of church divisions, which have persisted throughout European history, including the division between the Christian West and the Byzantine tradition of the Orthodox Church of the East as well as the Reformation and the Counter-Reformation. The schism between the West and the Byzantine East partly resulted from the defensive wars that the East has had to wage against Islam. Because the Christian West has left the East in a bind repeatedly, the East harbors an understandable distrust of the West.

The consequences of the church divisions of the sixteenth century have been more severe for the West. The sectarian wars that lasted until about 1650 played a crucial role in alienating Western culture. The warring denominations and all of Christendom contributed equally. Because of the difficulty in reconciling the confessional parties during the seventeenth century, the restoration of social peace is now only possible on a neutral foundation. This understanding of human nature has become foundational for the modern structural dynamic of European society. Thus the secularism of the modern European is a direct result of divisions in the Western church.

But a divided Christianity cannot convert the secular European. The ecumenical movement of our century points the way by which the European people can be reunified with Christianity. The Roman Catholic Church assumes falsely that it alone can call back the nations of Europe to an effective new consciousness of the church's Christian roots in history and culture. In today's Europe, the voice of Rome, when it speaks for itself without considering others, is easily heard as a manifestation of sectarian particularism that inspires anxious fears of claims for Roman supremacy. Modern European ideals of freedom, at least as far as its Christian roots have extended, have come out of Protestantism, not the Roman Catholic tradition.

Not until the Second Vatican Council did the Roman Catholic Church attempt to overcome its aloofness toward the modern European, at least verbally. A statement needs to be made, and it can only be accomplished through courageous steps in the direction of establishing an ecumenical community between the churches of the Reformation and the Roman Catholic Church. Unfortunately, recent years have not seen a conclusive breakthrough in the ecumenical movement, especially between Rome and Reformation churches. Not once have sixteenth-century pronouncements of mutual condemnation been recanted. Without renewed fellowship among the churches, the reasons that led to the sectarian wars of the sixteenth and seventeenth centuries have not been laid to rest. A mere amelioration of the ecumenical climate between the churches is not sufficient to change the basic situation. Only with the Christian churches together can the people of Europe remember their Christian origin as the reconciling bond of their cultural tradition. Such a memory can only have a reconciling effect when the wounds of confessional division are healed. The essential theological clarifications that support this view are widely followed today. One must, however, be willing to accept the consequences of this. Only through the renewing of the Christian ecclesial community can Christendom claim a fresh relevance for the consciousness of the unification of European culture over the diversity of national cultures.

Outlook for the Future

The future of the European people and their culture is not clear. Islamic populations are increasing throughout Europe. The distance between Christianity and Western culture may continue to grow. Such a future perspective appears threatening to me not so much for the churches as for the identity of European culture and for the survival of an independent Western society. The church must maintain its own identity. Above all, this concerns an awareness of faith and of the form of the faith well grounded in the way of life. The present social movement forces both kinds of churches into a sharper demarcation from their social context. Declining membership would not be a catastrophe for the churches as much as for a secular society that has separated itself from its religious ancestry. God becomes exclusively a private matter of one's individual faith orientation. The long-term consequence of such a trend may be an increase in anarchy. Today there is already a tendency toward this direction in that the principle of the self-realization of the individual is becoming ever more a central privilege for the secular societies of the West. Deferring to ethical norms and the rights of others is becoming a thing of the past. Tolerance will therefore become increasingly the supreme virtue in community life.

The courage to be tolerant is laudable. But this form of courage may be a function of indifference rather than tolerance, since the notion of tolerance presupposes the validity of norms, and in the present pluralistic society these always become uncertain. Thus the danger of a movement toward anarchy arises first within the ethical consciousness and then follows within societal conduct. Anarchy can only lead to a dictatorial form of government and must be avoided. It is high time that the relationship between society and religion be treated in public discussion with new sensitivity and as an issue that concerns all of society, not just the churches.

Meanwhile, Europe must become sensitive to the growing presence of Islam, possibly through action like that preached by Islamic missionaries who say that only Islam can save the people of Europe from secularism. Or, if we are to avoid this, Europe must remember that the foundation of its culture and social order rests in Christianity.

Chapter 22

New Dimensions in Spirituality & Christian Living

Bruce A. Demarest
·····························

I SALUTE MILLARD ERICKSON FOR HIS OUTSTANDING CONTRIBUTIONS to the cause of Christ and his church throughout a long and distinguished career. The example of his life, his commitment to Christian orthodoxy and the breadth and depth of his scholarship in theology and ethics reflected in numerous publications is of extraordinary value. The church has been greatly enriched by his faithful labors on behalf of the kingdom. The following essay on spirituality seeks to honor the faithful balance he has struck between the scholarly and the practical dimensions of Christian theology.

Introduction

Study of Scripture, cultivation of piety and dedicated service should unite in a seamless garment of personal devotion. Evangelical scholars have been productive in the theological disciplines, and many rank-and-file believers are involved in service and outreach. The integration of head and hands into the disciplines of the heart, however, remains an unfinished task for today's children of the Reformation. A recent study of two dozen evangelicals who left the church found that while most were active in church programs, many were starving spiritually.[1] A competent doctor of ministries student recently said to me, "Toward the end of seminary my spiritual

---

[1]William D. Hendricks, *Exit Interviews: Revealing Stories of Why People Are Leaving the Church* (Chicago: Moody Press, 1993).

life reached an all-time low. Seminary had put my prayer life in remission, and my first church nearly killed it altogether." Catholic seminaries offer well-defined curricula in spiritual formation and direction, and Catholic universities offer doctor's degrees in these disciplines. But until recently evangelicals had carved no place for spiritual formation in their taxonomy of disciplines, prompting Richard Lovelace to conclude that "spirituality is in many ways treated as the neglected stepchild of the Christian movement. It is often reduced to an emotional frosting spread over the surface of other parts of Christianity which are considered more substantial and important."[2]

The Murdock Charitable Trust (1994) surveyed more than eight hundred laypersons, pastors and seminary professors concerning their five priorities in pastoral training. Seminary educators identified these as (1) theological knowledge, (2) character, (3) leadership skills, (4) communication skills and (5) counseling skills.[3] Pastors placed spirituality in fourth place in their list of priorities, whereas seminary professors failed to include it at all. Few would argue that many professing biblical Christians are weak on the inner life. A. W. Tozer, a self-taught man who learned much from older Christian mystics, wrote:

> The simplicity which is in Christ is rarely found among us. In its stead are programs, methods, organizations and a world of nervous activities which occupy time and attention but can never satisfy the longing of the heart. The shallowness of our inner experience, the hollowness of our worship, and that sterile imitation of the world which marks our promotional methods all testify that we, in our day, know God only imperfectly, and the peace of God scarcely at all.[4]

More recently, McGrath has observed:

> Evangelicalism, particularly American evangelicalism, is failing the modern church. Evangelicals have done a superb job of evangelizing people, bringing them to a saving knowledge of Jesus Christ as Savior and Lord, but they are failing to provide believers with approaches to living that keep them going and growing in spiritual relationship with him.[5]

Interest in spirituality has mounted in our day, attested by the publication of many

---

[2]Richard F. Lovelace, *Dynamics of Spiritual Life* (Downers Grove, Ill.: InterVarsity Press, 1979), p. 12.

[3]"Re-engineering the Seminary," *Christianity Today*, October 24, 1994, p. 75. Walter L. Liefeld, "Spiritual Formation and Theological Education," in *Alive to God*, ed. J. I. Packer and Loren Wilkinson (Downers Grove, Ill.: InterVarsity Press, 1992), p. 245, comments, "Programs of spiritual formation are not as common in Protestant seminaries [as in Catholic seminaries]. The evangelical Protestant seminary does not welcome easily an emphasis on spiritual formation, nor, by and large, has it ever done so.... Cognitive instruction is thought of as the province of the seminary, with spiritual formation happening implicitly and informally." Fortunately, some evangelical seminaries are redressing this imbalance.

[4]A. W. Tozer, *The Pursuit of God* (Camp Hill, Penn.: Christian Publications, 1982), pp. 17-18.

[5]Alister E. McGrath, *Spirituality in an Age of Change* (Grand Rapids: Zondervan, 1994), p. 9.

treatises on spirituality from Christian, Jewish, Eastern monist and psychological perspectives.[6] We define Christian spirituality as the communion with God in which we, individually and corporately, live in response to the gracious work of the Spirit. The Reformers preferred the terms *piety* and *godly conversation.*[7] Christian spirituality includes, at a minimum, knowledge of biblical truth, communion with the triune God and service to a needy world. Evangelicals should not reject the term *mysticism,* which is defined as the believer's direct intuition or experience of God in the heart. The term has been so understood by many Christians, including John of the Cross, Teresa of Avila, the author of the *Cloud of Unknowing,* Thomas à Kempis, Bernard of Clairvaux and the Puritans. We reject as sub-Christian the speculative mysticism of Pseudo-Dionysius (about 500) and Meister Eckhardt (died 1327), who sought rapprochement between Neoplatonism and Christianity. Programs of spiritual revitalization must be conducted within the framework of historic Christian orthodoxy.

The Evangelical Consensus

Inspired Scripture is the primary guide to the spiritual life. The broad designation "Reformed" signifies belief and conduct reformed by the Word of God. The inspired Word is the principal instrument by which God makes himself known for salvation and growth. Biblical study and meditation facilitate the cognitive, affective and behavioral life of the growing Christian. Peter wrote, "Like newborn babies, crave pure spiritual milk, so that by it you may grow up in your salvation" (1 Pet 2:2). In the divine economy, Word precedes Spirit. Religious traditions that diminish the role of the enscripturated Word consign their adherents to a truncated spirituality.

The sine qua non of authentic spirituality is personal conversion. Persons enter into new spiritual life by faith in Jesus Christ as Savior and Lord. Salvation and growth in grace are achieved by faith, not by the mustering of our noblest human resources. A genuine spirituality begins with renouncing sinful ways and placing faith in the Savior. As Reformers, Puritans, Pietists and evangelicals insist, the first step toward authentic spirituality is that radical transformation of life known as the new birth.

Evangelicals further uphold the centrality of private and corporate prayer. Prayers of confession, praise, petition and intercession represent the lifeblood of Christian spirituality. Confession cleanses the heart of stains that impede fellowship with a holy God (Ps 32:5; 1 Jn 1:9). Praise and thanksgiving glorify God and refresh

---

[6]Note particularly the series Classics of Western Spirituality, ed. R. Payne, 86 vols. (New York: Paulist, 1978-). Also Cheslyn Jones, Geoffrey Wainwright and Edward Yarnold, eds., *The Study of Spirituality* (New York: Oxford University Press, 1986).

[7]John Calvin (*Institutes of the Christian Religion* 1.2.1) wrote, "I call 'piety' that reverence joined with love of God which the knowledge of his benefits induces."

the soul of the offerer (Ps 148; Heb 2:12). Petition implores God for personal needs (Mt 26:39-42; 2 Cor 12:7-9), and intercession beseeches God for the welfare of others (Ex 32:11-13; 2 Tim 1:3). Intercessory prayer enhances knowledge of God (Eph 1:17), increases love among the saints (1 Thess 3:12), fortifies believers against temptations (Mt 26:41), heals the sick (Jas 5:15) and advances the gospel (Col 4:3-4). Calvin devoted one of the longest chapters of the *Institutes of the Christian Religion* to an investigation of prayer. Every spiritual awakening has been preceded by fervent, believing prayer.

Evangelical spirituality likewise embraces the task of world evangelization. Following Christ's command, disciples engage the world in a life-saving mission (Jn 20:21). They take seriously Christ's command to bear the good news worldwide (Mt 28:18-20; Acts 1:8), and they present the gospel faithfully with the "offense of the cross" intact. Evangelicals have not lost their vision for evangelization in a world crowded with alternative agendas.

Finally, evangelicals have shown renewed commitment to programs of social concern, although frequently linked with a conservative political agenda. Seventeenth-century pietists withdrew from what they perceived to be a decadent society and church. Reacting against liberalism's humanistic agenda, fundamentalists earlier in this century disengaged from social concerns and focused on the salvation of the individual soul. Armed with a healthy kingdom vision, more evangelicals today labor on behalf of the indigent, the handicapped and the environment. Following Mather, Wesley, Wilberforce and others, evangelicals are making positive contributions in the areas of literacy, public health, peacemaking and social justice. A vibrant spirituality must embrace both personal renewal and social improvement.

Every Christian tradition, however, suffers from imbalances and deficiencies. We mention three deficiencies of evangelical spirituality. First, some evangelical spirituality suffers from the scourge of *intellectualism*, which holds that the heart can be satisfied by right thinking about God. Excessive rationalization puts God in a box and forfeits nourishing engagement with the divine Reality. Waltke observes that for some evangelicals their "spiritual life is brain deep rather than life deep."[8] Theological seminaries are vulnerable at this point, attested by the fact that some students struggle to maintain their walk with Christ. Calvin urged the need to bring head knowledge of God down to the heart. After receiving Christ, "it now remains to pour into the heart itself what the mind has absorbed. For the Word of God is not received by faith if it flits about in the top of the brain, but when it takes root in the depth of the heart that it may be an invisible defense to withstand and drive off all the stratagems of temptation."[9] Formal truth is

---

[8]Bruce Waltke, "Evangelical Spirituality: A Biblical Scholar's Perspective," *Journal of the Evangelical Theological Society* 31, no. 1 (March 1988): 16.
[9]Calvin *Institutes* 3.2.36.

necessary but not sufficient for spiritual health and vitality.

Second, evangelical spirituality suffers from the legacy of *legalism*, which teaches that mature spirituality results from following a set of rules. Some churches preach grace but practice works; they proclaim forgiveness but make people in the pew feel guilty. Embodying many strengths, the Puritans nevertheless fostered legalism by forbidding cosmetics, jewelry, dancing and theater attendance. Finney even banned coffee and tea. Carnell noted that "fundamentalists defend the gospel, to be sure, but they sometimes act as if the gospel read, 'Believe in the Lord Jesus Christ, don't smoke, don't go to the movies, and above all don't use the RSV—and you will be saved.' "[10] A pastor who was raised in a legalistic environment confided that God did not love him and, indeed, was against him rather than for him. Many Christians go through life spiritually crippled by the false message that they please God by fulfilling the letter of human regulations. McGrath calls this residual legalism "the dark side of Evangelicalism."[11]

Third, evangelical spirituality suffers from unhealthy *reactive postures*. The Puritans opposed the use of written prayers in public worship, notwithstanding the fact that when we sing the psalms we recite written prayers back to God. Owen held that liturgies stifle the work of the Spirit and engender false worship. Some evangelicals today take a dim view of charismatic brothers and sisters, many of whom gracefully exercise the Spirit's gifts. Still others claim that spiritual disciplines such as meditation and contemplative prayer are more Buddhist than Christian. The authors of *The Seduction of Christianity* inveigh against Christian psychology, claiming that it compromises the healing power of Scripture and promotes occult ideas in pseudoscientific language.[12]

While accepting *congratulatora* for our successes, we evangelicals must acknowledge the beams in our own eyes. Addressing deficiencies in evangelical spirituality, theologian John Stackhouse writes: "There is widespread discontent in North American Christianity. Many of us are being asked by churches to settle for life-support Christianity instead of thriving Christianity. We should be saying, 'Are we missing out on something?' "[13]

Contemporary Trends in Evangelical Spirituality

The Spirit of God is moving Christians to a recovery of spiritual discipline.

---

[10]Cited by George Marsden, *Reforming Fundamentalism* (Grand Rapids: Eerdmans, 1987), p. 189.

[11]Alister E. McGrath, *Evangelicalism and the Future of Christianity* (Downers Grove, Ill.: InterVarsity Press, 1995), chap. 8.

[12]Dave Hunt and T. A. McMahon, *The Seduction of Christianity* (Eugene, Ore.: Harvest House, 1985), chaps. 12-13. By the same authors, *America: The Sorcerer's New Apprentice* (Eugene, Ore.: Harvest House, 1988), chap. 8.

[13]As reported in "Toronto Blessing: Is It a Revival?" *Christianity Today*, May 15, 1995, p. 51.

Although we live in an age that rejects discipline,[14] evangelicals are rediscovering the classical spiritual disciplines. Books by Foster, Willard, Witney, Bridges and others helpfully interpret the disciplines for us today.[15] Physically, regular exercise produces healthy bodies; intellectually, mental powers develop through years of disciplined study. Likewise, spiritual maturity is a prize gained by lifelong habits (2 Pet 1:5-7; 1 Tim 4:7). Nouwen writes that "we cannot plan, organize or manipulate God; but without a careful discipline, we cannot receive him either."[16] The Christian journey is broken-field running rather than a stroll in the park, a battlefield rather than a bed of ease. Paul wrote, "I'm running hard for the finish line. I'm giving it everything I've got. No sloppy living for me! I'm staying alert and in top condition. I'm not going to get caught napping . . ." (1 Cor 9:26-27, *The Message*). The secular proverb applies to the spiritual life: "Sow an action and you reap a habit; sow a habit and you reap a character." A young man who left an evangelical megachurch testifies that the style "was too smooth for him, too slick. There was nothing hard about following Christ, nothing to work at."[17]

The exercise of spiritual discipline is not a reversion to earning merit. Howard Rice writes that "in our zeal as Reformed Christians to avoid any semblance of salvation by human works, we need to accept the fact that we have become overly negative about practices that were never intended to earn merit."[18] Private disciplines—such as quietness, contemplative prayer and journaling—and public disciplines—such as corporate worship, confession and service—constitute divinely appointed means of grace by which believers deepen friendship with God. Exercised in faith, the spiritual disciplines create an environment of availability to the Lord and an openness to his invitation for fellowship. As the psalmist wrote, "My heart says of you, 'Seek his face!' Your face, Lord, I will seek" (Ps 27:8). For both Rome and Geneva, the spiritual disciplines facilitate believers' sanctification rather than their justification.

To cite one private discipline, evangelicals are discovering the ancient Christian practice of contemplation. An evangelical comments that "meditation is the act of turning our attention from the things of the world to the things of God, but

---

[14]Albert Edward Day in *A Guide to Prayer* (Nashville: Upper Room, 1983), p. 385, writes, "We, Protestants, are an undisciplined people. Therein lies the reason for much dearth of spiritual insight and serious lack of moral power. Revolting, as we did, from the legalistic regimens of the medieval church, we have forgotten almost completely the necessity which inspired these regimens, and the faithful practices which have given to Christendom some of its noblest saints."

[15]Dallas Willard, *Spirit of the Disciplines* (San Francisco: Harper & Row, 1988), p. 68, defines the spiritual disciplines as "activities of mind and body, purposefully undertaken, to bring our personality and total being into effective cooperation with the divine order."

[16]Henri J. M. Nouwen, *Reaching Out* (Garden City, N.Y.: Doubleday, 1975), p. 89.

[17]As reported by Hendricks, *Exit Interviews*, p. 116.

[18]Howard L. Rice, *Reformed Spirituality* (Louisville, Ky.: Westminster/John Knox, 1991), p. 51.

contemplation involves turning our attention from the things of God to attend to God himself."[19] According to Richard of St. Victor, "Meditation investigates, contemplation wonders."[20] The purpose of contemplation—also called the prayer of simplicity or loving attention—is not to fashion speculative ideas about God; it is to be touched by the God who lives at the center of the believer's being (Rev 3:20). Contemplation involves practicing the presence of God with singular attentiveness; it means waiting before the Lord, listening to him and resting in his love. Like Mary in Luke 10, we devotedly sit at Jesus' feet and focus undivided attention on him.

Contemplation was widely practiced by Christians of old, including John Cassian, John of the Cross, Teresa of Ávila, Bernard of Clairvaux and Brother Lawrence. The Puritans practiced "extraordinary prayer"—distinguished from regular times of ordinary prayer—in which they fixed attention on God by repeating the name *Jesus* or a word such as *love.*[21] Evangelicals have neglected contemplative prayer by focusing primarily on verbal, audible prayer. In verbal prayer I tell God he is loved; in contemplation God tells me I am loved. Paul may have had the prayer of the heart in mind when he enjoined Christians to "pray continually" (1 Thess 5:17). The practice of contemplation is simple but not necessarily easy, for exchanging busyness and noise for quiet waiting on the Lord cuts against the grain of our hyperactive lifestyle.

As for the corporate disciplines, evangelicals today are reassessing the quality of their worship. Much evangelical worship is high on entertainment value and low on repentance for sins and adoration of the Lord. Kierkegaard observed that too often in worship the clergy and choir are the actors and the congregation is the audience. He suggested that in faithful, liturgical worship the worshipers are the actors, the worship leaders are the prompters and God is the audience.[22] James Torrance laments that much evangelical worship is superficial and ineffective:

> We sit in the pew watching the minister "doing his thing" and exhorting us "to do our thing," and go home thinking we have done our duty for another week! This kind of "do-it-yourself-with-the-help-of-the-minister" worship is what our forebears would have called "legal worship" as opposed to "evangelical" worship—what the ancient church would have described as

---

[19]R. Paul Stevens, "Poems for People Under Pressure: The Apocalypse of John and the Contemplative Life," in *Alive to God,* p. 87. Basil Pennington, *Centering Prayer* (Garden City, N.Y.: Doubleday/Image, 1980), p. 86, defines contemplation as "an opening, a response, a putting aside of all the debris that stands in the way of our being totally present to the present Lord, so that he can be present to us."

[20]Cited by Avery Brooke, "What Is Contemplation?" *Weavings* 7, no. 4 (July/August, 1992): 10. Meditation, whereby the mind reflects on biblical truths, is a necessary foundation for contemplation, where the heart focuses on God.

[21]See Rice, *Reformed Spirituality,* p. 88.

[22]See K. C. Ptomey Jr., "The Word of the People," *Weavings* 4, no. 4 (July/August 1989): 36.

"Arian" or "Pelagian," and not truly catholic.[23]
True worshipers do more than sit in the pews and take in the show. Worship involves the active service of the people, as the German word *Gottesdienst* ("service of God") indicates. The English word *liturgy* comes from the Greek noun *leitourgia* ("service," "ministry," "sacrifice," Luke 1:23; 2 Cor 9:12, Phil 2:17, 30; compare the adjective *leitourgikos*, "ministering," Heb 1:14). A root of these words is *ergon*, meaning "work." Liturgy thus is a spiritual work whereby the people of God celebrate what God has done in Christ. Liturgy includes reading Scripture, sharing in biblical responses (for example, the Magnificat, Benedictus and Nunc Dimittus), singing psalms, reciting ancient creeds, speaking prayers and celebrating the sacraments—all of which rehearse the faith of the people of God.[24] Many who have left evangelical churches relate that worship services were dull and sermons were boring. Hendricks observes, "I did not hear this as a call for more entertainment, but for more participation."[25]

Liturgy serves several valuable functions. First, it focuses on the central, rather than the trivial, aspects of the faith celebrated by Christians everywhere. The liturgy's set forms ensure that none of the essentials of worship are neglected. Second, whereas freeform worship can become individualistic, liturgy strengthens the communal dimension of worship. It provides structure and content that connect worshipers with the spiritual experience of Christians through the centuries. Third, liturgy forces us to worship and pray when we may not feel like it, thus priming the 'spiritual pump' in our often dry lives.[26] Foster comments that "liturgical prayer helps us articulate the yearnings of the heart that cry for expression."[27] Fourth, liturgy has the power to refresh believers' spirits deeply, much as a "soaker hose" applies water to the roots of plants. Far from being an obstacle to the Spirit's working, a scripturally based liturgy becomes a powerful tool of Spirit transformation.

> Liturgy is designed to penetrate past the surface level, allowing us to be available to the divine Presence in such a way that God can reach the depths of the human heart.... In the act of worship through the liturgy, we encounter a sacred structure which ultimately disciplines and forms us. Without such a spiritual formation we remain dispersed, unformed, and unmade.[28]

---

[23]James B. Torrance, "Contemplating the Trinitarian Mystery of Christ," in *Alive to God*, p. 142.
[24]For further explanation of the shape of the liturgy, see Lynn C. Bauman, "Spiritual Formation Through the Liturgy," in *The Christian Educator's Handbook on Spiritual Formation* (Wheaton, Ill.: Victor, 1994), pp. 104-6.
[25]Hendricks, *Exit Interviews*, p. 268.
[26]Eugene H. Peterson, *The Psalms as Tools for Prayer* (San Francisco: Harper & Row, 1984), p. 88, comments that "liturgy depsychologizes prayer. It removes prayer from the control of my emotions, my motivations, my physical energy, and my circumstances."
[27]Richard J. Foster, *Prayer: Finding the Heart's True Home* (San Francisco: HarperCollins, 1992), p. 107.
[28]Bauman, "Spiritual Formation Through the Liturgy," p. 104.

Jesus and the early Christians participated in the liturgy of the synagogue service (Lk 4:16), which included Scripture reading, praying the psalter (Lk 23:48) and teaching. With faithful Jews, Jesus recited twice daily the Shema of Israel (Deut 6:4; compare Mk 12:29-30) and participated in the three hours of prayer. The early church replaced the Shema with thrice daily repetition of the Lord's Prayer (*Didache* 8.2-3). The Reformers built on the structure of the Catholic liturgy found in the Mass.[29] Calvin included in his worship scheme the Kyrie Eleison ("Lord have mercy"), the Sursum Corda ("Lift up your hearts") and the Nunc Dimittus ("Dismiss us now") of the Catholic liturgy.[30] Calvin, Knox and Baxter employed fixed patterns of worship and prayer as well as spontaneous expressions. Following the Reformers, the optimal worship model may be a balance of liturgy and spontaneity—where spontaneity flows from the time-honored structure. Evangelicals may also need to achieve better balance between sermon and liturgy.

During the past two or three decades evangelicals have become more sensitive to the essential role of the Holy Spirit in Christian spirituality. A rigorously formulated theology or a carefully reasoned apologetic offers no guarantee of vital spiritual living. Evangelicals may subscribe to an impeccable theology but evidence little spiritual power in their lives, thereby becoming experiential deists.

Calvin emphasized the Spirit's essential ministry in the outworking of salvation, chiefly in regeneration and sanctification. But against "enthusiasts" who claimed to be inspired by the Spirit, the Reformers argued that the Spirit's extraordinary working ceased with the close of the apostolic age. Lovelace argues that sometimes "this failure to recognize the Holy Spirit . . . is intentional and theologically motivated, as in fundamentalist or confessional churches which are afraid that too much emphasis on conscious communion with the Holy Spirit will lead to a lessened regard for Christ, enthusiasm, mysticism or Pentecostalism."[31] In the early twentieth century Pentecostalism exceeded biblical warrant by claiming that the miraculous gifts constitute the sign attesting the postconversion experience of Spirit baptism. The Spirit-baptized Christian is said to live on a higher spiritual plane than believers lacking this second blessing. Pentecostal and charismatic churches, however, have honored the Holy Spirit and hence are among the most dynamic spiritual movements in the world today.

Careful exegesis of the major texts dealing with spiritual gifts (Rom 12:3-8; 1 Cor 12:7-11; 12:28-30; Eph 4:11-13) suggests that with the exception of the

---

[29]David G. Buttrick, "Liturgy, Reformed," in *Encyclopedia of the Reformed Faith*, ed. Donald K. McKim (Louisville, Ky.: Westminster/John Knox, 1992), p. 220, writes, "The basic movement of the Mass, from confessional rite to readings of Scripture to prayers of the faithful to eucharistic celebration, was preserved."

[30]Ibid., p. 222.

[31]Lovelace, *Dynamics of Spiritual Life*, p. 130.

office of apostle and the title of prophet,[32] Paul made no distinction between gifts that have been rescinded and gifts that are applicable to the entire church age.[33] All the gifts are valid in the present age when exercised in love (1 Cor 13:1-3). Paul wrote that "prophecies . . . will cease," "tongues . . . will be stilled" and "knowledge . . . will pass away" (v. 8). He added that "when perfection *[to teleion]* comes, the imperfect disappears" (v. 10). The context (vv. 8-12) has a strong eschatological focus. The "perfection" likely denotes the believers' exchange of immortality for mortality at the Second Advent (v. 12). " 'The perfect' means the future world, in which everything imperfect (v. 9) which distinguishes our present world is overcome."[34] Turner concludes that "the New Testament does not envisage the cessation of the prototypical gifts; on the contrary, every indication suggests that Luke and Paul expected them to continue."[35]

Evangelicals must give full weight to the Holy Spirit's gracious ministry. The exercise of the Spirit's gifts will not add new revelational content and will not be elevated above spiritual fruit (Gal 5:22-23). It will result in Christ-honoring kingdom ministry. We must petition the Father to bless us with the Holy Spirit (Lk 11:13). We must seek to "be filled with the Spirit" (Eph 5:18), to "pray in the Spirit" (Eph 6:18), to "live by the Spirit" (Gal 5:16), to show "the fruit of the Spirit" (Gal 5:22-23), to "keep in step with the Spirit" (Gal 5:25), and "not [to] put out the Spirit's fire" (1 Thess 5:19). Evangelicals must not confine the Spirit in a box but must allow the third person of the Godhead to do all that he longs to do in and through us.

The faithful exercise of the Spirit's gifts will keep orthodoxy open and connected to the transcendent in practice as well as in theory. We evangelicals must balance our propensity to cold rationality with the warm caress of the Spirit on our hearts. I witnessed a ministry of the Spirit at the Pecos Benedictine monastery charac-

---

[32]Today the word *apostle* may be used in the derivative sense of a pioneer church-planting missionary. C. Peter Wagner, *Your Spiritual Gifts* (Ventura, Calif.: Regal, 1994), pp. 181-82, 200. Wagner writes that "the gift of apostle is the special ability that God gives to certain members of the Body of Christ to assume and exercise general leadership over a number of churches with an extraordinary authority in spiritual matters that is spontaneously recognized and appreciated by those churches. . . . The gift of prophecy is the special ability that God gives to certain members of the Body of Christ to receive and communicate an immediate message of God to His people through a divinely anointed utterance."

[33]P. E. Hughes witnessed the Spirit and glossolalia firsthand and recorded his experiences in several Christian publications. Hughes concluded that "the breath of the loving God is stirring among the dry bones of the major, respectable denominations, and particularly within the Episcopal Church" (*Churchman* 76 [1962]: 131-35).

[34]R. Schippers, "Goal," in *New International Dictionary of New Testament Theology* (Grand Rapids: Zondervan, 1976), 2:62. D. A. Carson, *Showing the Spirit* (Grand Rapids: Baker, 1987), pp. 69-70, defines perfection as "the state of affairs brought about by the arrival of the parousia." So also F. F. Bruce, *I and II Corinthians*, New Century Bible Commentary (Grand Rapids: Eerdmans, 1980), p. 128; Max Turner, "Spiritual Gifts Then and Now," *Vox Evangelica* 15 (1985): 38-39.

[35]Turner, "Spiritual Gifts Then and Now," p. 41.

terized by a boldness, power and love seldom found in our churches. Spiritual gifts and graces were exercised in the community with great wisdom and sensitivity and were validated by lives of impeccable integrity. This reflects the power, joy and holy abandon that the early church must have experienced as it turned its world upside down for Christ.

A further trend in our day is hunger for direct experience of the living God. Believers often seek safe haven in theological studies, spiritual discussions or pious works. Some appear uncomfortable actually engaging the transcendent and mysterious Reality behind their God-talk. We fear that our emotions will get out of hand and we will lose control. We want to get on the right side of God, but we don't want to get too close. We need to supplement theological correctness with a transforming heart encounter with Christ. Orthodoxy and orthopraxy must be wedded to orthopathy—authentic experience of the living God in the heart.

The word *orthodoxy* comes from two Greek words meaning "right glory." Israel experienced Yahweh's glory during the Exodus (Ex 13:21-22), at Sinai (Ex 24:16-18), in the tent in the wilderness (Num 9:15-23) and in the temple (2 Chron 7:1-3). The disciples encountered the divine glory at Jesus' transfiguration (2 Pet 1:17) and ascension (Acts 1:9). Luke wrote of the early church that "everyone was filled with awe" (Acts 2:43). Paul believed that transforming encounter with the divine glory is the birthright of all God's people in the age of the Spirit: "We, who with unveiled faces all reflect the Lord's glory, are being transformed into his likeness with ever-increasing glory, which comes from the Lord, who is the Spirit" (2 Cor 3:18). Henri Nouwen articulated his passion for personal experience of the living God with the following prayer:

> Let me recognize you at the virginal point in the depth of my heart where you dwell and heal me. Let me experience you in that center of my being from which you want to teach and guide me. Let me know you as my loving brother who holds nothing—not even my worst sins—against me, but who wants to touch me in a gentle embrace.[36]

According to Hendricks, Christians who left the church lamented that they did not meet God in sermons or in the plethora of church programs. Hence they sought encounter with God outside the church's walls.[37] God will be found in solitude, contemplation and prayer rather than in frenetic activity. May we follow the lead of Augustine, Calvin and the Puritans and relate intimately to the God who engages our minds and lovingly touches our hearts. The quest for encounter with God is not self-absorption, irrationalism or mystical escapism. It is a fulfilling lived experience with the Lover of our souls. Those who fail to engage the true and living

---

[36]Henri Nouwen, *A Cry for Mercy* (Garden City, N.Y.: Doubleday, 1981), p. 24.
[37]Hendricks, *Exit Interviews*, p. 277.

God in a nourishing relation are vulnerable to transcendent experiences offered by the New Age movement and Eastern religions. Not mere head knowledge but the experience of the glory of God makes Christian people alive and whole.

Areas for Future Exploration

Spirituality may be enhanced through symbolism and the human senses. A symbol is a visible, material object that depicts an invisible, spiritual reality. By grace the imagination, focusing on God-given symbols that depict the spiritual world, draws the heart to intuitive and affective engagement with the supernatural. Symbolism and imagery in the fields of art, music and poetry take us deeper psychologically into the realm of the unconscious and deeper spiritually into the realm of God. In a July 1995 NBC special dealing with poetry, Bill Moyers noted what serious literary critics have long known, that "poetry does not so much announce truth as it reveals it." Metaphor, symbolism and imagery, as used by poets, reveal truth to the senses, whereas the reason and logic of philosophers demonstrate it to the mind. In this sense all Christians should be both poets and philosophers.

The Old Testament is filled with highly pictorial language. The image of a tree planted by streams of water (Ps 1:3; 92:12) vividly depicts the stability and prosperity of the righteous. The image of an infant nursing at its mother's breast (Is 49:15) conveys Yahweh's tender love for his covenant people. Jesus' teaching also employed rich symbolism and imagery. The Lord spoke of pouring new wine into old wineskins (Lk 5:37), building a house on a rock (6:48), lighting a lamp and placing it under a bowl (11:33), and so on. Paul represented death to sin through new birth by the water of baptism (Rom 6:4; Col 2:12) and Christ's atoning sacrifice by a broken loaf of bread and poured-out wine (1 Cor 10:16-17; 11:23-25). The Apocalypse is filled with dramatic images, such as a Lamb (Rev 5:6), a red dragon (12:3), a harlot (chap. 17), the wedding supper of the Lamb (19:9, 17) and the New Jerusalem (chap. 21).[38] Biblical imagery informs the mind, kindles the emotions and motivates the will more powerfully than propositional statements alone.

Evangelicals tend to pursue spirituality narrowly through the mind to the neglect of the senses. Overreacting to late medieval abuses, the Reformation tradition depreciated the concrete, material world and retreated into the realm of abstract ideas. Zwingli stripped the Zurich churches of ornamentation and whitewashed their walls. In order to "purify" worship, Zwingli removed the organ from the Great Minster. In Geneva Calvin eliminated physical objects, including religious art, from sanctuaries lest worshipers succumb to idolatry. The Puritans, reacting against Rome's rich symbolism expressed in architecture, art and liturgy, rejected sculptures,

---

[38]E. Schüssler Fiorenza, *Invitation to the Book of Revelation* (Garden City, N.Y.: Doubleday, 1981), p. 18, judges that "the strength of Revelation's language and images lies not in the theological argumentation or historical information but in their evocative power inviting imaginative participation."

wall paintings and clerical vestments. John Owen judged that pictorial displays in church buildings and pageantry in worship services were a great irreverence. I agree with Lovelace, who alleges that in their rejection of the visual and the symbolic

> the evangelical stream moved away from the sacramental vision of life in the Catholic tradition, in which the created world is not only celebrated as good but recognized as a constant symbolic message about spiritual reality. Evangelicals moved almost in a Manichaean direction, toward a frame of mind in which the objects of sense and sight could drag us away from what was "spiritual."[39]

God in his wisdom has willed that humans engage the invisible world through visible, material objects amenable to the five senses. God communicates spiritual reality to his image bearers through the "stuff" of the created order: sun, rain, trees, birds, sheep, incense, clay and mountains. God purposes that faith be nourished by common objects that can be seen, heard, felt, tasted and smelled.

We experience more of the world through the sense of sight than through any other faculty. The eyes perceive spiritual reality through a brightly colored banner depicting biblical scenes, a rough-hewn replica of the cross or an elegant work of religious art. Light, darkness and color transport our hearts deeper into the invisible world of the spirit. The chapel where the Pecos community and guests worship illustrates this principle. Entering the chapel, one immediately focuses on the Lord's Table, over which is hung a magnificently colored painting of the risen Christ in his ascension glory. Spotlights shining on the representation of the glorified Christ highlight its brilliance. Far from leading us away from spiritual realities, visual displays such as this powerfully draw the heart to spiritual reality. Edwards judges that

> authentic religious images have provided a vital way of training the contemplative eye and human affections and of concentrating the will. They provide an infinite subject worthy of the infinite longing within us (compared to the finite subjects of contemporary commercial and political images). . . . We need not have to choose between image and language (verbal images) . . . though. Both are needed if our means of formation are not to be impoverished.[40]

The sense of sound enriches our hearts spiritually. Ears receive grace through majestic pieces of music, such as Bach's *St. Matthew Passion*, Handel's *Messiah* or Verdi's *Requiem*. Barth sensed God's presence through the music of Mozart. The sensitive singing of a biblical psalm more often than not moves the heart in a significant spiritual experience. Similarly, grace is communicated through our sense of touch. Psychologists relate that an infant not held within two weeks of birth is damaged emotionally. Hugging is known to ease stress, lift depression and signifi-

---

[39]Lovelace, *Dynamics of Spiritual Life*, p. 345.
[40]Tilden Edwards, *Living in the Presence* (San Francisco: Harper & Row, 1987), p. 46.

cantly improve the quality of a person's life. Physical expressions of compassion were commonly employed in Israel and the church. Jacob embraced and kissed his grandsons (Gen 48:10); the prodigal hugged and kissed his father (Lk 15:20); and the Ephesian elders hugged and kissed Paul (Acts 20:37). The apostles commanded saints to share a "holy kiss" (Rom 16:16; 1 Cor 16:20; 2 Cor 13:12; 1 Thess 5:26) and a "kiss of love" (1 Pet 5:14).

The sense of smell likewise lifts believing hearts heavenward. Incense in Scripture signifies the pleasing sacrifice of Christ (2 Cor 2:14-15) and the prayers of God's people reaching to heaven (Ps 141:2; Rev 5:8; 8:3-4). Echoing biblical symbolism, Augustine wrote that "the pure prayer that ascends from a faithful heart will be like incense rising from a hallowed altar. No fragrance can be more pleasing to God than that of His own Son."[41] Liturgical worshipers testify that use of a censer in worship lifts their spirits in prayer to God. Finally, heaven's pleasures are mediated to us through our taste buds. At the Lord's Table when believers chew the bread and sip the wine, they "taste" spiritually the acceptance and peace that Christ has purchased through his death on the cross.

Sacred symbolic objects, mediated by the human senses, enhance holistic connectedness to God. Being neither Gnostics nor Manicheans, we evangelicals would be enriched by incorporating into our private devotion and corporate worship symbolic language, biblical imagery and sacred objects that communicate with our God-given senses. As we thereby give expression to our humanity, our entire beings will come alive and we will be lifted into God's glorious presence.

Bodily enactment is another area for exploration. Jesus' incarnation demonstrates that spirituality embraces the believer's entire being, including the body (Rom 12:1). The New Testament word for the propensity to sin is not *sōma* (body) but *sarx* (flesh). Whereas popular piety tends to regard the body as evil, Scripture depicts the body as an instrument of good as well as evil. Against the Gnostics, abundant life before God will involve the whole person, "spirit, soul and body" (1 Thess 5:23).

Bodily participation in symbolic actions lies at the warp and woof of Scripture. On the Day of Atonement the high priest laid hands on the scapegoat, symbolically transferring guilt to the animal, and then released it into the desert (Lev 16:20-22). Mary poured expensive perfume on Jesus' feet and wiped them with her hair (Jn 12:3). Jesus washed his disciples' feet, dried them with a towel and commanded his followers to do likewise (Jn 13:2-17). In the greatest sign/act of all, Jesus broke a loaf of bread and poured a cup of wine to depict his sacrifice for sins (Mt 26:26-29; 1 Cor 11:23-26). Apostles laid hands on missionaries (Acts 13:3), and elders anointed the sick with oil (Jas 5:14). Western evangelicals are strong in the auditory and cognitive functions. We approach spiritual truths abstractly and communicate

---

[41]Augustine *Commentary on the Psalms* 140.6.

the same by wordy discussion. Performance of a physical act, however, moves us from the abstract to the concrete more effectively than the utterance of words alone. Johnson comments that for reality to grip our beings, "it takes a physical act. When it registers physically, it also registers at the deepest levels of the psyche."[42] The old Anglican marriage vow, "With my body I thee worship," applies to one's spouse as well as to our heavenly Father.

A church I know creatively implements this principle of bodily enactment. While elders serve adult believers the Lord's Supper, the pastor invites children to the front of the sanctuary to receive grapes from a bowl. He informs the little ones that they will be served the bread and wine when they have personally trusted Jesus as Savior. But until they are old enough to make that decision, they receive the uncrushed grapes as a symbol of God's love. This physical act powerfully impacts the young boys and girls. A popular service of forgiveness and reconciliation at the Pecos monastery incorporates the same principle. Biblical instruction is given concerning the need to forgive those who have injured us. Prayer is offered for the grace to forgive and to allow God to heal. Those seeking release of grievances approach the altar, immerse their cupped hands into a bowl of water (symbolically "holding" the grievances) and then open their hands and bring them out of the water (symbolically "releasing" the grievances). Whatever faithful means we employ to put our bodies into worship will enhance the quality of our devotion.

Evangelicals need to recapture the spiritual and psychological power of biblically faithful ceremonies and rituals. One of the meanings of the Latin word behind the English word *ceremony* is "awe." "A ceremony was a way of behaving when one felt a sense of awe or stood in awe. All the set formality around a religious ceremony is an indication of the reverence and awe that people felt at one time regarding the object of the ceremony."[43] A ritual consists of a series of physical acts that express deeply held spiritual or emotional convictions. As long as the significance of the ceremony is preserved, it will not become a vehicle of superstition.

A woman I know has created a ritual to strengthen connectedness to her husband. Arriving home from work before her husband, she lights a candle to celebrate unity with her spouse. When her husband arrives, they greet one another with a kiss and blow out the candle. Simple rituals like this embody great power to cultivate positive attitudes and affections. Johnson concludes that "ritual, in its true form, is one of the most meaningful channels for our awe and sense of worship. . . . Modern people who are deprived of meaningful ritual feel a chronic sense of emptiness. They are denied contact with the great archetypes that nourish our soul life."[44]

---

[42]Robert A. Johnson, *Inner Work* (San Francisco: Harper & Row, 1986), pp. 100-101.
[43]Ibid., p. 102.
[44]Ibid.

A final area for exploration concerns the catholicity of spirituality. Spiritual renewal typically occurs in the context of trusting relationships within the Christian community. Today God's Spirit is bringing renewal to the historic Christian churches, leading many to personal faith in Christ and life in the Spirit. Christ's disciples grieve the Spirit when we hold at arm's length a brother or sister of another Christian tradition whom the Savior has accepted into his family.

We must set aside the sectarianism that eschews connectedness to the long history of Christian faith and spirituality. Two Southern Baptist authors observe that given the history of dissent in the Anabaptist tradition, Baptists and fundamentalists have been least favorable to transdenominational enrichment spiritually.[45] But they argue that in order to honor the Spirit's work among God's people,

> Baptists may more easily explore the vast resources of Christian spirituality . . . if we attempt to think of ourselves (at least experimentally) as (little c) catholic (little b) baptists. Catholic baptists are thus open, not only to be shaped by the spiritual pattern that was decisively present in the life of Jesus of Nazareth, but also to participate in the work of the Spirit that continues to be transformingly active in and through the whole church.[46]

The authors continue that we must listen carefully to the host of faithful voices from all the ages that can deepen life in the Spirit. They claim that

> our apostolic heritage cannot be reclaimed merely by returning to its origins in the English separatism of Smyth and Helwys or the Continental Anabaptism of Menno and the Brethren. The key to appropriating our heritage in a truly apostolic faith is learning to locate ourselves within the full history of the church—past and present—with all its richness and diversity.[47]

Furr and Freeman conclude:

> In this story we meet a host of faithful witnesses: martyrs and confessors, desert mothers and church fathers, scholastics and mystics, reformers and radicals, puritans and pietists. These and more are our spiritual heritage, too. They are the fount through which the apostolic spring flows.[48]

By way of illustration, we focus on what evangelicals can learn from Roman Catholics. When Catholicism has erred, it did so by appending traditions, not deleting essential doctrines. The magisterial Reformers viewed the Catholic Church as Christian but in need of reform. They valued many aspects of its spirituality, evidenced by many citations in Calvin and the Puritans from Catholic spiritual

---

[45]Gary A. Furr and Curtis W. Freeman, eds., *Ties That Bind: Life Together in the Baptist Vision* (Macon, Ga.: Smyth & Helwys, 1994).
[46]Ibid., p. 85.
[47]Ibid., pp. 93-94.
[48]Ibid., p. 94.

authorities.[49] Since Vatican II the Catholic Church in the United States has undergone significant reform. This is particularly evident in the charismatic renewal movement, where faith conversion, Bible study, devotion to Christ and evangelistic outreach are commonplace. While theological differences with Protestant evangelicals remain (chiefly concerning the nature of the church, the sacraments and Mary), evangelical emphases are mounting in the Catholic Church.[50] This trend is reflected in the 1994 document "Evangelicals and Catholics Together: The Christian Mission in the Third Millennium," signed by forty Catholic and evangelical leaders (including Charles Colson, Bill Bright, Pat Robertson, J. I. Packer, Richard Mouw, Os Guinness and Mark Noll), although sadly attacked by other evangelicals.[51]

I personally judge that Protestant evangelical theology is superior to Roman Catholic theology (although the latter varies from community to community). But in the Catholic renewal movements at least, spiritual discipline, engaging worship and consistent social voice may be superior to ours.[52] Vital spiritual life in Christ

---

[49]Lovelace, *Dynamics of Spiritual Life*, p. 302, writes, "It is also possible that the generation of Protestants following the Reformers gave up on Rome too quickly. . . . Rome has shown a surprising stability of commitment to supernatural Christianity and even a susceptibility to modern movements of Evangelical renewal such as the Charismatic movement."

[50]McGrath, *Evangelicalism and the Future of Christianity*, p. 180, predicts that in the next decade evangelicalism will become a significant force within the Catholic Church. Therefore, "at least in the short term, evangelicals would be well advised to encourage Roman Catholics to discover the vitality of evangelicalism without pressing them to leave their church."

[51]John MacArthur claims, wrongly, that "Roman Catholicism is another religion." Reported in "Evangelicals Clarify Accord with Catholics," *Christianity Today*, March 6, 1995, p. 53.

R. C. Sproul, *Faith Alone: The Evangelical Doctrine of Justification* (Grand Rapids: Baker, 1995), pp. 30, 42, 178-79, claims that Catholicism is "a non-Christian communion" and, indeed, is heretical and apostate. The differences between Rome and evangelicalism are "essential to true Christianity or to personal salvation." Sproul argues syllogistically (1) that justification by grace *alone* through faith *alone* is essential to salvation, (2) that Rome does not teach justification by grace *alone* through faith *alone*, therefore (3) a consistent Roman Catholic cannot be saved. Catholics who come to Christ do so by dissenting from official church teaching. We admit that some Catholics likely are saved in this manner, but certainly not all. Many Catholics, like a variety of other believers, come to Christ with less than a precise theology. Many in their distress cry out to Jesus, whom they believe to be the Son of God who died on the cross and rose from the grave for their sins.

A six- or seven-year-old child who gives her heart to Jesus knows nothing of the subtle interrelationship between the divine initiative in grace and the human response. Neither do most folks who in response to a gospel invitation come to the front of the church, talk briefly with the pastor and are received into membership on the spot. Luther, the great Reformational advocate of justification by faith alone, believed early on that infants are justified in baptism by the faith of sponsors and later by the nascent faith of the infant himself. Wesley and Finney viewed justification merely as the forgiveness of sins, judging that the imputation of Christ's righteousness to sinners is "fictional" and "absurd." Who doubts the salvation of these leading Protestants? Perhaps the fine distinctions Sproul highlights (with which I agree) come to be understood only after the person has received Christ and becomes familiar with the theology of the Pauline epistles.

[52]McGrath, *Evangelicalism*, p. 181, outlines five areas in which some evangelicals perceive Catholicism

may be as important in God's sight as precision on secondary and tertiary points of doctrine. Lovelace correctly suggests that "sheltered Evangelicals are surprised to find real and deep graces of Christ among many non-Evangelical Christians."[53] True believers in Christ, whatever their denominational labels, should be reconciled to one another without delay. We have much to learn from devout believers in other traditions. Furthermore, spiritual renewal and awakening have occurred when the body of Christ has been united in mutual respect, not behaving rancorously toward each other. Our Lord prayed that believers might be one "so that the world might believe" (Jn 17:22). Lovelace observes that

the great spiritual awakenings have come when both the ascetic and pentecostal models have been in force. . . . During almost every awakening Catholics and Protestants have drawn closer to one another as they are doing now, because they have been moving toward one another's partial models of spirituality to recover Scriptural balance.[54]

As we evangelicals pray about spiritual advance,

we need to listen carefully to other kinds of Christians. Mainline Protestants, Roman Catholics and Orthodox believers have preserved Biblical values that we lack. And they often have clear insights about our faults that could help us toward repentance.[55]

Our quest for spiritual renewal will be enhanced as we return, in the words of Packer, to "an historic Christian emphasis—Patristic, Medieval, Reformational, Puritan, Evangelical—with which the Protestantism that I know has largely lost touch."[56]

Concluding Reflections

Spiritual formation is an emphasis whose time has come. A staple for centuries in other Christian traditions, its influence is now being felt in evangelical circles. Evangelical seminaries are including courses of spiritual formation and guidance in their curricula. Parachurch organizations such as Young Life are providing staff with explicit training in the spiritual disciplines. Many evangelical presses—including Baker, Broadman, Crossway, Eerdmans, InterVarsity, Multnomah, NavPress, Victor, Word and Zondervan—are breaking new ground by publishing books in this

---

to be superior to their own tradition and thus appealing: (1) Catholicism's strong emphasis on the corporate Christian life; (2) its liturgy, which gives stability to public worship; (3) its strong commitment to the major doctrines of Christian orthodoxy; (4) its ministry of providing a haven for performance-oriented and burned-out Christians; and (5) its courageous stand on issues of social justice.

[53]Lovelace, *Dynamics of Spiritual Life,* p. 129.
[54]Lovelace, "Evangelical Spirituality: A Church Historian's Perspective," p. 34.
[55]Ibid., p. 35.
[56]J. I. Packer, *A Quest for Godliness: The Puritan Vision of the Christian Life* (Westchester, Ill.: Crossway, 1990), p. 13.

long-neglected field. The typical evangelical protocol has not lacked success in the cultivation of spiritual lives. But we must be honest enough to recognize blind spots and deficiencies that exist in this vital area. We also need to acknowledge imbalances in our schemes of Christian nurture. We do not always maintain the right proportions of intellect and affections, theology and experience, prayer of the lips and prayer of the heart, and structure and spontaneity in worship. Given historical conditioning, our models of devotion and formation are more or less partial and incomplete. From a biblical perspective individual believers, denominations and theological traditions "see but a poor reflection" (1 Cor 13:12).

We must continue to search the Scriptures to sharpen our perspective on the spiritual life. We must also be humble enough to learn from other Christians who have preserved values and practices that we lack. Many evangelicals are unaware of the vast spiritual treasures that lie untapped in other Christian traditions. We need to listen carefully to Christian visionaries and prophets who wear labels that differ from our own. We need to journey back into history and recapture the clear vision of the gospel, the deep passion for Christ and the joy and ecstasy owned by the early church. Leaders who connect up with their spiritual roots will encourage rank-and-file believers to go beyond the standard fare of church attendance, Bible reading and times of verbal prayer. We will encourage laypersons to explore neglected disciplines, such as solitude, fasting, contemplative prayer and journaling. We will find creative ways to employ our bodies in worship, such as liturgical dance and dramatization of biblical events. In what might become a significant paradigm shift, we ought to adopt a more incarnational and sacramental approach to the faith won by Christ. Certainly we will allow greater freedom for the working of divine Mystery in our lives and churches. We will view God less as a proposition to be scrutinized and more as a Person to be engaged in moments of loving awe and wonder.

For those who remain skeptical of the proposals presented in this essay, we encourage personal exploration through participation in programs and workshops offered by renewal communities in many parts of the country. Nothing will inform our ignorance, dissolve our prejudices and expand our horizons more than personal experience of what God is doing in our day through the Spirit. May we respond willingly and joyfully to the challenge issued in the words of the psalmist: "Taste and see that the LORD is good; happy are those who take refuge in him" (Ps 34:8). For each believer the clear goal of the spiritual quest is transformation into the image of our Lord Jesus Christ (2 Cor 3:18).

Resources for Additional Study

The church is blessed with a plethora of published materials, ancient and modern, that elucidate aspects of spirituality and Christian living. Among the most significant for evangelical readers are the following:

Foster, Richard J. *Celebration of Discipline.* Harper & Row, 1988; *Prayer: Finding the Heart's True Home.* San Francisco: HarperCollins, 1992. In the modern spiritual classic *Celebration of Discipline,* Foster interprets the fruitfulness of the inward, outward and corporate disciplines. In *Prayer: Finding the Heart's True Home* he describes the value of various prayer forms practiced by Christians throughout history that can deepen prayer experience today.

Foster, Richard J., and James B. Smith, eds. *Devotional Classics.* New York: Harper, 1993. This volume expounds important dimensions of the spiritual life from more than fifty leading writers in the field.

Hinson, E. Glenn. *Seekers After Mature Faith: A Historical Introduction to the Classics of Christian Devotion.* Dallas, Tex.: Word, 1968. In this volume Hinson examines Christian piety as practiced in several ecclesiastical traditions in various periods of church history.

Lovelace, Richard F. *Dynamics of Spiritual Life.* Downers Grove, Ill.: InterVarsity Press, 1979. Lovelace gleans valuable insights from past revivals and proposes guidelines that challenge us toward personal and corporate renewal today.

Magill, Frank, and Ian McGreal, eds. *Christian Spirituality: The Essential Guide to the Most Influential Spiritual Writings of the Christian Tradition.* New York: Harper & Row, 1988. This book comprehensively summarizes 120 spiritual classics, including information about each author and analysis of major themes.

Mulholland, Robert M., Jr. *Invitation to a Journey: A Road Map for Spiritual Formation.* Downers Grove, Ill.: InterVarsity Press, 1993. Mulholland likens the Christian life to a journey. Different personality types (as categorized by Jung) respond more readily to various spiritual regimens.

Nouwen, Henri J. M. *Making All Things New: An Invitation to the Spiritual Life.* New York: Harper & Row, 1981; *Reaching Out: The Three Movements of the Spiritual Life.* Garden City, N.Y.: Doubleday, 1975; *The Way of the Heart: Desert Spirituality and Contemporary Ministry.* New York: Harper, 1991. Read anything by this Roman Catholic clergyman, whose sensitive portrayal of the spiritual journey moves the hearts of all Christians.

Packer, J. I. *A Quest for Godliness: The Puritan Vision of the Christian Life.* Wheaton, Ill.: Crossway, 1990. Packer examines how the Puritans' pursuit of God can inform Christ-centered living today.

Peterson, Eugene H. *Answering God: The Psalms as Tools for Prayer.* San Francisco: Harper & Row, 1989; *The Contemplative Pastor: Returning to the Art of Spiritual Direction.* Dallas, Tex.: Word, 1989; *Working the Angles: The Shape of Pastoral Integrity.* Grand Rapids: Eerdmans, 1987. Peterson explores the believer's response to the movement of the Spirit vis-à-vis Christian life and ministry in these helpful books.

Tozer, A. W. *The Pursuit of God.* Camp Hill, Penn.: Christian Publications, 1982; *Keys to the Deeper Life.* Grand Rapids: Zondervan, 1984. Tozer integrates rich insights from classical spirituality into the evangelical tradition for fruitful Christian living.

Webber, Robert E. *Worship Old and New: A Biblical, Historical and Practical Introduction.* Grand Rapids: Zondervan, 1994. Webber summons evangelicals to recapture the power for renewal that is inherent in sacramental and liturgical worship.

Willard, Dallas. *The Spirit of the Disciplines: Understanding How God Changes Lives.* San Francisco: Harper & Row, 1988. Willard presents a wide-ranging exploration of the why and how of Christ-centered spiritual transformation.

Chapter 23

Christian Integrity
in a Postmodern World
(Theological Ethics)

Stanley J. Grenz

"A new command I give you: Love one another. As I have loved you,
so you must love one another. By this all ... will know that you
are my disciples, if you love one another."
JOHN 13:34-35

••••••••••••••••••••••••••

AN ACCIDENT HAS ROBBED LIEUTENANT WORF OF THE USE OF HIS LEGS.
In Klingon society, this means he is as good as dead. Therefore, in keeping with his
own cultural mores, Worf plans to end his life, and he has asked his good friend
Will Riker to assist him in the death ritual. Loath to participate in such a despicable
act, Riker has gone to the ship's captain, Jean-Luc Picard, for advice. The counsel
the good captain offers his second-in-command typifies contemporary ethical
thinking. Instead of invoking any idea of absolute right and wrong, Picard appeals
to the concept of friendship. He urges Riker to make his decision on the basis of
the fact that Worf is looking to him as a trusted friend.

We are living in a time of transition. From pop culture to academia, a new
intellectual and cultural ethos is emerging, one that now generally carries the
designation "postmodern." The central task we share as Christians is to embody the
gospel in the new postmodern context in which God has placed us. This task
demands that we think through the Christian ethic in a manner that takes seriously
the challenge of the postmodern ethos.

The Shape of the Postmodern Ethical Landscape
What exactly characterizes the postmodern ethical landscape in which God calls
us to live and minister? Two aspects of our changing intellectual context are

especially significant. We are witnessing the reemergence of public interest in ethics. This newer discussion, in turn, is resulting in the restructuring of the ethical quest toward a community-based ethic.

The reemerging public interest in ethics. By all outward appearances, the chief executive officer of the gigantic savings and loan association was a model citizen. He made generous gifts to worthwhile causes such as the work of Mother Teresa. He was an ardent crusader for social issues, opposing abortion and pornography.

Above all the CEO "cared for" his family, especially their financial needs. So prominent were his relatives on the corporation's payroll that during the 1980s the family took home some $34 million for their services. His oldest son was one such beneficiary of the CEO's position. Although a college dropout with little experience, the young man ascended to the helm of the business, enjoying annual reimbursement in the $1 million range.

The CEO's ardent conservative political loyalties did not prevent him from donating to the campaigns of those whose ideology differed from his own. One powerful liberal U.S. senator was the special beneficiary of his financial benevolence. When asked whether his generous contributions went to buy influence, he publicly replied, "I want to say in the most forceful way I can. I certainly hope so."[1]

If the 1980s were characterized by decadence and narcissism, the 1990s are turning out to be marked by an interest in ethics. People throughout our society are becoming aware of the ethical dimensions of contemporary life and are increasingly willing to speak the language of ethics. Christian moralists are not the only ones today who question the attitudes and actions of the CEO in our opening narrative. Many people who claim no connection to Christianity would label such conduct blatantly unethical.

The emergence of ethics as a concern throughout society is evidenced by front page news items that repeatedly deal with ethical problems or situations that carry ethical overtones. For example, a recent installment of *The Vancouver Sun* was awash in ethical issues. The featured stories covered elected officials receiving two pensions, whether or not a political party should nominate a self-proclaimed witch to run for public office, a scandal involving a well-known sports figure and the reflections of an AIDS patient who formerly was a pastor in a prominent conservative congregation.

Concern for ethics has also invaded the political realm. In fact, common parlance during election campaigns is the quest to gain the "ethical high ground" over one's opponents. The interest in ethics is likewise indicated by the recent inclusion of ethical aspects in public opinion polls. The November 1994 Maclean's/CTV poll of Canadians, published in the January 2, 1995, issue of *Maclean's* magazine,

---

[1]See Robert F. O'Neil and Darlene A. Pięnta, "Economic Criteria Versus Ethical Criteria: Toward Resolving a Basic Dilemma in Business," *Journal of Business Ethics* 13 (1994): 73.

included a section on ethics. Canadians were quizzed on issues ranging from cheating on exams to cheating on taxes and cheating on one's spouse. The poll's findings even brought out the moralistic sentiments of the reporter, for the article headline bemoans Canada's becoming "a nation of greedy, amoral self-promoters."

The blossoming of ethical concern is especially evident in the renewed interest in ethics as a field of inquiry. We are witnessing a renaissance of the classical study of ethics. More important, ethics has invaded a variety of academic disciplines. New specialties have grown up almost overnight. Medical ethics, business ethics, environmental ethics and legal ethics—which would have found few champions in academia a few decades ago—are not only serious endeavors but required curricular components in respected professional schools across the land. This interest, in turn, has produced new areas of specialization and new vocational opportunities. In short, these burgeoning fields have made ethics a "growth industry."

Underlying the mushrooming interest in the academic study of the ethical disciplines is a broadly based realization that ethics has gained a new sense of urgency. Wearing his prognosticator hat for the new year's weekend edition of *The Vancouver Sun*, columnist Douglas Todd joined many other voices in predicting that in the coming year public ethical discussion would "explode." This discussion, he predicted, would be fueled by the belief that our worsening situation requires concerted action: "More than four out of five North Americans believe a decline in morals is the continent's gravest problem."

Why a specifically *public* discussion? According to Todd, the old guardians of morality have lost credibility, a situation that forces us to hammer out a new ethic on our own: "Most people no longer believe a single religious institution can be the final authority on morality. So discussion of ethics will shift more to the wider, public domain." And what shape will this discussion take? Todd's answer is that "through thousands of courses, conferences, books, newspaper columns, government hearings and meetings, we'll struggle over values."[2]

Todd's remarks underscore the postmodern condition. The gravest ethical questions in the history of humankind are confronting us at a time when our society lacks any foundational moral consensus. An Anglican priest recently voiced what many people today sense. "We are bombarded with a host of problems," he said. "Every problem that comes our way has an answer that is simple, easy to understand and *wrong*."

As is illustrated in the episode of *Star Trek: The Next Generation* alluded to earlier (aptly entitled "Ethics"), there seems to be no shared fixed point of reference in the shifting seas of postmodernity from which to track our course, even if only theoretically. In view of the complexity of ethical issues and the feeling that beneath

---

[2]Douglas Todd, "What on Earth Happens Next?" *The Vancouver Sun*, December 31, 1994, p. D11.

our feet lies only sand, many people today seem to feel like Charlie Brown. The baseball game is nearly over. The comic strip character was getting ready to pitch the final "out." Then Lucy saunters to the mound. "If you strike out this last guy, Charlie Brown," she moralizes, "you're going to make him very, very unhappy." By this time, Linus has joined the party. "That's right," he agrees. "Are you sure you want to bring unexpected grief into that poor kid's life?" Faced with the burden posed by these questions, the hapless pitcher sighs, "Just what I need—ninth inning ethics."

The concern for a community-based ethic of being. Yet the recent resurgence of public interest in ethics does seem to lead somewhere. The public discussion has been paralleled by a reconsideration of the actual goal of the human ethical quest. In our day both professional and lay ethicists have grown increasingly uncomfortable with methods used by their immediate predecessors. Douglas Todd's remark "We'll struggle over values" bears witness to the nature of this transition. The renewed interest in ethical reflection has produced a reconceptualizing of the ethical task. A crucial dimension of this shift involves the move from the focus on "doing," which dominated Western ethical discourse during the modern era, to a concern for "being."[3]

Since the philosophical debates of ancient Greece, ethicists have been separated into two general camps: those who focus on what we might call an "ethic of doing" and those who elevate an "ethic of being." What divides them is their understanding of the basic goal of the ethical quest: Is ethical discourse primarily concerned with our actions—what we do—or with our character—who we are? In other words, should we focus our attention on right conduct or on the cultivation of virtue?

A way into this distinction is provided by an updated version of a question Aristotle posed in the fourth century B.C. Consider the case of a man who has lived in complete fidelity to his marriage vow for thirty years of marriage—except for one night. He was away from home on a business trip and met a woman in the bar at the hotel where he was staying. One thing led to another, and as we can well imagine, the night resulted in a sexual encounter in his hotel suite. Is this man an adulterer?

Proponents of an ethic of doing may be led to interpret the query as calling for an ethical judgment about the man's *action*. Many proponents would reformulate the question: Has the man through this act violated some ethical norm? Did his action transgress—say—the seventh commandment (Ex 20:14)? Posed in such a manner, the answer can only be yes. Other ethicists, in contrast, may follow Aristotle's own response. They interpret the question, Is the man an adulterer? as

---

[3]For examples of the turn-of-the-century focus on duty, see Henry E. Robins, *The Ethics of the Christian Life: The Science of Right Living* (Philadelphia: Griffith & Rowland, 1904); Newman Smyth, *Christian Ethics* (New York: Scribner's, 1906). Even some older works that speak of virtue in fact focus on duty. See, for example, A. D. Mattson, *Christian Ethics: The Basis and Content of the Christian Life*, rev. ed. (Rock Island, Ill.: Augustana Book Concern, 1947).

inquiring about his *character.* One act of adultery, they conclude, does not mark an otherwise faithful spouse as an adulterer. The man is a faithful husband who on one occasion acted out of character and against virtue.

The focus on "doing" has dominated Western ethical discourse during the modern era. Many contemporary ethicists today, however—as represented by secular voices such as Nel Noddings and Alasdair MacIntyre and by religious figures such as Stanley Hauerwas—no longer view the rightness or wrongness of specific actions as the central feature of the ethical task. Instead, they are concerned about character ideals—virtues—such as friendship and cooperation. Or they elevate the quest for "values" as the central ethical concern. In keeping with this shift, J. Philip Wogaman recently declared, "The question is, where do we *ultimately* get our values?" He then explained that "we do not have a basis for making ethical judgments until we can ground our conception of the good and of moral obligation on an ultimate framework of valuation."[4]

Paralleling this ethical revisioning is the advent of a new quest for spirituality. In the modern era, people expunged the remnants of the supernatural from their worldview and focused attention on the scientific method as the means to unlocking nature's secrets. In recent years, however, the children of the Enlightenment have launched a search for the key that can unlock the door to *spiritual* vitality and power. People today rush from guru to guru in an attempt to learn how to develop their own inner person. This search includes the goals of greater fortitude, higher virtue, personal character formation and enhanced relationships with others. In short, like the new ethical mood, it focuses on "being" instead of "doing."

The transition from doing to being has paralleled the philosophical shift away from the Enlightenment quest for knowledge understood as dispassionate, objective certainty. In the eighteenth century Immanuel Kant suggested that humans ask three central questions: What can I know? What should I do? What can I hope for?[5] Enlightenment ethics sought to answer the second question—the question of the ethical life—on the basis of a prior answer to the first. Thinkers today are no longer sure that this method is feasible. For a more promising alternative approach, many are looking to the third question, seeing in it a possible foundation for searching out answers to the question of ethics. Contrary to what we might expect, this proposal is not the exclusive domain of religious ethicists but is gaining adherents among secular thinkers as well.

Robert Kane provides a case in point. As a chastened secularist, Kane declares, "We simply do not know enough to ground ethics necessarily in human reason and knowledge alone; and centuries of failure in trying to do so have led many to

[4]J. Philip Wogaman, *Christian Moral Judgment* (Louisville, Ky.: Westminster/John Knox, 1989), pp. 13, 15.
[5]Immanuel Kant, *Critique of Pure Reason,* trans. Norman Kemp Smith (London: Macmillan, 1933), p. 635.

relativism, scepticism, and nihilism."[6] Kane rephrases Kant's third question to read "What should we aspire to?" in order to determine the guiding principles for a new, postmodern ethic. For his vision of the ethical life, he draws from the Latin root of the term. In that *aspiration* signifies a "going outward of the spirit," Kane proposes the image of "our spirits reaching beyond the finite perspectives we inhabit toward an objective reality and objective worth that are always only partly revealed to us."[7] He explains: "By living in certain ways, by loving and seeking excellences in our various practices and traditions, cultures and ways of life, we may 'embody the truth' in the sense of attaining objective worth, without being sure of having attained it."[8]

With the new focus on character and virtue, as well as images of aspiration, the center of ethics is shifting away from the individual actor and the quest for the one true, universal ethical theory. The new focus is on the community in the midst of which and according to the ideals of which personal character finds its reference point. In the end, the newer voices assert, ethical judgments arise from and must be articulated in accordance with the belief structures of the community in which a person lives. As Wayne Meeks remarked poignantly, "Making morals means making community."[9] Why? According to Meeks, "Individuals do not become moral agents except in the relationships, the transactions, the habits and reinforcements, the special uses of language and gesture that together constitute life in community."[10]

Thus the current restructuring of ethics pierces to the very heart of the modern "decisionist" ethic, with its focus on doing. The ethic of doing, communitarian thinkers argue, presupposed a basically Enlightenment view that understood the human person as a morally empty vessel waiting to be filled through the acts in which he or she chooses to engage. Communitarian ethicists repudiate this anthropology in favor of a community-based understanding of the moral life. They argue that personal identity and character do not first emerge as the product of choices we make as autonomous agents, but actually precede our acts. Mennonite thinker Harry Huebner states the point sharply: "When we engage in moral activity, we act on the basis of our perceptions and our beliefs. We act on the basis of who we are as social/moral beings and on the basis of the characters into which our communities/families have shaped us."[11]

---

[6]Robert Kane, *Through the Moral Maze: Searching for Absolute Values in a Pluralistic World* (New York: Paragon, 1994), p. 97.

[7]Kane, *Through the Moral Maze,* p. 98.

[8]Ibid.

[9]Wayne A. Meeks, *The Origins of Christian Morality: The First Two Centuries* (New Haven, Conn.: Yale University Press, 1993), p. 5.

[10]Meeks, *Origins of Christian Morality,* p. 8.

[11]Harry Huebner and David Schroeder, *Church as Parable: Whatever Happened to Ethics?* (Winnipeg: CMBC Publications, 1993), p. 79.

Communitarians do not deny the importance of the language of obligation. They are concerned instead that such language find its proper ground. In their thinking, obligation is not primarily connected to the individual agent or to the corollary concept of inherent individual rights. Obligation flows out of a person's presence in a community and the implications of this presence for being a person of character. Although reflecting a specifically Christian perspective, Huebner's words nevertheless articulate the more general communitarian view: "If obligation is a community matter, that is, if what we ought to do derives from the kind of people we have committed ourselves to be—the body of Christ—then what we do or do not do is not determined by the rights we and others as individuals have or do not have. Rather, our moral obligation then comes from the character of the community which we have given shaping power over us. Then what we do does not have its origin in what we can legitimately claim, but in what we have been graciously given and in turn are inspired to give."[12]

In a multicultural context, the focus on a community-based ethic leads in turn to the new ethical pluralism of the postmodern ethos. In a situation in which a multiplicity of communities exist side by side, ethical discourse becomes a discussion of the moral practices of differing communities. The underlying assumption, of course, is that what appears wrong from one vantage point, when viewed from within the community that practices the act, may actually be right.

The *Star Trek* episode noted earlier provides an especially illuminating illustration of this tendency. To Riker, Worf's proposed action constituted a reprehensible act of suicide. When Riker went to Picard for advice, however, the good captain sought to help him view the situation from Worf's perspective within the context of the Klingon community with its unique set of beliefs, mores and rituals. What appeared immoral to Riker, given his embeddedness in one particular moral community, was perfectly acceptable to the Klingon Worf.

But this community-based understanding of morality appears to lead to an impasse. Do postmodern ethicists offer any way to resolve the conflicts that would inevitably arise out of competing moral communities? Is there anything that transcends the multiplicity of social groups in our global village and can bring together people from differing communities? The *Star Trek* episode expressed one commonly presented postmodern response: "friendship." Picard appealed to Riker to remember that he was Worf's friend. Riker must do whatever act would be most in accordance with the ideal of friendship.

Douglas Todd concluded his essay by invoking a similar postmodern solution to the problem of multiculturalism. He wrote, "We'll debate everything from euthanasia to sexuality, poverty to business, in an effort to hammer out shared values that

---

[12]Huebner and Schroeder, *Church as Parable*, p. 82.

will enhance neighborliness and, let's hope, the common good." With these words, Todd inadvertently appealed to the one goal that all societies share. He used the word *neighborliness* to characterize that common goal.

We could draw Picard's advice and Todd's prognosis together by invoking the postmodern buzzword *community*. As terms like *neighborliness* and *friendship* suggest, all communities seek to foster a common goal—community. They want people to live together in a spirit of neighborliness and friendship. This goal is universal, even though the specific mores that determine what exactly community, neighborliness and friendship are may be culturally determined.

Christian Ethics as a Community-Based Ethic of Being

The public discussions of ethics today appear to be constructing a community-based ethic of being. What should we as Christians make of this development? Is the quest for a community-based ethic of being compatible with the Christian vision? And what specific perspective do we as Christians have to offer in the contemporary discussion?

The Christian vision of integrity. At first glance, we may be tempted to reject categorically the new emphasis on constructing an ethic of being. After all, isn't the Bible concerned with our conduct? Do we not find in Scripture a host of ethical imperatives? And will not the eschatological judgment be a divine appraisal of our works, that is, our conduct (Jer 17:10; 32:19; Mt 16:27; Rom 2:6; 2 Cor 5:10; Gal 6:7-8; Rev 22:12)?

Further, the interest in traits seems to move the focus of ethics away from the biblical emphasis on being concerned for the needs of others to a seemingly selfish desire for growth in personal character. Gilbert Meilaender capsulizes this difficulty: "The focus of one who trusts in God's pardoning grace must, especially in the exceptional moment, be not his own character but the neighbor's need; for, otherwise, his character cannot be fully shaped by the virtue of faith."[13]

While acknowledging the apparent biblical foundation for the interest in formulating an ethic of doing that dominated the modern era, we must place it in a broader scriptural context. Looking from the perspective of the whole, we must conclude that the biblical viewpoint does not lead to a concern solely for acts in themselves and hence for a pure ethic of doing.

In addition to an obvious interest in right actions, the biblical authors also display a great concern for what motivates conduct. This is evident in the repeated admonitions in Scripture that Christians seek God's glory (for example, 1 Cor 10:31). The important role of motivation likewise formed a central aspect of Jesus'

---

[13]Gilbert C. Meilaender, *Faith and Faithfulness: Basic Themes in Christian Ethics* (Notre Dame, Ind.: University of Notre Dame Press, 1991), p. 106.

critique of the religious leaders of his day. Outwardly they evidenced conformity to the Old Testament law, but their motives were wrong. They were only concerned about themselves; they were motivated by selfishness. This biblical concern has led certain ethicists to focus on the motivational foundation of conduct. Helmut Thielicke, for example, concludes, "The specifically 'Christian' element in ethics is rather to be sought explicitly and exclusively in the motivation of the action."[14]

But even the quest for right motives does not tap the central heartbeat of the New Testament conception of the ethical life. Motivation is itself related to something deeper. According to the New Testament writers, the ultimate wellspring of action is our "heart," or what Jonathan Edwards referred to as our "affections."[15] Jesus himself declared that God's intention for us does not stop with mere outward conformity to laws, especially humanly devised legal strictures. A focus on outward obedience fails to acknowledge that the human "heart" is the source of evil actions (Mt 12:33-37; Mk 7:14-23). For this reason, Jesus—echoing the Old Testament prophets before him—decried the condition of the religious leaders of his day. They honored God with their lips, but their hearts were far from his heavenly Father (Mt 15:8).

His focus on the heart as the wellspring of action led Jesus—again following the Old Testament itself—to conclude that the two greatest commandments were to love God and to love one's neighbor (Mt 22:37-40). In so doing, he reunited the inward and the outward. For Jesus, love meant an inward affection turned toward God and others, as well as the outward action such a godly affection produces.

This uniting of the inward and the outward that characterized Jesus' ethical teaching leads us to the concept of integrity. It suggests that a focus on integrity, and thus on character or virtue, must be central to our statement of the Christian ethic. For this reason we can readily find affinity with contemporary thinkers like Alasdair MacIntyre, who speaks about the ethical life as involving "singleness of purpose" or the virtue of integrity.[16]

But what is integrity? The common dictionary definition of the term characterizes it as "uprightness in character" and speaks of traits such as honesty.[17] Christian integrity goes even deeper. Fundamentally, integrity has to do with authenticity. Persons of integrity are free from duplicity: "what you see is what you get." You don't go away wondering whether they are motivated by "hidden agendas."

---

[14]Helmut Thielicke, *Theological Ethics*, ed. William H. Lazareth, 3 vols. (Grand Rapids: Eerdmans, 1979), 1:20.

[15]See, for example, Jonathan Edwards, *Religious Affections: How Man's Will Affects His Character Before God*, Classics of Faith and Devotion (Portland, Ore.: Multnomah, 1984).

[16]Alasdair MacIntyre, *After Virtue: A Study in Moral Theory*, 2nd ed. (Notre Dame, Ind.: University of Notre Dame Press, 1984), p. 203.

[17]See, for example, Sidney I. Landau and Ronald J. Bogus, eds., *The Doubleday Dictionary for Home, School and Office* (Garden City, N.Y.: Doubleday, 1975), p. 374.

Authenticity suggests that integrity means "acting in accordance with one's stated beliefs." People of integrity do what they say. To use the common parlance, they "walk" their "talk." They are free from hypocrisy. There is in their lives a congruence between the *confessio fidei* and actual conduct.[18] Likewise, integrity has to do with courage of conviction. Persons of integrity act on their beliefs, even when this exacts a great personal cost.

The wisdom literature of the Bible suggests that such integrity leads to a good reputation. The book of Proverbs points out the exceedingly great value of such a reputation: "A good name is more desirable than great riches; to be esteemed is better than silver or gold" (Prov 22:1).

But we have not yet reached our goal. The ethical life may be the life of integrity, the coherence of inner conviction and conduct and action. But what is the source of a person's inner convictions? Do they arise *sui generis* out of the individual moral agent?

Here again we can readily find ourselves in agreement with contemporary ethical thought and can profitably draw from it. As we noted earlier, communitarians are alerting us to the foundational role of the communities in which we participate in the building of personal identity and moral sensitivities. Communities, they argue, transmit from generation to generation traditions of virtue, common good and ultimate meaning.[19]

Thus communities are crucial to sustaining character and values. Ultimately we derive our personal convictions from the community that transmits to us an understanding of virtue and goodness. This suggests that the life of integrity entails living out the principles or worldview of that community of reference.

Viewed from this perspective, the ethical life is integrally linked to a communal vision, a shared worldview, or what we may even call a *theology*. This constitutes the great methodological innovation of postmodern ethics. In the postmodern world we are becoming increasingly aware that every ethical proposal—even ethics itself—is embedded in an interpretive framework that in the end makes up the shared belief structure—the theology—of a community. In short, every understanding of the ethical life is ultimately derived from a community-based vision that links the personal life with something beyond.[20]

---

[18]See Harmon L. Smith, *Where Two or Three Are Gathered: Liturgy and the Moral Life* (Cleveland: Pilgrim, 1995), p. 86.

[19]See, for example, George A. Lindbeck, "Confession and Community: An Israel-like View of the Church," *The Christian Century*, May 9, 1990, p. 495.

[20]The idea of an ethic of community has developed in the twentieth century. For example, already in the 1940s the British ethicist Sydney Cave spoke of ethics as "life in community." Yet for him the term *community* was merely a way of speaking about the older concept of the "orders of creation," which he divided into family, industry and the state. Sydney Cave, *The Christian Way: A Study of New Testament Ethics in Relation to Present Problems*, American ed. (New York: Philosophical Library, 1949), p. 175.

A Christian communitarian virtue ethic. These conclusions suggest that the contemporary quest for a community-based ethic of being has much to offer our reflections on the Christian ethic. Foundational to our understanding of the ethical life is the realization that as Christians we constitute a particular community. We are a people who confess together that Jesus is the Christ. This suggests that the Christian ethic, in turn, is the call to live out the worldview of the community that gathers around Jesus the Christ. It entails acting according to the foundational belief structure or convictions of this community, especially as derived from the Bible, the foundational text of the community of Christ.

In the ethical task, therefore, we are guided by the Christian vision, a vision that arises from the biblical narrative. At the heart of this narrative is the story of the God who is active in the world. This story plays a central role in Christian ethics. For example, it provides Christians a reference point from which to understand or define central ethical concepts. The biblical narrative depicts God's steadfast resoluteness toward humankind. The Scriptures speak of the God who enters into a special relationship—a covenant—with God's creation. Even in the face of human rebellion, God remains steadfast. God continues to act in accordance with God's good intentions for us. The biblical word for God's resoluteness is *faithfulness.*

One foundation for Christian integrity, therefore, lies in the God who is faithful to the divine covenant despite human failure and sin. Even as he lamented Jerusalem's falling to the invading Babylonian armies, the prophet Jeremiah reminded himself of God's faithfulness: "Because of the LORD's great love we are not consumed, for his compassions never fail. They are new every morning; great is your faithfulness" (Lam 3:22-23; see also Ps 94:14). As the one who is faithful to this covenant, God is trustworthy. We can entrust ourselves to God, knowing that God will fulfill the divine promises. And we know what true faithfulness is by our experience of God's own covenantal faithfulness.

The God who is faithful to this covenant is also just. The biblical authors narrate a divine justice that is impartial. God treats all persons fairly and shows favoritism to none. God extends grace to all, causing the sun "to rise on the evil and the good" and sending "rain on the righteous and the unrighteous" (Mt 5:45). God's impartiality also means that salvation is intended for all people, regardless of ethnic origin (Acts 10:34-35), social status or gender (Gal 3:28-29). Divine justice also entails compassion. All persons are the recipients of God's goodness (Ps 145:8-9), but God cares especially for the less fortunate (Ps 146:7-8).

In setting forth a biblical ethic of integrity, Christians can appeal to the ways of the God of the biblical story as a foundation for understanding concepts such as faithfulness and justice. This provides a solution to a perplexing problem introduced by the loss of moral consensus that characterizes contemporary society. In such a context, ethical terms no longer carry any agreed-on transcendent reference point.

For the Christian, in contrast, ideals like faithfulness, justice and even integrity itself can only be defined in connection with God's own character as depicted in the biblical description of the divine Covenant keeper.

Christians appeal to the example of the biblical God for another function as well. Perhaps even more important than serving as a transcendent reference point for ethical terms, God's way in the world forms a model for the Christian life in the world. For the Christian, integrity ultimately involves living in such a way that our lives mirror God's own nature and thereby show what God is like. In this task, Christians appeal above all to the life of Jesus the Christ, who is Immanuel, "God with us" (Mt 1:23), and the incarnate Word of God (Jn 1:14). To be an ethical Christian means to live consistently as Jesus' followers.

The foundation for the life of integrity is our personal sense of identity as derived from the community of Christ. The New Testament authors, especially Paul, describe the essence of the Christian life as union with Christ, or Christ in us, which constitutes our person (for example, Col 1:27). This means that we gain our foundational identity from the biblical narrative of Jesus. As we declare in baptism (Rom 6:1-8) and repeatedly reaffirm at the Lord's table (1 Cor 10:16), Christ's life *is* our life. Hence, our goal is to be formed by his values and ideals, to live in accordance with what motivated him and to love as he loved. We desire that our affections be set on things above (Rom 8:5), that is, that we be sincerely devoted to Christ and to the heavenly Father whom he loved and served. Thus, in all of life, we want to be conformed to his "image," both in our inward being and in our outward conduct (2 Cor 3:18).

On this basis the New Testament authors set forth a special concept of spirituality. The Christian life is "walking in the Spirit" (see Gal 5:16), that is, being imbued with the same Spirit who guided our Lord Jesus himself. This indwelling Holy Spirit, the Spirit of Christ, forms Christlike character within the disciple and thereby becomes the author of the life of integrity.

In this task, however, the Christian community plays an essential role.[21] The narrative of Jesus is passed from generation to generation by the historical community of which we are the contemporary expression. More important, however, the biblical narrative comes to be formed in us as the believing community becomes our primary social context, our ultimate community of reference. For the Christian, the life of integrity is more than merely "Jesus and me for each tomorrow." It is living according to the ideals of the Lord as embodied in the life of the community that lives out and transmits his vision.

For this reason, Christian integrity is never an isolated, purely personal ethic.

---

[21]For a recent philosophical discussion of this, see Alistair I. McFayden, *The Call to Personhood: A Christian Theory of the Individual in Social Relationships* (Cambridge, U.K.: Cambridge University Press, 1990), pp. 61-63.

Rather, the life of integrity begins as the Christian develops an awareness of personal identity within the context of the fellowship of believers. Indeed, integrity means living out a sense of foundational status (who I am as a child of God) and a sense of calling or vocation (who I am in the program of God). But even this identity cannot be isolated from that of the group. The Christian participates in a particular people. And even when living "in the world" we are responsible to be representatives of that people, the community of faith.

The potential pitfall of a communitarian Christian ethic. This short sketch of a Christian ethic of integrity suggests that the move to a communitarian understanding holds promise as a way of articulating the Christian ethic in the emerging postmodern context. But one potentially devastating problem surfaces immediately. The community-based approach seems to undercut any claim to express a universal ethic.

The loss of universality appears to be inherent in any understanding that views the ethical life as integrally embedded in the life of the social group. Such a focus serves to highlight the multiplicity of communities and hence the diversity of ethical visions present in our world. This multiplicity, in turn, seems to lead us headlong into a communitarian pluralism. The multiplicity of community-based ethical visions appears to call into question any attempt to claim that one is somehow more correct than the others. Rather than promoting the search for the one, universal human ethic, the various interpretative frameworks or theological visions seem to offer equally valid foundations for ethics in the postmodern context.

For this reason, embarking on the communitarian pathway may risk casting us into the murky waters of a new "conventionalism." In such a situation, each social group determines its own rules of conduct in accordance with its own customs (or conventions), which in turn are based on its own unique vision of reality. Taken to the extreme, such a conventionalism leaves each community with the prerogative of requiring uncritical conformity to such social authority.[22]

Forming the intellectual foundation for this new situation is what Jean-François Lyotard elevates as the defining characteristic of the postmodern condition: "incredulity toward metanarratives."[23] Postmodernism involves the rejection of all overarching stories. Its ethos emerges through the discounting of all claims to universality and every overarching belief system that attempts to encapsulate the story of all humankind.

This situation is especially grave for Christianity, with its inherent tendency to

---

[22]For a succinct summary of conventionalism, see Raziel Abelson, *Ethics and Metaethics: Readings in Ethical Philosophy* (New York: St. Martin's, 1963), pp. 303-4. See also Scott B. Rae, *Moral Choices: An Introduction to Ethics* (Grand Rapids: Zondervan, 1995), pp. 86-87.

[23]Jean-François Lyotard, *The Postmodern Condition: A Report on Knowledge*, trans. Geoff Bennington and Brian Massumi (Minneapolis: University of Minnesota Press, 1984), p. iv.

universalize its own transcendent narrative of the divine-human drama. To the postmodern mind, the Christian story is only one such imperialistic metanarrative. The categorical rejection of every metanarrative does not deny us as Christians the privilege of upholding the biblical story as the defining narrative for our specific community. But the postmodern ethos demands that we give up every ambition to bring all other communities under the umbrella of the biblical story of creation-fall-new creation. In this context, the Christian vision can be only one among the many.

By implication, the postmodern critique demands that Christians also refrain from subsuming all other visions of the ethical life under the rubric of "Christian ethics." Any talk of the universality of the Christian conception of the ethical life is abhorrent to the postmodern mind. Like the Christian narrative, the Christian vision is thereby reduced to being merely one of a manifold number of "tribal" ethical systems found in our global village.

The move to a communitarian ethic, therefore, raises perplexing questions for Christians. If every conception of the ethical life is imbedded in the belief structure of a community of reference, then which community? And whose theology should we "privilege"? In short, how do we deal with the seemingly unavoidable pluralistic conventionism of the postmodern ethos?

The Christian ethic and religious ethical traditions. Our response to the crucial challenge posed by the postmodern context requires that we tackle head-on the question of the relation between the Christian ethic and the ethical systems of the multiplicity of religious communities present in our global village.

Ethics and the religions. Our beginning point in addressing this question arises from the connection between ethics and the religions.[24] The foundation for such a connection lies in the crucial role in human life played by culture, understood—to quote Clifford Geertz—as "an historically transmitted pattern of meanings embodied in symbols, a system of inherited conceptions expressed in symbolic forms by means of which men communicate, perpetuate, and develop their knowledge about and attitudes toward life."[25] Religion, in turn, is a central, formative dimension of culture.

Modern sociologists have pointed out that all religions provide a foundation for ethics in that they mediate a sense of the transcendent both to the individual and to the social dimensions of life. According to Emile Durkheim, for example, religion creates and maintains social solidarity, for it provides the common symbols by means of which a specific people understand their world.[26] Further, it affords a sense of

---

[24]For a discussion of this topic from the perspective of philosophy of religion, see James F. Smurl, *Religious Ethics: A Systems Approach* (Englewood Cliffs, N.J.: Prentice-Hall, 1972).

[25]Clifford Geertz, *The Interpretation of Cultures: Selected Essays* (New York: Basic Books, 1973), p. 89.

[26]See, for example, Emile Durkheim, *The Elementary Forms of the Religious Life,* trans. Joseph Ward Swain (New York: Collier Books, 1961), pp. 463-87. For a helpful summary of Durkheim's view of religion,

cosmic unity necessary for such solidarity.[27] By furnishing the foundation for the social community in which we live, a specific religious tradition mediates to us the framework for group and personal identity formation. As a result, religion undergirds morality by providing a transcendent foundation for conceptions of the ethical life. In short, as Geertz succinctly states, "religion supports proper conduct by picturing a world in which such conduct is only common sense."[28]

The foundational role of religion to human society and by extension to ethics has led some thinkers to consider the possibility of developing a religiously based "global ethic."[29] This project would appear possible insofar as each of the many religions has a "community-producing" function. We could then hope to arrive at certain conclusions about a global ethic of community derived from the common vision of community that the religions share.

Although it originally arose as the outworking of the modern pluralist ethos, this goal looms even more conceivable in the postmodern climate. I noted earlier that contemporary thinkers seem quite able to close ranks around communitarian ideals such as friendship or neighborliness. In fact, if there is one nearly universally accepted guiding principle for ethics in the postmodern context, it is that the ethical life is the life that builds community. Douglas Todd spoke for many when he held out the hope that today's public ethical discussions would foster "neighborliness" and promote "the common good."

The seemingly universal quest for community and the social role of religion in human life lends us the criterion by which we can appraise all religious visions. The common goal of community suggests that to evaluate the transcendent vision of every community (including Christianity) we need to determine the extent to which the beliefs it inculcates and the practices it fosters promote social cohesion.

While appeal to a universal criterion such as the promotion of community is plausible in our postmodern world, the construction of a global ethic—a universally acknowledged understanding of the ethical life—remains difficult. As the postmodern focus on "difference" or multiplicity reminds us, despite their common quest for community, the various communities remain quite different from each other. They espouse differing transcendent visions, and consequently they embody differing understandings of what actually constitutes true community.

Such divergence reintroduces the "impolite" question of truth. It leads us to ask,

---

see Robert N. Bellah, introduction to *On Morality and Society: Selected Writings*, by Emile Durkheim, ed. Robert N. Bellah (Chicago: University of Chicago Press, 1973), pp. lv-lii.

[27]This is most obviously the case with monotheistic religions, which look to the one God as the foundation of cosmic and hence social unity. But polytheistic religions can likewise offer a unified cosmic vision insofar as they elevate one god above the others.

[28]Geertz, *Interpretation of Cultures*, p. 129. See also Geertz's classic definition of religion on page 90.

[29]This possibility was discussed at the Parliament of the World's Religions, which met in Chicago in 1993.

Which religious vision carries within itself the foundation for the community-building role of a transcendent religious vision?

The uniqueness of the Christian ethical vision. At this point, the Christian gospel provides a unique answer. Like other community-based visions, a central goal of the Christian ethic is the advancement of social cohesion. And in keeping with other community-based ethical proposals, it speaks of this goal as "community" (or fellowship). Taken as a whole, the biblical narrative speaks of God at work establishing community. God's *telos* is nothing less than gathering a reconciled people, nurtured in a renewed creation and enjoying fellowship with the eternal God (Rev 21:1-5).

This biblical vision of community suggests that Christians can affirm all religious traditions to the extent that they provide social cohesion (and hence some measure of "community"). We might also admit that the various religions can even mediate to their devotees fellowship with God to the extent that through the religious practices they come to know the only God as the Most High God. Thus we can affirm each social group insofar as it fosters the one divine goal of establishing community and thus becomes a community of people that gathers around a vision of the only true God.

The Christian message does not stop with any such generic vision of the transcendent, however. We firmly believe that the Christian ethic reveals more clearly God's goal for humankind and hence the nature of both the community and the good life that all human ethical systems seek to foster. In addition, we humbly declare that the religions cannot provide community in its ultimate sense because they are beset with a theological problem. They do not embody the highest vision of who God is, namely, God as the triune One.

Foundational to the specifically Christian theological vision is the acknowledgment of God in God's triune fullness. We declare that the only true God is none other than the social Trinity. The Christian vision speaks of humankind, in turn, as "created in God's image." The divine design is that we mirror within creation what God is like in God's own eternal reality. The goal of human existence has been revealed most completely in Jesus Christ, who in his life, death and resurrection modeled the divine principle of life, namely, life in intimate fellowship with his heavenly Father by the Holy Spirit who indwelled him.

In this manner, the Christian vision of God as the social Trinity and our creation to be the imago Dei provides the transcendent basis for the human ethical ideal as life in community. Consequently, the reciprocal, perichoric life of the triune God is the cosmic reference point for the idea of society itself. Just as God is a plurality in unity, to be human means to be persons in community. The task of every society, therefore, is to bring a higher unity out of the multiplicity of individuals, as is reflected so well in the motto of the United States—"e pluribus unum" (out of the many, one).

In short, the biblical vision of God at work establishing community is not merely a great idea that God devised in all eternity. Instead, it is an outworking of God's own eternal reality. As a result, the human quest for community, often expressed today as "neighborliness" or "the common good," is not misguided. At its heart it is nothing less than the quest to mirror in the midst of all creation the eternal reality of God and thereby to be the image of God. Ultimately, this vision lies at the heart of the Christian ethic of integrity. And it is this vision of the human community living together in the midst of the new creation in full integrity—humankind showing forth the eternal fellowship of the triune God—that Christians have to offer as the foundation of a truly constructive ethic in the postmodern context.

Chapter 24

New Dimensions in Evangelism & Church Growth

Thom S. Rainer
....

T HE YEAR 1955 MARKED THE BIRTH OF THE CHURCH GROWTH MOVE-
ment. In that year Donald A. McGavran wrote a defining work on people
movements, *The Bridges of God*.[1] The "father of the church growth movement"
wanted to identify the most effective means to reach different people groups for
Christ. In his mission in India, McGavran noted many ineffective evangelistic
efforts. How, he asked, can we be better stewards of time, people and money as we
work to reach people for Christ?

In our fascination with the methodologies, the theories and the social sciences
of church growth, we sometimes forget that the movement began as a concern for
evangelism. The disciplines of evangelism and church growth are closely related. In
this chapter we will examine the nature of their relationship and then survey a
history of the church growth movement to determine points of departure and
common ground between evangelism and church growth. Finally we will look at
major developing trends with a view to determining implications for ministry today.

The Relationship Between Evangelism and Church Growth
One of the most significant trends in evangelical ministry in the last half-century
has been a perception of incongruence between evangelism and church growth.

---

[1]Donald A. McGavran, *The Bridges of God*, rev. ed. (New York: Friendship, 1981). The first edition was
published in 1955.

Such a view has potentially dangerous implications for ministry. If evangelism is not connected with the growth of the local church, disciple making becomes nothing more than convert making. The new Christian has no ties to a local body of believers for spiritual growth and accountability. The biblical mandate to become a part of the body of Christ is deemphasized at best and ignored at worst.

If, however, church growth is not connected to conversion, the growth of the kingdom may be forsaken for the transfer of saints from one local fellowship to another. The North American Society for Church Growth (now the American Society for Church Growth) included a definition of church growth that began,

> Church growth is that discipline which investigates the nature, expansion, planting, multiplication, functioning and health of Christian churches as they relate to the effective implementation of God's commission to "make disciples of all peoples" (Matthew 28:18-20).[2]

Without an explicit reference to evangelism, church growth can lose its kingdom focus. Some early leaders in the church growth movement expressed that very concern as church growth literature focused on total numerical growth, not evangelistic growth. Some of their comments are insightful.

C. Peter Wagner on Evangelism

C. Peter Wagner notes that we can look at the relationship between evangelism and church growth in terms of (1) organization, (2) education and (3) definition. First, each field is organized and has its own professional society. The Academy for Evangelism in Theological Education was founded in 1973. The North American Society for Church Growth (now the American Society for Church Growth) was founded in 1985. Furthermore, many denominational and parachurch agencies have emphases or directorships in either evangelism or church growth, or both. Typically, the church growth positions include evangelism, "but evangelism traditionally has not included church growth."[3]

Second, chairs and professorships of evangelism have been part of seminaries and Bible colleges for generations. But church growth positions are relatively new, though increasing at a steady pace. An institution's view of the two disciplines is typically reflected in its organization. For example, the fields of evangelism and church growth are in separate graduate schools at Fuller Theological Seminary. But at the Southern Baptist Theological Seminary, where I serve as dean, the two disciplines are in the same school *and* the same department.

Third, the two are alike only when evangelism includes bringing new believers beyond conversion into responsible church membership. Some argue that evangel-

---

[2]C. Peter Wagner, *Strategies for Church Growth* (Ventura, Calif.: Regal, 1987), p. 114.
[3]C. Peter Wagner, "Evangelism and the Church Growth Movement," in *Evangelism in the Twenty-first Century*, ed. Thom S. Rainer (Wheaton, Ill.: Harold Shaw, 1989), p. 26.

ism as a discipline does not include responsible church membership. But if we are to use the Great Commission (Mt 28:19-20) as a central evangelistic proof text, we must have as our goal not only "convert making" but "disciple making" as well. And disciples may best be understood in today's world as "responsible church members." Thus the "church" element, or ecclesiological element of church growth, becomes critically important.

Wagner summarized his thoughts on the subject in this manner:

The fields of evangelism and church growth are distinct, but they enjoy a close and often symbiotic relationship. The field of evangelism is broader than church growth in educational, theological, social, and methodological aspects. The two intersect and become synonymous when the goal of evangelism—the bottom line on which success or failure is evaluated—is to bring unbelievers into a personal relationship with Jesus Christ and into responsible church member-ship.[4]

McGavran on Evangelism

McGavran, it seems, was not consciously birthing a movement when he wrote *The Bridges of God* in 1955. Nor was he intentionally perpetuating a movement in 1970 when he wrote *Understanding Church Growth*, the Magna Carta[5] of the movement. McGavran began using the term *church growth* in the late fifties and early sixties when he recognized that much of the activity that missions and churches were engaging in and calling evangelism was not evangelism.

McGavran's heart for effective evangelism remained his life's passion. In one of his final works, *Effective Evangelism*,[6] he used the terms *evangelism* and *church growth* almost interchangeably. He did not change disciplines; he simply and pragmatically sought real evangelistic results.

The Church Growth Movement

Americanizing and pragmatizing evangelism. A historical survey of the church growth movement can help us understand better how the two disciplines became, at least in the minds of many, distinct and separate. Perhaps this overview can also assist us in evaluating the wisdom of continuing to look at church growth and evangelism as separate fields.

The McGavran era (1955-70). The church growth movement began with *The Bridges of God* in 1955. Before writing that book, McGavran extensively studied

---

[4]Ibid., p. 33.

[5]C. Peter Wagner, *Your Church Can Grow* (Glendale, Calif.: Regal, 1976), p. 14. This book was revised in 1980.

[6]Donald A. McGavran, *Effective Evangelism: A Theological Mandate* (Phillipsburg, N.J.: Presbyterian & Reformed, 1988).

numerous mission stations in central India where he served. Some of the mission stations were evangelistically effective, but the great majority were not. Why, McGavran asked, are some churches growing while others are not, when the factors of leadership, faithfulness and demographics cannot explain the differences?

The Bridges of God was a noble attempt to provide both theological and methodological answers to this question. The book evoked emotional responses from its readers, and debate continues to this day on what may be only peripheral issues. The major issue—factors that engender effective evangelism—was obscured by the sometimes heated discussions of relatively insignificant details.

The McGavran era also saw the institutionalization of the church growth movement. In 1960 McGavran was invited to locate his Institute of Church Growth on the campus of Northwest Christian College in Eugene, Oregon, and it began full operation in 1961. Perhaps the single most important development in the institutionalization of the movement transpired in 1965. McGavran was invited to Fuller Theological Seminary in Pasadena, California. He reestablished the Institute of Church Growth there and became the founding dean of Fuller's School of World Mission. The Pasadena area soon became a hub for American church growth activities. These years were critical for the establishment of a relationship between evangelism and church growth. McGavran's ultimate concern was growth in the church that resulted from Great Commission evangelism and disciple making. His passion was to win the lost and incorporate them into the fellowship of a local church. Numbers never enamored him. For McGavran, church growth and evangelism were so closely related that one was the extension of the other.

Yet the two disciplines were drifting away from each other organizationally. Perhaps the Pasadena leadership unintentionally allowed this chasm to grow. When McGavran founded the new school at Fuller Seminary, the disciplines of missions and church growth were together in the pioneer endeavor. But evangelism was taught in Fuller's School of Theology. Instead of bringing evangelism into McGavran's new school, it remained a separate and distinct discipline, although closely related to church growth. In later years tensions grew between the two schools for various reasons, the chasm between evangelism and church growth widened.

In 1970 McGavran completed his definitive work on church growth, *Understanding Church Growth*. Wagner called this volume the "Magna Carta of the church growth movement."[7] It provided the movement with clarity of direction that included both theological and methodological insight. Strangely, however, McGavran then directed his attention away from American church growth to missions in Third World nations and other areas outside the United States. The father of the church growth movement was no longer totally involved in the

---

[7] See note 5.

movement. McGavran's passion for evangelism that results in real church growth no longer informed writings about American church growth. The movement was in real danger of losing its evangelistic impetus.

The identity-crisis era (1970-1981). The 1970s witnessed both rapid growth and defensive retreat for the church growth movement. This paradoxical situation resulted from some church growth advocates promoting their mission unapologetically while others used their works to defend church growth concepts that were being harshly criticized. With the exception of McGavran, no leader emerged in this decade as the primary spokesperson for the movement. McGavran himself did not write much about the American church, focusing instead on missions and church growth in other parts of the world.

The "Pasadena gang" was the group most clearly identified with church growth. This group included some of the first faculty members at Fuller's School of World Mission: McGavran, Ralph Winter, Arthur Glasser, Charles Kraft, Allen Tippett and C. Peter Wagner. Win Arn founded the Institute of American Church Growth in 1972, and John Wimber became founding director of the Department of Church Growth at Fuller Evangelistic Association (now known as the Charles E. Fuller Institute of Evangelism and Church Growth).

The 1970s produced some church growth advocates outside the Pasadena area as well. Kent R. Hunter founded the Church Growth Center in 1977 in Corunna, Indiana. Elmer Towns, now at Liberty University in Lynchburg, Virginia, made contributions in the area of Sunday school growth. In Southern Baptist circles Charles Chaney and Ron Lewis coauthored the book *Design for Church Growth*.

McGavran's second major contribution to American church growth in the 1970s was the book *How to Grow a Church*, coauthored with Win Arn in 1973. The book was written as an easy-to-understand dialogue between McGavran and Arn. The highly technical language of earlier books was conspicuously absent, and many church growth principles were applied to the American scene.

Other events helped shape church growth during this time. In 1972 Paul Benjamin founded the National Church Growth Research Center, an organization devoted to church growth in America. Also in 1972 the publication of *Why Conservative Churches Are Growing* generated much discussion and debate. The author was Dean Kelley, an executive with the National Council of Churches. His presentation of evidence that conservative churches were growing faster than liberal churches complemented church growth precepts, but it drew the criticism of many of his peers.

Despite all the writings about church growth, the movement failed to establish a clear identity. Church growth material began to be published from so many different perspectives that it was difficult to answer the question, Who speaks for church growth?

Another confusing factor was the movement's response to criticism. McGavran was the aggressive protagonist of the movement. His writings were straightforward and unapologetic. The candid and sometimes polemical tone of McGavran's views set the pace by which church growth boldly asserted itself.

Critics of church growth began to gather momentum by the beginning of the 1970s, and the movement began to devote significant time and resources to responding to criticism. A sampling of the criticisms provides the general milieu in which church growth found itself in the 1970s.

Some critics showed disdain for the kind of evangelism inherent in some church growth models. Commenting on the concept of the homogeneous unit, one critic concluded that church growth was "evangelism without the gospel."[8] Church growth, he said, has a theology of evangelism that "reduces initial Christian commitment to an inoffensive appeal, avoiding the suggestion that to become a Christian one must turn from a social order that perpetuates injustice."[9] Archbishop William Temple's definition of evangelism had been a standard among evangelicals for years, but when McGavran affirmed the definition, he was criticized for having a "narrow description of . . . evangelism."[10]

Wagner received the brunt of the criticism after the furor over *Understanding Church Growth* subsided. Wagner's approach to church growth and development, said one critic, "is precariously deficient as a strategy for evangelism."[11] Kenneth L. Smith of Colgate Rochester-Bexley-Crozier found fault with Wagner's strategy of evangelism because it concentrated on evangelism "in the narrow sense of 'saving souls.' "[12] Smith further characterized Wagner's methodology as "a mixture of theological absolutism (i.e., the necessity for a born-again experience) and sociological utilitarianism."[13]

Also in the seventies Wagner began receiving the theology of the rapidly growing Pentecostal movement more warmly, which did not escape the notice of the critics. After Wagner wrote *Look Out! The Pentecostals Are Coming*, one reviewer said that his "book tends to read like a propaganda piece."[14]

---

[8]Tom Nees, review of *Our Kind of People: The Ethical Dimensions of Church Growth*, by C. Peter Wagner, *Sojourners* 9 (February 1980): 27. Nees closely examines the sociological precepts of church growth.

[9]Ibid., p. 29.

[10]John H. Piet, review of *Understanding Church Growth*, by Donald A. McGavran, *Reformed Review* 25 (Fall 1971): 30. Archbishop Temple's definition: "Evangelism is the winning of men to acknowledge Christ as their Savior and King, so that they give themselves to His service in the fellowship of His Church."

[11]David L. Watson, review of *Our Kind of People: The Ethical Dimensions of Church Growth*, by C. Peter Wagner, *Perkins Journal* 33 (Winter 1979): 33.

[12]Kenneth L. Smith, review of *Our Kind of People: The Ethical Dimensions of Church Growth*, by C. Peter Wagner, *Review of Religious Research* 22 (September 1980): 100.

[13]Ibid.

[14]James Patterson, review of *Look Out! The Pentecostals Are Coming*, by C. Peter Wagner, *Christianity Today*, June 21, 1974, p. 30.

The definition of evangelism, which remains a point of contention to this day, was debated as early as 1971, the publication date of Wagner's *Frontiers in Missionary Strategy*. Again, Wagner was the chief recipient of the criticisms, one reviewer claiming that theologically Wagner fell "dangerously close to Pelagianism."[15]

Criticism also came from those who viewed church growth as a misguided theology/sociology that overemphasized numbers. Opposing the concept that mission should emphasize "the actual number of souls gained," Sabbas J. Kilian retorted, "If one continues to look at church growth exclusively as saving souls and at theology as feeding the people with the one formula allowed, one can hardly speak of an understanding of church growth today. In a diaspora situation, numbers reveal nothing at all."[16]

While not every critic summarily rejected the importance of numerical increase in mission, Robert K. Hundnut wrote a book-length repudiation of the quantitative approach to mission.

> People are leaving the church. It could not be a better sign. Indeed, while they are leaving church income is growing. It was up 5.2 percent in 1973, according to the National Council of Churches. This proves that the more serious the membership, the more substantial the church. . . . Most churches could be two-thirds smaller and lose nothing in power. In most churches, the first third are committed, the second third are peripheral, and the third third are out.[17]

Some antagonists of church growth were less irritated at the quantitative emphasis of the movement than at the perception that church growth alone claimed exclusive rights to this emphasis. In a review of *Understanding Church Growth*, James Scherer wrote that "[McGavran] would have us believe that numerical increase is rejected by the majority of persons concerned with mission work—a view that many readers are not likely to accept—and that he alone remains faithful to the commission to disciple the nations, while others have gone whoring after the *Baalim* of social relevance, ecumenical relations, institutional witness, and so on."[18]

Still others totally rejected church growth as a legitimate missiological movement. Shortly after *Understanding Church Growth* appeared, Kilian stated that he "disagree[d] with M[cGavran] on almost everything."[19] Alfred C. Krass questioned

[15]Roger S. Greenway, review of *Frontiers in Missionary Strategy*, by C. Peter Wagner, *Westminster Theological Journal* 35 (Fall/Spring 1972-73): 373.

[16]Sabbas J. Kilian, review of *Understanding Church Growth*, by Donald A. McGavran, *Theological Studies* 33 (1972): 182.

[17]Robert K. Hundnut, *Church Growth Is Not the Point* (New York: Harper & Row, 1975), p. xi. Hundnut rejects growth as the purpose of the church and offers fourteen alternative purposes.

[18]James A. Scherer, review of *Understanding Church Growth*, by Donald A. McGavran, *International Review of Mission* 60 (January 1971): 127.

[19]Kilian, review of *Understanding Church Growth*, p. 182.

the legitimacy of church growth as a movement:

> They have lost the woods for the sake of trees which they did not need to climb. In trying to develop a psychology of mission, a sociology of mission, an ethnotheology of mission, they have had a necessity to start from scratch with each new synthesis. They have picked up the relevant secular discipline at a certain point and tried to mate it with a real mission-theological concern—and rarely do they seem to go back to that secular discipline again, but labor on, patiently shouldering an immense burden trying to develop a new science.[20]

Other critics in the 1970s attempted to accept the contributions of church growth, yet they encountered serious hermeneutical and theological problems. "One problem area with church growth theory," said Third World missiologist Orlando E. Costas, "is the fact that its theorists have not been able to come up with a sound hermeneutic for their theological endeavors."[21] Costas and other critics charged that the church growth movement had "failed . . . to interpret the text in the light of the many situations of contemporary man."[22] The church growth approach to Scriptures was thus seen to be primarily, perhaps solely, concerned with correct strategies for best results. As a consequence, church growth advocates were accused of ignoring poverty and oppression, as well as social, economic and political problems.

As a result of its shallow hermeneutic, the critics charged, the movement developed a concept of mission that was incomplete and unbiblical. They believed that advocates of church growth had a narrow missiology so focused on results and conversions that Christian social ministry was all but forgotten; propagation of the faith completely overshadowed the whole gospel of Jesus Christ.

Thus Rodger Bassham argued in 1979 that "church growth theology has some serious weakness . . . the narrow conception of mission as evangelism."[23] He concluded that the church growth movement "appears to have neglected a substantial discussion which has taken place over the past twenty-five years, in which the meaning of mission, evangelism, witness, service, and salvation have been explored and developed."[24]

Such was the milieu in which church growth struggled in the 1970s. Criticisms were hurled at the movement with increasing frequency and intensity. The reactions of the church growth advocates were mixed. McGavran and Wagner continued to affirm boldly the basic tenets of the movement. Still others were involved in writing

---

[20]Alfred C. Krass, review of *God, Man and Church Growth: A Festschrift in Honor of Donald Anderson McGavran*, ed. A. R. Tippett, *Missiology* 3 (January, 1975): 118.

[21]Orlando E. Costas, *The Church and Its Mission: A Shattering Critique from the Third World* (Wheaton, Ill.: Tyndale, 1974), p. 131.

[22]Ibid., p. 132.

[23]Rodger C. Bassham, *Mission Theology: 1948-1975, Years of Worldwide Creative Tension—Ecumenical, Evangelical and Roman Catholic* (Pasadena, Calif.: William Carey Library, 1979), pp. 194-95.

[24]Ibid.

a mix of both defensive and affirmative statements about church growth.

During this critical period, however, the chasm between evangelism and church growth grew. Church growth proponents were busy defending their methodologies. Consequently the heart of McGavran—growing churches by effective evangelism—was overshadowed by peripheral issues. The disciplines may have been divorced irreconcilably had it not been for the efforts of the leader of the second generation of the church growth movement.

The Wagner era (1981-1988). While the church growth movement was struggling for identity and acceptance in the 1970s, one man was steadily rising to the top as the chief spokesperson for American church growth. C. Peter Wagner is now the Donald McGavran Professor of Church Growth at Fuller Theological Seminary. Whereas Fuller Seminary gave the movement its institutional staying power, Wagner provided the personal leadership to maintain church growth as a recognized movement in evangelical Christianity.

Wagner had written numerous books prior to 1981, most of which addressed methodological concerns. In 1981, however, *Church Growth and the Whole Gospel: A Biblical Mandate* was published. In the book Wagner responded to the plethora of criticisms of the movement over the past two decades. The tone of this book was much less polemical than the tone of most earlier church growth writings. Openness to criticisms and new input marked the book. One example of many demonstrates the irenic spirit of *Church Growth and the Whole Gospel:*

> I feel like a candidate for the "how my mind has changed" series. Not that I have taken a complete 180 degree turn. In fact I am reasonably sure that some readers of this new book will say that the leopard has not changed his spots. But today I would no longer argue as I did that "one searches the Scriptures in vain to find a commandment that would have Christians move into the world with a mission designed to create peace and order, justice and liberty, dignity and community."[25]

What characterized this book more than other factors was the asking of *theological* questions. Wagner was attempting to place the movement in its proper biblical and theological context. This book and other writings[26] would continue to seek and to state biblical directions for the movement. In essence the church growth movement, an *ecclesiological* movement, was becoming a *soteriological* movement. Growth for growth's sake was not the critical issue. *Kingdom* growth was as important as *church* growth. Issues of adding people to God's kingdom become issues of evangelism. The two disciplines, church growth and evangelism, were starting to be understood as what they really are—siblings.

Had Wagner continued to ask these theological questions, I believe, he would

---

[25]C. Peter Wagner, *Church Growth and the Whole Gospel: A Biblical Mandate* (San Francisco: Harper & Row, 1981), p. xii.

[26]See, for example, C. Peter Wagner, *Strategies for Church Growth* (Ventura, Calif.: Regal, 1987).

have exerted significant impact on the church growth movement of the twenty-first century. But Wagner's calling and interests moved him to a new and controversial area: the "third wave," an evangelical signs-and-wonders movement promoted largely by John Wimber and Vineyard churches. Wagner's definitive treatment of his pilgrimage can be found in his book *How to Have a Healing Ministry Without Making Your Church Sick.*[27] The publication of that book in 1988 marked the end of Wagner's leadership in mainstream church growth. His recent ventures into another important worldwide movement, the great prayer movement, have further diminished his identification with church growth. Since 1988 the church growth movement has been without a clear leader, a clear direction or a clear purpose.

Evangelism and Church Growth: A Proposal for the Twenty-first Century

When Donald McGavran began asking questions about church growth in the 1930s and 1940s, his primary concern was ineffective evangelism that engendered anemic church growth in India. McGavran's church growth questions were largely evangelism questions. His first concern was not right methodologies but effective evangelism. The evangelism that asked no ecclesiological questions was at best conversion evangelism. It certainly was not the disciple-making evangelism mandated by the Great Commission. The church growth movement thus began as a movement that saw itself as related to the venerable field of evangelism. In the years since the early 1980s, the relationship between the two disciplines seems tenuous at best. A "family reunion" is in order to restore the evangelistic fervor that marked the church growth movement in its early years.

The church growth movement grew out of one man's concern for evangelism in the local church. Its acceptance as a legitimate discipline is the result of the movement's emphasis on conversion growth, which brought disciples into the local church. The future of church growth as a discipline hinges on its ability to reestablish ties with the field of evangelism.

The reunion of evangelism and church growth. In 1975 Lewis A. Drummond proposed a definition for evangelism that departed from traditional conversion-only meanings. He defined evangelism as a "concerted effort to confront the unbeliever with the truth about and claims of Jesus Christ and to challenge him with the view of leading him into repentance toward God and faith in our Lord Jesus Christ, and thus, into the fellowship of the church."[28]

Drummond's definition of evangelism was not accepted by everyone in evangelism. Some struggled with the concept of "fellowship of the church" being a true concern of evangelism. Was Drummond advocating a works salvation implicitly in

---

[27]C. Peter Wagner, *How to Have a Healing Ministry Without Making Your Church Sick* (Ventura, Calif.: Regal, 1988).

[28]Lewis A. Drummond, *Leading Your Church in Evangelism* (Nashville: Broadman, 1975), p. 21.

his definition? Must one become active in a local church to be saved?

C. Peter Wagner was confronted with the same issue as he debated the meaning of evangelism with peers serving on the theology working group on the International Congress of World Evangelization in Lausanne, Switzerland, in 1974. The theology working group was assigned the task of developing a covenant of theology for evangelicals around the world who have a passion for world evangelization. That included incorporation of the new convert into the local church. Though such language was included in the definition of evangelism per se, Wagner won a partial victory when the statement included "The results of evangelism include obedience to Christ, incorporation into his church and responsible service in the world."[29]

Wagner realized that "a disciple is made when the power of the Holy Spirit comes and makes that person a new creature. 'Therefore, if anyone is in Christ, he is a new creation; old things have passed away; behold, all things become new' (2 Corinthians 5:17). This is salvation. The new birth."[30] But Wagner also knew that many who verbally profess Christ are not Christians. How can we know, he asked, when our evangelistic efforts are complete with any given individual?

Wagner asserts that although we cannot "look up anyone's name in the Lamb's Book of Life,"[31] we can at least have some assurance of their salvation if they are bearing fruit in a local church. He continues, "But the test used by the church growth movement is responsible church membership. A person's commitment to Christ may be invisible, but the same person's commitment to the Body of Christ is visible and measurable. The two commandments should not be separated."[32] Wagner thus refused to separate evangelism and church growth. They were inextricably tied together. "If a person who professes to be a Christian is not a responsible church member, I need at least to raise questions about the validity of the profession."[33]

Although Wagner's concern about the bond between the two disciplines was stated clearly, the church growth movement as a whole began to drift away from its evangelism sibling in the 1980s. Church growth came to be measured by total numerical growth rather than conversion growth. And when *all* types of growth are equally heralded, the importance of conversion growth is diminished.

A healthy trend that may be gaining momentum in the church growth movement is a reestablished relationship between evangelism and church growth. A family reunion is in order. Leaders in both disciplines need to acknowledge their dependence on each other. Evangelism needs church growth and church growth

---

[29]See Thom S. Rainer, *The Book of Church Growth: History, Theology and Principles* (Nashville: Broadman & Holman, 1993), pp. 75-85, for the complete text of the Lausanne Covenant. The quote cited is on page 78.
[30]Wagner, *Strategies for Church Growth*, p. 54.
[31]Ibid.
[32]Ibid.
[33]Ibid.

needs evangelism. The Great Commission cannot be fulfilled without both.

A church growth theology of conversion. The church growth movement should state clearly the "entrance requirements for membership" into the kingdom. A church growth theology of conversion would include some of the following affirmations:

> Church growth results from new believers who are added to God's kingdom and to the local church. These new believers have experienced the incursion of divine grace into their lives, the resurrection from spiritual death to eternal life. This conversion occurred not through any human power but through repenting from sin and turning to Christ through the power of his Spirit.

Thus church growth excludes other types of growth, such as biological growth and transfer growth. The heart of church growth becomes evangelism, which results in fruit-bearing disciples being added to the local church.

Organizational reunion. Many of the leaders and writers of church growth and evangelism are affiliated with either the Academy for Evangelism in Theological Education or the American Society for Church Growth. These leaders set the pace and establish the tone for much of the literature that emanates from the disciplines. But very few people belong to or participate in both organizations. The resources of each group are needed by the other. The collective insights of both the academy and the society could prove invaluable.

While a merger between the two groups is unlikely, bridges must be built. A symbiotic relationship would be best for the kingdom. Each has an annual meeting. Could they meet together in alternating years? Each publishes its own journal or newsletter. Could they publish jointly? The leaders of each group could produce materials focused on conversionary disciple making. Obedience to the Great Commission would come from the passion of evangelism and the passion of discipleship in a body of believers.

Conclusion: Implications for Ministry

The proposed reunion of evangelism and church growth is more than an academic exercise performed by elites. What these leaders advocate will be received by eager pastors and other church leaders who desire more than the latest methodological growth fad. The reunion thus has several implications for ministry.

Evangelistic intentionality. As leaders in both disciplines promote evangelism as the key emphasis of church growth, church leaders will become more evangelistically intentional. For example, the Billy Graham School of Missions, Evangelism, and Church Growth of the Southern Baptist Theological Seminary recently conducted an expansive study of 583 of the most evangelistic churches in America.[34]

---

[34] I have compiled the results, interpretation and implications of this study in Thom S. Rainer, *Effective*

A key factor in the evangelistic successes of the churches was the intentionality of evangelism in most of their ministries. For example, nearly one-half of these churches view youth ministry as a unique opportunity for evangelism. The adolescent years are among the most receptive years of a person's life. These churches focused on reaching youth for Christ. A youth lock-in, therefore, becomes an explicitly evangelistic event. Church leaders are concerned more to reach youth for Christ than to entertain Christians. They send invitations to unchurched youth in the public schools and encourage Christian young people to invite their lost friends. The gospel is clearly proclaimed in a context of fun and games.

The church growth movement of recent years has not explicitly advocated evangelistic intentionality. Churches have given more attention to drawing a crowd, regardless of the salvific state of the individuals. In the youth lock-in example, the goal becomes a crowd rather than reaching lost persons for Christ.

As evangelism and church growth become more interrelated, growth methodologies will emphasize conversion growth rather than total growth. Disciples cannot be made unless they are first introduced to the Savior whom they will follow.

New "rewards." In our human fallibility, we tend to attempt that which is rewarded. For four decades we have rewarded leaders whose churches have experienced significant numerical growth. These leaders speak in conferences, share their success stories with peers and have articles written about them in books and magazines. For example, a recent book highlighting the growth stories of several churches provided an appendix of ten years' statistical data. But only one of the churches was reaching any significant numbers for Christ. The reward system has favored total growth, often at the expense of conversion growth.

When evangelistic growth becomes the "reward," church leaders will become more intentional about their efforts to evangelize the lost. A new genre of church growth literature is needed that offers such rewards.[35]

Heightened awareness of the importance of the local church. One of the church growth movement's most significant contributions to evangelistic ministries is its focus on the local church. The New Testament pattern of evangelism includes a clear presentation of the gospel message, a decision by an unbeliever to repent from sin and turn to God through Jesus Christ, and assimilation and discipleship in a local fellowship of believers. But assimilation and discipleship in a local church have often been neglected by some enthusiasts for evangelism.

Such was McGavran's concern as he observed churches in India in the 1940s.

Evangelistic Churches: Surprising Insights from Churches That Reach the Lost (Nashville: Broadman & Holman, 1996).

[35] Such is the emphasis of my book *Effective Evangelistic Churches* (see note 34). The 583 churches studied and their pastors were "rewarded" for having annual baptisms of at least twenty-five *and* a baptismal ratio (resident church members/total baptisms) of less than 20:1.

Some churches were not evangelistic in any of their ministries. But evangelism supposedly was taking place. The new Christians, however, were not assimilated into a local church. Thus McGavran argued that *evangelistic* growth must result in *church* growth. The evangelistic process is not complete until the new believer is a fruit-bearing Christian in a local congregation.

The concerns that McGavran had more than a half-century ago must be our concerns as well. As the disciplines of evangelism and church growth work in dependency on one another, evangelism will have an ecclesiocentric emphasis. The local church will once again play a key role in successful evangelism. We will again make disciples, not just converts.

Reduction of competition and "turfism" between churches. An unspoken issue among most church leaders is the issue of competition, or "turfism," as it is commonly called. Very few pastors remain emotionless when church members move to another church in the same area. Jealousy and anger are more common than most leaders would like to admit. This "sheep shuffling" or "saint circulating" has created bad feelings and unhealthy competition among churches. Some facets of the church growth movement have encouraged this competitive spirit. Since total growth is rewarded, it matters little what the source of the growth is. But a church that adds one hundred Christian churchgoers to its rolls annually has not been used to increase the rolls of the kingdom.

If the emphasis of church growth becomes conversion growth, however, winning saints to a church will become far less important than winning a soul to Christ. Competition will diminish and resources will be directed toward more healthy endeavors.

Increased church planting. Church planting has been cited in numerous studies as the most effective evangelistic tool available.[36] If all empirical evidence points to the value of church planting for evangelism, why are so few churches starting new churches? The dearth of new church starts is exacerbated by the reward system cited earlier, among other reasons. If total growth or numerical size is our standard of success, the likelihood of churches giving away resources to start new works diminishes.

One anecdote derived from the study of evangelistic churches referred to earlier illustrates this point. A pastor in Texas led a church to a record year in evangelism, as measured by total baptisms. In our interview with him, we discovered that the community in which the church was located was 70 percent unchurched. All demographic indicators pointed to an exciting opportunity to start new churches. Although the pastor agreed, he admitted candidly that such an endeavor by his church was unlikely. "Success today is measured by your church's total growth and

---

[36]For example, C. Peter Wagner, *Church Planting for a Greater Harvest* (Ventura, Calif.: Regal, 1990).

the rate of that growth," he said. "I just can't see our church sacrificing people and money for a new church, even in the short term. The pressure is just too great to grow every year."

While few church leaders are as forthright as this Texas pastor, he is not alone in thinking such thoughts. Until we change the reward system, a surge in church planting by existing churches will be unlikely. The task of church planting will remain primarily in the hands of denominational leaders and entities other than local churches. But if evangelistic growth becomes our goal, church planting will expand.

A sharper focus on eternal matters instead of the latest trends. When evangelism is excluded from the definition of church growth, matters of immediate concern become more pressing than those of eternal significance. When total church growth is the primary concern, the issues of greatest interest are tools, methodologies and trends that can engender greater growth. In the seventies and eighties we thus saw a proliferation of seminars, conferences and books concerned with the latest pragmatic tool to grow a church. While methodologies and trends are not inherently evil, a focus on such issues detracts from greater issues, such as a person's eternal destiny. But when evangelism becomes the most important issue in church growth, the focus becomes eternal rather than peripheral.

Conclusion: The Challenge of Evangelism and Church Growth in the Twenty-first Century

In the 1940s Donald McGavran was concerned that churches were involved in seemingly evangelistic activities that produced no growth in the local church. He thus exhorted Christians to focus on ecclesiocentric evangelism, or evangelism that results in church growth. Today the concern is similar, but from a different perspective. Many churches are growing, but few are growing as the result of evangelistic activities. The call to churches today is for growth that is soteriocentric.

The Great Commission commanded us to make disciples of all peoples. To be a disciple is first of all to be a Christian. But discipleship is more. It is being a Christian in the New Testament pattern of bearing fruit in the local church. The call today is for evangelism *and* church growth. And such is the right response to the Great Commission.

Resources for Additional Study

Hemphill, Ken. *The Antioch Effect.* Nashville: Broadman & Holman, 1994.

Hunter, George G., III. *How to Reach Secular People.* Nashville: Abingdon, 1992.

Kelley, Dean M. *Why Conservative Churches Are Growing.* Rev. ed. Macon, Ga.: Mercer, 1986.

McGavran, Donald A. *The Bridges of God.* Rev. ed. New York: Friendship, 1981.

———. *Understanding Church Growth.* 2nd rev. ed. Edited by C. Peter Wagner. Grand Rapids, Eerdmans, 1990.

Miles, Delos. *Church Growth: A Mighty River.* Nashville: Broadman, 1981.

Mims, Gene. *Kingdom Principles for Church Growth.* Nashville: Convention, 1994.

Rainer, Thom S. *The Book of Church Growth: History, Theology and Principles.* Nashville: Broadman & Holman, 1993.

Towns, Elmer L. *Ten of Today's Most Innovative Churches.* Ventura, Calif,: Regal, 1990.

Wagner, C. Peter. *Church Growth and the Whole Gospel: A Biblical Mandate.* San Francisco: Harper & Row, 1981.

———. *Leading Your Church to Growth.* Ventura, Calif.: Regal, 1984.

———. *Strategies for Church Growth.* Ventura, Calif.: Regal, 1987.

Chapter 25

New Dimensions in Worship & Ministry

Harry L. Poe

·····························

Since 1960, worship in American churches has undergone a revolution that cuts across denominational and geographical boundaries. Following Vatican II the Latin Mass disappeared as the norm in Catholic parishes as the vernacular language replaced the ancient language of the church for the first time in centuries. Many Catholic churches then moved the altar from the eastern wall to the crossing, so that the priest celebrates Mass facing toward the people instead of facing away from them. If these changes were not enough, a folk Mass appeared, complete with guitars. With these changes came a new involvement of the laity in the worship service. An entirely new body of hymns also came into being.

During the same period the Protestant Episcopal Church in the United States revised the Book of Common Prayer, which dated for the most part from the time of Henry VIII and was written in the English of the Tudor period, antedating the Authorized Version of the Bible. The changes involved more than modernizing the language, however, completely revising the service and doing away with what had been a central element of the Anglican Communion for over four hundred years. Other mainline churches have made changes of a similar magnitude. Incorporating gender-neutral language into hymns and the lectionary has been a major focus of the changes in mainline worship.

Restoration movements have arisen in some places that have led to formal denominational splits. Pockets of conservative resistance have clung to the Latin Mass. A growing number of Episcopal churches have been organized that use the old prayer book. They have left the authority of the Protestant Episcopal Church.

Bishops and clergy of these new denominational groups are intent on preserving traditions that were discarded by the denomination from which they separated.

Evangelicals are also changing traditional patterns of worship. The most well-known challenge to the peace and security of the traditional service comes from the seeker service associated with Willow Creek Church in suburban Chicago and with Saddleback Valley Church in Orange County, California. The dramatic growth of these churches, under Bill Hybels at Willow Creek and under Rick Warren at Saddleback, has elicited the interest of evangelicals and has inspired a significant number of imitations. Millard Erickson has observed of this phenomenon:

> Anyone alert to what is going on in evangelical American churches is aware of the shift toward a more informal, experience-centered style of religion. Celebration is replacing meditation, praise choruses are supplanting hymns, worship teams have succeeded robed choirs, organs are sitting unused in favor of guitars, hymnals are replaced by words projected on a screen or inserted in the worship folder, casual attire is worn instead of Sunday-go-to-meeting clothes. One church leader, observing that a change-oriented congregation had just installed an organ costing over one million dollars in its new sanctuary, commented, "Think how many guitars that would have bought." This youth-oriented trend is gaining momentum.[1]

The seeker service as a major trend has sparked conflict in evangelical ranks, some believing that this worship style is the wave of the future and others holding that it constitutes "dining with the devil."

Dining with the Devil

Os Guinness opens his book *Dining with the Devil* with a description of a worship service conducted by Leith Anderson (whom Guinness does not mention by name) in Minneapolis's Mall of America shortly after it opened. Guinness makes the point that "the problem is not the presence of a church in a mall but the presence of the mall in the church."[2] He warns of the dangers of modernity (or what others might call postmodernity). This warning finds its greatest sounding in relation to the challenge to truth as an eternal constant as pastors abandon theology for "the latest insights of sociology."[3] Guinness illustrates the lack of communication that exists between church growth advocates and its critics with his systematic demolition of the "new ground" Peter Wagner has advocated as a basis for new churches. For Wagner, starting churches on "new ground" means starting a church in an area where no church has been. Like Origen of old, however, Guinness develops an elaborate

---

[1] Millard J. Erickson, *Where Is Theology Going?* (Grand Rapids: Baker, 1994), p. 41.
[2] Os Guinness, *Dining with the Devil* (Grand Rapids: Baker, 1993), p. 12.
[3] Ibid., p. 29.

allegory to describe "new ground" as the insights and techniques of modernity, which he devotes his book to demolishing.[4]

Guinness believes that the "sovereign audience" and "audience-driven" preaching constitute a great threat to truth. He argues that the church growth movement breeds unintended consequences through "the uncritical espousal of the ideal of 'relevance' and its companion slogans 'seeker-friendly,' 'audience-driven,' and 'full-service churches.'"[5] Guinness explains that "when 'Saturday Night Live' becomes a church's seeker-friendly 'Sunday Morning Live' and 'The Best Show in Town,' the typical church staff question after worship becomes 'How did it go?'"[6]

The danger of programming to "felt needs," which Guinness and other critics raise, reflects the rationale of Islamic governments that ban Christian ministries out of a fear that Christians will gain adherents through "bribery." Guinness approaches the issue from an entirely different perspective, of course, but he has a genuine concern that people may "affiliate" who have no faith. He challenges the validity of what he refers to as one of the "defining features of church-growth rhetoric." This rhetoric asserts that "we have shifted decisively . . . from an era of proclamation to one of incarnation, from product-centered thinking to audience-centered thinking, from a focus on tradition to one of change, from a concern for theology to one for doing, and so on."[7]

Douglas Webster develops this concern in *Selling Jesus: What's Wrong with Marketing the Church*. He criticizes what he describes as a "market-driven" model of church growth made popular by people like George Barna, Leith Anderson and Elmer Towns.[8] He objects to speaking of worship in terms of "quality of performance" and warns of the danger in an entertainment view of worship. Entertaining sermons aim to present the Christian life as an "attractive, relevant, compelling" alternative to the competition.[9] He views with disdain George Barna's encouragement of churches to "shed existing attitudes of piety and solemnness, in favor of attitudes of anticipation, joy and fulfillment."[10] The tone of worship itself is a point at issue between the advocates and critics of innovative approaches to worship. The discussion is reminiscent of the debate between the English Puritans and Archbishop Laud, who believed that worship must take place with a lofty "spirit of holiness" instead of the Puritan approach, which focused on "plain preaching."

Webster stresses the nature of the church in his argument, declaring that

---

[4]Ibid., pp. 13-14, 41.
[5]Ibid., p. 62.
[6]Ibid., p. 64.
[7]Ibid., p. 79.
[8]Douglas D. Webster, *Selling Jesus: What's Wrong with Marketing the Church* (Downers Grove, Ill.: InterVarsity Press, 1992), p. 10-13.
[9]Ibid., pp. 13-14.
[10]Ibid., quoting George Barna, *The Frog in the Kettle* (Ventura, Calif.: Regal, 1990), pp. 62-63, 153.

the church is not based on human opinions, no matter how positive. It is not an audience positively inclined toward Jesus, but a company of committed individuals whose lives depend upon the truth that Jesus Christ is Lord. The church must not obscure this truth by transforming a congregation into an audience, transforming proclamation into performance or transforming worship into entertainment.[11]

In terms of the tone set by the style of worship, the metaphors of worship and the order of worship, Webster declares that "if 'unchurched Harry' feels perfectly at home in our churches, then the chances are that we have no longer an authentic household of faith, but a popular cultural religion."[12]

Webster continually argues that his opponents are driven by "popular opinion about Jesus" and that they market a picture of Jesus that people will feel comfortable with. This criticism of marketing seems focused on the church that wants "unchurched Harry" to feel at home. This terminology is the terminology of Willow Creek Church, the originator of the seeker service, but Webster seems unaware that Willow Creek refuses to market itself, relying instead on the commitment of its members to do personal evangelism and to bring people to their outreach service. Nonetheless, Webster is concerned with an extremely important issue. He is not opposed to enlarging the church or even to developing strategies for reaching the lost. He is concerned that people experience true confession instead of mere affiliation.

Many who criticize innovations in worship join Michael Horton, who identifies the new worship styles with the shallowness of postmodernism. Horton particularly condemns the pragmatism that he detects in his opponents' methodology:

> If the success of Christianity depends on whether it can sell, or whether it works, or whether it feels good or provides meaningful experiences, then that success is threatened by exposure to the critical judgment of Scripture, not to mention of life's daily pressures.[13]

Horton joins Bloesch in arguing that the evangelical faith he defends is "the historic Christian faith grounded in apostolic witness, reaffirmed by Augustine in his battle with Pelagius, and rediscovered by the Reformers and the Puritans."[14] Horton traces the shift to secularization in society and in the church, from the abandonment of Reformed theology and the "apostasy" of Arminianism.[15]

Horton attributes the pragmatism that he observes dominating evangelical life to the Second Great Awakening, when "a whole system of techniques and methods

---

[11]Ibid., p. 16.
[12]Ibid., p. 17.
[13]Michael Scott Horton, *Made in America* (Grand Rapids: Baker, 1991), p. 8.
[14]Ibid., p. 13.
[15]Ibid., pp. 21, 32, 35.

emerges in order to assist (some said manipulate) audiences into doing what they must do in order to achieve salvation."[16] In the evangelism of Moody and Sunday, "the gospel not only had to work; it had to sell."[17] Thus by the mid-nineteenth century, evangelicals had embraced consumerism. Horton insists, in contrast to this tradition, that the church should not try to attract a large hearing for the gospel because he believes Jesus did not.

Evangelicals who stress self-esteem have given in to Lucifer's illusion of self-fulfillment, which appears as hedonism, narcissism and materialism.[18] Horton traces this tendency among evangelicals to seventeenth-century English Arminianism. He decries concern for feelings or religious experience among evangelicals with the assertion that "today's pietists are tomorrow's liberals."[19] Feelings breed the same subjectivism as existentialism and are destructive to rational faith. By shifting its focus from God to human beings, Arminianism paved the way for the development of the New Age movement through subjective personal experience.[20] Evangelicals also bear the responsibility for the relativism of the postmodern world. By abandoning Reformation orthodoxy, evangelicals opened the door to relativism. By tolerating differences of opinion on the interpretation of Scripture, evangelicals have abandoned theology.[21]

David Wells came to the controversy to defend his academic specialty (theology) against the charge of irrelevancy. Wells maintains that the sorry state of theology has been brought about by pastors and laity in the churches, not theologians. Wells complains that evangelization does not provide a sufficiently broad basis for unity to give evangelicalism a sense of direction. What evangelicalism requires is theological unity in order to have the *esprit* necessary to constitute a vibrant movement.[22]

Wells views culture as the enemy of faith, for it is "laden with values, many of which work to rearrange the substance of faith, even when they are mediated to us through the benefits that the modern world also bestows upon us."[23] Evangelicals have by and large embraced the modern world, but Wells argues that evangelicals should adopt an antimodern stance. He attributes the divergence of contemporary evangelicalism from historic orthodoxy to the acceptance of modernity by evangelicals.[24] Wells seems to identify "truth" with "the structures of the historic Protestant faith" rather than with the confession of Jesus Christ. Wells is horrified that

---

[16]Ibid., p. 42.
[17]Ibid., p. 61.
[18]Ibid., p. 74.
[19]Ibid., p. 93.
[20]Ibid., p. 120.
[21]Ibid., pp. 141-54.
[22]David F. Wells, *No Place for Truth* (Grand Rapids: Eerdmans, 1993), pp. 1-9.
[23]Ibid., p. 11.
[24]Ibid., p. 12.

evangelicals can hold to the creeds and the Bible but use methods and practices that are new.[25]

Wells sees the disappearance of theology "in the vacuous worship that is so prevalent, for example, in the shift from God to the self as the central focus of faith, in the psychologized preaching that follows this shift, in the erosion of its conviction, in its strident pragmatism, in its inability to think incisively about the culture, in its reveling in the irrational."[26] This slippage would never have occurred if evangelicals had remained committed to truth. It has led to a "technology of practice" that aims at expanding the church and a self-mastery based on ideas gleaned from business management and psychology. Thus the pastoral role has been redefined from dispenser of truth to management specialist and psychologist.[27]

Wells argues that the disappearance of theology among evangelicals may be traced to trading Calvinistic spirituality for pietism, which marked the passage from the First Great Awakening to the Second Great Awakening. With this passage, Wells argues, evangelicals developed a "passion for souls" that undermined their "passion for truth."[28] Wells ridicules the pastoral concern for practical skills and the kind of seminary education that prepares ministers to do something other than obtain "scholarly expertise in theological sciences."[29] The shift in the nineteenth century from a predominantly Calvinistic orientation to an Arminian orientation speeded the decline of truth. It led to such suspect features of worship as testimonies of personal experience of Christ, which offer a "seductive" appeal for those who yearn for a personal experience with God.[30]

The rise of "everyperson," or radical egalitarianism, accompanied the rejection of Calvinistic orthodoxy, which was seen as being of a piece with power and privilege, and the ascendancy of Arminianism. This trend has led to the tyranny of popular opinion and a "truth" based on majority rule. By conforming itself to American culture, evangelicalism takes on the values of that culture and unconsciously reshapes its theology, which may not become apparent until the next generation comes of age with no evident knowledge of a holy God and sinful humanity.[31]

Reaching Secular People

In articulating the need to adapt ministry to cultural context, George Hunter asserts

---

[25]Ibid., p. 108-9.
[26]Ibid., p. 95.
[27]Ibid., p. 101.
[28]Ibid., p. 110.
[29]Ibid., p. 112.
[30]Ibid., p. 172.
[31]Ibid., p. 298.

that secular people are ignorant of basic Christianity, are oriented toward life, are conscious of doubt more than guilt, have a negative image of the church, experience multiple alienation, are untrusting, have low self-esteem, feel out of control and cannot find "the door" to Christ.[32] These assumptions mandate a ministry designed to bring the gospel to the lost rather than to make the saints feel comfortable.

Churches that are highly effective in reaching secular people tend to have a working understanding of how the different dimensions of ministry relate to each other. They do not expect any one ministry to bear the full weight of being the church. They understand that each element of a church should have a clear purpose with a spiritual mandate and that when the purpose of a church function becomes lost, then the function becomes ineffective. This understanding results in a strategic approach to ministry.[33] The presence of strategy for ministry would constitute one of the major institutional differences between innovative churches and traditional churches.

If a church intends to present the gospel in an evangelistic meeting to non-Christians with the desire for them to come to faith, then the church must plan a service to which non-Christians will come. Lee Strobel has observed that "unless Christians make a conscious effort to create programs that will appeal to unbelievers, they naturally default to designing events that reflect their own tastes."[34] On the other hand, a church that intends to reach unchurched Christians will plan different kinds of services. Strobel argues that one church cannot reach all people and should identify the ones God intends for them to reach in particular. This identification of an audience provides the context for developing a total ministry strategy.[35]

In regard to designing ministry, Leonard Sweet has identified what he calls "designerquakes" as one of the spiritual earthquakes that the church faces today. The designer church arises in response to the "egonomics" phenomenon whereby people want a church that "fits" them. The form and style of a church represent the package rather than its contents. As people in the broad culture become increasingly concerned with their own style and identity, Sweet suggests that churches must respond to this reality and create distinct identities for themselves. This approach creates more personal ownership of the church by the laity because the church is truly their community. Nevertheless, Sweet warns that the style is just wrapping and can warp the content if given too much emphasis.[36] In his critique of traditional evangelical and mainline churches, George Barna observes that few are prepared for the challenge:

---

[32]George G. Hunter III, *How to Reach Secular People* (Nashville: Abingdon, 1992), pp. 44-54.
[33]Ibid., pp. 154-71.
[34]Lee Strobel, *Inside the Mind of Unchurched Harry and Mary* (Grand Rapids: Zondervan, 1993), p. 161.
[35]Ibid., pp. 162-65.
[36]Leonard Sweet, *Faithquakes* (Nashville: Abingdon, 1994), pp. 95-123.

Realize that Americans most readily accept institutions, philosophies, programs or individuals that respond to our felt needs through highly personalized and relevant messages. We are looking for that which is fresh and exciting, but credible and substantive. We are interested in that which is solid but flexible. The Christian faith, as promoted in our churches today, offers few of these traits.[37]

Barna is a leading advocate of not only designing ministries to reach secular people but also marketing the church to the lost.

While Barna is a theorist, Leith Anderson represents a group of pastors who are actually trying to market the church to particular segments of the population. In the past, church growth has focused on homogeneous units or people groups in a missiological sense—racial groups, language groups or castes within a distinct society. Anderson more than any other traditional, evangelical pastor represents the American adaptation of the people group to generational segmentation. Baby boomers live in a culture that differs from their parents'. Baby busters live in yet another culture. Anderson does not prescribe what churches ought to do in the current environment of change. Rather, he describes the nature of change and advocates that churches respond appropriately.

When Anderson speaks of a church that targets baby boomers, he speaks of holding "high expectations of its people, including church membership and attendance, devotional disciplines, service inside and outside the church, financial support, social responsibility, and Christian lifestyle."[38] Baby boomers will feel "at home" in such a church because one of the "felt needs" of boomers is to be challenged. With these high expectations, however, boomers also expect teaching and the full range of discipleship training.

Anderson does not downplay the essential message of truth that the church proclaims about Jesus Christ, but he does declare that the medium of the message will change:

They will become open to the message of Jesus Christ during the transition times of their lives, such as divorce, remarriage, the birth of a child, unemployment, or the death of a parent. But that message will probably get to them through a divorce recovery workshop, an unemployment support group, or a workshop on grief rather than through a sermon.[39]

Anderson advocates sociological adaptation rather than theological bending or compromise. For Anderson, the starting point of reaching others for Christ begins with Christ and the truth of the gospel. He speaks of clearly establishing the "nonnegotiables." He speaks of understanding why the church exists. He speaks of

---

[37]Barna, *Frog in the Kettle*, p. 119.
[38]Leith Anderson, *Dying for Change* (Minneapolis: Bethany House, 1990), p. 85.
[39]Ibid., p. 95.

maintaining spiritual values as the determining factors in a church.[40]

Though Anderson does not advocate any particular shape for worship or ministry, he does advocate a process for change:

1. decide who is to be reached
2. learn about these people
3. discover the most effective means of reaching them
4. change the church or other Christian organization accordingly[41]

Anderson speaks freely of churches and their "customers," "salespersons," "consumers," "market" and "employees."[42] The larger churches that have succeeded in becoming "full service churches" manage to reach people through offering a wide range of ministries, including "variety in music, extensive youth programs, diverse educational opportunities, a counseling staff, support groups, singles' ministry, athletic activities, multiple Sunday morning services, a modern nursery," and other programs and ministries that meet felt needs.[43] Anderson argues that evangelicals must change their ways if they expect to evangelize the next generation. Evangelicals have "done well on revelation (the Bible) but poorly on relevance (the culture)."[44]

Historical Perspective

Scripture provides for a wide range of acceptable worship styles, from the liturgical features of the Mosaic law to the spontaneity of David dancing before the ark to the quietist admonition to be still and know the Lord. One searches the New Testament in vain for a rule of worship, though informality seems to be the mode in contrast to the formality of the law. The early church had a participatory character. Anyone who had a song or a testimony or other contribution to make was encouraged to do so (Col 3:16; Eph 5:19). The governing principles of worship seem to have been that it be carried on "in spirit and truth" (Jn 4:23) and "in a fitting and orderly way" (1 Cor 14:40). In the present, traditionalists contend that the innovators have abandoned truth while the innovators contend that the traditionalists have neglected spirit in worship.

Controversy over worship is hardly new to the people of God. As often as not, the controversy has involved God as much as people. Cain may have had the form of worship, but his worship was not acceptable to God. The acceptability of worship constituted a major issue in the message of the prophets to Israel. Though Israel observed the form of the law and rightly constituted worship, the form was meaningless to God, who despised the spirit in which the form was carried out

---

[40]Ibid., pp. 167, 150, 118.
[41]Ibid., p. 99.
[42]Ibid., pp. 121, 132, 164.
[43]Ibid., p. 51.
[44]Ibid., p. 17.

(Amos 5:21; Mal 1:6). Some advocates of innovative service point to passages like these as proof that traditional forms of worship should be abandoned. These texts do not advocate abandoning the traditional forms, however, so much as they express the view that true worship involves something other than the external form. Innovative worship can be as guilty as traditional worship of the flaw that God despises. Worship borders on idolatry when the form of worship becomes the object of worship and the experience of worship makes no difference in the life of a person before God.

Major changes in the style or form of worship have occurred over the last two thousand years in periods of dramatic and cataclysmic change in the broader society. The first major change for the church came in moving from the worship of the temple to the worship of the house church. Initially, Christians worshiped in the temple with the rest of the children of Abraham (Acts 2:46; 3:1; 5:12; 5:25; 5:42; 21:26). At the same time, however, they began meeting in their houses in small groups to pray, study the Scriptures, maintain fellowship and learn the apostles' teachings, which they had received from Jesus (Acts 2:42-47). It would be difficult to say from the text whether the worship of God took place in the temple or in the homes at the beginning of the book of Acts. As the church moved out of Palestine, however, Christians abandoned the old forms of worship. In the Gentile world, new forms emerged that had more continuity with the synagogue than with the temple. Jesus himself radically changed the meaning and observance of the Passover. With the change in form came a change in theology. The confrontation between Paul and the Judaizers represented a change of theology symbolized by the form of ritual observances related to worship. With the destruction of Jerusalem and the temple in A.D. 70, the change in worship was complete. The innovation with its change in theology became the tradition. The church with its devotion to Jesus Christ was severed from the synagogue and its devotion to the law. Both were severed from the ceremonial law of Moses and the sacrificial system. Judaism underwent as dramatic a change in theology as Christianity.

The next major revolution in worship occurred for the church when Christianity received official sanction from Constantine in the fourth century and the church moved from private homes to the public basilica. The informality and variety that had characterized the regional worship practices of the church began to take on a more formal and unified tone as Christianity became the state religion of the decaying empire. The liturgy of John Chrysostom became the liturgy for the Eastern church. Worship would play a key role in the evangelistic ministry of the church throughout the first two major epochs of the church. While it might be argued that what happened on the day of Pentecost does not correspond to what is meant by worship today, it might just as easily be asserted that nothing in the New Testament corresponds exactly to what is meant by worship today.

On the anniversary of the death of the martyrs, the early church would gather at the tombs or the repositories of whatever might remain of the martyrs for a worship service that had an evangelistic emphasis. Because of the noble way in which the martyrs had met their death, the Roman world could not help but exhibit some curiosity in what prompted them to die for this Jesus they worshiped. Augustine himself testified about the impact of the martyrs on his own conversion. Before this evangelistic dimension developed, however, the church had celebrated the anniversary of the death of the martyrs as a means of encouraging those left behind in their hour of trial. Because God had given the martyrs the grace to endure, the early church believed that the martyrs stood in a special relationship to the Lord. After the persecutions ended, those who had failed to keep the faith in the hour of trial sought out martyrs who had suffered for their faith although not to the point of death. Those who lapsed sought the forgiveness of the martyrs. After a thousand years of practice lost from its original purpose, the church developed its understanding of merit and prayer through the sainted martyrs.

Worship held a particularly powerful evangelistic sway over the Celtic peoples of western Europe. Druidism, that often romanticized religion of the Celts, included human sacrifice and cannibalism. Believing that gods inhabited the trees, the Celts sacrificed their victims on trees. They thought that the god entered the body of the sacrifice to receive it. The Celts then drank the blood and ate the flesh of the sacrifice to receive the power of the god. Though the Romans began suppressing this practice in Gaul as early as the time of Julius Caesar, it persisted in the Celtic regions that never came under the jurisdiction of the Empire, notably Ireland, Scotland and Germany. Martin of Tours and generations of monks after him challenged the druids and set up places of Christian worship at the pagan holy sites of druidism. There they offered the sacrifice of the flesh and blood of Jesus. They obtained immortality by drinking Jesus' blood and eating his flesh. It is not surprising that the Catholic doctrine of transubstantiation emerged from the Celtic church in northern Europe, not the Latin church.

In its efforts to win the Arian church of Visigothic Spain to orthodox Christianity, the church of Charlemagne's empire altered the creed that had been established by a universal council. To help people understand that the relationship between the Father and the Son was a matter of their nature, not an adoption, Charlemagne's church added that the Holy Spirit proceeds not only from the Father but also from the Son. This alteration helped the Franks deal with the Arian heresy of the Spanish church and led to the ultimate embrace of Roman Christianity by the Spanish. The alteration in the formula of worship by a synod without the benefit of a universal council, however, did not sit well with the Eastern church. The addition of the famous *filioque* phrase resulted in the initial break between the Eastern church and the Western church.

In the East, orthodoxy means right praise *(doxa)*, not right belief. The right praise of the church had been finalized in the liturgy of John Chrysostom, and the Eastern church could not tolerate the heretical innovations of the Roman church. With its otherworldly tone, the worship of the Eastern church became the central element in the evangelization of Russia beginning in the late tenth century. The Russian church attributed Islam's conquest of Byzantium to the negotiations that the emperor and the patriarch were carrying on with what good Orthodox Christians considered an apostate church. The integrity of traditional worship continued to be a major theme in the Russian church. When Patriarch Nikon in the seventeenth century introduced liturgical reforms that brought the Russian church into conformity with the Greek church, a large group of priests and monks known as Old Believers rebelled. Thousands died at the hands of the tsar's army rather than conform to the abominable practices that the Russians believed had contaminated the Greek church. Many more died by locking themselves within their monasteries and setting the buildings afire.

The controversy between Rome and the Reformers had as much to do with worship as it had to do with theology, since worship and theology are inseparable. Worship determines theology and theology determines worship. Worship is never neutral. It always represents one's experience with or knowledge of God. Much of the worship tradition that the Reformers rejected represented innovations of a thousand years earlier. In the English church, the Puritan movement arose initially because the worship of the English church did not represent the theology of the Reformation, which the Thirty-nine Articles espoused. By continuing to maintain a stone altar against the eastern wall instead of serving the sacrament from a wooden table, the English church perpetuated the theology of the Mass through the symbols of worship, even though the English church had rejected the Mass.

Most efforts to change worship have an emotional component as well as a rational reaction. The efforts of the Eastern emperor to abolish the use of icons in the Eastern church met with violent riots. The efforts of Archbishop Laud to change the worship of Scotland to conform to the style of worship he was imposing in England resulted in riot and war. The interplay between intellect and emotions can often cloud the essential issues in controversy over matters of worship. People may argue from a rational perspective when their underlying issues are actually emotional. The same dynamic is at work when a small congregation meeting in a mammoth old sanctuary is spread throughout the huge room. Even though they may be intimate friends, they do not sit together in a group. The frustrated transient pastor who rails against their lack of spirituality has missed the dynamic involved. They are operating out of an ancient theology of place, worshiping where their family worshiped years ago when it was still together. Eighty-year-old women sit where they sat as young mothers with their children and husbands. Any changes in familiar patterns touch deep emotional chords because the familiar represents the context in which people have had their most significant spiritual experiences.

Toward a Resolution

A number of matters require clarification if there is to be any resolution to the brewing controversy over worship. The use of hyperbole, characterization and generalization by the adversaries has not helped. The rationalists wax emotional on the subject, and the experientialists tend toward rationalism. Neither side seems particularly interested in conversation.

The historiographic justification for the criticism of the innovators tends to be built on a denial of the Puritan heritage and a surrender to the Arminian extremes of Charles Finney. This argument tends to ignore the Puritan revolution in worship. The Puritans rejected choirs and organs and the old style of music altogether. They rejected the old style of preaching that tended toward the pedantic in its analysis of the text. The Puritans insisted on what they called "plain preaching." This style of preaching spoke to the everyday experience of people and demonstrated the relevance of God's Word for each life. In criticizing the current emphasis on experience, the critics of innovation once again point to the excesses of revivalism but ignore the Puritan emphasis on religious experience. The Pietists derived their concern for religion of the heart from the Puritans. William Perkins developed Puritan casuistry as a means of helping people deal with their spiritual experiences. This concern for experience forms a major thread of Reformed ministry throughout the seventeenth century, from Perkins through Bunyan and Baxter.

Critics also charge that pietistic influence has led to a passion for souls that undermines sound theology. Once again, this criticism ignores the entire Puritan agenda, which aimed at the conversion of England. William Perkins himself declared that the commission of a preacher is "to deliver a man from going to hell."[45] This concern led to the extensive practice of lectureships by the Puritans. As often as not, the lectureship would take place away from the parish church building. The lectureship competed with productions of Shakespeare's plays and with bear baiting, one of the most popular forms of entertainment. The Puritans made no bones about their desire to draw a crowd because preaching is "the chief and ordinary means God hath ordained for the salvation of sinners." Though the expression was coined by the apostle Paul, Perkins popularized the expression "to win souls" in his book *The Calling of the Ministry.*[46] Through the lectureships the Puritans hoped to reach with the gospel people who would not normally have gone to church.

George Whitefield and Jonathan Edwards carried the Reformed revolution

---

[45]John Brown, *Puritan Preaching in England* (New York: Scribner's, 1900), pp. 75-76.
[46]Ibid.

forward into the eighteenth century and even influenced Arminians, such as John Wesley, who were reluctant to take up such innovative and unseemly practices as preaching outdoors. Whitefield introduced the concept of mass marketing through the new institution of the newspaper. He resorted to extraordinary means to attract large crowds, going to the coal mines and to the carnival atmosphere of the market days in order to gain a crowd.[47] Edwards stressed the importance of the emotional dimension in faith in his *Treatise on Religious Affections*. In the nineteenth century, Charles Spurgeon self-consciously continued this Puritan tradition in his London ministry. In doing so, he labored to develop a ministry which would reach the teeming masses of metropolitan London.

This brief survey simply serves to illustrate that the current debate has become littered with inappropriate historical arguments mustered by both sides to rationalize their positions. Instead of pursuing these excursions, we ought to focus on answering several fundamental questions. What kind of worship pleases God? Were the Puritans right when they said that the chief responsibility of a minister is to deliver a person from going to hell? What relationship, if any, exists between worship and evangelism? What limits does God place on innovation, and how can they be known? These seem to be the fundamental questions at issue, yet the disputants do not seem to have the disposition to consider them.

To a certain extent, contemporary evangelical life represents the era of specialization gone to seed. The theological church is as guilty of this rarefied specialization as the innovative church, which markets to a particular felt need. Traditionalists do theology, innovators do experience. This dichotomy between heart and mind reflects a danger that Millard Erickson has warned about on numerous occasions. Notably in his inaugural sermon as dean of Bethel Theological Seminary, Erickson envisioned a school that would strive to bring these two dimensions of faith together. If traditionalists refuse to innovate, they have denied their Lord's commission. If innovators refuse to consider the theological implications of their innovations, they have denied their Lord's commands.

The style and form of worship have been in a state of constant change since the first century. As a culture changes, so the way Christians worship in that culture will change. The gospel must always address a world in rebellion against God. Augustine understood that the world in which he had grown up was in a state of collapse. The old culture was being replaced by something he did not yet know, but in the midst of the collapse of Roman civilization and the emergence of Christendom, he wrote *The City of God*. He may not have cared for the barbarians, but he knew God was doing something far greater than the fall of Rome meant to him.

[47]For a recent study of George Whitefield's creative use of mass marketing in his ministry, see Frank Lambert, *Pedlar in Divinity: George Whitefield and the Transatlantic Revivals, 1737-1770* (Princeton, N.J.: Princeton University Press, 1994).

The Western world appears to be in the midst of another great collapse. Consider that at the beginning of the twentieth century, most of the world was controlled by a few monarchical empires: Britain, Russia, Austro-Hungary, Ottoman Turk, China, Japan, Spain and the emerging empires of Italy and Germany. Within fifty years all of these empires had collapsed, and of all the monarchies, only a few remained. With the collapse of the Christian empire came the collapse of Christian identity.

Whether we like it or not, the church now ministers in a neopagan, postliterate society in the West. Delivering people from going to hell is still the commission. That being so, however, is ministry a no-holds-barred exercise? The church has two thousand years of experience in engaging different cultures with the gospel. It is strange to be engaging one's own culture as a new and different culture, but that is the case. We do not yet know what postmodernity is or will be. Currently the expression is a fad, but it reflects a true situation of perhaps eschatological significance. While we cannot predict with accuracy what the world will be like in the future, it is possible to take some lessons from the experience of the saints. This exercise differs somewhat from the debate over which side has the true apostolic lineage.

If the innovators are correct that the church has the responsibility to bring the gospel to a generation that does not go to church, then the traditionalists are correct in observing that some successful methods can actually undermine the gospel while producing large numerical responses. The evangelization of Europe and South America resulted in a number of accommodations that altered the theology of salvation, prayer, the sacraments, the saints and a vast array of related matters. Innovators do not have the luxury of ignoring the theological implications of their innovations. Neither do the traditionalists have the luxury of fighting innovation instead of helping those who are blessed with the energy and creativity needed to carry the gospel into the next century.

In his sobering critique of the church, *The Body*, Charles Colson applauds Willow Creek Church for recognizing the difference between a worship service for Christians and an evangelistic service for non-Christians. By keeping the services separate and focused on their distinct purposes, Willow Creek has succeeded in raising the faithfulness of each.[48] Willow Creek has done nothing but take the old Sunday-evening service and move it to Sunday morning while moving the Sunday-morning service to Wednesday night. Most evangelical churches have forgotten that the evening service was begun at the end of the last century as an alternative outreach service. It was more informal, with upbeat music and testimonies designed for non-Christians. It works like a Billy Graham crusade or an inner-city rescue

---

[48]Charles Colson with Ellen Santilli Vaughn, *The Body* (Dallas: Word, 1992), p. 343.

mission. It corresponds to holding a revival meeting every Sunday, but it looks different because the people for whom it is intended are a different generation.

While Willow Creek Church and Saddleback Valley do an outstanding job of attending to the theological foundations for their ministries, their imitators do not always have the same concern. In this regard, imitation rather than innovation is the danger. Bill Hybels warns those who would imitate Willow Creek that the "formula" cannot be reproduced. The underlying principles that involve personal evangelism, an outreach meeting, a service for believers, discipleship groups, involvement in ministry and stewardship toward God are reproducible. Those who neglect the underlying principles or strategy are not doing the Willow Creek model. They are merely doing a weekly rally.

Change in worship will continue. Some of what happens today will pass away as fad. Other things will become the sacred traditions against which future generations will rebel. The music will change. The instrumentation will change. The style of preaching will change. The arrangement of sanctuaries will change. The old songs I love will be forgotten. Old churches will die. New churches will repeat mistakes made by their forebears. New denominations will form. Intergenerational conflict will continue. But the gospel of Jesus Christ will go forward.

Chapter 26

Bibliographic Essay on the Works of Millard J. Erickson

Arnold Hustad

••••••••••••••••••••••••••••

As A YOUNG SEMINARY STUDENT SEARCHING FOR A MAJOR, I HEADED for the office of the adviser for majors in historical-theological studies. After I explained my theological and philosophical interests, I wondered aloud whether his department would be practical for pastoral ministry. Millard Erickson leaned back in his chair and suggested that it depended on what I meant by practical. My misgivings were soon put to rest.

Shaped in the classroom and tested in the church, Erickson's writings effectively join a scholar's mind and a pastor's heart. This chapter neither catalogs nor reviews Erickson's numerous works. Rather, it samples his principal works and attempts to capture the flavor of over twenty-five years of scholarly production.

Erickson's Early Works

It is fitting that Erickson's first book clarifies the setting for much of his later writing. Published in 1968, while Erickson was associate professor of Bible and apologetics at Wheaton College, *The New Evangelical Theology* recounts the historical and doctrinal context of the burgeoning movement. With fundamentalism as a backdrop, the tenets of the new evangelical theology are drawn primarily from Edward John Carnell, Bernard Ramm and Carl F. H. Henry.

In the late 1960s evangelicals were debating the issue of authority, so it is not surprising that Erickson devotes an entire chapter to it. Subsequent sections introduce the doctrinal content and apologetic emphases of new evangelical doctrine. Anticipating the author's growing interest in ethics, it applies new evangelical doctrine to personal and social ethics. Outlined in the concluding chapter are characteristics of the movement, including its positive attitude toward culture, the place of reason as a judicial rather than a legislative authority, and the return by new evangelicals to a breadth found among early fundamentalists. In some respects, Erickson's description of new evangelicalism prefigured many of the personal convictions expressed in *Christian Theology*, written almost twenty years later.

While he was at Wheaton, Erickson participated in a discussion group for a Chicago television program on Joseph Fletcher's *Situation Ethics* and experienced a growing interest in the subject. The resulting research, along with courses taught on ethics at Bethel Theological Seminary, culminated in *Relativism in Contemporary Christian Ethics*. Erickson asserts that theology, and thereby Christian ethics, was influenced by developments in culture and theology that undermined commonsense beliefs in absolutes. Relativity in physics and mathematics, for example, though not logically correlated to ethics, created a mood in which relativism became more acceptable. Cultural relativism, however, has had a direct impact on ethical thinking. Theological influences, including various forms of biblical higher criticism, have cast doubts on the authenticity of some sayings attributed to Jesus, and thus on commonly held biblical teachings. Existentialism undermined universal values by asserting that values do not exist until the individual creates them. Given this milieu, ethical relativism is hardly surprising.

After introducing and assessing Fletcher's system, in which love is the only norm, Erickson proposes principialism as an alternative. Good is the expression of God's nature, conveyed as cognitive truth through revelation. This yields objective principles that may have different applications in various situations. Principialism thus avoids the vacuous nature of situationism and the rigidity of legalism. Though brief, a useful method of application follows, including suggestions for handling exceptional cases.

Growing out of student requests for a course on eschatological alternatives, *Contemporary Options in Eschatology: A Study of the Millennium* was published in 1977. Though some reviewers noted that nonconservatives would have appreciated more extensive treatment of their positions,[1] such an approach would have betrayed the students' desire for an objective treatment of the types of views often encountered in the context of ministry. Nonconservative historical and, more important, thematic backgrounds to contemporary eschatology are introduced in two brief chapters. Albert Schweitzer's consistent eschatology is contrasted to the realized eschatology of C. H. Dodd. Rudolf Bultmann is selected to represent the existential approach, and Jürgen Moltmann the theology of hope in which eschatology is the

---

[1] For example, see Douglas K. Erlandson's review of *Contemporary Options in Eschatology*, by Millard J. Erickson, *Christian Scholar's Review* 9, no. 2 (1979): 186-87.

motif around which all theology ought to be framed.

The remainder of the book consists of an overview of the millennial and tribulational views that, for many lay readers, constitute eschatology. Each view is delineated through a brief history, major tenets and evaluation. Only in the conclusion does Erickson reveal his own posttribulational and premillennial position. The scope of the book is limited. Those searching for a discussion of personal eschatology, including resurrection, intermediate and final states, must look elsewhere. The brief chapter on dispensationalism is dated, especially in light of recent developments. Nonetheless, Erickson's side-by-side comparison has proved useful to many.

The Tools of Systematic Theology

The name Millard Erickson came to prominence through the tools he devised for teaching systematic theology at Bethel Seminary. The first was a trilogy of anthologies published in the 1970s. *The Living God, Man's Need and God's Gift* and *The New Life* stemmed from a conviction that students of systematic theology ought to be exposed to a variety of theological outlooks. Thus authors as diverse as Augustine, John Wesley, Karl Barth, Harry Emerson Fosdick, Paul Tillich and Carl Henry are included. An editor's introduction to each unit assists the reader in identifing the perspective of each excerpt.

The anthologies were intended to supplement the widely used text *Christian Theology*. First published in three volumes between 1983 and 1985 and in a one-volume format in 1986, it received the Gold Medallion Book Award in the theology/doctrine category, presented by the Evangelical Christian Publishers Association. In 1992 an abridged version for undergraduates, *Introducing Christian Doctrine*, eliminated much of the critical and philosophical material. *Does It Matter What I Believe?*—published in the same year—is a simplified survey of doctrine for laypersons. Related topical studies, *Salvation: God's Amazing Plan* and *Responsive Faith* (reprinted as *Does It Matter How I Live?*) represent several recent volumes designed for lay audiences. Also produced during this period was the *Concise Dictionary of Christian Theology*, which provides succinct definitions of many of the terms used in these volumes.

Readers get to know Millard Erickson in the pages of *Christian Theology*. He identifies his theology as "classical" (p. 11), fashioned around the motif of the magnificence of God (p. 78). Although he is not as thorough as some want him to be, Erickson is clearly aware of critical biblical issues and the daunting philosophical and theological obstacles facing systematic theologians. Despite the difficulty of the concepts, however, his style is lucid and often pastoral. He respected Clark Pinnock's counsel to "let it sing like a hymn, not read like a telephone book" (p. 12). Erickson also credits his pastoral ministry, which served as a laboratory in which to refine some of his views, and acknowledges the church of which he was interim pastor during part of the time of writing.

Of particular value in *Christian Theology* are several introductory chapters dealing with the definition, relationships and method of theology. There is a useful step-by-step procedure of actually doing theology, from the initial collection of biblical materials to the final stratification of topics on the basis of relative importance. Especially noteworthy is a section on contemporizing the Christian message. Employing William Hordern's distinction between "transformers" and "translators," Erickson sides with the translators, who wish to reexpress the biblical message without altering its essence. Also provided is a list of criteria for identifying the permanent factors of a doctrine.

A recurring theme in *Christian Theology*, as well as in the notations of its reviewers, is Erickson's self-described "moderate Calvinism." Based on the philosophical concept of "compatibilism," Erickson argues that although God renders events certain, he does not render them necessary. Individuals thus act freely, within the limitations that God created. Accordingly, election is the act of God bringing into existence those whom he knows will freely choose him. The elect will also persevere to the end, for while they could apostatize, they will not.

Christian Theology firmly maintains the evangelical insistence on Scripture as the primary source for theology. The book is replete with scriptural references, but it also reflects the author's conviction that theology is more than a compendium of Bible verses. Where Scripture is not explicit on an issue or offers no resolution to a problem, Erickson does not appear averse to pressing beyond biblical assertion to discover a reasonable solution. This is evident in the explanation that he gives of the age of responsibility (pp. 637-39) and his proposal of a two-stage glorification of Christ (p. 777).

Several More Books

In the preface to *Christian Theology*, noting the danger of superficiality in an introductory text, Erickson hints of things to come when he speaks of "gaining an agenda of several more books" (p. 9). One item on that agenda was another Gold Medallion Book Award winner, *The Word Became Flesh: A Contemporary Incarnational Christology*. Since the intention is to develop a contemporary christology, review of ancient formulations is kept to a minimum. Erickson depicts and evaluates various approaches to Christology, such as the historical, the sociological and the metaphysical, categorized according to the types of problems they are designed to solve.

For example, liberation theology attempts to solve a sociological problem, oppression, by understanding Christ through praxis. The metaphysical problem of Christ's natures might be alleviated by adopting a functional Christology that affirms that the only concern of the biblical writers was the work of Christ. A process metaphysic, on the other hand, views Christ through the nature of God in process. Quite useful, in light of recent developments, is the chapter on postmodern Christology, featuring the theology of Mark C. Taylor. Other types of Christology evaluated include critical, existential, black, feminist, universalistic, mythological and narrative.

In the last part of *The Word Became Flesh* Erickson develops an incarnational Christology intended to do for our time what the Chalcedonian statement did for its time, and perhaps go beyond it. Erickson first establishes the biblical basis, demonstrating the historical reliability of Jesus' existence and the New Testament witness to the deity of Christ. Affirming that the incarnation requires a metaphysical basis, the author suggests factors that reduce, to some extent, certain difficulties that some have perceived in the event. For example, since humans are created in the image of God, there exists already an affinity between a human being and God. That the human nature of Jesus was sinless diminishes further the distance between the two natures.

Erickson adopts a view of kenosis by addition, in which attributes of each nature are added to the other. Thus Christ did not surrender his divine qualities but chose not to exercise them. For example, the incarnate Christ was omniscient, but the attribute remained latent unless the Father granted access. Concluding chapters take up the objection that Jesus cannot be the Savior of all people and explain how incarnational Christology helps us address the problem of evil.

God in Three Persons: A Contemporary Interpretation of the Trinity follows a similar format. Though ancient formulations receive only summary treatment, the book's agenda is established through a discussion of several problems raised by current debate. Included are questions regarding the metaphysical and logical objections to the Trinity, whether a trinitarian Christianity is the way of salvation for everyone and whether the Trinity is even biblical or practical. These questions are explored through representative theologians such as Cyril C. Richardson, Karl Rahner, Sally McFague and Raimundo Panikkar.

Acknowledging the questions raised by biblical criticism, Erickson nevertheless affirms that the concept of the Trinity is revealed in Scripture. However, a contemporary statement of the doctrine's metaphysical elements requires an appropriate set of categories. Metaphysically basic to all that exists is the spiritual dimension, for God is the one uncreated reality. The creation reflects the Creator in that it is fundamentally personal and social. Erickson concludes that the Trinity must, therefore, be understood as a society, bound together in genuine *agapē*.

Crucial to his logical formulation of the doctrine is the distinction between the *is* of identity, for example, God *is* God, and the *is* of predication, for example, the Father *is* God or the Son *is* God. No one member of the Trinity, therefore, is identical to God without the other two, and several analogies are offered for clarification. Concluding chapters respond to questions of whether the triune God, portrayed as masculine, can be the God of all people, the nature of internal relations within the Trinity, and the appropriateness of praying to and worshiping all three members of the Godhead.

Erickson's Trilogy

As esteem grew for Erickson as a scholar and an effective communicator, he was invited to lecture in a variety of colleges and seminaries. The three books published in 1993-94 are largely the fruit of such ventures. The trilogy explores a multiplicity of theoretical and practical issues to which evangelicals must respond.

If there is a theme to the first of these, *The Evangelical Mind and Heart: Perspectives on Theological and Practical Issues,* it appears to be evangelicalism itself. An assortment of topics are investigated, including the movement's influence on society, its obligation to the environment, the doctrine of Christ and issues of salvation and the Christian life. A clue to Erickson's concerns is found in a chapter titled "The Challenge." Noting the lure of culture, the author concludes that "evangelicalism is in danger of losing its vitality and ability to influence society, and is instead being influenced by society" (p. 39). The suggested corrective steps effectively balance the themes of mind and heart. Evangelicals ought to reemphasize the distinction between Christianity and secularism, develop a complete herme-neutic and return to true theocentrism. They must also take sin seriously and accept the unpopularity that may result, timely counsel for a movement currently engaged in marketing itself. Readers are further admonished to realign, if necessary, their personal lifestyle with expressed social values. This list of challenges concludes on a note of encouragement to emphasize evangelicalism's positive heritage and tradition.

Subsequent chapters address controversial issues currently debated among evan-gelicals. Regarding the dispute over the place of Christ's lordship, both the "free grace" and "lordship" views may profit, says Erickson, from a greater emphasis on union with Christ as a basic quality of salvation. In the chapter "Will Anyone Be Finally Lost?" some evangelicals' departure from traditional exclusivism is evalu-ated. Responding to recent suggestions by Clark Pinnock, Erickson cautions that this shift toward a more relaxed approach regarding positions such as annihilation-ism could have a damaging effect on the next generation of believers, who may be tempted to take these positions even further. Other sections assess the signs and wonders movement and the potential of an impending shortage of qualified clergy for evangelical churches.

Evangelical Interpretation: Perspectives on Hermeneutical Issues permits Erickson to tackle topics frequently relegated to biblical theologians. The initial section on the nature of authorial intent sets the tone. The focus of his analysis is the view that a given passage of Scripture has only one meaning, the one intended by the original author. In the terminology of E. D. Hirsch Jr., adopted by Walter C. Kaiser Jr. and others, "meaning" refers to what the authors intended to say, and "significance" pertains to the application made by readers who relate what was said to their own situation. Though Erickson is in fundamental agreement with Hirsch and Kaiser in their rejection of subjective, or reader-response, approaches to biblical interpretation, he identifies several ambiguities and suggests alternative terminology. For example, he finds "affirmation" an appropriate substitute for the more ambiguous "intention." He prefers "meaning" as an inclusive term, favoring "signification and significance" for "meaning and significance" as used by Hirsch and Kaiser.

Other issues raised by the initial chapter are subsequently addressed. Included is a critique of Daniel P. Fuller's assertion that the role of the Holy Spirit is not to provide understanding of the biblical text but to make reception of the truth possible. Although recognizing the Holy Spirit as the author of Scripture, Erickson asserts that the Holy Spirit now functions as a tutor instead of a lecturer, illumining the reader with insight and understanding. This does not negate the need for proper exegetical method but may extend understanding more deeply than mere method makes possible.

In "Getting from There to Here," Erickson proposes adding a third step, in which the permanent (or timeless) meaning of a passage is identified, to the commonly accepted two-step hermeneutic of exegesis and exposition. By noting these timeless principles, one may then translate the message in such a way that the impact on hearers today will be what was intended for the original recipients. The book concludes with a set of guidelines for a postmodern hermeneutic designed to preserve the evangelical nature of the task while taking postmodernism seriously.

The third volume of the trilogy, *Where Is Theology Going? Issues and Perspectives on the Future of Theology,* scans the theological horizon to predict what trends may continue and what shifts may occur within evangelicalism. Organized according to selected doctrinal categories, such forecasting is not simply theological fortunetelling. Specific tools are utilized, including the projection of identified trends within culture, theology and nontheological disciplines. Indicators for the future range from philosophical developments to the content of popular Christian music.

The final chapter, "Influencing the Direction of Theology," is worth considering. Erickson exhorts evangelicals to maintain attitudes and values that are consonant with Christian faith. Several recommendations pertain to improving theological education in the church and seminary and to influencing society by penetrating its structures. Interspersed with personal references and illustrations, the chapter reflects the concerns of one who has invested a lifetime of effort in both church and classroom. It is thus not surprising that many of his recommendations parallel his own career and ministry.

Recent projects continue to reflect the breadth of Erickson's concerns. He engages current evangelical debates in *How Shall They Be Saved? The Destiny of Those Who Do Not Hear of Jesus* (1996) and in *The Evangelical Left: Encountering Postconservative Evangelical Theology* (1997). Works still in process will assess evangelical responses to postmodernism and will explore the attributes of God. In *Old Wine in New Wineskins: Doctrinal Preaching in a Changing World* (1997), written with James L. Heflin, the reader is reminded that for Erickson theological formulation and expression are not reserved for the seminary or the university but fundamentally belong to the church.

In addition to Erickson's numerous book chapters, articles and reviews, several essays provide a more personal acquaintance with the man and his work. Leslie R. Keylock's brief biographical sketch "Meet Millard J. Erickson" appeared in *Moody Monthly* as part of the series Evangelical Leaders You Should Know. Focus on one aspect of Erickson's thought is found in James Emery White's *What Is Truth? A Comparative Study of the Positions of Cornelius Van Til, Francis Schaeffer, Carl F. H. Henry, Donald Bloesch, Millard Erickson.* A broader survey is David S. Dockery's essay in *Baptist Theologians,* edited by Dockery and Timothy George. He emphasizes the Baptist heritage of Erickson's theology and evaluates it within that tradition. A similar treatment by L. Arnold Hustad appears in *Handbook of Evangelical Theologians,* edited by Walter Elwell. From these sources emerges a portrait of a scholar and an educator who is foremost a pastor whose ministry continues to challenge, encourage and exhort a generation of evangelical minds and hearts.

Complete Bibliography of Works by Millard J. Erickson

Books

Christian Theology. 3 vols. Grand Rapids: Baker, 1983-1985. One-volume edition, 1986. Rev. ed. 1998.

Concise Dictionary of Christian Theology. Grand Rapids: Baker, 1986. In Portuguese: *Conciso dicionário de teologia Cristã.* Rio de Janeiro: Junta de Educação Religiosa e Publicaç Çes da Convenção Batista Brasileira, 1990.

Contemporary Options in Eschatology: A Study of the Millennium. Grand Rapids: Baker, 1977. Also in Portuguese: *Opcoes contemporaneas na escatologia: Um estudo do milenio.* São Paulo: Sociedade Religios Edicoes Vida Nova, 1982. In Swedish: *Tusen Årsriket Dröm eller Verklighet.* Falun: ICI, Dagengruppen AB, 1992.

Does It Matter How I Live? Applying Biblical Beliefs to Your Daily Life. Grand Rapids: Baker, 1994. Reissue of *Responsive Faith.*

Does It Matter If God Exists? Understanding Who God Is and What He Does for Us. Grand Rapids: Baker, 1996.

Does It Matter That I'm Saved? What the Bible Teaches About Salvation. Grand Rapids: Baker, 1996.

Does It Matter What I Believe? What the Bible Teaches and Why We Should Believe It. Grand Rapids: Baker, 1992. Also in Korean: Seoul: Joy Mission Press, 1994.

Evangelical Interpretation: Perspectives on Hermeneutical Issues. Grand Rapids: Baker, 1993.

The Evangelical Left: Encountering Postconservative Evangelical Theology. Grand Rapids: Baker, 1997.

The Evangelical Mind and Heart: Perspectives on Theological and Practical Issues. Grand Rapids: Baker, 1993.

God in Three Persons: A Contemporary Understanding of the Trinity. Grand Rapids: Baker, 1995.

How Shall They Be Saved? The Destiny of Those Who Do Not Hear of Jesus. Grand Rapids: Baker, 1996.

Introducing Christian Doctrine. Abridgment of *Christian Theology.* Edited by L. Arnold Hustad. Grand Rapids: Baker, 1992.

The New Evangelical Theology. Westwood, N.J.: Fleming H. Revell, 1968; London: Marshall, Morgan and Scott, 1969.

Old Wine in New Wineskins: Doctrinal Preaching in a Changing World. With James L. Heflin. Grand Rapids: Baker, 1997.

Relativism in Contemporary Christian Ethics. Grand Rapids: Baker, 1974.

Responsive Faith. Arlington Heights, Ill.: Harvest Publications, 1987.

Salvation: God's Amazing Plan. Wheaton, Ill.: Victor Books, 1978

Where Is Theology Going? Issues and Perspectives on the Future of Theology. Grand Rapids: Baker, 1994.

The Word Became Flesh: A Contemporary Incarnational Christology. Grand Rapids: Baker, 1991.

Edited Volumes

The Living God: Readings in Christian Theology. Grand Rapids: Baker, 1973. Part one also in Chinese: Hong Kong: Seed Press, 1982.

Man's Need and God's Gift: Readings in Christian Theology. Grand Rapids: Baker, 1976.

The New Life: Readings in Christian Theology. Grand Rapids: Baker, 1979.

Journal and Periodical Articles and Book Chapters

"Apologetics Today: Its Task and Shape." *Bethel Seminary Journal* 18, no. 1 (1969): 1-13.

"Authority of the Bible—Historical Basis." In *Old Drums to March By,* pp. 6-14. St. Paul, Minn.: Bethel College and Seminary, 1971.

"The Baptist Doctrine of Baptism in the Context of Interchurch Relations." In *Baptist Faith and Witness: The Papers of the Study and Research Division of the Baptist World Alliance 1990-1995,* pp. 29-38. Edited by William H. Brackney and L. A. Tony Cupitt. Birmingham, Ala.: Samford University Press, 1995.

"The Basis of Our Hope." *The Standard* 61, no. 17 (1971): 20-21.

"The Bible, Science and Creation—How to Interpret the Evidence." *The Standard* 58, no. 15 (1968): 23-24.

"Biblical Ethics of Ecology." In *The Earth Is the Lord's: Christians and the Environment,* pp. 70-90. Edited by Richard D. Land and Louis A. Moore. Nashville: Broadman, 1992.

"Biblical Inerrancy: The Last Twenty-five Years." *Journal of the Evangelical Theological Society* 25, no. 4 (1982): 387-94.

"Biblical Theology of Ecology." In *The Earth Is the Lord's: Christians and the Environment,* pp. 36-54. Edited by Richard D. Land and Louis A. Moore. Nashville: Broadman, 1992.

"Carl F. H. Henry." In *A New Handbook of Christian Theologians,* pp. 214-20. Edited by Donald W. Musser and Joseph L. Price. Nashville: Abingdon, 1996.

"Christ Says, 'Go!' " *The Standard* 47, no. 43 (1957): 3, 15.

"Christology from Above and Christology from Below: A Study in Contrasting Methodologies." *Perspectives on Evangelical Theology,* pp. 43-55. Edited by Kenneth S. Kantzer and Stanley N. Gundry. Grand Rapids: Baker, 1979.

"Christology from an Evangelical Perspective." *Review and Expositor* 88, no. 4 (1991): 379-97.

"The Church and Stable Motion." *Bethel Seminary Journal* 20, no. 3 (1972): 9-17; *Christianity Today* 18, no. 1 (1973).

"Doctrine, Preaching and the Preacher." In *Proclaim the Good News: Essays in Honor of Gordon G. Johnson,* pp. 43-57. Edited by Norris Magnuson. Arlington Heights, Ill.: Harvest, 1986.

"Euthanasia and Christian Ethics." With Ines E. Bowers. *Journal of the Evangelical Theological Society* 19, no. 1 (1976): 15-24.

"Evangelical Christology and Soteriology Today." *Interpretation* 49, no. 3 (1995): 255-66.

"The Fate of Those Who Never Hear." *Bibliotheca Sacra* 152, no. 605 (1995): 3-15.

"The Foundation Does Not Move." *The Standard* 61, no. 13 (1971): 15-18.

"The Holy Spirit and the Church Today." *The Standard* 65, no. 9 (1975): 14-15.

"Hope for Those Who Haven't Heard? Yes, But . . . " *Evangelical Missions Quarterly* 11, no. 2 (1975): 122-26.

"How Do I Become Wise?" *Decision* 38, no. 2 (1997): 13-14.

"How Do You Deal with Doubt?" *The Standard* 77, no. 7 (1987): 21-23.

"Human Engineering and Christian Ethical Values." *Journal of the American Scientific*

Affiliation 30, no. 1 (1978): 16-20.

"Human Language: Human Vehicle for Divine Truth." In *Biblical Hermeneutics: A Comprehensive Introduction to Interpreting Scripture,* pp. 180-89. Edited by Bruce Corley, Steve Lemke and Grant Lovejoy. Nashville: Broadman-Holman, 1996.

"Immanence, Transcendence and the Doctrine of Scripture." In *The Living and Active Word of God,* pp. 193-205. Edited by Morris Inch and Ronald Youngblood. Winona Lake, Ind.: Eisenbrauns, 1983.

"Implications of Biblical Inerrancy for the Christian Mission." In *The Proceedings of the Conference on Biblical Inerrancy 1987,* pp. 233-36. Nashville: Broadman, 1987.

"The Inspiration and Authority of the Bible." In *The Holman Bible Handbook,* pp. 5-11. Edited by David S. Dockery. Nashville: Holman, 1992.

"Is Hell Forever?" *Bibliotheca Sacra* 152, no. 607 (1995): 259-72.

"Is There Opportunity for Salvation After Death?" *Bibliotheca Sacra* 152, no. 606 (1995): 131-44.

"Is Tongues-Speaking for Today?" *The Standard* 63, no. 18 (1973): 18-19; 63, no. 19 (1973): 20-21.

"Is Universalistic Thinking Now Appearing Among Evangelicals?" *United Evangelical ACTION* 48, no. 5 (1989): 4-6.

"Jesus Christ—Still the Hope of the World." *Evangelical Missions Quarterly* 9, no. 4 (1973): 237-42.

"The Lord's Supper." In *People of God: Essays on the Believer's Church,* pp. 51-62. Edited by Paul Basdon and David Dockery. Nashville: Broadman, 1990.

"Lordship Theology: The Current Controversy." *Southwestern Journal of Theology* 33, no. 2 (1991): 5-15.

"Narrative Theology: Translation or Transformation?" In *Festschrift: A Tribute to William Hordern,* pp. 29-39. Edited by Walter Freitag. Saskatoon: University of Saskatchewan Press, 1985.

"The New Birth Today." *Christianity Today* 18, no. 22 (1974): 8-10.

"A New Look at Various Aspects of Inspiration." *Bethel Seminary Journal* 15, no. 1 (1966): 16-26.

"Pannenberg's Use of History as a Solution to the Religious Language Problem." *Journal of the Evangelical Theological Society* 17, no. 2 (1974): 99-105.

"The Potential of Apologetics." *Christianity Today* 14, no. 21 (1970): 6-8; 14, no. 22 (1970): 13-15.

"Presuppositions of Non-evangelical Hermeneutics." *Hermeneutics, Inerrancy and the Bible,* pp. 591-612. Edited by Earl Radmacher and Robert D. Preus. Grand Rapids: Zondervan, 1984.

"Principles, Permanence and Future Divine Judgment: A Case Study in Theological Method." *Journal of the Evangelical Theological Society* 28, no. 3 (1985): 317-25.

"Problem Areas Related to Biblical Inerrancy." In *The Proceedings of the Conference on Biblical Inerrancy 1987,* pp. 175-89. Nashville: Broadman, 1987.

"The Real Issue in Christian Leadership." *Moody Monthly* 87, no. 10 (1987): 72-73. Condensation of article from *The Standard.*

"The Real Issue in Christian Leadership." *The Standard* 72, no. 5 (1982): 28-29.

"Revelation." In *Foundations for Biblical Interpretation: A Complete Library of Tools and Resources,* pp. 3-18. Edited by David S. Dockery, Kenneth A. Matthews and Robert B. Sloan. Nashville: Broadman and Holman, 1994.

"The State of the Question." In *Through No Fault of Their Own,* pp. 23-33. Edited by William Crockett and James Sigountos. Grand Rapids: Baker, 1990.

"The Sting Is Gone." Sermon excerpt in *The Minister's Manual,* p. 314. Edited by Charles L. Wallis. 1972 edition. New York: Harper and Row, 1972.

"The Sting Is Gone." *The Standard* 60, no. 6 (1970): 4-5.

"This Talk About the Millennium and the Tribulation—What's It All About?" *The Standard* 64, no. 15 (1974): 16-17.

"What Conference Baptists Want in a Pastor." *The Standard* 69, no. 9 (1979): 22-23.

"Why I Believe in Jesus Christ." *The Standard* 60, no. 19 (1970): 24-25.

"You Bet Your Life." *The Standard* 51, no. 13 (1961): 6, 20, 26.

Dictionary and Encyclopedia Articles

"Absolutes, Moral," "Act Ethics," "Joseph Fletcher," "Norms," "Principles," "Rule Ethics." In *Baker's Dictionary of Christian Ethics.* Edited by Carl F. H. Henry. Grand Rapids: Baker, 1973.

"Baptism," "Image of God," "Man." In *Nelson's Illustrated Bible Dictionary.* Edited by Herbert Lockyer Sr. Nashville: Thomas Nelson, 1986.

"Bethel Academy," "Bethel Seminary," "Edgren, John Alexis," "Gordh, Arvid." In *Dictionary of Baptists in America.* Edited by Bill J. Leonard. Downers Grove, Ill.: InterVarsity Press, 1994.

"Christology in America," "Theories of Atonement in America." In *Dictionary of Christianity in America.* Edited by Daniel G. Reid et al. Downers Grove, Ill.: InterVarsity Press, 1990.

"Euthanasia," "Millennial Views," "Separation." In *Evangelical Dictionary of Theology.* Edited by Walter A. Elwell. Grand Rapids: Baker, 1984.

"Evangelicalism, USA." In *The Blackwell Encyclopedia of Modern Christian Thought.* Edited by Alister E. McGrath. Cambridge, Mass: Blackwell, 1993.

"Jealousy," "Joy." In *Zondervan's New Pictorial Bible Encyclopedia.* Edited by Merrill E. Tenney. Grand Rapids: Zondervan, 1974.

Reviews

Review of *The Bible and the Future,* by Anthony Hoekema. *Eternity* 30, no. 10 (1974): 62-63.

Review of *Christian Apologetics,* by J. K. S. Reid. *Christian Scholar's Review* 1, no. 3 (1971): 260-62.

Review of *Christian Apologetics in a World Community,* by William Dyrness, and *Challenge and Response: A Handbook of Christian Apologetics,* by Frederic R. Howe. *Christian Scholar's Review* 13, no. 3 (1984): 302-3.

Review of *Contextualization of Theology: An Evangelical Assessment,* by Bruce C. E. Fleming. *Eternity* 32, no. 11 (1981): 44.

Review of *The Creative Word: Canon as a Model for Biblical Education,* by Walter Brueggemann. *Journal of the Evangelical Theological Society* 26, no. 4 (1983): 485-86.

"Careful: Demons at Work." Review of *Demons in the World Today,* by Merrill F. Unger. *The Standard* 63, no. 2 (1973): 18.

"One for the Bookshelf." Review of *The Epistle to the Romans,* by Leon Morris. *Eternity* 39, no. 10 (1988): 46-47.

"Another Look at Christian Ethics." Review of *Ethics: Issues and Alternatives,* by Norman L. Geisler. *The Standard* 62, no. 14 (1972): 4.

Review of *Faith Under Scrutiny,* by Tibor Horvath. *Christian Scholar's Review* 6, nos. 2-3

(1976): 208-9.

Review of *Friendship: A Study in Theological Ethics,* by Gilbert Meilander. *TSF Bulletin* 7, no. 2 (1983): 30.

Review of *General Revelation; Historical Views and ⌐ontemporary Issues,* by Bruce Demarest. *Themelios* 8, no. 2 (1983): 32-33.

Review of *Hermeneutics: Principles and Processes of Biblical Interpretation,* by Henry A. Virkler. *Journal of the Evangelical Theological Society* 27, no. 1 (1984): 106-7.

Review of *Horizons of Science: Christian Scholars Speak Out,* edited by Carl F. H. Henry. *Eternity* 30, no. 2 (1979): 50.

"Against One-Sided Extremism." Review of *In Search of Balance,* by Virginia Mollenkott. *Christianity Today* 14, no. 19 (1970): 27-28.

Review of *Integrative Theology,* vol. 1, by Bruce Demarest and Gordon Lewis. *Trinity Journal* 8 n.s., no. 2 (1987): 235-39.

Review of *No Place for Truth: Or, Whatever Happened to Evangelical Theology?* by David Wells. *Southwestern Journal of Theology* 36, no. 3 (1994): 58.

Review of *Organ Transplants: The Moral Issues,* by Catherine Lyons. *Bethel Seminary Journal* 20, no. 2 (1972): 24.

Review of *Sacred Discontent, the Bible and Western Tradition,* by Herbert N. Schneidau. *Christian Scholar's Review* 9, no. 1 (1979): 89-90.

Review of *Southern Baptists and American Evangelicals: The Conversation Continues,* edited by David S. Dockery. *Review and Expositor* 92, no. 2 (1995): 237-39.

Review of *Theology for the Community of God,* by Stanley Grenz. *Southwestern Journal of Theology* 38, no. 2 (1996): 45.

Review of *Understanding and Applying the Bible,* by Robertson McQuilken. *Journal of the Evangelical Theological Society* 27, no. 1 (1984): 107-8.

Review of *What Are They Saying About Euthanasia?* by Richard M. Gula. *TSF Bulletin* 10, no. 5 (1987): 40-42.

Forthcoming

"Bloesch's Doctrine of Holy Scripture." In a festschrift for Donald Bloesch. Edited by Elmer Colyer. Downers Grove, Ill.: InterVarsity Press, forthcoming.

God the Father Almighty: A Contemporary Exploration of the Divine Attributes. Grand Rapids: Baker, 1998.

Postmodernizing the Faith: Evangelical Responses to the Challenge of Postmodernism. Grand Rapids: Baker, 1998.

Works About Millard Erickson

Dockery, David S. "Millard J. Erickson." In *Baptist Theologians,* pp. 640-59. Edited by Timothy George and David S. Dockery. Nashville: Broadman, 1990.

Hustad, L. Arnold. "Millard J. Erickson." In *Handbook of Evangelical Theologians,* pp. 412-26. Edited by Walter A. Elwell. Grand Rapids: Baker, 1993.

Keylock, Leslie R. "Evangelical Leaders You Should Know: Meet Millard J. Erickson." *Moody Monthly* 87, no. 10 (1987): 71-73.

White, James Emery. *What Is Truth? A Comparative Study of the Positions of Cornelius Van Til, Francis Schaeffer, Carl F. H. Henry, Donald Bloesch, Millard Erickson.* Nashville: Broadman & Holman, 1994.

Scripture Index

The indexes were
prepared by:
Angela Earl
Tobie Hannah
Lyle Larson